The Battle for Asia

Asia has been a crucial ideological battleground between capitalism and communism, between nationalism and Anglo-American liberalism and between the nation-state and globalization. This book is a history of the Asian region from 1945 to the present day. It delineates the various ideological battles over Asia's development by combining a critical perspective on the transformation of the region over the past fifty years with a fresh interpretation of the shift towards globalization.

Subjects covered include:

- theories of development;
- decolonization and the nation-state system;
- geo-politics of nation-building;
- US political and economic intervention;
- the effects of communism;
- the end of the Cold War;
- discussion of specific national trajectories in the context of regional and international history;
- the rise of neo-liberalism;
- the dynamics of the 'Asian Miracle';
- the Asian crisis and after;
- Asia in the era of globalization.

Broad in sweep and rich in theory and empirical detail, this is an essential account of the turbulent ascent of Asia and the region's position in the global political economy of the twenty-first Century.

Mark T. Berger is Senior Lecturer in International Studies at the University of New South Wales. He has published widely in international journals and is the co-editor of *The Rise of East Asia: Critical Visions of the Pacific Century*.

Asia's Transformations

Edited by Mark Selden

Binghamton University and Cornell University, USA

The books in this series explore the political, social, economic and cultural consequences of Asia's transformations in the twentieth and twenty-first centuries. The series emphasizes the tumultuous interplay of local, national, regional and global forces as Asia bids to become the hub of the world economy. While focusing on the contemporary, it also looks back to analyze the antecedents of Asia's contested rise.

This series comprises several strands:

Asia's Transformations aims to address the needs of students and teachers, and the titles will be published in hardback and paperback. Titles include:

Asia's Great Cities: Each volume aims to capture the heartbeat of the contemporary city from multiple perspectives emblematic of the authors' own deep familiarity with the distinctive faces of the city, its history, society, culture, politics and economics, and its evolving position in national, regional and global frameworks. While most volumes emphasize urban developments since the Second World War, some pay close attention to the legacy of the longue durée in shaping the contemporary. Thematic and comparative volumes address such themes as urbanization, economic and financial linkages, architecture and space, wealth and power, gendered relationships, planning and anarchy, and ethnographies in national and regional perspective. Titles include:

Hong Kong
Global city
Stephen Chiu and Tai-Lok Lui

Shanghai
Global city
Jeff Wasserstrom

Singapore
Carl Trocki

Beijing in the Modern World
David Strand and Madeline Yue Dong

Bangkok
Place, practice and representation
Marc Askew

Asia.com is a series which focuses on the ways in which new information and communication technologies are influencing politics, society and culture in Asia. Titles include:

Asia.com
Asia encounters the internet
Edited by K. C. Ho, Randolph Kluver and Kenneth C. C. Yang

Japanese Cybercultures
Edited by Mark McLelland and Nanette Gottlieb

RoutledgeCurzon Studies in Asia's Transformations is a forum for innovative new research intended for a high-level specialist readership, and the titles will be available in hardback only. Titles include:

Chinese Media, Global Contexts
Edited by Chin-Chuan Lee

Imperialism in South East Asia
"A fleeting, passing phase"
Nicholas Tarling

Internationalizing the Pacific
The United States, Japan and the Institute of Pacific Relations in War and Peace, 1919–1945
Tomoko Akami

Koreans in Japan
Critical voices from the margin
Edited by Sonia Ryang

The American Occupation of Japan and Okinawa *
Literature and Memory
Michael Molasky

* *Now available in paperback*

Critical Asian Scholarship is a series intended to showcase the most important individual contributions to scholarship in Asian Studies. Each of the volumes presents a leading Asian scholar addressing themes that are central to his or her most significant and lasting contribution to Asian studies. The series is committed to the rich variety of research and writing on Asia, and is not restricted to any particular discipline, theoretical approach or geographical expertise.

China's Past, China's Future
Energy, food, environment
Vaclav Smil

China Unbound
Evolving perspectives on the
Chinese past
Paul A. Cohen

**Women and the Family in
Chinese History**
Patricia Buckley Ebrey

Southeast Asia
A testament
George McT. Kahin

The Battle for Asia

From decolonization to globalization

Mark T. Berger

RoutledgeCurzon
Taylor & Francis Group

LONDON AND NEW YORK

First published 2004
by RoutledgeCurzon
11 New Fetter Lane, London EC4P 4EE

Simultaneously published in the USA and Canada
by RoutledgeCurzon
29 West 35th Street, New York, NY 10001

RoutledgeCurzon is an imprint of the Taylor & Francis Group

© 2004 Mark T. Berger

Typeset in Baskerville by
Taylor & Francis Books Ltd

Printed and bound in Great Britain by
MPG Books Ltd, Bodmin

British Library Cataloguing in Publication Data
A catalogue record for this book is available from the British Library

Library of Congress Cataloging in Publication Data
A catalog record for this book has been requested

ISBN 0–415–32528–5 (hbk)
ISBN 0–415–32529–3 (pbk)

For Brooke, Paige, Bailey, Carter, Chad and
Devin ... and Madison

The "problem" in the Orient is indissolubly connected with the "problem" in the Occident and it is useless to try to seek a solution of one without the other.

Contents

Preface and acknowledgements

This book is the product of fifteen years of research and teaching on the modern history, geo-politics and economic development of Asia. It also flows from over two decades of visits to, and travels in, various parts of what is a large and diverse region – stretching from the Indian sub-continent in the west to the Japanese islands in the northeast. The immediate origins of the book, however, go back to the early post-Cold War era. It began as an attempt to engage critically with both the liberal "triumphalism" that attended the end of the Cold War and the East Asian "triumphalism" that flowed from the surging industrial dynamism of Northeast and Southeast Asia by the late 1980s and early 1990s. Over time this study broadened into an effort to synthesize and come to grips with the ongoing debate about the post-1945 history of Asia generally, and the phenomenon that was increasingly known as the (East) Asian Miracle – until it was supplanted in 1997–1998 by the (East) Asian Crisis – more specifically. This book is about the geo-politics of economic development. At the same time, it is a sustained effort to argue that although the waning days of the Second World War and the dramatic era of decolonization and the early Cold War now appear to be in the distant past, there is more than ever a need to adopt an historical perspective to understand contemporary Asia and the changing global order at the start of the twenty-first century.

This book can be read in a sequential and cumulative fashion as the chapters move chronologically and thematically from the 1940s to the 1990s. At the same time, some readers may want to focus on certain issues or themes: chapters 1 and 4 provide a broad overview of the geo-politics of development at a global level over the entire post-1945 period. Chapters 2 and 3, meanwhile, are more focused in both geographical and thematic terms. The former provides a history of development economics with a particular emphasis on South Asia, while the latter provides a detailed history of modernization theory as it relates to Asia generally and Southeast Asia more specifically. Chapters 5, 6 and 7 also focus in detail on the geo-politics of development and theories of development in relation to Asia – neo-liberalism and the East Asian Miracle, the debate over the cultural roots and contours of the East Asian Miracle, and the rise and fall of the developmental state, respectively. Chapters 8 and 9, by contrast, provide a synthetic overview of the historical political economy of the transformation of Asia from decolonization to globalization.

I started preliminary work on this book while I was employed in the Asian Studies and Development Studies Programs in the School of Humanities at Murdoch University. From 1994 to 1997 the School of Humanities at Murdoch provided a particularly congenial and exciting intellectual and pedagogical setting and I feel privileged to have worked there in that period. Since 1998 I have been based in the School of Modern Language Studies in the Faculty of Arts and Social Sciences at UNSW, where my involvement with the International Studies Program, the Comparative Development Program, not to mention the School of History, the School of Politics and International Relations and the Department of Spanish and Latin American Studies, has provided an exciting and dynamic context for inter-disciplinary research and teaching.

A number of research centers and institutes also provided support for this project at various stages. I would like to thank the Asia Research Centre at Murdoch University (where I have been a Research Fellow since 1997) and its former Director, Professor Richard Robison. In June–July 1997 I spent a very useful period as a Visiting Researcher at the East–West Centre at the University of Hawaii in Honolulu, and I thank the head of Development Studies, Dr Elizabeth Buck, in particular, for making my visit possible. I was also a Visiting Scholar at the Centre for Advanced Studies (CAS) at the National University of Singapore (NUS) during a key period (January–February 2000) in the early preparation of this book, and I would like to thank the then-Director of CAS, Professor Deborah Yeoh. From March to June 2000 I was a Visiting Fellow at the Institute of International Studies at the University of Technology in Sydney, and I thank the Director, Professor David Goodman. For the past couple of years, when I am not at UNSW, I have been a Visiting Fellow at the Institute of Commonwealth Studies (ICS) in the School of Advanced Study at the University of London. In particular, I thank the Director of ICS, Professor Tim Shaw, for his and the Institute's support in the final stages of this book.

Given the broad and synthetic character of this book, the list of individuals who have helped along the way, indirectly and directly, is, of course, a long one. At the risk of leaving some of them out I would still like to name those friends and colleagues who contributed to this project in significant and direct ways or in a more indirect fashion. My thanks go to: Mengistu Amberber, William Armour, Ed Aspinall, Mark Beeson, John Brotherton, Kerstin Calley, Bruce Cumings, Arif Dirlik, Nick Doumanis, David C. Engerman, Marc Frey, Stephen Frost, Devleena Ghosh, Nils Gilman, Jasper Goss, Sarah Graham, Gerard Greenfield, Vedi Hadiz, Max Harcourt, Sebastian Job, Irvin Lim, Andrew Mitchell, David Moore, Ravi Arvind Palat, Diana Palaversich, Michael Pearson, Simon Philpott, Shahid Qadir, David Reeve, Jonathan Schrag, Mark Selden, Tim Shaw, Alvin Y. So, Tay Cheng Cheng, Yao Souchou, Jing Wang, Carol Warren, Jim Warren, C. J. W.-L. Wee, and Marc Williams. At Routledge I would like to thank Craig Fowlie and Zoe Botterill for the expeditious way in which they shepherded this manuscript through to publication. My primary debt, however, goes to Catherine Waldby – thanks for everything, Cathy.

Introduction

Theories of progress and the nation-state system

When future historians look back at the twentieth century, they will no doubt view the decades from the 1940s to the 1970s as the high period of the nation-state system. It was in these decades that the nation-state system was universalized and the idea that the nation-state was the primary, if not the exclusive vehicle for achieving progress was consolidated worldwide. In fact many of the big questions about the changing role of the nation-state in the global political economy of the early twenty-first century, and important debates about the significance of influential contemporary theories of development, are best understood against the backdrop of the world-historical shift towards decolonization and the rise and transformation of the nation-state system during the Cold War.[1] In particular the limitations of the dominant theories of progress, as they emerged in the Cold War era, and as they have been continuously revised into the post-Cold War era, can be traced to the way in which they routinized the nation-state as their key unit, or sub-unit, of analysis. Between the 1940s and the 1970s a growing array of theories and policies of development (capitalist and socialist) were outlined and implemented on the assumption that nation-states could be treated as natural units of a wider international order. Despite both the complex history of nation-state formation and consolidation following decolonization and the onset of the Cold War, and the significant changes associated with the reorientation of the global political economy since the 1970s, the routinization of the nation-state has remained central to the dominant narratives of progress at the start of the twenty-first century.

Between the 1940s and the 1970s virtually all the main theories of development assumed that the "state" had a central and legitimate role to play in the process of development and, at least in theory, development involved some form of state-mediated, if not state-directed, national redistribution and even restructuring that sought to incorporate the poorer and disenfranchised citizens into a national development project. However, in the 1980s and then into the post-Cold War era, the profit-maximizing consumption-oriented individual was increasingly enshrined as the universal subject of development and the idea of state-mediated national development as the key to prosperity was increasingly challenged by the rise of neo-liberalism.[2] A rising neo-liberalism was central to the emergence of the US-led globalization project.[3] Despite this shift, national leaders have continued to mobilize the citizens of many nation-states in the name of nationalism and the "national interest", while dismantling many of the public institutions and state-owned enterprises that, at least in theory, had under-pinned the social and economic cohesion and developmental initiatives of these nation-states in an earlier era. And many economists and other social scientists continue to treat nations as the unproblematic beneficiaries of globalization. Meanwhile, most intellectuals and politicians who seek to challenge the global-ization project still do so primarily at the level of the nation-state or via the promotion of an alliance of nation-states. The fear of many is that the globaliza-tion project represents the demise of the nation-state. While nation-states in many parts of the world are in crisis, and in some cases have already failed, the globalization project as it emerged by the 1980s signalled the waning of state-mediated national development rather than the end of the nation-state in the foreseeable future. It needs to be emphasized that the globalization project is currently being constituted via the nation-state system at the same time as it is radically transforming both the character of that system and the trajectories of specific nation-states. Nation-states around the world have increasingly taken on the role of globalizers in contrast to an earlier emphasis on state-mediated national development. Thus, in many parts of the world the changes to the global order since the 1980s have resulted in the uneven reorientation of erst-while state-mediated national development projects into globalizing states. However, in other parts of the world, nation-states are not simply being reori-ented from national development to globalization. In these cases the experience of state-mediated national development was either very attenuated or profoundly flawed and these polities are now in the throes of crises of the nation-state and are failing, or have already failed, as nation-states.[4]

The connection between the changing global political economy, the univer-salization and transformation of the nation-state system and the vicissitudes of theories of development is an important but neglected area of study. There are, of course, important articles and books on various aspects of the relationship between US geo-politics and the theory and practice of development.[5] And there are numerous studies of the international development debate and devel-opment theory more generally.[6] There are also a number of articles and books (many of which will be discussed and examined in the pages that follow) on theories of development and Asia.[7] However, the most common approach to understanding the international development debate generally and the Asian development debate more specifically (and this is apparent in most studies of Asian development), is for commentators to begin books or articles on various aspects of economic and political development with a brief summary of what are understood as the main theories of development. Far less common, by contrast, are efforts to explain the competing narratives on development in Asia and beyond with an emphasis on the wider geo-political context in which they are produced. The dominant narratives on economic development in Asia flow in significant measure from the disciplines of economics and political science. This is despite the important role of interdisciplinary settings such as Asian

Studies and Development Studies, and the important, but very secondary role of disciplines such as anthropology, sociology and history in development theory. The dominant development discourse, centered on economics and political science and closely linked to the economic policy process, continues to rest on assumptions about the rationality and objectivity of their methodologies and analyses. To understand the international development debate generally, and the debate about Asian development more specifically, there is a need to place the production and revision of theories of progress in the context of the universalization of the nation-state system and the changing global political economy since 1945. This book explores the main theories of development, with a focus on Asia, via a sustained emphasis on the wider context in which they are produced. It draws attention to the important connection between academic approaches and popular debates about economic growth and political change in Asia. It emphasizes the central role of US foreign policy and the wider geopolitical struggles that have conditioned approaches to, and debates about, economic and political development between the 1940s and the 1990s. At the very center of this effort to trace the history and geo-politics of the Asian development debate is a critical perspective on the question of the changing significance of the nation-state in the second half of the twentieth century. At the outset this introduction outlines some of the main thematic and conceptual issues and then sets out a framework for the discussion of theories of development and the nation-state system in relation to the transformation of Asia and the changing global order.

The transformation of Asia and the changing global order I

Asia and the development debate I: neo-liberalism and history

By the end of the Cold War, decades of sustained economic development in Japan, South Korea, Taiwan, Hong Kong and Singapore, and the growing capitalist dynamism of Thailand, Malaysia, Indonesia and coastal China, had catapulted the region to global prominence. The dominant international image of East Asia in this period was that decades of sustained economic growth in an increasing number of nation-states, variously known as Newly Industrializing Countries (NICs), Newly Industrializing Economies (NIEs), High Performing Asian Economies (HPAEs), or simply as the Asian Dragons or Asian Tigers, had resulted in the "East Asian Miracle". The rise of East Asia was also often seen to herald the coming of a Pacific Century and the debate about the sources of the region's economic dynamism was at the center of the development debate worldwide. While the most influential explanations for the East Asian Miracle represented the region's economic success as a vindication of neo-liberalism, this interpretation was increasingly challenged by a number of interpreters who emphasized the role of the state and/or cultural/national/racial characteristics particular to the social formations of Northeast and Southeast Asia. From the latter perspective the coming of the Pacific Century represented a New Asian Renaissance rather than the triumph of neo-liberalism and Anglo-American capitalism. But much of the anticipation of, or the concern about, the twenty-first century being the Pacific Century dissipated rapidly with the onset of the Asian crisis (1997–1998).[8] Of course, the increasing economic and politico-military significance of the People's Republic of China by the second half of the 1990s has ensured that great expectations continue to prevail about China's significant, even central, role in the region and the world in the twenty-first century.[9] The growing displacement of the Asia-Pacific Economic Cooperation forum (APEC) by ASEAN+3 (the Association of Southeast Asian Nations, China, Japan and South Korea) in the wake of the Asian crisis, meanwhile, has also provided some support for exclusive and celebratory forms of regionalism.[10] Nevertheless, the East Asian Miracle of an earlier era has passed into history and the US remains the hegemonic power in the region and worldwide in the short-to medium-term. Furthermore, as will be argued in chapter 4, the wider changes to the global order of the past three decades mean that conventional conceptions of the rise and fall of Great Powers shed less light on US relations with East Asia generally, and between Washington and Beijing more specifically, in the era of the US-led globalization project than in an earlier era.

The rise of the US-led globalization project and the transformation of the nation-state system are bound up in part with the diffusion of neo-liberalism and the growing prominence of neo-classical economics in the last decade of the Cold War. By the 1980s the main policy conclusions of neo-classical economics were becoming, or had already become, received wisdom among most of the senior officials in the OECD nations and at the International Monetary Fund (IMF) and the World Bank.[11] The central prescription that the IMF and the World Bank increasingly offered to governments around the world was that underdevelopment was caused by excessive state intervention in the economy. They argued that selling state-owned corporations, opening up to foreign investment and getting rid of government regulations on prices and markets would encourage economic growth and efficiency. While the shift to neo-liberalism was not nearly as pronounced in Asia as in other parts of the world, such as Latin America, efforts to promote neo-liberal economic policies were on the rise in the region by the 1980s. In fact, the rise and diffusion of neo-liberal ideas paralleled the growing interest in the economic dynamism of East Asia. By the end of the 1970s, Japan, South Korea, Taiwan, Hong Kong and Singapore, because of their success with export-oriented industrialization (EOI) starting in the 1960s, had been identified by proponents of neo-classical economics as exemplars of *laissez-faire*. Having conflated EOI with free-trade, neo-classical economists pointed to the experience of post-1945 state-mediated national development in Latin America and Africa not only as evidence of the failure of the import-substitution industrialization (ISI) model, but as evidence of the failure of state intervention more generally. By the 1980s, advocates of neo-liberalism were seeking ever more assiduously to incorporate the rise of Asia into a neo-classical narrative on Asian capitalism specifically and capitalist transformation more generally. For example, Deepak Lal, a prominent exponent of neo-liberalism, went so far as to argue in 1983 that South Korea's "success" as a Newly Industrializing Country had not only *not* been a result of state intervention but that its "success" had been "achieved despite" state "intervention".[12] A decade later the lead article in a special edition of the *Far Eastern Economic Review*, celebrating twenty years of "Asian Growth", argued that the key to the region's "economic boom" was a combination of "hard work, low taxes, high savings rates" and "minimal government".[13]

However, the late 1980s and early 1990s also saw the emergence of a growing challenge to neo-liberalism on the part of the government of Japan.[14] In fact, in part as a result of the September 1985 Plaza Accord, the "external reach" of the Japanese state, via foreign investment and aid programs, had increased significantly by the end of the Cold War. This resulted in a range of attempts by the Japanese government to encourage governing elites in the nation-states in which Tokyo enjoyed growing influence to view economic development in more strategic and interventionist ways than was advocated by influential institutions such as the World Bank.[15] Nevertheless, the early post-Cold War era saw the consolidation of the "Washington Consensus", centered on the acceptance (enthusiastic or reluctant) of the neo-liberal reform package promoted by organizations such as the International Monetary Fund (IMF) and World Bank.[16] More broadly, the demise of the Soviet Union reinvigorated support for, and resulted in the unalloyed celebration of, the particular neo-liberal form of capitalism, which had emerged in the 1980s, as both universally applicable and superior to all other modes of economic development. By the early 1990s, however, the World Bank was increasingly seeking to accommodate the Japanese challenge, while retaining its basic commitment to neo-liberalism. The effort to at least gesture towards the important role of government (emphasized by Tokyo) was reflected in the opening address of the annual World Bank and IMF meeting in Bangkok, in October 1991. In this address, the new president of the World Bank, Lewis Preston, asserted that the demise of the Soviet Bloc had led to "the broad convergence of development thinking which has replaced ideological conflict". He asserted that there was now a consensus spreading around the globe based on the free-market, a balance between the private sector and government and sustainable economic growth.[17]

This was the setting for the publication of the influential 1993 World Bank Report on East Asia.[18] The 1993 study, which was funded by the Japanese Ministry of Finance (MOF), was a profoundly political document that reluctantly conceded that government intervention had played some role in economic development in East Asia. Despite its concessions to government intervention, the report was criticized by the Japanese Ministry of Finance and by proponents of the developmental state for still not placing nearly enough emphasis on state intervention and industrial policy.[19] The effort to domesticate the Japanese challenge to the dominant neo-liberal conception of capitalist transformation was taken further in the *World Development Report 1997*.[20] Overall, however, this study (which emphasized the need for an "effective state" that could act as an ostensibly neutral arbiter) remained inoculated from political questions, while the wider historical context was sidestepped and the authoritarian character of most of the developmental states in Asia was given implicit, if not explicit, legitimacy. The report's appearance coincided with the start of the Asian financial crisis in mid-1997 and efforts to learn the lessons and significance of the East Asian Miracle quickly gave way to a new debate about the causes and consequences of the Asian crisis. With the Asian crisis, there was also a further assertion of US hegemony, via the International Monetary Fund (IMF) in particular, and neo-liberal economic policies were further imposed/embraced, at the same time as they were represented more than ever as the key to universal prosperity.[21] Ultimately, efforts by the Japanese government (which will be examined in more detail in chapter 5, not to mention advocates of industrial policy and the developmental state who will be discussed in chapter 7) to challenge a neo-classical reading of the East Asian Miracle were domesticated on terms set by the liberal institutions and discourses of the global political economy and the nation-state system. In the aftermath of the Asian crisis the one-time developmental states of East Asia have been increasingly subordinated to the post-Cold War neo-liberal order. By the end of the 1990s the dominant neo-liberal narratives had undergone considerable revision, while remaining committed to a Eurocentric and technocratic approach to capitalist development. As will be outlined in more detail in the book that follows, the dominant interpretations of capitalist development have increasingly retreated from a historically grounded understanding of the transformation of Asia. By contrast, the emphasis throughout this book will be on the need to historicize development and historicize theories of development.

Theories of capitalism I: "The Great Transformation"

To a considerable extent, liberal and neo-liberal interpretations of nation-states and capitalist development in Asia and beyond not only remain grounded in a routinized notion of the nation-state, but are also centered on a romanticized and naturalized conception of the history of capitalism in Western Europe (and latterly North America).[22] The national industrial paths followed by England and the United States, in particular, and the rationality and reason of the Enlightenment more generally, are often still implicitly assumed to be, or explicitly represented as, providing lessons in development for the rest of the world.[23] Even though economic history has been increasingly marginalized by the rise of neo-classical economics, in part because the former represents a challenge to the ahistorical character of the latter, the evolutionary and celebratory assumptions on which neo-classical economics rests are supported and reinforced by the work of a range of historians of capitalism.[24] For example, Alan Macfarlane approvingly prefaces his analysis of the English trajectory with the comment by Adam Smith that "little else is required to carry a state to the highest degree of opulence from the lowest barbarism, but peace, easy taxes, and a tolerable administration of justice; all the rest being brought about by the natural order of things". Macfarlane then goes on to argue that between the thirteenth and the eighteenth centuries "the English political system ... guaranteed peace through the control of feuding, taxes were light and justice was uniform and firmly administered", providing the framework for the development of "competitive individualism".[25]

Such an approach, however, gives insufficient weight to the wider social conflict and political struggles that were central to the rise of capitalism and the emergence of the modern state system in Western Europe and North America. It also assumes the prior existence of, or fails to problematize, the nation-state. Modern territorial states, and then nation-states, emerged as an integral part of the rise of capitalism, and were a key element in the consolidation and reproduction of the social forces unleashed by mercantile and then industrial capitalism. The centralized-absolutist state forms that emerged in Western Europe in the early modern era transcended and mediated rival social forces, providing a partial solution to the social and political crises connected to the rise of capitalism.[26] Over the course of the shift from dynastic sovereignty to territorial sovereignty and then to national sovereignty the state forms changed, but sovereignty remained grounded in the state.[27] The rise of capitalism and the formation of sovereign states in Western Europe (contrary to Macfarlane's analysis of England) also interacted directly with the history of commercial and colonial expansion. Between 1415 and the 1770s European conquerors, traders, missionaries and settlers expanded overseas, aided by the growing political, naval and military power of the rising states of Europe. This period saw major territorial as well as commercial expansion in the Americas, but prior to the nineteenth century most of Asia and Africa was much less directly affected by the changes that were remaking the Americas. The industrial revolution, however, was not only facilitated by commercial and colonial expansion, it also dramatically transformed the character of states in Europe and dramatically shaped the pace, extent and form of subsequent European expansion.[28] During the late eighteenth century, and over the course of the nineteenth century, many of the modern states in Western Europe emerged, or were consolidated, as industrializing national-imperial-states acquiring both the impetus and the capability to embark on a process of worldwide economic integration.[29] By the end of this period, Germany and France (as well as the United States and Japan) in particular, began to successfully challenge Britain's primacy as the "workshop of the world". After 1870 these increasingly powerful industrialized and imperial states sought to expand markets and access to raw materials through the annexation of territory. The so-called "New Imperialism" involved an unprecedented scramble for empire in Africa, Asia and the Pacific between 1870 and 1914. During this period about one quarter of the surface of the globe was distributed or re-distributed as colonies among half a dozen imperial powers.[30] The "New Imperialism" reached its apogee on the eve of the First World War. However, within two decades of the end of the 1914–1918 conflagration, the failure of Imperial Germany to attain a "place in the sun" was revisited with even more ferocity as a new global battle for empire raged from the end of the 1930s until 1945. Hitler's particularly violent, racist and genocidal effort to create a German colonial empire in Europe in the late 1930s and early 1940s was as grounded in previous European colonial activities in Asia, Africa and the Americas as it was in earlier attempts, by the Habsburgs (1519–1659) and Revolutionary France (1792–1815), to dominate Europe.[31] The rise of Hitler's colonial project in Europe was connected to the wider crisis of colonialism that afflicted the established European colonial powers as a result of economic depression, rising nationalist movements and the dramatic encroachment in Asia of an expanding Japanese empire.[32] This was the wider backdrop for the cataclysm of the Second World War and the effective passing, in decades, of empires that had, in some cases, been built up over centuries.

This brief critical counter-point to the liberal and neo-liberal narrative on the history of capitalism outlined above is reflected in a wealth of detail in the work of historians and political economists writing in the Marxist tradition, or drawing on theories of historical change derived from Marxism (the Marxist tradition is defined very broadly here to include dependency theories and world-system theory). These writers have emphasized class structure and social conflict, at the same time as they have highlighted the expansionary and transformative (creative and destructive) character of capitalism. These themes are readily apparent in Karl Marx and Friedrich Engels' famous observation in the second half of the nineteenth century that the rising bourgeoisie of North America and Western Europe were bringing "civilization" to "even the most barbarian" parts of the world, battering down the "Chinese walls" and compelling "all nations" to embrace the "bourgeois mode of production" in order to create "a world after its own image".[33] Since Marx and Engels, many historians and social scientists have continued to conceptualize capitalist development generally and capitalism in Asia more specifically, in terms that reflect the main themes of Marx's work. Apart from Marx, a list of the studies that have become cornerstones of the critical history of capitalism would run from Karl Polanyi's *The Great Transformation* (1944) to Barrington Moore's *Social Origins of Dictatorship and Democracy* (1966).[34] More recently the history of capitalism has been illuminated by, and the liberal and neo-liberal understanding of capitalist transformation has been challenged by, the work of Perry Anderson, Giovanni Arrighi, Fernand Braudel, Robert Brenner, T. J. Byres, Robert W. Cox, Bruce Cumings, Hill Gates, Michael Mann, Jeffrey M. Paige, Dietrich Rueschemeyer, Evelyne Huber Stephens and John D. Stephens, Immanuel Wallerstein, Eric Wolf and Ellen Meiksins Wood, among others.[35] In general terms these authors attempt to theorize the historical development of capitalism in various parts of the world, although the European and North American experience tends to get more coverage – Bruce Cumings is the most grounded in the East Asian experience and his work will be discussed in more detail below. At the same time, much of this work uses European national trajectories as implicit, if not explicit measures, of capitalist transformation in Asia and elsewhere. All these writers have sought to explain the variations of capitalist development with an emphasis on the impact of colonialism and other historical factors, paying particular attention to the relationship between social forces and state formation. For example, Michael Hardt and Antonio Negri have conceptualized the rise of capitalism in Western Europe as the onset of a crisis of authority in the context of the interplay between revolution and reaction. They argue that in this situation the emergence of the modern state, as a "locus of sovereignty" that mediated and transcended rival social forces, represented the temporary and partial solution to the crisis of modernity. Furthermore, modern national sovereignty, as it emerged in Western Europe, and was then universalized over the past two centuries, was grounded in an implicit "affirmation of the market" as the basis of social, cultural and political life, ensuring that, despite major challenges during the twentieth century, the sovereignty of modern nation-states, within the wider nation-state system, was consolidated as "capitalist sovereignty".[36]

As Hardt and Negri's analysis suggests, the work of proponents of a historically grounded perspective on capitalism intersects with the Marxist tradition in political economy, particularly in relation to the importance of the connection between state formation and the social dynamics of capitalist development.[37] And over the years a number of Marxist political economists working on Asia and Africa have emphasized the historic role of the state in mediating the emergence and consolidation of capitalism (much of this work has built on, while also often departing dramatically from, dependency theory and world-system theory).[38] In his important 1986 study, *Indonesia: The Rise of Capital*, Richard Robison linked historical materialism to the insights of the dependency debate, but placed his major emphasis on state and class structures in the periphery, pointing to the relative potential for autonomous capitalist development, and emphasizing that politics in Indonesia and elsewhere still enjoyed a degree of freedom from external pressures. Robison argued that the emergence and transformation of the nation-state of Indonesia after 1945 could "only be understood and explained within its specific historical and social context" in which "class" was a "crucial factor".[39] A key aspect of this process was the way in which "political power" flowed from "within the state apparatus". At the same time, he emphasized that the institutions and language of Suharto's New Order as it was consolidated after 1965 were corporatist: they placed considerable emphasis on the "common national good" and on the need to organize politics along consensual and functional rather than competitive lines. He located the "ideological basis" of the New Order state in a form of cultural nationalism that juxtaposed Eastern harmony and consensus with Western confrontation and individualism (among other things this meant that under the Suharto government engaging in work stoppages and strikes was illegal at the same time as the banning of these practices was justified on the grounds that they were alien to the harmonious and communal character of Indonesian culture). Robison also emphasized that the emergence of a state-sponsored organicist ideology was linked to the thinking of influential Javanese aristocratic officials in post-1945 Indonesia who held up authority and hierarchy, along with the concept of aristocratic obligation, as key values. He noted that these ideas had considerable overlap with the "conservative, organic political theories of the declining aristocracy of Bismarckian Germany and other European authoritarian monarchies". Writing in the early 1990s Robison concluded that, contrary to the "liberal democratic model" that was and is widely deployed to explain the political prospects for post-Suharto Indonesia, a "more helpful model" could be found in "post-Bismarckian Germany".[40]

While the prism of Anglo-American liberalism does little to illuminate the Indonesian trajectory, there are also serious limits to examining the rise and transformation of Indonesia through the prism of late-nineteenth century Germany. As Robison's analysis makes clear, there are key differences between liberal and Marxist approaches to the dynamics of capitalist development. At the same time, his analysis also exemplifies the Eurocentrism characteristic of Marxism and of the dominant development discourse, which entails the evaluation and naturalization of national paths to modernity in terms of their apparent success or failure to follow a relatively limited number of idealized North American or Western European trajectories. While, as we have seen, liberal and neo-liberal analyses make virtually no effort to conceptualize power relations and often treat culture in a static or deterministic fashion, Marxist observers tend to view power in centralized terms as embedded in class relations and state structures, while representing culture as an unproblematic ideological function of the dominant elites. For example, while Robison addresses the issue of culture, he deals with it in a mechanistic fashion effectively linking the culture of capitalism in Indonesia to a particular stage in history, equating the Suharto era (1965–1998) with late-nineteenth-century Germany. This type of approach fails to draw out the temporal and spatial particularity of capitalist transformation.[41] Furthermore it treats the nation-state as a natural unit of analysis rather than viewing the nation-state itself as a historically contingent and changing entity.[42] If it had been possible for Otto von Bismarck – who presided over the unification of Germany and its rise as an industrial and imperial power between the 1860s and the 1880s – to visit Indonesia between the 1960s and the 1980s, it is not at all clear that he would have taken Robison's view that life in the archipelago was at the same "stage" as his homeland. Nor would a person from Suharto's Indonesia who was transported halfway around the world and 100 years into the past find anything particularly familiar about Bismarck's Germany.

Theories of capitalism II: "the New Asian Industrialism"

The state-centered approach adopted by Robison, which was an explicit response to both modernization theory and the rise of dependency and world-system theories in the 1970s, ultimately deflected attention from the wider context in which the Indonesian nation-state or other nation-states in Asia emerged and were consolidated (or failed to be consolidated) following decolonization. As Meredith Woo-Cumings has noted, observers who assign a marginal role to "external considerations" and emphasize the importance of the state generally, and the developmental state more specifically, tend to focus on "a world of bureaucrats who, along with business leaders and politicians, pursue a 'national interest' that is assumed away in a realm devoid of world politics, the strategic goals of superpowers, the actions of multinational corporations, foreign aid, and so on".[43] In part as a reaction to this trend, there are now a growing number of writers (influenced by Marxism and world-system theory) who have adopted an explicitly regional approach to the history of capitalism in East Asia, while linking their analysis to global trends at the same time as they emphasize historical specificity.[44] An influential article by Bruce Cumings, which appeared in the 1980s in an edited collection by Frederic C. Deyo (*The Political Economy of the New Asian Industrialism*, 1987), drew attention to the regional character and significance of capitalist dynamism in East Asia. Cumings also emphasized the way in which economic growth and integration after 1945 was increasingly centered on Japan and the US–Japan alliance. He pointed to the way in which the Japanese colonial foundations, particularly in South Korea and Taiwan, interacted with the imperatives of the Cold War to produce what he called a bureaucratic-authoritarian industrializing regime (BAIR). In his analysis the US-led push to contain communism and secure a capitalist economic order in Asia during the Cold War increasingly combined with the resurgence of Japanese corporate activity in the region to provide the overall framework for the "Northeast Asian Political Economy".[45] By the late 1980s and 1990s, the overall approach popularized by Cumings had directly influenced, or was more indirectly reflected in, the work of a growing number of historians and political economists.[46] This trend also sometimes involved a critical reworking of Japanese economic ideas associated with the work of Akamatsu Kaname in the 1930s and 1940s and predicated on the "flying geese" (later reworked as "product cycles") that postulated the various colonies/nation-states of the region and beyond, following the lead (and/or leadership) of Western Europe, the US and Japan through successive stages of industrial development and technological transformation.[47]

The work of Mitchell Bernard reflects an avowedly Marxist strand within this wider effort to take a regional–global approach and to critically engage with the Japanese "flying geese" theory.[48] For Bernard, the Asian crisis and its aftermath need to be located in a broad regional and global perspective. The events of 1997–1998 did not just involve a financial crisis, but were also a "crisis of production and political regulation", which signalled the demise of the "export-oriented" dependent capitalist development that had emerged in a variety of historically specific ways in Asia during the Cold War. Bernard was particularly concerned to distinguish his approach from that taken by dependency theorists. He emphasized that, despite the importance of transnational influences, "dependent capitalist development" can only be understood with reference to the particular national "configuration of class forces and form of state". This specificity was, in his view, grounded in the localized character of "class struggles" and the processes whereby the "internal balance of social forces" conditioned the "production, appropriation and distribution of surplus in relation to the local ecological base". He argued, however, that this should not be understood as the "structural dependence" on a state in the core by a state on the periphery. For Bernard, the dependent element of the form of capitalism he was trying to conceptualize referred particularly to how the "state elites and the dominant classes or class fractions within states" retain and "reproduce their own social control through specific relationships with agents of transnational capital or with state elites in advanced capitalist countries". The national elites depend on technology, military assistance, financial support and investment, as well as "legitimating ideologies" provided by the "advanced capitalist countries"; however, they also "possess an autonomous local base of political and social power". This includes the "power to regulate the exploitation of local workers or peasants and the appropriation of local ecological assets to maintain levels of profit as well as levels of consumption, both in the advanced capitalist world and among local urban-based elites". Following this definition Bernard argues that the rise of dependent capitalism in East Asia after 1945 was grounded in the "confluence" of three related "processes": (a) "the particular forms of state and class configurations that emerged from de-colonisation"; (b) the onset of the Cold War in the region "which enmeshed the state elites" in anti-communist alliances with the United States; and (c) "the regionalisation of Japanese industrial capital in a manner that integrated fractions of local capital with their Japanese counterparts".[49]

This type of approach is fruitful but, despite its historical emphasis, Bernard like Robison (discussed earlier) conflates class analysis with historical analysis. They both represent class and state as universal categories that are the only salient axes of power. They also demonstrate that, while Marxism and radical political economy approaches challenge the naturalization of capitalism by liberal theory and neo-classical economics, they still routinize the nation-state. As a result of these methodological shortcomings these approaches, despite their claims to the contrary, do not draw out the historical particularity of capitalist integration and differentiation and the role of cultural change in that process against the backdrop of wider regional and global changes. By contrast, the work of anthropologists, such as Robert Hefner and the other contributors to *Market Cultures: Society and Morality in the New Asian Capitalisms* (1998), represents an effort to re-establish the importance of culture in the development of capitalism in Northeast and Southeast Asia. They avoid the reductionist cultural formulations that were in the ascendant prior to 1997, which will be discussed in chapter 6. They also attempt to skirt the pitfalls of the universalizing and ethnocentric descriptions and prescriptions associated with neo-classical economics and with those strands of political economy and history, exemplified by Robison and Bernard, that conceptualize capitalism in excessively unitary terms. They do this by reintroducing the concept of "embeddedness" to examine the different ways in which capitalism is domesticated to specific historical circumstances. The conceptualization of culture at the center of their approach is one that presents culture "in pluralistic and contingent terms, examining its history and social genesis, its dependency on different social carriers and its interaction with other forces in Asia's ongoing transformation". At the outset Hefner argues that:

"culture and social relations are intrinsic to politics and the economy, not free-standing social spheres".[50] At the same time, Hefner's analysis operates within a revised theory of modernization that still conceptualizes change as gradual and evolutionary. Furthermore, this approach, with its emphasis on pluralism, down-plays, or ignores, power relations and the role of the state in the wider process of capitalist development and also routinizes the nation as a unit of analysis. Michael Pinches, for example, has mapped out a more useful approach to the role of culture in the wider history of capitalism. He has argued for the need to "conceive of the relationship between" the discursive "sphere of symbols and meanings" and the material sphere as "a broadly dialectical one, whose path is historical and largely indeterminant". In this context he has emphasized that regardless of how "problematic" class relations and class differences "may be conceptually and analytically" they remain "fundamental to an understanding of the cultural construction" of the identities and subjectivities integral to the wider dynamics of capitalism in Asia and beyond.[51]

The transformation of Asia and the changing global order II

Asia and the development debate II: Eurocentrism and history

By the 1980s the growing academic interest in the role of culture in the capitalist transformation of Asia coincided with, and was in part a response to, the rise of vigorous forms of cultural nationalism and Pan Asianism. These rising cultural nationalisms and Pan Asian narratives explicitly sought to challenge the Eurocentrism and power of the "West". A number of prominent politicians and intellectuals in the region increasingly explained the rise of Asia in terms of cultural/national/racial characteristics and values that were distinct from and superior to the institutions and practices associated with what was often perceived as a decadent West.[52] These popular Asian narratives were complemented by a range of academic studies that also explained East Asia's industrial dynamism in terms of reductionist conceptions of Confucianism and Asian values.[53] These attempts were also more indirectly complemented by efforts to trace the limits or failure of national development in much of the rest of the world to the Eurocentrism of dominant economic and political discourses and/or of the nation-state system itself.[54] A particularly influential example of this approach is to be found in Arturo Escobar's 1995 study in which he argued that the dominant development discourse centered on North America and Western Europe, which emerged in the late 1940s and early 1950s, had less to do with development and more to do with "the exercise of power over the Third World". Escobar argued that both the post-1945 modernization project and the subsequent globalization project (although he did not use these terms) were "the last and failed attempt to complete the Enlightenment in Asia, Africa and Latin America".[55] Escobar drew particular attention to the way in which the idea and practice of development was consolidated after 1945 as part of the ongoing effort to manage the contradictions of capitalism in the Cold War era. At the same time, his overall approach to the development discourse completely failed to capture the broader historical changes of the post-1945 era and the relationship between these changes and changes to the dominant idea of development. In particular Escobar neglected the way in which the modern idea of development was consolidated as national development during the Cold War, and the way in which between the 1940s and the 1970s the nation-state became the universal unit of development. He also overlooked the shift, beginning in the 1970s, from state-mediated national development to globalization. Furthermore, and this is of particular relevance here, there is no discussion (or even acknowledgement) in his book of the rise of East Asia or the significance of the end of the Cold War. These shortcomings are all connected to the fact that, although Escobar acknowledged the imprecision of the term "the West", his analysis represented the West as an undifferentiated motor of a destructive modernity sweeping Latin America, Africa and Asia.[56]

In defense of the critical use of the term the West, writers such as Stuart Hall have emphasized that "the 'West' is an *historical*, not a geographical, construct". Hall argued that the usage of the term refers to the "effects of hegemonic representations of the Western self rather than its subjugated traditions".[57] However, usage of the term by its defenders and its challengers also serves to reinforce a reductionist conception of the West that obscures rather than clarifies what is at stake. For example, Ozay Mehmet, like Escobar, provides a unitary and a profoundly static conception of the Western idea of development when he argues that "central" to "Westernization is the idea of economic development as 'progress' determined according to the market forces of supply and demand which emerged in the West".[58] This conflates the dominant neo-liberal conception of development of the last twenty years with an immutable Western idea of development. This homogenizes the West as much as the most ardent proponent of Western civilization, and simplifies the complex processes whereby theories and practices that apparently originated in Western Europe have been increasingly universalized and domesticated in a wide range of different contexts around the world. Thus, while it is common, as with Mehmet and Escobar, to represent the dominant idea and practice of development as Western, instead of something more specific, such as "liberal", to do so is problematic for at least two reasons. First, while the central role of the West in the making of the contemporary global liberal order is beyond dispute, describing nation-states and social formations around the world as Westernized implies that the rest of the world has become, or is becoming, similar to the West when the process is actually a complex one of resistance and accommodation.[59] Second, economic, and political, liberalism is not the only element in the Western tradition. Authoritarianism, Fascism and state-socialism are "nonliberal", but clearly as central to the history of the West as the "liberal tradition".[60] As Mark Mazower has argued: it is comforting to believe that the apparent triumph of liberalism with the end of the Cold War "proves" that economic and political liberalism have "deep roots in Europe's soil", but the history of twentieth-century Europe "tells us otherwise".[61]

The nation-state increasingly emerged in the late-colonial and early Cold War era as the main vehicle for various efforts to challenge the power of the West; however, the idea and structure of the modern nation-state itself is grounded in Western European history and the universalization of the nation-state system after 1945 points to the ultimately illusory character of efforts to overcome Eurocentrism.[62] While nationalism emerged in the colonies as a reaction against colonialism, and even against Eurocentrism, colonialism provided the overall context for the rise of the new nation-states. This has meant that the possibility of the new nations of Asia, Africa, or the Middle East transcending their Eurocentric foundations is more circumscribed than has often been asserted.[63] This issue is addressed in the work of Akhil Gupta, who emphasizes that with decolonization it was assumed that national development involved the "mimicking" of the historical path of the former colonial powers. However, he also emphasizes that the "underdevelopment" that the state-guided national development projects were supposed to address was not simply a "structural location in the global community of nations", but also an important "form of identity in the postcolonial world". He argues that the post-1945 "apparatus of development" produced a "new mode of global governmentality" that formally arranged the world into a system of "equal nation-states", at the same time as it positioned the nation-states of the emergent Third World spatially on the "periphery" and temporally "behind" the First World. At the heart of Gupta's book is the argument that the dominant development discourse (that enshrined national development as the key to progress), and the wider global political economy in which it operates, are key elements in "the postcolonial condition". Furthermore, while the concept of the postcolonial is often deployed to signify the period immediately following formal decolonization, in his view, it is the "decline of the *order* of nation-states" even more than decolonization that represents a "fundamental shift that might justify the use of the 'post' as a temporal marker". While the globalization project will continue to reconfigure postcolonial subjectivities, the new forms of "global governmentality" (embodied by a growing array of international accords, treaties, and institutions) point, in his view, to a "deeper transformation in the order of nation-states that underlay colonialism". For Gupta this shift means that the notion of the "postcolonial" is a "more appropriate modifier to forms of identity, states of being, and modes of analysis than ever before".[64]

Gupta's analysis is insightful; however, there are major problems involved in deploying the notion of the postcolonial condition as a means of conceptualizing much, if not all, of the world in the late twentieth and early twenty-first centuries. First, in the immediate post-1945 period the new nation-state of India was central to the emergent idea of national development. It was also central to the rise of postcolonial theory, and post-1947 India's position as a paradigmatic developing and postcolonial nation-state has meant that it has become a normative model of the transition from colony to postcolonial nation-state. Postcolonial theory and the notion of a postcolonial condition do not fit quite as well with the history, and contemporary circumstances, of other parts of Asia.[65] Such an approach can obscure the different pre-colonial histories and the way they inter-acted with the differences in the timing and pace of colonial conquest. The important differences in the length of colonial rule, the differing degrees and forms of formal and informal rule and the pace and dynamics of decolonization all contribute to the specificity of the postcolonial experience. In South Korea, for example, there was a "direct handover" from Japanese colonialism to US hegemony, while North Korea entered the Soviet orbit simultaneously.[66] The timing and character of decolonization and the dynamics of the Cold War in Southeast Asia also varied.[67] More importantly still the relevance of the concept of the postcolonial condition, even in the case of India, has been weakened by the rise of the globalization project and the end of the Cold War. The world-historical changes of the last twenty-five years have dramatically altered the context in which the postcolonial critique of the rise and demise of national development operates. That is, with the ascendancy of the globalization project and the passing of the Cold War, the very terrain on which efforts to challenge Eurocentrism now operate has shifted so as to render problematic the idea that the present world-historical conjuncture can be conceptualized as postcolonial. Postcolonialism as a political-theoretical project, or series of projects, emerged in the 1970s from diverse origins. By the 1980s postcolonial theory increasingly provided the means for a thorough questioning and critique of the degree to which, and the way in which, nationalist ideas and practices generally, and state-guided national development projects more specifically, were implicated in, and reproduced knowledges and practices that were grounded in European history. In contrast to the 1980s, however, postcolonial theorists now operate on the terrain created by the partial displacement of an earlier anti-colonial nation-alism. At this juncture a point of diminishing returns has been reached. Postcolonial theory provided an important point of departure for examining the history of the transition from colonies to nation-states, but it is of less relevance when grappling with the changing post-Cold War order.[68]

Postcolonial theory emerged as a critique of the Enlightenment project gener-ally, and the failure of the national development projects between the 1940s and the 1970s more specifically; however, it has remained bounded by both those projects in important ways. Postcolonial theory often still implicitly accepts the framework of national politics established by the earlier national development projects. During the Cold War anti-liberalism and anti-capitalism were implicit in much postcolonial theory and political alternatives were regularly assumed to involve some form of socialism.[69] Thus, the postcolonial era is defined not only by the colonial legacy, but also by the Cold War and the rise and fall, after decol-onization, of the "great experiments with socialism" of the "Bandung Era" (1955–1975), which will be discussed in chapter 1. With the rise of the globaliza-tion project, the passing of the state-mediated national developmentalism of the Bandung Era, followed by the collapse of the international communist move-ment (centered in complex ways on the Soviet Union), "it is no longer clear what 'overcoming' Western power actually means".[70] Eurocentrism is embedded in the very fabric of the contemporary nation-state system and the global political economy of the post-Cold War era, and challenging it as part of a search for progressive alternatives to the US-led globalization project has lost much of its salience. The new and reconfigured national trajectories of the post-1945 era have emerged in a fashion that has meant they remain implicated in various forms of Eurocentrism that are embedded in the vicissitudes of the nation-state system and the changing global order. Individual and collective efforts to over-come Eurocentrism are contaminated from the outset.[71] For example, in the case of East Asia, although powerful Asian narratives deployed ideas about Confucian or Asian values to explain the industrialization of the region, these formulations were produced within a wider framework that immediately and always meant that its effort to generate what Arif Dirlik has called "alternative values to those of EuroAmerican origin" did not represent the triumph of Eastern values, but the successful "articulation" of East Asian cultures "into a capitalist narrative".[72] The view taken here is that the most problematic aspect of the dominant theories of progress is not their Eurocentrism, but the way in which they continue to assume an easy commensurability between the interests of national elites on the one hand and those of the majority of the peoples of the modern nation-states that have emerged in Asia and elsewhere on the other hand. For example, as Thongchai Winichakul has argued, the effort to address the long history of Eurocentrism and adopt a more culturally sensitive position by many "Western" observers and academics has often resulted in the accep-tance of "the established views of the Siamese elite as *the* legitimate discourse about Thailand".[73]

Power and progress I: the modernization project and the nation-state system

A key focus of this book is the way that the idea of development was universal-ized as national development against the backdrop of the establishment of the United Nations (UN), a major wave of decolonization in Asia and Africa, and rising US and Soviet power after 1945.[74] With the increasingly global reach of the nation-state system, the nation-state emerged as the central element in a new development discourse and a high modernist vision that targeted parts of the world (such as Asia and Africa) for national development and nation-building, where nation-states had often been non-existent prior to the Second World War.[75] The idea of national development and a concern with nation-building as an ostensibly capitalist endeavor was centered on what is being characterized here as the US-led modernization project. The content of national development and the main elements of the US-led modernization project were conditioned by a number of major trends that were specific to the period from the 1940s to the 1970s. To begin with, national development after 1945 increasingly involved the representation and promotion by the US and its allies of what were originally Western European and North American measures of, and approaches to, polit-ical, social and economic progress as increasingly universal solutions for large areas of the world that had previously been under direct colonial rule. Although, as we will see, many of these particular measures and approaches had their origins in the nineteenth and early twentieth centuries, a number of them were only consolidated in Western Europe and North America, along with parts of Latin America, Eastern Europe and Japan in the 1930s or even the 1940s. After 1945 these measures and approaches increasingly involved a universal emphasis, in theory, on the national economy and national industrialization, as well as agrarian reform and agrarian modernization within a national framework. As also already suggested, an absolutely crucial element was the privileging of the role of the state (or the government) in the management of economic development. In a wider sense, national development increasingly involved, again in theory, a "social democratic" (the term socialism was also widely used by governments still committed to some form of capitalism) emphasis on the provision of public education, health care and other public institutions to facilitate social advance and the incorporation of the majority of the population into the process of national development. More broadly, development and progress became central elements in national narratives and in the lexicon of national leaders around the world.[76]

This emphasis was also readily apparent, albeit in different ways, in the state-socialist versions of national development that emerged with the growing influence of the Soviet Union.[77] The new global order of the Cold War era (increasingly framed in terms of the First World, the Second World and the Third World) congealed around the universalization and stabilization of the pursuit of historically specific national development projects worldwide. Outside Europe and Latin America, not to mention a small number of nation-states in Asia, such as Japan and Thailand, new nations were generally created following existing colonial boundaries. Between the 1940s and the 1970s the Cold War, and the UN-centered system of nation-states, facilitated the construction or reconstruction of nation-states and national identities within a global framework that allowed for the dramatic addition of a range of new nations based on the former colonies.[78] This involved the simultaneous reconfiguration of imperial nation-states, such as Great Britain, France, Portugal, Holland and Belgium, as well as Japan and the United States, into nation-states shorn of most of their formal colonial possessions. Most importantly, the global spread of nationalism involved the universalization, in theory, of the idea of the equality of all nations and the equality of all citizens within all nations. The idea of nationhood carried with it a commitment, at least in the abstract, to democracy, human rights and universal suffrage. The UN Charter explicitly envisioned a global community of formally equal nation-states that were expected to observe the democratic sentiments expressed in that Charter, as well as a range of conventions on human rights. This assumption and the conflation of development with national development and the naturalization of the nation is encapsulated in the Declaration on the Right to Development passed by the United Nations General Assembly in the mid-1970s, at the very moment when the idea of development as some sort of state-guided national process had been universalized and was starting to be challenged. In 1976 the General Assembly resolved that all developing nations had the right to levels of material prosperity and consumption commensurate with that enjoyed in the developed nations.[79] However, regardless of the claims to liberty, freedom and democracy that accompanied the founding and consolidation of a growing number of nation-states after 1945, sovereignty continued to lie with the states rather than with the people who inhabited the modern nations. The diverse, and often profoundly flawed, versions of national development that had emerged and/or been consolidated after 1945 failed to live up to ideals of the UN vision or the expectations of their own citizens at the same time as they were increasingly challenged in the 1970s by the incipient globalization project.[80]

A key weakness of the dominant theories of progress is the way in which they uncritically took and continue to take the nation-state as the key unit of analysis. Between the 1940s and the 1970s an increasingly elaborate international framework for national development emerged. This framework assumed that nations could be treated as homogenous and natural units of a wider capitalist order and development planning by national governments could, should or would lead to outcomes beneficial to all. The routinization of the nation was reinforced by a great deal of social science work on development. Most social scientists took for granted that social boundaries were coterminous with the boundaries of nation-states. In political theory, globalization and the end of the Cold War has encouraged the problematization of the boundaries between national and international political space; however, more empirically oriented practitioners of political science, international relations and comparative politics have generally continued to accept the international and national as unproblematic foundations for their work. Meanwhile, the most pronounced contradiction may lie with the discipline of economics. While economic forces are widely agreed to be at the center of any effort to understand globalization, professional economists play virtually no significant role in seeking to critically theorize globalization.[81] A classic example of this is the influential study by Michael Porter, entitled *The Competitive Advantage of Nations* (1990).[82] A key text in the wider celebratory narrative on globalization, it conflates corporations with the citizenry of nation-states in which they are based and assumes that national economic growth benefits all citizens of the nation. While the emergence of the globalization project dramatically reconfigured the nation-state (and undermined the idea of national development that had been consolidated between the 1940s and the 1970s), economists such as Porter have continued to treat the nation-state as an unproblematic and routine unit of analysis.

Power and progress II: the globalization project and the nation-state system

The reorientation of US hegemony in the 1970s paved the way for the reconfiguration of the role of the state in the global political economy of the Cold War and challenged the idea of development as a state-guided national modernization project. The end of the Cold War further strengthened the worldwide trend from the project of national development (in its various capitalist and socialist forms) to what is being characterized here as the globalization project. With the end of the Cold War there has been a proliferation of studies of virtually every aspect of what is now widely termed globalization. There are now a wide range of theories and definitions of globalization. A great deal of the debate about globalization has focused on the relationship between globalization and the nation-state. Some commentators emphasize, for example, that the global order is being reconstituted. In this context, although the nation-state remains significant, they conclude that it may increasingly "lose out" to supra-national organizations and transnational corporations. From this perspective, "there is a shadow over the capacity of the nation-state to exercise autonomy" as the world economy becomes increasingly centered on private corporations.[83] Other commentators, particularly journalists and management consultants, have gone even further and anticipate the "end of the nation-state".[84] However, this type of analysis fails to emphasize sufficiently that the nation-state system is both being transformed by and playing a key role in the rise of the globalization project. Furthermore, this is a highly uneven, and unfinished process. As James H. Mittelman has argued, while globalization is often perceived "as a totalising or homogenising force" it involves an ongoing process of articulation "with local structures in diverse ways", often "accentuating" rather than "eroding" differences.[85]

In his polemic on "globalisation theory" (as distinct from "theories of globalisation") Justin Rosenberg has argued that some of the key academic proponents of globalization theory have exaggerated the extent of the changes in the past few decades and have become proponents of globalization rather than critical evaluators of it.[86] While this is no doubt the case for some of the theorists that he targets, such as Anthony Giddens, Rosenberg's own analysis neglects the complexities of the relationship between nation-states and the changing global order. Nevertheless, his critique of key proponents of "globalization theory" points to the way that globalization is best understood as a project. From this perspective a central element of the globalization project is its focus on the promotion of liberal economic policies and the reconfiguration of state-mediated national development efforts into neo-liberal states. Also central to the globalization project are the technological changes of the past few decades, which have under-girded the instantaneous character of a growing range of financial, economic, social, political and cultural "transactions". The globalization project, as conceptualized here, is centered on the US, but it is also being pursued at a wide range of sites by increasingly unaccountable transnationalized and overlapping elites.[87] The globalization project is linked, in particular, to the growing concentration of control over the global economy by a relatively small number of large oligopolistic transnational corporations that have emerged from merger-driven and technology-facilitated changes to the global political economy of the last few decades.[88] However, despite the increasingly oligopolistic character of global business operations the US-led globalization project is legitimated by, and promoted in the name of, a free enterprise and free trade vision of the global economy.[89]

The globalization project was erected on and increasingly mediated by a range of international institutions and in a global context centered on US power. Given the central role of the United States in the globalization project, the historian David Reynolds has suggested that globalization is not "the interpretive key to the last half-century", but merely "cold war victor's history conceptualized in a wider frame".[90] However, I wish to argue that beneath the post-Cold War triumphalism and the uncritical celebration of globalization there are important changes that can still be most usefully identified and understood, in a critical fashion, as the globalization project. The emergence and unfolding of the globalization project is very uneven. There have been a number of turning points and important moments of consolidation and crisis that have facilitated the emergence and reorientation of the US-led globalization project, as it is being defined and periodized here. My periodization, which situates the immediate origins of globalization in important changes in the 1970s, is meant to imply that globalization is one of the main, although not the only, interpretive keys to the last quarter-century, not the last half-century, regardless of the fact that it is also, on one level, "cold war victor's history conceptualized in a wider frame". As such a periodization suggests I also take issue with those historians and social scientists that move in the opposite direction and conflate globalization with the rise of capitalism and the expansion of Europe beginning in the early modern era.[91] Finally, I disagree with John Gray who has argued that: "globalisation", broadly defined, "dates back at least to the late nineteenth century, when transatlantic telegraph cables provided, for the first time, an instant link between markets in Europe and North America".[92]

The immediate origins of the globalization project should not be traced to the rise of capitalism in the early modern era, or to the late nineteenth century, or to the 1990s, but to a number of interconnected trends that became apparent in the 1970s and coincided with the effective universalization of the nation-state system by this period. This latter emphasis is important. In order for the concept of globalization to avoid being stretched by historians and other observers to refer to virtually any activity that involves crossing some sort of frontier or border, we need to locate it as a project that only emerges after the nation-state system has been universalized regardless of how far back its antecedents might reach. The rise of information technology in the 1970s, which was directly grounded in the military-oriented research and development of the Cold War, was a central trend in the emergent globalization project. The globalization project must also be traced directly to the modifications of the overall shape of the political economy of the Cold War by the administration of US president Richard Nixon (1969–1974). These modifications were linked to the US crisis of hegemony centered on the Vietnam War and involved the US rapprochement with China, détente with the USSR, the end of the Bretton Woods system and the waning of Fordism in North America, Western Europe, and to a lesser extent Japan in the 1970s. These shifts signalled the end of the high-modernist period of state-guided national development and paved the way for the elaboration and promotion of the US-led globalization project. A second major turning point, facilitating the deepening and clarification of the globalization project, was the installation of the Reagan administration (1981–1988) in the US and the election of the government of Margaret Thatcher in Great Britain (1979–1990). Their governments were profoundly influenced by, and major facilitators of, the rise of neo-liberalism. Washington and London played a key role in the onset of the New Cold War and the promotion of "structural adjustment" in Latin America, Africa and Asia in the wake of the Debt Crisis in the early 1980s. A third major turning point was the end of the Cold War. This led to the enthusiastic promotion of the globalization project by the Clinton administration (1993–2000) as part of the wider US economic boom. The promulgation of the North American Free Trade Agreement (NAFTA) in 1994 represented a key building block, or anchor, of the globalization project in this period. A central characteristic of the post-Cold War era, meanwhile, was the dwindling of systemic political and economic challengers to the globalization project. With the end of the Cold War the challenge of state-socialism (centered on the Soviet Union and its allies) passed into history.[93] The Asian crisis of the late 1990s represented another turning point for the globalization project, undermining the threat that was thought, by some observers, to be posed by the Japan-led developmental states of East Asia. In fact the Japanese national development project had been in serious decline since the end of the Cold War.[94] Of course, the growing economic and military significance of China in post-crisis Asia and the complexities of the United States–Japan–China triangle mean that the "battle for Asia" will continue.[95]

In world-historical terms, the present juncture is one in which, in many quarters, no serious systemic alternative to the US-led globalization project is regarded as necessary, nor does one currently exist. Of course, some observers hope that the European Union (EU) will emerge as a social democratic counter-weight to the United States.[96] Meanwhile, for a growing number of commentators and activists the very early stirrings of a progressive systemic challenge were discerned in the demonstrations and mobilizations (globalization-from-below) that followed in the wake of the "Battle for Seattle" at the World Trade Organization (WTO) meeting in October 1999.[97] However, this latter prospect was weakened by the September 11 2001 terrorist attacks on the World Trade Center and the Pentagon. The suicide attacks on the US by Al Qaeda led to a strengthening of the coercive capacities of many states around the world and greater support for the use of repression and the military against opponents which readily fell, or could be made to fall, under the general rubric of "terrorist". This combined with a new awareness in Washington and elsewhere of the security problems associated with globalization. However, although the US-centered economic boom over which Clinton presided has ended and September 11 has posed new challenges for proponents of the free market, the changes to the global configuration of financial and corporate power over the past thirty years mean that the US government will be unable and unwilling to engineer a reversal of the globalization project even as Washington increases its emphasis on security and the war on terrorism. In fact, the response has not been to close borders but to find new ways of making open borders more secure. For example, in the case of the massive movement of containers by ship, rail and road, around the world, the effort to improve surveillance of their content (at a time when only 2 percent of containers entering the United States were inspected) has focused on global solutions.[98] September 11 also appears to have crystallized a new concern about the unevenness of the way in which the benefits of globalization have been disbursed.[99] In the lead up to the UN conference on financing development, held in Monterrey, Mexico, in late March 2002, World Bank president, James Wolfensohn, reiterated his call for the US and other OECD nation-states to increase their foreign aid budgets by at least 50 percent.[100] The Bush administration surprised most observers when it announced at Monterrey that US foreign aid spending would in fact be increased by 50 percent within three years with the additional funds going to a new "Millennium Challenge Account". Although it garnered most of the publicity, the US announcement of a dramatic increase (from a very low base) in aid spending was exceeded by the European Union's pledge to increase European government spending on foreign aid from 0.33 percent on average to 0.39 percent of GNP.[101] At the same time, the increased emphasis on, and the direct use of, military power by the US and its allies in Afghanistan and Iraq has resulted, or will result in, the economic opening of polities that had resisted neo-liberal economic policies helping to destabilize rather than stabilize these crisis-ridden nation-states, regardless of how much foreign aid is disbursed. The momentum for globalization-from-below, meanwhile, may have been weakened in the short term by September 11 (and the dramatic rise of a global peace movement following the US-led invasion of Iraq underlines the short-term character of the set-back), but many of the organizations and individuals involved are asking the right questions and pointing in the right direction. A number of these movements are drawing attention to the fact that the nation-state has always had serious limitations as an instrument for universal liberation and progress and those limitations have become even more apparent in the past few decades in many parts of the world. The changes of the past twenty or thirty years have highlighted the need to reorient progressive politics in ways that directly address the serious constraints on national politics and/or the politics of the nation-state system. As the US-led globalization project has reoriented the nation-state system, and nation-states have shifted increasingly from a focus on national development to globalization, progressive responses are increasingly acting on this new global political terrain.

Conclusion: theories of progress and the nation-state system

At the center of this book is the question of relationship between the nation-state system and influential theories of progress. To this end this study provides a historically grounded examination of theories of development as they relate to the transformation of Asia from the 1940s to the 1990s against the backdrop of the changing global order. This involves a focus on the history of the universal-ization of the nation-state system in the context of decolonization and the Cold War. It looks closely at the central role of US foreign policy and wider geo-polit-ical struggles in changing approaches to development. It also seeks to come to grips with the relationship between academic and popular theories of develop-ment. Part I, which contains three chapters, begins with a historical overview of influential theories of progress and then turns to specific examinations of, partic-ularly, development economics and theories of modernization and nation-building, which emerged, and were revised, between the 1940s and 1970s. It assesses the links between these theories and US geo-political strategy in Asia. Part II, which contains four chapters, looks at the way in which, before the 1980s and then even more significantly in the post-Cold War era, the inter-play between geo-politics and development shifted. In this period development policies were changing their focus from state-mediated national development to globalization, at the same time as a dynamic new Asian industrialism attracted increasing interest and/or concern in North America and Western Europe. East Asia became a major site for the wider development debate in the 1980s and 1990s. This occurred against the backdrop of the end of the Cold War and the consolidation of the US-led globalization project. More specifically, chapter 4 explores the complex relationship between the globalization project and the nation-state system as part of a wider discussion of the debate about the role of the US in post-Cold War Asia and beyond. Chapter 5 looks at the way that neo-liberalism was promoted and revised in the 1980s and 1990s, with particular reference to Asia. Chapters 6 and 7 examine the main challenges to neo-liberal ideas and the globalization project in the form of cultural explanations (the New Asian Renaissance) and state-centered explanations (developmental state theory) for the East Asian Miracle. Finally, part III, which contains two chapters, provides an integrated history of the interplay between geo-politics and the prac-tice of development from 1947 to 1997 via an examination of global and regional history and specific national trajectories, especially Japan, South Korea, Indonesia and the People's Republic of China. Of particular importance to this section is the discussion of the relationship between the new regionalism and the changes to nation-states and to the nation-state system in the context of the rise of the globalization project, the end of the Cold War and the onset of the Asian crisis. The regional and global shifts of the past four or five years appear to be carrying Asia and the world into a new era very different from the world of only a decade ago, but we continue to live in the receding but still long shadow of the era of decolonization and the Cold War and it is this history that we examine in chapter 1.

Notes

1 The term the Cold War, which was first used on April 16 1947 in a speech by Bernard Baruch (a former adviser to President Franklin Delano Roosevelt), is gener-ally understood to refer to the period stretching from 1947 to the collapse of the state-socialist regimes in Eastern Europe in 1989 and/or the subsequent disintegra-

tion of the Soviet Union by 1991. The "Cold War Recognition Certificates", distributed by the US Department of Defense, date the start of the Cold War as September 2 1945 (the day Imperial Japan surrendered ending the Second World War in the Pacific) and its end as December 26 1991 (the first day of the Commonwealth of Independent States, the successor to the USSR).

2 Neo-liberalism is defined here as a fundamentalist version of classical liberalism. Classical liberalism is centered on a commitment to individualism, gradual political and social change, representative government, free trade, and the sanctity of private property and the market. Since the end of the eighteenth century, liberalism has been an overarching element of political, economic and intellectual life in Great Britain and North America. It shaped and was linked to the rise of the "Second" British empire in the nineteenth century and the emergence of the US as a great power by the end of the nineteenth century. Since the turn of the century, and particularly since 1945, liberalism has become an increasingly dominant force in the international political economy, reinforcing and informing US hegemony. Neo-liberalism, by contrast, is primarily associated with political and intellectual shifts from the 1970s onwards and is directly linked to the resurgence of neo-classical economics and the waning of Keynesianism. This definition is different from the way the term is generally used in the United States itself, where liberalism has come to be associated with the social democratic policies of successive US governments from the 1930s to the 1960s in general, and the Kennedy and Johnson administrations in particular. For example, H. W. Brands defines liberalism in the US context as being "premised on a prevailing confidence in the ability of government – preeminently the federal government – to accomplish substantial good on behalf of the American people" (H. W. Brands, *The Strange Death of American Liberalism*, New Haven: Yale University Press, 2001, p. viii; see also I. Wallerstein, *After Liberalism*, New York: New Press, 1995).

3 The notion of a US-led globalization project (and the idea of national development that it overlaid) will be defined in detail below. I build on Philip McMichael's idea of a globalization project and his notion of an earlier, post-1945 development project. See P. McMichael, *Development and Social Change: A Global Perspective*, 2nd edn, Thousand Oaks: Pine Forge Press, 2000, pp. 7, 17, 25–41, 43–76, 350, 354.

4 M. T. Berger, "The Nation-State and the Challenge of Global Capitalism" *Third World Quarterly: Journal of Emerging Areas* vol. 22, no. 6, 2001.

5 For example, see D. A. Baldwin, *Economic Development and American Foreign Policy 1943–1962*, Chicago: University of Chicago Press, 1966; I. L. Horowitz, ed., *The Rise and Fall of Project Camelot: Studies in the Relationship between Social Science and Practical Politics*, Cambridge, MA: MIT Press, 1967; R. A. Packenham, *Liberal America and the Third World: Political Development Ideas in Foreign Aid and Social Science*, Princeton: Princeton University Press, 1973; S. L. Baily, *The United States and the Development of South America 1945–1975*, New York: Franklin Watts, 1976; I. L. Gendzier, *Managing Political Change: Social Scientists and the Third World*, Boulder: Westview, 1985; D. Merrill, *Bread and the Ballot: The United States and India's Economic Development, 1947–1963*, Chapel Hill: University of North Carolina Press, 1990; M. T. Berger, *Under Northern Eyes: Latin American Studies and US Hegemony in the Americas 1898–1990*, Bloomington: Indiana University Press, 1995; M. E. Latham, *Modernization as Ideology: American Social Science and "Nation Building" in the Kennedy Era*, Chapel Hill: University of North Carolina Press, 2000; K. C. Pearce, *Rostow, Kennedy, and the Rhetoric of Foreign Aid*, East Lansing: Michigan State University Press, 2001; D. Engerman, ed., *Staging Growth: Modernization, Development and the Global Cold War*, Amherst: University of Massachusetts Press, 2003; N. Gilman, *Mandarins of the Future: Modernization Theory in Cold War America*, Baltimore: Johns Hopkins University Press, 2003. On the intersection between US diplomatic history and development studies see N. Cullather, "Development? Its History" *Diplomatic History* vol. 24, no. 4, 2000.

6 For example, see I. L. Horowitz, *Beyond Empire and Revolution: Militarization and Consolidation in the Third World*, New York: Oxford University Press, 1982; G. M. Meier and D. Seers, eds, *Pioneers in Development*, Oxford: Oxford University Press for the World Bank, 1984; G. Rosen, *Western Economists and Eastern Societies: Agents of Change in South Asia, 1950–1970*, Baltimore: Johns Hopkins University Press, 1985; H. W. Arndt, *Economic Development: The History of an Idea*, Chicago: University of Chicago Press, 1987; D. Hunt, *Economic Theories of Development: An Analysis of Competing Paradigms*, Brighton: Harvester Wheatsheaf, 1989; J. Larrain, *Theories of Development: Capitalism, Colonialism and Dependency*, London: Polity Press, 1989; B. Hettne, *Development Theory and the Three Worlds*, London: Longman, 1990; C. Ramirez-Faria, *The Origins of Economic Inequality Between Nations: A Critique of Western Theories of Development and Underdevelopment*, London: Unwin Hyman, 1991; W. W. Rostow, *Theories of Economic Growth From David Hume to the Present*, New York: Oxford University Press, 1992 (first published 1990); R. A. Packenham, *The Dependency Movement: Scholarship and Politics in Development Studies*, Cambridge, MA: Harvard University Press, 1992; D. B. Moore and G. J. Schmitz, eds, *Debating Development Discourse: Institutional and Popular Perspectives*, London: Macmillan, 1995; C. Leys, *The Rise and Fall of Development Theory*, Bloomington: Indiana University Press, 1996; M. P. Cowen and R. W. Shenton, *Doctrines of Development*, New York: Routledge 1996; J. L. Love, *Crafting the Third World: Theorizing Underdevelopment in Rumania and Brazil*, Stanford: Stanford University Press, 1996; F. Cooper and R. Packard, eds, *International Development and the Social Sciences: Essays on the History and Politics of Knowledge*, Berkeley: University of California Press, 1997; P. Cammack, *Capitalism and Democracy in the Third World: The Doctrine of Political Development*, London: Leicester University Press, 1997; J. Martinussen, *Society, State and Market: A Guide to Competing Theories of Development*, London: Zed Books, 1997; M. Woo-Cumings, ed., *The Developmental State*, Ithaca: Cornell University Press, 1999; W. Easterly, *The Elusive Quest for Growth: Economists' Adventures and Misadventures in the Tropics*, Cambridge, MA: MIT Press, 2001.

7 "Asia" generally refers to South Asia, Southeast Asia and Northeast Asia. East Asia, which is often used to mean Northeast Asia, will be used here to refer to Northeast and Southeast Asia. At times Asia will also be used to refer primarily to East Asia, in which case the meaning will be clear from the usage. The term Asia-Pacific will also be used at times. This latter term has only entered general usage in the post-Cold War era. It will be used here to refer primarily to East Asia, but it also implies the wider region covered by the Asia-Pacific Economic Cooperation forum (APEC).

8 A comprehensive examination of the Asian crisis and the debate it generated is beyond the scope of this book. At the same time, the Asian crisis can only be understood against the backdrop of the wider history and theories of development that are examined here. For a particularly systematic attempt to examine the post-Asian crisis debates see I. Islam and A. Chowdhury, *The Political Economy of East Asia: Post-Crisis Debates*, New York: Oxford University Press, 2000.

9 A. Goldstein, "Great Expectations: Interpreting China's Arrival" in M. E. Brown, O. R. Coté, Jr, S. M. Lynn-Jones and S. E. Miller, eds, *The Rise of China*, Cambridge, MA: MIT Press, 2000.

10 M. T. Berger and M. Beeson, "APEC, ASEAN+3 and American Power: The Limits of the New Regionalism in the Asia-Pacific" in M. Boas, M. Marchand and T. Shaw, eds, *The Political Economy of Regions and Regionalisms*, Basingstoke: Palgrave Macmillan, 2003.

11 M. Finnemore, "Redefining Development at the World Bank" in F. Cooper and R. Packard, eds, *International Development and the Social Sciences*, Berkeley: University of California Press, 1997.

12 D. Lal, *The Poverty of Development Economics*, Cambridge, MA: Harvard University Press, 1985 (first published 1983), p. 46.

13 J. M. Leger, "The Boom: How Asians Started the 'Pacific Century' Early" *Far Eastern Economic Review* November 24, 1994, pp. 43–9.

14 M. T. Berger and M. Beeson, "Lineages of Liberalism and Miracles of Modernisation: The World Bank, the East Asian Trajectory and the International Development Debate" *Third World Quarterly: Journal of Emerging Areas* vol. 19, no. 3, 1998.

15 R. Wade, "Japan, the World Bank, and the Art of Paradigm Maintenance: The East Asian Miracle in Political Perspective" *New Left Review (I)* no. 217, 1996, pp. 6–7.

16 John Williamson is often seen as the originator of the term "Washington Consensus". See especially, J. Williamson, "The Progress of Policy Reform in Latin America" in J. Williamson, ed., *Latin American Adjustment: How Much Has Happened?*, Washington, DC: Institute for International Economics, 1990, pp. 351–420.

17 Cited in B. Rich, *Mortgaging the Earth: The World Bank, Environmental Impoverishment and the Crisis of Development*, Boston: Beacon Press, 1994, pp. 22–3.

18 World Bank, *The East Asian Miracle: Economic Growth and Public Policy*, Oxford: Oxford University Press for the World Bank, 1993.

19 A. Amsden, "Why Isn't the Whole World Experimenting with the East Asian Model to Develop? Review of The East Asian Miracle" *World Development* vol. 22, no. 4, 1994.

20 World Bank *World Development Report: 1997 The State in a Changing World*, Oxford: Oxford University Press, 1997.

21 See, for example, C. Wolf, "Blame Government for the Asian Meltdown" *Asian Wall Street Journal* February 5, 1998; P. Woodall, "Frozen Miracle: A Survey of East Asian Economies" *The Economist* March 7, 1998.

22 P. Mirowski, "Doing What Comes Naturally: Four Metanarratives on What Metaphors Are For" in P. Mirowski, ed., *Natural Images in Economic Thought: "Markets Read in Tooth and Claw"*, Cambridge: Cambridge University Press, 1994. Also see G. M. Hodgson, *Economics and Evolution: Bringing Life Back into Economics*, Ann Arbor: University of Michigan Press, 1993; G. M. Hodgson, *How Economics Forgot History*, London: Routledge, 2001.

23 For an elaborate and explicit example of such an approach see E. B. Haas, *Nationalism, Liberalism and Progress: (Volume 1) The Rise and Decline of Nationalism*, Ithaca: Cornell University Press, 1997; E. B. Haas, *Nationalism, Liberalism and Progress: (Volume 2) The Dismal Fate of New Nations*, Ithaca: Cornell University Press, 2000.

24 For a book-length critique of romantic liberal readings of the rise of capitalism that focuses on the work and lives of the classical political economists see M. Perelman, *The Invention of Capitalism: Classical Political Economy and the Secret History of Primitive Accumulation*, Durham: Duke University Press, 2000.

25 A. Macfarlane, "The Cradle of Capitalism: The Case of England" in J. Baechler, J. A. Hall and M. Mann, eds, *Europe and the Rise of Capitalism*, 2nd edn, Oxford: Basil Blackwell, 1989, pp. 201–2. Also see A. Macfarlane, *The Origins of English Individualism: The Family, Property and Social Transition*, Oxford: Blackwell, 1978; A. Macfarlane, *The Culture of Capitalism*, Oxford: Blackwell, 1987; A. Macfarlane, *The Riddle of the Modern World: Of Liberty, Wealth and Equality*, Basingstoke: Palgrave, 2001. For related approaches see T. Bethell, *The Noblest Triumph: Property and Prosperity Through the Ages*, New York: St Martin's Press, 1998; E. L. Jones, *The European Miracle: Environments, Economies and Geopolitics in the History of Europe and Asia*, 2nd edn, Cambridge: Cambridge University Press, 1992; D. Lal, *Unintended Consequences: The Impact of Factor Endowments, Culture and Politics in Long-Run Economic Performance*, Cambridge, MA: MIT Press, 1998; D. S. Landes, *The Unbound Prometheus: Technological Change and Industrial Development in Western Europe from 1750 to the Present*, Cambridge: Cambridge University Press, 1969; D. S. Landes, *The Wealth and Poverty of Nations: Why Some Are So Rich and Some So Poor*, New York: W. W. Norton, 1998; J. Mokyr, *The Lever of Riches: Technological Creativity and Economic Progress*, New York:

Oxford University Press, 1990; D. C. North and R. Paul, *The Rise of the Western World: A New Economic History*, Cambridge: Cambridge University Press, 1973; D. C. North, *Understanding the Process of Economic Change*, London: Institute of Economic Affairs, 1999; J. P. Powelson, *Centuries of Economic Endeavor: Parallel Paths in Japan and Europe and Their Contrast with the Third World*, Ann Arbor: University of Michigan Press, 1994; N. Rosenberg and L. E. Birdzell, Jr, *How the West Grew Rich: The Economic Transformation of the Industrial World*, New York: Basic Books, 1986; D. Yergin and J. Stanislaw, *The Commanding Heights: The Battle between Government and the Marketplace that is Remaking the Modern World*, New York: Simon and Schuster, 1998.

26 T. Ertman, *Birth of the Leviathan: Building States and Regimes in Medieval and Early Modern Europe*, Cambridge: Cambridge University Press, 1997.

27 R. B. Hall, *National Collective Identity: Social Constructs and International Systems*, Columbia, 1999, p. 6.

28 For a good overview of the ongoing debate about, and the wider significance of, the industrial revolution in England see J. E. Inikori, *Africans and the Industrial Revolution in England: A Study in International Trade and Economic Development*, Cambridge: Cambridge University Press, 2002, pp. 89–155.

29 D. B. Abernethy, *The Dynamics of Global Dominance: European Overseas Empires 1415–1980*, New Haven: Yale University Press, 2000, pp. 45–63, 81–103.

30 Britain increased its colonial holdings by some 4 million square miles, France by 3.5 million square miles, while Germany acquired a little more than 1 million square miles and Belgium and Italy just under 1 million each. The United States acquired some 100,000 square miles, mainly from Spain, while Japan acquired something like the same amount from China, Russia and Korea. Portugal expanded its colonies by about 300,000 square miles. Of the major colonial empires, the Dutch were the only ones who failed to, or refused to, acquire new territory, although they did consolidate control over those parts of the Netherlands East Indies which they had long controlled in a more indirect way. E. Hobsbawm, *The Age of Empire 1875–1914*, London: Abacus, 1994 (first published 1987), pp. 61–2.

31 M. Mazower, *Dark Continent: Europe's Twentieth Century*, London: Allen Lane, 1998, p. 184; P. Kennedy, *The Rise and Fall of the Great Powers: Economic Change and Military Conflict 1500 to 2000*, 2nd edn, London: Fontana Press, 1989, pp. 39–93, 149–80.

32 P. Darby, *Three Faces of Imperialism: British and American Approaches to Asia and Africa 1870–1970*, New Haven: Yale University Press, 1987, pp. 106–17, 132–40.

33 K. Marx and F. Engels, *The Communist Manifesto*, New York: Penguin, 1986 (this translation first published 1888), p. 84.

34 K. Polanyi, *The Great Transformation*, Boston: Beacon Press, 1944; B. Moore, Jr, *Social Origins of Dictatorship and Democracy: Lord and Peasant in the Making of the Modern World*, Boston: Beacon Press, 1966.

35 P. Anderson, *Lineages of the Absolutist State*, London: New Left Books, 1974; P. Anderson, *The Origins of Postmodernity*, London: Verso, 1998; G. Arrighi, *The Long Twentieth Century: Money, Power, and the Origins of Our Times*, London: Verso, 1994; F. Braudel, *Civilization and Capitalism 15th–18th Century: Volume One, The Structures of Everyday Life*, New York: Harper and Row, 1981; F. Braudel, *Civilization and Capitalism 15th–18th Century: Volume Two, The Wheels of Commerce*, New York: Harper and Row, 1982; F. Braudel, *Civilization and Capitalism 15th–18th Century: Volume Three, The Perspective of the World*, New York: Harper and Row, 1984; R. Brenner, "Agrarian Class Structure and Economic Development in Pre-Industrial Europe" in T. H. Aston and C. H. E. Philpin, eds, *The Brenner Debate: Agrarian Class Structure and Economic Development in Pre-Industrial Europe*, Cambridge: Cambridge University Press, 1987; T. J. Byres, "The Agrarian Question and Differing Forms of Capitalist Agrarian Transitions: An Essay with Reference to Asia" in Jan Breman and Sudipto Mundle, eds, *Rural Transformation in Asia*, New Delhi: Oxford University Press, 1991; R. W. Cox, *Power, Production and World Order: Social Forces in the Making of History*, New

York: Columbia University Press, 1987; H. Gates, *China's Motor: A Thousand Years of Petty Capitalism*, Ithaca: Cornell University Press, 1996; M. Mann, *The Sources of Social Power Volume I: A History of Power from the Beginning to A.D. 1760*, Cambridge: Cambridge University Press, 1986; M. Mann, *The Sources of Social Power Volume II: The Rise of Classes and Nation-States, 1760–1914*, Cambridge: Cambridge University Press, 1993; J. M. Paige, *Agrarian Revolution: Social Movements and Export Agriculture in the Underdeveloped World*, New York: Free Press, 1978; J. M. Paige, *Coffee and Power: Revolution and the Rise of Democracy in Central America*, Cambridge, MA: Harvard University Press, 1997; D. Rueschemeyer, E. H. Stephens and J. D. Stephens, *Capitalist Development and Democracy*, Chicago: University of Chicago Press, 1992; I. Wallerstein, *The Modern World-System – I: Capitalist Agriculture and the Origins of the European World-Economy in the Sixteenth Century*, New York: Academic Press, 1974; I. Wallerstein, *The Modern World-System – II: Mercantilism and the Consolidation of the European World-Economy 1600–1750*, New York: Academic Press, 1980; I. Wallerstein, *The Modern World-System – III: The Second Era of Great Expansion of the Capitalist World-Economy 1730–1840s*, San Diego: Academic Press, 1989; I. Wallerstein, *Historical Capitalism with Capitalist Civilization*, London: Verso, 1995; E. Wolf, *Europe and the Peoples Without History*, Berkeley: University of California Press, 1982; E. Meiksins Wood, *The Pristine Culture of Capitalism*, London: Verso, 1991; E. Meiksins Wood, *The Origin of Capitalism: A Longer View*, London: Verso, 2002.

36 M. Hardt and A. Negri, *Empire*, Cambridge, MA: Harvard University Press, 2000, pp. 70, 74–8.

37 N. Poulantzas, *Political Power and Social Classes*, London: Verso, 1973 (first published in French in 1968 as *Pouvoir politique et classes sociales*); R. Miliband, *The State in Capitalist Society*, London: Weidenfeld and Nicolson, 1969. For a critical review of theories of the capitalist state see B. Jessop, *State Theory: Putting Capitalist States in Their Place*, University Park: Pennsylvania University Press, 1990; B. Jessop, *The Future of the Capitalist State*, Cambridge: Cambridge University Press, 2003.

38 For example, see R. Mortimer, *Showcase State: The Illusion of Indonesia's 'Accelerated Modernisation'*, Sydney: Angus and Robertson, 1973; G. Rodan, *The Political Economy of Singapore's Industrialization*, London: Macmillan, 1989; K. Hewison, *Bankers and Bureaucrats: Capital and the Role of the State in Thailand*, New Haven: Yale University Press, 1989. For an overview in relation to Southeast Asia, see R. Higgott and R. Robison, "Theories of Development and Underdevelopment: Implications for the Study of Southeast Asia" in R. Higgott and R. Robison, eds, *Southeast Asia: Essays in the Political Economy of Structural Change*, London: Routledge and Kegan Paul, 1985. For an African-oriented overview, see J.-F. Bayart, *The State in Africa: The Politics of the Belly*, London: Longman, 1993 (first published in 1989 in French as *L'Etat en Afrique*).

39 R. Robison, *Indonesia: The Rise of Capital*, Sydney: Allen and Unwin, 1986, pp. 117–26.

40 R. Robison, "Indonesia: Tensions in State and Regime" in K. Hewison, R. Robison and G. Rodan, eds, *Southeast Asia in the 1990s: Authoritarianism, Democracy and Capitalism*, Sydney: Allen and Unwin, 1993, pp. 41–3, 45, 49, 70–2. Also see R. Robison, "Indonesia: Crisis, Oligarchy and Reform" in G. Rodan, K. Hewison and R. Robison, eds, *The Political Economy of South-East Asia: Conflicts, Crises and Change*, 2nd edn, New York: Oxford University Press, 2001.

41 P. McMichael, "Rethinking Comparative Analysis in a Post-Develolpmentalist Context" *International Social Science Journal* no. 133, 1992.

42 Some important steps toward problematizing the nation-state as a unit of analysis are apparent in Jeffrey Winters' work on Indonesia. He rejects conventional categories of foreign and domestic capital (international and national) in favor of an approach that focuses on the structural power of capital in terms of its relative mobility rather than its nationality. J. A. Winters, *Power in Motion: Capital Mobility and the Indonesian State*, Ithaca: Cornell University Press, 1996.

43 M. Woo-Cumings, "The Political Economy of Growth in East Asia: A Perspective on the State, Market, and Ideology" in M. Aoki, H.-K. Kim and M. Okuno-Fujiwara, eds, *The Role of Government in East Asian Economic Development: Comparative Institutional Analysis*, New York: Oxford University Press, 1997, p. 333.

44 For an early example of such an approach, that focuses on the period prior to the First World War, see F. V. Moulder, *Japan, China and the Modern World Economy: Toward a Reinterpretation of East Asian Development ca. 1600 to ca. 1918*, 2nd edn, Cambridge: Cambridge University Press, 1979. Also see J. Abu-Lughod, *Before European Hegemony: The World System A.D. 1250–1350*, New York: Oxford University Press, 1989. Abu-Lughod's approach challenged the retrospective periodization that overlooked the way in which the transition to capitalism in Western Europe may have been linked to earlier commercial connections to a pre-modern world-system centered on China. She also emphasized that if one went back far enough the Chinese-centered world-system appeared to have as much, if not more, potential for outward and even global expansion than the emerging commercial networks and state-system of Western Europe. These overall concerns have been revived in an important new effort to frame and debate contemporary change and development in East Asia not only in terms of the colonial and Cold War era, but in terms of the much longer history of the region and the world economy. See R. B. Wong, *China Transformed: Historical Change and the Limits of European Experience*, Ithaca: Cornell University Press, 1997; A. G. Frank, *ReOrient: Global Economy in the Asian Age*, Berkeley: University of California Press, 1998; K. Pomeranz, *The Great Divergence: China, Europe and the Making of the Modern World Economy*, Princeton: Princeton University Press, 2001; G. Arrighi, T. Hamashita and M. Selden, *The Resurgence of East Asia: 500, 150 and 50 Year Perspectives*, London: RoutledgeCurzon, 2003. On this debate see G. Stokes, "The Fate of Human Societies: A Review of Recent Macrohistories" *The American Historical Review* vol. 106, no. 2, 2001.

45 B. Cumings, "The Origins and Development of the Northeast Asian Political Economy: Industrial Sectors, Product Cycles and Political Consequences" *International Organization* vol. 38, no. 1, 1984 (reprinted in F. C. Deyo, ed., *The Political Economy of the New Asian Industrialism*, Ithaca: Cornell University Press, 1987). Also see B. Cumings, "Japan in the World-System" in A. Gordon, ed., *Post-War Japan as History*, Berkeley: University of California Press, 1993; B. Cumings, "Japan and Northeast Asia into the Twenty-First Century" in P. J. Katzenstein and T. Shiraishi, eds, *Network Power: Japan and Asia*, Ithaca: Cornell University Press, 1997.

46 U. Menzel, "The Newly Industrialising Countries of East Asia: Imperialist Continuity or a Case of Catching Up?" in W. J. Mommsen and J. Osterhammel, eds, *Imperialism and After: Continuities and Discontinuities*, London: Allen and Unwin, 1986; F. C. Deyo, *Beneath the Miracle: Labor Subordination in the New Asian Industrialism*, Berkeley: University of California Press, 1989; R. Steven, *Japan's New Imperialism*, Armonk: M. E. Sharpe, 1990; G. Arrighi, S. Ikeda and A. Irwan, "The Rise of East Asia: One Miracle or Many?" in R. A. Palat, ed., *Pacific-Asia and the Future of the World-System*, Westport: Greenwood Press, 1993; B. Gills, "The Hegemonic Transition in East Asia: A Historical Perspective" in S. Gill, ed., *Gramsci, Historical Materialism and International Relations*, Cambridge: Cambridge University Press, 1993; R. Stubbs, "The Political Economy of the Asia-Pacific Region" in R. Stubbs and G. R. D. Underhill, eds, *Political Economy and the Changing Global Order*, London: Macmillan, 1994; A. Y. So and S. W. K. Chiu, *East Asia and the World Economy*, Thousand Oaks: Sage, 1995; R. A. Palat, "Pacific Century: Myth or Reality?" *Theory and Society* vol. 25, no. 3, 1996; W. Hatch and K. Yamamura, *Asia in Japan's Embrace: Building a Regional Production Alliance*, Cambridge: Cambridge University Press, 1996; M. Selden, "China, Japan, and the Regional Political Economy of East Asia, 1945–1995" in P. J. Katzenstein and T. Shiraishi, eds, *Network Power: Japan and Asia*, Ithaca: Cornell University Press, 1997; M. T. Berger and D. A.

Borer, "Introduction: The Rise of East Asia: Critical Visions of the Pacific Century" in M. T. Berger and D. A. Borer, eds, *The Rise of East Asia: Critical Visions of the Pacific Century*, London: Routledge, 1997; B. Anderson, *The Spectre of Comparison: Nationalism, Southeast Asia and the World*, London: Verso, 1998; R. Stubbs, "War and Economic Development: Export-Oriented Industrialization in East and Southeast Asia" *Comparative Politics* vol. 31, no. 3, 1999; T. J. Pempel, "Regional Ups, Regional Downs" in T. J. Pempel, ed., *The Politics of the Asian Economic Crisis*, Ithaca: Cornell University Press, 1999; M. T. Berger, "Bringing History Back In: The Making and Unmaking of the East Asian Miracle" *Internationale Politik Und Gesellschaft* no. 3, 1999; M. T. Berger, "Battering Down the Chinese Walls: The Antinomies of Anglo-American Liberalism and the History of East Asian Capitalism in the Shadow of the Cold War" in C. J. W.-L. Wee, ed., *Local Cultures and the "New Asia": The State, Culture and Capitalism in Southeast Asia*, Singapore: Institute of Southeast Asian Studies, 2002; D. Kelly, *Japan and the Reconstruction of East Asia*, Basingstoke: Palgrave, 2002; G. Arrighi, "The Rise of East Asia and the Withering Away of the Interstate System" in C. Bartolovich and N. Lazarus, eds, *Marxism, Modernity and Postcolonial Studies*, Cambridge: Cambridge University Press, 2002.

47 M. Bernard and J. Ravenhill, "Beyond Product Cycles and Flying Geese: Regionalisation, Hierarchy and the Industrialisation of East Asia" *World Politics* vol. 47, no. 1, 1995. In fact, the idea of the developmental state is also traced to the "flying geese" theory, the formulation of which in the 1930s coincided with increased interest in Japan and (Germany) in the work of Friedrich List. P. Korhonen, "The Theory of the Flying Geese Pattern of Development and Its Interpretations" *Journal of Peace Research* vol. 31, no. 1, 1994. Also see E. Terry, *How Asia Got Rich: Japan, China and the Asian Miracle*, Armonk: M. E. Sharpe, 2002, pp. 46–101.

48 M. Bernard, "States, Social Forces, Regions and Historical Time in the Industrialization of Eastern Asia" *Third World Quarterly: Journal of Emerging Areas* vol. 17, no. 4, 1996.

49 M. Bernard, "East Asia's Tumbling Dominoes: Financial Crises and the Myth of the Regional Model" in L. Panitch and C. Leys, eds, *Socialist Register 1999: Global Capitalism Versus Democracy*, New York: Monthly Review Press, 1999, pp. 178, 181–2, 184.

50 R. W. Hefner, "Introduction: Society and Morality in the New Asian Capitalisms" in R. W. Hefner, ed., *Market Cultures: Society and Morality in the New Asian Capitalisms*, Boulder: Westview, 1998, pp. 2–5.

51 M. Pinches, "Cultural Relations, Class and the New Rich in Asia" in M. Pinches, ed., *Culture and Privilege in Capitalist Asia*, London: Routledge, 1999, pp. 2–5. Also see, C. J. W.-L. Wee, "Introduction: Local Cultures, Economic Development and Southeast Asia" in C. J. W.-L. Wee, ed., *Local Cultures and the "New Asia": The State, Culture and Capitalism in Southeast Asia*, Singapore: Institute of Southeast Asian Studies, 2002.

52 M. T. Berger, "Yellow Mythologies: The East Asian Miracle and Post-Cold War Capitalism" *positions: east asia cultures critique* vol. 4, no. 1, 1996.

53 S. Yao, *Confucian Capitalism: Discourse, Practice and the Myth of Chinese Enterprise*, London: Routledge 2002.

54 For example, see S. Latouche, *The Westernization of the World: The Significance, Scope and Limits of the Drive towards Global Uniformity*, Cambridge: Polity Press, 1996; G. Rist *The History of Development: From Western Origins to Global Faith*, London: Zed Books, 1997; V. Tucker, "The Myth of Development: A Critique of a Eurocentric Discourse" in R. Munck and D. O'Hearn, eds, *Critical Development: Contributions to a New Paradigm*, London: Zed Books, 1999; B. Badie, *The Imported State: The Westernization of the Political Order*, Stanford: Stanford University Press, 2000.

55 A. Escobar, *Encountering Development: The Making and Unmaking of the Third World*, Princeton: Princeton University Press, 1995, pp. 3–4, 9–12, 21–2, 221, 224.

56 For a critique of Escobar see M. T. Berger, "Post-Cold War Capitalism: Modernization and Modes of Resistance After the Fall" *Third World Quarterly: Journal of Emerging Areas* vol. 16, no. 4, 1995.

57 S. Hall, "The West and the Rest: Discourse and Power" in S. Hall and B. Gieben, eds, *Formations of Modernity*, Milton Keynes: Open University Press, 1992, pp. 276–8.

58 O. Mehmet, *Westernizing the Third World: The Eurocentricity of Economic Development Theories*, 2nd edn, London: Routledge, 1999, p. 2.

59 A. Appadurai, *Modernity at Large: Cultural Dimensions of Globalization*, Minneapolis: University of Minnesota Press, 1996.

60 R. Latham, *The Liberal Moment: Modernity, Security and the Making of Postwar International Order*, New York: Columbia University Press, 1997, pp. 16–17.

61 M. Mazower, *Dark Continent: Europe's Twentieth Century*, London: Allen Lane, 1998, p. 3.

62 A. Dirlik, *After the Revolution: Waking to Global Capitalism*, London: Wesleyan University Press, 1994, pp. 51–2, 96–7.

63 M. T. Berger, "Southeast Asian Trajectories: Eurocentrism and the History of the Modern Nation-State" *Bulletin of Concerned Asian Scholars* vol. 28, nos. 3–4, 1996.

64 A. Gupta, *Postcolonial Developments: Agriculture in the Making of Modern India*, Durham: Duke University Press, 1998, pp. 9–14, 22–4, 39–42, 338–9.

65 J. Goss, "Postcolonialism: Subverting Whose Empire?" *Third World Quarterly: Journal of Emerging Areas* vol. 17, no. 2, 1996.

66 K.-H. Chen, "America in East Asia" *New Left Review (II)* no. 12, 2001, pp. 81–3.

67 While Thailand was never formally colonized, it increasingly fell under British influence and more briefly under Japanese influence in the first half of the twentieth century, and with the end of the Second World War it became an important client/ally of the United States. The Philippines meanwhile, emerged as an independent polity in 1946, but the influence of its former colonizer, the US, remained particularly marked. The dynamics of decolonization in erstwhile French Indochina were soon deeply enmeshed with the Cold War and the French defeat and departure in 1954 was followed by the former colony becoming a key battleground of the Cold War. In the Malay Peninsula a major anti-communist counter-insurgency effort preceded independence by almost a decade, and continued into the independence period. Meanwhile, in the sprawling Dutch-ruled archipelago that became Indonesia, independence flowed from a lengthy military struggle between 1945 and 1949, while Indonesian politics were directly implicated in the Cold War by the late 1940s. M. T. Berger, "Decolonizing Southeast Asia: Nationalism, Revolution and the Cold War" in M. Beeson, ed., *Contemporary Southeast Asia: Regional Dynamics, National Differences*, Basingstoke: Palgrave Macmillan, 2003.

68 Hardt and Negri, *Empire*, pp. 137–9, 143–6.

69 For a recent, and particularly thorough overview that emphasizes the Marxist roots of postcolonialism generally see R. J. C. Young, *Postcolonialism: An Historical Introduction*, Oxford: Blackwell, 2001.

70 D. Scott, *Refashioning Futures: Criticism After Postcoloniality*, Princeton: Princeton University Press, 1999, pp. 12–15, 143–4, 221–4.

71 Dipesh Chakrabarty has argued that challenging Eurocentrism "cannot ever be a project of shunning European thought. For at the end of European imperialism, European thought is a gift to us all." D. Chakrabarty, *Provincializing Europe: Postcolonial Thought and Historical Difference*, Princeton: Princeton University Press, 2000, p. 255.

72 Dirlik, *After the Revolution*, pp. 51–2, 74. Also see L. Ching, "Globalizing the Regional, Regionalizing the Global: Mass Culture and Asianism in the Age of Late Capital" *Public Culture* vol. 12, no. 1, 2000, p. 236.

73 T. Winichakul, *Siam Mapped: A History of the Geo-Body of A Nation*, Honolulu: University of Hawaii Press, 1994, p. 7.

74 For recent analyses that emphasize the important and ideologically transformative character of decolonization and the universalization of the nation-state system, see J. D. Kelly and M. Kaplan, *Represented Communities: Fiji and World Decolonization*, Chicago: University of Chicago Press, 2001, pp. 1–26; D. Philpott, *Revolutions in Sovereignty: How Ideas Shaped Modern International Relations*, Princeton: Princeton University Press, 2001, pp. 151–250; R. H. Wiebe, *Who We Are: A History of Popular Nationalism*, Princeton: Princeton University Press, 2002, pp. 127–210.

75 The term high modernism is used here, following David Harvey, to refer particularly to the period running from around 1945 to the 1960s. D. Harvey, *The Condition of Postmodernity: An Enquiry into the Origins of Cultural Change*, London: Basil Blackwell, 1989, p. 35. For a much broader usage see J. C. Scott, *Seeing Like A State: How Certain Schemes to Improve the Human Condition Have Failed*, New Haven: Yale University Press, 1998, pp. 87–90, 377.

76 B. Jessop, "Narrating the Future of the National Economy and the National State: Remarks on Remapping Regulation and Reinventing Governance" in G. Steinmetz, ed., *State/Culture: State-Formation after the Cultural Turn*, Ithaca: Cornell University Press, 1999, pp. 380–4; D. Coates, *Models of Capitalism: Growth and Stagnation in the Modern Era*, Cambridge: Polity Press, 2000.

77 N. P. Halpern, "Creating Socialist Economies: Stalinist Political Economy and the Impact of Ideas" in J. Goldstein and R. O. Keohane, eds, *Ideas and Foreign Policy: Beliefs, Institutions and Political Change*, Ithaca: Cornell University Press, 1993.

78 F. Ansprenger, *The Dissolution of the Colonial Empires*, London: Routledge, 1989; M. E. Chamberlain, *Decolonization: The Fall of the European Empires*, 2nd edn, Oxford: Blackwell, 1999 (first published 1985).

79 United Nations, *Declaration on the Right to Development* (Resolution 41/128 of the United Nations General Assembly, 1976). Also see O. De Rivero, *The Myth of Development: The Non-Viable Economies of the 21st Century*, London: Zed Books, 2001, pp. 113–14.

80 M. T. Berger, "The Rise and Demise of National Development and the Origins of Post-Cold War Capitalism" *Millennium: Journal of International Studies* vol. 30, no. 2, 2001.

81 M. Shaw, *Theory of the Global State: Globality as an Unfinished Revolution*, Cambridge: Cambridge University Press, 2000, pp. 68–9, 72–3, 75.

82 M. Porter, *The Competitive Advantage of Nations*, London: Macmillan, 1990.

83 M. Schudson, "Culture and the Integration of National Societies" *International Social Science Journal* no. 139, 1994, pp. 77–8.

84 M. Horsman and A. Marshall, *After the Nation-State: Citizens, Tribalism and the New World Disorder*, London: HarperCollins, 1994; K. Ohmae, *The End of the Nation-State: The Rise of Regional Economies*, London: HarperCollins, 1995.

85 J. H. Mittelman, "The Globalization Challenge: Surviving at the Margins" *Third World Quarterly: Journal of Emerging Areas* vol. 15, no. 3, 1994, p. 428. Also see J. H. Mittelman, *The Globalization Syndrome: Transformation and Resistance*, Princeton: Princeton University Press, 2000.

86 J. Rosenberg, *The Follies of Globalisation Theory: Polemical Essays*, London: Verso, 2000.

87 L. Sklair, *The Transnational Capitalist Class*, Oxford: Blackwell, 2001.

88 S. Gill, *Power and Resistance in the New World Order*, Basingstoke: Palgrave Macmillan, 2003, pp. 116–42.

89 McMichael, *Development and Social Change*, pp. 350, 354.

90 D. Reynolds, *One World Divisible: A Global History since 1945*, New York: W. W. Norton, 2000, pp. 3–4.

91 There are numerous studies that do this. For example, see G. Raudzens, *Empires: Europe and Globalization 1492–1788*, Gloucestershire: Sutton, 1999.

92 Gray also argues that: "the global free market is a political project that is not much more than a decade old". And, for Gray, September 11 has precipitated the

subordination of "market forces" to the "imperatives of war and politics". J. Gray, "The Decay of the Free Market" *New Statesman* March 25, 2002, p. 25. Also see J. Gray, "Goodbye to Globalisation" *The Guardian Weekly* March 14, 2001, p. 13; J. Gray, *False Dawn: The Delusions of Global Capitalism*, 2nd edn, New York: New Press, 2000.

93 J. P. Arnason, *The Future That Failed: Origins and Destinies of the Soviet Model*, London: Routledge, 1993.

94 W. W. Grimes, *Unmaking the Japanese Miracle: Macroeconomic Politics, 1985–2000*, Ithaca: Cornell University Press, 2001.

95 M. Beeson and M. T. Berger, "The Paradoxes of Paramountcy: Regional Rivalries and the Dynamics of US Hegemony in East Asia" *Global Change, Peace & Security* vol. 15. no. 1, 2003.

96 W. Hutton, *The World We're In*, Boston: Little Brown, 2002.

97 W. K. Tabb, *The Amoral Elephant: Globalization and the Struggle for Social Justice in the Twenty-First Century*, New York: Monthly Review Press, 2001.

98 "When Trade and Security Clash" *The Economist* April 6, 2002, pp. 73–5.

99 In the wake of September 11, for example, former US president Bill Clinton has repeatedly pointed to the need to "close the gap between rich and poor" in order to "defeat global terrorism". For example, see B. Clinton, "World Without Walls: How Do We Defeat Global Terrorism?" *The Guardian (Saturday Review)* January 26, 2002, pp. 1–2.

100 "Help in the Right Places" *The Economist* March 16, 2002, pp. 91–2.

101 "Foreign Aid: A Feast of Giving" *The Economist* March 23, 2002, p. 93.

Part I
The modernization project

When in the nineteenth and twentieth centuries the concept of the nation was taken up in very different ideological contexts and led to popular mobilizations in regions and countries within and outside Europe that had experienced neither the liberal revolution nor the same level of primitive accumulation, it still always was presented as a concept of capitalist modernization, which aimed to bring together the interclass demands for political unity and the needs of economic development. In other words, the nation was posed as the one and only active vehicle that could deliver modernity and development.

Michael Hardt and Antonio Negri, *Empire*,
Harvard: Harvard University Press, 2000, p. 96

The postwar "naturalization" of the relatively closed national economy as the taken-for-granted object of economic regulation can be seen as a product of convergent public narratives about the nature of key economic and political changes facing postwar Europe and North America … Although this constitution of national economies and national modes of growth was mediated through national states, it was closely connected with the "making of an Atlantic ruling class" under US hegemony.

Bob Jessop, "Narrating the Future of the
National Economy and the National State:
Remarks on Remapping Regulation and
Reinventing Governance" in George Steinmetz, ed.,
State/Culture: State-Formation after the Cultural Turn,
Ithaca: Cornell University Press, 1999, p. 397

1 US hegemony and national development

The new global order that emerged in the Cold War era was premised on the sovereign equality of all nation-states, despite the substantial inequalities between and within them. Against this backdrop the nation-state was naturalized as the key unit of (capitalist and socialist) development worldwide. The idea and practice of development was enshrined between the 1940s and the 1970s as a national and state-guided process of modernization. Decolonization and the universalization of the nation-state system brought the leadership (and even the general population) of diverse postcolonial polities in Asia and Africa (as well as the older nation-states of Latin America and Europe, not to mention the mandates and/or nation-states that had emerged in the Middle East after the First World War) into increasingly direct relations with the main protagonists of the Cold War – the United States of America and the Union of Soviet Socialist Republics. Apart from growing links with one or the other (or both) super-powers, the leadership of the new nations interacted with each other in a range of new international organizations such as the United Nations (UN). In the Cold War era, the US was central to the elaboration in many parts of the world of an anti-communist modernization project centered on state-guided national development.

The primary challenge to the US-led modernization project came from the USSR and its allies. However, it was also challenged by particular radical nationalist regimes and movements, often as part of a wider series of Third Worldist initiatives in the Bandung Era (1955–1975). Specific national and regional initiatives, and Third Worldism as an international movement, ultimately failed. But, in part, as a result of the various challenges, the US-led modernization project had entered a period of transition, by the late 1960s, symbolized most powerfully by the Vietnam War. The reorientation of US hegemony in the late 1960s and early 1970s paved the way for the uneven reconfiguration of the role of nation-states in the global political economy of the Cold War, a process that increasingly challenged the idea of development as a state-led national project by the beginning of the 1980s. This chapter discusses decolonization, the Cold War and the elaboration of the nation-state system in an effort to situate US hegemony in relation to the rise and decline of national development between the 1940s and the 1970s. It then turns to an examination of Bandung regimes and

Third Worldism in this period as a way of clarifying the contradictions of national development and the paradox of the nation-state in the Cold War era. What is particularly salient in retrospect is the fact that even as these regimes and movements sought alternative development paths and alliance arrangements to those being offered by the US and the USSR, they always accepted that the nation-state was the vehicle for liberation and that development should involve some form of state-mediated national process.

Decolonization, the Cold War and the nation-state system I

The origins of national development

Many observers trace the roots of the dominant post-1945 idea and practice of development as *national* development to the transition to industrial capitalism and the consolidation of nation-states in Western Europe in the late eighteenth century and the first half of the nineteenth century. For example, M. P. Cowen and R. W. Shenton regard the work of Friedrich List, the influential German nationalist and political economist, as "the fountainhead of 'national development'".[1] However, any attempt to locate the origins of the modern notion of national development also needs to look further east, particularly to Russia and Japan where, by the nineteenth century, nationalist politicians and policy-makers were increasingly seeking to emulate the nation-states of Western Europe via state-directed economic growth.[2] Following the Russian Revolution and the US entry into the First World War in 1917, the debate about the form that national development should take was an important element in the wider struggle between Wilsonianism and Leninism.[3] The Russian Revolution ensured that an increasingly state-socialist version of national development became central to the Soviet project. By the 1930s the late-industrializing efforts of the USSR were attracting the attention of economists and policy-makers in North America, Western Europe and beyond.[4] In fact, it was during the 1930s that the idea of development as a state-mediated and economically redistributive (although not necessarily politically democratic) process of national mobilization and development was consolidated in the United States, parts of Latin America and, of course, Western, Central and Eastern Europe.

The rise of the new or reconfigured nation-states of East Central Europe after the First World War is, in fact, widely regarded as the *locus classicus* of the practice of national development as it was elaborated after the Second World War. A significant number of the pioneers of development economics (the intellectual anchor of national development efforts in many of the nation-states of the developing world after 1945) were born in East Central Europe, and their early research focused on national development in the region. For example, Paul Rosenstein-Rodan (who played a particularly important role in the establishment of development economics in Britain and the US in the 1940s), along with a number of other economists, sought to prescribe ways in which the nation-states of East Central Europe could be developed following the nineteenth- and early twentieth-century German experience. The idea that industrialization was the key to national development, and that government planning was necessary for this to take place, was the central element in the work of virtually all of these economists. Between the 1930s and the 1960s their views also meshed with the developmental preoccupations of Latin American economists and policy-makers.[5] For example, Raúl Prebisch, Under Secretary of Finance in Argentina in the early 1930s, emerged as a key figure in development economics and a major promoter of state-guided national development after the Second World War. In the post-1945 era Prebisch served as Director-General of the UN-sponsored Economic Commission for Latin America (Comisión Economica para América Latina – CEPAL) from 1948 to 1962. He also founded and then headed the United Nations Conference on Trade and Development (UNCTAD) from 1964 to 1969, a position from which he sought to encourage preferential tariffs for the exports of late-industrializing nation-states.[6]

The consolidation of the idea of national development, centered intellectu-ally on development economics, was also an outgrowth of the late-colonial era in Asia and Africa.[7] In the late-colonial era the idea of development was increas-ingly used by the British Colonial Office as a framework for a series of policy interventions and metropolitan financial initiatives that were aimed at improving living standards in the colonies and re-legitimizing empire. A similar pattern, with a somewhat different timeframe was also apparent in the case of French colonialism.[8] The emergence of the idea of development as state-mediated national development was also linked to greater regulation and control over the economy as part of the war effort during the Second World War. This was certainly the case in the Middle East.[9] Following the Colonial Development and Welfare Act of 1940, the British government used this new conception of devel-opment to try and revitalize its colonial project in Africa and parts of Asia at the very moment when it was under siege from within and without.[10] This eventu-ally led to the establishment of the Colonial Development Corporation in 1948. It was renamed the Commonwealth Development Corporation in the mid-1960s.[11] The British were also committed to retaining imperial influence in the Middle East in the post-1945 era, but did not necessarily see the Colonial Development and Welfare Act as having much relevance to their relations with the region.[12] At the same time, the ideas associated with the colonial develop-ment initiative still impacted on the Middle East. The intrusive character of this new found developmentalism (whether as part of the direct effort by colonial officials or the more indirect result of war-time exigencies) resulted in, or at least contributed to, increased conflict in the late-colonial era as nationalists and trade-unionists in Asia, Africa and the Middle East appropriated the language and concepts of state-mediated development escalating their demands for better wages, social services and improved living standards as well as political power and national sovereignty or independence.[13]

It was increasingly clear that, in contrast to earlier efforts to justify empire, the post-1940 idea and practice of colonial development, and the Keynesian instrumentalities that went with it, appealed strongly to nationalist elites in Asia, Africa and the Middle East. As decolonization gained momentum, it became apparent that by attempting to use the idea of development to bolster their influence and power, British colonial officials had helped to fatally undermine the powerful metropolitan view that the British empire was primarily about the elaboration and maintenance of a finely graded social hierarchy grounded in the semi-feudal and agrarian vision of the British aristocracy. This vision, and the increasingly complex array of honors and pageants on which it rested, had helped to link the British ruling elite to the traditional chiefs and princes of Africa, Asia and the Middle East.[14] With some exceptions (mainly in the Middle East and Oceania), it was not a framework that could contain the young, often urbanized, and educated nationalists who increasingly took over both the newly established colonial development projects and the more long-standing machinery of the colonial or semi-colonial states in the 1950s and 1960s.[15] Ultimately the developmentalism promoted by the colonial officials had undermined the long-standing colonial claim to be bringing civilization and order to savage peoples whose backwardness was thought to be grounded in distinct cultures and/or immutable racial shortcomings. The idea of development that emerged in the 1940s out of the crisis of colonialism increasingly assumed that all colonial subjects could operate as modern subjects.[16] This was a central thread in the shift from a global order of colonial empires to a worldwide system of nation-states.

US hegemony and the creation of an international framework for national development I

The United States played a key role in the consolidation of the nation-state system after 1945, with the Soviet Union emerging as its only significant rival. During the Cold War, both the position of the US in the nation-state system and the foreign policies and practices of the USSR still bore significant traces of the colonialism and imperialism practiced by the European powers and Imperial Japan, as well as by the United States (in places such as the Philippines and the Caribbean) in an earlier era. It should be emphasized, however, that despite continuities the Cold War "empires" of both the US and the Soviet Union departed in important ways from earlier colonial or imperial projects. Most significantly, in political and administrative terms both the United States and the Soviet Union presided over empires that were made up more or less entirely of formally independent and sovereign nation-states, rather than colonies. The role of the US in Latin America by the early twentieth century and the role of Britain in Latin America, as well as Britain and France in the Middle East after the First World War had foreshadowed this form of indirect rule. In the Cold War era the relationship between the respective superpowers and their allies was increasingly mediated by systems of military alliances, regional organizations, and new international institutions such as the United Nations. In economic terms, meanwhile, US hegemony in the second half of the twentieth century can be, and has been, characterized as "postimperial". This was particularly the case by the 1970s, by which time the nation-state system had been universalized and the overall contours of the globalization project were just beginning, at least in retrospect, to become apparent. The key point is that while the empires of the late-colonial and pre-Second World War era were grounded to a great degree in the regulation and control of colonial markets by the metropolitan powers, in the interests of corporations and investors based in the colonial metropolis, the economic arrangements that were put in place under US auspices after the Second World War paved the way for large corporations to increasingly transcend any dependence on particular metropolitan nation-states for regulatory and other support.[17] This trend became most apparent in the 1980s and 1990s, but it is grounded in the post-1945 settlement that sought to "reconcile openness" with the Keynesian orientation of national leaders to ensure national and international economic stability and full employment.[18] With the onset of the Cold War in the late 1940s the US was increasingly animated by a commitment to construct an open world economy, while promoting state-mediated national development as part of its wider effort to contain the USSR and its allies. The protection of private property and the interests of capital were an essential part of the wider fabric of the anti-communist internationalism that increasingly informed US foreign policy.[19] As George Kennan (who was Director of Policy Planning at the State Department at the time) observed in a now well-known 1948 planning document, "We have 50 percent of the world's wealth, but only 6.3 percent of its population" and "Our real task in the coming period is to devise a pattern of relationships which will allow us to maintain this position of disparity."[20]

Kennan was writing shortly after the promulgation of the Truman Doctrine. Formally announced on March 12 1947 by President Harry S. Truman (1944–1952), it represented an important turning point in the onset of the Cold War. The Truman Doctrine was a response to the growing influence of communist parties in Greece and Turkey and included the extension, after approval by the US Congress on May 15 1947, of US$400 million in economic and military aid to the Greek and Turkish governments. This was followed on June 5 1947 by Secretary of State George C. Marshall's famous speech announcing what would become the Marshall Plan for Western Europe.[21] On April 3 1948 Truman signed the Economic Cooperation Act (Marshall Plan) creating the Economic Cooperation Administration, an initiative that represented an important precedent for subsequent US aid to Asia, Africa, the Middle East and Latin America (in fact Japan, South Korea and Saudi Arabia also received aid under the Marshall Plan). The Marshall Plan was aimed at preventing any further worsening of the post-1945 economic and political crisis in post-1945 Europe. In particular it was aimed at preventing or containing the emergence in Europe of governments, or groupings of governments, that would threaten the geo-political and security interests of the United States. It involved the disbursement of US$12.5 billion towards the reconstruction of Western Europe over a four-year period. Although it was initially offered to the USSR and Eastern Europe, Moscow and its client regimes found the conditions that went with it unacceptable and rejected the Plan. By the early 1950s the Marshall Plan was a key factor in increasing

Western European industrial production to 35 percent and agricultural production to 18 percent above the levels they had been at before the Second World War. The Marshall Plan also drew attention to the benefits of foreign aid for the US economy. One of the requirements of the Marshall Plan had been that the bulk of the aid money had to be used to purchase US exports and this provided an important stimulus to the US economy, while bolstering trade linkages that favored US manufacturers.[22] At the end of the 1940s the US had not only embarked on a full-scale program of industrial reconstruction and national development in Western Europe, but also in Northeast Asia, as part of an attempt to turn Japan and key nation-states, such as South Korea and Taiwan, into capitalist bulwarks against the Soviet Union and the People's Republic of China.[23] By the time of the CCP's victory in China in October 1949, followed soon after by the Korean War (1950–1953), the US defense industry, and a range of new or revitalized civilian and military agencies, had been organized into a US national security state that became the backbone of the US-led modernization project that emerged between the 1940s and the 1970s.[24]

A number of new international institutions were also central to the generation of the international framework for the US-led modernization project and the promotion of national, and capitalist, development in the Cold War era. For example, the International Monetary Fund (IMF), which sought to curtail foreign exchange difficulties, and the International Bank for Reconstruction and Development (the World Bank), which dispensed loans to encourage private foreign investment around the world, had been established on December 27 1945 following a high-level meeting in Bretton Woods, New Hampshire, in 1944. With the start of the Cold War the Bretton Woods institutions (which were ostensibly part of the United Nations, but in practice operated beyond UN control) became central to US international economic predominance and the international framework for national development. The arrangements laid down at Bretton Woods produced an "informal bargain". On the one side, the US (with the dollar providing the central currency for the post-war order) accepted the increasingly large balance of payments deficits necessary to pay for its expanding network of military bases and the large quantities of foreign aid it was disbursing, which were paralleled by high-levels of foreign investments made by US-based companies. On the other side, the United States' allies (particularly key anti-communist nation-states such as West Germany and Japan, which also became its main economic competitors) were allowed to retain high levels of control over their economies in terms of things such as the flow of capital and commodities. Furthermore, with the implicit agreement that its allies would not attempt to convert large amounts of their US dollar holdings to gold (which was technically permitted by the gold standard), Washington threw open important North American markets, while tolerating and even encouraging the protectionist trading practices and restrictions on capital movement of its more important Cold War allies.[25] While the World Bank and the International Monetary Fund had been established with a view to the post-war reconstruction of Western Europe, by the 1950s they had clearly expanded their activities to include the encouragement and facilitation of capitalist development and anti-communist stability in Asia and elsewhere.[26] In 1952 Chile, which became an important Cold War battleground in the 1960s and 1970s, was the first nation-state outside of Western Europe to receive a World Bank loan.[27]

Also of significance in creating an international framework for capitalist forms of national development was the network of regional development banks, such as the Inter-American Development Bank (IDB) and the Asian Development Bank (ADB). The administration of President Dwight D. Eisenhower (1953–1960) established the Inter-American Development Bank in 1959, while the Asian Development Bank was not set up until 1966, primarily under the auspices of the Japanese government. The US initially opposed the establishment of the ADB, but, in the context of the escalating war in Vietnam, Washington accepted that there was a need for a regional development bank in Asia.[28] There are also a range of development-related organizations that grew up around the United Nations. While the UN Security Council's focus was on issues of peace and war, the General Assembly was given particular responsibility from the outset for social and economic issues. Over the years, as this brief grew, an array of, often semi-autonomous, specialized agencies (besides the already mentioned IMF and World Bank) emerged. For example, the International Labor Organization (ILO), which had been set up by the League of Nations, was revitalized. The UN also established the World Health Organization (WHO), the United Nations Educational, Scientific and Cultural Organization (UNESCO) and the Food and Agriculture Organization (FAO), not to mention the United Nations Conference on Trade and Development (UNCTAD), the United Nations Development Programme (UNDP) and the Expanded Programme of Technical Assistance.[29]

These initiatives followed on from President Truman's Point IV Program. On January 20 1949 Truman delivered his inaugural address at the start of his second term as president, during which he sketched out an expanded foreign aid policy in the fourth and final point of the address. Point I pledged continuing US support for the United Nations. Point II emphasized US support for world economic recovery, while Point III reiterated the US commitment to supporting "freedom loving nations". Point IV set out a US commitment to providing technical and scientific expertise, and capital, to "underdeveloped" nations in an effort to improve their living standards. Point IV led to the Act for International Development in June 1950 that allowed for the creation of a Technical Cooperation Administration. The program started with a budget of US$45 million. By early 1951 there were 350 technicians working under US auspices and engaged in over 100 cooperation projects in almost 30 countries. In 1953 the US Congress increased the budget of the Point IV program to US$155 million. With the outbreak of the Korean War, Washington also sought, via the establishment of the Mutual Security Agency on October 31 1951, to directly link economic programs and technical assistance to military initiatives, while the passage of Public Law 480 (PL 480) on July 10 1954 provided the authority for surplus food in the US to be purchased by Washington and used for economic development purposes.[30]

While Washington was elaborating the various initiatives that flowed from Point IV, the British government, in concert with the leadership of a number of its former colonies in Asia, was launching the Colombo Plan, formally known as the Colombo Plan For Cooperative Economic Development in Asia and the Pacific, to coordinate the disbursement of development aid to governments in the region. Established in 1950 and emerging directly out of the spread of the Cold War to Asia by the late 1940s, the Colombo Plan represented a significant foreign aid effort. Centered initially on the British Commonwealth and initiated by the British Foreign Secretary, Ernest Bevin, the British hoped that the promotion of the developmental and technical elements of the Colombo Plan would demonstrate to the peoples of South and Southeast Asia that there were viable alternatives to those provided by state-socialism in China and the various visions of a socialist future being promoted by the communist parties of the region. It was also hoped that the Plan would provide a focus for the Indian and other Commonwealth governments and increase US and British cooperation. The Plan was drawn up by an assembled group of Commonwealth delegates at the Colombo Conference (held in the capital of Ceylon, renamed Sri Lanka in 1972) in January 1950. It formally began operation in July 1951.[31] The United States joined the Colombo Plan in 1951 (as did Japan, somewhat later), dramatically increasing its resources and reach. There were two overarching and interconnected components of the Plan. The first was a program of technical cooperation that sought to provide expertise and equipment to the recipient nations and bring students to the donor countries for training. The second part of the Plan was a broad program of economic development directed at major public investment and infrastructure projects, including roads, railways, irrigation, electricity and communications, as well as various other services. By 1956 the United States had contributed at least US$2 billion worth of aid to the governments of South and Southeast Asia and was the single biggest donor government to the region inside and outside the Colombo Plan. Against the backdrop of the Cold War, US$72 billion was disbursed via the Colombo Plan between 1950 and 1983 and over 50 percent of that amount (US$41.2 billion) came from the United States.[32] As these new organizations and initiatives illustrate, the contours of an international framework for national development and the US-led modernization project, under the stewardship of the Truman administration and then the Eisenhower administration, were taking shape by the late 1940s and 1950s.

US hegemony and the creation of an international framework for national development II

It was, however, during the administration of John F. Kennedy (1961–1963) and his immediate successor, Lyndon B. Johnson (1963–1968), that the US-led modernization project reached its apex.[33] Following the Cuban revolution in 1959 there was a dramatic increase in US interest in Latin America.[34] This was part of a wider concern in the US in the second half of the 1950s and the 1960s that the USSR was gaining ground in the Third World.[35] This was a key concern of Kennedy's while he was still a senator and was something he followed up with a number of major symbolic and substantive initiatives. As part of its wider emphasis on foreign aid and national development, the Kennedy adminis- tration formed the Peace Corps on March 1 1961 and set up the US Agency for International Development (USAID) in November 1961. USAID followed on from the passage of the Foreign Assistance Act on September 4 1961 and sought to coordinate and combine government foreign aid initiatives, such as the International Cooperation Administration and the Development Loan Fund. Established as a semi-autonomous body operating in the State Department, USAID was responsible for disbursing and administering aid around the world. Apart from South Vietnam, which was emerging as a major focus of aid, a large percentage of the aid this new body disbursed went initially to the Alliance for Progress, which had been set up following a famous speech by Kennedy on March 13 1961 in which he called for all the people and governments of the Western Hemisphere to participate in an ambitious modernizing initiative that he hoped would transform Latin America in a decade and contain the commu- nist threat to the region represented by the emergence of state-socialism in Cuba. The Alliance for Progress, which saw political stability and democracy as flowing from economic development, embodied the "full flowering" of the "liberal developmentalism" that was at the core of the US-led modernization project.[36]

The Alliance for Progress began as a decade-long program of land and economic reform that was expected to cost US$100 billion. The US made an initial contribution of US$1 billion and a commitment to raise another US$20 billion overall from both public and private sources. The US set the achievement of an annual economic growth rate for Latin America of at least 2.5 percent as one of the main goals of the Alliance. Emphasizing the importance of national development planning, the Alliance, under US leadership, sought to achieve greater productivity in the agricultural sector, eradicate illiteracy, stimulate trade diversification and industrialization, generate improvements in housing and bring about improved income distribution in the region. A key contradiction of the US-led modernization project in Latin America centered on the fact that successful trade diversification would undermine the monopoly of primary agri- cultural products and mineral extraction enjoyed by a number of US-based transnationals, while any significant land reform threatened the power of the still largely land-based ruling elites in Latin America. By the late 1960s, high rates of economic growth in many Latin American countries had been achieved. However, high growth rates had served primarily to increase social inequality, while the middle classes moved to side with the ruling elites as politics, instead of becoming more democratic, moved increasingly towards authoritarianism and military dictatorship. By the time of Kennedy's assassination in late 1963, in the context of a growing emphasis on the important role the military could play in providing order and guiding national development, the reformist elements of the Alliance for Progress had been displaced by a more straightforward focus on military and economic aid to any regime, regardless of how draconian, which was committed to the maintenance of US hegemony in the region.[37]

US support for military establishments and authoritarian governments in Latin America and beyond grew significantly in the 1960s. Apart from economic aid this support took the form of US military, CIA or civilian advisers, training programs for the police and the military, or military aid and technical assistance for counter-insurgency and stabilization programs. This is not to mention the direct deployment of troops temporarily or indefinitely, such as in South Korea, or the massive troop deployment in South Vietnam by the late 1960s. Increasing US support for anti-communist dictatorships in Asia, the Middle East, Latin America and Africa reflected the updating of a long-standing practice, exemplified, for example, by support for Rafael Trujillo (1930–1961) in the Dominican Republic and Fulgencio Batista (1934–1958) in Cuba.[38] In the 1960s and 1970s (and beyond) entrenched, or new, authoritarian governments, such as the Somoza family in Nicaragua (1937–1979), the Shah of Iran (1953–1979), Park Chung Hee in South Korea (1961–1979), Joseph Désiré Mobutu (Mobutu Sese Seko) in Congo/Zaire (1965–1997), Ferdinand Marcos in the Philippines (1965–1986) and General Suharto in Indonesia (1965–1998), could be relied upon to, by and large, support the US in its effort to maintain a regional and international order that can be characterized as "really existing liberalism".[39] The relative strategic importance of the nation-states concerned ensured a greater or lesser degree of tolerance by the US of the illiberal economic and political practices of its clients. While the US-backed dictatorships were clearly not liberal, they were partially incorporated into a liberal world order centered on the United States, which was itself a liberal democracy that still tolerated apartheid-style arrangements for the black population in its southern states into the 1960s. The successful imposition of US power flowed from both the appeal and malleability of liberal values.[40] It was these liberal values that underpinned the universalization of the nation-state system and the idea of development as national development worldwide.

The creation of a US-centered international framework for the promotion of really existing liberal-capitalist versions of national development was part of the wider struggle between rival capitalist and socialist models of modernization that was central to the Cold War, even as all participants in the debate accepted the nation-state as the key unit of development. It is worth emphasizing that up to the 1970s, the Soviet Union specifically and various forms of state-socialism more generally were still viewed in many parts of the world as serious alternatives to the liberal capitalist model of national development sponsored by the US. In response, the various efforts at anti-communist reconstruction and national development spearheaded by the US, beginning in Western Europe and Japan after 1945, involved promoting a vision of modernity based in part on many of the socially and politically reformist ideas and practices that had taken shape in the 1930s. The earlier North American, Western European and Japanese forms of state corporatism and state-directed social welfarism (both liberal and national-socialist versions) were built on and transformed after 1945 under US leadership.[41] While the experiences of the 1930s were an important influence, the post-1945 US-led modernization project was also clearly grounded in the culture of Cold War North America where there was, particularly in the Eisenhower years, considerable opposition to the social democratic legacy of the 1930s. The high modernist vision that was ascendant in post-1945 North America distinguished between backward and advanced regions, representing the United States as the "summit of modernity" with a "mission to transform a world eager to learn the lessons only America could teach".[42] The model that was promoted by the US and allied nation-states of Western Europe, included an emphasis on Fordist pay and production arrangements, Taylorist forms of labor organization, and a "paternalistic and protective", but modernizing, state. Of course, in practice, the vision of global Fordist modernity was reproduced in a highly uneven and fragmented fashion in the emerging Third World. At the same time, in the 1950s and 1960s the promise of global Fordism and national development provided the ideological content for the US-led modernization project.[43]

Throughout the Cold War era the contradiction between the US as a repressive military power and guardian of the interests of capital on the one hand, and liberal anti-communist defender of freedom and promoter of progressive forms of state-mediated national development on the other hand became more pronounced. The lengthy US intervention in Vietnam was "the pinnacle of this tendency".[44] In the early 1950s Washington's assistance to France's increasingly embattled effort to hold on to its colonial empire in Indochina had become a major facet of the wider commitment to containing communism in Southeast Asia.[45] Following the collapse of French power in 1954, the US role in South Vietnam was gradually, but inexorably expanded, increasingly placing Washington in a relationship with Vietnamese nationalism analogous to that occupied earlier by the French colonizers. Communism in Southeast Asia was eventually contained within the boundaries of the former French colonial possessions in the region, but the US effort at nation-building in South Vietnam between the late 1950s and the early 1970s (which will be discussed in more detail in chapters 3 and 8) was an unalloyed failure. The inability of the US to turn South Vietnam into a Southeast Asian version of South Korea, despite a truly massive military and economic commitment, highlighted the limits of Washington's ability to achieve its goals via an approach which, although postcolonial in its emphasis on modernization and nation-building was still often grounded in colonial frameworks and methods.[46] The Vietnam War, which was central to the reorientation of US hegemony in the late 1960s and early 1970s, threw the limits of the US-led modernization project into particularly stark relief.

Decolonization, the Cold War and the nation-state system II

The Bandung Spirit

The Vietnam War was also a pivot of the wider rise and fall of Third Worldism and the various efforts in the so-called Third World to pursue forms of state-guided national development that sought to challenge the overall structure of the

Cold War order and avoid relying on the models of development being promoted by the US or the Soviet Union. Of course, no government in the Third World ever pursued a consistently or genuinely non-aligned policy. Furthermore, even less surprisingly, none of the main challengers to the international order that emerged questioned the centrality of the nation-state to this system, nor did they question the equation of development with some form of state-mediated national process.[47] In an effort to clarify the dynamics of the contest over the most appropriate forms of national development in the Cold War era, this section turns to a closer examination of the rise and decline of state-guided national development in the context of the emergence of Third Worldism in the Bandung Era (1955–1975).[48] The Bandung Era takes its name from the Bandung Conference, formally known as the Asian–African Conference, which was held in the town of Bandung, Indonesia from April 17 to April 24 1955.[49] The conference, which was sponsored by the governments of Indonesia, Burma, Ceylon, India and Pakistan, reflected their dissatisfaction with the slow pace of decolonization in the early 1950s and the assertion on the part of President Eisenhower that the nation-states of Asia should not try and remain neutral in the Cold War.[50]

Attended by delegations from twenty-nine, primarily new, nation-states or nationalist movements in Asia and Africa, the meeting in Bandung also included members of the African National Congress, as well as observers from Greek Cypriot and African American organizations. The key figures at the conference were Sukarno, President of Indonesia (1945–1965), Jawaharlal Nehru, Prime Minister of India (1947–1964), Ho Chi Minh, leader of the Democratic Republic of Vietnam (1954–1969), Gamal Abdel Nasser, President of Egypt (1954–1970), Kwame Nkrumah, the future Prime Minister of Ghana (1957–1966), and Chou En-Lai, the Prime Minister (1949–1976) and Foreign Minister (1949–1958) of the People's Republic of China. The assembled delegates also emphasized their opposition to colonialism, singling out French colonialism in North Africa for particular criticism. Furthermore there was a major debate as to whether Soviet domination of Eastern Europe was equivalent to Western European colonialism in Asia and Africa. The final communiqué of the conference condemned all "manifestations" of colonialism and was viewed as an attack on the formal colonialism of the Western European powers, the Soviet occupation of Eastern Europe and the informal colonialism of the United States. The proceedings ended with a call for: increased technical and cultural cooperation between the governments in attendance; the establishment of an economic development fund to be operated by the United Nations; increased support for human rights and the "self-determination of peoples and nations" singling out South Africa and Israel for their failure in this regard; and negotiations to reduce the building and stockpiling of nuclear weapons.[51]

The Bandung Conference represented a precursor to the formation of the Movement of Non-Aligned Countries. In September 1961 the First Conference of Heads of State or Government of Non-Aligned Countries was held in

Belgrade, Yugoslavia. Hosted by Josip Broz Tito, President of Yugoslavia (1953–1980), it was attended by officials from only twenty-five governments; however, representatives from nineteen different national liberation movements were also in attendance.[52] A number of governments that had been in attendance in Bandung were excluded if they were seen to be clearly oriented towards the US or the Soviet Union. A number of former French colonies that were closely tied to Paris were also excluded, while representatives from Yugoslavia and Cuba were in attendance. The complicated and conflicting interests of the governments of the new nations in Asia and Africa increasingly worked to undermine the establishment of a strong coalition of non-aligned governments.[53] For example, the second Asian–African Conference, which had been scheduled to meet in Algeria in June 1965 (a decade after the first meeting in Bandung), was cancelled when the machinations of the Sino-Soviet split undermined the planning of the event. Between 1961 and the end of the 1990s there were a total of twelve non-aligned conferences. The Belgrade Conference was followed by Cairo (Egypt) in 1964, then Lusaka (Zambia) in 1970 and Algiers (Algeria) in 1973. In 1976 the venue was Colombo (Sri Lanka), followed by Havana (Cuba) in 1979, New Delhi (India) in 1983, Harare (Zimbabwe) in 1986, with a return to Belgrade in 1989. A meeting in Jakarta (Indonesia) in 1992 was followed by Cartagena (Colombia) in 1995 and Durban (South Africa) in 1998. The most recent meeting was in Kuala Lumpur (Malaysia) in early 2003.[54] However, as an international organization the Movement of Non-Aligned Countries has never played a role of any great significance. By the 1990s, when the Indonesian government, under President Suharto, took over as chairman, the Non-Aligned Movement was effectively moribund and the Bandung Era had been over for at least a decade. In broader terms, however, one of the main results of the Bandung Conference was symbolic. It was the first major international conference that sought to bring together the governments of the newly independent nations of Asia and Africa. In the view of one observer, Bandung was "the first blueprint for solidarity between the colonized countries".[55] And, despite the profound organizational and strategic weaknesses that plagued Third Worldism and the Non-Aligned Movement, it is clear that the Bandung Spirit captured the imagination of an entire generation between the 1950s and the 1970s.[56]

The Bandung Era and Third Worldism I

In the 1950s and the 1960s the Bandung Spirit interacted with the enthusiasm and optimism of decolonization and national liberation as the nation-state system was universalized and consolidated. In Asia, the Philippines became independent of the United States in 1946, the new nations of India and Pakistan emerged out of the break-up of British India in 1947, while the British transfer of power to an independent government in Burma occurred in 1948. The onetime British colony of Ceylon also achieved independence in 1948, changing its name to Sri Lanka in 1972. Sukarno presided over the establishment of an independent Indonesia in 1945; however, the new government's control of the former Netherlands East Indies was not achieved until 1949, by which time the war with the Dutch had run its course. British Malaya achieved independence in the late 1950s, a process that had resulted by the mid-1960s in the consolidation of the nation-states of Malaysia and Singapore. The French became embroiled in a major military effort to hold on to French Indochina between 1946 and 1954 against a determined national liberation movement led by Ho Chi Minh and the Vietnamese Communist Party.[57] In fact, the First Indochina War (1946–1954) and the Second Indochina War (1965–1975) draw particular attention to the way in which the Cold War increasingly conditioned the overall direction of decolonization and the elaboration of the nation-state system after 1945.[58] This trend is also apparent in the establishment (on the economic and administrative foundations of Japanese colonialism) of South Korea and Taiwan by the end of the 1940s. These truncated polities rapidly emerged as key allies/clients of the United States by the 1950s, while their Cold War *doppelgängers*, North Korea and the People's Republic of China, entered into a complex triangle of alliance/client relationships with the USSR.[59]

By the end of the 1950s a range of African colonies (beginning in 1957 with Ghana, formerly the Gold Coast) were also moving towards or had already achieved independence. In 1960 sixteen new nations in Africa joined the United Nations, including Nigeria, and the Republic of the Congo (formerly the Belgian Congo). Decolonization in Africa culminated with the emergence of Angola, Mozambique, Guinea-Bissau, Cape Verde and Sao Tome out of the collapse of the Portuguese empire in 1974. The dynamics of the Cold War interacted brutally with decolonization and national liberation in southern Africa, facilitating the rise and consolidation after 1965 of the predatory Mobutu dictatorship in the Congo (renamed Zaire in 1971). Meanwhile, postcolonial Angola and Mozambique were riven by externally funded guerrilla insurgencies seeking to topple the nationalist-Marxist leadership of these new nation-states. These conflicts ground on into the post-Cold War era.[60] Part of this process, but also distinct in important ways, were the paths taken in the settler colonies of southern Africa. Rhodesia gained a second independence in 1980, becoming Zimbabwe, following the end of fifteen years of direct rule by European settlers, and the cessation of a struggle that had been deeply enmeshed in the wider Cold War in the region.[61] Meanwhile, the South African government withdrew from South-West Africa (Namibia) in 1990 and apartheid gave way to majority rule in South Africa itself in 1994.[62]

In the Middle East, the timing and character of decolonization was somewhat different, but as elsewhere, nation-states that emerged from the complex interaction between colonial frameworks and localized political dynamics were often presented by nationalist leaders as natural and liberating vehicles for development, in the context of the expanding system of nation-states. Britain and France had exercised indirect forms of rule in parts of the Middle East, via support for and intervention in the declining Ottoman Empire prior to 1914, and then via a range of mandates and alliance arrangements following the

Ottoman collapse and the emergence of the nation-state of Turkey after the Great War of 1914–1918. The Paris Peace Conference in January 1919 and the establishment of the League of Nations saw former provinces of the Ottoman Empire turned over to Britain and France as mandates. While France assumed control of Syria and Lebanon, Britain took over Iraq and Palestine. They were all designated as "Class A" mandates with the expectation that independence would be granted in short order.[63] In the case of Iraq, for example, London did not even set up a formal mandate, preferring to negotiate a treaty in 1922 that gave Britain the prerogative to appoint financial and foreign policy advisers, as well as play a role in the armed forces. This treaty was ratified in 1924, but it was a source of continuing nationalist dissatisfaction and a much weaker version was promulgated when Iraq was declared formally independent in 1930. With Britain's support, Iraq joined the League of Nations in 1932. British influence over Baghdad remained significant until the Iraqi revolution of July 1958, which signalled the wider decline of British power in the region that had begun in the early 1950s.[64] For example, in Iran, Britain had exerted considerable indirect influence in the early decades of the twentieth century; however, by the 1950s, the United States had displaced Britain, symbolized by the prominent, albeit covert, US role in the overthrow of the Musaddiq government and the installa- tion of the Shah in 1953.[65] At the same time, by 1954, the French were involved in an escalating military struggle against a determined nationalist movement (the FLN) in Algeria that would culminate in Algerian independence in July 1962.[66] Meanwhile, Egypt, which had been a protectorate of Britain since the 1880s, emerged as a formally independent monarchy after the First World War, with links to Britain that were perceived by some Egyptian nationalists as neo-colo- nial. It was not until over thirty years later that the ouster on July 23 1952 of the British-backed King Farouk in a bloodless coup initiated a process that soon led to the departure of all British troops from Egypt and the Egyptian takeover of the Suez Canal by 1956.[67] These events catapulted Nasser to prominence as a major figure not only in Egyptian nationalism, but also in Arab nationalism and Third Worldism.

As has been suggested, regimes such as Nasser's in Egypt were at the center of an intense debate by the 1950s about the most appropriate form of state-guided national development to be followed in the Bandung Era. Egypt under Nasser, along with India under Nehru, Indonesia under Sukarno, and Ghana under Nkrumah, initially sought to anchor a wider effort to steer national development in the Third World between the capitalism of the United States (and the First World) and the communism of the Soviet Bloc (and the Second World). India, which will be discussed in more detail in chapter 2, provides a clear example of an effort to pursue state-guided national development that sought to draw on development experiences in Western Europe, the USSR, Japan and post-1949 China to pursue industrialization and national development along socialist lines. Because of India's sheer size, its appearance as a new nation at the very begin- ning of the wider post-1945 wave of decolonization, its democratic credentials and its government's efforts to maintain a non-aligned stance in the emerging

Cold War, it occupied a key position in relation to the consolidation and universalization of the idea of national development. However, by the time Nehru died in May 1964, the notion that a benevolent technocratic elite could successfully guide the nation to modernity and that India could serve as a model for other parts of the Third World was already in crisis.[68] Meanwhile, in September 1965, a little over a year after Nehru's death, the Indonesian president Sukarno (the sponsor of the 1955 Bandung Conference and another major leader of the Bandung Era) was gradually displaced by General Suharto, in a process carried out against the backdrop of a prolonged and bloody anti-communist campaign. Suharto presided over an increasingly conservative anti-communist and authoritarian version of national developmentalism in Indonesia, erected on the foundations of Sukarno's failed national development project.[69]

While the causes of the failure of national development projects in Indonesia and elsewhere in the Bandung Era are complex, the key to that failure can be traced to the way in which the institution of the nation-state was universally seen as the main vehicle for liberation and development in the non-European world. While nationalism emerged in the colonies as a reaction against colonialism, the colonial order provided the overall foundation for the rise of new nation-states. This meant that the ability of the new nations to transcend their colonial histories was always more circumscribed than was often anticipated by leaders in the Bandung Era. Between the 1940s and the 1970s the new nation-states in Asia and Africa (and elsewhere) grounded their legitimacy in, and built directly on, the former colonial states. Despite a range of different historical contexts, in the Bandung era the nation-state was universally presented as a constitutive element of freedom, self-determination and modernization that would unite its inhabitants and carry them towards development. However, the progressive aspects of the nation-state were constrained by powerful institutional and structural legacies that flowed (in the case of Asia, Africa and the Middle East) from the colonial era, and from the hierarchical character of the nation-state system conditioned by the deepening of the Cold War. It is particularly important to draw a distinction between state and nation, as many observers now do.[70] This is especially relevant to understanding the way in which sovereignty, especially national sovereignty, resides with the state rather than with the people who inhabit the nation. Regardless, of the particular political system of the nation-states that have emerged, "modern sovereignty" has a solitary "political figure: a single transcendent power" centered on the state.[71] This is readily apparent in the way in which, under the post-1945 dispensation of the United Nations, self-determination and sovereignty are primarily, if not exclusively, the right of the state.[72] Contrary to the roseate image promoted by the UN, which views the post-1945 nation-state system as "a harmonious concert of equal and autonomous national subjects", the terms on which the newly sovereign nation-states were both consolidated, and then incorporated into the wider global order, ensured that the "*state*", often a direct inheritance of the colonial era, was "*the poisoned gift of national liberation*" at the same time as "*the nation*" became the prescribed, if not "*the only way to imagine community*".[73]

The Bandung Era and Third Worldism II

While the erstwhile colonial empires framed the territorial boundaries of the new nations that emerged after 1945, and the nationalist leadership built their states on colonial foundations, the dynamics of the Cold War increasingly conditioned national trajectories worldwide into the 1970s. What would be the last two decades of the Cold War provided the backdrop for a second generation of Bandung regimes, such as Chile under Salvador Allende (1970–73), Tanzania under Julius Nyerere (1965–85), and Jamaica under Michael Manley (1972–80), not to mention Libya under Muammar Gaddafi after 1969, and Nicaragua under the Sandinistas (1979–1990). In contrast to the first generation, the second generation of Bandung regimes reflected a more radical, explicitly socialist Third Worldist agenda, sometimes known as tricontinentalism, which emerged in the wake of the Tricontinental Conference of Solidarity of the Peoples of Africa, Asia and Latin America, that was held in Havana in January 1966. While the Bandung Conference had brought together a relatively small number of leaders from mainly recently independent nation-states in Asia and Africa in order to stake out a non-aligned position in the Cold War, the 1966 Tricontinental Conference in Havana involved delegates from throughout Asia, Africa, the Middle East and Latin America, and articulated a radical anti-imperial agenda that located the participants firmly in the socialist camp at the same time as they formally emphasized their independence from the USSR and Maoist China.[74] Second generation Bandung regimes, directly or indirectly linked to the tricontinentalism of the late 1960s and 1970s, represented the practical complement to the rise and spread of dependency theory (along with other revitalized Marxist theories of development).[75] In this era second generation Bandung regimes and their supporters attempted to radicalize national development efforts in various ways in the name of socialism and national liberation, remaining firmly committed to the view that the nation-state was the primary vehicle by which to achieve freedom and prosperity.

The second generation of Bandung regimes emerged as a reaction to the relative or absolute failure of most forms of state-guided national development in many parts of the world by the 1970s. And even where state-guided national development had been relatively successful it was under increasing pressure. The rise of the Newly Industrializing Countries (NICs) in East Asia (and the more short-lived enthusiasm for the Mexican and Brazilian Miracles) by the 1970s highlighted both the potential, and the limits, of state-guided national development in the post-1945 era. Mexico and Brazil were initially grouped as NICs, but the Debt Crisis of the 1980s ended their reputation as miracle economies and developmental states.[76] As will be discussed in later chapters, the East Asian NICs emerged in the 1970s and even more in the 1980s as key sites for the relocation of production activity and the geographical restructuring of the world economy precipitated by the combination of the waning of the Fordist era in North America, Western Europe and Japan (not to mention Australia) and the rise of the US-led globalization project.[77] The geographical unevenness of the global politico-economic shifts of the 1970s (which also saw a number of oil-rich states, in the Middle East, gain economic prominence and influence) and the conservative and anti-communist character of the developmental states of East Asia and their strong links to the US represented a major obstacle to any attempt to build a Third World alliance aimed at restructuring the world economy in a way that challenged US hegemony. By the 1980s, the developmental states of East Asia were also increasingly subjected to internal (as well as external) pressure for economic and political liberalization, and they too had clearly reached the limits of state-guided national development by the post-Cold War era.

The socialist-oriented national development efforts of the Bandung Era, such as India, Egypt and Tanzania, which emerged in Asia, the Middle East and Africa (not to mention Latin America), as well as more explicitly Marxist efforts in China and Vietnam (as well as Cuba), had sought to remake often heavily populated and deeply hierarchical rural societies, at the same time as they had usually tried to industrialize. However, despite these efforts, long-standing divisions in most of these peasants societies were reinforced and reconfigured rather than undermined, and capitalist and socialist national development in Asia and Africa (as well as elsewhere) was clearly in crisis by the 1970s.[78] Like the Bandung regimes, the Soviet Bloc (as well as those state-socialist countries not allied with the USSR, but not readily located with the Bandung regimes), took the nation as the natural unit of development. In fact, state-socialist regimes in the Soviet Bloc and elsewhere not only embraced the nation-state as the key to modernity, but also sought from the outset to emulate the economic advancements of the most successful capitalist states; setting goals that capitalism was ultimately "much better equipped than socialism to achieve".[79] By the 1980s, by which time the post-1945 model of national development in the capitalist world was also in crisis, the leaders of most of the state-socialist regimes had begun to make important accommodations to the shifts in the global political economy of the Cold War that flowed from the changes in the 1970s, a trend that accelerated dramatically with the end of the Cold War.[80]

It is now clear that Third Worldism peaked in the 1970s.[81] For example, in April 1974 the Sixth Special Session of the General Assembly of the United Nations passed the Declaration and Programme of Action for the Establishment of a New Economic Order.[82] This was directly linked to the non-aligned movement's earlier call for a New International Economic Order (NIEO) that would improve the terms under which the nation-states of the Third World, or what was increasingly characterized as the South, participated in the world economy.[83] In his first two years in office, meanwhile, US president Jimmy Carter (1977–1980) drew attention to the North–South divide and advocated cooperation with the governments of the Third World. However, by the beginning of the 1980s the emphasis on restructuring the world economy to address the North–South divide was increasingly being challenged by the emergent US-led globalization project. With the world recession and the Debt Crisis at the start of the 1980s, and the subsequent spread of neo-liberal economic policies and practices, the idea of a New International Economic Order quickly disappeared from view. The International Monetary Fund and the World Bank, supported by the administration of Ronald Reagan (1981–1988) and the governments of Margaret Thatcher in Britain (1979–1990) and Helmut Kohl in West Germany/Germany (1982–1998), encouraged the governments of the erstwhile Third World to liberalize trade, privatize their public sectors and deregulate their financial sectors. This trend also coincided with the renewal of the Cold War. From the end of the 1970s to the late 1980s the Reagan administration presided over an unprecedented military build-up and a reinvigorated anti-communist crusade directed at the Soviet bloc and the state-socialist model that it embodied.[84] Against this backdrop neo-classical economics and a romanticized vision of *laissez-faire* capitalism increasingly emerged to challenge the idea of state-guided national development that had been consolidated as an integral part of the universalization of the nation-state system in the first three decades of the Cold War era.

Conclusion: US hegemony and national development

This chapter has outlined the way in which the crisis of colonialism, the deepening of the Cold War, and the global spread of the nation-state system provided the context for the emergence of an international framework and a powerful vision of development as a series of state-mediated national projects. It was emphasized that between the 1940s and the 1970s the nation-state was routinized as the main object of development in its capitalist and socialist forms. The United States was central to, and a key promoter of, an international framework for capitalist versions of state-mediated national development. In the Bandung Era, in what became known as the Third World, there were numerous attempts to counter the US-led modernization project, while also attempting to avoid both alignment with the Soviet Union and explicit emulation of the particular state-socialist model of development that Moscow promoted. Important challenges to US hegemony resulted in the reorientation of US foreign policy in Asia and beyond. At the same time, despite intense disagreements over the form that development should take, there was virtually universal agreement that the state had a role to play in economic development and that the nation-state was the primary vehicle for the pursuit of progress. Throughout this period, influential theories of development and modernization, with direct and indirect links to US power, played a central role in elaborating and consolidating the idea of development as national development. The emergent sub-discipline of development economics has a particularly close connection with, and played a key role in, the rise and universalization and subsequent decline of national development. It is to the history of development economics in this period that we now turn.

Notes

1 List, who was influenced in part (as a result of political exile in the United States) by the protectionist ideas of Alexander Hamilton, advocated state-guided industrialization as a way for a rising German polity to catch up with Britain. M. P. Cowen and R. W. Shenton, *Doctrines of Development*, New York: Routledge, 1996, pp. 12–13, 60–75; F. List, *The National System of Political Economy*, London: Longmans, Green and Company,

1916 (first published 1844). Also see L. Greenfeld, *The Spirit of Capitalism: Nationalism and Economic Growth*, Cambridge, MA: Harvard University Press, 2002, pp. 199–214.

2 E. Kingston-Mann, *In Search of the True West: Culture, Economics and Problems of Russian Development*, Princeton: Princeton University Press, 1999; T. Morris-Suzuki, *A History of Japanese Economic Thought*, 2nd edn, London: Routledge, 1991, pp. 44–70.

3 I. Wallerstein, "The Concept of National Development 1917–1989" *American Behavioural Scientist* vol. 35, nos. 4–5, 1992, pp. 518, 528.

4 On the interaction between North American approaches to modernization and the Soviet trajectory between the two World Wars see D. C. Engerman, *Modernization from the Other Shore: American Intellectuals and Russian Development*, Cambridge, MA: Harvard University Press, 2003.

5 J. L. Love, *Crafting the Third World: Theorizing Underdevelopment in Rumania and Brazil*, Stanford: Stanford University Press, 1996, pp. 6–7, 112–13, 213–14.

6 R. Prebisch, "Five Stages in My Thinking on Development" in G. M. Meier and D. Seers, eds, *Pioneers in Development*, New York: Oxford University Press, 1984 (published for the World Bank), pp. 175–91.

7 S. Constantine, *The Making of British Colonial Development Policy 1914–1940*, London: Frank Cass, 1984.

8 F. Cooper, *Africa Since 1940: The Past of the Present*, Cambridge: Cambridge University Press, 2002, pp. 38–65.

9 R. Vitalis and S. Heydemann, "War, Keynesianism and Colonialism: Explaining State–Market Relations in the Postwar Middle East" in S. Heydemann, ed., *War, Institutions, and Social Change in the Middle East*, Berkeley: University of California Press, 2000, pp. 100–2.

10 J. M. Lee, *The Colonial Office, War, and Development Policy: Organisation and the Planning of A Metropolitan Initiative, 1939–1945*, London: Institute of Commonwealth Studies, 1982; J. M. Lee, *Colonial Development and Good Government: A Study of the Ideas Expressed by the British Official Classes in Planning Decolonization 1939–1964*, Oxford: Clarendon Press, 1967; L. J. Butler, *Britain and Empire: Adjusting to a Post-Imperial World*, London: I. B. Tauris, 2002, especially pp. 18–24, 34–5, 47–51, 81–5, 107–9.

11 M. McWilliam, *The Development Business: A History of the Commonwealth Development Corporation*, London: Palgrave, 2001. More generally see D. J. Morgan, *The Official History of Colonial Development* (five volumes), London: Macmillan, 1980.

12 W. R. Louis, *The British Empire in the Middle East 1945–1951: Arab Nationalism, the United States and Postwar Imperialism*, Oxford: Clarendon Press, 1984, pp. 50, 181–2.

13 F. Cooper and R. Packard, "Introduction" in F. Cooper and R. Packard, eds, *International Development and the Social Sciences: Essays on the History and Politics of Knowledge*, Berkeley: University of California Press, 1997, pp. 6–7; Vitalis and Heydemann, "War, Keynesianism and Colonialism", pp. 100–2.

14 D. Cannadine, *Ornamentalism: How the British Saw their Empire*, London: Penguin, 2001.

15 H. Tinker, *Men Who Overturned Empires: Fighters, Dreamers and Schemers*, Madison: University of Wisconsin Press, 1987.

16 F. Cooper, "Modernizing Bureaucrats, Backward Africans, and the Development Concept" in F. Cooper and R. Packard, eds, *International Development and the Social Sciences: Essays on the History and Politics of Knowledge*, Berkeley: University of California Press, 1997, pp. 64, 75–6; F. Cooper, *Decolonization and African Society: The Labor Question in French and British Africa*, Cambridge: Cambridge University Press, 1996.

17 D. G. Becker and R. L. Sklar, "Introduction" in D. G. Becker and R. L. Sklar, eds, *Postimperialism in World Politics*, New York: Praeger, 1999. Also see D. G. Becker, J. Frieden, S. P. Schartz and R. L. Sklar, *Postimperialism: International Capitalism and Development in the Late Twentieth Century*, Boulder: Lynne Rienner, 1987.

18 G. J. Ikenberry, "Creating Yesterday's New World Order: Keynesian 'New Thinking' and the Anglo-American Postwar Settlement" in J. Goldstein and R. O. Keohane,

eds, *Ideas and Foreign Policy: Beliefs, Institutions and Political Change*, Ithaca: Cornell University Press, 1993, p. 57.

19 R. W. Cox, *Production, Power and World Order: Social Forces in the Making of History*, New York: Columbia University Press, 1987, pp. 211–67; S. Gill, *American Hegemony and the Trilateral Commission*, Cambridge: Cambridge University Press, 1990.

20 G. F. Kennan "Review of Current Trends, U.S. Foreign Policy" PPS/23 (Top Secret) in *Department of State, Foreign Relations of the United States, 1948*, Washington, DC: Government Printing Office, 1976, pp. 509–29. Cited in W. I. Robinson, *Promoting Polyarchy: Globalization, US Intervention and Hegemony*, Cambridge: Cambridge University Press, 1996, p. 1.

21 The governments that received Marshall Plan aid in Europe were, Austria, Belgium, Denmark, Finland, France, Greece, Ireland, Italy, Luxembourg, Norway, Portugal, Spain, Sweden, Turkey and the United Kingdom. Australia and Canada also received some Marshall Plan aid.

22 M. J. Hogan, *The Marshall Plan: America, Britain, and the Reconstruction of Western Europe, 1947–1952*, 2nd edn, Cambridge: Cambridge University Press, 1989. The Organization for European Economic Cooperation (OEEC) was set up to coordinate the Marshall Plan. With the cessation of aid in 1950, it continued to operate as a focus of economic cooperation amongst the governments of Europe. The OEEC changed its name to the Organization for Economic Cooperation and Development (OECD) in 1961. The US and Canada joined the OECD. Through its Development Assistance Committee (DAC) the OECD increasingly began to act as a vehicle for the distribution of foreign aid from North America and Western Europe to the so-called developing nations of the Third World.

23 B. Cumings, "Japan in the World-System" in A. Gordon, ed., *Post-War Japan as History*, Berkeley: University of California Press, 1993; W. S. Borden, *The Pacific Alliance: United States Foreign Economic Policy and Japanese Trade Recovery, 1947–1955*, Madison: University of Wisconsin Press, 1984; R. L. McGlothlen, *Controlling the Waves: Dean Acheson and U.S. Foreign Policy in Asia*, New York: W. W. Norton, 1993.

24 M. P. Leffler, *A Preponderance of Power: National Security, the Truman Administration and the Cold War*, Stanford: Stanford University Press, 1992; M. J. Hogan, *A Cross of Iron: Harry S. Truman and the Origins of the National Security State, 1945–1954*, Cambridge: Cambridge University Press, 1998.

25 R. Brenner, "Uneven Development and the Long Downturn: The Advanced Capitalist Economies from Boom to Stagnation, 1950–1998" *New Left Review (I)* no. 229, 1998, pp. 43, 47. Both West Germany and Japan's dramatic industrial success after 1945 built on important economic policies and arrangements laid down in the pre-1945 era. See S. Reich, *The Fruits of Fascism: Postwar Prosperity in Historical Perspective*, Ithaca: Cornell University Press, 1990.

26 D. Kapur, J. Lewis and R. Webb, *The World Bank: Its First Half-Century, Volume 1: History*, Washington, DC: Brookings Institution, 1997, pp. 57–138.

27 J. V. Kofas, "Stabilization and Class Conflict: The State Department, the IMF and the IBRD in Chile, 1952–1958" *The International History Review* vol. 21, no. 2 (June), 1999.

28 N. K. Dutt, "The United States and the Asian Development Bank" *Journal of Contemporary Asia* vol. 27, no. 1, 1997.

29 F. Cooper and R. Packard, "Introduction" in F. Cooper and R. Packard, eds, *International Development and the Social Sciences: Essays on the History and Politics of Knowledge*, Berkeley: University of California Press, 1997, pp. 8–9, 13.

30 Some writers, such as Gilbert Rist, go so far as to represent Truman's Point IV as "the opening act" of "the 'Development' Age". G. Rist, *The History of Development: From Western Origins to Global Faith*, London: Zed Books, 1997, p. 68.

31 N. Tarling, *Britain, Southeast Asia and the Onset of the Cold War 1945–1950*, Cambridge: Cambridge University Press, 1998, pp. 336–42.

32 J. E. Williams, "The Colombo Conference and Communist Insurgency in South and South East Asia" *International Relations* vol. 4, no. 1, 1972, pp. 94–107.

33 M. E. Latham, *Modernization as Ideology: American Social Science and "Nation-Building" in the Kennedy Era*, Chapel Hill: University of North Carolina Press, 2000.

34 S. G. Rabe, *The Most Dangerous Area in the World: John F. Kennedy Confronts Communist Revolution in Latin America*, Chapel Hill: University of North Carolina Press, 1999.

35 G. Kolko, *Confronting the Third World: United States Foreign Policy 1945–1980*, New York: Pantheon, 1988.

36 J. R. Benjamin, "The Framework of US Relations with Latin America in the Twentieth Century: An Interpretive Essay" *Diplomatic History* vol. 11, no. 2, 1987, pp. 107–8. On the intellectual origins of the Alliance for Progress see M. E. Latham, "Ideology, Social Science and Destiny: Modernization and the Kennedy-Era Alliance for Progress" *Diplomatic History* vol. 22, no. 2, 1998.

37 M. T. Berger, *Under Northern Eyes: Latin American Studies and US Hegemony in the Americas 1898–1990*, Bloomington: Indiana University Press, 1995, pp. 87–8; K. C. Pearce, *Rostow, Kennedy, and the Rhetoric of Foreign Aid*, East Lansing: Michigan State University Press, 2001, pp. 103–16.

38 E. P. Roorda, *The Dictator Next Door: The Good Neighbor Policy and the Trujillo Regime in the Dominican Republic, 1930–1945*, Durham: Duke University Press, 1998; D. F. Schmitz, *Thank God They're On Our Side: The United States and Right-Wing Dictatorships, 1921–1965*, Chapel Hill: University of North Carolina Press, 1999.

39 C. Brown, "'Really Existing Liberalism' and International Order" *Millennium: Journal of International Studies* vol. 21, no. 3, 1992.

40 B. Cumings, "Still the American Century" *Review of International Studies* vol. 25, supplement, 1999, p. 286.

41 A. Glyn, A. Hughes, A. Lipietz and A. Singh, "The Rise and Fall of the Golden Age" in S. A. Marglin and J. B. Schor, eds, *The Golden Age of Capitalism: Interpreting the Postwar Experience*, 2nd edn, New York: Oxford University Press, 1991.

42 Latham, *Modernization as Ideology*, pp. 14–15, 58–9, 68, 153, 211–15.

43 B. Jessop, "Narrating the Future of the National Economy and the National State: Remarks on Remapping Regulation and Reinventing Governance" in G. Steinmetz, ed., *State/Culture: State-Formation after the Cultural Turn*, Ithaca: Cornell University Press, 1999.

44 M. Hardt and A. Negri, *Empire*, Cambridge, MA: Harvard University Press, 2000, pp. 178–9.

45 L. C. Gardner, *Approaching Vietnam: From World War II Through Dienbienphu*, New York: W. W. Norton, 1988.

46 G. Kolko, *Anatomy of a War: Vietnam, the United States and the Modern Historical Experience*, 2nd edn, New York: New Press, 1994, p. 545.

47 M. T. Berger, "After the Third World? History, Destiny and the Fate of Third Worldism" *Third World Quarterly: Journal of Emerging Areas*, vol. 25, no. 1, 2004.

48 For the notion of the Bandung Era see S. Amin, *Re-reading the Postwar Period: An Intellectual Itinerary*, New York: Monthly Review Press, 1994.

49 A. Appadorai, *The Bandung Conference*, New Delhi: Indian Council of World Affairs, 1955; G. McTurnan Kahin, *The Asian-African Conference, Bandung, Indonesia, April 1955*, Ithaca: Cornell University Press, 1956.

50 H. W. Brands, *The Specter of Neutralism: The United States and the Emergence of the Third World, 1947–1960*, New York: Columbia University Press, 1990.

51 R. J. C. Young, *Postcolonialism: An Historical Introduction*, Oxford: Blackwell, 2001, pp. 191–2.

52 R. F. Betts, *Decolonization*, London: Routledge, 1998, p. 43.

53 P. Willetts, *The Non-Aligned Movement: The Origins of a Third World Alliance*, London: Macmillan, 1978.

54 G. Lundestad, *East, West, North, South: Major Developments in International Politics Since 1945*, 4th edn, New York: Oxford University Press, 1999, pp. 296–8. Also see R. A. Mortimer, *The Third World Coalition in World Politics*, Boulder: Westview, 1984.

55 A. Abdel-Malek cited in Young, *Postcolonialism*, p. 191.

56 R. Abdulgani, *Bandung Spirit: Moving on the Tide of History*, Djakarta: Prapantja, 1964. Also see C. P. Romulo, *The Meaning of Bandung*, Chapel Hill: University of North Carolina Press, 1956.

57 D. A. Low, *Eclipse of Empire*, Cambridge: Cambridge University Press, 1991, pp. 22–57.

58 In Vietnam the former is sometimes called the "War of National Liberation" and the latter is often known as the "American War", while in the United States the latter is known as the "Vietnam War".

59 Kuan-Hsing Chen has argued that in East Asia "there was a direct relay between an older kind of colonialism and new Cold War structures after 1945". In East Asia, he says, the US "took over from former territorial empires, and established a vast arc of strategic protectorates, mobilized to form a defensive bloc against Communism". He emphasizes that "there was a direct handover from Japanese imperialism to the US", and as a result "the decolonization that unfolded elsewhere after the Second World War never occurred. Instead a Cold War system effectively took over the structures of colonialism, intercepting any possibility of decolonization taking place. For fifty years the predominant world view and traditions of popular knowledge were generated out of systems of power and production at the intersection of colonialism and the Cold War." K.-H. Chen, "America in East Asia" *New Left Review (II)* no. 12, 2001, pp. 81–3. Also see K.-H. Chen, "Introduction: The Decolonization Question" in K-H. Chen, ed., *Trajectories: Inter-Asia Cultural Studies*, London: Routledge, 1998. While this represents an incisive interpretation of the shift from colonialism to the Cold War in East Asia, it downplays the way in which decolonization elsewhere in the region and beyond intersected and interacted with the Cold War. Although the speed of the transition and the intensity of the experience varied, all efforts at decolonization were quickly overlaid by the Cold War and postcolonial nation-states everywhere embraced, or were domesticated by, the wider structures of the Cold War. M. T. Berger, "Decolonizing Southeast Asia: Nationalism, Revolution and the Cold War" in M. Beeson, ed., *Contemporary Southeast Asia: Regional Dynamics, National Differences*, Basingstoke: Palgrave Macmillan, 2003.

60 H. S. Wilson, *African Decolonization*, London: Edward Arnold, 1994.

61 M. T. Berger, "The Cold War and National Liberation in Southern Africa: The United States and the Emergence of Zimbabwe" *Intelligence and National Security: An Inter-Disciplinary Journal* vol. 18, no. 1, 2003.

62 J. Springhall, *Decolonization Since 1945: The Collapse of European Overseas Empires*, Basingstoke: Palgrave Macmillan, 2001, pp. 182–4.

63 D. Fromkin, *A Peace to End All Peace: The Fall of the Ottoman Empire and the Creation of the Modern Middle East*, 2nd edn, New York: Henry Holt, 2001. For a good study of the dynamics of this process, which emphasizes local actors, see E. Karsh and I. Karsh, *Empires of the Sand: The Struggle for Mastery in the Middle East, 1789–1923*, Cambridge, MA: Harvard University Press, 1999. Also see J. McCarthy, *The Ottoman Peoples and the End of Empire*, New York: Oxford University Press, 2001.

64 C. A. Tripp, *A History of Iraq*, Cambridge: Cambridge University Press, 2000.

65 M. A. Heiss, *Empire and Nationhood: The United States, Great Britain, and Iranian Oil, 1950–1954*, New York: Columbia University Press, 1997.

66 I. M. Wall, *France, the United States and the Algerian War*, Berkeley: University of California Press, 2001.

67 P. L. Hahn, *The United States, Great Britain and Egypt, 1945–1956: Strategy and Diplomacy in the Early Cold War*, Chapel Hill: University of North Carolina Press, 1991.

68 S. Khilnani, *The Idea of India*, New York: Farrar Straus Giroux, 1997, pp. 81–6.

60 *The modernization project*

69 M. T. Berger, "Old State and New Empire in Indonesia: Debating the Rise and Decline of Suharto's New Order" *Third World Quarterly: Journal of Emerging Areas* vol. 18, no. 2, 1997.

70 B. Anderson, "Old State, New Society: Indonesia's New Order in Comparative Historical Perspective" *Journal of Asian Studies* vol. 42, no. 2, 1983 (reprinted in B. Anderson, *Language and Power: Exploring Political Cultures in Indonesia*, Ithaca: Cornell University Press, 1990).

71 Hardt and Negri, *Empire*, pp. 69–77, 83–8, 96 (authors' italics).

72 For example, Articles 1 and 55 of the UN Charter enshrined the principle of "self-determination of peoples", and this was reaffirmed in both *The Declaration on the Granting of Independence to Colonial Countries and Peoples* in 1960 and in *The Covenant on Civil and Political Rights* in 1966; however, these pronouncements say nothing about how to define "peoples". R. H. Jackson, *Quasi-states: Sovereignty, International Relations and the Third World*, Cambridge: Cambridge University Press, 1993 (first published 1990), pp. 151–2.

73 Hardt and Negri, *Empire*, pp. 105–9, 132–4 (authors' italics).

74 Young, *Postcolonialism*, p. 213.

75 On the history and politics of dependency theory see Berger, *Under Northern Eyes*, pp. 106–21.

76 P. H. Smith, "The Rise and Fall of the Developmental State in Latin America" in M. Vellinga, ed., *The Changing Role of the State in Latin America*, Boulder: Westview, 1998.

77 I. Wallerstein, "The Rise of East Asia, or the World-System in the Twenty-First Century" in I. Wallerstein, *The End of the World As We Know It: Social Science for the Twenty-First Century*, Minneapolis: University of Minnesota Press, 1999, pp. 36–7.

78 D. A. Low, *The Egalitarian Moment: Asia and Africa 1950–1980*, Cambridge: Cambridge University Press, 1996, pp. 1–2.

79 A. Dirlik, *After the Revolution: Waking to Global Capitalism*, Hanover: Wesleyan University Press, 1994, p. 44.

80 P. Desai, "Introduction" in P. Desai, ed., *Going Global: Transition from Plan to Market in the World Economy*, Cambridge, MA: MIT Press, 1997.

81 N. Harris, *The End of the Third World: Newly Industrializing Countries and the Decline of an Ideology*, London: I. B. Tauris, 1986.

82 Third World governments gained greater numerical influence at the UN in the 1970s. The UN's membership rose from 51 nation-states in 1945 to 156 nation-states in 1980. The vast majority of the new members were from Asia and Africa. P. McMichael, *Development and Social Change: A Global Perspective*, 2nd edn, Thousand Oaks: Pine Forge Press, 2000, p. 17.

83 At the end of the 1970s the UN set-up the Independent Commission on International Development (the Brandt Commission) chaired by former West German Chancellor Willy Brandt to address the North–South conflict. W. Brandt, *North–South: A Programme for Survival – Report of the Independent Commission on International Development Issues*, London: Pan, 1980.

84 F. Halliday, *The Making of the Second Cold War*, London: Verso, 1986.

2   Development economics

The rise of development economics was an important complement to the consolidation of the idea of national development in the Cold War era. This chapter focuses on the rise and fall of development economics and the relationship between this process and the elaboration of the US-led modernization project via a particular emphasis on the major state-guided national development effort in India up to the 1970s. This focus draws attention to the fact that in the 1950s and early 1960s, before the escalation of US involvement in Vietnam in the mid- and late 1960s and the dramatic emergence of the newly industrializing nation-states of East Asia in the 1970s, the developmental prospects of the Indian sub-continent and the geo-political significance of the new nation-states of India and Pakistan were the subject of considerable international attention (including a great deal of attention from the US). India in particular – because of its sheer size, its appearance as a new nation at the very beginning of the wider post-1945 wave of decolonization, and because of its government's efforts to maintain a non-aligned stance in the emerging Cold War (particularly under Prime Minister Jawaharlal Nehru 1947–1964) – occupied a key position in relation to the consolidation and universalization of the idea of development as national development. Within and outside of India there were great expectations that the new government's efforts to deliver material improvement and prosperity to its citizens could serve as a model of national development throughout the emerging Third World.[1]

This chapter begins with a discussion of the emergence of development economics and the part it played in the promotion and consolidation of the idea of national development. The role of the US in the rise of development economics is then explored via an examination of the Center for International Studies (CENIS) at the Massachusetts Institute of Technology (MIT) and its activities in India between 1955 and 1965, particularly its involvement with the Planning Commission. After 1945, development economics (like modernization theory and the social sciences more generally) conflated capitalist development with national development and turned nation-states that flowed from complex and contested histories into unproblematic units to be developed and modernized, equating the governments of those nations with the nations themselves. This is directly linked to the way in which development economics and the idea of national development rested on an elitist and technocratic approach that conceived of development as a technical problem outside of history and politics. The 1960s saw the waning of the high modernist approach to national development associated, for example, with the Planning Commission in India. Development economics itself was also in decline by this period. Development economics had been displaced by neo-classical economics by the end of the 1970s. This was part of the wider trend in which the post-1945 idea of national development was increasingly challenged by the globalization project. However, this process was uneven and the legacy of the ideas and instrumentalities associated with development economics, and the high modernist approach to national development, continued to exert a significant, albeit declining, influence in the context of shifting visions of the nation and its future in India and elsewhere.

The spectre of communism and the pursuit of progress I: the rise of development economics

The golden age of development economics

Before and after the Second World War the discipline of economics was preoccupied with understanding economic growth (and was focused on the nation-states of North America and Western Europe), while in the Cold War era the emergent sub-discipline of development economics explicitly sought to understand the causes of poverty and underdevelopment (and to generate policies that would address these problems) in what became known as the developing nation-states of the Third World. Following on from growing state intervention in economic matters in Western Europe and North America in the 1930s, the post-1945 influence of Keynesian ideas and the Marshall Plan meshed with the generally social-democratic character of the era in Great Britain and Western Europe (and to a lesser extent the United States) and legitimated an emphasis on planning and the assumption that economic development problems could be overcome when government action was combined with the necessary expertise and capital. The immediate origins of development economics, however, are usually traced to a group of economists working in Britain during the Second World War. In particular, for many observers and for many development economists, it was Paul N. Rosenstein-Rodan (who was born in Poland in 1902 and emigrated to Britain in the 1930s) who launched development economics with his essay on the "Problems of Industrialization of Eastern and South-Eastern Europe" in 1943.[2] During the Second World War Rosenstein-Rodan encouraged research on economic development (at the Royal Institute of International Affairs, Nuffield College, where he was secretary of the committee on post-war reconstruction) and subsequently, from his base at the Massachusetts Institute of Technology (MIT) in the 1950s (from where he presided over the major economic development initiative carried out by CENIS in India).[3]

For Rosenstein-Rodan and his colleagues, industrialization was the key to national development (this was the main theme of Rosenstein-Rodan's 1943 essay), and government planning was necessary for this to take place. As we have seen, this view overlapped with the developmental preoccupations of economists and politicians in Latin America by the 1930s and 1940s.[4] The 1930s was also a turning point for the US civilizing mission, especially in the Caribbean and Central America. A central goal of Washington's Good Neighbor Policy (1933) was to substitute the outdated policy of "punishing" Washington's southern neighbors for "uncivilized behavior" with a Pan-American policy that emphasized a program of hemispheric political and economic integration under US leadership. This approach increasingly assumed that Latin Americans could and should follow the road to national development charted by the United States.[5] As suggested in chapter 1, development economics was also an outgrowth of the effort by British colonial officials in the 1930s to recast the civilizing mission.[6] A new awareness of the importance of economic development in the colonies was particularly apparent by the eve of the Second World War. This shift began with Lord Hailey's confidential report to the Colonial Office that led to the Colonial Development and Welfare Act of 1940.[7] This was a manifestation of the fact that a growing number of government officials, colonial administrators and politicians had been converted to the "doctrines of a managed economy" and the "development idea".[8] At the same time, it needs to be emphasized that the idea and practice of development that emerged in the late-colonial context was an explicit attempt by British and French colonial officials to stabilize the colonial order. It was clearly linked to the paternalistic and racist notions of trusteeship of an earlier era; however, it also represented a new departure.[9]

The rise of development economics was directly linked to the wider process of decolonization, the onset of the Cold War and the universalization of the idea of development as national development after 1945. Development economics provided an increasingly substantial body of ideas and policies concerned with national development that could be used by postcolonial elites in Asia, Africa and the Middle East, and by those politicians, economists and industrialists in Latin America seeking a late-industrializing path to national development and modernity. An emphasis on government planning, foreign aid and an active effort at industrialization emerged as the dominant approach; however, there were some development economists, such as Peter T. Bauer (who eventually played a role in the "neo-classical counter-revolution" of the 1970s and 1980s), who remained committed to neo-classical economics.[10] But, despite dissenters, the key assumptions that underpinned the work of the vast majority of development economists by the 1950s included a commitment to the idea that economic development in the developing nations of the Third World was an uneven process (of structural change) that required active government efforts to facilitate increases in national levels of capital accumulation. It was assumed that, once a certain level of capital investment had been achieved within a particular developing nation, economic development would be self-sustaining; however, at the outset a "big push" by the state was required. The big push included a dramatic change to the ratio of national income to capital investment. It was expected that increases in national rates of economic growth would be parallelled by increases in the share of GDP that was invested. It was assumed that the expansion of the industrial sector and the growth of the urban population would ensure a growing market for agriculture, while providing an increased range of consumer goods that both the urban and rural population would purchase.[11]

In the golden age of development economics, industrialization was viewed as the linchpin of national development. The emphasis was on import-substitution industrialization (ISI). The centrality of industrialization to development economics and to the idea of national development was exemplified by W. Arthur Lewis's insistence, in a 1946 report on Jamaica, that it was as "clear as daylight" that industrialization was the cornerstone of national development.[12] Lewis was one of the most influential development economists of the 1950s and early 1960s. He embodied the way in which the late colonial era and the early Cold War provided the immediate context for the rise of development economics.[13] Born on Saint Lucia, in the British Caribbean, in 1915, Lewis served on the Colonial Research Committee, chaired by Lord Hailey, which was established in the wake of the Colonial Development and Welfare Act of 1940. Many of his later ideas about the role of government and the need for the movement of labor out of agriculture and into industry were already apparent in his contributions to the Committee.[14] He was eventually knighted and received the Nobel Memorial Prize in Economic Science in 1979 for his contribution to development economics. Apart from writing a number of influential works in development economics in the 1950s, Lewis also made a major contribution to the 1951 United Nations report on *Measures for the Economic Development of Underdeveloped Countries*.[15]

Lewis's work and outlook encapsulated the growing concern of many North American and Western European policy-makers and development economists, that the Soviet model of national development was gaining support in Asia, Africa, the Middle East and Latin America. In his influential 1955 work, *The Theory of Economic Growth*, Lewis expressed particular concern about the appeal the Soviet Union had to nationalist leaders seeking rapid industrialization. He lamented that "it has been demonstrated by the USSR that a ruthless government can raise real output very rapidly" and "underdeveloped countries" were "being invited, by Communist or other propaganda, to yield up their liberties in return for a promise of rapid economic growth".[16] More broadly, for some observers, Lewis's work, which emphasized the enabling role of the state in capitalist development, represented a major point of departure for W. W. Rostow's efforts to articulate a developmental alternative to Marxism.[17] This effort was famously embodied by his publication of *The Stages of Economic Growth: A Non-Communist Manifesto* in 1960.[18] Influential development economists, such as Lewis and Rostow, played an important role in the study of, and the macroeconomic policies followed by, the developing nations of the Third World in the 1950s and early 1960s.[19]

The Center for International Studies and the Cold War in Asia I

While Lewis embodied the connection between the crisis of British colonialism and the rise of development economics in the early Cold War era, Rostow's career signified the important connection between development economics and US geo-political strategy after 1945. In the 1950s Rostow was closely associated with the Center for International Studies (CENIS), an important nexus for development economics and modernization theory that was established at the Massachusetts Institute of Technology (MIT) in 1951.[20] MIT had already emerged as the biggest defense contractor of any university in the United States by the end of the Second World War, a position it occupied, followed closely by Stanford University, throughout the Cold War (and into the post-Cold War) era.[21] Following CENIS's establishment at MIT, it initially focused its research activities, according to Rostow, on the "study of communist societies and the study of problems of development – economic, social and political".[22] At the end of the 1950s Rostow, who served in the research and analysis branch of the Office of Strategic Services (OSS) during the Second World War, became an adviser to Senator John F. Kennedy. He went on to be chair of the Policy Planning Staff in the State Department during the Kennedy administration, as well as an adviser to President Johnson during the Vietnam War (he was appointed National Security Advisor in 1966).[23] Meanwhile, Max Millikan, who like Rostow had studied in Britain in the 1930s, was on leave from MIT in the late 1940s and early 1950s in order to serve as assistant director (of economic research) at the Central Intelligence Agency. Millikan returned to MIT in 1952 to become the director of CENIS, remaining director until his death in 1969.[24]

By the late 1950s CENIS luminaries such as Rostow increasingly advocated and symbolized the shift in US foreign policy away from containing the Soviet Union with direct military force (at a time when the Soviet Union had begun developing atomic weaponry), and towards taking the initiative in Asia, Africa and Latin America via infusions of economic and military aid as part of an increasingly ambitious set of national development and counter-insurgency programs.[25] Rostow's book, *The Stages of Economic Growth: A Non-Communist Manifesto*, encapsulated, more than any other single text, the high modernist and anti-communist approach to national development emanating from Washington in the early 1960s. First published in 1960, it argued that "Communism" was "a kind of disease which can befall a transitional society if it fails to organize effectively those elements within it which are prepared to get on the with the job of modernization". He called on "we of the democratic north" to "face and deal with the challenge implicit in the stages-of-growth … at the full stretch of our moral commitment, our energy, and our resources".[26] Rostow advocated government planning and state intervention to facilitate the movement of a developing nation-state through his five stages to reach "take off". However, in contrast to some of the more structuralist proponents of development economics, his approach tended to ignore the hierarchical character of the historical and contemporary world economy. Of course, like virtually all development economists, his approach was ahistorical and technocratic. He took nation-states as routine units of a wider international order, while overlooking the numerous historical changes that distinguished the industrialization of emergent imperial nation-states in the eighteenth- and nineteenth-centuries from developing nation-states of the twentieth century. When *The Stages of Economic Growth* was published, Rostow, Millikan and Rosenstein-Rodan were already serving as advisers to Senator, soon to be President, John F. Kennedy. In January 1960, the US Senate Committee on Foreign Relations (of which Kennedy was a member) received (at the committee's request) a report from CENIS entitled "Economic, Social and Political Change in the Underdeveloped Countries and Its Implications for United States Policy". The authors expounded CENIS's view on the importance of the developing nations for US foreign policy. The report's main recommendations were that US foreign economic aid should be disbursed on a "long-term" and "unlinked" basis following clear economic criteria. Technical assistance, particularly in agriculture, needed to continue and land reform needed to be promoted. It emphasized that the US needed to coordinate the distribution of aid with other aid-donor governments in the developed world and a corps of development professionals should be established. Aid for particular capital-intensive projects, it was argued, should be increased and it needed to be spread over a number of projects to facilitate a "big push" in the developing nations.[27] A revised and expanded version of the report was published in 1961 as *The Emerging Nations: Their Growth and United States Policy*. It was edited by Millikan and Donald Blackmer, and included chapters by Rosenstein-Rodan and Rostow, as well as Lucian Pye, and Daniel Lerner, among others.[28]

By the time President Kennedy had established USAID and the Peace Corps, which were both initiatives that had been proposed in the CENIS report, Rostow in particular was well on his way to becoming a major figure in the new administration, where he could continue to put his and CENIS's ideas into practice. For example, shortly after joining the Kennedy administration, Rostow (along with Robert Komer) scrutinized the situation in South Korea and concluded that Washington's focus, which emphasized military and security questions, was too narrow. In a June 12 1961 memo, Komer (who had served in the Directorate of Intelligence and Office of National Estimates at the CIA from 1957 until he joined the National Security Council as a senior staff member in 1961) argued that "one of the basic reasons why we have accomplished so little in Korea since 1953 has been our predominantly military focus". In March 1961, an earlier memorandum, also written by Komer, had already mapped out a new US policy for South Korea that attached greater weight to economic development. He emphasized the need for "crash economic development", the "creation of light labor-intensive industry" and "much more vigorous" and "imaginative US action in directing and supervising ROK economic development".[29] Of course, this shift coincided with the rise of the Park Chung Hee dictatorship in South Korea and it is clear that Park, who was profoundly influenced by the Japanese experience of industrialization, required no encouragement from the US to embark on a major state-directed national development initiative, which is not to say that, as we shall see in chapter eight, the Park regime did not reap considerable developmental benefits from its close alliance with the United States. At any rate, regardless of its provenance, General Park's grand vision of national development meshed with the preoccupation of Rostow and other development economists with a "big push" rather than with incremental change. By the late 1960s, South Korea and Taiwan (which had become major US military redoubts against international communism) were already being held up by some observers as possible examples of successful "non-Communist" modernization and nation-building in the Third World.[30] However, it was not until the second half of the 1970s – as we will see in chapters 5 to 7 – that the East Asian NICs (South Korea, Taiwan, Hong Kong and Singapore) began to attract sustained attention.

The Center for International Studies and the Cold War in Asia II

US support for national development in the Third World in the 1960s burgeoned. Washington's primary geographical concern, immediately after 1945, had been Western Europe, Greece, Turkey and Northeast Asia. For example, Southeast Asia did not attract sustained attention until at least the 1950s. Washington had also taken a limited interest in the new nation-states of India and Pakistan that emerged in South Asia in 1947. However, as with Southeast Asia (which will be discussed in more detail in chapter 3), the US began to change its assessment of South Asia with the establishment of the Peoples' Republic of China in late 1949 and the start of the Korean War in 1950. By the beginning of the 1950s some policy-makers, politicians and journalists were arguing that South Asia was of central importance to a range of key US foreign policy goals.[31] As noted above, India, under the charismatic leadership of Jawaharlal Nehru, was increasingly viewed as a possible political and economic model for Asia and the Third World. By the 1950s, Nehru's international profile and his commitment to a combination of parliamentary democracy, economic planning and socialist principles which drew on Soviet, Western European and Chinese experience had helped to focus considerable world attention on India as a laboratory for national development. For some observers in the US by this time, India was regarded as an important prize: they conjured with the political and ideological benefits for Washington that an alliance with the most influential non-aligned government in Asia would bring. According to this vision, if the US strengthened ties with Nehru's government, Washington could help ensure that India would serve as an anchor for, and model of, democratic capitalist development in the Third World to counter the explicitly anti-capitalist and state-socialist alternatives exemplified by China and the Soviet Union. However, for other US strategists Pakistan was the most important nation-state in the region for military-strategic reasons: they emphasized its proximity to the Soviet Union and its position in relation to the Middle East. By 1954 the emphasis on the relative importance of Pakistan had led to the decision to enter into a mutual security agreement between the US and the government of Pakistan. At the same time, Pakistan also became a founding member of the South-East Asia Treaty Organization (SEATO) that was formally established in February 1955.[32]

Nehru concluded that the move by the Eisenhower administration to provide significant quantities of military assistance to Pakistan necessitated that the Indian government make substantial increases in defense spending. It was also assumed that this would mean that the government of Pakistan would be more opposed to the settlement of a range of bilateral issues, such as Kashmir. In this period the government in New Delhi also set about balancing its relationship with Washington by deepening its economic and military links to Moscow and maintaining good relations with the Chinese government. In part, as a result of these changes, by the end of the 1950s the US approach to South Asia had shifted away from an emphasis on Pakistan and towards an emphasis on India. Worried that the USSR, in particular, was gaining influence in Indian government circles, via its generous trade and aid arrangements, and concerned that if the Indian government failed to achieve its national development plans the strength of the country's communist movement would increase, President Eisenhower expanded his administration's economic aid program to India in his final years in office. Meanwhile, Senator John F. Kennedy, from his position on the Senate Foreign Relations Committee, increasingly emphasized the centrality of India to US foreign policy. By the end of the 1950s the Eisenhower administration also shared the concern, voiced by Kennedy and others, that economic decline in India could enhance the Chinese government's prestige in international affairs, undermining the US claim that the democratic-capitalist model was superior to the state-socialist model of national development.[33]

CENIS's effort to redirect US foreign policy towards India gained new impetus with the election of Kennedy as president at the end of 1960.[34] Apart from key CENIS figures, such as Rostow (and Millikan, who was an adviser on foreign aid), Kennedy's new ambassador to India, John Kenneth Galbraith, as well as Chester Bowles, who succeeded Galbraith as ambassador to India in 1963, along with John Lewis (who took up the post of chief of USAID in New Delhi under Kennedy), were all in general agreement with the importance CENIS attached to foreign aid and national development. Meanwhile, CENIS had been running a major economic development project in India since the mid-1950s. The US government, especially the Central Intelligence Agency (CIA), financed CENIS's research on communist countries; however, private foundations, especially the Ford Foundation, were the primary financial backers of its research on economic development.[35] In the 1950s, the Ford Foundation's activities in India had grown to the point where they were bigger than all of its other programs outside of the continental United States.[36] In July 1952 the Ford Foundation gave CENIS US$125,000 for preliminary research, to be followed in 1953 by another interim grant of US$175,000 for the project as a whole, and US$50,000 for Indonesian fieldwork. Then, in June 1954 CENIS was given a long-term grant of US$750,000 for a four- to five-year study of economic and political development in Italy, Indonesia and India; however, the Center's project eventually focused exclusively on India (for which two more grants of US$750,000 and approximately US$560,000 each were disbursed) and operated from 1955 to 1965. The major concern of the MIT project, directed by Rosenstein-Rodan for much of its existence, was the preparation of development plans and the estimation of the quantity of foreign aid needed for the realization of those plans. The Planning Commission, chaired by Prime Minister Nehru, emerged as the main focus of cooperation between the MIT development economists and the Indian government.[37]

The spectre of communism and the pursuit of progress II: the fall of development economics

The "Gradual Revolution" I: Nehruvian socialism and national development in India

By the mid-1950s the Planning Commission was the key site for the articulation of Nehru's high modernist vision of national development and the pursuit of Nehruvian socialism and the "Gradual Revolution" in India.[38] The origins of the Planning Commission specifically, and development planning in India more generally, are usually traced to the ferment of nationalist politics in the sub-continent in the 1930s.[39] In particular, in 1938 (two years prior to the promulgation of the Colonial Development and Welfare Act and almost a decade before formal independence from Britain) the Indian National Congress established a National Planning Committee that was charged with drawing up a blueprint for the social and economic reconstruction of post-independence India. Unlike Africa and other parts of Asia, the institutional and intellectual manifestations of the idea of national development in India clearly preceded and/or at least parallelled the rise of the idea of colonial development in Britain. However, the initial efforts at development planning carried out by the state in postcolonial India relied far more on the Planning and Development Department set up in 1944 and centered on the Indian Civil Service (ICS), than they did on the work of the National Planning Committee established by the Indian National Congress in 1938. The First Five-Year Plan (1950–55) was primarily an array of public works projects that had been in the planning stages in the final years of British rule.[40] In fact, when India became independent in 1947 there was considerable uncertainty about the new government's overall approach to national development. At the outset, Prime Minister Nehru had to contend with the conservative Home Minister and Deputy Prime Minister, Vallabhabhai Patel (the most powerful figure in the complex bureaucratic politics of the Congress Party), who was opposed to Nehru's high modernist and socialist vision of national development. It was not until Patel's death in 1950 that Nehru was able to set about more effectively asserting his control over the state apparatus and the party organization.[41]

While Nehru's high modernist conception of state-guided national development, which reached its peak during the second half of the 1950s and early 1960s, is often seen as being shaped by the Soviet model, this was always tempered by a critique of the lack of democracy in the Soviet Union and the human cost of Soviet industrialization. For some observers Nehru's views by the 1950s had much more in common with social democracy in post-1945 Western Europe than they did with state-socialism in the Soviet Union, despite the much-publicized Soviet support for national development in India.[42] Nehru certainly rejected key aspects of the Soviet model and his perspective bore similarities to social democratic currents in Western Europe; however, Nehru and the Planning Commission also drew on China's post-1949 approach to national development, especially its approach to agriculture.[43] Furthermore, although there is clearly no direct parallel between the practice of national development in India and the path followed in the Soviet Union and Mao's China, it is possible to see Nehruvian socialism as more explicitly grounded in Marxism than writers such as Partha Chatterjee (who views Nehru's "appropriation" of Marxism as "selective") have implied.[44] It can be argued that Marxism was a constitutive aspect of Nehru's high modernist and statist nationalism. The domestication of Marxism (as a broader politico-intellectual frame of reference) to Indian nationalism carried out by Nehru in the 1930s flowed directly from the trajectory Marxism took after Marx, particularly after Lenin's reformulation of the colonial question as the national question. Marxism became national in India and elsewhere, regardless of whether formal communist movements were successful or unsuccessful in coming to power. Marxism was established as a vibrant, although not hegemonic, intellectual force in India, at the same time as its formally organized political position in the subcontinent was relatively weak. Marxism has historically been heavily implicated in both nationalism and the expanding nation-state system, and the rise and vicissitudes of Nehruvian socialism exemplify the way in which Marxism was assimilated to national circumstances against the background of an international Marxist discourse that often privileged nationalist struggles over class struggles, and actively participated in the routinization of the nation-state.[45]

The Indian government under Nehru clearly articulated a vision of development that was socialist and nationalist, as well as technocratic and paternalistic. This was apparent in the operation of the Planning Commission, the main instrument of national development in this period.[46] Its influence, which was paramount in this period, was grounded directly in Nehru's patronage. Key players, such as Prasanta Chandra Mahalanobis – who was a chief adviser to, and after 1955 a *de facto* member of, the Commission – had Nehru's unwavering support. Mahalanobis was undoubtedly the main author of the Second Five-Year Plan (1955–1960), which was a variant of the "Lewis Model" (named after and grounded in the ideas of W. Arthur Lewis discussed above) and privileged heavy industry with particular zeal. The Planning Commission and its operations had a profound impact on the idea and practice of national development in India; however, its ascendancy was relatively short-lived and the implementation of its policies never transcended the complexities of national and regional politics and bureaucratic rivalries. By the time Nehru died in May 1964, the notion that a benevolent technocratic elite, centered on the Planning Commission, could guide the national development of India was in crisis in the context of a wider crisis of Congress Party rule.[47] The Nehru era had been characterized by the consolidation of state power and the strengthening of the reach of the Congress Party via myriad local and regional political compromises. In this situation, the pursuit of socialism generally, and the goal of industrialization more specifically, increasingly involved government support for private interests, rather than the public sector approach to industrialization that was Nehru's ideal. It was clear by the mid-1960s that the majority of the population actually saw few benefits from national development, which went primarily to the private commercial and industrial groups and bureaucratic and professional interests directly or indirectly connected to the political leadership.[48] By the second half of the 1960s the diminution of the Planning Commission's power coincided and combined with the failure of the monsoons in 1965–1966 and 1966–1967 to usher in a turn to the scientific, technical and capital-intensive food production methods and practices associated with the Green Revolution. This, as we shall see, significantly altered the balance between industrialization and agricultural production in India by the end of the 1960s.[49]

The "Gradual Revolution" II: the Center for International Studies and the Cold War in India

The Center for International Studies and the United States played a much-debated role in this shift in the balance between industry and agriculture in this period. A key activity of CENIS by the early 1960s was the development of a multi-sector planning model for the Indian economy spearheaded by MIT development economist Richard Eckhaus.[50] The model was eventually used to evaluate the Third Five-Year Plan (1960–1965). The results suggested a need to redirect investment away from capital goods and towards consumer goods, especially in agriculture, calling into question the emphasis on industrialization, particularly the preoccupation with heavy industry associated with Nehru and the Planning Commission's vision of national development. It also represented a departure from the emphasis of many development economists in the 1950s. However, it meshed with the view articulated by the US government that had been arguing for a number of years that agriculture should be given much greater priority in terms of resources and that farmers should be given a range of incentives to embrace more capital-intensive methods. In fact, World Bank officials had been making this point and also insisting since the late 1950s that the Planning Commission's public-sector program was too large and the domestic and foreign private sector needed to be given a bigger role. These criticisms took on new significance, however, once Nehru was dead. The new Prime Minister, Lal Bahadur Shastri (1964–1966), did not have Nehru's authority and the Planning Commission was the object of growing criticism in the context of a deepening political and economic crisis.[51]

By the mid-1960s, meanwhile, it was clear that CENIS was an important player in the US policy-making process. In 1964, a new book, *The Invisible Government*, by David Wise and Thomas B. Ross made public the fact that the CIA had assisted in funding the establishment of CENIS (and continued to fund some of its projects afterwards). The book also drew attention to the fact that Max Millikan had been employed at the CIA before he took up the director's job at CENIS. Although the CIA had apparently not directly funded any of the center's projects in India, the suggestion of a CIA connection had already undermined an earlier Ford Foundation-funded social science project operated by Cornell University in the sub-continent.[52] Meanwhile, on October 14 1964 the Indian ambassador to the United States, B. K. Nehru, visited MIT where he met with Millikan, Rosenstein-Rodan and, briefly, Eckaus. The implications of the Center's modelling of the Indian economy were the main topic of discussion. The ambassador subsequently wrote a letter to Ashok Mehta, the new Deputy Chairman of the Planning Commission, drawing his attention to the fact that the development economists at MIT felt that there needed to be a change in emphasis in development planning away from heavy industry and towards light industry and consumer goods. In the politically fractious post-Nehru era the contents of the letter were quickly construed as a direct attack on the Planning Commission.[53] Because of growing tension, Millikan and Rosenstein-Rodan decided that CENIS would suspend the work it had planned to carry out in the second half of 1965; however, they were still thinking of despatching a new group of development economists to India the following year. The Ford Foundation thought such plans were no longer appropriate and decided to let the CENIS grant end in 1965. The main concern was that if CENIS work continued it would not only cast a shadow over the rest of the MIT presence in India, but spread to the Ford Foundation's other operations in the sub-continent.[54]

This affair was unfolding in the context of an overall deterioration in relations between the Indian government and Washington as the exaggerated geo-strategic and developmental aims of the Kennedy era, like Nehru's high modernist vision of national development, fell well short of expectations. Following the outbreak of war between India and Pakistan in 1965, Washington suspended all aid to both sides indefinitely and even food aid under Public Law 480 (PL480) was disbursed via a "short tether" policy, which involved shipping only enough food to last a couple of months. By 1966 the continuation of US food aid had been made dependent on the Indian government adopting policies in the countryside that were directed towards lowering population growth rates and increasing agricultural production.[55] In the 1950s and early 1960s US policy-makers had assigned great significance to South Asia generally, and India more specifically, in relation to wider US geo-political calculations. Between 1947 and 1965 the US disbursed US$12 billion worth of military and economic aid to South Asia. Ultimately, with the support of organizations such as CENIS, the US government had pursued a course of action that rested on an inflated estimate of the degree to which it could facilitate the transformation of India and Pakistan into stable Cold War military allies and paragons of national development. As its approach to military and economic aid following the war between Pakistan and India in 1965 suggests, the Johnson administration (1963–1968) sought to limit US direct involvement in South Asia relative to the earlier period.[56]

The Green Revolution: the waning of Nehruvian socialism in India

As development economics generally, and Nehru's Planning Commission more specifically, fell into disrepute by the second half of the 1960s, the Green Revolution moved to the center of the development debate in India and elsewhere in Asia and the Third World. In effect the myth that the technical and scientific knowledge and expertise of state planners and development economists could rapidly industrialize the new nations gave way to a new mythology about the way in which technology and science could once again come to the rescue by transforming agriculture and solving the problems of poverty, famine and hunger in the rural regions of the new nation-states.[57] Reports of the new high-yielding varieties of wheat and rice, the magic key to the Green Revolution, had begun to appear in 1964. In that year it was announced that scientists working with the backing of the Indian Council of Agricultural Research and the Rockefeller Foundation had successfully developed new varieties of maize and that plant geneticists, also supported by the Rockefeller Foundation, had created a hybrid wheat variety, based on Mexican and Japanese strains, that could generate double the output of existing Indian wheat types.[58] Meanwhile, in October 1964 a high profile World Bank mission, led by US economist, Bernard Bell, arrived in India to carry out a review of India's "development performance". Bell and his colleagues focused on the agricultural sector, arguing that there was a need to increase fertilizer use and domestic fertilizer production. They also drew attention to the need for improved distribution of inputs and outputs in the rural sector generally. None of these ideas were new, but the Bell Mission added weight to the pressure for a greater emphasis on agriculture that had been emanating from the Ford and Rockefeller Foundations, and USAID, not to mention from CENIS. In fact, at the end of 1964, USAID started to use conditional loans to encourage reform in the agricultural sector. This was done with the support of C. Subramaniam, who had become India's new Minister of Food and Agriculture in the government of Nehru's successor, Lal Bahadur Shastri.[59]

The appointment of Subramaniam as Minister of Food and Agriculture was particularly significant. It was the first change Shastri made to the Cabinet he inherited from Nehru, a cabinet in which Subramaniam had been head of the Steel ministry.[60] While this appointment signalled Shastri's own willingness to place greater emphasis on agriculture, Subramaniam was himself a keen advocate of the use of the new high-yielding rice and wheat and the various institutional and technological changes, and economic reforms, that went with the Green Revolution package. This approach was accepted in principle by the Indian cabinet and Parliament by the end of 1965 and this paved the way for its introduction and spread in the second half of the 1960s.[61] In fact, in the twenty months that Shastri served as Prime Minister the overall approach to national development in India shifted. Apart from the weakening of the Planning Commission, incentives rather than controls were adopted in development planning, and public investment was reoriented towards agriculture and away from basic industries. In this period a new approach to agriculture, which focused on capital-intensive efforts in rural areas that already had irrigation infrastructure, was introduced, while the role of private domestic and overseas investors in industrialization was enlarged. By the time of Shastri's death in January 1966 the key elements of Nehru's conception of national development (an emphasis on public sector heavy industries and land reform and the cooperative reorganization of agriculture), which had fallen well short in practice, were in decline.[62] Ironically, the general direction that the CENIS model had been suggesting was followed even as CENIS ended its project in India. In a wider sense the Indian government clearly moved towards a "production-oriented agricultural strategy" in the mid-1960s because of pressure from the United States (more specifically from USAID, the US Embassy and the World Bank); however, this pressure probably reinforced rather than caused an emerging post-Nehru consensus, between the Prime Minister and most chief ministers of the various states, as well as economists and intellectuals, that led to the Green Revolution in India.[63]

The introduction of Green Revolution practices was a response to the fact that from independence to the mid-1960s there was no sustained growth in rural India. During the heyday of the Planning Commission long-standing subsistence agricultural practices had undergone a "fine tuning" rather than a transformation. The more immediate roots of the Green Revolution in India are to be found in the major climatic downturn in 1965 that led to a crisis in the countryside, especially in the heavily populated states of Uttar Pradesh and Bihar. Only large purchases of food from overseas and an influx of US food aid prevented a significant death toll. The agrarian crisis was an important reason behind the electoral defeat of the Congress party in eight states in 1967. Its majority in the national legislature was also reduced significantly. The crises of 1965–1967 encouraged Prime Minister Indira Gandhi (1966–1977), Nehru's daughter, who had emerged from the Congress party's internal power struggles as successor to Shastri, to push ahead with the Green Revolution. At the same time, the Congress Party split into the Organisation Congress and the Indira Congress in 1969. Over the next two years Mrs Gandhi attempted to link the rich peasantry, who were the main beneficiaries of the Green Revolution, to her family's traditional support base amongst the poor peasantry, Muslims and Harijans. To do this she adopted an increasingly populist nationalism, that involved, among other things, nationalizing over a dozen private banking institutions and directing lines of credit away from urban areas and towards the rural sector. When these initiatives were combined with campaign promises to bring an end to poverty, the result was a landslide victory in the 1971 general election.[64] Indira Gandhi's populist nationalism signalled a quantitative and qualitative change in the idea of national development in India. Her vision of national development was far more widely disseminated as a result of more effective use of the mass media and because she was able to bring new constituencies under the banner of a more populist nationalism. Her populism altered the content of national development from the high modernist industrializing vision articulated by her father to a grand narrative of India as a modernizing, but still agricultural, nation. This shift led to an increase in both the degree, and the extent, to which the idea of national development, in its populist agrarian form, became part of the quotidian existence of the poor in the Indian countryside.[65]

By the mid-1970s, however, Indira Gandhi's government was foundering. The growing contradiction between the centralization of power and the weakening authority of the postcolonial Indian state that was well advanced by the 1970s had its roots in the shortcomings of national development in the Nehru years.[66] However, the failure of Mrs Gandhi's version of national development was also closely connected to the more immediate political economy and social dynamics of the Green Revolution.[67] The wheat yields in areas where the new techniques were embraced with the most enthusiasm had risen dramatically by the 1970s and the government developed a major buffer stock capacity from the resulting surplus. However, the use of Green Revolution production methods for wheat was still primarily taking place in the plains of the northwest, while Green Revolution methods for producing rice had only been established in a handful of southern agricultural zones. When the monsoons failed in 1972–1973, widespread starvation was only averted by massive food imports, triggering a dramatic rise in inflation. At the same time, some of the new inputs were imported. This put pressure on the country's foreign exchange reserves, a situation that became much worse after the 1973 oil crisis, because fertilizers that were crucial to the Green Revolution were petroleum-based. Also, the need for large agricultural holdings, to maximize the economic rewards promised by the Green Revolution, sparked a dramatic increase in the eviction of sharecroppers and tenants, as well as a significant rise in mortgage foreclosures. Meanwhile, the increasingly capital-intensive character of farming, including mechanization, broke down the "semi-feudal ties" that had often connected rich peasants to their agricultural workers (either poor peasants or landless laborers). As the paternal obligations of the rich peasants towards their former retainers faded and the size of the landless rural population increased, against the backdrop of an increasingly unequal distribution of wealth, social tensions in the countryside were exacerbated. The contradictions of the Green Revolution and of the populist nationalism that had briefly united the poor and the wealthy peasants behind Indira Gandhi in the late 1960s and early 1970s had been laid bare by the mid-1970s. Mrs Gandhi's rejection by the rural poor combined with charges of electoral malpractice (that could have led to her being excluded from holding public office for at least six years) encouraged her to declare a State of Emergency on June 26 1975 which allowed her to retain the Prime Ministership via martial law until 1977.[68]

The end of the golden age of development economics

The modernizing optimism that had pervaded development economics (and had been manifested in the grandiose plans to transform the Third World that characterized the Kennedy administration and the technocratic and high modernist vision of national development of Nehru's Planning Commission) had clearly passed by the end of the 1960s. According to Paul Krugman, the golden age of development economics, or what he calls the era of "high development theory" (which he dates very precisely from 1943 to 1958), had ended before the 1960s even began.[69] In contrast to Krugman, Robert Gilpin dates the ascendancy of development economics more generously from 1945 to 1970.[70] Meanwhile, H. W. Arndt argues that the "orthodoxy of the first phase of post-war thinking about economic development" (an orthodoxy that he argues coalesced around the general "structuralist approach" outlined by development economists such as Hollis B. Chenery, a key figure at the World Bank in the 1970s who will be discussed in chapter 5) began to fragment in the 1960s.[71] Carlos Ramirez-Faria agrees with Arndt that there was an "orthodoxy of development economics or economic development"; however, he argues that the "orthodoxy was not successfully challenged in the West from within or from without until the 1970s", while in the Third World it still reflected "the dominant outlook on development" at the beginning of the 1990s.[72] Despite these very significant differences over periodization and geographical purchase, all observers agree that development economics had clearly lost or was at least losing its influence by the 1970s, if not before.[73]

The reasons for the decline of development economics, like the precise periodization, are contested. It is now clear that a central factor in the decline of development economics was that the political complexities that development economists, such as those operating in India, faced were not given sufficient consideration at the outset, when a commitment to state-guided planning and industrialization, along with foreign aid and increased levels of capital accumulation had been seen as a veritable magic formula. Nor had the deeper assumptions on which their analyses and prescriptions rested ever been scrutinized. The work of Gunnar Myrdal, for example, makes clear the limitations of development economics in this period. In the 1950s Myrdal's work exemplified the view, central to development economics and embodied in concepts such as the "big push", that underdeveloped nations could not escape from poverty unless they embarked on major state-guided national development efforts, supported by substantial foreign aid.[74] Writing many years later, Myrdal reiterated that what had been needed in India and other underdeveloped nations "in order to raise the miserable living levels of the poor masses" was "radical institutional reforms" and the governments of the new nations had not been able to bring these about.[75] This concern that the state in India and elsewhere was unable to act as a disciplined arbiter of national development was one of the main themes of *Asian Drama* that appeared in 1968. In this now-famous three-volume work he noted that, while the governments of India and other new nations in South and Southeast Asia were formally committed to promoting economic development in a coordinated and planned fashion (often described in India as "democratic planning") "even India has been unable to register a rate of progress comparable to that in the Western countries". This failure, said Myrdal, was "rooted in the inefficiency, rigidity, and inequality of the established institutions and attitudes, and in the economic and social power relations embodied in this framework of institutions and attitudes". Ultimately, for Myrdal, India and other new nation-states in South and Southeast Asia had failed to develop because they were "soft states". What he meant was: "policies decided on are often not enforced, if they are enacted at all", while "the authorities, even when framing policies, are reluctant to place obligations on people". He was particularly critical of the way in which "democratic planning" had come to mean that the implementation of policies "should not require compulsion" and that "abstention from compulsion" was "permitted to masquerade as part" of the ideal of modernization.[76]

This analysis highlights the array of issues that fell outside the expertise and concern of development economics – even development economists such as Myrdal, whose analysis was particularly comprehensive – in the heyday of national development. In the process of systematizing development economics the question of why social formations and political systems might not respond in the anticipated fashion once the prescriptions of development economists were applied had been neglected. Nevertheless Myrdal grappled tentatively with these issues, arguing that there was a need for a "hard state". This led to the worrying conclusion that in the case of Indonesia for example: "only the army could conceivably carry out" the "relentless but benevolent and enlightened dictatorship" that he thought was required.[77] This view foreshadowed the theory of the developmental state and the legitimation of authoritarian developmentalism that emerged in later years, which will be discussed in detail in chapter 7. The most influential response to the question of political capacity and institutional effectiveness in the 1950s and 1960s, however, was provided by North American political scientists in the form of modernization theory, or political development theory, which is the subject of the next chapter.[78] Unlike development economists, political development theorists were more concerned from the outset with political order than economic development.[79] At the same time, development economics and political development theory were more technocratic than democratic (Myrdal's call for a "hard state" meshed nicely with the militarization of modernization theory in the 1960s), and neither addressed more basic issues to do with the way in which nation-states, regardless of their complex history, were/are taken as routine objects of analysis that should develop, or could be made to develop.[80] Thus, one of the most basic assumptions on which development economics rested went, and in many cases continues to go, unchallenged. Taking the nation-state as the unquestioned object of their technocratic and paternalistic efforts was one of the most significant weaknesses of development economics and of a wide range of theories of modernization in the high period of national development.

Despite its decline in the 1960s, many of the ideas associated with development economics, such as state intervention, planning, and the relative
importance of industrialization, continued, as Ramirez-Faria has argued, to have
considerable, albeit decreasing, purchase in the theory and the practice of
national development into the 1970s and beyond. In some governing circles the
importance of the role of the state in economic development remained widely
accepted. For example, the Indian government did not signal a significant break
with the legacy of development economics and national planning until the
much-celebrated liberalizing initiatives of 1991.[81] Most nation-states in the
Middle East, in large part because of oil wealth and/or their geo-political significance, have also been able to resist pressure for both economic and political
liberalism.[82] In East Asia, meanwhile, the waning of ideas loosely connected to
development economics was, as we shall see in later chapters, a very uneven
process. Furthermore, although development economics was in full retreat from
the international economic policy high ground by the beginning of the 1980s,
many of its key ideas, along with its overall status as a body of economic theory
and practice, survived in a range of university settings. W. Arthur Lewis pointed
out in a 1983 address to the American Economic Association that the dramatic
resurgence of neo-classical economics was not an immediately universal
phenomenon and development economics continued to attract students from the
so-called Third World.[83] In the second half of the 1980s, Gustav Ranis and John
Fei insisted that "reports of the death of development economics have been
greatly exaggerated", although they acknowledged that a process of reorientation had taken place.[84] More recently, Michael Carter has also argued that
reports of the demise of development economics are overstated. Although the
"ascendance of a policy orthodoxy of development liberalism" is beyond
dispute, he insisted that development economics has continued to participate in
the process of revision within economics.[85] Furthermore, the rise of a state-
centered challenge to neo-classical economics, with a focus on Northeast (and to
a lesser extent Southeast) Asia, meant that development economics underwent a
revival and revision in the 1980s, in the guise of theories of the developmental
state.[86] Development economics may also have had some influence on the new
institutional economics that appeared as a revisionist outgrowth of neo-classical
economics by the second half of the 1980s.[87] It is also possible to discern the
influence of development economics on the new political economy associated
with writers such as Robert Bates, which emerged in the 1980s and 1990s and
will be discussed in chapter 5. Meanwhile, in 2000, the World Bank sponsored a
major retrospective and prospective on development economics, under the
editorship of Gerald Meier, Joseph Stiglitz and Nicholas Stern. This massive
volume clearly sought to critically examine but also breathe new life into what is
now a much-revised and long-marginalized sub-discipline of economics.[88]

Significantly, the failure in the 1960s of development economics, and the
declining fortunes of an array of state-mediated national development projects
in the so-called Third World, also paved the way for a more radical challenge,
symbolized by Cuba and the other second-generation Bandung regimes that

were discussed briefly in chapter 1.[89] The rise and spread of dependency theory (along with other revitalized Marxist theories of development) in the second half of the 1960s and 1970s was an explicit reaction to both development economics and political development theory; however, as has been emphasized, these radical challengers also accepted nation-states as natural units of the wider international political economy. In this regard it should also be noted that one of the lines of descent of dependency theory is the work in the 1940s and 1950s of the influential development economist, Raul Prebisch. In the 1940s and 1950s Prebisch, as head of the United Nations-sponsored *Comisión Economica para América Latina* (CEPAL), articulated a conservative version of dependency theory, in the context of the shift to an import-substitution industrialization policy in Latin America. Beginning as Director of Research for CEPAL in Chile in 1949, Prebisch, as we have seen, was in charge of the United Nations Conference on Trade and Development in the second half of the 1960s, a position from which he sought to encourage preferential tariffs for the exports of late-industrializing nation-states.[90] In fact, as we shall see in later chapters, theories of the developmental state grew in part, not only out of development economics but also from various strands of dependency theory.[91]

Conclusion: development economics

This chapter has looked at the rise and fall of development economics and the dynamics of national development in Asia with particular emphasis on India between the 1940s and the 1970s. The vicissitudes of state-guided national development in India in this period make clear both the specificity of the meanings of national development and the way in which the content of the idea of national development changed in important ways over time. The national development project under Nehru was reoriented under his immediate successor (Lal Bahadur Shastri) and then reconfigured in a populist and increasingly authoritarian direction under Indira Gandhi. More broadly, the "Gradual Revolution" in India was perceived at the time as a potential model for efforts to steer national development in the Third World between the capitalism of the First World and the state-socialism of the Second World. This chapter has emphasized that the contradictions of state-guided national development in India and beyond flow from the complex history of colonialism, decolonization, national liberation and the US-led modernization project in the Cold War. The rise and decline of development economics was embedded in this wider history. Development economics was implicated in the failure of national development in India and elsewhere in significant measure because of its unwillingness to historicize the nation-state. The acceptance of nation-states as natural units to be developed and their universal enshrinement as sovereign vehicles for the achievement of modernity was a central contradiction of development economics, of US foreign policy and of state-guided national development in this period. Furthermore, development economics ultimately reinforced the way that sovereignty in a wide array of nation-states continued to lay with the states rather than with the people who inhabited the modern nations. In the next chapter we turn to an examination of the other main theoretical approach that acted as a key complement to national development in this period. Like development economics, political development theory specifically, and modernization theory more generally, played an important role in the routinization of the nation-state as the unquestioned unit of development between the 1940s and the 1970s.

Notes

1 The Indian government was probably the first government in the emerging Third World to draw up a detailed planning document, producing a development plan of over 600 pages in 1952. I. Islam and A. Chowdhury, *The Political Economy of East Asia: Post-Crisis Debates*, New York: Oxford University Press, 2000, p. 5.

2 P. N. Rosenstein-Rodan, "Problems of Industrialization of Eastern and South-Eastern Europe" *Economic Journal* vol. 53, 1943. Also see P. N. Rosenstein-Rodan, "The International Development of Economically Backward Areas" *International Affairs* vol. 20, no. 2, 1944.

3 The Oxford Institute of Statistics, as well as the Political and Economic Planning (PEP) group also provided important springboards for development economics after 1941. H. W. Arndt, *Economic Development: The History of an Idea*, Chicago: University of Chicago Press, 1987, pp. 47–8.

4 In the 1930s and 1940s economists and political leaders in Latin America, particularly in Mexico, Chile, Brazil and Argentina, focused with increasing energy on state-directed national development and industrialization strategies. V. Bulmer-Thomas, *The Economic History of Latin America since Independence*, Cambridge: Cambridge University Press, 1994, pp. 194–275.

5 M. T. Berger, *Under Northern Eyes: Latin American Studies and US Hegemony in the Americas 1898–1990*, Bloomington: Indiana University Press, 1995, p. 50.

6 P. Darby, *Three Faces of Imperialism: British and American Approaches to Asia and Africa 1870–1970*, New Haven: Yale University Press, 1987, pp. 106–17, 132–40.

7 D. K. Fieldhouse, "Decolonization, Development, and Dependence: A Survey of Changing Attitudes" in P. Gifford and W. R. Louis, eds, *The Transfer of Power in Africa: Decolonization, 1940–1960*, New Haven: Yale University Press, 1982, p. 486.

8 J. M. Lee, *Colonial Development and Good Government: A Study of the Ideas Expressed by the British Official Classes in Planning Decolonization 1939–1964*, Oxford: Clarendon Press, 1967, pp. 39–41.

9 F. Cooper and R. Packard, "Introduction" in F. Cooper and R. Packard, eds, *International Development and the Social Sciences: Essays on the History and Politics of Knowledge*, Berkeley: University of California Press, 1997, pp. 6–7.

10 P. T. Bauer, *The Rubber Industry: A Study in Competition and Monopoly*, Cambridge, MA: Harvard University Press, 1948; P. T. Bauer, *West African Trade: A Study of Competition, Oligopoly and Monopoly in a Changing Economy*, Cambridge: Cambridge University Press, 1954; P. T. Bauer, "'Remembrance of Studies Past: Retracing First Steps" in G. M. Meier and D. Seers, eds, *Pioneers in Development*, Oxford: Oxford University Press for the World Bank, 1984.

11 The key assumptions of development economics are summarized in a schematic but accurate fashion by neo-classical critic Deepak Lal as: (a) "that the price mechanism, or the working of a market economy, needs to be supplanted (and not merely supplemented) by various forms of direct government control, both national and international, to promote economic development"; (b) that "[t]he essential task of governments is … charting and implementing a 'strategy' for rapid and equitable growth which attaches prime importance to macro-economic accounting aggregates

such as savings, the balance of payments, and the relative balance between broadly defined 'sectors' such as 'industry' and 'agriculture'"; (c) "that the classical 19th-century liberal case for free trade is invalid for developing countries, and thus government restriction of international trade and payments is necessary for development"; and (d) that the alleviation of poverty and the improvement of income distribution necessitates "massive and continuing government intervention ... to redistribute assets and to manipulate the returns to different types of labor and capital through pervasive price and (if possible) wage controls ... so that scarce resources are used to meet the so-called 'basic needs' of the poor rather than the luxurious 'wants' of the rich". D. Lal, *The Poverty of Development Economics*, 2nd edn, Cambridge, MA: Harvard University Press, 1985, p. 5

12 W. A. Lewis (1946) cited in A. Escobar, *Encountering Development: The Making and Unmaking of the Third World*, Princeton: Princeton University Press, 1995, p. 74.
13 For a good summary of Lewis's contribution to development economics see M. P. Todaro, *Economic Development*, 5th edn, New York: Longman, 1994, pp. 74–81. Also see W. A. Lewis, "Development Economics in the 1950s" in G. M. Meier and D. Seers, eds, *Pioneers in Development*, Oxford: Oxford University Press for the World Bank, 1984.
14 M. Havinden and D. Meredith, *Colonialism and Development: Britain and its Tropical Colonies 1850–1960*, London: Routledge, 1993, pp. 215–17.
15 W. A. Lewis, "Economic Development with Unlimited Supplies of Labour" *Manchester School* May 22, 1954; United Nations, *Measures for the Economic Development of Underdeveloped Countries*, New York: United Nations, 1951.
16 W. A. Lewis, *The Theory of Economic Growth*, London: Allen and Unwin, 1955, p. 431.
17 J. Martinussen, *Society, State and Market*, London: Zed Books, 1997, pp. 61–3.
18 W. W. Rostow, *The Stages of Economic Growth: A Non-Communist Manifesto*, New York: Cambridge University Press, 1960.
19 M. E. Latham, *Modernization as Ideology: American Social Science and "Nation Building" in the Kennedy Era*, Chapel Hill: University of North Carolina Press, 2000, pp. 41–6.
20 An immediate catalyst for CENIS was provided by Project Troy, which was conducted at MIT at the beginning of the 1950s. A. Needell, "Project Troy and the Cold War Annexation of the Social Sciences" in C. Simpson, ed., *Universities and Empire: Money and Politics in the Social Sciences During the Cold War*, New York: New Press, 1998, pp. 3–4, 23–4.
21 S. W. Leslie, *The Cold War and American Science: The Military–Industrial–Academic Complex at MIT and Stanford*, New York: Columbia University Press, 1993, pp. 11–12.
22 W. W. Rostow, "Development: The Political Economy of the Marshallian Long Period" in G. M. Meier and D. Seers, eds, *Pioneers in Development*, Oxford: Oxford University Press for the World Bank, 1984, p. 241.
23 See K. C. Pearce, *Rostow, Kennedy, and the Rhetoric of Foreign Aid*, East Lansing: Michigan State University Press, 2001.
24 G. Rosen, *Western Economists and Eastern Societies: Agents of Change in South Asia, 1950–1970*, Baltimore: Johns Hopkins University Press, 1985, pp. 27–9.
25 L. Freedman, *Kennedy's Wars: Berlin, Cuba, Laos and Vietnam*, New York: Oxford University Press, 2000, pp. 27–31.
26 Rostow, *The Stages of Economic Growth*, pp. 162–7.
27 N. Gilman, *Mandarins of the Future: Modernization Theory in Cold War America*, Baltimore: Johns Hopkins University Press, 2003.
28 M. F. Millikan and D. L. M. Blackmer, eds, *The Emerging Nations: Their Growth and United States Policy*, Boston: Little, Brown and Company, 1961.
29 Robert Komer cited in J.-E. Woo (M. Woo-Cumings), *Race to the Swift: State and Finance in Korean Industrialization*, New York: Columbia University Press, 1991, pp. 75–7. Komer went on to spend three years in South Vietnam (1966–1968) where he served as chief pacification advisor and rose to the position of Deputy to the Commander of

US Military Forces in Vietnam. R. W. Komer, *Bureaucracy At War: U.S. Performance in the Vietnam Conflict*, Boulder: Westview, 1986; R. A. Hunt, *Pacification: The American Struggle for Vietnam's Hearts and Minds*, Boulder: Westview, 1995.

30 For example, see D. C. Cole and P. N. Lyman, *Korean Development: The Interplay of Politics and Economics*, Cambridge, MA: Harvard University Press, 1971. For a discussion of US views of Korea in this period see B. Cumings, "Bringing Korea Back In: Structured Absence, Glaring Presence, and Invisibility" in W. I. Cohen, *Pacific Passage: The Study of American–East Asian Relations on the Eve of the Twenty-First Century*, New York: Columbia University Press, 1996, pp. 352–3.

31 In 1951 the journalist, W. Gordon Graham, warned that Marxism was the "only philosophy of natural appeal to India's awakening masses". W. G. Graham, "Communism in South Asia" *The Pacific Spectator: A Journal of Interpretation* vol. 5, no. 2, 1951, p. 230.

32 R. J. McMahon, *The Cold War on the Periphery: The United States, India and Pakistan*, New York: Columbia University Press, 1994, pp. 7, 337–8.

33 McMahon, *The Cold War on the Periphery*, pp. 261–3, 338–9. For a history of US relations with India that focuses on economic development in the 1950s and early 1960s see D. Merrill, *Bread and the Ballot: The United States and India's Economic Development, 1947–1963*, Chapel Hill: University of North Carolina Press, 1990. Also see A. J. Rotter, *Comrades at Odds: The United States and India, 1947–1964*, Ithaca: Cornell University Press, 2000.

34 D. Engerman, "West Meets East: The Center for International Studies and Indian Economic Development" in D. Engerman, N. Gilman, M. Haefele and M. Latham, eds, *Staging Growth: Modernization, Development and the Global Cold War*, Amherst: University of Massachusetts Press, 2003.

35 Rosen, *Western Economists and Eastern Societies*, pp. 27, 113–14, 121–2.

36 E. B. Ross, *The Malthus Factor: Poverty, Politics and Population in Capitalist Development*, London: Zed Books, 1998, p. 148.

37 Rosen, *Western Economists and Eastern Societies*, pp. 27, 29–36, 101, 127.

38 F. R. Frankel, *India's Political Economy, 1947–1977: The Gradual Revolution*, Princeton: Princeton University Press, 1978, pp. 113–15. More generally see R. J. Herring, "Embedded Particularism: India's Failed Developmental State" in M. Woo-Cumings, ed., *The Developmental State*, Ithaca: Cornell University Press, 1999.

39 As the Indian National Congress emerged as a mass organization there was growing debate between those in the sub-continent who viewed industrialization as central to their vision of independent India and those who shared Gandhi's rejection of industrial modernity in favor of a revitalized agricultural society grounded in the sub-continent's pre-colonial past. The industrializers, who would eventually win this debate, could themselves be divided into at least three groups. The first group was a powerful circle of industrialists and businessmen that had emerged in the late colonial period and was based in Bombay (Mumbai). In the final years before independence this group put forward *A Plan for Economic Development for India* .Popularly known as the "Bombay Plan", this document emphasized that the economic development of an independent India should be grounded in the expansion of textile and consumer goods industries that were already well established in cities such as Bombay. This plan also outlined the need for the state to take the lead in investing in infrastructure and heavy industries and providing the protective framework that would keep foreign capital at bay. This group saw little or no need for redistributive policies or a public sector. The second group in this debate included a number of technocratic Indians who occupied senior positions in the Indian Civil Service (ICS) and/or were members of the Planning and Development Department set up by the British in 1944. This group wanted to give the responsibility for national development to a council of experts made up of businessmen, economists and officials. The third group, represented most prominently by Jawaharlal Nehru and Subhas Chandra

Bose, also favored planned industrialization, but they envisioned a far more redistributive role for the state, including land reform. They also emphasized heavy industry, which they wanted under public ownership for reasons of national development and national security. S. Khilnani, *The Idea of India*, New York: Farrar Straus Giroux, 1997, pp. 69–75; B. Chandra, "Colonial India: British versus Indian Views of Development" *Review: A Journal of the Fernand Braudel Center* vol. 14, no. 1, 1991, pp. 134–60.

40 S. Bose, "Instruments and Idioms of Colonial and National Development: India's Historical Experience in Comparative Perspective" in F. Cooper and R. Packard, eds, *International Development and the Social Sciences: Essays on the History and Politics of Knowledge*, Berkeley: University of California Press, 1997, pp. 47–8, 53–4.

41 S. Corbridge and J. Harriss, *Reinventing India: Liberalization, Hindu Nationalism and Popular Democracy*, Cambridge: Polity Press, 2000, pp. 43–4.

42 Khilnani, *The Idea of India*, pp. 75–7.

43 Frankel, *India's Political Economy, 1947–1977*, pp. 124–5.

44 P. Chatterjee *Nationalist Thought and Colonial World: A Derivative Discourse?*, London: Zed Books, 1986, pp. 140, 145.

45 S. Seth, *Marxist Theory and Nationalist Politics: The Case of Colonial India*, New Delhi: Sage, 1995, pp. 215–18, 221–2, 232–6.

46 For a good general account of the Planning Commission see S. Chakravarty, *Development Planning: The Indian Experience*, Oxford: Clarendon Press, 1987.

47 Khilnani, *The Idea of India*, pp. 81–6.

48 A. Kohli, *The State and Poverty in India: The Politics of Reform*, London: Cambridge University Press, 1987, p. 61.

49 A. Gupta, *Postcolonial Developments: Agriculture in the Making of Modern India*, Durham: Duke University Press, 1998, pp. 33, 48–52, 59–63.

50 Work on modelling by CENIS, using new econometric methods, began with the arrival of Richard Eckhaus in New Delhi in 1961. Eckhaus's enthusiasm for modelling was greeted with ambivalence by Tarlok Singh (Secretary of the Planning Commission), but with considerable interest by K. S. Krishnaswamy (Director of the recently established Economic Research Division of the Planning Commission). Meanwhile, Pitamber Pant (head of the Perspective Planning Division and close to Nehru and Mahalanobis) reacted negatively to the idea. At the beginning of 1962 the CENIS development economists in Delhi began work with Krishnaswamy's research unit on the construction of an input–output model of India's economy. Eckhaus went back to MIT in the middle of 1962 where, along with Louis Lafeber, he continued to work on the model. Additionally money was provided by the US Agency for International Development (USAID). Kirit Parikh (who had recently completed his PhD in Engineering at MIT) and Sukhamoy Chakravarty (a former economics student at MIT who came back as a visiting professor in 1963) also worked on the model. The model that emerged was named the CELP model after Chakravarty, Eckhaus, Lafeber and Parikh. Rosen, *Western Economists and Eastern Societies*, pp. 123, 124, 128–30.

51 Frankel, *India's Political Economy, 1947–1977*, p. 269.

52 Rosen, *Western Economists and Eastern Societies*, pp. 101, 130–1; D. Wise and T. B. Ross, *The Invisible Government: The CIA and US Intelligence*, New York: Vintage, 1974 (first published 1964).

53 Meanwhile, at the end of 1964 a prominent left-wing journal (*Now*) in Calcutta published an article that characterized CENIS as "an extended arm of the CIA research division". It said that the MIT development economists had used "highly classified information" in their economic modelling work to challenge "the major postulates of Indian planning". The Center's model was represented as a "deliberate attempt" to "sabotage the country's long-term development plan". "Indian Plan, U.S. Model" *Now* December 25, 1964, pp. 3–4. Cited in Rosen, *Western Economists and Eastern Societies*, pp. 133–7.

54 Rosen, *Western Economists and Eastern Societies*, pp. 137–9.
55 Frankel, *India's Political Economy, 1947–1977*, p. 286.
56 McMahon, *The Cold War on the Periphery*, pp. 6, 8, 340, 346.
57 The myth-making that was central to the Green Revolution needs to be set against the fact that many, if not all, of its main claims do not stand up to close scrutiny. For a good critique see N. Cullather, "Parable of Seeds: The Green Revolution in the Modernizing Imagination" in M. Frey, R. W. Pruessen and T. T. Yong, eds, *The Transformation in Southeast Asia: International Perspectives on Decolonization*, Armonk: M. E. Sharpe, 2003.
58 L. I. Rudolph and S. H. Rudolph, *In Pursuit of Lakshmi: The Political Economy of the Indian State*, Chicago: University of Chicago Press, 1987, p. 320.
59 D. Kapur, J. Lewis and R. Webb, *The World Bank: Its First Half-Century, Volume 1: History*, Washington, DC: Brookings Institution, 1997, pp. 388–9.
60 Frankel, *India's Political Economy, 1947–1977*, p. 252.
61 Kapur, Lewis and Webb, *The World Bank*, pp. 389–90.
62 Frankel, *India's Political Economy, 1947–1977*, pp. 246–7.
63 Rudolph and Rudolph, *In Pursuit of Lakshmi*, pp. 322–3.
64 M. Harcourt, "India: From Stable Underdevelopment to Turbulent Growth" in J. Ingleson, ed., *Third World Update*, Sydney: University of New South Wales, 1986.
65 Gupta, *Postcolonial Developments*, pp. 62–3.
66 Corbridge and Harriss, *Reinventing India*, p. 45.
67 F. R. Frankel, *India's Green Revolution: Economic Gains and Political Costs*, Princeton: Princeton University Press, 1973.
68 Harcourt, "India".
69 P. Krugman, "The Fall and Rise of Development Economics" in P. Krugman, *Development, Geography and Economic Theory*, Cambridge, MA: MIT Press, 1999 (first published 1995), pp. 6–7.
70 R. Gilpin, *Global Political Economy: Understanding the International Economic Order*, Princeton: Princeton University Press, 2001, pp. 305–6.
71 H. W. Arndt, *Economic Development: The History of an Idea*, Chicago: University of Chicago Press, 1987, pp. 122–6.
72 C. Ramirez-Faria, *The Origins of Economic Inequality Between Nations: A Critique of Western Theories of Development and Underdevelopment*, London: Unwin Hyman, 1991, pp. 98–101.
73 D. Seers, "The Birth, Life, and Death of Development Economics" *Development and Change* vol. 10, no. 4, 1979; A. O. Hirschman, "The Rise and Decline of Development Economics" in A. O. Hirschman, *Essays in Trespassing: Economics to Politics and Beyond*, Cambridge: Cambridge University Press, 1981, p. 23. Also see I. M. D. Little, *Economic Development: Theory, Policy and International Relations*, New York: Basic Books, A Twentieth Century Fund Book, 1982, pp. 16–18; W. W. Rostow, *Theories of Economic Growth from David Hume to the Present*, 2nd edn, New York: Oxford University Press, 1992, p. 373.
74 G. Myrdal, *Economic Theory and Underdeveloped Regions*, New York: Harper, 1957.
75 G. Myrdal, "International Inequality and Foreign Aid in Retrospect" in G. M. Meier and D. Seers, eds, *Pioneers in Development*, Oxford: Oxford University Press for the World Bank, 1984, p. 153.
76 G. Myrdal, *Asian Drama: An Inquiry into the Poverty of Nations*, volume I, London: Penguin, in association with the Twentieth Century Fund, 1968, pp. 47, 66–7.
77 Myrdal, *Asian Drama* (vol. I), p. 380.
78 An important figure in political development theory who worked on India was political scientist Myron Weiner of the University of Chicago's South Asia Center. Closely involved with the Committee for Comparative Politics, which will also be discussed in chapter 3, Weiner was the author of the chapter on South Asia in Gabriel A. Almond and James S. Coleman's *The Politics of Developing Areas*, and a number of other works

on India in this period. M. Weiner, "The Politics of South Asia" in G. A. Almond and J. S. Coleman, eds, *The Politics of Developing Areas*, Princeton: Princeton University Press, 1960; M. Weiner, *Party Politics in India: The Development of a Multi-Party System*, Princeton: Princeton University Press, 1957; M. Weiner, *The Politics of Scarcity: Public Pressure and Political Response in India*, 3rd edn, Chicago: University of Chicago Press, 1968; M. Weiner, *Party Building in a New Nation: The Indian National Congress*, Chicago: University of Chicago Press, 1967.

79 For example, see R. L. Hardgrave, Jr, *India Under Pressure: Prospects for Political Stability*, Boulder: Westview, 1984.

80 A very partial exception might be *The Political Economy of Nationalism* by Dudley Seers, which remained committed to state-mediated ideas of development, but saw supra-national or regional blocs as more appropriate units via which to pursue development. However, his approach still assumed that nations were the natural sub-units of supra-national or regional blocs. See D. Seers, *The Political Economy of Nationalism*, Oxford: Oxford University Press, 1983.

81 Corbridge and Harriss, *Reinventing India*, pp. 143–72.

82 C. M. Henry and R. Springborg, *Globalization and the Politics of Development in the Middle East*, Cambridge: Cambridge University Press, 2001.

83 W. A. Lewis, "The State of Development Theory" *American Economic Review* vol. 74, no. 1, 1984.

84 G. Ranis and J. C. H. Fei, "Development Economics: What Next?" in G. Ranis and T. P. Schultz, eds, *The State of Development Economics: Progress and Perspectives*, Oxford: Basil Blackwell, 1988, pp. 100–1, 132.

85 M. R. Carter, "Intellectual Openings and Policy Closures: Disequilibria in Contemporary Development Economics" in F. Cooper and R. Packard, eds, *International Development and the Social Sciences: Essays on the History and Politics of Knowledge*, Berkeley: University of California Press, 1997, pp. 119, 121.

86 H.-J. Chang, "The Economic Theory of the Developmental State" in M. Woo-Cumings, ed., *The Developmental State*, Ithaca: Cornell University Press, 1999, pp. 182–3.

87 J. Harriss, J. Hunter and C. M. Lewis, "Introduction: Development and the Significance of New Institutional Economics" in J. Harriss, J. Hunter and C. M. Lewis, eds, *The New Institutional Economics and Third World Development*, London: Routledge, 1997 (first published 1995), pp. 2–3.

88 G. M. Meier, J. E. Stiglitz and N. Stern, eds, *The Frontiers of Development Economics: The Future in Perspective*, New York: Oxford University Press, 2000.

89 A detailed treatment of the significant array of radical theories of development that have risen and fallen since the 1960s and the political context that informed them is beyond the scope of this book. Two recent studies provide very good overviews of key nationalist, Third Worldist and postcolonial intellectuals and political leaders and their ideas. See R. Young, *Postcolonialism: An Historical Introduction*, Oxford: Blackwell, 2001; C. J. Christie, *Ideology and Revolution in Southeast Asia 1900–1980*, Richmond: Curzon, 2001.

90 R. Prebisch (United Nations Economic Commission for Latin America), *The Economic Development of Latin America and Its Principal Problems*, New York: United Nations, 1949.

91 On the rise and revision of dependency theory in relation to Latin American studies see M. T. Berger, *Under Northern Eyes: Latin American Studies and US Hegemony in the Americas, 1898–1990*, Bloomington: Indiana University Press, 1995, pp. 106–21.

3 Modernization theory

Like development economists, political scientists and historians also turned their attention to Asia, Africa, the Middle East and Latin America after the Second World War. The Cold War provided the crucial backdrop for the rise and elaboration of modernization theory and closely related theories of political development and nation-building that were centered on direct or indirect US involvement in the formation and consolidation of stable anti-communist national political systems. Important early US efforts at nation-building in Japan and West Germany, which were directed at building anti-communist and democratic polities, foreshadowed later concerns with modernization and nation-building, in South Vietnam and elsewhere in what became known as the Third World, where the emphasis was on a stable anti-communist, although not necessarily democratic, government.[1] Modernization theory and theories of nation-building exercised a profound influence on, and were bound up with the rise and transformation of, Asian Studies and area studies more generally.[2] The dominant discourse within Asian Studies between the 1940s and the 1970s emphasized the need for the various nations of Asia to develop gradually towards a relatively universal form of liberal capitalist modernity. In the context of the universalization of the nation-state system, the nation-state became the unquestioned unit of study for proponents of modernization. Modernization theorists sometimes conceived of the new nation-states in ways that at least implicitly acknowledged that they were historically constructed and contingent, but like development economists their work generally treated the new nations as natural units that should and would, or at least ought to, evolve along a single, or at best a limited number of, paths towards modernity. Meanwhile, the use of political models (and lessons) with little or no regard to questions of time and place further undermined modernization theory's relationship to the spatial and temporal specificity of the formation and consolidation, or failure (in the case of South Vietnam, for example) of nation-states in this period.

This chapter begins by discussing briefly the rise of modernization theory. This is followed by a discussion of area studies generally and Asian Studies more specifically. It then looks at Japan as an early focus of work in Asian Studies and its emergence as a model of modernization in the 1950s and 1960s. This is followed by an examination of the role of the Committee on Comparative

Politics (which was established by the Social Science Research Council in 1954) in the rise and consolidation of modernization theory. This leads to a discussion of the work of modernization theorists, such as Lucian W. Pye, who was closely associated with the Committee on Comparative Politics and the Center for International Studies (CENIS) at MIT – the latter organization was discussed in some detail in the previous chapter. This is followed by an examination of the changes to modernization theory in the 1960s and early 1970s, with a particular emphasis on the US-backed nation-building effort in South Vietnam (which had become the fulcrum of US policy in Asia by the 1960s) and on the work of Samuel Huntington. The changes to modernization theory in this period were intimately connected to the challenges to, and shifts in orientation of, US foreign policy in Asia and beyond in the Cold War era. Too much emphasis, however, on the perceived shift in modernization theory in the 1960s away from a focus on democracy to a preoccupation with order, in the context of the reorientation of US hegemony, is no longer warranted. As recent observers have argued, a close examination of the modernization literature makes clear that order and stability were always more important than democracy as far as most modernization theo- rists were concerned. Nevertheless, modernization theory was subject to revision in the 1960s and early 1970s in the context of growing challenges to its explana- tory and prescriptive aspirations. The most obvious shift was a retreat from the relative optimism of the late 1950s and early 1960s, which credited the US with considerable power to shape events and encourage nation-building in the so- called Third World in its own image, to a concern, by the late 1960s and early 1970s, with order and the limits of Washington's power. However, this did not involve a dramatic rethinking of the basic assumptions that underpinned the work of modernization theorists and US policy-makers: assumptions that had facilitated Washington's slide into full-scale war in Vietnam in the 1960s.[3]

The Cold War and nation-building I: the making of modernization theory

The origins of modernization theory

Many observers define modernization theory in a way that includes development economics.[4] However, others, such as Colin Leys (and this is reinforced by Nils Gilman's recent intellectual history of modernization theory), argue that it is more precise to view development economics as having provided the earliest systematic formulations of development theory generally, while modernization theory is best viewed as having appeared in the late 1950s as a particularly North American response by political scientists to the incipient failure of many of the prescriptions of development economists.[5] Other observers prefer to use the term political development theory, rather than modernization theory, to describe the work on modernization by North American political scientists in the late 1950s and 1960s. In the view of Paul Cammack, political development theory "drew heavily upon modernization theory" (which Cammack attributes primarily to the sociological tradition running from Max Weber to Talcott Parsons and Edward Shils), "but at the same time engaged in a critical dialogue with it".[6] While political development theory played an important role in the rise and or revision of modernization theory, the latter term can still be seen to encompass conceptions of political, social, and cultural change that extend beyond political development theory as such. At the same time, I agree that development economics should be regarded as an early form of development theory that is distinct from modernization theory. However, while I will use the term modernization theory to refer primarily to political development theory, I also use it more broadly, as is widely accepted, to describe the growing array of liberal theories of modernization that emerged after 1945 and took nation-states in the Third World as their main objects. Thus, modernization theory will be viewed as centered on political development theory, but also reaching across the social sciences to encompass political science generally, as well as history, sociology and area studies.

This formulation allows the Social Science Research Council's (SSRC) Committee on Comparative Politics, which was the key site for the production of political development theory, to be seen as an important force behind modernization theory in the 1950s and early 1960s whether the latter term is defined narrowly or broadly.[7] Chaired by Gabriel Almond from 1954 to 1963 (the other founding members of the committee were Lucian W. Pye, Guy J. Pauker, Taylor Cole, Roy Macridis and George McTurnan Kahin), this committee provided a key focus for the production and dissemination of modernization theory. The Committee sponsored a wide range of academic and policy-oriented publications, as well as a number of conferences and seminars. The goal of the Committee on Comparative Politics was to come up with a theory of political development; however, over time many crucial concepts were used inconsistently, while no full-blown theory could be said to have emerged.[8] Despite its scientific aspirations and despite the widespread usage of the word "theory" to describe modernization theory, what the Committee on Comparative Politics provided was primarily an outlook or approach to, rather than a theory of, modernization. The Committee also played an important role in the establishment of the acceptable parameters of the professional study of politics. Like historians, such as John K. Fairbanks and Edwin O. Reischauer who will be discussed below, the political scientists associated with the Committee were aware that they were engaged in the production of a theoretical alternative to Marxism. For example, in the early 1980s a former member of the Committee asserted that its "purpose" had been to "formulate a non-Communist theory of change and thus to provide a non-Marxian alternative for the developing nations".[9]

The desire to generate an alternative theoretical apparatus to Marxism is nicely encapsulated by the Committee on Comparative Politics' efforts to marginalize the conceptual use of the state. Of course, the foundations for such an effort had already been laid by the 1920s. After the First World War, the concept of the state was increasingly displaced as political science was consolidated and professionalized around pluralism as both the basis of US politics and the norm by which political theory and practice elsewhere was to be measured.[10]

In the 1950s Gabriel Almond and his fellow scholars avoided using the term "state", favoring the term political system, because, in their view the former was afflicted with at least two important and connected shortcomings. First of all it was felt that it was a vague term and it would be difficult to reach agreement as to what exactly it meant. At the same time, it was felt that even if an agreed definition of the state could be found any such definition would marginalize or exclude important elements of the political process. Writing later, Almond argued more broadly that it had been felt at the time that the dramatic social and political changes which had occurred since the industrial revolution meant that identifying the boundaries between state and society had become ever more difficult.[11] However, these reasons for avoiding the notion of the state appear less persuasive than the fact that the Second World War and the Cold War had placed new constraints on North American political science. For example, in a 1944 report on the future of comparative politics, Karl Loewenstein argued that political scientists should dispense with any narrow focus on the state and become "a conscious instrument of social engineering" for "imparting" the US "experience to other nations" and the scientific integration of "their institutions into a universal pattern of government". He envisioned the emergence of a "total science", arguing that the "frontier posts of comparative government must be moved boldly" to include both the entire world and a range of other academic disciplines, which would ensure "access to the true Gestalt of foreign political civilizations".[12] In 1953 David Easton argued that the Cold War made the clarification of the political lexicon, the purging of the concept of the state and the production of general laws, which would encompass all important political activities and transcend specific cultures, a national and international imperative.[13]

While modernization theorists sought to find alternatives to the "state" and articulate "a non-Marxian alternative for the developing nations", they were also attempting (as Easton's comments suggest) to shift anti-communism away from the populist hysteria of the McCarthy era, towards a far more scientifically grounded political position. Modernization theory was, as Nils Gilman has suggested, a "high-concept version" of Americanism that involved "materialism without class conflict, secularism without irreverence, democracy without disobedience". Although modernization theory was clearly anti-communist in its political outlook, it rested on a deeper set of assumptions about progress and modernity that overlapped with Marxism. In particular industrialization and urbanization were central to both liberal and Marxist visions of modernity and national development. Furthermore, modernization theorists acknowledged the modernity of the USSR, representing communism as a perverted version of modernity, while hoping that the Soviet Union would eventually converge with the democratic and capitalist type of modernity exemplified by the United States.[14] Ultimately, modernization theory privileged an evolutionary conception of political change and development grounded in a romanticized vision of the history of the United States of America. Early modernization theorists were at least rhetorically committed to democracy, often seeing it as the direct result of economic development and the key to political stability. For example, James Coleman discerned a "positive relationship between economic development" and competitive and democratic political systems.[15] At the same time, this conception of political development was elitist and technocratic and even in the 1950s stability was regarded as more important than democracy, an emphasis that would become more pronounced in the 1960s.

The rise of Asian Studies

In the 1950s and 1960s Asian Studies generally, and the Association for Asian Studies (AAS) more specifically, were strongly influenced by modernization theory, while playing a complementary role in the wider US-led modernization project of the Cold War era. The Second World War had brought a large number of academics into direct contact with the US government. This provided the foundation for a wave of institutional growth and expansion that began during the Second World War but was facilitated over a much longer period by the Cold War. Political scientists and historians established closer links with the US government during the Second World War and the subsequent Cold War than virtually any other academic disciplines except physics. The linkages emerged in a number of ways, and although not all political scientists and historians participated, the senior members of the political science and historical professions were very well represented. Many academics took up full-time posts with government agencies, while others did so part-time or irregularly, while many others consciously allowed Second World War and later Cold War imperatives to influence their work. The Office of Strategic Services (OSS), the forerunner of the Central Intelligence Agency (CIA), was one of the most well-known postings for political scientists and historians, and one of the most significant for area studies generally (and Asian Studies more specifically).[16] W. Norman Brown, who is credited with founding and guiding South Asian Studies in North America after the Second World War, was employed by the OSS, as was John K. Fairbank, who worked as an information officer at the US embassy in Chongqing (Chungking) after the US entered the Second World War. Fairbank went on to become professor of history at Harvard and is regarded as the effective founder of modern Chinese studies in North America.[17] Shortly after the Second World War, Brown and Fairbank both wrote influential historical surveys in the American Foreign Policy Library series about US relations with India, Pakistan and China respectively.[18] McGeorge Bundy, one-time president of the Ford Foundation, which provided considerable support for area studies in the 1950s and 1960s through its International Training and Research Program among other initiatives, characterized the Office of Strategic Services as the "first great center of area studies in the United States".[19]

In the 1950s and 1960s large amounts of money from government and private foundations, such as the Ford Foundation, became available with the intention of enhancing the North American understanding of Asia and beyond.[20] At the same time, the disciplinary range of area studies grew dramatically as a new generation of academics entered new or revised fields of study that emerged with the expansion and diversification of the social sciences after 1945. This was the context in which Asian Studies was consolidated. The main North American-based professional organization for the study of Asia came into existence in 1948 as the Far Eastern Association – around the *Far Eastern Quarterly*, which had first appeared in 1941. The Far Eastern Association became the Association for Asian Studies in 1958. Although the Asian Studies profession increasingly emerged as a result of, and tended to complement, the Cold War policies of the US, a number of important Asian Studies specialists were badly treated by the government in the early Cold War era. In the 1950s, the reputation of the Institute for Pacific Relations, which had provided an important pre-1945 institutional focus for Asian experts, suffered irreparable damage after the Senate Internal Security Subcommittee concluded that the organization had been instrumental in the so-called "loss" of China. The tensions surrounding the debate over the loss of China, and the Institute for Pacific Relations controversy complicated the emergence of the Association for Asian Studies in the 1950s.[21] For example, John King Fairbank came under scrutiny in the McCarthy years and did not have a particularly good relationship with the State Department until the 1960s. In the early 1950s Fairbank's services as a State Department consultant were discontinued. In 1951 he was refused a passport by the US government, placing a year and a half delay on a planned trip to Japan, at the same time as he was called to appear before a number of Congressional hearings that scrutinized his loyalty.[22]

In the 1950s a geographically grounded academic division of labor emerged within the US-centered Asian Studies profession. The professional study of Asia was increasingly divided into, and institutionalized as, East Asian Studies, Southeast Asian Studies and South Asian Studies, with the regional groupings being further divided into their national components.[23] Between the 1950s and the 1970s the dominant narrative within East Asian Studies, reflected in the work of John King Fairbank (along with his fellow Harvard historian, Edwin O. Reischauer who went on to be US ambassador to Japan from 1961 to 1966), naturalized China, Japan and Korea as parts of an historically more or less unitary and long-standing regional civilization. The knowledge they produced about East Asia was descriptive and their approach framed the modern history of the region in terms of the tension between tradition and modernity, a dichotomy that was/is central to modernization theory in all its forms. Even though, as noted, academics such as Fairbank and Reischauer were not always in favor with the government of the day, their work, along with that of most other North American scholars, on the history and politics of East Asia reflected an overall congruence with US geo-political concerns in the region even if they disagreed with particular strategies and tactics.[24] For example, Reischauer, the son of missionary parents, who spent most of the first two decades of his life in Japan at the start of the twentieth century (he was born in 1910), actively promoted US–Japanese partnership from the outset of his career after 1945. This view meshed with US policy by the late 1940s; it was also grounded directly in Reischauer's liberal universalism. He was unwavering in the view, as expressed years later in his autobiography, that Japan and the United States "shared common basic ideals of democracy, human rights and egalitarianism, and yearned alike for a peaceful world order made up of truly independent nations bound together by as free and open world trade as possible".[25]

The Japanese model I: "a web with no spider"

Against this background, Reischauer had been an enthusiastic supporter of US efforts to transform Japan into a liberal democratic nation-state after the Second World War.[26] While working for General MacArthur during the occupation of Japan, Reischauer (who had spent the Second World War training US military officers in the Japanese language and deciphering/translating Japanese cables) persistently advocated that Japan could be returned to the path of liberal democracy from which it had ostensibly strayed in the 1930s. In a policy document written at the end of 1945 Reischauer argued that the institution of the emperor could be made to be compatible with democracy and turned into a symbol of modern Japan. In his view, no profound changes were required to bring the Japanese political system into line with the standard now being set by the victorious United States. This perspective was grounded in what would become known disparagingly as the "Reischauer Line".[27] In the 1950s and 1960s Reischauer took the view that, "using nineteenth-century China instead of the West as the yardstick, Japan's social and economic modernization and remarkable progress toward democracy appeared to be an amazing success story".[28] This complemented US policy, particularly following the so-called "reverse course" after 1947. With the onset of the Cold War Washington's fear of social upheaval and even revolution in Japan ensured the effective restoration of the old order minus the most notorious militarists. In the Japanese case, as with West Germany, the US initially expected formal occupation would be relatively brief, but it ended up assuming the responsibilities of an occupying power for a number of years with General MacArthur and the majority of US occupation troops remaining until 1952. (Of course, Japan remains a major base for US troops in East Asia down to the present). In Japan, nation-building included the reconstruction and reform of the education system, the press, industry and the legal system, as well as the retraining of the police, and major disarmament, demobilization and demilitarization initiatives; however, more significant changes were increasingly subordinated to the imperatives of the Cold War. US efforts to stabilize the Japanese political system by retaining and using the emperor and facilitating a conservative political restoration under the Liberal Democratic Party (which has ruled Japan since 1955, apart from a brief hiatus in the early 1990s) became central to turning Japan into a bastion of the US-centered Cold War order in the region.[29]

Tokyo's position as a pivot of US hegemony in East Asia increasingly meshed, by the late 1950s and early 1960s, with Japan's elevation to the status of an Asian model of successful national development and evolutionary capitalist modernization. The profound social costs of Japan's emergence as a modern nation-state prior to 1945 were routinely overlooked or downplayed. This led to the effective marginalization of a great deal of Japanese language work in the Marxist tradition, not to mention the work of pre-1945 North American scholars of Japan, such as E. H. Norman (a Canadian academic and diplomat).[30] One site where the implicit, if not the explicit, effort to produce a conception of modernization that would provide an alternative to Marxism was apparent was the Conference on Modern Japan, set up as a special project of the Association of Asian Studies at the University of Michigan in 1958. It became a key vehicle for the study of the modernization of Japan in the 1960s. Its main goals were to facilitate the dissemination of recent scholarship and the articulation of new perspectives on modern Japan. Under the stewardship of an executive committee, chaired by John Whitney Hall, which included Ronald P. Dore, Marius B. Jansen, William W. Lockwood, Donald H. Shively and Robert E. Ward, and with the financial support of the Ford Foundation, the Conference on Modern Japan conducted five annual seminars on various aspects of "the problem of Japan's modern development". It was hoped that the volumes that resulted from the Conference on Modern Japan project would "prove both representative of current scholarship on Japan and comprehensive in their coverage of one of the most fascinating stories of national development in recent history". The Conference on Modern Japan also involved two more informal theoretical discussions on modernization.[31] As will be discussed in more detail in chapter 6, an influential understanding of the role of government in the process of modernization flowed from this nexus. The analysis provided by William Lockwood in this period reflected the general consensus on state-guided national development that prevailed. Lockwood's edited volume in the series was entitled *The State and Economic Enterprise in Japan* (1965) (despite the efforts of the Committee on Comparative Politics to discourage the use of the term in this period). He argued that the economic modernization of post-1945 Japan was driven by a "web of influences and pressures interweaving through government and business, rather than a streamlined pyramid of authoritarian control". It was, said Lockwood, a "web with no spider".[32] This interpretation meshed with the analysis of the role of the government in Japanese modernization provided by the standard and exceedingly influential text, *East Asia: Tradition and Transformation*, by Reischauer, Fairbank and Albert Craig. They pointed to the "particular Japanese combination of free enterprise and government guidance", arguing that the government "was more deeply involved in planning than the government of any other nonsocialist state".[33]

More broadly, Reischauer's writings helped by the 1960s and early 1970s to promote the Japanese trajectory as an example of successful modernization with lessons for developing nations. He deployed the pre-1945 Japanese trajectory as a cautionary tale for those governments pursuing modernization in the post-1945 era. Writing in the early 1970s, he observed that "growth in any society is likely to be uneven, thus producing new imbalances" and that this "seems to be true even when growth has been a relatively slow, evolutionary process". He argued, however, that "imbalances are more likely to become dangerously pronounced when growth has been artificially forced, as in Meiji Japan, by a strong leadership utilizing the experience and patterns of more developed societies". The precise result, he observed, was "unpredictable", however, "there seems to be a broad causal relationship between imbalanced growth and eventual instability". In his view this was "one conclusion to be derived from modern Japanese history that seems relevant for the many other countries which are undergoing rapid and usually forced change today".[34] At the same time, Reischauer's work generally sought to normalize the pre-1945 Japanese trajectory. This was embedded in his wider concern to present Japanese history as part of world history emphasizing what Japan had in common with the histories of other nations rather than what made it unique.[35] It was this kind of universalism that allowed Reischauer, and most other modernization theorists, to assume that development lessons from the experience of pre-1945 Japan, or from the US, were readily transferable to other parts of the world in the post-1945 era.[36]

The challenge of "guerrilla communism" in Southeast Asia I: Malaysia

While Japan emerged as central to US hegemony in East Asia after 1945 and became an important focus of wider attempts to theorize the process of modernization, increasing US involvement in Southeast Asia in the 1950s ensured that the region also attracted the interest of a significant and growing number of North American political scientists by the 1960s. George McTurnan Kahin, who had played a founding role in the Committee on Comparative Politics, but parted company with the Committee early on, was a central figure in the creation and consolidation of Southeast Asian Studies in this early period.[37] After finishing a bachelor's degree at Harvard University in 1940, Kahin entered the US army. During the Second World War he was part of a contingent of paratroopers who were trained for insertion behind enemy lines in the Netherlands East Indies, which was then occupied by Japan. However, by the time US forces under General MacArthur began rolling back the Japanese empire, it had been decided that the erstwhile Dutch colony would not be a direct focus of the campaign. Kahin ended up in Europe instead, but rekindled his interest in Southeast Asia after the war. He received an MA from Stanford University in 1946 and then went on to Johns Hopkins University. He did graduate research in Indonesia during the final period of the Indonesian nationalist movement's struggle against Dutch colonialism in 1948–1949. After finishing his PhD in 1951 he took up the post of assistant professor of government and executive director of the recently established Southeast Asia Program at Cornell University. Kahin was a driving force in Southeast Asian Studies at Cornell in the 1950s and 1960s (he was director of the program between 1961 and 1970). Meanwhile, in 1954 he established the Cornell Modern Indonesia Project, which he ran until his retirement in 1988. In the early 1960s Kahin rose to prominence because of his outspoken opposition to US policy in South Vietnam. He was the main speaker at the first National Teach-in in Washington, DC in April 1964.[38] Kahin played a key role in the 1950s in consolidating Southeast Asian Studies in the North American university system. He edited an influential general study of Asian politics and another on Southeast Asian politics, both of which were widely used as textbooks in this period.[39] Kahin's classic early study, *Nationalism and Revolution in Indonesia* (1952), which was based on his doctoral research in Indonesia in the late 1940s, reflected the early optimism about decolonization, modernization and nation-building. In the case of Indonesia and the rest of Southeast Asia and beyond it was hoped, if not confidently expected in the 1950s that ethnic loyalties, and so-called primordial sentiments, would fade and new loyalties to the modern nation would become the central aspect of every citizen's identity.[40]

Kahin's work reflected a particularly early interest in Southeast Asia after 1945 by a political scientist. By the time his book was published, however, Southeast Asia was becoming a major arena of the Cold War. Policy-makers in Washington were increasingly concerned about the stability of the colonies and/or new nations in the context of the consolidation of the People's Republic of China and the growing significance of "guerrilla communism" in the region. Signalling this shift, at the end of the 1950s, Guy Pauker, a founding member of the Committee on Comparative Politics, warned that Southeast Asia was going to be a "Problem Area in the Next Decade".[41] In the early 1960s Pauker was head of the Asian Section of the Social Science Division at the Rand Corporation and an important figure in what Ron Robin has characterized as the "Military-Intellectual Complex".[42] The geo-strategic importance of Southeast Asia and the importance of political science to the study of the region are reflected in the disciplinary and regional breakdown of recipients of the Ford Foundation-funded Foreign Area Fellowship Program (FAFP). The FAFP, which was managed by the Social Science Research Council, awarded 2,050 fellowships between 1952 and 1972. As a group political scientists received 439 of these awards, more than any other discipline, while 8 percent of the fellowships were disbursed for political science research on Southeast Asia.[43]

The rising interest in Southeast Asia, in the context of the growing concern with developing areas generally, is apparent in the work of Lucian W. Pye, also a founding member of the Committee on Comparative Politics, who emerged as a particularly influential advocate of modernization theory in the 1950s and early 1960s. Pye, who was born in China in 1921 of missionary parents, served as an intelligence officer in the Marine Corps in Asia during the Second World War. Following the end of the war he did graduate studies in political science at Yale University where he studied with Gabriel Almond. Pye succeeded Almond as head of the Committee in 1963, a post he held until it ceased operation in 1972. Pye's work combined an explicitly psychological approach to political behaviour with the examination of political change in the emerging nation-states of Asia and Africa.[44] His first book, which was published in 1956, was on "guerrilla communism" in British Malaya.[45] It built on Almond's 1954 study, which was preoccupied with the psychological "appeal" of communism. Almond had concluded that the communist parties of Western Europe, which were the focus of his study, drew their recruits from members of the population who were "alienated", "deviational" or "psychologically maladjusted". Under these circumstances the new recruits were attracted to the structure provided by the communist parties primarily as a means to resolve personal identity crises.[46]

Pye's book on the communist insurgency in British Malaya linked Almond's ideas to an explicitly developmental approach that identified late-colonial Malaya as a "transitional" society.[47] He argued that the fundamental basis of the appeal of communism in Malaya and other underdeveloped nation-states was the insecurity experienced by people who had lost their "traditional way of life" and were undergoing psychological stress as part of their effort to achieve a "modern" existence. Pye, who conducted his fieldwork in 1952 and 1953 in Malaya, where he interviewed sixty former members of the Malayan Communist Party with the cooperation of the Malayan authorities, concluded that those who joined the MCP did so because the organization represented a "stable element in their otherwise highly unstable societies". He argued that "in the structure of the party" the recruits could find "a closer relationship between effort and reward than anything they have known in either the static old society or the unstable, unpredictable new one".[48] Harry J. Benda outlined a similar perspective on the "appeals of communism" when he observed that: "Communist movements" in Asia and other parts of the developing world "provide a substitute for decayed or vanishing institutions".[49]

This kind of work reinforced the outlook that underpinned the counter-insurgency and nation-building efforts of the colonial government in Malaya (as manifested in the writings of British officials such as Sir Robert Thompson).[50] Like Thompson (who was head of the British Advisory Mission to South Vietnam between 1961 and 1965), Pye's analysis also meshed with the thinking that increasingly underpinned the US modernizing and counter-insurgency efforts in South Vietnam by the early 1960s. According to Pye, if peasants in "transitional societies" joined guerrilla movements to acquire a modern identity then the way to defeat the guerrillas was to establish governing institutions that were more effective, more appealing and more modern than those provided by the communists. In November 1963 Pye presented a paper at a United States Agency for International Development (USAID) advisory committee meeting that argued that all governments in the new nations confronted profound crises of "participation" and "legitimacy". In order to resolve these crises, he advised that the governments concerned should seek to gain greater control over their citizens by mobilizing them for a more active role in national politics.[51]

The Cold War and nation-building II: the militarization of modernization theory

The "search for identity" in Southeast Asia: Burma and Indonesia

As his presentation to USAID made clear, Pye and other modernization theorists were expressing growing concern by the early 1960s about whether the incipient or recently established nation-states in Asia and Africa would successfully make the transition to modernity. For example, in 1960 Pye lamented that the "transitional societies of Southeast Asia have not fully incorporated the view common to rational-legal systems of authority that the appropriate goal of politics is the production of public policy in the form of laws". He noted that, in Southeast Asia, "power and prestige" were still regularly regarded as "values to be fully enjoyed for their own sake".[52] In 1962 Pye published a major study (supported by the Center for International Studies at MIT) that focused on the "problems of building a modern nation-state". His book, *Politics, Personality and Nation-Building: Burma's Search for Identity*, used Burma as a case study, but drew examples from a wide range of emergent nation-states in Asia and Africa. A central concern was why "transitional societies have such great difficulties in creating an effective modern state system?" At the outset he remonstrated that the "shocking fact has been that in the last decade the new countries of Asia have had more difficulties with the psychological than with the objective economic problems basic to nation-building". He argued that, as colonies in Africa increasingly moved towards decolonization, it would "become more apparent" that they, like the new nations of Asia, are "crucially affected by deep psychological conflicts". Making clear the concern with order that was central to modernization theory from the outset, he lamented the apparent lack of "doctrines on nation-building". The formulation of such a doctrine, he argued, had been "inhibited primarily" by an "unreasoned expectation" that democracy was "inevitable" and by the "belief that political development is a natural and even automatic phenomenon which cannot be rationally planned or directed". Pye emphasized that there was a "need to create more effective, more adaptive, more complex, and more rationalized organizations" to facilitate nation-building. However, the "heart" of the nation-building "problem", for Pye, still centered on the "interrelationships among personality, culture, and the polity".[53]

The preoccupation with personality that characterized Pye's work is reflected in his assertion that the "hope" for "transitional peoples" rested in their search "for new collective as well as individual identities". He was adamant that the successful national development depended upon the realization of a "greater sense of order" at both the personal and national political levels. Pye proffered two broad approaches to make this happen, arguing that for transitional societies to "advance" they would have to successfully combine both of these. The first involved a "grand ideological solution" where a leader would emerge who, "out of the depths of his own personal experience", would be "able to give his people an understanding of the new sentiments and values necessary for national development". The second lay in "assisting individuals as individuals", helping them "to find their sense of identity through the mastery of demanding skills". In this way national development would be advanced "as ever increasing numbers of competent people meet in their daily lives the exacting but also psychologically reassuring standards of professional performance basic to the modern world".[54] These prescriptions clearly reflect the evolutionary and universalized character of modernization theory, assuming that modernization is about making a transition from tradition to modernity and that transition is made at the level of individual change under a leadership with a modernizing vision.

Pye's work clearly demonstrated the way in which modernization theorists expected, or at least remained confident, that the right nation-building strategies would ensure that traditional loyalties, such as ethnic allegiance, would fade and new loyalties to the modern nation would become the central element of every citizen's identity. By the beginning of the 1960s a growing number of new nation-states were experiencing instability related to ethnic conflict; however, despite this trend and despite its significance for Burma in particular, Pye's book avoids the question of ethnic conflict. For a decade since independence from Britain in 1948 the Burmese state, controlled by the politically dominant Burmans, had been engaged in more or less ongoing warfare with the former colony's ethnic minorities. Most of the insurgencies had wound down by 1958 (only the Karens remained in open rebellion), but it was not at all clear that these conflicts had been resolved. That they had not been resolved became clear in subsequent decades.[55] These ongoing ethnic insurgencies represented what Walker Connor has described as the postcolonial Burmese state's "most visible and significant barrier to integration"; however, Pye makes only one passing reference to minorities in a book of 300 pages (nor does it figure in his earlier work on Malaya), and his neglect of ethnicized conflict was not particularly unusual for modernization theorists in this period.[56]

By contrast, Clifford Geertz – who served in the US Navy during the Second World War before embarking on an academic career – addressed the question of ethnic differences more directly in a 1963 book sponsored by the Committee for the Comparative Study of New Nations at the University of Chicago.[57] Although his analysis reflected an awareness of ethnic differences, in his contribution to *Old Societies and New States: The Quest for Modernity in Asia and Africa*, Geertz tended to treat cultural and religious sentiments as relatively fixed and even "primordial". In his chapter on "The Integrative Revolution", Geertz (an anthropologist, rather than a political scientist, by training) expressed a significant degree of concern about the chances for success of what he called the "integrative revolution" (this was represented as a process by which "primordial" loyalties to region, race, kinship group, custom, religion and language were subsumed into a wider national consciousness) that was underway in the new nations of Asia and Africa. His chapter dealt with a range of examples, including Burma, Malaya and Indonesia. Despite the differences between Burma, Malaya and Indonesia, he argued that they, and other new nation-states, shared a "common problem – the political normalization of primordial discontent". Geertz compared the "new states" to "naïve or apprentice painters or poets or composers, seeking their own proper style". He then described the "new states" as "imitative, poorly organized, eclectic, opportunistic, subject to fads, ill-defined" and "uncertain". In the case of Burma, Geertz warned that the government did not have the loyalty of non-Burmans during much of the 1950s and "if its ethnic enthusiasm is not contained, it may not have it a decade hence either". Writing at the time of the rebellions in the Outer Islands and the trend towards authoritarianism under Sukarno in the late 1950s and early 1960s, Geertz perceived Indonesia as "an almost classic case of integrative failure". He lamented that "every step toward modernity" in Indonesia had simply strengthened the tendency towards "an unstable amalgam of military coercion and ideological revivalism".[58] The increasing perception, by the early 1960s, that Southeast Asian nation-states, such as Burma and Indonesia, were drifting from the modern democratic path was apparent in the detailed empirical work of Herbert Feith and Daniel Lev on Indonesia. At the same time, their analysis reflected the elitist orientation of modernization theory and its ahistorical and universalizing approach, evaluating the Indonesian trajectory in terms of its inability to recapitulate an idealized version of the North American path to modernity.[59]

While North American social scientists, such as Geertz, were concerned with the integrative prospects of an independent Indonesia, the US government was playing a key role in supporting the rebellions of the late 1950s as part of its efforts to destabilize the Sukarno government. The so-called "loss" of China in 1949 had a powerful impact on the thinking of President Eisenhower and his Secretary of State John Foster Dulles. In particular, they thought the victory of the Chinese revolution flowed in large measure from the Truman administration's preoccupation with maintaining the territorial integrity of China when confronted with the obvious military and political superiority of the communists. This outlook, combined with the assumption that Sukarno's non-aligned policy, and his alliance with the Indonesian Communist Party, were evidence that he was leading Indonesia into the communist bloc, formed the centerpiece of the Eisenhower administration's approach to a series of rebellions in the archipelago in the late 1950s. The emergence of *Pemerintahan Revolusioner Republik Indonesia* (Revolutionary Government of the Republic of Indonesia – PRRI) in Sumatra and *Piagam Perjuangan Semesta Alam* (Universal Struggle Charter – *Permesta*) in Sulawesi, primarily under the leadership of disgruntled army officers, were driven to a significant degree by the struggle between "left" and "right" in Indonesia. In particular the PRRI and *Permesta* revolts were a response to the resurgence of the *Partai Komunis Indonesia* (Communist Party of Indonesia – PKI), which was growing in influence by the late 1950s. In this period, the PKI was increasingly arguing that the national revolution needed to be completed by breaking the nation's ties with imperialism and its dependence on comprador elements. Viewing the rebellions as an opportunity to destabilize and possibly even topple the increasingly left-leaning government of Sukarno, Washington provided considerable covert support to the ultimately unsuccessful rebellions. In 1957 and 1958 the US initiated a CIA-led covert operation, involving the US Navy and elements of the US Airforce, which was larger in scale and scope than the much better-known, although no more successful, Bay of Pigs operation against Castro's Cuba in the early 1960s.[60] However, these conflicts in Indonesia, while certainly having an ethnic component, were not secessionist as such and were still primarily about reconfiguring the Indonesian nation-state rather than (in contrast to Burma, for example) breaking it up. Throughout this period, and in contrast to the later period, a strong commitment to national unity survived across the political spectrum in Indonesia.[61]

The challenge of "guerrilla communism" in Southeast Asia
II: South Vietnam

The work on nation-building and national development by Pye and Geertz, as well as other modernization theorists, reflected the growing concern in the 1960s about the future of the new nation-states in Asia and the emerging Third World. This intersected with an increased emphasis in US foreign policy circles (symbolized by the election to the US presidency of John F. Kennedy) on the need for a more ambitious nation-building strategy. As we have seen, this involved taking the initiative in Asia (as well as Latin America, the Middle East and Africa) to counter the communist threat via the infusion of increased levels of military and economic aid, advice and support. As already empha-sized, the country that encapsulated US nation-building efforts in the early 1960s was South Vietnam. In a major address to a conference at West Point on April 18 1963, attended by Lucian Pye among others, Walt Whitman Rostow declared that the key to winning the guerrilla war in South Vietnam was to "create at forced-draft the bone structure of a modern nation".[62] In the context of the Kennedy administration's wider effort to bring modernity to the Third World, the US-backed nation-building initiative in South Vietnam had entered a new phase by the early 1960s. This new phase also flowed in signifi-cant measure from changes to the situation in South Vietnam itself by the end of the 1950s. Following the Geneva Conference in 1954, which temporarily divided Vietnam between North and South, the Viet Minh had withdrawn militarily to the north, but a large number of its members and supporters continued to live in the south. In 1959 the Communist party leadership in Hanoi, in part as a result of growing pressure from its southern members, took the decision to support armed struggle in South Vietnam. In December 1960 the National Liberation Front of South Vietnam (NLF), a popular front orga-nization modelled on the Viet Minh, was established to spearhead the guerrilla war. By 1961 the fighting between the NLF and the South Vietnamese regime was increasing steadily.[63]

In response, the Strategic Hamlet Program became the "centerpiece" of Washington's policy towards South Vietnam in 1962 and 1963. Drawing on the experience of previous French colonial initiatives, earlier efforts by the regime of Ngo Dinh Diem (1955–1963), as well as British counter-insurgency programs in Malaya in the 1950s, the Kennedy administration encouraged and facilitated the removal of peasants from widely dispersed villages, placing them in concentrated settlements which could be controlled more directly by the government in Saigon. Washington's commitment to this program was apparent in the fact that the State Department scheduled almost US$90 million to be spent on strategic hamlet programs for fiscal year 1963. Using this strategy the US Military Assistance Command (MACV) and USAID sought to prevent, or at least seri-ously weaken the NLF's ability to get intelligence, food and other supplies, as well as recruits from the southern population. They also sought to inculcate new ideas about national citizenship that were centered on loyalty to the government of South Vietnam. In 1962 it initially appeared as if the strategic hamlets were undermining the influence of the NLF; however, the guerrillas acted rapidly and effectively to counter this trend. The NLF promised the peasants (many of whom were, not surprisingly, hostile to resettlement, as well as the forced labor demands and other coercive aspects of the US-backed program) that following the revolution they would be allowed to return to their old villages. The NLF also intensified military attacks on and recruitment in the strategic hamlets. In a wider sense, however, the Strategic Hamlet Program failed because US officials and advisors were unable or unwilling to examine the ideas it rested on. The assumption that rural practices and values could be eradicated, or at least revised, to fit anti-communist modernizing and nation-building goals remained entrenched as the war deepened. After Diem's ouster and death, the term strategic hamlet was excised from counterinsurgency discourse, but subsequent efforts to resettle and control the rural population did little but rework the basic modernization framework that underpinned the failed Strategic Hamlet Program of 1962–1963.[64]

After the overthrow and assassination of Diem and his brother Ngo Dinh Nhu Diem in a military coup in October 1963, the Strategic Hamlet Program's successors were increasingly overshadowed by full-scale warfare. The US had hoped that the overthrow of the Diem regime would improve the stability of South Vietnam; however, the deterioration in the military situation following the coup paved the way for the escalation of US involvement and direct military intervention by 1965. This led, in turn, to immense human, material and environmental destruction, but failed to solve the fundamental political problems of the Saigon regime and the fragile nation-state of South Vietnam. The pervasive reliance on the US, economically, militarily and politically, generated growing possibilities for government and private corruption that completely shredded the South Vietnamese government's nationalist credentials. The war became a business opportunity for many members of the wealthy and well-connected elite in Saigon. While a significant number of people in the south were hostile to the communists, they also lost interest in fighting for the increasingly corrupt and despotic US-backed regime.[65] Furthermore, in their effort to build a modern nation-state in the southern half of Vietnam (something that will be discussed in more detail in chapter 8), US policy-makers overlooked the fact that many southerners identified with the culturally and historically delineated Vietnamese "nation" that was larger than the post-1954 polity presided over by Diem and his successors.[66] At no point were the assumptions about modernization, or the viability of South Vietnam as a nation-state, ever seriously questioned by US policy-makers or advocates of modernization theory. This is reflected in the relative acquiescence to the imperatives of the Cold War on the part of the majority of the members of the Asian Studies profession in the 1960s and early 1970s. In the Vietnam era, the Association for Asian Studies, which had almost 5,000 members in 1970, adopted a relatively detached majority stance on the war in Southeast Asia. At the end of the 1960s AAS president, William Theodore de Bary of Columbia

University, called for a position on the war in Vietnam that was "nonpolitical but not unconcerned".[67] The active academic opposition to the war was left to the much smaller Committee of Concerned Asian Scholars, which broke from the Association for Asian Studies in the late 1960s.[68]

The politics of order and nation-building I: reorientation and revision

In the late 1960s and 1970s a continued commitment to the search for theories of modernization and strategies of nation-building with universal relevance was apparent in the work of a number of modernization theorists who were much more overtly political than the non-political position advocated by AAS president de Bary. A number of observers have argued that the war in Vietnam provided the backdrop for the consolidation of what is sometimes called the politics-of-order approach, or military modernization theory. In particular it is often argued that, as a result of an increasing number of challenges to US nation-building efforts, the creation of institutions and organizations that could provide order became the key issue for modernization theorists during the 1960s.[69] In the context of the prominent role of the military in politics in Asia and beyond this led to growing interest in the "military as a modernizing force".[70] In 1959, in an article that sought to direct attention to Southeast Asia, Guy Pauker had warned that the "liberal tradition" of the United States made "it repugnant to contemplate regimes controlled by military elements".[71] By 1962 Pauker's views had become more explicit in their emphasis on a military solution, rejecting psychological theories of nation-building and the preoccupation with winning "hearts and minds" that was ostensibly the key to "constructive counterinsurgency" in the late 1950s and early 1960s. At a conference on "The U.S. Army's Limited War Mission and Social Science Research" in mid-1962, which was held at American University in Washington DC, Pauker told those in attendance about new research at the Rand Corporation that challenged the prevailing emphasis on social and economic reform in, and psychological approaches to, counterinsurgency. While Pauker's views were apparently out of step with those of the other participants in the conference, the shift in emphasis from "constructive counterinsurgency" to "coercive counterinsurgency" that was being advocated by the social science division at the Rand Corporation eventually became the "intellectual prop" for direct US intervention in South Vietnam by the Johnson administration after 1965.[72] As the 1960s unfolded the US government, with the support of policy-intellectuals based at, or affiliated with, the Rand Corporation, along with other modernization theorists, were increasingly formulating and/or acting on what some observers have called "military modernization theory".[73] As the 1960s progressed, proponents of the modernizing role of the military in Asia and elsewhere increasingly emphasized the importance of cultivating military officers, and pointed to the central role the military as an organization could play in nation-building and the provision of order.[74]

Samuel Huntington is generally seen as one of the most prominent exponents of the need to shift from classical modernization theory, with its psychological orientation and its ostensible emphasis on democracy, to the politics of order and military modernization theory.[75] A major figure in North American political science, Huntington began his career as an undergraduate at Yale in the 1940s.[76] He then completed an MA at the University of Chicago in 1948. He did his PhD at Harvard, graduating in 1951, and remaining as a member of staff. In the 1950s and 1960s he acted in various consultant and advisory capacities to the US government and to the Democratic Party. In the 1970s he developed close links with the Trilateral Commission. He was on the Trilateral Task Force on the Governability of Democracies and authored the section on the United States in the well-known Task Force report, *The Crisis of Democracy*. Huntington served as the Coordinator of National Security on the National Security Council during the Carter administration, a post he resigned from in August 1978 in order to become the Director of the Center for International Affairs at Harvard University.[77] In the 1950s and early 1960s Huntington wrote about the military in politics.[78] His reputation as a theorist of political development and modernization – a reputation that had first been established with *The Soldier and the State* in 1957 – was consolidated with *Political Order in Changing Societies*, which first appeared in 1968.[79]

Political Order in Changing Societies was exceedingly influential.[80] However, as Paul Cammack and Irene L. Gendzier have argued, it was not as dramatic a departure from earlier trends in modernization theory as either Huntington, or many other observers, have suggested.[81] Many of its main ideas and propositions are to be found in earlier books on modernization theory. What Huntington did, however, was to synthesize this earlier work while focusing on predicting what might or might not be necessary to ensure continued political order and social stability. He held up political order as the ultimate goal of any society.[82] In an implicit critique of development economics and Cold War policy-makers he argued that, contrary to earlier expectations, the instability in Asia and the rest of the Third World since the Second World War was primarily the result of "rapid social change and the rapid mobilization of new groups into politics coupled with the slow development of political institutions". In his view, US foreign policy since 1945 had missed this point, because Washington had focused on the "economic gap" and ignored the "political gap". He emphasized that the political gap had been ignored because of the assumption in North America that political stability flowed from "social reform" stimulated by economic development. However, in his view it was actually the process of modernization that resulted in political instability. For Huntington organization was the "road to political power" as well as the "foundation of political stability". While the "vacuum of power and authority" which was seen to exist in "so many modernizing countries may be filled temporarily by charismatic leadership or by military force", he argued that it could only "be filled permanently" by "political organization".[83]

Much of this emphasis can already be discerned in the writing of earlier modernization theorists such as Pye and Almond. For example, as we have seen a concern about the neglect of the political side of development, and the emphasis on building institutions and creating organizations, was present in Pye's book on Burma, which was cited approvingly by Huntington in relation to his discussion of the need for building political organizations.[84] At the same time, despite growing evidence to the contrary, the assumption that economic development produced political stability continued to prevail in US government circles into the mid-1960s. In fact, Secretary of Defense, Robert S. McNamara's articulation of this view in 1966 was challenged directly by Huntington.[85] As his criticisms of McNamara's views on the causal link between poverty and instability suggest, there was a connection between Huntington's conclusions in *Political Order in Changing Societies* and his work for the US government in the second half of the 1960s.[86] From 1966 to 1969 Huntington was chairman of the Council on Vietnamese Studies of USAID's South East Asian Advisory Group. In 1967 he spent time in South Vietnam, and in 1968 he wrote an article that explained the communist success there in terms of their "ability to impose authority in rural areas where authority was lacking". In his view – and this was a major theme of his book as well – the appeals of communism in South Vietnam did not stem from material poverty, but from "political deprivation", that is, the lack of an "effective structure of authority". In Huntington's estimation, and in contrast to earlier writers on the subject, the rural areas could not be retaken from the communists. In the three years between 1965 and 1968, approximately 3 million Vietnamese had already fled to the urban areas, especially Saigon. In South Vietnam and elsewhere the key to combating wars of national liberation, according to Huntington, was to adopt a policy of "forced-draft urbanization" and "modernization", which would quickly shift the nation-state in question beyond the stage where a rural-based revolution had any chance of building up enough support to capture national political power.[87]

The draconian prescriptions of Huntington, and other modernization theorists who viewed order as the primary objective, held out the possibility that successful nation-building in South Vietnam and elsewhere remained within Washington's power. However, with the Tet Offensive in early 1968, any idea that US power could turn South Vietnam into a viable capitalist nation-state and achieve military victory against the North had already disappeared. For the architects of the US war in Vietnam, the Tet Offensive represented what Gabriel Kolko has described as "a long-postponed confrontation with reality".[88] Against the backdrop of the failing US effort to turn South Vietnam into a Southeast Asian version of South Korea or Taiwan (which, in Cold War terms, were superficially similar to South Vietnam and each other, but, as we will see in chapter 8, have different histories), Huntington's book represented an important reorientation and revision of modernization theory. It also represented an inability, or an unwillingness, to probe the deeper assumptions on which the US-led modernization project rested. *Political Order in Changing Societies* highlighted the close connection between political science and the "policy concerns of the day".[89] The assumptions and concerns of the officials who carried the US into full-scale war in Vietnam were closely connected to the theories of modernization that emerged in the 1950s and 1960s.[90] Despite revisions, modernization theory continued to be constrained by the way in which change was conceptualized as a process in which nation-states evolve, ought to evolve, or can be made to evolve, along a single path, or at best a limited number of paths, towards capitalist modernity. This outlook was grounded implicitly, and often explicitly, in romanticized visions of the history of North America and Western Europe (especially the US and Great Britain). The routinization of the nation-state system also meshed with and reinforced the wider organic metaphors that had come to underpin a great deal of work on modernization. Organic and evolutionary conceptions of development glossed over the uneven and destructive aspects of capitalist development. Meanwhile, the use of economic and political models with little regard to questions of time and place facilitated the consolidation between the 1940s and the 1970s of a shifting but consistently technocratic and elitist approach to national development and universalized nation-building lessons based on selective readings of particular cases of nation-state formation and consolidation. At the same time, as we will see, the Committee on Comparative Politics did not survive the 1970s, and part of its undoing flowed from a growing challenge to its pretensions to produce a universal theory of modernization.

By the late 1960s, political development theorists such as Huntington had completely subordinated democracy to a concern with order and stability. The politics-of-order approach treated the emergence of authoritarian regimes, such as Suharto's New Order (1966–1998) in Indonesia that followed the displacement of Sukarno in 1965–1966, as a necessary response to instability, and focused on the need for and the ability of centralized authoritarian states (although the term state was not usually used) to better pursue capitalist development.[91] This understanding of the emergence of the New Order in Indonesia was apparent, for example, in an article in *Asian Survey* by Guy Pauker in the late 1960s.[92] Not surprisingly, ideas about the functional need for a military-led technocracy to oversee the process of development were also popular with members of the Indonesian military. For example, Huntington's ideas, as well as those of earlier North American modernization theorists, are readily apparent in the writings of Ali Moertopo, who served as Suharto's intelligence chief for many years.[93] In South Korea, meanwhile, Huntington's book was widely read in translation by the 1970s, and provided legitimation for the authoritarian regime of Park Chung Hee (1961–1979).[94] More broadly, political scientists, such as John P. Lovell and C. I. Eugene Kim, drew attention to the role of the military in politics and education in the communist states of Asia, before emphasizing the "political relevance of military education, training and indoctrination" in the non-communist nation-states of the region. For example, they held out the "system of military education in South Korea" as important because "of both the politically relevant substance of military education and the numbers of persons in the society exposed to such education". By 1967 over 300,000 South Koreans had received basic military training and also completed at least one of the many courses run by the military.[95]

The politics of order and nation-building II: diversification and decline

By the 1970s the elaboration of the politics-of-order approach was part of a much wider process of diversification and decline as various new radical and moderate theoretical challengers to modernization theory emerged, including the theory of bureaucratic-authoritarianism. Associated initially with the work of Guillermo A. O'Donnell, the idea of bureaucratic-authoritarianism had gained some prominence by the 1970s.[96] O'Donnell argued that, in late-industrializing nation-states, economic development intersected with the end of democracy and greater, rather than less, inequality. His approach drew on Weberian sociology, Marxism and corporatist concepts. More specifically he built critically on Huntington's approach and on the early historical critique of modernization theory articulated by Barrington Moore.[97] Central to O'Donnell's analysis was the argument that a bureaucratic-authoritarian state emerged when the limits of import-substitution industrialization were reached. At this point the alliance, which had been forged between the working class and the bourgeoisie, broke down and the national bourgeoisie moved to form an alliance with the military and the technocracy resulting in bureaucratic-authoritarianism. A central characteristic of a bureaucratic-authoritarian regime, as defined by O'Donnell, was that it was an attempt by the national bourgeoisie, linked to transnational capital, to protect their interests and guide the economy in a direction commensurate with their needs. The more deterministic elements of the theory of bureaucratic-authoritarianism were increasingly challenged (even by O'Donnell himself) by the second half of the 1970s, at the same time as it was used as a relatively open conceptual framework that provided more of a guide for research than a verifiable theory.[98] The concept of bureaucratic-authoritarianism represented a particularly critical revision of modernization theory that went much further than Huntington in the way that it incorporated insights from Marxist and Marxist-derived theories. Although its primary impact was in Latin American studies, bureaucratic-authoritarianism had a broad influence on the study of modernization and political development. It played a role in, or was connected to, the shift in political science towards "bringing the state back in", a shift that had important implications for the analysis of political and economic change in Northeast and Southeast Asia.

The shift towards "bringing the state back in" followed on from the diversification of modernization theory generally and from the decline of the Committee on Comparative Politics more specifically. These changes are reflected by Charles Tilly's work on state formation in Western Europe, which was sponsored by the Committee.[99] The Committee had apparently hoped that Western European examples could be used to "test and refine" the theories of modernization and political development they had generated in relation to the developing world. The Committee was also concerned that the study of European politics was declining in significance within the sub-discipline of comparative politics. The proposed project on Europe was, at least partially, an attempt to rejuvenate European political studies via its inclusion in the study of political development in the non-European world. Lucian Pye, who was by this point chair of the Committee, argued in the foreword to Tilly's book that one of its goals "was to discover the extent to which" the study of state formation in Western Europe "could usefully inform contemporary efforts at advancing both the practice and theories of political development". However, Tilly's study was a disappointment for Pye, particularly because of its failure to provide sustenance for the universalizing and ahistorical approach that was the hallmark of political development theory. Tilly's study crystallized the tension between political science and history in relation to the study of state formation and nation-building. By the time the project was underway the field of political development theory was breaking down. In fact the Committee on Comparative Politics was wound up in 1972, while *The Formation of National States in Western Europe* was not published until 1975. Ultimately Tilly's study symbolized the growing interest by the 1970s on the part of North American social scientists and historians generally, and political scientists specifically, in state-centered approaches to historical and political change.[100] This shift was formalized with the establishment of the SSRC's Committee on States and Social Structures in 1983, the body that sponsored the 1985 edited volume entitled *Bringing the State Back In*.[101]

The publication of Tilly's book coincided with the fall of Saigon, by which time Southeast Asian Studies in general had declined in significance in North America. However, it was specific disciplines within Southeast Asian Studies, such as political science, that were the most dramatically affected. Between 1962 and 1964 political science applications for work on Southeast Asia were by far the most numerous to be received by the Foreign Area Fellowship Program (FAFP) run by the SSRC. As US involvement in Vietnam deepened in 1965–1967, political science proposals represented at least 50 percent of all applications. Between 1968 and 1970 political science applications remained as numerous as in the previous three-year period; however between 1971 and 1973, proposals from anthropologists overtook those from political scientists. Political science applications to the FAFP for support for work on Southeast Asia then descended to a historically low level in 1974–1976. The relative retreat of North American political scientists from Southeast Asia by the end of the Vietnam War points to the way in which US failure in Vietnam led to the redirection of the modernizing expectations of political scientists. In effect, for its practitioners it was not modernization theory that was seen to have failed, but South Vietnam specifically, and even Southeast Asia more generally. Instead of exploring the reasons for that failure, political scientists turned their attention elsewhere, either geographically or thematically.[102] By the late 1970s, the Newly Industrializing Countries (NICs) of East Asia, South Korea, Taiwan, Hong Kong and Singapore were attracting growing interest. By the 1980s the economic success of Thailand and Malaysia (and latterly Indonesia and coastal China) was being studied and celebrated, often via revised theories of modernization, including an effort by Lucian Pye to vindicate earlier modernization theory.[103] By the end of the Cold War Vietnam, which had in an earlier era been a key geo-political factor behind the wider effort to produce a non-communist theory of modernization, was also increasingly represented as having finally discovered the path to capitalist modernity, although the Vietnamese leadership looked to Japan far more than the United States as the model of national development to emulate.[104]

Conclusion: modernization theory

In the 1950s modernization theory generally, and political development theory more specifically, emerged as one of the most significant trends in political science and area studies. The rise and transformation of modernization theory was linked in important ways to decolonization, the Cold War and US policy in Asia (and beyond). This chapter has examined the history of modernization theory from the 1940s to the 1970s with a focus on Japan and Southeast Asia, emphasizing the way in which decolonization, the Cold War and the growing power of the US were linked to the emergence and consolidation of the modern idea of development as national development. Using Northeast Asian and Southeast Asian examples it has been argued that a central contradiction of modernization theory, and of the wider US-sponsored modernization project, was the way in which they uncritically took the nation-state as the key unit of analysis. It has also been emphasized that the work of North American political scientists writing about modernization intersected with the concerns of US policy-makers. Ultimately the assumptions that these groups shared played an important role in Washington's deepening involvement in Vietnam in the 1960s. At the same time, the war in Vietnam was also central to the changes to modernization theory and the overall reorientation of US hegemony that occurred in this period. The reorientation of US hegemony provided the overall context for the decline of national development and the emergence and consolidation of the US-led globalization project after 1975.

Notes

1   Nation-building in the Cold War era is being defined here primarily as a US- or Soviet-sponsored effort, with important relative exceptions such as United Nations involvement in the Congo from July 1960 to June 1964. The *Operation des Nations Unies au Congo* (ONUC) was the biggest UN action since the Korean War (1950–1953). The latter had formally been a UN initiative despite the fact that it was an overwhelming US operation in practice. Furthermore, it was not until the post-Cold War era, when the United Nations again began to play a somewhat more significant role in nation-building efforts, that the UN intervened on the scale of its operation in the Congo in the early 1960s. K. von Hippel, *Democracy By Force: US Military Intervention in the Post-Cold War World*, Cambridge: Cambridge University Press, 2000.
2   The history of Asian Studies is an important topic. Unfortunately it falls outside of the scope of this book. For background on area studies generally and Asian Studies more specifically see R. A. McCaughey, *International Studies and Academic Enterprise: A Chapter in the Enclosure of American Learning*, New York: Columbia University Press, 1984; I. Wallerstein, "The Unintended Consequences of Cold War Area Studies" in A. Schiffrin, ed., *The Cold War and the University: Toward an Intellectual History of the*

Postwar Years, New York: New Press, 1997; B. Cumings, "Boundary Displacement: Area Studies and International Studies During and After the Cold War" in C. Simpson, ed., *Universities and Empire: Money and Politics in the Social Sciences During the Cold War*, New York: New Press, 1998.

3 N. Gilman, *Mandarins of the Future: Modernization Theory in Cold War America*, Baltimore: Johns Hopkins University Press, 2003.

4 For example, see J. Martinussen, *Society, State and Market*, London: Zed Books, 1997, pp. 61–6, 167–72; P. W. Preston, *Development Theory: An Introduction*, Oxford: Blackwell, 1996, pp. 153–78; M. E. Latham, *Modernization as Ideology: American Social Science and "Nation Building" in the Kennedy Era*, Chapel Hill: University of North Carolina Press, 2000, pp. 30–46.

5 C. Leys, *The Rise and Fall of Development Theory*, Bloomington: Indiana University Press, 1996, pp. 8–9. Nils Gilman identifies *The Passing of Traditional Society: Modernizing the Middle East* by Daniel Lerner, which was published in 1958 and jointly sponsored by the Center for International Studies at MIT and the Bureau of Applied Social Research at Columbia University, as the first clear articulation by a North American social scientist of what would become modernization theory. See D. Lerner, *The Passing of Traditional Society: Modernizing the Middle East*, New York: Free Press, 1958; Gilman, *Mandarins of the Future*.

6 P. Cammack, *Capitalism and Democracy in the Third World: The Doctrine of Political Development*, London: Leicester University Press, 1997, pp. 44–5.

7 On the origins and early history of the Social Science Research Council see D. Fisher, *Fundamental Development of the Social Sciences: Rockefeller Philanthropy and the United States Social Science Research Council*, Ann Arbor: University of Michigan Press, 1993. For background on the Committee on Comparative Politics see I. L. Gendzier, *Managing Political Change: Social Scientists and the Third World*, Boulder: Westview, 1985, pp. 84–5, 109–47.

8 D. M. Ricci, *The Tragedy of Political Science: Politics, Scholarship, and Democracy*, New Haven: Yale University Press, 1984, pp. 263–4.

9 Cited in H. Wiarda, *Ethnocentrism in Foreign Policy: Can We Understand the Third World?*, Washington, DC: American Enterprise Institute, 1985, p. 63.

10 J. G. Gunnell, "The Declination of the 'State' and the Origins of American Pluralism" in J. Farr, J. S. Dryzek and S. T. Leonard, eds, *Political Science in History: Research Programs and Political Traditions*, Cambridge: Cambridge University Press, 1995, pp. 19–23, 29–30, 39–40.

11 T. Mitchell, "The Limits of the State: Beyond Statist Approaches and their Critics" *American Political Science Review* vol. 85, no. 1 (March), 1991, pp. 78–9.

12 K. Loewenstein, "Report on the Research Panel on Comparative Government" *American Political Science Review* vol. 38, no. 2, 1944, pp. 541–3, 547. Cited in T. Mitchell, "Society, Economy, and the State Effect" in G. Steinmetz, ed., *State/Culture: State-Formation after the Cultural Turn*, Ithaca: Cornell University Press, 1999, p. 78.

13 D. Easton, *The Political System: An Inquiry into the State of Political Science*, 2nd edn, Chicago: University of Chicago Press, 1981, pp. 1–4.

14 Gilman, *Mandarins of the Future*. Also see Latham, *Modernization as Ideology*.

15 J. S. Coleman, "The Political Systems of the Developing Areas" in G. Almond and J. S. Coleman, eds, *The Politics of the Developing Areas*, Princeton: Princeton University Press, 1960, pp. 537–9.

16 McCaughey, *International Studies and Academic Enterprise*, pp. 102–3, 114.

17 P. M. Evans, *John Fairbank and the American Understanding of Modern China*, Oxford: Basil Blackwell, 1988; R. W. Winks, *Cloak and Gown: Scholars in the Secret War 1939–1961*, New Haven: Yale University Press, 1987, pp. 495–8.

18 W. N. Brown, *The United States and India and Pakistan*, Cambridge, MA: Harvard University Press, 1953; J. K. Fairbank, *The United States and China*, Cambridge, MA: Harvard University Press, 1948.

19 M. Bundy, "The Battlefields of Power and the Searchlights of the Academy" in E. A. G. Johnson, ed., *Dimensions of Diplomacy*, Baltimore: Johns Hopkins University Press, 1964, pp. 2–3.

20 P. J. Seybold, "The Ford Foundation and the Triumph of Behavioralism in American Political Science" in R. F. Arnove, ed., *Philanthropy and Cultural Imperialism: The Foundations at Home and Abroad*, Bloomington: Indiana University Press, 1982, pp. 269–303.

21 J. N. Thomas, *The Institute of Pacific Relations: Asian Scholars and American Politics*, Seattle: University of Washington Press, 1974; R. P. Newman, *Owen Lattimore and the "Loss" of China*, Berkeley: University of California Press, 1992.

22 Evans, *John Fairbank and the American Understanding of Modern China*, pp. 64, 206–13.

23 The Association for Asian Studies is currently subdivided into four councils: the China and Inner Asia Council; the Northeast Asia Council; the South Asia Council and the Southeast Asia Council.

24 For a detailed critique of Fairbank's work see T. E. Barlow, "Colonialism's Career in Postwar China Studies" in T. E. Barlow, ed., *Formations of Colonial Modernity in East Asia*, Durham: Duke University Press, 1997.

25 E. O. Reischauer, *My Life Between Japan and America*, New York: Harper and Row, 1986, p. 196.

26 H. B. Schonberger, *Aftermath of War: Americans and the Remaking of Japan 1945–1952*, Kent: Kent State University Press, 1989.

27 For upwards of twenty years after the "modernization argument" (*kindaikaron*) was introduced to Japan, progressive and Marxist Japanese scholars rejected the "Reischauer Line", as they called it. They attacked "its positive appraisal of Japan's modernization, its view of the (Meiji) Restoration as a peaceful, pragmatic, and nonrevolutionary 'revolution from above', and its suggestion that Japan was a model for Asian development". C. Gluck, "The Past in the Present" in A. Gordon, ed., *Postwar Japan as History*, Berkeley: University of California Press, 1993, pp. 80–1.

28 Reischauer, *My Life Between Japan and America*, p. 118.

29 J. W. Dower, *Embracing Defeat: Japan in the Wake of World War II*, New York: W. W. Norton, 1999.

30 Those elements of pre-1945 Japanese history that Norman had assigned primary importance to, such as uneven economic development, a lack of freedom, the poverty and misery of much of the population, as well as the militarism and the revision of feudal institutions and practices, were at odds with the post-1945 need to promote Japan as an exemplar of evolutionary modernization that had made a sharp break with tradition. J. W. Dower, "E. H. Norman, Japan and the Uses of History" in J. W. Dower, *Origins of the Modern Japanese State: Selected Writings of E. H. Norman*, New York: Pantheon, 1975, pp. 33–4.

31 J. Whitney Hall, "Foreword" in M. B. Jansen, ed., *Changing Japanese Attitudes toward Modernization*, Princeton: Princeton University Press, 1965, pp. v–vii. See J. W. Hall, "Changing Conceptions of the Modernization of Japan" in M. B. Jansen, ed., *Changing Japanese Attitudes toward Modernization*, Princeton: Princeton University Press, 1965. The other volumes in the series are W. W. Lockwood, ed., *The State and Economic Enterprise in Japan*, Princeton: Princeton University Press, 1965; R. P. Dore, ed., *Aspects of Social Change in Modern Japan*, Princeton: Princeton University Press, 1967; R. E. Ward, *Political Development in Modern Japan*, Princeton: Princeton University Press, 1968; D. H. Shively, ed., *Tradition and Modernization in Japanese Culture*, Princeton: Princeton University Press, 1971; J. W. Morley, ed., *Dilemmas of Growth in Prewar Japan*, Princeton: Princeton University Press, 1971.

32 He emphasized the central role of MITI, noting "business makes few major decisions without consulting the appropriate governmental authority"; however, the "same" was also "true in reverse". W. W. Lockwood, "Japan's New Capitalism" in

W. W. Lockwood, ed., *The State and Economic Enterprise in Japan*, Princeton: Princeton University Press, 1965, p. 503.

33 E. O. Reischauer, J. K. Fairbank and A. Craig, *East Asia: Tradition and Transformation*, Boston: Houghton Mifflin, 1973, pp. 829–30.

34 E. O. Reischauer, "What Went Wrong?" in J. W. Morley, ed., *Dilemmas of Growth in Prewar Japan*, Princeton: Princeton University Press, 1971, pp. 489–90, 509–10.

35 A. Iriye, "Reischauer, Fairbank and American–Asian Relations" *Diplomatic History* vol. 12, no. 3, 1988, p. 335.

36 For a concerted attempt to relate pre-1945 Japan's history to the contemporary Third World see E. W. Nafziger, *Learning from the Japanese: Japan's Pre-War Development and the Third World*, Armonk: M. E. Sharpe, 1995.

37 G. McT. Kahin, *Southeast Asia: A Testament*, London: RoutledgeCurzon, 2003.

38 See G. McT. Kahin and J. W. Lewis, *The United States in Vietnam*, 2nd edn, New York: Dial Press, 1969; G. McT. Kahin, *Intervention: How America Became Involved in Vietnam*, New York: Alfred A. Knopf, 1986.

39 G. McT. Kahin, ed., *Major Governments of Asia*, 2nd edn, Ithaca: Cornell University Press, 1963; G. McT. Kahin, ed., *Governments and Politics of Southeast Asia*, 2nd edn, Ithaca: Cornell University Press, 1964.

40 G. McT. Kahin, *Nationalism and Revolution in Indonesia*, Ithaca: Cornell University Press, 1952.

41 G. J. Pauker, "Southeast Asia as Problem Area in the Next Decade" *World Politics* vol. 11, no. 3, 1959.

42 R. Robin, *The Making of the Cold War Enemy: Culture and Politics in the Military-Intellectual Complex*, Princeton: Princeton University Press, 2001, p. 189.

43 Prior to 1974 political science proposals for the FAFP represented over 30 percent of all applications, but between 1975 and 1977 they declined dramatically, accounting for only 6 percent of all proposals. S. Philpott, *Rethinking Indonesia: Postcolonial Theory, Authoritarianism and Identity*, London: Macmillan, 2000, p. 115.

44 See Gilman, *Mandarins of the Future*.

45 L. Pye, *Guerrilla Communism in Malaya: Its Social and Political Meaning*, Princeton: Princeton University Press, 1956.

46 G. A. Almond, *The Appeals of Communism*, Princeton: Princeton University Press, 1954, pp. 234, 370, 380.

47 See Gilman, *Mandarins of the Future*.

48 Pye, *Guerrilla Communism in Malaya*, pp. 3, 7, 201–2.

49 H. J. Benda, "Reflections on Asian Communism" *The Yale Review* vol. 56, 1966, pp. 1–16, especially 12–13. Also see H. J. Benda, "Communism in Southeast Asia" *The Yale Review* vol. 45, 1956, pp. 417–29.

50 R. Thompson, *Defeating Communist Insurgency: Experiences from Malaya and Vietnam*, London: Chatto and Windus, 1966. Thompson joined the Malayan Civil Service in 1938 and, following a number of years in Burma during the Second World War, he returned to Malaya where he worked on security questions. Between 1957 and 1961 he served as Deputy Secretary and then Secretary of Defense in the Federation of Malaya.

51 L. W. Pye, "Political Development and Foreign Aid", November 1963, Bell Papers, box 23, "AID's Advisory Committee on Economic Development (Mason Committee), 1963–1964" JFKL. Cited in Latham, *Modernization as Ideology*, pp. 176–8.

52 L. W. Pye, "The Politics of Southeast Asia" in G. A. Almond and J. S. Coleman, eds, *The Politics of Developing Areas*, Princeton: Princeton University Press, 1960, pp. 142–3.

53 L. W. Pye, *Politics, Personality and Nation-Building: Burma's Search for Identity*, New Haven: Yale University Press, 1962, pp. xv–xvi, 6–8, 13, 15–31, 38–9, 42.

54 Pye, *Politics, Personality and Nation-Building*, pp. 287–91, 297–9, 301.

55 M. Smith, *Burma: Insurgency and the Politics of Ethnicity*, 2nd edn, London: Zed Books, 1999, pp. 170–9.

56 W. Connor, *Ethnonationalism: The Quest for Understanding*, Princeton: Princeton University Press, 1990, pp. 57–9.

57 Geertz was a member of the Committee for the Comparative Study of New Nations from 1962 to 1970, serving as Executive Secretary from 1964 to 1966 and Chairman from 1968 to 1970. Other prominent modernization theorists on the Committee in this period included Lloyd I. Rudolph, who was a member from 1964 to 1972, and Aristide Zolberg, who was a member from 1963 to 1976 and Executive Secretary from 1966 to 1969 and 1973 to 1976. L. I. Rudolph and S. H. Rudolph, "Generals and Politicians in Indian" in W. C. McWilliams, ed., *Garrisons and Governments: Politics and the Military in New States*, San Francisco: Chandler, 1967; A. Zolberg, *Creating Political Order: The Party-States of West Africa*, New York: Rand McNally, 1965.

58 C. Geertz, "The Integrative Revolution: Primordial Sentiments and Civil Politics in the New States" in C. Geertz, ed., *Old Societies and New States: The Quest for Modernity in Asia and Africa*, London: Macmillan, 1963, pp. 128–39, 153–7.

59 H. Feith, *The Decline of Constitutional Democracy in Indonesia*, Ithaca: Cornell University Press, 1962; D. S. Lev, *The Transition to Guided Democracy: Indonesian Politics 1957–1959*, Ithaca: Cornell Modern Indonesia Project Monograph, 1966.

60 See A. R. Kahin and G. McT. Kahin, *Subversion as Foreign Policy: The Secret Eisenhower and Dulles Debacle in Indonesia*, New York: New Press, 1995, p. 75.

61 There was only one significant revolt by a group that rejected the new state of Indonesia outright: that was a short-lived movement in 1950 to establish the Republic of the South Moluccas, led primarily by troops from the old Dutch colonial army. E. Aspinall and M. T. Berger, "The Breakup of Indonesia? Nationalisms after Decolonization and the Limits of the Nation-State in Post-Cold War Southeast Asia" *Third World Quarterly: Journal of Emerging Areas* vol. 22, no. 6, 2001, p. 1006.

62 Cited in Gilman, *Mandarins of the Future*.

63 G. Kolko, *Anatomy of a War: Vietnam, the United States and Modern Historical Experience*, 2nd edn, New York: New Press, 1994, pp. 80–108.

64 Latham, *Modernization as Ideology*, pp. 153–4, 180–2, 197–8, 203–4. See R. A. Hunt, *Pacification: The American Struggle for Vietnam's Hearts and Minds*, Boulder: Westview, 1995.

65 Kolko, *Anatomy of A War*, pp. 111–25, 208–30, 654–7.

66 Latham, *Modernization as Ideology*, p. 161.

67 See W. T. de Bary, "The Association for Asian Studies: Nonpolitical but Not Unconcerned" *Journal of Asian Studies* vol. 29, no. 4, 1970.

68 D. Allen, "Antiwar Asian Scholars and the Vietnam/Indochina War" *Bulletin of Concerned Asian Scholars* vol. 21, nos. 2–4, 1989.

69 For example, see D. C. O'Brien, "Modernization, Order, and the Erosion of a Democratic Ideal: American Political Science 1960–1970" in D. Lehmann, ed., *Development Theory: Four Critical Essays*, London: Frank Cass, 1979, p. 50.

70 H. Bienen, "The Background to Contemporary Study of Militaries and Modernization" in H. Bienen, ed., *The Military and Modernization*, Chicago: Aldine Atherton, 1971, p. 7.

71 Pauker, "Southeast Asia as Problem Area in the Next Decade", p. 343.

72 Robin, *The Making of the Cold War Enemy*, pp. 189–90, 192–9.

73 G. Kolko, *Confronting the Third World: United States Foreign Policy 1945–1980*, New York: Pantheon, 1988, pp. 132–4.

74 For example, see W. Gutteridge, *Armed Forces in the New States*, London: Oxford University Press, 1962; J. J. Johnson, ed., *The Role of the Military in Underdeveloped Countries*, Princeton: Princeton University Press, 1962; M. Janowitz, *The Military in the Political Development of New Nations: An Essay in Comparative Analysis*, Chicago:

University of Chicago Press, 1964; W. Gutteridge, *Military Institutions and Power in the New States*, New York: Praeger, 1965.

75 C. Leys, "Samuel Huntington and the End of Classical Modernization Theory" in H. Alavi and T. Shanin, eds, *Introduction to the Sociology of "Developing Societies"*, London: Macmillan, 1983; V. Randall and R. Theobald, *Political Change and Underdevelopment: A Critical Introduction to Third World Politics*, London: Macmillan, 1985, pp. 67–98. M. T. Berger, *Under Northern Eyes: Latin American Studies and US Hegemony in the Americas 1898–1990*, Bloomington: Indiana University Press, 1995, pp. 129–30.

76 For biographical background and a brief discussion of Huntington's main works see R. D. Kaplan, "Looking the World In The Eye" *The Atlantic Monthly* vol. 288, no. 5, 2001, pp. 68–82.

77 S. P. Huntington, M. Crozier and J. Watanuki, *The Crisis of Democracy: Report on the Governability of Democracies to the Trilateral Commission*, New York: New York University Press, 1975.

78 S. P. Huntington, *The Soldier and the State: The Theory and Politics of Civil–Military Relations*, Cambridge, MA: Harvard University Press, 1957; S. P. Huntington, ed., *Changing Patterns of Military Politics*, New York: Free Press, 1962.

79 S. P. Huntington, *Political Order in Changing Societies*, New Haven: Yale University Press, 1968.

80 In the early 1970s almost 60 percent of North American academics surveyed regarded *Political Order in Changing Societies* as the "most important" book on political development and modernization theory available. H. C. Kenski and M. G. Kenski, *Teaching Political Development and Modernization at American Universities: A Survey*, Tucson: University of Arizona Press, 1974, pp. 9–10.

81 Cammack, *Capitalism and Democracy in the Third World*, pp. 2, 36–7, 52–4; Gendzier, *Managing Political Change*, pp. 130, 142–7.

82 The argument of his 1968 book was foreshadowed in S. P. Huntington, "Political Development and Political Decay" *World Politics* vol. 17, no. 3, 1965.

83 Huntington, *Political Order in Changing Societies*, pp. vii, 4–5, 40–1, 43–5, 460–1.

84 Huntington, *Political Order in Changing Societies*, pp. 30–1.

85 Huntington, *Political Order in Changing Societies*, pp. 40–1.

86 For a good discussion of Huntington's work and the Vietnam War see Leys, "Samuel Huntington and the End of Classical Modernization Theory".

87 S. P. Huntington, "The Bases of Accommodation" *Foreign Affairs* vol. 46, no. 3, 1968, p. 644. See S. P. Huntington, "Social Science and Vietnam" *Asian Survey* vol. 7, no. 8, 1967.

88 Kolko, *Anatomy of A War*, pp. 303–37, 341–55.

89 D. M. Shafer, *Deadly Paradigms: The Failure of US Counterinsurgency Policy*, Princeton: Princeton University Press, 1988, p. 12.

90 See Gilman, *Mandarins of the Future*. The Vietnam War has been the subject of a massive amount of historical scholarship, including considerable evaluation of the assumptions that underpinned US policy in that era. On this immense literature see R. J. McMahon, "U.S.–Vietnamese Relations: A Historiographical Survey" in W. I. Cohen, ed., *Pacific Passage: The Study of American–East Asian Relations on the Eve of the Twenty-First Century*, New York: Columbia University Press, 1996.

91 B. Glassburner, "Economic Policy-Making in Indonesia, 1950–1957" and "Indonesian Economic Policy after Sukarno" in B. Glassburner, ed., *The Economy of Indonesia: Selected Readings*, Ithaca: Cornell University Press, 1971; B. Glassburner, "Political Economy and the Suharto Regime" *Bulletin of Indonesian Economic Studies* vol. 14, no. 3, 1978.

92 G. J. Pauker, "Indonesia: The Age of Reason?" *Asian Survey* vol. 8, no. 2, 1968. Also see an article by the former US ambassador to Indonesia, John M. Allison, who enthused that the "greatest encouragement for the future" of Indonesia "remains

the character and intelligence of the leaders of the New Order". J. M. Allison, "Indonesia: Year of the Pragmatists" *Asian Survey* vol. 9, no. 2, 1969, p. 137. Allison was less optimistic, but still very supportive, a year later. See J. M. Allison, "Indonesia: The End of the Beginning?" *Asian Survey* vol. 10, no. 2, 1970.

93 See A. Moertopo, *Some Basic Thoughts on the Acceleration and Modernization of 25 Years' Development*, Jakarta: Centre for Strategic and International Studies, 1972.

94 B. Cumings, "The Origins and Development of the Northeast Asian Political Economy: Industrial Sectors, Product Cycles and Political Consequences" in F. C. Deyo, ed., *The Political Economy of the New Asian Industrialism*, Ithaca: Cornell University Press, 1987, p. 72.

95 J. P. Lovell and C. I. E. Kim, "The Military and Political Change in Asia" in H. Bienen, ed., *The Military and Modernization*, Chicago: Aldine Atherton, 1971, pp. 108–11.

96 G. A. O'Donnell, *Modernization and Bureaucratic-Authoritarianism: Studies in South American Politics*, Berkeley: University of California Institute of International Studies, 1973; G. A. O'Donnell, "Modernization and Military Coups: Theory, Comparisons and the Argentine Case" in A. F. Lowenthal, ed., *Armies and Politics in Latin America*, New York: Holmes and Meier, 1976; G. A. O'Donnell, "Corporatism and the Question of the State" in J. M. Malloy, ed., *Authoritarianism and Corporatism in Latin America*, Pittsburgh: University of Pittsburgh Press, 1977; G. A. O'Donnell, "Reflections on the Patterns of Change in the Bureaucratic-Authoritarian State" *Latin American Research Review* vol. 13, no. 1, 1978; G. A. O'Donnell, "Tensions in the Bureaucratic-Authoritarian State and the Question of Democracy" in D. Collier, ed., *The New Authoritarianism in Latin America*, New York: Columbia University Press, 1979; G. A. O'Donnell, *Bureaucratic-Authoritarianism: Argentina, 1966–1973, in Comparative Perspective*, Berkeley: University of California Press, 1988.

97 B. Moore, Jr, *Social Origins of Dictatorship and Democracy: Lord and Peasant in the Making of the Modern World*, Boston: Beacon Press, 1966.

98 See D. Collier, "The Bureaucratic-Authoritarian Model: Synthesis and Priorities for Future Research" in D. Collier, ed., *The New Authoritarianism in Latin America*, New York: Columbia University Press, 1979; K. L. Remmer and G. W. Merkx, "Bureaucratic-Authoritarianism Revisited" *Latin American Research Review* vol. 17, no. 2, 1982; D. Y. King, "Indonesia's New Order as a Bureaucratic Polity, a Neopatrimonial Regime, or a Bureaucratic-Authoritarian Regime: What Difference Does It Make?" in B. Anderson and A. Kahin, eds, *Interpreting Indonesian Politics: Thirteen Contributions to the Debate*, Ithaca: Cornell Modern Indonesia Project, Cornell University, 1982; F. D. Adriano, "A Critique of the Bureaucratic Authoritarian State Thesis: The Case of the Philippines" *Journal of Contemporary Asia* vol. 14, no. 4, 1984; A. Budiman, "The State and Industrialisation in Indonesia" in K. Kyong-Dong, ed., *Dependency Issues in Korean Development*, Seoul: National University Press, 1987; S. Haggard, *Pathways From the Periphery: The Politics of Growth in the Newly Industrializing Countries*, Ithaca: Cornell University Press, 1990, pp. 254–70.

99 C. Tilly, ed., *The Formation of National States in Western Europe*, Princeton: Princeton University Press, 1975.

100 Pye, cited in S. Heydemann, "War, Institutions, and Social Change in the Middle East" in S. Heydemann, ed., *War, Institutions, and Social Change in the Middle East*, Berkeley: University of California Press, 2000, pp. 5–7, 28–9. Of course other important revisions of modernization theory were also more historically grounded and challenged the tradition–modernity dichotomy and earlier assumptions about unilinear cultural transformation, emphasizing the persistence of traditional institutions and outlooks and the historical specificity of political cultures. This approach was often more historically grounded, arguing that modernization was not simply about the transition from tradition to modernity, but the modernizing and adapting of tradition, and that all modern societies are a mix of traditional and modern. For

example, see L. I. Rudolph and S. H. Rudolph, *The Modernity of Tradition: Political Development in India*, Chicago: University of Chicago Press, 1967; B. Geddes, "Paradigms and Sand Castles in Comparative Politics of Developing Areas" in W. Crotty, ed., *Comparative Politics, Policy, and International Relations (Political Science: Looking to the Future, vol. 2)*, Evanston: Northwestern University Press, 1991, p. 49.

101 T. Skocpol, "Bringing the State Back In: Strategies of Analysis in Current Research" in P. B. Evans, D. Rueshemeyer and T. Skocpol, eds, *Bringing the State Back In*, New York: Cambridge University Press, 1985.
102 Philpott, *Rethinking Indonesia*, pp. 115–17.
103 L. W. Pye, *Asian Power and Politics: The Cultural Dimensions of Authority*, Cambridge, MA: Harvard University Press, 1985.
104 G. Greenfield, "Fragmented Visions of Asia's Next Tiger: Vietnam and the Pacific Century" in M. T. Berger and D. A. Borer, eds, *The Rise of East Asia: Critical Visions of the Pacific Century*, London: Routledge, 1997.

Part II
The globalization project

It may be the case that the heroic age of building national champions through state-supported industrial policy is over. If this is indeed the case, the idea will not have been defeated by the triumph of small-scale perfectly competitive firms. Rather it will have been defeated by the full flowering of global oligopolistic capitalism.

Peter Nolan,
China and the Global Economy,
London: Palgrave, 2001, p. 188

As the bloody twentieth century drew to a close, God's promise of peace on earth remained unfulfilled; it was now incumbent upon the United States, having ascended to the status of sole superpower, to complete God's work – or, as members of a largely secularized elite preferred it, to guide history toward its intended destination.

Andrew J. Bacevich,
American Empire: The Realities and Consequences of U.S. Diplomacy,
Cambridge, MA: Harvard University Press, 2002, p. 1

4 US hegemony and the passing of national development

The waning of the high modernist era of national development in the 1970s is grounded in the shifts in the global political economy of the Cold War and the emergence of the US-led globalization project.[1] However, the consolidation of the globalization project in the 1980s coincided with the revival of the Cold War, which meant that the long-term significance of the changes to the global political economy and to the nation-state system in this period remained partially obscured by the continued centrality of the US–Soviet rivalry to international relations.[2] With the end of the Cold War the shift from state-mediated national development (in its various capitalist and socialist forms) to the US-led globalization project was dramatically strengthened. By the 1990s the globalization project was being pursued at multiple sites, but remained centered on US power. It is an unfinished, and unfinishable project of political, social and cultural transformation that, in the context of dramatic technological changes, is profoundly conditioned, but not determined, by processes of financial deregulation, trade liberalization and privatization in which nation-states and the nation-state system play an increasingly important globalizing, rather than their earlier ostensibly national developmental, role. By the end of the Cold War there was a clear overall pattern, with considerable historical variation, of a sustained, but uneven, transformation of state-mediated national development projects (of all politico-ideological types) into neo-liberal states. This was reinforced by increasingly uneven economic development within and between nation-states and within and between regions against the backdrop of the transformation of the nation-state system and the elaboration of the globalization project.

The globalization project and the nation-state system I

The rise of the globalization project I: the financial revolution and the changing global order

The rise of the US-led globalization project is grounded to a considerable degree in the financial revolution of the 1970s. At the same time, the dramatic changes in international finance in this period flowed directly from the shifts in the global political economy that occurred during the administration of US president

Richard M. Nixon (1969–1974). The reorientation of the political economy of the Cold War spearheaded by Nixon was, in large measure, a result of geo-political calculations and economic problems that flowed from the Vietnam War. Meanwhile, by the end of the 1960s, West Germany's and Japan's economic advances had also become a source of growing concern in Washington. As we have seen in chapter 1, West Germany and Japan were crucial anti-communist nation-states that pursued national development paths that placed significant restrictions on foreign investment and trade after 1945, while being allowed privileged access to the US market. By the late 1960s these key Cold War allies had emerged as increasingly dynamic and globally competitive industrial nation-states. This situation, combined with the financial burden of the war in Vietnam, prompted Nixon to end the gold standard, initiate the winding back of fixed exchange rates and begin a process of dramatically liberalizing the international financial regulatory order, all of which were a legacy of the Bretton Woods meeting in 1944. In 1971 he floated the US dollar and suspended its convertibility to gold, at the same time as he introduced a new 10 percent surcharge on all imports into the United States. This eventually led to the Smithsonian Agreement that re-valued the yen by 16.88 percent against the dollar, while the deutschmark was re-valued by 13.5 percent against the dollar.[3]

Nixon's de-linking of the dollar in 1971 was a decisive moment, but the dramatic rise in the price of oil in late 1973 also marked another important shift in the political economy of the Cold War. It is generally assumed that the rise in oil prices at the end of 1973 was driven by the oil-states of the Middle East and their opposition to Israel, and to US support of Israel in the Yom Kippur War (October 1973). However, despite Washington's public remonstrances against increases in the price of oil, there is evidence to suggest that the Nixon administration had earlier pressured the OPEC states to increase oil prices in order to undermine the economic advances of Japan and Washington's Western European allies, particularly West Germany. This was not necessarily the reason why prices were increased, but it does suggest that the Nixon administration thought that the US, with far more significant oil reserves, was better positioned than Western Europe and Japan to cope with a rise in the price of oil. The oil crisis and Nixon's termination of the global financial protocols associated with the Bretton Woods system had at least four crucial results. First, they ensured that private banks (particularly US-based banks) began to play a much greater role in global finance. Second, government supervision of global financial organizations was dramatically weakened. Third, the currency exchange rates and financial systems of other nation-states, particularly in Latin America, Africa and Asia, were increasingly influenced by trends in the financial markets in the United States. Fourth, growing competition within the banking systems of the various countries in the OECD was encouraged, while the government of the US was increasingly able to more or less determine the regulatory framework for global financial markets.[4]

The financial revolution was also facilitated by technological change, particularly in relation to advances in what became known as information technology. At the same time, the rise of information technology is directly linked to the research and development in the 1970s that was connected to the military imperatives of the Cold War. The combination of computer chips and innovative new forms of communication, centered on the Internet, have proved, in the view of one historian of the period, to be the most significant "technological innovation of the Cold War".[5] In fact, as the Cold War came to an end it was this technological transformation, applied to the financial sector, that increasingly bound together the major centers of capitalist activity in North America, Western Europe and East Asia, even as it also reinforced the exclusion of those parts of the world that were marginal to, or being marginalized by, the globalization project. Thus the rise of the US-led globalization project is clearly centered on the dramatic technological changes in which the information economy has emerged as the leading sector of the world economy, increasingly shaping and facilitating the reordering of industrial and agricultural production, political activity and social and cultural life.[6] More broadly, the emergent US-led globalization project was also increasingly reinforced and carried forward by a complex array of transnational socio-economic forces.[7] As has been suggested, the globalization project is linked, in particular, to the growing concentration of control over the global economy by a relatively small number of large oligopolistic transnational corporations that emerged by the 1990s from the dramatic merger-driven and technology-facilitated changes to the global political economy. Regardless of the increasingly oligopolistic character of global business operations, the US-led globalization project is legitimated by, and promoted in the name of, a free enterprise vision of the global economy.[8]

Despite the widening, although still highly concentrated, array of transnational socio-economic forces and institutions driving the globalization project, Washington was, and continues to be, central to the creation of an international framework for globalization. A centerpiece of the new post-Bretton Woods order was the way in which, between 1975 and the end of the Cold War, Washington moved towards the creation of what has been termed the "Dollar Wall Street Regime" (DWSR). No consistent use of the DWSR by Washington emerged until the administration of Bill Clinton (1993–2000). Nevertheless, by the Reagan era (1981–1988) the overall direction was, in retrospect at least, becoming increasingly clear. Concerned about inflation and industrial overcapacity in the US, the Chairman of the US Federal Reserve, Paul Volcker, who was also wary of the dollar losing too much value, embarked on his now well-known increase in interest rates in an effort to strengthen the dollar. Volcker took this path before Reagan came to office, but once Reagan became president in 1981 these measures were dramatically extended. The key elements of the Reagan administration's economic policy shift were: to conduct economic policy on behalf of finance capital and to expand and utilize the new DWSR for the benefit of the US government. The former meant driving down inflation (thus strengthening the profits of financiers), deregulating the banking and financial system and dispensing major cuts in taxes to the wealthy, while attempting to drive up the value of the dollar. Meanwhile, the DWSR provided the leverage to stimulate US industrial expansion via a dramatic increase in defense spending, which was carried out against the backdrop of the Cold War revivalism of the Reagan administration. This involved pulling in large amounts of capital from overseas while running a rising budget deficit. This put the US state in the position of "surrogate export market" for a number of major US-based manufacturers of defense-related equipment.[9] Furthermore, it is worth noting that every year from the beginning of the Korean War to the end of the Cold War the budget of the US Defense Department was greater than the "combined net profits" of all US-based corporations.[10] At the same time, Reagan administration officials began to extend the DWSR in an effort to address specific problems. To begin with, keeping the dollar high could have involved maintaining high interest rates in the US, unless major new sources of external funds could be attracted to invest in North American financial markets. It was under the Reagan administration that the attempt to ensure high levels of inward investment led to a major effort to wind back or eliminate capital controls in the OECD, particularly the nation-states of Western Europe and Japan.[11]

The rise of the globalization project II: the Debt Crisis and the changing global order

The Debt Crisis of the 1980s (triggered in part by the economic policies of Volcker and the early Reagan administration) was also central to the consolidation of the globalization project. It was a key lever for the Reagan administration, with the support of the governments of Margaret Thatcher in Britain (1979–1990) and Helmut Kohl (1982–1998) in West Germany/Germany, in its effort to accelerate and deepen financial deregulation, trade liberalization, and privatization well beyond North America and Western Europe. The Debt Crisis flowed from the rise in oil prices and the liberalization of the international financial system in the 1970s. Many of the petroleum-exporting nations, particularly in the Middle East, had acquired massive profits following the dramatic increase in oil prices in the 1970s. They deposited these petro-dollars in banks in Western Europe and North America, especially in the United States. The banks in turn attempted to find borrowers, turning to the governments of the nation-states in Asia, Latin America and Africa. While some countries in Asia, such as South Korea (which will be discussed in chapter 8), accumulated a high level of foreign debt during the 1970s, Latin America, where economic growth had been significant in the 1960s and 1970s, was a particular focus of international bankers. By the start of the 1980s, more than 60 percent of the total foreign debt that was owed to private banks worldwide was owed by the governments of Latin America. In 1970 the combined foreign debt for all governments in Latin America was US$2.3 billion. By 1975 the figure was US$75 billion, rising precipitously to US$229 billion by 1980 (it was US$340 billion by 1983). The global recession of the early 1980s led to a major reduction in the demand for exports from Latin America at the very moment when exports were crucial to the acquisition of the foreign exchange that was needed to make even minimal payments on the rising foreign debt. Meanwhile, by 1982 more capital was leaving Latin America in the form of interest and/or principal payments on this debt than was entering the region. This massive outflow of capital helped, among other things, to finance the escalating US budget deficit that had resulted from Reagan's tax cuts and increased defense spending. By the end of 1982, most governments in Latin America were in arrears on their debt payments. There was some concern on the part of the bankers, and some hope on the part of their critics, that governments in the region would form debtor cartels and refuse to pay their debts. However, such a Third Worldist initiative did not materialize and it was abundantly clear that by the 1980s the Bandung Era had ended. The various indebted governments were unable and unwilling to unite in the face of strong bilateral pressure from the US and its main allies. Beginning in the early 1980s various debtor clubs were institutionalized as the IMF and the World Bank increasingly took on a central role in Latin America and beyond. The meetings of the debtor clubs, which were usually attended by IMF and/or World Bank representatives, rescheduled loans in the context of various structural adjustment agreements aimed at liberalizing, privatizing and deregulating the economies concerned.[12]

Mexico is a particularly important example of the connection between the Debt Crisis and the passing of national development. In fact, the Mexican trajectory represents a paradigmatic example of the overall shift from state-mediated national development to the globalization project.[13] In the Mexican case this shift was consolidated with the implementation of the North American Free Trade Agreement (NAFTA) in January 1994. NAFTA was a major turning point in the overall transformation of the political economy of Mexico and the realignment of US–Mexican relations over the previous two decades. More broadly, the incorporation of the United States, Canada and Mexico into a continent-wide free trade zone helped to anchor the post-Cold War deepening of the US-led globalization project. By the 1990s the *Partido Revolucionaria Institucional* (Institutional Revolutionary Party – PRI), which ruled Mexico under one name or another for over seventy years, had dismantled most of the institutional structures of the state-guided national development project that it had built up since the 1930s. The redistributive elements of state-mediated national development were manifested dramatically during President Lázaro Cárdenas's rule (1934–1940). During his six years in office, he redistributed 47 million acres of land among over 1 million peasant families as well as establishing farming collectives, and a national bank to assist peasants. Meanwhile, Cárdenas's successors established and pursued a concerted state-guided import-substitution industrialization program. Between 1940 and the end of the 1960s the Mexican economy grew at 6 percent a year and a significant percentage of the population experienced improved standards of living. However, by the late 1960s cracks in the national development project were becoming increasingly apparent and the policies pursued by the governments of President Luis Echeverría (1970–1976) and his immediate successor, José Lopez Portillo (1976–1982), reflected an incoherent effort to keep the national development project alive in the context of rising social tensions and pressure for political and economic reform. The PRI-led national development project in Mexico entered its most acute crisis in 1982. The price of oil fell by more than 50 percent in a couple of months, dramatically exacerbating the closely entwined trends of devaluation, inflation and capital flight, along with steadily rising foreign debt repayments (the total foreign debt for Mexico by 1982 was US$85.5 billion). During the presidency of Miguel de la Madrid Hurtado (1982–1988) the Mexican government applied the structural adjustment programme that was being encouraged throughout the region and beyond. To this end, Mexico's currency, the peso, was devalued, government spending on education and health care was reduced, as was the subsidization of staple foods, while expensive imports were also cut back. Public sector companies were sold or wound up by the hundreds. Meanwhile, wage controls and dramatically rising prices reduced the purchasing power of the peso for ordinary Mexicans by at least 50 percent.[14] However, it was during the administration of President Carlos Salinas de Gortari (1988–1994), that the state-guided model of national development, which had emerged in the 1930s, definitely gave way to the privatization of state enterprises and the pursuit of export-led growth. The result, in the late 1980s and 1990s, was considerable economic growth in tandem with steadily rising levels of poverty and inequality along social, ethnic and regional lines, and the weakening and eventual end of one-party rule.[15]

The shift to neo-liberal economic policies and the elaboration of the US-led globalization project was not as pronounced in Asia as it was in Latin America or Africa. Latin American nation-states such as Mexico and Brazil had briefly been grouped with the Newly Industrializing Countries (NICs) of East Asia (South Korea, Taiwan, Hong Kong and Singapore) in the 1970s. While the Debt Crisis quickly undermined Mexico's and Brazil's status as economic miracles, the East Asian NICs, and particularly, the newly emergent second-wave NICs of Thailand, Malaysia, Indonesia and coastal China, although affected by the Debt Crisis, benefited far more than Latin America from the relative decline of Fordist-style production in Japan, as well as in North America and Western Europe, and the resulting relocation of manufacturing operations.[16] Nevertheless, the changes of the 1980s coincided with and were connected to the uneven spread of neo-liberalism in the region. In the context of the Debt Crisis the pressure to liberalize being exerted on governments in Asia certainly increased. For example, in Thailand, in the early 1980s, the IMF and the World Bank presided over a comprehensive structural adjustment program. This was aimed at stabilizing the Thai economy and opening it up further to foreign investment, paving the way for the continued growth of the manufacturing sector as major Japanese corporations in particular expanded their operations southward. The structural adjustment program in Thailand was followed in the 1980s by reform packages for other governments in the region.[17] At the same time, governments in Asia, as elsewhere, were increasingly subject to bilateral pressure from the office of the United States' Special Trade Representative on a wide range of issues including increased access to domestic markets.[18] In Indonesia, as in Mexico, the decline in oil prices in the 1980s resulted in increasing debt and a decreased capacity on the part of the state to facilitate local capital accumulation, while greater use of foreign loans and foreign aid led to greater leverage on the part of the World Bank, the IMF and foreign investors. By the second half of the 1980s, important liberalizing reforms were under way in Indonesia. This shift in economic policy facilitated an increase in the influx of foreign capital into Indonesia in the late 1980s, much of it from Japan (as well as from South Korea and Taiwan), and the rapid rise of an export-industry sector, especially on Java.[19] Meanwhile, in South Korea (also a major debtor by the 1980s), the rapid economic growth and the dramatic social changes of the previous twenty years had paved the way for the relative decline of the developmental state during the regime of General Chun Doo Hwan (1980–1988). Although the US reinvigorated the security alliance with Seoul in the Reagan era, Washington increasingly began to question South Korea's financial and trading practices. Chun Doo Hwan responded to mounting foreign and domestic pressure by embarking on a process of economic and political liberalization. As we will see in chapter 8, the liberalization of the political system was closely connected to the liberalization of the economy.[20] In India, meanwhile, as discussed in chapter 2, the high period of national development had passed by the 1960s, but considerable commitment to the ideas and instrumentalities associated with state-guided national development remained in place until at least the end of the 1980s.[21]

Security, development and foreign aid I: the Cold War order

The waning of the high modern era of national development and the rise of the US-led globalization project was also linked to a reorientation in the approach to and disbursement of US foreign aid. In the context of the US defeat in Vietnam and the wider debate about US foreign policy that resulted from the failed anticommunist modernizing mission in one-time French Indochina, there was growing pressure to rethink US economic assistance programs. This resulted in the passage of various reformist pieces of legislation under the heading of "New Directions" in the 1970s. This led briefly to an emphasis on both the basic needs of the poor and direct grassroots participation in the process of development. At the same time, the Foreign Assistance Act was amended to provide for an increased focus on human rights in the disbursement of foreign aid. However, by the late 1970s, influential free-market critics of "New Directions" were in the ascendant. Their views were consolidated during the Reagan administration. In the 1980s USAID's main focus was the Private Enterprise Initiative (PEI), which promoted private sector development and encouraged market-oriented reform.[22] For example, in a 1984 policy paper on "Private Enterprise Development", USAID asserted that:

a society in which individuals have freedom of economic choice, freedom to own the means of production, freedom to compete in the market place, freedom to take economic risk for profit and freedom to receive and retain the rewards of economic decisions is a fundamental objective of the A.I.D. program in less developed countries.

The policy document went on to argue that: "such a private enterprise economy is held to be the most efficient means of achieving broad-based economic development". The main goals of USAID were said to be: "To encourage LDCs to open their economies to a greater reliance on competitive markets and private enterprise in order to meet the basic human needs of their poor majorities through broadly-based self-sustained economic growth". Closely connected to this was an injunction about the need: "to foster the growth of productive, self-sustaining income and job producing private enterprises in developing countries".[23] At the same time, US foreign assistance policy in the 1980s, as in earlier periods, remained firmly grounded in geo-political calculations and strategic interests, with the percentage of foreign assistance going to development-related programs declining and the amount spent on security-related projects rising.[24]

This trend was readily apparent in Washington's growing involvement in Central America, following the revolutionary overthrow in 1979 of the Somoza regime in Nicaragua. In the 1980s Central America became a crucial focus of the Reagan administration's effort to "exorcise the ghosts of Vietnam".[25] The nation-states of Central America were the recipients of more US economic and military aid during Reagan's first term (1981–1984) than they had received in the preceding thirty years (1950–1980). For example, between 1981 and 1984 the El Salvadoran government received US$758 million in economic aid and US$396 million in military aid (compared to only US$6 million in military aid in 1980). El Salvador had emerged as the recipient of more US aid than any other country in Latin America by the middle of Reagan's first term. In fact, in this period El Salvador was the third-largest US aid recipient worldwide, behind Israel and Egypt. Reflecting the ongoing strategic significance of the Middle East, Israel and Egypt received about one-third of all US foreign aid disbursed in the 1980s. Ultimately, the level of foreign aid for El Salvador in the 1980s was on a scale reminiscent of the US nation-building effort in South Vietnam in the 1960s, minus the direct US military intervention. By the end of the 1980s the US had disbursed upwards of US$3 billion in economic and military aid to El Salvador (the equivalent of about US$800,000 a day for ten years).[26] While the economic aid to Central America in this period was driven by geo-political considerations this did not negate its focus on the liberalization of the economies of the region. In the 1980s the US combined its support for the military and proxy warfare with pressure on the governments of Central America to adopt neo-liberal economic policies. This led, among other things, to the dismantling of national institutions that had bolstered almost fifty years of Costa Rican social democracy. In El Salvador and Nicaragua, it threatened even the very limited popular economic and political gains made during the 1980s.[27] This shift contributed to the rising levels of social inequality and privatized violence in the region in the 1990s that have continued since the electoral defeat of the Sandinistas in 1990 and the finalization of peace agreements in El Salvador in 1992 and in Guatemala in 1996.[28]

Following the Soviet invasion in late 1979, Afghanistan also became an important focus for Washington. This was reflected in the dramatic reorientation of economic and military aid to Pakistan and to a lesser extent India. As we have seen, after 1965 President Lyndon Johnson (1963–1968) sought to limit Washington's direct involvement in, and aid to, South Asia in comparison to the importance that had been attached to the region in the late 1950s and early 1960s.[29] In 1978 US relations with Pakistan had been weakened by the criticisms made by President Jimmy Carter (1977–1980) of the human rights violations of the military government of General Zia ul-Haq (1977–1988) following its ouster and execution of President Zulfikar Ali Bhutto (1971–1977). The relationship between the US and Pakistan had also been undermined by Pakistan's efforts to develop nuclear weapons. In April 1979, in response to the Pakistani government's nuclear weapons initiative, the Carter administration suspended US aid to Pakistan. However, once the Soviet Union entered Afghanistan, US aid to Pakistan was restored and then significantly increased.[30] In the 1980s the Pakistani military, and its main intelligence organization, the Inter-Services Intelligence directorate (ISI), played an important role (along with the Saudi Arabian and Chinese governments) in supporting the loose coalition of resistance groups (Islamic Unity of Afghan Mujahideen) fighting the Soviet occupation.[31] The Carter administration also attempted to improve its relations with the Indian government, under Prime Minister Morarji Desai (1977–1980), who was trying to lessen reliance on the USSR. Desai and Carter signed the Delhi Declaration in 1977, which restated both governments' commitment to democracy and human rights. Washington also waived restrictions on uranium sales to India. These efforts failed to put US–Indian relations on a more stable footing, once the US resumed military and economic aid to Pakistan and increasingly tilted towards China in the context of Washington and Beijing's rapprochement in the 1970s and the war in Afghanistan after 1979. In 1980, Prime Minister Indira Gandhi, who had replaced Desai, moved to improve Indian relations with the USSR. She announced a major arms deal, worth US$1.6 billion, with the Soviet Union in May 1980. Then in December, Leonid Brezhnev visited India and Mrs. Gandhi and the Soviet leader issued a public statement that condemned outside involvement in Southwest Asia, a clear reference to US involvement in the war in Afghanistan. The withdrawal of Soviet military forces from Afghanistan (between May 1988 and February 1989) and the subsequent end of the Cold War led to a significant geo-political reorientation in South Asia. The end of all US aid to Pakistan by 1990 (in the context of renewed US concern about Pakistan's clandestine nuclear weapons program) and the general deterioration of US relations with Pakistan were parallelled by improvements in US relations with India.[32]

Security, development and foreign aid II: the post-Cold War order

With the end of the Cold War, there was a further shift in the overall direction, geographical orientation and quantity of US foreign assistance, in the context of important changes and equally important continuities in US foreign policy.[33] While still seeking to promote economic development via market-oriented reform, USAID revised its programs to encompass the goal of encouraging political reform and democracy as part of a wider emphasis by the Clinton administration on democratization. The Clinton administration introduced a range of reforms that were ostensibly aimed at replacing security as the key focus of foreign aid and "enlarging the community of democratic nations worldwide".[34] In particular four main goals for US foreign aid in the post-Cold War era were outlined. The 1997 USAID Strategic Plan identified these goals as being: the promotion of the rule of law; the promotion of electoral politics; building and expanding civil society; and improving governance. Movement towards all of these objectives was regarded by USAID as "necessary to achieve sustainable democracy".[35] A greater emphasis was also placed on humanitarian assistance and sustainable development. However, the foreign aid bill that was passed by the US Congress in 1994 continued, not surprisingly, to reflect a commitment to geo-political concerns. This was readily apparent, for example, in the way in which, in the year the bill was passed, Israel and Egypt received over one-third of all US foreign aid. The figure for Israel was US$3 billion and for Egypt it was US$2.1 billion, while the 1994 figure for sub-Saharan Africa as a whole was US$800 million.[36] This was more or less the same percentage for Israel and Egypt as they had received in the 1980s. Israel's importance to US foreign policy (and to domestic US politics) goes back decades, while Egypt has been a major strategic outpost since 1977 when President Anwar Sadat ended his government's ties to the USSR and became a central player in the US-sponsored peace process in the region. From the time of this reorientation to the end of the 1990s Cairo received at least US$46 billion in military and economic aid from Washington. Since the late 1970s US policy towards Egypt has viewed it as the key to making and expanding peace and political stability in the region.[37] With the end of the Cold War, foreign aid was also directed increasingly at the former Soviet bloc, again for broad geo-political reasons, related particularly to a concern to improve relations with, and enhance the political stability of, a post-communist Russia that still possesses a major capacity for nuclear warfare and is the world's second largest oil exporter after Saudi Arabia.[38] For example, more than US$2.2 billion of foreign aid was disbursed to Russia between 1992 and 1997 under the Freedom Support Act (FSA). Over the same period over US$2.6 billion was also disbursed to Russia via programs not covered by the FSA. The figures for the Ukraine were over US$1 billion FSA funds and US$652 million worth of non-FSA funds, while the former Soviet republics in the Caucus and Central Asia together received over US$1.9 billion in FSA funds and US$2.4 billion in non-FSA funds between 1992 and 1997 inclusive.[39]

The redirection of, but limited changes to the basis of, US foreign aid policy after the Cold War reflected the relative continuity in US strategic thinking in the 1990s. For example, planning documents and the public pronouncements that emanated from the administration of President George Bush (1989–1992) reflected a preoccupation with Russia and some of the other successor states, such as the Ukraine, that had emerged from the collapse of the Soviet Union. There was also a continued focus on the Middle East, at the same time as Central America and Afghanistan quickly dropped from view. In contrast to the global orientation of the Cold War era, policy-makers also emphasized the regional character of strategic planning and threat assessment.[40] For example, in the aftermath of the Gulf War, Colin Powell (then chairman of the Joint Chiefs of Staff and now Secretary of State in the administration of George W. Bush) observed that US "plans and resources are primarily focused on deterring and fighting regional rather than global wars".[41] The Gulf War also highlighted the continued centrality of Saudi Arabia to US policy in the Middle East and the centrality of the Middle East to US policy. Along with Israel and Egypt, Saudi Arabia is one of the three most important US allies in the region. Saudi Arabia, which along with Japan and South Korea was one of the few non-European countries that received Marshall Plan assistance in the late 1940s, has the biggest oil reserves in the world. It is by far the most significant of the various oil-states of the Persian Gulf at the same time as it has a shared border with Iraq and is just across the Gulf from Iran, both of which continued to be viewed by the US, in this period, as "hostile" states.[42] (At the time of writing – early 2003 – Iraq's status as a "hostile" state, was something Washington and its allies were attempting to change.)

Despite the high degree of continuity in US foreign policy in the 1990s, the Clinton administration emphasized at the outset that it intended to shift from "containment to enlargement".[43] Clinton advised that his administration's main goal was not just to "secure the peace won in the Cold War", but to strengthen the country's "national security" by "enlarging the community of market democracies".[44] However, like the administration of his predecessor, the Clinton team understood that the immediate post-Cold War world conferred clear geo-political and economic advantages on the United States and they sought primarily to both manage and wherever possible to enhance and extend US preponderance.[45] Like the Bush administration, Clinton remained focused on the major powers: Britain, Germany, France, Russia, Japan and China. Clinton, like Bush before him, also attempted to maintain as high a level of defense spending as possible. Throughout the 1990s, rhetoric about humanitarian intervention to the contrary, the Clinton administration clearly viewed Europe, East Asia/the Asia-Pacific and the Middle East/Southwest Asia as the three most important regions in the world in terms of US strategy and security. Meanwhile, Latin America, Africa and South Asia were perceived as regions where no vital US security interests were at stake. Europe was apparently at the top of the list, while the Middle East/Southwest Asia was third. In the 1990s East Asia/the Asia-Pacific was regarded as number two and rising. The interconnection between security and economic development was also particularly obvious in the thinking of defense planners in relation to East Asia. For example, a 1995 Department of Defense document described the US miliary operations in the Asia-Pacific as the "foundation for economic growth" and the "oxygen" of "development".[46] This also highlighted the connection between China's economic development on the one hand and US geo-political concerns on the other, as the search for threats to the US position in the world shifted increasingly to East Asia following the collapse of the USSR and the US victory in the First Gulf War (1990–1991). By the second half of the 1990s, if not before, Washington had clearly fastened on the geo-political implications of the economic rise of China against the wider backdrop of the transformation of Asia.

The globalization project and the nation-state system II

The post-Cold War order and the nation-state system I: "The End of History" or "The Clash of Civilizations"?

Despite post-Cold War concerns about a rising China, the demise of the Soviet Union and the dramatic transfer of political power and attendant shifts in economic orientation in Eastern Europe at the beginning of the 1990s were, as we have seen, understood and celebrated by many observers as a moment of triumph for the United States.[47] Furthermore, the decolonization of the Soviet empire was widely, albeit often implicitly, read not just as a victory for the United States, or for capitalism, but for the neo-liberal form of capitalism that emerged in the 1980s at the center of the US-led globalization project.[48] The end of Soviet imperium and the passing of the state-socialist model of development, of which it was the most celebrated example, were quickly and readily used to strengthen the case for the global applicability of neo-liberal economic policies and the benevolence of the US-led globalization project. Undoubtedly one of the most well-known proponents of the US as global benefactor in the post-Cold War era is the *New York Times* journalist, Thomas Friedman. In fact, Friedman's best-selling book, *The Lexus and the Olive Tree* (1999) (which, as the title suggests, rests on the same dubious distinction between modernity and tradition that informed modernization theory in the Cold War era), nicely encapsulates virtually all the main elements of US post-Cold War triumphalism and the dominant neo-liberal narrative on globalization. In his influential book, Friedman argues that "America, at its best, is not just a country", but "a spiritual value and role model" for the rest of the world. According to Friedman, the post-Cold War order is more complicated than the international system of the Cold War era. While the Cold War order, he says, was constructed "exclusively around nation-states" and "balanced at the center by two superpowers", the post-Cold War age of globalization is based on "three balances". The first is the "traditional balance between nation-states" in a wider "globalization system" in which the US has emerged as the "sole and dominant superpower". The second balance is "between nation-states and global markets", while the third balance is the "newest of all": the "balance between individuals and nation-states".[49]

Friedman's book has been widely celebrated and criticized.[50] Many observers, for example, have challenged or ridiculed his "Gold Arches Theory of Conflict Prevention", which postulates that nation-states that have McDonald's restaurants will not attack one another.[51] Of course, the bombing of Belgrade (which boasted a McDonald's) undermined this populist version of the theory that democratic nation-states do not go to war with each other, insofar as Slobodan Milosevic was an unpopular, but still elected president.[52] At the same time, what Friedman completely fails to address is the way in which globalization has exacerbated conflict within nation-states and these latter struggles are far more of a problem than conflict between nation-states in many parts of the world in the post-Cold War era. This shortcoming also points to a key element of Friedman's approach that has attracted less attention. This is the way in which, like the dominant narratives on development and globalization generally, Friedman routinizes the nation-state and the nation-state system.[53] Friedman, and other celebratory accounts of post-Cold War US power, fail to address the transformation of the nation-state system that has taken place as a key aspect of the rise of the US-led globalization project. The way in which the globalization project emerged following the universalization of the nation-state system, dramatically reorienting nation-states in the process, is absent from this vision of globalization as the pursuit of the American Dream on a global scale. His account glosses over the contradictions of a post-Cold War era in which the market-oriented self-interested individual has been elevated to the status of the universal subject at the same time as people continue to be mobilized by and derive their sense of identity from culturally specific collectivities that interact and overlap with, or come into conflict with, the myriad nation-states that make up the nation-state system in the post-Cold War era.

In contrast to commentators such as Friedman, Samuel Huntington sought to address the question of the relationship between cultural/national specificity and liberal universalism. Since the end of the Cold War Huntington has argued against the triumphalism of the era, emphasizing that there were major limits to the Americanization of the world and serious challenges to US hegemony in the post-Cold War era. For Huntington, as for other realists, US foreign policy after the Cold War should continue to focus on vital national interests and recognize the serious constraints on trying to create a global order in its own image.[54] These concerns were apparent in Huntington's 1996 book, *The Clash of Civilizations and the Remaking of World Order*, which also exemplified the culturally reductionist view that had emerged in North America and Western Europe towards various perceived civilizational threats to the West in the post-Cold War era.[55] His 1993 article in *Foreign Affairs* foreshadowed the main arguments of the 1996 book. It is thought to be the most widely discussed and influential article in that journal since the anonymous article by George Kennan in the late 1940s that paved the way for Washington's containment strategy towards the USSR and international communism. Huntington's approach rested heavily on a sharp and dubious distinction between the West and the non-West. In his view international politics was increasingly converging on the conflict between the West and the rest of the world and on the reaction of "non-Western civilizations to Western power and values".[56] This reflects a point of view that has enjoyed a resurgence in the wake of September 11 and has allowed Huntington's views to be seen as prescient.[57] However, there are major difficulties involved in interpreting the terrorist bombings of the World Trade Center and the Pentagon and their aftermath in terms of a primarily cultural or civilizational struggle between a monolithic Islam and a homogenous West (the interpretation those who engineered the terrorist attacks are trying to promote). The tendency of many influential observers and policy-makers to view the Cold War as a struggle against a homogenous and monolithic communist movement was politically appealing. However, this kind of approach was also a major obstacle to understanding. The same type of appeal and problem is central to Huntington's vision of the post-Cold War era.[58]

Huntington has clearly advocated an approach that views culture and civilization as the relatively fixed and even immutable key to international relations in the post-Cold War era.[59] The premise of his 1993 article and of the 1996 book as a whole was that the overall context of post-Cold War international relations is one in which "states increasingly define their interests in civilizational terms". He argued that states "cooperate with and ally themselves with states with similar or common culture and are more often in conflict with countries of different culture".[60] According to Huntington, for example, "Japan is a society and civilization unique to itself" and regardless of the strength of investment and trading linkages it forms with the rest of East Asia, the "cultural differences" between Japan and the rest of the region represent a serious obstacle and may well "preclude" the economic integration of the region to the degree that is occurring in North America and Europe. At the same time, in his view, cultural similarities were hastening the steady increase in economic relations between Singapore, Hong Kong, Taiwan, China and the overseas Chinese throughout the region. As a result, says Huntington, the main "East Asian economic bloc" could well coalesce around China rather than Japan.[61] Elsewhere, Huntington has also argued that "the rise of China" brings with it the possibility of "a big intercivilizational war of core states".[62] While there is no disputing the growing significance of China in the region, Huntington has tended to represent China and the Chinese Diaspora as a monolithic entity, and to overlook the innumerable lines of tension and fracture within China and between the mainland and the Chinese inhabitants elsewhere in the region, not to mention the fissures and complicated loyalties within the wider Chinese Diaspora. While Huntington's approach may reflect the way many influential political leaders and policy-makers around the globe approach international affairs, in particular the way they seek to mobilize political support, it completely overlooks the way in which civilizations, cultures and nation-states are reconfigured and reinvented, a process in which these elites play an important role. At the same time, despite the provocative title of his book (and the apparent importance of civilizational conflict to Huntington's argument), it should be emphasized that Huntington did not represent conflict as inevitable. He offered some fairly explicit policy prescriptions that suggested various ways in which the West needed to revitalize itself, while continuing to reach out to other civilizations in an effort to manage the global political economy within which US and Western power was perceived to be diminishing.[63]

Another problem with the approach taken by Huntington, and this is something he shares with many other observers, is a tendency to exaggerate the stability of the Cold War era. For example, at the end of the 1990s, the prominent US historian of the Cold War, John Lewis Gaddis, lamented the growing disorder of the post-Cold War era and warned of a possible return of empires ("the form of governance that hardly dares speak its name") as a means of restoring regional and international order.[64] However, the Cold War era was not as orderly as commentators such as Gaddis (who famously characterized it as a "long peace") have implied.[65] Gaddis's approach reflects a Eurocentric, or more accurately an Atlantic-centered, perspective.[66] Such an approach neglects the instability, revolution and warfare of the Cold War era, particularly beyond North America and Europe, and the way in which, despite incredible power, Washington's efforts to remake the world in its own image were regularly and severely constrained (the Korean War and the Vietnam War, not to mention the Cuban revolution and its aftermath, being good examples). Furthermore, some of the most perilous and destabilizing events since 1945 coincided with the apex of US power in the early 1960s. In this period, the USSR, under Khrushchev, believed that it was on track to overtake the US and the Chinese government acquired nuclear capability. At the same time, nationalist leaders at the head of major mass movements had toppled or were about to topple colonial governments in Asia and Africa. Decolonization and the Cold War catapulted a number of these leaders and their governments into positions as important players in international politics in the context of a wider effort to mobilize around reformist or revolutionary Third Worldist initiatives that challenged a Cold War international order centered on the rivalry between Washington and Moscow. In the 1990s, by contrast, the US position in the world was apparently so secure, or was regarded as so secure, that in the same year (1997) as the Asian crisis began to wreak havoc in South Korea, Thailand and Indonesia (later spreading to Russia and Brazil), the US government and the media appeared to be primarily concerned, not to say obsessed, with the Monica Lewinsky scandal.[67] This kind of parochialism is a luxury that can only be afforded when the nation-state concerned occupies a position of unrivalled global power.

The post-Cold War order and the nation-state system II: "The Rise and Fall of the Great Powers" or a "New World Order"?

Also a key weakness of Huntington's approach, along with other writers in the late 1980s and 1990s who reported that US hegemony was in decline, under threat and/or could be renewed, was their continued conceptualization of the US role in the late Cold War, or post-Cold War, era in terms grounded not only in the early Cold War, but in a cyclical conception of the rise and fall of Great

Powers as a process that stretched back to the early modern era, if not before.[68] For example, writing in 1989, Thomas J. McCormick characterized the US as "a hegemonic power in decline". He ended his book with Henry Kissinger's 1988 observation that "we have neither the resources nor the stomach for" hegemony, and "the only question is how much we have to suffer before we realize this". This led McCormick to observe that, "[i]t took Britain fifty years and two world wars, following its Vietnam (the Boer War), to reach that realization" and "[i]t remains to be seen whether the American timetable will be shorter or its consequences more benign".[69] Of course the classic example of this approach is Paul Kennedy's *The Rise and Fall of the Great Powers: Economic Change and Military Conflict from 1500 to 2000*.[70] In this highly influential study, Kennedy famously and wrongly anticipated that US "imperial overstretch" in the 1980s was signalling the relative decline of the US in much the same way as an excess of geo-political, military and economic commitments had undermined Great Powers, such as Napoleonic France, in an earlier era.[71] Of course, Kennedy's view that the United States had entered a period of relative, although not absolute decline, was challenged by influential observers, such as Henry R. Nau and Joseph S. Nye. At the beginning of the 1990s they both argued that the US position as a global power was not under serious threat and that the US could even enjoy a resurgence based on a renewed sense of "national purpose" and economic liberalization.[72]

Despite Kennedy's historical sweep and his important emphasis on the interplay between geo-politics and industrialization, and despite the apparent general veracity of Nau and Nye's analysis of the prospects for US power in the 1990s, there is something distinctly ahistorical about the realist conception of a Great Power and of a nation-state that underpins their work.[73] To begin with, Kennedy locates the rise of nation-states and talks of "national power" in Western Europe in a period when by a stricter definition there were no nation-states as such, but monarchical states and absolutist empires, not to mention the feudal remnants that these larger polities were seeking with uneven success to incorporate into new conceptions and new structures of centralized power and territoriality.[74] It was only in the late eighteenth and early nineteenth centuries that the process of forming monarchical states in Western Europe was accommodated to, or marginalized by, the rise of nationalism and growing efforts to realize the idea of the nation via the reconfiguration, or establishment, of sovereign national states. This points towards the wider weakness of Kennedy's analysis, which is the neglect of the complex history behind the emergence and universalization of the system of modern nation-states against the backdrop of which his Great Powers have risen and fallen. This weakness is closely connected to his treatment of successive Great Powers as unproblematic units of national power.[75] A good example of this problem, with particular relevance to this study, is the way in which, by the mid-1990s, the rise of China was increasingly compared to the rise of Germany in the late nineteenth century (and even to Nazi Germany in the early twentieth century). In 1996, Fareed Zakaria, observed that: "Like Germany in the late nineteenth century, China is also growing rapidly but uncertainly into a global system in which it feels it deserves more attention and honor".[76] However, the challenge to the US-led globalization project does not necessarily come from a rival Great Power and even if it does the entire context for such a challenge has changed in important ways.[77]

The rise of the US-led globalization project and the transformation of the nation-state system is not just the latest round in a cycle of the rise and fall of Great Powers.[78] Of course, this is not to deny that the US has emerged as *the* global hegemon in the post-Cold War era, or that it possesses some of the key characteristics that exemplified Great Power status in an earlier era. For example, the dramatic increase in the US defense budget in the wake of September 11, and the subsequent scale and scope of the US-led military intervention in Afghanistan and Iraq, make clear that US hegemony, like the influence of Great Powers before it, is still ultimately grounded in military power. Even before September 11, the Pentagon's budget represented over 30 percent of global arms expenditures and US defense spending is greater than the total combined defense budgets of the nine nation-states that along with the US are the top ten military powers in the world.[79] Nevertheless, US hegemony, as opposed to US dominance, is based on far more than military power and the US reach has become increasingly diffuse with the end of the Cold War. Even though Washington's disregard for the United Nations and its invasion of Iraq in early 2003 – combined with the global economic downturn that began before, but was aggravated by, September 11, and the global economic impact of the war in the Middle East – have weakened Washington's political influence and the overall economic appeal of the US model, the global economy and the nation-state system continues to be a unipolar order centered on US power. Despite the possibility that we are on the cusp of or have entered an incipient crisis of neo-liberalism and of the US-led globalization project more generally, the form of capitalism at the center of the globalization project, which is concerned with spending rather than saving, continues to have mass appeal in many parts of the world for those who can participate in it and even for those who cannot, but continue to dream of doing so. At the same time the widening gyre of mass consumption and mass culture feeds off and is rein-forced by a broad North American middle class with a stake in high levels of consumption and directly or indirectly (via pension plans and the like) involved in the stock market. Second, as emphasized at the beginning of this chapter, infor-mation technology has increasingly emerged as, and remains, the new "leading sector" of the US and the world economy, despite the bursting of the information technology bubble in 2000–2001. The US government and US-based companies have played a key role in this technological transformation and the information economy remains centered on the US. In geographical terms US hegemony is girded by the continental size and location of the US, facilitating its position and engagement with both the Asia-Pacific and Europe. Importantly, the "liberal" character of US hegemony has also contributed to its strength and its diffusion. The liberal ideas and practices that the US embodies are promoted and mediated through a growing range of international networks. The spread of liberal ideas and practices across a range of international institutions such as the UN, which will be discussed below, has reinforced US leadership. As Bruce Cumings has observed, US hegemony "is potent, and it has a message: in the 1940s it crushed" Nazi Germany and Imperial Japan. In the 1980s it dispatched another threat to freedom and democracy in the form of the Soviet Union. By the end of the 1990s it was undermining if not eliminating the "last formidable alternative system", the "state-directed neomercantilism" of Japan and South Korea, an alternative that had been profoundly constrained from the outset by its incubation and inclusion in the US-centered order in Cold War Asia.[80] The shift from national development to globalization, and the universalization and transformation of the nation-state system, represent the appearance of a new system, which retains important elements of Great Power rivalry, but also contains equally important, even crucial, new elements, that set US hegemony in the post-Cold War era apart from the structures and sinews that supported Great Powers in an earlier era.[81] The "New World Order", proclaimed on September 11 1990 – exactly eleven years before Al Qaeda's devastating suicide attack on the World Trade Center and the Pentagon and just days before the US began "Operation Desert Storm" to drive the Iraqi army out of Kuwait – by President George Bush, was "new" in important ways that were not neccessarilty understood or foreseen by the forty-first president of the United States.

Elaborating the globalization project I: US hegemony and the nation-state system after the Cold War

What is also important here is the way in which the universalization of the nation-state system and the rise of the globalization project have, in an increasingly uneven fashion, pushed the nation-state in many parts of the world to the limits of its potential as a vehicle for progress and prosperity. Central to the rise of the US-led globalization project in the post-Cold War era is the dramatic reorientation of nation-states and the nation-state system. As the global market unfolds the territorial boundaries of nation-states become more porous, while national sovereignty is reconfigured and diluted.[82] The US trajectory is both a driving force of, and a template for, this wider process. Since the 1980s the orientation of the US government has increasingly been towards the redirection of government funds away from social programs and towards the promotion of economic and geo-political initiatives overseas. This is linked to the ongoing efforts to bring down domestic wages and standards of living in support of higher profits and the pursuit of increased global market share for US-based corporations. Successive governments, that are profoundly influenced by, and well integrated with, an externally oriented elite that is the primary beneficiary of a regressive tax system that effectively redistributes income upwards, are carrying this out. The socio-economic order in North America is one in which large numbers of people are connected to declining national institutions and economic networks at the same time as transnationalized elites and an important section of the middle class are benefiting dramatically from the economic boom of the 1990s.[83] As Jeffrey E. Garten, Dean of the Yale School of Management and former Undersecretary of Commerce for International Trade in the first Clinton administration, has argued, US companies "have internationalised" in the past twenty or thirty years "more than is generally acknowledged". At the beginning of the twenty-first century, their supply networks, production systems, labor forces, management and financing are increasingly globalized. A significant number of Fortune 500 companies now receive over 50 percent of their income from overseas, while "global diversification" continues to be a key goal of most of the remaining companies in this group. Although the orientation of the Bush administration after September 11 2001 may have shifted (and it should be emphasized that what has occurred is a reorientation, or a military deepening of, rather than a retreat from, the globalization project, which – as outlined at the beginning of this study – has been consolidated and carried forward in the past by political and economic crisis), US companies will continue to "have much more interest in an open world economy than in one focused on increasing regulation".[84] Nevertheless this emergent and uneven new order, based on a new relationship between the global political economy and the nation-state system, has transformed rather than obviated the role of nation-states. While the rise of the globalization project has dramatically reoriented the state away from national development, state intervention continues to be necessary in order to successfully realize the globalization project. Ultimately, the nation-state system itself has been transformed by and has provided the framework for the emergence of the US-led globalization project. For example, the elimination of constraints on international financial flows, the privatization of public sectors and a whole range of changes to financial and economic regulation and control have occurred as a result of interventions by states across the nation-state system. This process demanded new, or reconfigured, state-provided legal frameworks and new relationships between national governments and/or international bodies. In practice this has meant that one of the main objectives of the US has been to promote the "Americanization" of international and national legal frameworks for the regulation of financial activities.[85]

Despite the historical specificity of the sustained, but still uneven, transformation of particular state-mediated national development projects into globalizing states against the backdrop of the transformation of the nation-state system, two generalized trajectories can be suggested. The first involves a process of national reorientation and a crisis of national development. Apart from South Korea and Japan, the nation-states included in this category range from Thailand, Malaysia and Singapore to the OECD.[86] This is in contrast to some nation-states where the end of the high period of state-mediated national development has increasingly coincided not only with dramatic national reorientation, but with sometimes violent struggles over the ethnic or religious content and/or territorial boundaries (usually, but not always, at the margins rather than the center) of the nation itself. This has been the case for India and even more dramatically for Indonesia.[87] As will be suggested in chapter 9, China also has the potential to follow this second path. Other countries more obviously included in the category of polities undergoing a crisis of the nation-state (or that are already "failed states") might be Burma, Pakistan, Afghanistan, or Colombia.[88] This is not to mention the Democratic Republic of the Congo and numerous other nation-states in sub-Saharan Africa.[89] The often complete inability of nation-states generally, and various earlier state-mediated national development projects more specifically, to emerge as stable and socially inclusive polities, is a particularly tragic theme in Africa's postcolonial history.[90] But, the nation-states that have emerged in Africa since decolonization are quantitatively rather than qualitatively different from those in other parts of the world, such as Asia. The vast majority of national trajectories in Africa draw attention to the more general limits on the nation-state's ability to deliver the prosperity and freedom that it was thought to embody even in the heyday of state-mediated national development.

Up to the 1970s, the US-led modernization project, centered on the promotion of national development, involved the deepening of the liberal capitalist order and the universalization of the nation-state system. With the shift from the modernization project to the globalization project, and the waning of national development, beginning in the 1970s, the deepening of global capitalism has been even more geographically uneven than in the 1950s and 1960s, when development strategies were (as we have seen in earlier chapters), in theory, more attuned to questions of redistribution and the need to address the uneven development that was taking place within nation-states and between them. In much of the world, governments and ruling elites now increasingly use the institutions of the state to advance the process of globalization (and their own interests) and undermine or rollback whatever institutions, if any, of national development were erected in earlier decades. A key characteristic of the US-led globalization project by the 1990s was the growing concentration of economic power in the hands of a small number of large oligopolistic corporations.[91] The rise of the globalization project has involved the coalescence of regionalized economic systems that provide the main motors of the global economy. These regions are North America, Western Europe and East Asia. Instead of the international economy expanding in spatial terms, since the 1970s the various financial, trading and production networks that connect these economic regions have been getting deeper and stronger. The economic elites of these regions can increasingly take advantage of the broad range of connections to diversify their investments and business operations within and between these main regions. The rapid movement of capital also allows for a quick exit, by local or transnational investors from those regions, or those parts of regions, where the risks are seen as too great.[92] The particularly uneven territorial character of globalization and the process of regional exclusion is clearly reflected in the way that, in the 1990s, the most economically significant post-communist nation-states that arose following the collapse of Soviet power (including Russia itself), were reconfigured as part of the "emerging economies" or "emerging markets".[93] The idea of emerging markets, as applied to the major developing nations of the one-time Third World, had first appeared in the early 1980s. In 1981, at the same time as neo-liberal economic policies and structural adjustment were gaining

momentum, the International Finance Corporation (IFC), an organization affiliated with the World Bank, introduced the idea of the emerging market. The
main factor used to identify an emerging market was relative wealth. By the
1990s nation-states, from South Africa to Russia, were identified by the World
Bank as emerging markets because their average annual per capita incomes were
above the mean world annual income. In this formulation, the remaining nation-
states of the erstwhile Second and Third Worlds (the "least developed nations")
are implicitly, if not explicitly, viewed as unimportant or irrelevant to the wider
world economy unless they are seen to directly threaten the security of the core
regions.[94]

Elaborating the globalization project II: US hegemony and the United Nations after the Cold War

The process of regional exclusion, however, does not just involve the economic
neglect of a particular region or economies, even though that is a key trend. It
also entails the increasing elaboration of humanitarian networks and activities by
the United Nations (UN) and a range of aid organizations. There are also
important military interventions by outside governments in the marginalized
regions sometimes under UN auspices and at other times operating under the
authority of a particular national government or group of national governments,
or a regional organization.[95] The UN was central to the elaboration of the
nation-state system after 1945 and to the diffusion of the ideas and practices
associated with state-mediated national development up to the 1970s. At the
same time, the UN and its various agencies have been major sites for the elaboration of the globalization project since the 1980s. The history of US hegemony
in the second half of the twentieth century is closely bound up with the United
Nations. The United States was a key force behind the establishment of the
United Nations at the end of the Second World War and the actual Charter of
the United Nations that was finalized in 1945 was effectively a US document, in
contrast to the Covenant of the League of Nations that had been based on both
US and British drafts. The UN Charter flowed from discussions at Dumbarton
Oaks (outside Washington, DC) in 1944 between the US, Britain, the Soviet
Union and, later, China. Fifty-one governments signed the Charter in June 1945.
By the early 1970s UN membership exceeded 120 and was over 150 by 1980,
reaching 185 nation-states by the end of the 1990s. Despite the central role of
the US in the establishment, and many of the subsequent operations, of the UN,
Washington's relationship with the organization has not been without friction
over the years, as evidenced most spectacularly by Washington's decision in early
2003 to ignore the UN Security Council's opposition to the invasion of Iraq in
March 2003. In the late 1940s and early 1950s the Cold War undermined the
expectation that the United Nations, centered on the Security Council, would
provide the overall framework for international security after 1945. The Security
Council was established with five permanent members and ten rotating
members. The permanent members are the major allied powers that won the

Second World War: the US, the USSR (now Russia), Great Britain, France and China (Taiwan held the Chinese seat until 1971). After 1945 international politics, as played out at the UN, was directly linked to the centrality of these five states to UN security decisions and initiatives. The veto also meant that although these five powers were prevented, in theory, from using force in a fashion that went against the UN Charter, their veto in the Security Council protected them from sanction or censure if they did engage in unilateral action. The Security Council thus represented a major arena for Cold War politics at the same time as the Cold War ensured that the ability of the Security Council to act was often profoundly constrained.[96]

With the end of the Cold War, however, the UN was presented with an opportunity to revive the major peacekeeping and security activities that many of its early proponents had anticipated. For example, while the UN dispatched a total of 10,000 peacekeepers to five operations (with an annual budget of about US$233 million) in 1987, by 1995 the total number of troops acting as peacekeepers, under UN auspices, was 72,000. They were operating in eighteen different countries and the total cost of these operations was over US$3 billion. Early post-Cold War initiatives were thought to augur well for the UN's new role. The major civil war in El Salvador, which had been fuelled by the Cold War, came to a negotiated end in 1992 under the auspices of the United Nations. Apart from El Salvador, the countries in which the UN has provided peacekeepers and election monitors include Angola, Bosnia-Herzegovina, Cambodia, Croatia, East Timor, Macedonia, Mozambique, Rwanda, Somalia and the Western Sahara. While East Timor, for example, is seen as a UN success story thus far, the abject failure of the United Nations in Angola and Somalia and its more qualified failure in places such as Cambodia highlight the constraints on the UN's role in the post-Cold War era.[97] The UN's new peacekeeping activities in the post-Cold War era were closely connected to the appointment of Boutros Boutros-Ghali as Secretary General at the beginning of 1992. Shortly after taking up the new post, Boutros-Ghali presented the Security Council with his "Agenda for Peace". Boutros-Ghali wanted member states to provide permanently designated military units that could be deployed quickly and overcome the UN's well-known inability to act with alacrity in a time of crisis. A number of states expressed an interest in such an arrangement at the same time as changes were made at UN headquarters in New York. There was even some talk of forming a multinational military establishment, made up of volunteers that would be under the direct control of the UN. These initiatives made little progress, however, in the context of an organization comprised of sovereign nation-states that were very wary of providing soldiers and equipment in ways that might diminish their sovereignty. Furthermore, there was little or no possibility of a more effective and united intervention by the UN in situations where the national interests of the major powers were thought to be at stake. At the same time, the fact that a number of countries, including the US and Russia, fell behind in their payment of dues to the UN suggested the prospects for a more activist and revamped UN were still limited.[98]

As a result of concerted US opposition, Boutros-Ghali was not reappointed as Secretary-General for a second term, further dampening the momentum towards a more assertive United Nations in the post-Cold War era. His replacement, Kofi Annan, has emerged as a much more cautious and conciliatory Secretary-General. By the end of the 1990s the United Nations was a central, albeit profoundly constrained, player in a wider post-Cold War order centered on the United States. This is a post-Cold War order in which instability, terrorism and criminality in the marginalized regions and failing nation-states in various parts of the world have precipitated the emergence (even before September 11 2001) of a renewed emphasis on the connection between security and development, viewing poverty and underdevelopment as a threat to global order. This shift is embodied in the growing links between strategies of conflict resolution, social reconstruction and foreign aid policies. While the United States and other OECD governments have been engaged in the post-Cold War nation-building effort that this reorientation represents, this task is also being shifted to new or reconfigured networks that combine national governments, military establishments, myriad private companies and contractors and NGOs.[99] This new merging of security and development in a distinct post-Cold War form is reminiscent, although not the same as, the anti-communist nation-building and poverty-alleviating strategies and efforts that rose and fell during the Cold War. The new, more privatized and more decentralized approach to nation-building reflects the shift from state-guided national development to globalization that was consolidated in the 1980s. Like earlier nation-building efforts, the chances of success (measured in terms of the genuine social and economic uplift and political enfranchisement of the majority of the citizens of a given nation-state, as opposed to a more minimal goal of political stability – the former being a standard by which the United States itself can be found wanting) for nation-building in the early twenty-first century remain seriously constrained. In fact, the instrumentalities available in theory and in practice to carry out nation-building in the post-Cold War era are even more limited than they were at the height of the Cold War.

Conclusion: US hegemony and the passing of national development

This chapter has looked at the reorientation of US hegemony and the passing of state-guided national development. It has located the rise of the US-led globalization project in the shifts in the global political economy and the transformation of the nation-state system during the Cold War and after. This chapter has also discussed the post-Cold War debate about the role of the US in the world. It has attempted to move beyond the main positions in that debate, which still tend to conceive of the US as the latest Great Power in a historic cycle of the rise and fall of Great Powers. It has emphasized the way in which the debate about US hegemony in the post-Cold War era has often failed to take account of the important, even fundamental, differences between US hegemony in the past few decades and the position of Great Powers in an earlier era.

Central to this difference has been the rise, universalization and changing character of the nation-state system. Of particular importance is the relationship between globalization and the nation-state system. By the 1990s the globalization project was being pursued at multiple sites, but remained grounded in US hegemony. The globalization project is being constituted via the nation-state system at the same time as it is transforming the character of that system and its constituent elements. A theoretical and policy trend that was central to this shift was the growing ascendancy of neo-liberalism by the 1980s. Neo-liberalism generally, and neo-classical economics more specifically, played a key role in challenging the very idea of state-guided national development. It is to the promotion and revision of neo-liberalism in the 1980s and 1990s and the relationship between that trend and the transformation of Asia that we now turn.

Notes

1 P. McMichael, *Development and Social Change: A Global Perspective*, 2nd edn, Thousand Oaks: Pine Forge Press, 2000, pp. 147–237.
2 J. E. Cronin, *The World the Cold War Made: Order, Chaos and the Return of History*, London: Routledge, 1996, pp. 195–6.
3 R. Brenner, "Uneven Development and the Long Downturn: The Advanced Capitalist Economies from Boom to Stagnation, 1950–1998" *New Left Review (I)* no. 229, 1998, pp. 43, 47, 116–24.
4 P. Gowan, *The Global Gamble: Washington's Faustian Bid for World Dominance*, London: Verso, 1999, pp. 4–5, 19–26.
5 Odd Arne Westad has argued that: "the market revolution of the late twentieth century – or globalization if one prefers to use that term – would not have been possible without the advances in communications that the Cold War competition brought on". O. A. Westad, "The New International History of the Cold War" *Diplomatic History* vol. 24, no. 4, 2000, p. 559.
6 On these changes generally see, of course, M. Castells, *The Rise of Network Society (The Information Age: Economy, Society and Culture*, volume 1), Oxford: Blackwell, 1996; M. Castells, *The Power of Identity (The Information Age: Economy, Society and Culture*, volume 2), Oxford: Blackwell, 1997; M. Castells, *End of Millennium (The Information Age: Economy, Society and Culture*, volume 3), Oxford: Blackwell, 1998.
7 L. Sklair, *The Transnational Capitalist Class*, Oxford: Blackwell, 2001.
8 McMichael, *Development and Social Change*, pp. 350, 354.
9 Gowan, *The Global Gamble*, pp. 26–39.
10 During the Cold War the Pentagon's budget was important, and often crucial to the fortunes of over 30,000 contractors and at least 100,000 subcontractors in the United States. M. Miyoshi, "A Borderless World? From Colonialism to Transnationalism and the Decline of the Nation-State" *Critical Inquiry* vol. 19, no. 4, 1993, p. 733. In fact, the "military-industrial complex" was also the single biggest US employer throughout the Cold War. M. Walker, "Pentagon Trapped in Political Crossfire" *The Guardian Weekly* July 16, 1995, p. 6.
11 Prior to the Reagan era, the Carter administration (1977–1980) made an effort to keep the value of the dollar low as part of a national economic growth strategy that remained focused on US industries and retained "quasi-Keynesian" characteristics. In the second half of the 1970s the dollar dropped by over 25 percent of its value in relation to the deutschmark and the yen, as Washington attempted to increase US manufacturing exports. However, while it used the new flexibility that went with the de-linking of the dollar to complement a politically driven national industrial policy, the Carter administration was apparently unaware of, or uninterested in exploiting,

the wider possibilities that went with the emerging DWSR. Gowan, *The Global Gamble*, pp. 39, 40–1.

12 Furthermore, almost 40 percent of the total foreign debt of the governments of the region was owed to US-based private banks. These loans were dollar dominated and had variable interest rates. This meant that any increase in interest rates immediately affected the size of the debt. For a critique of the US role see L. Whitehead, "Debt, Diversification and Dependency: Latin America's International Political Relations" in K. J. Middlebrook and C. Rico, eds, *The United States and Latin America in the 1980s: Contending Perspectives on a Decade of Crisis*, Pittsburgh: University of Pittsburgh Press, 1986. For a more sympathetic treatment see R. A. Pastor, *Latin America's Debt Crisis: Adjusting to the Past or Planning for the Future*, Boulder: Lynne Rienner, 1987.

13 S. Babb, *Managing Mexico: Economists from Nationalism to Neoliberalism*, Princeton: Princeton University Press, 2001.

14 P. Beaucage, "The Third Wave of Modernization: Liberalism, Salinismo, and Indigenous Peasants in Mexico" in L. Philips, ed., *The Third Wave of Modernization in Latin America: Cultural Perspectives on Neoliberalism*, Wilmington, DE: Scholarly Resources, 1998, pp. 13–16.

15 N. Lustig, *Mexico: The Remaking of an Economy*, Washington, DC: Brookings Institution, 1998, pp. 201–12.

16 I. Wallerstein, "The Rise of East Asia, or the World-System in the Twenty-First Century" in I. Wallerstein, *The End of the World As We Know It: Social Science for the Twenty-First Century*, Minneapolis: University of Minnesota Press, 1999, pp. 36–7.

17 C. Dixon, *South East Asia in the World Economy: A Regional Geography*, Cambridge: Cambridge University Press, 1991, pp. 33–4, 217–18.

18 A. MacIntyre, "South-East Asia and the Political Economy of APEC" in G. Rodan, K. Hewison and R. Robison, eds, *The Political Economy of South-East Asia: An Introduction*, Melbourne: Oxford University Press, 1997, pp. 237–8.

19 J. Bresnan, *Managing Indonesia: The Modern Political Economy*, New York: Columbia University Press, 1993, p. 83.

20 S. S. Kim, "Korea and Globalization (*Segyehwa*): A Framework for Analysis" in S. S. Kim, ed., *Korea's Globalization*, Cambridge: Cambridge University Press, 2000, pp. 2–4.

21 S. Corbridge and J. Harriss, *Reinventing India: Liberalization, Hindu Nationalism and Popular Democracy*, Cambridge: Polity Press, 2000, 143–72, 192–9.

22 F. Adams, *Dollar Diplomacy: United States Economic Assistance to Latin America*, Aldershot: Ashgate, 2000, pp. 53–4, 68–70, 75.

23 United States Agency for International Development, *Private Enterprise Development*, Washington, DC: Bureau for Program and Policy Coordination, US Agency for International Development, November 9, 1984. Online at http://www.usaid.gov

24 Adams, *Dollar Diplomacy*, pp. 90–1.

25 W. M. LeoGrande, *Our Own Backyard: The United States in Central America, 1977–1992*, Chapel Hill: University of North Carolina Press, 1998, pp. 583–91.

26 W. LaFeber, *Inevitable Revolutions: The United States in Central America*, 2nd edn, New York: W. W. Norton, 1993, pp. 353–8.

27 J. M. Paige, *Coffee and Power: Revolution and the Rise of Democracy in Central America*, Cambridge, MA: Harvard University Press, 1997, p. 51.

28 J. Dunkerley, *The Pacification of Central America: Political Change in the Isthmus 1987–1993*, London: Verso, 1994. By the end of the 1990s, 58 percent of the Guatemalan population live below the national poverty line (53.3 percent live on one US dollar a day or less). In El Salvador 38 percent live below the national poverty line. In Nicaragua 50 percent of the population live below the national poverty line (43.8 percent live on one US dollar a day or less). On the UNDP's Human Development Index, El Salvador ranks 107, Guatemala 117 and Nicaragua 121. United Nations

Development Programme, *Human Development Report 1999*, New York: Oxford University Press, 1999, p. 147.

29 R. J. McMahon, *The Cold War on the Periphery: The United States, India and Pakistan*, New York: Columbia University Press, 1994.

30 A. Jalal, *The State of Martial Rule: The Origins of Pakistan's Political Economy of Defence*, Cambridge: Cambridge University Press, 1990.

31 O. Roy, *Islam and Resistance in Afghanistan*, Cambridge: Cambridge University Press, 1986.

32 S. R. Tahir-Kheli, *India, Pakistan, and the United States: Breaking with the Past*, New York: Council on Foreign Relations Press, 1997.

33 K. Griffin, "Foreign Aid After the Cold War" *Development and Change* vol. 22, no. 4 (October), 1991, pp. 647–8.

34 See W. I. Robinson, *Promoting Polyarchy: Globalization, US Intervention and Hegemony*, Cambridge: Cambridge University Press, 1996; T. Carothers, *Aiding Democracy Abroad: The Learning Curve*, Washington, DC: Brookings Institution, 1999.

35 United States Agency for International Development, "Agency Objectives". Online at http://www.usaid.gov/democracy/dgso.html

36 Adams, *Dollar Diplomacy*, pp. 110–11.

37 This has resulted in the emergence in Cairo of the "biggest USAID program in the world" and the "largest U.S. diplomatic complex in the world". R. Owen, "Egypt" in R. Chase, E. Hill and P. Kennedy, eds, *The Pivotal States: A New Framework for U.S. Policy in the Developing World*, New York: W. W. Norton, 1999, pp. 120–1, 133.

38 In fact, by the beginning of the twenty-first century there was a steady and significant increase in oil output in Russia. E. L. Morse and J. Richard, "The Battle for Energy Dominance" *Foreign Affairs* vol. 81, no. 2, 2002, pp. 16–17.

39 See J. R. Wedel, *Collision and Collusion: The Strange Case of Western Aid to Eastern Europe 1989–1998*, New York: St. Martin's Press, 1998.

40 D. C. F. Daniel and A. L. Ross, "U.S. Strategic Planning and the Pivotal States" in R. Chase, E. Hill and P. Kennedy, eds, *The Pivotal States: A New Framework for U.S. Policy in the Developing World*, New York: W. W. Norton, 1999, pp. 385–7.

41 United States Department of Defense, *National Military Strategy of the United States*, Washington, DC: US Government Printing Office, January, 1992, p. 11. Cited in Daniel and Ross, "U.S. Strategic Planning and the Pivotal States", p. 387.

42 Daniel and Ross, "U.S. Strategic Planning and the Pivotal States", pp. 397–9; N. J. Citino, *From Arab Nationalism to OPEC: Eisenhower, King Saud, and the Making of U.S.–Saudi Relations*, Bloomington: Indiana University Press, 2002.

43 A. Lake, "From Containment to Enlargement" *U.S. Department of State Dispatch* vol. 4, no. 39 (September 27), 1993.

44 Office of the President of the United States, *A National Security Strategy of Engagement and Enlargement*, Washington, DC: US Government Printing Office, 1996. Online at http://www.fas.org/spp/military/docops/national/1996stra.htm, p. 2.

45 A. J. Bacevich, *American Empire: The Realities and Consequences of U.S. Diplomacy*, Cambridge, MA: Harvard University Press, 2002, pp. 2–3, 32 and 43.

46 Daniel and Ross, "U.S. Strategic Planning and the Pivotal States", pp. 388–92, 402; United States Department of Defense, Office of International Security Affairs, *United States Security Strategy for the East Asia and Pacific Region*, Washington, DC: US Department of Defense, February 1995, pp. 1–2.

47 J. Muravchik, *Exporting Democracy: Fulfilling America's Destiny*, Washington, DC: American Enterprise Institute, 1991; F. Fukuyama, *The End of History and the Last Man*, London: Hamish Hamilton, 1992; T. Smith, *America's Mission: The United States and the Worldwide Struggle for Democracy in the Twentieth Century*, Princeton: Princeton University Press, 1994; D. Yergin and J. Stanislaw, *The Commanding Heights: The Battle between Government and the Marketplace that is Remaking the Modern World*, New York: Simon and Schuster, 1998.

48 W. Keegan, *The Spectre of Capitalism: The Future of the World Economy After the Fall of Communism*, 2nd edn, London: Vintage, 1993 (first published 1992), p. 4.

49 T. Friedman, *The Lexus and the Olive Tree*, New York: HarperCollins, 1999, pp. 8, 11–12, 378.

50 For example, see N. Guyatt, *Another American Century? The United States and the World After 2000*, London: Zed Books, 2000, pp. 187–9, 199–200, 210–11, 238–40.

51 Friedman, *The Lexus and the Olive Tree*, pp. 195–8.

52 M. E. Brown, S. M. Lynn-Jones and S. E. Miller, eds, *Debating the Democratic Peace*, Cambridge, MA: MIT Press, 1996.

53 For a sustained attempt to address this problem, in relation to international relations theory in particular, see R. B. Hall, *National Collective Identity: Social Constructs and International Systems*, New York: Columbia University Press, 1999.

54 S. P. Huntington, "The West: Unique, not Universal" *Foreign Affairs* vol. 75. no. 6 (November/December), 1996, pp. 28–46.

55 S. P. Huntington, *The Clash of Civilizations and the Remaking of World Order*, New York: Simon and Schuster, 1996.

56 S. P. Huntington, "The Clash of Civilizations?" *Foreign Affairs* vol. 72, no. 3, 1993, p. 41.

57 According to Robert Kaplan, "the terrorist attacks on the World Trade Center and Pentagon highlight the tragic relevance not just of Huntington's ideas about a clash of civilizations but of his entire life's work". R. D. Kaplan, "Looking the World In The Eye" *The Atlantic Monthly* vol. 288, no. 5, 2001, pp. 70, 81.

58 For thorough critiques of the "clash of civilizations" as a way of understanding post-Cold War international relations see M. B. Salter, *Barbarians and Civilization in International Relations*, London: Pluto Press, 2002. G. Achcar, *The Clash of Barbarisms: Sept 11 and the Making of the New World Disorder*, New York: Monthly Review Press, 2002.

59 Numerous other writers parallel the realist and culturally deterministic views that are a hallmark of Huntington's work. For example, see R. D. Kaplan, *Balkan Ghosts: A Journey through History*, New York: Vintage, 1994; R. D. Kaplan, *The Ends of the Earth: A Journey to the Frontiers of Anarchy*, New York: Vintage, 1997; R. D. Kaplan, *The Coming Anarchy: Shattering the Dreams of the Post-Cold War*, New York: Vintage, 2000; R. D. Kaplan, *Soldiers of God: With Islamic Warriors in Afghanistan and Pakistan*, 2nd edn, New York: Vintage, 2001 (first published in 1990); R. D. Kaplan, *Warrior Politics: Why Leadership Demands a Pagan Ethos*, New York: Random House, 2001.

60 Huntington, *The Clash of Civilizations and the Remaking of World Order*, pp. 34, 209.

61 Huntington, "The Clash of Civilizations?", pp. 22–8. In support of this argument Huntington cited M. Weidenbaum, *Greater China: The Next Economic Superpower?*, St. Louis: Washington University Center for the Study of American Business, Contemporary Issues Series 57, February 1993, pp. 2–3. Also see M. Weidenbaum and S. Hughes, *The Bamboo Network: How Expatriate Chinese Entrepreneurs are Creating a New Economic Superpower in Asia*, New York: Martin Kessler Books, 1996.

62 Huntington, *The Clash of Civilizations and the Remaking of World Order*, pp. 34, 209.

63 Huntington's warning about a potential clash of civilizations and his call to revitalize the West were linked to his concern, voiced in the final years of the Clinton administration, that Washington policy-makers had been seduced by what he called the "'benign hegemon' syndrome". S. P. Huntington, "The Lonely Superpower" *Foreign Affairs* vol. 78, no 2, 1999, pp. 37–8, 40–1.

64 J. L. Gaddis, "Living in Candlestick Park" *The Atlantic Monthly* vol. 283, no. 4, 1999, pp. 73–4.

65 J. L. Gaddis, *The Long Peace: Inquiries into the History of the Cold War*, New York: Oxford University Press, 1987.

66 B. Cumings, "The Wicked Witch of the West is Dead. Long Live the Wicked Witch of the East" in M. J. Hogan, ed., *The End of the Cold War: Its Meaning and Implications*, Cambridge: Cambridge University Press, 1992, p. 87; T. R. Gurr argues that, contrary to the "conventional wisdom", the "rash of ethnic warfare peaked in the

early 1990s" as a result of greater resort to strategies of accommodation by the holders of state power. T. R. Gurr, "Ethnic Warfare on the Wane" *Foreign Affairs* vol. 79, no. 3, 2000, p. 52.

67 B. Cumings, "Still the American Century" *Review of International Studies* vol. 25, supplement, 1999, pp. 271–2, 274–5.

68 S. P. Huntington, "The U.S. – Decline or Renewal?" *Foreign Affairs* vol. 67, no. 2 (Winter), 1988/1989; S. P. Huntington, "The Erosion of American National Interests" *Foreign Affairs* vol. 76, no. 5 (September/October), 1997; D. W. White, *The American Century: The Rise and Decline of the United States as a World Power*, New Haven: Yale University Press, 1996; S. Hoffmann, *World Disorders: Troubled Peace in the Post-Cold War Era*, Lanham: Rowman and Littlefield, 1998.

69 Kissinger cited in T. J. McCormick, *America's Half Century: United States Foreign Policy in the Cold War*, Baltimore: Johns Hopkins University Press, 1989, pp. 216, 243.

70 P. Kennedy, *The Rise and Fall of the Great Powers: Economic Change and Military Conflict from 1500 to 2000*, 2nd edn, London: HarperCollins, 1989 (first published 1987).

71 In recent years there has been a revival of Kennedy's argument, with variations. For example, see C. Kupchan, *The End of the American Era: U.S. Foreign Policy After the Cold War*, New York: Alfred A. Knopf, 2002. Some world-system theorists have also paralleled Kennedy's earlier argument emphasizing that US hegemony is in decline. Terry Boswell and Christopher Chase-Dunn posit one possible scenario in which the US "continues its relative decline", but "remains the world's dominant power" for the next couple of decades. At the same time they suggest that by the 2020s "a new world leader" will emerge "with a preponderance of military power". T. Boswell and C. Chase-Dunn, *The Spiral of Capitalism and Socialism: Toward Global Democracy*, Boulder: Lynne Rienner, 2000, pp. 201–2. I. Wallerstein, "The Eagle Has Crash Landed" *Foreign Policy*, July/August, 2002.

72 H. R. Nau, *The Myth of America's Decline: Leading the World Economy into the 1990s*, New York: Oxford University Press, 1990; J. S. Nye, Jr, *Bound to Lead: The Changing Nature of American Power*, New York: Basic Books, 1990.

73 Kennedy, *The Rise and Fall of the Great Powers*, pp. 44, 55, 70–1, 76, 135.

74 T. Ertman, *Birth of the Leviathan: Building States and Regimes in Medieval and Early Modern Europe*, Cambridge: Cambridge University Press, 1997. Also see P. Anderson, *Lineages of the Absolutist State*, London: New Left Books, 1974; M. Van Creveld, *The Rise and Decline of the State*, Cambridge: Cambridge University Press, 1999, pp. 59–188.

75 In the wake of September 11 2001, Kennedy acknowledged that there are problems involved with assuming that "the nature of power itself has not changed since Roosevelt and Churchill's time". But, despite that concession, and the observation that the terrorist attacks sponsored by Osama bin Laden suggested that "force and power and threat have become much more diffuse", Kennedy quickly returned to the selective use of the history of the rise and fall of Great Powers in earlier eras to illuminate the position of the US in the world in the early twenty-first century. For example, he noted that "[f]or the U.S. to lose its share of global productive power and prosperity in the years to come would be *the same as* Spain's losing ground to the Dutch republic in the seventeenth century, or the overtaking of Britain's position by both Germany and America early in the twentieth century" P. Kennedy, "Maintaining American Power: From Injury to Recovery" in S. Talbott and N. Chanda, eds, *The Age of Terror: America and the World After September 11*, Oxford: Perseus Press, 2001, pp. 60–1, 71; italics added.

76 F. Zakaria, "Speak Softly, Carry a Veiled Threat" *New York Times Magazine* February 18, 1996, pp. 36–7. Also see A. Waldon, "Deterring China" *Commentary* vol. 100, no. 4, 1995. For the analogy with Nazi Germany see G. Rachman, "Containing China" *Washington Quarterly* vol. 19, no. 1, 1996. For a discussion of this issue see E. Friedman, "The Challenge of a Rising China: Another Germany?" in R. J. Lieber, ed., *Eagle Adrift: American Foreign Policy at the End of the Century*, New York: Longman, 1997.

77 Furthermore, a conception of international relations as primarily about the rise and fall of Great Powers fails to provide a template for the "new wars" of the twenty-first century generally and the war on terrorism more specifically. See M. Kaldor, *New and Old Wars: Organized Violence in a Global Era*, 2nd edn, Cambridge: Polity Press, 2001.

78 Meanwhile, as emphasized in chapter 1, some observers argue that US hegemony by the late twentieth century was complemented by fundamentally different sets of economic and business arrangements in contrast to an earlier era in which imperial powers dominated the world economy. This approach postulates the present era as "postimperial". See D. G. Becker, J. Frieden, S. P. Schartz and R. L. Sklar, *Postimperialism: International Capitalism and Development in the Late Twentieth Century*, Boulder: Lynne Rienner, 1987.

79 P. Gowan, "After America?" *New Left Review (II)* no. 13, 2002, p. 136.

80 B. Cumings, "Still the American Century", pp. 275, 277–8, 282, 285–6, 289. Also see T. L. Knutsen, *The Rise and Fall of World Orders*, Manchester: Manchester University Press, 1999, pp. 9–12, 212–14.

81 J. S. Nye, now Dean of the Kennedy School of Government at Harvard University, has characterized the wider acceptance of, and even enthusiasm for, a liberal world order centered on the US as "soft power". Oddly, however, Nye argues that given the "widely dispersed" character of "soft power", it should not be understood as hegemony. J. S. Nye, Jr, "America's Power: The New Rome Meets the New Barbarians" *The Economist* March 23, 2002, pp. 23–5. J. S. Nye, Jr, *The Paradox of American Power: Why the World's Only Superpower Can't Go It Alone*, New York: Oxford University Press, 2002." By contrast, it can be argued that the "ability to get others to want what you want" (the essence of "soft power" according to Nye) is also a precise definition of hegemony.

82 M. A. Bamyeh, *The Ends of Globalization*, Minneapolis: University of Minnesota Press, 2000, pp. 1–8, 52–8. M. Hardt and A. Negri, *Empire*, Cambridge, MA: Harvard University Press, 2000, pp. xii–xiii, 150–1, 178–9, 197, 201–3.

83 For a variation on this argument see J. Petras and M. Morley, *Empire or Republic? American Global Power and Domestic Decay*, New York: Routledge, 1995, pp. xi–xii, xv–xvi, 24.

84 J. E. Garten, "From New Economy to Siege Economy: Globalization, Foreign Policy and the CEO Agenda" *Business and Strategy* no. 26, 2002, pp. 46–7.

85 L. Panitch, "The New Imperial State" *New Left Review (II)* no. 2 (March–April), 2000, pp. 6–8, 14–15; S. Sassen, *Losing Control: Sovereignty in an Age of Globalization*, New York: Columbia University Press, 1996, p. 18.

86 J. Goss and D. Burch, "From Agricultural Modernisation to Agri-Food Globalisation: The Waning of National Development in Thailand" *Third World Quarterly: Journal of Emerging Areas* vol. 22, no. 6, 2001; C. J. W.-L. Wee, "The End of Disciplinary Modernisation? The Asian Economic Crisis and the Ongoing Re-Invention of Singapore" *Third World Quarterly: Journal of Emerging Areas* vol. 22, no. 6, 2001.

87 S. P. Cohen and S. Ganguly, "India" in R. Chase, E. Hill and P. Kennedy, eds, *The Pivotal States: A New Framework for U.S. Policy in the Developing World*, New York: W. W. Norton, 1999; E. Aspinall and M. T. Berger, "The Breakup of Indonesia? Nationalisms After Decolonisation and the Limits of the Nation-State in Post-Cold War Southeast Asia" *Third World Quarterly: Journal of Emerging Areas* vol. 22, no. 6, 2001.

88 M. Smith, *Burma: Insurgency and the Politics of Ethnicity*, 2nd edn, London: Zed Books, 1999 (first published 1991); H.-A. Rizvi, "Pakistan" in R. Chase, E. Hill and P. Kennedy, eds, *The Pivotal States: A New Framework for U.S. Policy in the Developing World*, New York: W. W. Norton, 1999; L. P. Goodson, *Afghanistan's Endless War: State Failure, Regional Politics, and the Rise of the Taliban*, Seattle: University of Washington Press, 2001; J. Browitt, "Capital Punishment: The Fragmentation of Colombia and the

Crisis of the Nation-State" *Third World Quarterly: Journal of Emerging Areas* vol. 22, no. 6, 2001.

89 G. Nzongola-Ntalaja, *The Congo From Leopold to Kabila: A People's History*, London: Zed Books, 2002.

90 D. Moore, "Neo-Liberal Globalisation and the Triple Crisis of 'Modernisation' in Africa: Zimbabwe, The Democratic Republic of the Congo and South Africa" *Third World Quarterly: Journal of Emerging Areas* vol. 22, no. 6, 2001.

91 As Peter Nolan has observed, "the role played by big business is even more important in the late 1990s than it was at any previous point in the history of capitalism. Large capitalist firms now stand at the centre of a vast network of outsourced businesses" that "are highly dependent on the core big businesses for their survival. Using new information technology, the core firm links together on a global scale a large number of related businesses." P. Nolan, *China and the Global Economy*, Basingstoke: Palgrave, 2001. Or, as Stephen Gill argued in the mid-1990s, "the current phase of economic globalisation has come to be characterised increasingly not by free competition as idealised in neoclassical theory, but by *oligopolistic neoliberalism*: oligopoly and protection for the strong and a socialisation of their risks, market discipline for the weak". For example, by 1992, "the 300 largest transnational firms controlled about 25 per cent of the worlds' $20 trillion stock of productive assets; the top 600 corporations with annual sales over $1 billion accounted for over 20 per cent of the world's total value-added in manufacturing and agriculture. There were about 37,000 transnational corportations by 1992, with 170,000 affiliates (up from 7,000 in the early 1970s). These firms had cumulative foreign direct investment of about $2 trillion, one-third of which was controlled by the 100 largest corporations. The top 100 had global sales of $5.5 trillion, a sum roughly equal to the GNP of the United States. ... Directly and indirectly, transnationals account for around five per cent of the global work force, although they control over 33 per cent of global assets. In the financial markets, by 1994 the daily flow of foreign exchange transactions world wide may have exceeded $1 trillion or 'roughly the foreign exchange holdings of all the central banks of the major industrialized nations' ". At the same time, "no more than 10 per cent of all financial transactions are related to real economic activity (that is, to finance trade flows or capital movements). Much of the rest is related to speculative activity, money laundering, and tax evasion, as well as the offsetting of risk". S. Gill, "Globalisation, Market Civilisation, and Disciplinary Neo-Liberalism" *Millennium: Journal of International Studies* vol. 24, no. 3, 1995, pp. 405–6.

92 Gowan, "After America?", pp. 139–40.

93 The most important twenty-five "emerging markets" that *The Economist* tracks are: China, Hong Kong, India, Indonesia, Malaysia, Philippines, Singapore, South Korea, Taiwan, Thailand, Argentina, Brazil, Chile, Colombia, Mexico, Peru, Venezuela, Egypt, Israel, South Africa, Turkey, Czech Republic, Hungary, Poland, Russia. See "Emerging-Market Indicators" on the last page of *The Economist* every week. Also see J. E. Garten, *The Big Ten: The Big Emerging Markets and How They Will Change Our Lives*, New York: Basic Books, 1997.

94 R. J. C. Young, *Postcolonialism: An Historical Introduction*, Oxford: Blackwell, 2001, p. 53–4.

95 M. Duffield, *Global Governance and the New Wars: The Merging of Development and Security*, London: Zed Books, 2001, pp. 2–5.

96 R. C. Hilderbrand, *Dumbarton Oaks: The Origins of the United Nations and the Search for Postwar Security*, Chapel Hill: University of North Carolina Press, 1990.

97 M. Wesley, *Casualties of the New World Order: The Causes of Failure of UN Missions to Civil Wars*, London: Macmillan, 1997; P. P. Lizée, *Peace, Power and Resistance in Cambodia: Global Governance and the Failure of International Conflict Resolution*, London: Macmillan, 2000.

98 Kaldor, *New and Old Wars*, pp. 112–13.

99 Duffield, *Global Governance and the New Wars*, pp. 1–2.

5 The neo-liberal ascendancy and the East Asian Miracle

The reorientation of US hegemony in the 1970s, and the consolidation of the globalization project in the 1980s, was complemented by the rise of neo-liberalism as a sustained and organized attempt to challenge the influence of ideas about state-directed national development. By the early 1980s neo-liberalism was in the ascendant in North America and Western Europe. This had major implications for theories of development as they had emerged and been elaborated after 1945. In particular neo-liberalism was a direct challenge to development economics, which had been central to development theory in the 1950s and 1960s and one of the main sources of economic policies for Asia and the Third World. This chapter starts with a discussion of the origins of neo-liberalism. This is followed by an examination of the consolidation of the neo-liberal ascendancy at the World Bank and the role of the World Bank in the promotion and revision of neo-liberalism in the 1980s and 1990s. Central to this process was the articulation of a reading of the East Asian Miracle that meshed with the increasingly dominant neo-liberal approach to capitalist development. In fact, the World Bank was central to the popularization of the term "East Asian Miracle" in the 1990s. This trend and the efforts of the Japanese government to counter the neo-liberal conception of the East Asian Miracle precipitated a major political battle over the causes and lessons of the East Asian Miracle. The effort to defend the theory and the practice of state-centered versions of the Asian Model was met with a process of accommodation, against the backdrop of unequal international power relations and the end of the Cold War. This conjuncture ensured that opposition to the neo-liberal ascendancy was increasingly domesticated to the liberal institutions and discourses of the nation-state system and the global political economy centered on US power. By the second half of the 1990s the dominant neo-liberal narrative had undergone some revision. The rise of rational choice theory, the new institutionalism and the new political economy were an important part of this process. However, despite revisions, neo-liberalism continued to privilege a technocratic understanding of development grounded in ahistorical assumptions about the dynamics of capitalism in the Asia-Pacific and beyond. These trends were reinforced by the Asian crisis of 1997–1998.

Promoting neo-liberalism

Think tanks and the "neo-classical counter-revolution"

The leaders of the counter-revolution that carried neo-liberalism to the highest political heights in Washington and London and then beyond were primarily economists, policy-intellectuals and, of course, politicians, whose first, but not their only, concern was to influence the political struggles and policy debates in North America and Western Europe.[1] Since the 1940s (if not earlier) economists and intellectuals in the United States and Great Britain had been engaged in the concerted promotion of neo-classical economics via a growing network of political organizations and what would become known as think tanks.[2] In Britain, in the latter years of the Second World War, exponents of economic and political liberalism, such as Friedrich Hayek and Karl Popper, had already published books that would become key texts in an ongoing challenge to national economic planning and social democracy between the 1940s and the 1970s.[3] In 1947 Hayek established the Mont Pélerin Society (named after the Swiss resort town where like-minded economic liberals from North America, Britain and continental Europe held their first meeting). Meanwhile, organizations such as the Institute of Economic Affairs (IEA), which was set up in 1955 by Antony Fisher and was inspired by Hayek's writings, went on to eventually play an important role in the rise of Thatcherism in Britain in the 1970s. One of the IEA's most famous publications was a paper on monetary policy by the inveterate North American advocate of free trade, Milton Friedman of the University of Chicago. Friedman's links to the IEA reflected the way that North American think tanks, such as the American Enterprise Institute (AEI), with which Friedman was also connected, often worked closely with their counterparts in Great Britain.[4]

Although the American Enterprise Institute was founded in 1943, it was a relatively marginal organization for at least the first twenty-five years of its existence. By the 1970s, however, it was receiving greater corporate support, and its reputation grew when former president Gerald Ford (1974–1976), as well as other members of his administration, spent time as resident fellows at the AEI. From the mid-1970s the AEI gained influence by establishing a dialogue with, and supporting the research of, prominent academics and policy-intellectuals. By reaching out to influential participants in the major policy debates the AEI, whose publications were widely distributed, sought to achieve a position of authority. The AEI played an important role in the neo-liberal shift in North America. By the end of the 1970s the AEI was a major source of policy advice for the US presidential candidate, Ronald Reagan (1981–1988). When Reagan took office in early 1981, thirty-four of his administration's new staff-members came from the American Enterprise Institute. Another conservative think tank, the Heritage Foundation, which was established in 1973, provided the Reagan administration with thirty-six staff members in 1981, while eighteen people from the Center for Strategic and International Studies (CSIS) also set up operations at the White House. The much older conservative think tank, the Hoover

Institution, provided the administration with at least fifty academics or former academics by 1985.[5]

With its conquest of political power in the United States and Great Britain by the beginning of the 1980s, neo-liberalism increasingly extended its reach.[6] As we have seen, in much of Asia, Africa, the Middle East and Latin America, development economics, or more radical Marxist and dependency theories of development, provided an important body of ideas and policies that were used by nationalist political and economic elites seeking a state-guided late-industrializing path to national development between the 1940s and the 1970s. With the rise of neo-liberalism, individuals and organizations that worked in development studies or were practitioners of development were often already part of the bureaucracy of the state or were dependent on the state for funding, and this constrained their ability to respond critically to neo-liberal policies. At the same time, Washington and London exercised predominant influence over the World Bank and the International Monetary Fund (IMF), and decisively shifted the emphasis of international and domestic economic policy-making. As we have seen, the World Bank and the IMF, supported by the Reagan administration, Margaret Thatcher's government in Britain (1979–1990) and the lengthy administration of Helmut Kohl (1982–1998) in West Germany/Germany, increasingly encouraged governments in Asia, Africa and Latin America to liberalize trade, privatize their public sectors and deregulate their financial sectors. This trend also coincided with the renewal of the Cold War. From the end of the 1970s to the late 1980s the Reagan administration presided over an unprecedented military build-up and a reinvigorated anti-communist crusade directed at the Soviet bloc and the state-socialist model that it embodied. Against this backdrop neo-classical economics and a romanticized version of *laissez-faire* capitalism increasingly provided the intellectual and imaginative framework for the US-led globalization project. In this context many development economists who were committed to, or had been converted to, neo-classical economics, emerged from relative obscurity. Collectively, their view was that none of the explanations and policy prescriptions provided by post-war development economics specifically, and post-war development theory more generally, had the answer to the problem of development in Asia, Africa and Latin America. From their perspective the notion that development could be achieved via state intervention was quite simply wrong.[7]

This is certainly apparent in Deepak Lal's influential and scathing critique of development economics (which was first published in 1983 by the Institute of Economic Affairs). A prominent exponent of neo-liberalism, Lal argued that the case for state intervention in the economy had been undermined by the post-1945 economic history of nation-states in the Third World. From his point of view the economic problems in the developing world did not result from "the inevitable imperfections of a market economy", but from the policy-induced, and thus "far from inevitable, distortions created by irrational *dirigisme*". He concluded that the governments of the Third World had to choose between "a necessarily imperfect planning mechanism" and "a necessarily imperfect market mechanism", arguing that "the latter is likely to perform better in practice".[8] Meanwhile, as noted briefly in chapter 2, P. T. Bauer, who was one of the more famous long-time advocates of the neo-classical approach to development in the Third World, gained new stature and authority in the 1980s with the rise of neo-liberalism.[9] Bauer's career as a dissenting development economist stretched back to the late colonial era. With the end of the Second World War, he was based at the London School of Economics and Political Science. He was a member of the Mont Pélerin Society from its inception in 1947. He also had close links with the Institute of Economic Affairs, following its establishment in 1955, and with the Conservative Philosophy Group (CPG), which was set up in the 1970s by members of the Conservative Party who emphasized the merits of *laissez faire*. The CPG eventually provided staff and policy advice to Margaret Thatcher's government.[10] The work of Bauer (Lord Bauer by the 1980s) and a large number of other neo-classical economists who participated in the rise of neo-liberalism contributed to the overall intellectual framework for the neo-liberal reforms that were increasingly promoted by the IMF and the World Bank.

Power and knowledge at the World Bank I

An important disseminator of development ideas, the World Bank is significant both as the source of authoritative knowledge about economic development and because of its key role in setting the agenda in the international development debate. This flows from its unrivalled budget for research and extensive policy-formulation capacity. At the same time, the World Bank is able to attract a high degree of international media attention for its pronouncements and major reports. This intellectual influence is directly reinforced by its economic leverage with governments around the world looking for investment, loans and foreign aid.[11] The ideas that have shaped the Bank's policy agenda over the years are also produced and disseminated in part by its own think tank, which was set up in 1956, using financial support from the Rockefeller and Ford Foundations. The organization was named the Economic Development Institute (EDI) and it instructed people from a wide range of developing countries in the creation and management of projects commensurate with the Bank's overall conception of development. According to its first director, Sir Alexander Cairncross, the inten-tion of the EDI was to ensure that by associating with and studying at the Bank, students "would carry with them ideas that were more congenial to the Bank when they went back to their own country". Certainly, a number of EDI gradu-ates achieved positions of prominence in their nations of origin. In the late 1970s Cairncross argued that EDI graduates "more or less ran" South Korea, and in Pakistan there were "a great many ex-EDI men who quite consciously were pulling together and having an influence on development".[12]

Up to the 1970s, of course, the dominant conception of development that prevailed at the World Bank had been grounded in development economics and focused on state-mediated national development against the backdrop of the

Cold War. These influences were readily apparent during Robert McNamara's tenure as president of the Bank from 1968 to 1981. McNamara had served as Secretary of Defense in both the Kennedy and Johnson administrations, and was one of the key architects of the Vietnam War until his resignation in 1968. The overall approach of McNamara, and other Cold War warriors of his generation, was conditioned by the idea that the poverty of nation-states in Asia, Africa and Latin America was the main underlying cause of the spread of communism.[13] Into the 1970s the presumption that there was a direct link between poverty and revolution, and that the communist threat could be contained and eliminated via the eradication of poverty, was at the heart of the dominant development discourse. As we have seen in chapter 3, McNamara also continued to be committed to the idea that economic development led more or less directly to political stability and democracy.[14] Under McNamara the World Bank significantly expanded its lending at the same time as "the alleviation of poverty" was promoted as a major focus of the organization's activity. And for most of the McNamara era the Bank reflected the enthusiastic and optimistic pursuit of the US-led modernization project via state-mediated national development that had already reached its apex in the 1960s.

In the mid-1970s, for example, Hollis Chenery, a prominent development economist and the World Bank's Vice-President for Development Policy, initiated a study of the Bank's record on economic development since 1950. David Morawetz, an outside consultant, conducted the study, but the conclusions he drew crystallized the official viewpoint of the Bank in this period. Overall, the study, like the Bank in the 1970s, took the view that on a global scale economic growth had been rapid and dramatic; however, this growth continued to be very poorly distributed. Nevertheless, the Morawetz Report was confident to the point of complacency that poverty elimination would continue to be the central concern of the Bank, that the limitations of monocrop-agriculture in many nation-states could be mitigated, that excessive concern about debt was misplaced, and that the dramatic growth in commercial lending in the 1970s was not a cause for concern.[15] Only with the second oil crisis (1979–1980) did the Bank express any public reservations about the ability of the changing international financial system to recycle enough funds to maintain economic growth and systemic stability.[16] This, combined with anti-inflation policies of recently elected neo-liberal governments, such as the Thatcher administration in Britain, and the anticipation that energy prices might continue to rise dramatically throughout the 1980s, convinced McNamara that the world economy had undergone a permanent change. Once the perception of permanent change in the world economy took hold of the Bank in 1980, various other policy conclusions followed. While financial assistance to governments of developing countries had been used in the past as a "substitute for structural adjustment", it was increasingly used to "support structural adjustment".[17] Thus, in the early 1980s, the Bank began to use structural adjustment loans to lock recipient governments into the economic policies that were central to the neo-liberal ascendancy.

Power and knowledge at the World Bank II

The shift to the promotion of neo-liberalism at the World Bank by the early 1980s
was clearly bound up with the wider geo-political and economic changes in the
1970s.[18] Symbolically, the shift was reflected by McNamara's departure from the
presidency in 1981. McNamara's successor was Alden Winship (Tom) Clausen
(1981–1986). Clausen ensured that the conception of development (and the
emphasis on alleviating poverty) that had predominated during the McNamara era
was more or less erased. Clausen, whose previous position had been at the head of
the Bank of America – the largest commercial bank in the world – made it clear to
the World Bank's top executives at the outset that he had no intention of maintaining his predecessor's focus on poverty alleviation. Clausen was primarily
concerned with making sure that the Bank continued to be, and became even
more, responsive to the concerns and priorities of the US government. As we have
seen the World Bank came into existence as part of the overall Bretton Woods
system that emerged from the capitalist crisis, global war and reconstruction of the
1930s and 1940s. The Bank (and the IMF) was envisioned by the victorious allied
powers as an instrument that could be used to both consolidate and manage the
post-war international political economy. From its inception, therefore, the Bank
was grounded in the wider power relations of the emerging Cold War. By the late
Cold War, early post-Cold War era the United States continued to be the Bank's
most powerful member, although its position as a Bank shareholder relative to
other key governments, such as the major European nation-states and Japan, had
declined. However, the US is the only country with a veto over amendments to the
Articles of Agreement. Furthermore, the US closely monitors Bank activities, and
is the only member to review all loan proposals in detail; officials of the Treasury
Department are in daily contact not only with the US executive director, but also
with other Bank officials.[19] By the 1980s US influence was also increasingly
grounded in the Bank's dependence on world financial markets, the central position of the US as a global financial center, and the closely aligned interests of key
financial actors with those of US foreign policy. Meanwhile, at least 80 percent of
the economists working for the World Bank are trained in Britain or North
America. In the 1980s and early 1990s, their outlook, and that of virtually all of
the remaining 20 percent, was increasingly based on the assumptions and methodologies of neo-classical economics. Economists who do not subscribe to the main
precepts of neo-classical economics are unlikely even to be employed by the Bank,
while social scientists from other disciplines who work for the Bank on peripheral
projects have no influence over economic policy formulation.[20]

In this context it was no surprise that poverty alleviation disappeared from
view and structural adjustment became the centerpiece of World Bank policies
in the 1980s. This shift in development thinking was clearly manifested by the
Berg Report, published in 1981. Written by Elliot Berg, the official title of the
Report was *Accelerated Development in Sub-Saharan Africa: An Agenda for Action*.[21] The
Berg Report relied on insights drawn from rational choice theory to evaluate the
developmental record of governments in Sub-Saharan Africa. Its prescriptions
centered on the need for a greatly reduced role for the state in the economy and

much greater reliance on the market as a means of accelerating economic activity, particularly in the agricultural sector. However, it is misleading to view the Bank during Clausen's presidency as being united from the outset around the neo-liberalism reflected in the Berg Report. Against the backdrop of the wider shift from development economics to neo-classical economics, the Bank under Clausen experienced greater policy fragmentation and diversity within still limited parameters than was the case during the McNamara era. In this period, for example, the Research Department of the World Bank was characterized by a particularly devout commitment to the free market and an intolerance of dissent that was not necessarily shared by other sections of the Bank. After 1981 the research department's operations and activities were devoted increasingly to "large projects designed to substantiate what everyone knew in their hearts already: that economic liberalization was right".[22] The head of the Research Department was Anne Krueger, who Clausen had hired to replace Hollis Chenery, the Bank's chief economic theorist in the McNamara era. Chenery was a major figure in development economics whose work was anathema to advocates of neo-classical economics.[23] According to one insider, Krueger was not interested in debating economic policy and "cut off" anyone "who ever had any relationship" with Chenery.[24]

The high period of neo-classical fundamentalism at the World Bank had peaked by the second half of the 1980s, coinciding with a shift in the approach to the world economy by the Reagan administration as ideologues gave way to technocrats in Washington. At the World Bank, this shift was marked by the change of presidents from Clausen to Barber Conable (1986–1991). With Conable at the helm, the organization's public image was seen to be more consensual than under Clausen, while poverty alleviation and the mitigation of the social costs of structural adjustment were given greater prominence. The neo-classical ideologues in the Research Department departed and the Department itself disappeared as a separate Vice-Presidency, following the reorganization of the Bank in 1987.[25] However, this reorganization, during Conable's tenure as president, was primarily aimed at making the Bank more effective and smaller. Conable sought to reduce the organization's 6,000 employees by 10 percent. It was also part of an effort to break the influence of powerful long-time managers, particularly Ernest Stern, the economist who had been with the Bank during the McNamara era and remained an important "de facto power" during the 1980s. The Bank certainly was shaken up in the months after Conable first took over, but even before Conable left the size of the staff had returned to 6,000 and most of the powerful and long-serving senior officials at the Bank remained in place. Stern, for example, remained at the Bank long after Conable had retired.[26] Nevertheless, the World Bank's understanding of development into the 1990s continued to be, or increasingly became, influenced by rational choice theory (the new institutionalism and the new political economy), resulting in a highly mechanistic approach to the dynamics of political and economic change in the various countries that the researchers at the Bank sought to understand.[27]

The lessons of the East Asian Miracle

East Asia occupied a pivotal, albeit contradictory, position in the wider neo-liberal ascendancy. As one of the few regions of the world outside North America and Western Europe that still appeared by the end of the 1970s and early 1980s to be undergoing successful economic development, it is not surprising that the lessons of what became widely known as the East Asian Miracle were central to the wider geo-political struggle that attended the rise of neo-liberalism. In the late 1970s and early 1980s a growing number of commentators found free-trade, or at least market-oriented policies, particularly export-oriented industrialization (EOI), to be the key to the economic dynamism of East Asia (South Korea, Taiwan, Hong Kong and Singapore), while pointing to the apparent failure of import-substitution industrialization (ISI) in nation-states in Latin America and Africa.[28] More broadly, the rise of the miracle economies of East Asia, or what were variously known as the Newly Industrializing Countries (NICs) or Newly Industrializing Economies (NIEs) of East Asia (not to mention enthusiastic references to the Asian Dragons and Asian Tigers), was increasingly interpreted as a natural outgrowth of liberal capitalist expansion. For example, in 1979, Edward Chen argued that in the case of what he called the "hyper-growth" of Japan, South Korea, Taiwan, Hong Kong and Singapore, "state intervention" was "largely absent". From his point of view all that the state had "provided" was "a suitable environment for the entrepreneurs to perform their functions".[29]

Milton Friedman (whose stature increased dramatically in the 1980s) offered a similar interpretation the following year in a book, co-authored with Rose Friedman, which sought explicitly to popularize neo-classical economics. In *Free to Choose* (1980) they argued that as a result of extensive reliance on "private markets", Japan, South Korea, Taiwan, Hong Kong and Singapore were "thriving", while China, Indonesia and India, "all relying heavily on central planning", were experiencing "economic stagnation".[30] This continued to be a particularly influential interpretation of East Asian capitalism throughout the 1980s. For example, according to David Aikman, the industrial dynamism of East Asia demonstrated "just how faithful, consciously or not" many of the NICs had been "to American conceptions of free enterprise".[31] In 1986 Staffan Burenstam Linder asserted that the rise of East Asia flowed from "the very policies" that had earlier given "the rich countries their affluence".[32] These observations nicely capture the way in which a growing number of commentators discovered policies and practices in East Asia that were similar to the values and virtues perceived to have underpinned the rise of the West in an earlier era. For example, in a short article in the *Far Eastern Economic Review* (one of the most influential English-language business and news magazines in the region) the former Prime Minister of Britain, Margaret Thatcher, argued in 1993 that: "such success as Asia now enjoys is the result of unremitting hard work, an unquenchable spirit of enterprise, and sound economic policies".[33]

Against the background of the end of the Cold War, the neo-liberal ascendancy increasingly sought to appropriate East Asian capitalism. The East Asian Miracle was promoted as a recapitulation of a romanticized liberal version of the earlier rise of the West providing confirmation and comfort to those who believed that the accumulation of wealth was primarily the result of hard work and virtuous conduct. At the end of the twentieth century the histories of a variety of national trajectories in Asia continued to be widely interpreted as belated versions of the rise of the West (or more particularly the rise of the United States and Britain). This approach was manifested clearly, at the end of the 1980s, in the argument by Francis Fukuyama – a RAND consultant and former US State Department employee – that the end of the Cold War might well be the "end of history". In a now-famous article he characterized the waning of the conflict between Washington and Moscow as the "end point of mankind's ideological evolution and the universalization of Western liberal democracy as the final form of human government". He emphasized that the liberal "victory" was still unfinished, and it had occurred mainly "in the realm of ideas or consciousness". The process was "as yet incomplete in the real or material world". However, with regard to East Asia he saw liberalization as well advanced. In Japan, where "the essential elements of economic and political liberalism" had been "successfully grafted onto uniquely Japanese traditions and institutions", he was confident that liberalism's "survival in the long run" was assured. In the case of South Korea he argued that "political liberalism" had been trailing "economic liberalism, more slowly than many had hoped but with seeming inevitability" and South Korea "could not possibly be isolated from the larger democratic trends" which were sweeping the globe.[34]

Then, in 1992, Fukuyama argued that East Asia's "postwar economic miracle" makes clear that "capitalism is a path toward economic development that is potentially available to all countries". More specifically, he argued that: "the established industrial powers" had not been "capable of blocking the development of a latecomer, provided that country plays by the rules of economic liberalism". From his point of view the newly industrializing economies (NIEs) of Asia, "repeating the experiences of Germany and Japan in the late nineteenth and early twentieth centuries, have proven that economic liberalism allows late modernizers to catch up with and even overtake" established industrial powers. Fukuyama's emphasis on the inexorable rise of liberal economic and political ideas, and his dubious effort to fit the pre-1945 Japanese and German trajectories into a neo-liberal understanding of economic transformation (an exercise that is hard enough for post-1945 Japan and Germany) clearly reflects the wider effort in the post-Cold War era to find in the East Asian Miracle confirmation of the superiority of the modes of political and economic organization associated with an idealized conception of Anglo-American liberalism. At the same time, Fukuyama acknowledged in passing that the development model emanating from a resurgent Asia, apparently led by Japan, might in fact embody a major challenge to, rather than a recapitulation of, the Anglo-American model.[35]

One of the first professional economists, with experience in the developing world, to attempt to systematize a neo-liberal understanding of the industrialization of East Asia was the development economist, Ian Little. He emphasized the way in which South Korea, Taiwan, Hong Kong and Singapore had briefly pursued import-substitution industrialization (ISI), shifting in the early 1960s to export-oriented industrialization (EOI). Reflecting what would become the established neo-classical explanation for East Asian success, he saw this policy reorientation as the key. Focusing his analysis on South Korea, Taiwan and Singapore, Little argued that from about 1960, the governments of these nation-states embarked on a reorientation in economic policy that resulted by the mid-1960s in an overall approach to economic development that "combined selective protection for certain import competing sectors with a virtual free trade regime for exporters". He emphasized that exporters were able to purchase inputs at international market prices and the "effective exchange rate for exporters" was more or less the same as the rate that would have prevailed "under free trade". Little argued that "overall effective protection for industry was zero" in the case of South Korea and Hong Kong, while it was "low" in Singapore and Taiwan. He concluded that the "consequential growth of exports was phenomenal, far exceeding what anyone could have predicted or did predict".[36] Writing in 1981 he argued that: "labour-intensive export-oriented policies, which amounted to almost free trade conditions for exporters", and "nothing else", explain the industrial transformation of Asia after 1960.[37] Of course, such a narrow focus on export-oriented industrialization as the key to the East Asian Miracle results in an ahistorical and technocratic explanation for, and decontextualized lessons from, the transformation of Asia.[38]

In the 1980s other neo-classical economists with direct and indirect links to the World Bank produced studies that reinforced Little's conclusion about EOI and the East Asian Miracle.[39] One of the more influential World Bank economists to consistently articulate a neo-classical interpretation of industrialization in East Asia in this period that complemented Little's emphasis on EOI was Bela Balassa. From Balassa's perspective, comparative advantage (or the idea that nation-states should specialize in what they are naturally best at) was a key factor in economic development. From this point of view the natural unfolding of the world economy results in the movement of national economies from the production of low technology goods to the manufacture of higher technology goods, as a particular country's comparative advantage shifts from unskilled labor-intensive manufacturing to skilled, capital-intensive production.[40] In the late 1980s Balassa argued that with the exception of Hong Kong, the NICs had all gone through an initial stage of import-substitution industrialization, but in contrast to late-industrializing nation-states in Latin America, the East Asian NICs had subsequently and successfully embraced export-oriented industrialization. For Balassa, this external orientation was a central and dynamic element of the comparative advantage framework, insofar as an external orientation facilitated the overcoming of domestic constraints, undercutting monopolistic and protectionist economic arrangements, and encouraging competition and the pursuit of technological improvement.[41] These kinds of lessons were also adumbrated in World Bank publications such as *Korea's Experience with the Development of Trade and Industry: Lessons for Latin America*.[42] What is readily apparent in the wider neo-classical/neo-liberal narrative on East Asia that emerged in the 1980s is the way in which it naturalized discrete national trajectories. What is also apparent is that the ahistorical and technocratic understanding of capitalist transformation that underpinned neo-classical economics not only involved the naturalization of nation-states but also involved the naturalization of liberal capitalism itself.

Revising neo-liberalism

Japan, the United States and the World Bank

The World Bank, as the above discussion implies, was an important site by the 1980s for the promotion of an interpretation of the East Asian Miracle that conformed to the main tenets of neo-classical economics.[43] This was linked to a wider effort by the World Bank to promote a normative vision of capitalist trans-formation as the unfolding of a natural and liberal process.[44] This project was increasingly challenged by the Japanese government – throughout the 1980s pressure from Tokyo on the World Bank for greater acknowledgement of the role of the state in economic development had been building.[45] Despite the growing influence of neo-liberalism, the Japanese government continued to intervene in economic activity in a manner that flouted the neo-liberal ascen-dancy, while unlike other governments it generally failed even to pay lip-service to free trade. This ensured that Japan was increasingly subject to criticism in the context of ongoing trade disputes with the United States. During the 1980s the Japanese government continued to direct or assist the expansion of Japanese corporations overseas.[46] In 1987, for example, the Ministry of International Trade and Industry (MITI) planned a regional industrialization strategy for the governments of Southeast Asia, a key element of which was the allocation of directed credit. The Japanese Ministry of Finance (MOF), meanwhile, set up the ASEAN–Japan Development Fund at the end of the 1980s. It was administered by Japan's main aid agency and sought to provide credit to Japanese companies operating in Southeast Asia. Officials at the World Bank conveyed their concern about this approach through informal channels, but this had no discernible effect. In fact, by June 1989, Masaki Shiratori, a senior MOF official who was well known for his dedication to making the World Bank rethink direct credit policies specifically and take the role of the state in East Asia into account gener-ally, had become the World Bank's new Executive Director for Japan.[47]

The end of the Cold War, and increased friction with the US government over the perceived unfair trading practices of Japanese companies, provided the back-drop for the Japanese government's growing efforts to challenge neo-liberalism. At the same time, with the end of the Cold War, elites and governments in the Asia-Pacific more generally expressed concern that the world economy might shift, or was shifting, towards economic blocs centered on Western Europe and North America.[48] While European economic integration and the North American Free Trade Agreement (NAFTA) were represented by many of their proponents as liberalizing rather than protectionist initiatives, there was scepticism about this inside and outside of East Asia. There were also some observers who perceived the Asia-Pacific Economic Cooperation forum (APEC), which was set-up in 1989, as a possible vehicle for US domination.[49] It was clear from the outset that there were divergent views about the orientation and even the appropriate membership of APEC.[50] In terms of orientation it was clear that the US and other key players envisioned APEC, in the words of C. Fred Bergsten, a member of the Eminent Persons Group commissioned to draw up the founding documents, as "a force for worldwide liberalisation".[51] While the Australian government is often seen as the originator of APEC, the Japanese Ministry for International Trade and Industry (MITI) was also an early advocate of a post-Cold War Asia-Pacific trade organization. However, MITI envisioned that such an organization would provide a venue for trade cooperation rather than free trade. At the same time, it encouraged the Australian government (which clearly emphasized that APEC should be about free trade) to take the initiative because the Japanese government felt that the idea of a regional economic organization would be better received in the region if it came from Australia rather than from the country that had been the promoter, in an earlier era, of the erstwhile "Greater East Asia Co-Prosperity Sphere".[52]

In December 1990, a year after APEC had been formally established, Prime Minister Mahathir Mohamad of Malaysia sought to explicitly counter the EU, NAFTA and the APEC initiative with a proposal that Japan and other East Asian countries form an East Asian Economic Bloc (EAEB). The following year his idea of an exclusive regional bloc was presented to a post-ministerial meeting of ASEAN, by which time it was being called an East Asian Economic Group (EAEG). While some Southeast Asian governments were wary of Mahathir's proposal, it did lead directly to the formation of the ASEAN Free Trade Area (AFTA) that was set up in June 1991 with the goal of eliminating tariff barriers between the members of ASEAN. The EAEG continued as an agenda item within ASEAN, with its name being changed again in October 1991 to the less threatening East Asian Economic Caucus (EAEC).[53] At the beginning of the 1990s the Japanese government is reported to have seriously considered joining Mahathir's EAEC.[54] This did not come to pass, and by 1994 Mahathir had reluctantly agreed to make the EAEC a component of APEC.[55] Nevertheless, as we will see in chapter 6, Mahathir's views enjoyed wide, although not necessarily deep, appeal amongst the general population in Japan and beyond. And his "Asia-first" approach continued to mesh with the views of some influential members of the Japanese elite in this period.[56] In fact, the Asian crisis at the end of the decade resulted in the weakening of APEC and the strengthening of ASEAN+3 (the Association of Southeast Asian Nations, South Korea, Japan and China). For some observers the latter organization represents a close approximation of Mathathir's Pan-Asian vision.[57]

Meanwhile, at the World Bank, the potential for increased conflict over competing visions of regional development was exacerbated by the appointment, in January 1991, of Lawrence Summers to the position of chief economist and vice-president at the Bank. Summers (who later went on to be Deputy Treasury

Secretary, then Treasury Secretary in the Clinton administration and is now president of Harvard University) was well known for regarding Japanese economists as "second rate". He came up with the term "market friendly" that was used to soften the overall free-market approach of the final version of the 1991 *World Development Report*. It emphasized that "market-friendly policies", which it characterized as "neither complete laissez faire nor interventionism", were "optimal for growth and income distribution".[58] This terminological change did little, however, to ameliorate the concerns of the Japanese government. Tokyo continued to promote its own model of economic development using its increasing influence at the Bank and the IMF as leverage. For example, in an address at the World Bank and the IMF's Board of Governors annual meeting in October 1991, Yasushi Mieno, then head of the Bank of Japan, argued that the East Asian experience demonstrated the significance of government intervention. In his speech, which had been drafted by the Ministry of Finance's International Finance Bureau, he made an explicit appeal for the IMF and the World Bank to produce a study that would directly address the question of states and markets in East Asia and the lessons from the region for the rest of the world.[59] At the same meeting the World Bank's vice-president and managing director, Attila Karaosmanoglu, suggested that the NICs of East Asia were a "powerful argument" for "a more activist, positive governmental role" in industrialization. He insisted, furthermore, that "what is replicable and transferable" in the East Asian experience "must be brought to light and shared with others".[60]

This was the context in which the World Bank's now famous 1993 Report, entitled *The East Asian Miracle* and funded by the Japanese Ministry of Finance, appeared. The report set out to examine the eight High Performing Asian Economies (HPAEs), which were identified as Japan, South Korea, Taiwan, Hong Kong, Thailand, Malaysia, Singapore and Indonesia. It was concluded that they all shared "some economic characteristics that set them apart from most other developing countries". Their success, according to the report, was grounded in "a combination of sound, market-based, foreign investment-friendly, export-oriented, and generally equitable policies". The report also distilled what was regarded as the "essence of the miracle". This involved a number of basic elements, but it boiled down to an emphasis on the need to "get the basics right". The report went out of its way to extract a range of ahistorical and technocratic economic lessons from the diverse national trajectories of the HPAEs. In particular, it emphasized that government intervention aimed at promoting exports was the form of intervention most "compatible with a wide diversity of economic circumstances".[61] While the Japanese government was not happy with the final product, the 1993 Report was significant in that, for the first time since the start of the "neo-classical counter-revolution", a major Bank publication had conceded that government intervention played some role in economic development in East Asia.[62] However, it continued to treat economic development as a technical policy question, and the role of the state (or government institutions) as well as wider historical considerations were not seen as particularly relevant to an overall understanding of successful capitalist development.

One of the most prominent series of reactions to, and criticisms of, the 1993 Report, appeared under the editorship of Alice Amsden in a special section of the April 1994 issue of the influential journal, *World Development.*[63] In his contribution Sanjaya Lall, a well-known development economist who served as a staff member (1965–1968 and 1985–1987) and a consultant with the World Bank, described the report as "flawed". He argued that the methodology used to "evaluate the effectiveness of the study's version of industrial strategy" (which the study defined as "government efforts to alter industrial structure to promote productivity-based growth") failed even to begin to assess industrial strategies "as they were conceived and implemented by the governments concerned". This resulted in the conclusion that "industrial policy had little structural effect"; however, this is contrary to "overwhelming micro-level evidence" that indicated the vast majority of economic initiatives that East Asian governments promoted would not have occurred without government encouragement. Another problem, for Lall, was the way that the Report examined "selective interventions" as separate phenomena rather than as elements in a broad strategy. This ensured that the Report failed to assess the overall contribution made by government intervention. For example, argued Lall, government intervention in the credit market would not have been effective if the interventions had not been part of a wider strategy of technological promotion, market protection and selective skill creation. Ultimately, in his view, the Report drew anodyne and "partisan" lessons from the capitalist transformation of East Asia.[64] Some proponents of industrial policy, and of the development state, such as Lall, clearly found little of significance in the Report. But, as we will see in chapter 7, advocates of revised versions of the developmental state, such as Peter Evans, were more forgiving of the World Bank's assessment of the role of the state in the East Asian Miracle.[65] This was part of an effort by Evans and others writing in the developmental state tradition to move beyond the sharply drawn positions of state versus market as they had crystallized in the 1980s and early 1990s. Evan's outlook reflected the way in which, even as the role of the state was being acknowledged but downplayed by the World Bank, the way had already been paved for greater accommodation of the state-centered perspective by the rise of new trade theory (or new growth theory) and rational choice theory as part an effort to revise neo-classical economics.

"The Myth of Asia's Miracle"

In 1994 the prominent North American economist Paul Krugman (whose name is widely associated with new trade theory) sought to puncture the more enthusiastic assessments of the East Asian Miracle proffered by all sides in the debate. His intervention also had important implications for the debate over industrial policy, which, as we have seen, had been a key focus of the World Bank Report and its critics. In a now well-known article entitled "The Myth of Asia's Miracle", Krugman argued that the high rates of growth in East Asia in the 1980s and 1990s were not sustainable. He also argued that the high growth rates were primarily a function of the movement of large numbers of people out of low-productivity agricultural work into the industry and service sectors, combined with high rates of savings and investment. This meant that there had not been, and had been no need for, major improvements in productivity. In Krugman's view, explanations for the transformation of Asia that focused on the efficient allocation of resources (neo-liberalism) or effective industrial strategies (developmental state theory) were overlooking a more prosaic explanation. From his perspective, "Asia's Miracle" flowed from the expansion of industrial capacity as a result of increasing investment and abundant labor and when demand dropped, growth would also drop.[66] At the same time, as Krugman himself has subsequently noted, his 1994 article, which was based on the work of Alwyn Young, should not be construed as anticipating the Asian crisis (1997–1998).[67] The crisis was not a result of a decline in demand, but a much more complicated shift centered on the banking and financial sector in the region and beyond.

Krugman's equally significant, if somewhat more indirect, contribution to the debate about the East Asian Miracle was probably his work on new trade theory. He was already well known in the 1980s for his efforts, along with others, to revise the neo-classical approach to international trade with important implications for the question of state intervention that was at the center of the battle for the East Asian Miracle. In the second half of the 1980s he argued that domestic markets did not function nearly as well as was assumed by neo-classical economists. His work challenged the comparative advantage approach to trade, emphasizing that nation-states did not simply specialize in an effort to exploit particular advantages *vis-à-vis* other nation-states, they also specialized because specialization over time produces its own advantages simply as a result of specialization, regardless of whether there were distinctive comparative advantages that flowed from specialization initially. Krugman, along with other proponents of the new trade theory, argued that when this was combined with the presence of market distortions, there was a case for the state to intervene to produce and facilitate "*dynamic* advantages" via the support of things such as technological improvements. From this point of view some countries may well experience higher rates of economic growth if trade restrictions are applied. In Krugman's view "one thing" was very "clear: the idealized theoretical model on which the classical case for free trade is based will not serve us anymore" in the face of the complexity of the "real world".[68] While new trade theory (or new growth theory) had limited initial impact on the neoclassical approach generally and the policy debate about East Asia more specifically, its ideas gradually impacted on the work of economists, such as Sanjaya Lal, and it was used to challenge or revise neo-liberalism.[69]

"The Key to the Asian Miracle"

The revision of neo-liberalism was, as already suggested, also facilitated by the rise of rational choice theory in North American political science in the 1980s.[70] Like the approach to economic behaviour taken by neo-classical economics, rational choice theory built its explanations for political behaviour on assumptions about the rational calculations that informed the policies and actions of the individuals and groups concerned. There is only limited agreement as to how to categorize and identify the various tendencies in rational choice theory as they relate to the study of development.[71] Some observers identify three major strands within the institutionally oriented rational choice analysis based on their relative distance from neo-classical economics. The first strand is the new institutional economics, which is effectively a sub-discipline of neo-classical economics.[72] The second strand is the new institutionalism. Within this strand authors from a variety of disciplines seek to use rational choice theory to evaluate the operation of a range of institutions: everything from finance to irrigation projects. The third strand takes what is called the new political economy approach to the application of rational choice theory to institutions and economic development. The difference between the new institutionalism and the new political economy revolves primarily around the latter's greater sensitivity to politics.[73] Douglass C. North is widely perceived as a key figure in the new institutionalism.[74] The influence of North's work was already apparent in a number of World Bank reports by the second half of the 1980s. By the 1990s he had emerged as a major proponent of the view that rational choice theory could be deployed to ground a new theory of development. Meanwhile, the US-based political scientist Robert H. Bates is widely perceived as a key figure in the new political economy. His work also exercised a direct influence on a number of reports produced by the World Bank by the second half of the 1980s.[75] For example, the World Bank's annual *World Development Report* for 1986 embraced Bates's approach to agricultural policy. The 1991 Report rested on a synthesis of North and Bates to bolster its main prescriptions. Meanwhile, the 1994 *World Development Report* on infrastructure clearly owed its major debt to North and a growing number of proponents of the new institutionalism. By the 1990s, the terminology of rational choice theory, if not the more rigorous versions of its conceptual framework, was being widely deployed, facilitating the revision and strengthening of the neo-liberal ascendancy.[76]

The role of rational choice theory in revising and bolstering neo-liberalism generally, and in accommodating the state-led development trajectory of East Asia to neo-classical economics more specifically, is apparent in *The Key to the Asian Miracle*, which was published in 1996. Although not a World Bank publication as such, the book was written by Jose Edgardo Campos, a World Bank economist and co-author of the 1993 Miracle Report, and Hilton L. Root, an economic historian based at the Hoover Institution at Stanford University. In their book, they attempted to outline "concrete lessons for the rest of the developing world" by examining "the rationality of the structure and performance" of key institutions in East Asia. From their point of view, although East Asian institutions were not necessarily "directly transferable" to other nation-states, knowing how they operated could still provide a "guide" for other governments facing similar economic problems.[77] Their analysis, which clearly reflected the influence of rational choice theory, represented Japan, South Korea, Taiwan, Hong Kong, Singapore, Thailand, Malaysia and Indonesia as variations of a generalized form of enlightened and paternalistic authoritarianism. They argued that the governments of the HPAEs were aware that successful economic development necessitated coordinating the "expectations" of various groups. This led, they said, to the crafting of institutional arrangements that sought to distribute "the benefits of growth-enhancing policies widely", while reassuring businesses and individuals "that they would share the growth dividend". They emphasized that: "sharing gave the less fortunate a stake in the economy". This worked to discourage "disruptive activities" and reduced "the risk of regime failure". Importantly, it also allowed the various governments to focus "on promoting rational economic policies by reducing the need to constantly contend with issues of redistribution".[78]

The authors observed that many of the regimes that presided over successful economic growth in East Asia between the 1970s and the 1990s are regularly regarded "as authoritarian, even dictatorial". They argued that this perception is misleading and "occurs largely because of the failure of Western observers to recognize in East Asia systems for ensuring accountability and consensus building that differ from Western-style institutions". They emphasized that "the mechanisms that Westerners expect to see – written constitutions, elected legislators, a formal system of checks and balances – are but one set of solutions to establishing regime legitimacy and guaranteeing limits on government action". From their point of view there are "other ways of" mobilizing "public support" and "restraining ruling cliques from overriding the economic rights of others". Furthermore, although the different HPAEs vary significantly from each other they "share enough common elements to suggest a developmental model that differs from the trajectory of the Western democracies and from the autocracies of the past and present". According to the authors, instead of behaving "like roving bandits" the regimes of the HPAEs "have considered the future output of society and have offered incentives to productive investment (physical and human) that are typically found only in the Western democracies". They conclude that, while the future for the HPAEs is uncertain and the historical context (the Cold War in particular) has altered, the governments of developing nations around the world can still benefit from an examination of the HPAEs as a way of finding "their own best starting points".[79] Ultimately their analysis of the HPAEs legitimated authoritarianism and endeavoured to accommodate the developmental state and ideas about Asian democracy and Asian values to the dominant neo-liberal discourse on development. At the same time, Campos and Root produced a homogenous image of East Asia (which lumped Indonesia with Japan) conflating historically distinct national trajectories and reinforcing a dubious distinction between East and West which will be taken up in more detail in chapter 6.

"The State in a Changing World"

The revision of neo-liberalism, reflected in *The Key to the Asian Miracle* and in the earlier East Asian Miracle Report, was also apparent in *The State in a Changing*

World, published with much fanfare in 1997 by the World Bank.[80] This study reflected the influence of rational choice theory and the new institutionalism discussed previously. The report was a significant departure from the organization's earlier position, and it provides an obvious marker of the ongoing revision of neo-liberalism in which the Bank played an important role. *The State in a Changing World* was a product of the increasing economic significance, and therefore political influence, of the governments of East Asia, particularly Japan, by the first half of the 1990s. The 1997 report exemplified the World Bank's shifting position on the role of the state. Indeed, the entire report is premised on the idea that the state is not just a necessarily important determinant of national economic welfare, but that "its capability – *defined as the ability to undertake and promote collective actions efficiently* – must be increased".[81] Although the report was at pains to describe the actions of Japan and the East Asian states more generally as "market enhancing", it also clearly conceded that the "state" was fundamentally implicated in defining the structure of market-mediated economic relations. In other words, intervention *per se* was not necessarily a problem. Indeed, according to the report "development without an effective state is impossible". East Asia took on a particular significance in this regard as it demonstrated, in the words of the Report, "how government and the private sector can cooperate to achieve rapid growth and shared development". What this amounted to was a heavily qualified endorsement of the close relationships between government and business that characterized the nation-states of Asia. For the late-industrializing nations of East Asia, and by implication for their counterparts in the rest of the so-called developing world, the Report concluded that the state was capable of "not merely laying the foundations of industrial development but actually accelerating it".[82] At the same time, the World Bank's 1997 Report defined an "effective state" in a way that bypassed the wider social context and the social impact of the developmental states in the region. Not surprisingly, as with Campos and Root's 1996 study, the conception of an effective state in East Asia presented in *The State in a Changing World* was grounded in an elite-centered approach to political and economic change that implicitly, if not explicitly, valorized authoritarianism.[83] This is a question to which we will return in chapter 7, on the rise and decline of the developmental state.

The publication of the World Bank's 1997 Report coincided with the onset of the Asian crisis and the discrediting of the very state-guided model that the World Bank had partially accommodated during the 1990s. The Asian crisis will be taken up in the final chapters and the conclusion, but it is worth noting here that the dominant interpretation of the Asian crisis effectively attributed it to the types of relationships between government and business that the World Bank had slowly begun to endorse during the 1990s. Rather than being seen as a source of effective planning and economic development, the governments of East Asia in the wake of the 1997–1998 financial crisis were routinely associated with cronyism, corruption and inefficiency. The Bank's post-crisis position, however, did not involve a reversion to the neo-liberal model of development and the free-trade understanding of the East Asian trajectory it had championed in the early 1980s. Significantly, during the crisis and subsequently there was a marked divergence between the approach taken by the Bank and that of the IMF (the latter organization took a much more prominent role in the management of the Asian crisis). These differences should not be exaggerated. The Bank remains central to the general trend toward market-oriented reform in the region.[84] However, the Bank did question the IMF's handling of the crisis. In the second half of 1997, the IMF embarked on major efforts to restore financial stability to the region via loan packages to the governments of Thailand, Indonesia and South Korea. Its overall approach was premised on the widespread neo-liberal view that the crisis flowed from the distortions and inefficiencies that were characteristic of state-guided capitalism in East Asia. In this context IMF loans were conditional on the implementation of a range of austerity measures and liberalizing initiatives. However, by 1998, the IMF was increasingly being seen as having failed, and/or aggravated a worsening situation, at the same time as other parts of the world were catching the so-called "Asian Flu".[85] Already in late 1997, Joseph Stiglitz, Chief Economist at the World Bank, was challenging the IMF's approach. He argued that the East Asian crisis flowed from poor oversight rather than over-regulation, and the solution was to find the appropriate regulatory arrangements, not to dispense with regulation, a critique that he subsequently outlined in a book-length study.[86]

This critique of the IMF plan for the region by a senior official at the World Bank was soon followed by others also emanating from the World Bank, as well as elsewhere.[87] In fact, the World Bank was in good company, as a growing number of influential policy-makers and economists (including writers such as Jeffrey Sachs, who had played an important role in the spread of neo-liberal ideas and policies, and Paul Krugman) increasingly argued that the crisis in East Asia was the result of a "financial panic" that fuelled a dramatic and unnecessary shift in investor confidence and market expectation, which led to the rapid movement of capital out of the region and the resultant currency collapses.[88] In September 1998 *The Wall Street Journal* described the growing reaction against IMF prescriptions in Asia emanating from the World Bank and elsewhere, and the drift towards capital controls, as "the most serious challenge yet to the free-market orthodoxy that the globe has embraced since the end of the Cold War".[89] At one level, meanwhile, the president of the World Bank, James Wolfensohn – who joined his Chief Economist, Joseph Stiglitz, in criticizing the IMF and criticizing the way the Bank itself had operated, particularly its alienation from those whom it is supposedly intended to help – simply reflected the wider shift that attended the end of the East Asian Miracle as promoters of neo-liberalism sought to respond to criticisms and problems by further revising neo-liberalism.[90] By the end of the 1990s, the World Bank had ostensibly made a shift from "structural adjustment" to a focus on a "comprehensive development framework" that again foregrounded poverty alleviation, the latter having been the stated focus of the Bank's efforts up to the end of the 1970s.[91] This shift has been reinforced by a renewed emphasis, in some quarters, in the wake of the terrorist bombings in New York and Washington on September 11 2001, on the importance of foreign aid and poverty alleviation to engender economic and political stability and undercut the appeal of fundamentalist Islam. However, these reorientations do not represent a retreat from any of the core elements of the US-led globalization project within which the World Bank plays a central role.[92] The World Bank remains profoundly implicated in the dominant technocratic and ahistorical conception of development that is grounded in the naturalization of both distinct and historically contingent national trajectories and the wider process of capitalist transformation itself.

Conclusion: the neo-liberal ascendancy and the East Asian Miracle

The rise of neo-liberalism, which emerged as a complement to, and flowed out of, the reorientation of US hegemony in the 1970s, was central to the wider and increasingly global challenge to state-guided national development by the 1980s. In this chapter the intellectual origins of neo-liberalism have been traced to economists and politicians committed to neo-classical economics that sought to transform the economic policy process in North America and Western Europe (especially in the United States and Great Britain). In the context of the wider shifts of the 1970s, proponents of neo-liberalism became key players in the Thatcher and Reagan administrations. At the same time, this chapter has focused in particular on the neo-liberal ascendancy at the World Bank and the relationship between the changes at the World Bank in the 1980s and the promotion of an understanding of the East Asian Miracle that accorded with the main precepts of neo-classical economics. This led to a major battle for the East Asian Miracle as the Japanese government in particular sought to challenge the dominant interpretation being promoted by the World Bank. The Japanese government's challenge was accommodated to the neo-liberal approach to the East Asian Miracle in the context of the unequal power relations that had framed US–Japan relations throughout the Cold War and into the post-Cold War era. During the 1980s and 1990s the dominant neo-liberal narrative underwent a process of revision, complemented by the growing influence of rational choice theory and the new institutionalism. However, these revisions served primarily to contain the challenge to neo-liberalism represented by the Japanese government and the state-centered Asian model it promoted. The revisions also served to strengthen the technocratic and ahistorical understanding of development central to the dominant narrative on capitalism in Asia and beyond.

Notes

1 John Toye characterized the rise of neo-liberalism as "the counter-revolution in development theory and policy". J. Toye, *Dilemmas of Development*, Oxford: Blackwell, 1987. Michael Todaro represented it as the "neo-classical counter-revolution". M. P. Todaro, *Economic Development in the Third World*, 4th edn, London: Longman, 1989.

2 D. Stone, *Capturing the Political Imagination: Think Tanks and the Policy Process*, London: Frank Cass, 1997. Also see R. Desai, "Second-Hand Dealers in Ideas: Think-Tanks and Thatcherite Hegemony" *New Left Review (I)* no. 203, 1994.

3 F. A. Hayek, *The Road to Serfdom*, Chicago: University of Chicago Press, 1994 (first published 1944); K. R. Popper, *The Open Society and Its Enemies: Volume I Plato*, 5th edn, Princeton: Princeton University Press, 1966; K. R. Popper, *The Open Society and Its Enemies: Volume II Hegel and Marx*, 5th edn, Princeton: Princeton University Press, 1966.

4 R. Cockett, *Thinking the Unthinkable: Think-Tanks and the Economic Counter-Revolution 1931–1983*, Hammersmith: HarperCollins, 1995, pp. 77–85, 97–9, 122–58, 281.

5 S. Blumenthal, *The Rise of the Counter-Establishment: From Conservative Ideology to Political Power*, New York: Times Books, 1986, pp. 4–5, 32–45; J. A. Smith, *The Idea Brokers: Think Tanks and the Rise of the New Policy Elite*, New York: Free Press, 1991, pp. 174–80, 270–1.

6 A particularly early turn to neo-liberalism occurred in Chile, where the economic policies crafted by the so-called Chicago Boys (Chilean economists and technocrats educated at the University of Chicago and other major US universities) were enthusiastically pursued during the dictatorship of General Augusto Pinochet Ugarte (1973–1990) using the not-so-invisible hand of the authoritarian state to dramatically liberalize the economy. J. G. Valdés, *Pinochet's Economists: The Chicago School in Chile*, Cambridge: Cambridge University Press, 1995. At the same time, Margaret Thatcher and other early proponents of neo-liberalism in Britain took a keen interest in Pinochet's experiment in authoritarian neo-liberalism. For example, the British economist Alan Walters visited Chile a number of times in the 1970s and characterized himself as an "honorary Chicago boy". It is now apparent that the economic "shock therapy" carried out in post-1973 Chile directly inspired Thatcher's own experiment in neo-liberalism when she came to power in Britain in 1979. See A. Beckett, *Pinochet in Piccadilly: Britain and Chile's Hidden History*, London: Faber, 2002.

7 C. Leys, *The Rise and Fall of Development Theory*, Bloomington: Indiana University Press, 1996, pp. 17–19.

8 D. Lal, *The Poverty of Development Economics*, 2nd edn, Cambridge, MA: Harvard University Press, 1985 (first published in 1983 by the Institute of Economic Affairs), pp. 103–6.

9 P. T. Bauer, *Equality, the Third World, and Economic Delusion*, Cambridge, MA: Harvard University Press, 1981; P. T. Bauer, *Reality and Rhetoric: Studies in the Economics of Development*, London: Weidenfeld and Nicolson, 1984.

10 Cockett, *Thinking the Unthinkable*, pp. 30, 109, 116, 119, 143, 153, 218, 265, 281.

11 R. Wade, "Japan, the World Bank, and the Art of Paradigm Maintenance: The East Asian Miracle in Political Perspective", *New Left Review (I)* no. 217, 1996, p. 5. Also see C. Payer, *The World Bank: A Critical Analysis*, New York: Monthly Review Press, 1982, pp. 15–21.

12 Alexander Cairncross cited in C. Caufield, *Masters of Illusion: The World Bank and the Poverty of Nations*, New York: Henry Holt, 1996, pp. 62–3, 196–7.

13 R. S. McNamara, *One Hundred Countries, Two Billion People: The Dimensions of Development*, New York: Henry Holt, 1973.

14 R. A. Packenham, *Liberal America and the Third World: Political Development Ideas in Foreign Aid and Social Science*, Princeton: Princeton University Press, 1973, pp. 52–3.

15 D. Morawetz, *Twenty-Five Years of Economic Development 1950–1975*, Baltimore: Johns Hopkins University Press for the World Bank, 1977.

16 World Bank, *World Development Report 1980*, Washington, DC: World Bank, 1980, p. 3.

17 For a detailed analysis of the move to Structural Adjustment Loans (SALs) and Sectoral Adjustment Loans (SECALs) by the World Bank see P. Mosley, J. Harrigan and J. Toye, *Aid and Power: The World Bank and Policy-Based Lending* (volume 1: Analysis and Policy Proposals), London: Routledge, 1991, pp. 21–3, 27–61. Also see P. Mosley, J. Harrigan and J. Toye, *Aid and Power: The World Bank and Policy-based Lending* (volume 2: Case Studies), London: Routledge, 1991.

18 On the history of the World Bank in the 1960s and 1970s and the shift to neo-liberalism in the 1980s see D. Kapur, J. Lewis and R. Webb, *The World Bank: Its First Half-Century, Volume 1: History*, Washington, DC: Brookings Institution, 1997, pp. 1–379.

19 Caufield, *Masters of Illusion*, pp. 144–5, 178, 197.

20 Wade, "Japan, the World Bank, and the Art of Paradigm Maintenance", pp. 16, 30–1, 35–6.

21 World Bank, *Accelerated Development in Sub-Saharan Africa: An Agenda for Action*, Washington, DC: World Bank, 1981.

22 Mosley, Harrigan and Toye, *Aid and Power* (volume 1), pp. 23–4.

23 J. Martinussen, *Society, State and Market*, London: Zed Books, 1997, pp. 51–2, 66–70.

24 Cited in Caufield, *Masters of Illusion*, pp. 144–5.

25 Mosley, Harrigan and Toye, *Aid and Power* (volume 1), pp. 24–5.

26 Caufield, *Masters of Illusion*, pp. 178–80, 266.

27 Mosley, Harrigan and Toye, *Aid and Power* (volume 1), pp. 24–5.

28 Todaro, *Economic Development in the Third World*, pp. 83–4; M. B. Brown, *Africa's Choices: After Thirty Years of the World Bank*, London: Penguin, 1995, pp. 5–6, 29–49.

29 E. K. Y. Chen, *Hyper-Growth in Asian Economies: A Comparative Study of Hong Kong, Japan, Korea, Singapore and Taiwan*, London: Macmillan, 1979, p. 41.

30 M. Friedman and R. Friedman, *Free to Choose: A Personal Statement*, New York: Harcourt Brace Jovanovich, 1980, p. 57.

31 D. Aikman, *The Pacific Rim: Area of Change, Area of Opportunity*, Boston: Little Brown, 1986, p. 116.

32 S. B. Linder, *The Pacific Century: Economic and Political Consequences of Asian-Pacific Dynamism*, Stanford: Stanford University Press, 1986, p. 4.

33 M. Thatcher, "The Triumph of Trade" *Far Eastern Economic Review* September 2, 1993, p. 23.

34 F. Fukuyama, "The End of History?" *The National Interest* vol. 16, no. 8, 1989, pp. 3–4, 15.

35 F. Fukuyama *The End of History and the Last Man*, London: Hamish Hamilton, 1992, pp. 101–7, 243.

36 I. M. D. Little, *Economic Development: Theory, Policy and International Relations*, New York: Basic Books, A Twentieth Century Fund Book, 1982, p. 141.

37 I. M. D. Little, "The Experiences and Causes of Labour-Intensive Development in Korea, Taiwan Province, Hong Kong and Singapore and the Possibilities of Emulation" in E. Lee, ed., *Export Processing Zones and Industrial Employment in Asia*, Bangkok: International Labour Organization/Artep, 1981. Also see I. M. D. Little, "An Economic Reconnaissance" in W. Galenson, ed., *Economic Growth and Structural Change in Taiwan: The Post-War Experience of the Republic of China*, Ithaca: Cornell University Press, 1979.

38 I. Islam and A. Chowdhury, *The Political Economy of East Asia: Post-Crisis Debates*, New York: Oxford University Press, 2000, pp. 6–7.

39 See W. Galenson, ed., *Foreign Trade and Investment: Economic Growth in the Newly Industrializing Asian Countries*, Madison: University of Wisconsin Press, 1985; V. Corbo, A. O. Krueger and F. Ossa, *Export-Oriented Development Strategies*, Boulder: Westview, 1985; H. Hughes, ed., *Achieving Industrialization in East Asia*, Cambridge: Cambridge University Press, 1988; W. E. James, S. Naya and G. M. Meier, *Asian Development: Economic Success and Policy Lessons*, Madison: University of Wisconsin Press, 1989; A. O. Krueger, "Asian Trade and Growth Lessons" *American Economic Review* vol. 80, no. 2, 1990.

40 B. Balassa, *The Newly Industrializing Countries in the World Economy*, New York: Pergamon Press, 1981.

41 B. Balassa, "The Lessons of East Asian Development: An Overview" *Economic Development and Cultural Change* vol. 36, no. 3, supplement, 1988, pp. S280–1, S286–8.

42 See World Bank, *Korea's Experience with the Development of Trade and Industry: Lessons for Latin America*, Washington, DC: World Bank, 1988.
43 M. T. Berger and M. Beeson, "Lineages of Liberalism and Miracles of Modernisation: The World Bank, the East Asian Trajectory and the International Development Debate" *Third World Quarterly: Journal of Emerging Areas* vol. 19, no. 3, 1998.
44 D. Williams, "Constructing the Economic Space: The World Bank and the Making of *Homo Oeconomicus*" *Millennium: Journal of International Studies* vol. 28, no. 1, 1999, pp. 79–81.
45 T. Gyohten, "Japan and the World Bank" in D. Kapur, J. P. Lewis and R. Webb, eds, *The World Bank: Its First Half Century, Volume 2: Perspectives*, Washington, DC: Brookings Institution, 1997, pp. 298–303. For an exhaustive journalistic analysis of this challenge see E. Terry, *How Asia Got Rich: Japan, China and the Asian Miracle*, Armonk: M. E. Sharpe, 2002, especially pp. 238–334.
46 W. Hatch and K. Yamamura, *Asia in Japan's Embrace: Building a Regional Production Alliance*, Cambridge: Cambridge University Press, 1996.
47 Wade, "Japan, the World Bank, and the Art of Paradigm Maintenance" , pp. 6–9.
48 L. Thurow, *Head To Head: The Coming Economic Battle Among Japan, Europe and America*, Sydney: Allen and Unwin, 1992.
49 H. E. S. Nesadurai, "APEC: a tool for US regional domination?" *The Pacific Review* vol. 9, no. 1, 1996, p. 52.
50 For an overview of APEC's history see J. Ravenhill, *APEC and the Construction of Pacific Rim Regionalism*, Cambridge: Cambridge University Press, 2001.
51 C. F. Bergsten, "APEC and the World Economy: A Force for Worldwide Liberalisation" *Foreign Affairs* vol. 73, no. 3, 1994. For a similar perspective see R. Garnaut, *Open Regionalism and Trade Liberalization: An Asia-Pacific Contribution to the World Trade System*, Singapore: Institute of Southeast Asia Studies, 1996. Also see APEC Eminent Persons Group, *A Vision for APEC: Towards an Asia Pacific Economic Community*, Singapore: APEC Secretariat, October 1993; APEC Eminent Persons Group, *Achieving the APEC Vision: Free and Open Trade in the Asia Pacific*, Singapore: APEC Secretariat, August 1994; APEC Eminent Persons Group, *Implementing the APEC Vision*, Singapore: APEC Secretariat, August 1995.
52 Y. Funabashi, *Asia Pacific Fusion: Japan's Role in APEC*, Washington, DC: Institute for International Economics, 1995, pp. 58–69.
53 S. Abe, "Prospects for Asian Economic Integration" in S. Nishijima and P. H. Smith, eds, *Cooperation or Rivalry? Regional Integration in the Americas and the Pacific Rim*, Boulder: Westview, 1996, pp. 244–5.
54 Wade, "Japan, the World Bank, and the Art of Paradigm Maintenance", p. 9.
55 Funabashi, *Asia Pacific Fusion*, pp. 68–9.
56 "Saying No" *The Economist* November 25, p. 31.
57 M. T. Berger, "The New Asian Renaissance and Its Discontents: National Narratives, Pan-Asian Visions and the Changing Post-Cold War Order" *International Politics: A Journal of Transnational Issues and Global Problems* vol. 40, no. 2, 2003.
58 World Bank, *World Development Report 1991: The Challenge of Development*, Washington, DC: World Bank, 1991; Wade, "Japan, the World Bank, and the Art of Paradigm Maintenance", p. 10.
59 Wade, "Japan, the World Bank, and the Art of Paradigm Maintenance", pp. 10–11.
60 Cited in P. Evans, *Embedded Autonomy: States and Industrial Transformation*, Princeton: Princeton University Press, 1995, p. 21.
61 World Bank, *The East Asian Miracle: Economic Growth and Public Policy*, Oxford: Oxford University Press for the World Bank, 1993, pp. 2, 347, 366–8.
62 Wade, "Japan, the World Bank, and the Art of Paradigm Maintenance", p. 23.
63 A. Amsden, "Why Isn't the Whole World Experimenting with the East Asian Model to Develop? Review of the East Asian Miracle" *World Development* vol. 22, no. 4, 1994;

J. Kwon, "The East Asian Challenge to Neoclassical Orthodoxy" *World Development* vol. 22, no. 4, 1994; J. M. Page, "The East Asian Miracle: An Introduction" *World Development* vol. 22, no. 4, 1994; D. Perkins, "There Are At Least Three Models of East Asian Development" *World Development* vol. 22, no. 4, 1994; T. Yanagihara, "Anything New in the *Miracle* Report? Yes and No" *World Development* vol. 22, no. 4, 1994.

64 S. Lall, " 'The East Asian Miracle' Study: Does the Bell Toll for Industrial Strategy?" *World Development* vol. 22, no. 4, 1994, pp. 646, 651–2.

65 Evans, *Embedded Autonomy*, p. 28.

66 P. Krugman, "The Myth of Asia's Miracle" *Foreign Affairs* vol. 73, no. 6, 1994, pp. 62–78.

67 A. Young, "A Tale of Two Cities: Factor Accumulation and Technical Change in Hong Kong and Singapore" in O. J. Blanchard and S. Fischer, eds, *NBER Macroeconomics Annual 1992*, Cambridge, MA: MIT Press, 1992; A. Young, "Lessons from the East Asian NICs: A Contrarian View" *European Economic Review* no. 38, 1994.

68 P. Krugman, *Strategic Trade Policy and the New International Economics*, Cambridge, MA: MIT Press, 1986, p. 15 (italics in original). Also see P. Krugman, *Pop Internationalism*, 2nd edn, Cambridge, MA: MIT Press, 1997, pp. 108–16.

69 S. Lall, *Learning from the Asian Tigers: Studies in Technology and Industrial Policy*, London: Macmillan, 1996, pp. 4, 215.

70 D. P. Green and I. Shapiro, *Pathologies of Rational Choice Theory: A Critique of Applications in Political Science*, New Haven: Yale University Press, 1994.

71 For example, some critics treat the rational choice trend in development theory as a relatively homogenous perspective (the "new institutional political economy") that they differentiate from neo-classical economics on the one hand and Marxist-derived political economy on the other. R. Robison, G. Rodan and K. Hewison, "Introduction" in G. Rodan, K. Hewison and R. Robison, eds, *The Political Economy of South-East Asia: An Introduction*, Melbourne: Oxford University Press, 1997, pp. 9–15.

72 J. Harriss, J. Hunter and C. M. Lewis, "Introduction: Development and the Significance of New Institutional Economics" in J. Harriss, J. Hunter and C. M. Lewis, eds, *The New Institutional Economics and Third World Development*, 2nd edn, London: Routledge, 1997.

73 Leys, *The Rise and Fall of Development Theory*, pp. 82–4.

74 D. C. North, *Structure and Change in Economic History*, New York: W. W. Norton, 1981; D. C. North, *Institutional Change and Economic Performance*, Cambridge: Cambridge University Press, 1990.

75 R. H. Bates, *Markets and States in Tropical Africa: The Political Basis of Agricultural Policies*, Berkeley: University of California Press, 1981; R. H. Bates, *Essays on the Political Economy of Rural Africa*, Berkeley: University of California Press, 1987; R. H. Bates, *Beyond the Miracle of the Market: The Political Economy of Agrarian Development in Kenya*, Cambridge: Cambridge University Press 1989.

76 Leys, *The Rise and Fall of Development Theory*, pp. 36–7, 80–2.

77 J. E. Campos and H. L. Root, *The Key to the Asian Miracle: Making Shared Growth Credible*, Washington, DC: Brookings Institution, 1996, p. viii.

78 Campos and Root, *The Key to the Asian Miracle*, pp. 1–3.

79 Campos and Root, *The Key to the Asian Miracle*, pp. 174–7.

80 World Bank, *World Development Report 1997: The State in a Changing World*, New York: Oxford University Press, 1997.

81 World Bank, *World Development Report 1997*, p. 3 (italics in original).

82 World Bank, *World Development Report 1997*, pp. 6, 24, 46, 61.

83 Asia Monitor Resource Centre, *Everyone's State? Redefining an "Effective State" in East Asia*, Hong Kong: Asia Monitor Resource Centre, 1997, pp. 6, 24–6.

84 M. T. Berger and M. Beeson, "Miracles of Modernisation and Crises of Capitalism: The World Bank, Liberal Hegemony and East Asian Development" in D. Moore, ed.,

Banking on Hegemony: Critical Essays on the World Bank's Development Discourse, Pietermaritzburg: University of Natal Press/London: Zed Press, 2003.
85 J. Sachs, "The IMF and the Asian Flu" *The American Prospect* no. 37, 1998.
86 J. E. Stiglitz, *Globalisation and Its Discontents*, New York: W. W. Norton, 2002. Also see J. E. Stiglitz and S. Yusuf, eds, *Rethinking the East Asian Miracle*, New York: Oxford University Press, 2001; H.-J. Chang, ed., *Joseph Stiglitz and the World Bank: The Rebel Within*, London: Anthem, 2002.
87 For an overview of this trend see R. Wade and F. Veneroso, "The Resources Lie Within" *The Economist* November 7, 1998, pp. 19–21. Also see R. Wade and F. Veneroso, "The Gathering World Slump and the Battle Over Capital Controls" *New Left Review (I)* no. 231, 1998; R. Wade, "The Asian Crisis and the Global Economy: Causes, Consequences, and Cure" *Current History* vol. 97, no. 622, 1998.
88 For example see J. Sachs, "Global Capitalism: Making It Work" *The Economist* September 12, 1998, pp. 19–23; P. Krugman, "Saving Asia: It's Time to Get Radical" *Fortune* September 7, 1998, pp. 32–7.
89 D. Wessell and B. Davis, "Currency Controls Gain a Hearing as Crisis in Asia Takes Its Toll" *The Wall Street Journal* September 4, 1998, pp. A1–A2.
90 For example, see J. D. Wolfensohn, "People First", Paul Hoffman Lecture, New York, May 29, 1997. Online at http://www.worldbank.org
91 J. Pender, "From 'Structural Adjustment' to 'Comprehensive Development Framework': Conditionality Transformed?" *Third World Quarterly: Journal of Emerging Areas* vol. 22, no. 3 (June), 2001, pp. 397–411.
92 P. Cammack, "Attacking the Global Poor" *New Left Review (II)* no. 13, 2002, pp. 125–32.

6 The vicissitudes of the New Asian Renaissance

The revision of neo-liberalism in the 1980s and 1990s and the effort by the Japanese government to defend state-guided national development were paralleled by, and overlapped with, the emergence of culturally and racially oriented explanations for the East Asian Miracle inside and outside of the Asia-Pacific. Linked to these approaches were increasingly strident concerns that the rise of East Asia, especially Japan (and latterly China) was a threat to the "West".[1] By the early 1990s, the notion of a "New Asian Renaissance" had emerged as a somewhat amorphous term that captured the dramatic economic, political and cultural changes transforming the region.[2] For some commentators the New Asian Renaissance encompassed the many "non-Asian" nation-states and peoples in the Asia-Pacific, while for others it encapsulated a more exclusive Pan-Asianism.[3] East Asian commentators and political leaders also increasingly held up Asian values and virtues as not only the key to the region's success but also as a model for the West. This chapter begins by looking briefly at the question of culture and race in the debate about the causes of Japan's post-1945 economic success. This is followed by an examination of the popular debate inside and outside of the region about the cultural roots of Asian capitalism generally. It then turns to a discussion of key strands of the narratives about Asian values and neo-Confucianism in the late Cold War and early post-Cold War era, looking particularly at Singapore and Malaysia, which were the sites for, and the sources of, the most influential and sustained articulation of Asian values and/or the idea of a New Asian Renaissance. This section ends with a short discussion of the possible re-emergence, in the wake of the Asian crisis, of the more exclusive Asian regional organization that many of the promoters of the New Asian Renaissance, such as Prime Minister Mahathir Mohamad of Malaysia, sought, unsuccessfully, to establish as an alternative to APEC at the very beginning of the 1990s. The final section looks at the significance of cultural nationalism in the economic rise of China after 1978. This chapter emphasizes that both the dominant East Asian-based narratives and many of the cultural explanations provided by commentators outside the region rested, and/or continue to rest on a dubious distinction between East and West and on generally fixed notions of culture/race. At the same time, the continued, but changing, salience of racialized politics, and fixed conceptions of culture in Asia, can only be understood in terms of the dynamics of both specific national trajectories and their wider geo-political and economic context. The deployment of Asian values and neo-Confucian ideas in the 1980s and 1990s, against the backdrop of new regional initiatives, reflected an important attempt by national elites in East Asia to reposition themselves and retain, or strengthen, the legitimacy of often authoritarian political arrangements in the context of the dramatic capitalist transformation of the Asia-Pacific over the preceding decades.

Promoting the New Asian Renaissance I

The Japanese model II: "Asia's New Giant"

With the rise of Japan as an economic challenge to the US in the 1970s, the debate about its development and its position as an exemplar of modernization took on new significance.[4] This was parallelled by a renewed interest in the cultural dynamics of Japan's post-1945 resurgence. Interestingly, the debate about Japan's economic success was far less contentious in the 1950s and 1960s than it became in the 1970s and 1980s. In the 1960s influential observers such as William Lockwood emphasized an "interweaving" network "of influences and pressures" connecting government and business ("a web without a spider") that underpinned the Japanese trajectory.[5] Meanwhile, in *East Asia: Tradition and Transformation* (1973), which was – as has already been noted – a key English language text on East Asia in the 1970s and 1980s, Edwin O. Reischauer, John K. Fairbank and Albert Craig identified a "particular Japanese combination of free enterprise and government guidance", noting that the government played more of a role in economic planning in Japan than anywhere else in the capi-talist world.[6] Up to the 1970s government/state intervention to facilitate modernization was far more acceptable in the United States itself, making this analysis of the role of the state in Japanese economic development relatively uncontentious. Japan was also a key ally in the wider US containment strategy in Asia. Furthermore, post-1945 Japan was widely perceived as a developing, rather than a developed, nation-state and the degree of state intervention that was viewed as necessary for developing nations was even greater than that required for developed nations such as the United States.[7]

In the context of the incipient rise of neo-liberalism, however, influential commentators challenged the view that Japanese economic growth was a result of a *dirigiste* history. The effort to encourage the Japanese government to adopt more liberal economic policies was clearly linked to attempts to challenge the view that illiberal economic policies were the key to Japan's success. An early and influential example of this view is to be found in the massive edited collection by Hugh Patrick and Henry Rosovsky, entitled *Asia's New Giant* (1976). This book brought together a group of neo-classical economists who expressed scepticism about the importance of industrial policy in Japan's post-1945 phoenix-like rise from the ashes of defeat.[8] In a 1977 article that reiterated the main thrust of *Asia's New Giant*, Hugh Patrick argued that Japan's impressive economic performance was "due primarily to the actions and efforts of private individuals and enterprises responding to the opportunities provided in quite free markets for commodities and labor". He emphasized that, although "the government has been supportive and indeed has done much to create the environment of growth, its role has often been exaggerated".[9] By contrast other academics and journalists, writing in the late 1970s and 1980s, rejected neo-classical explanations and built on Lockwood's assessment to present Japan as a new type of capitalism that involved a high degree of state intervention characterized by steady economic growth and political stability.[10] While some observers tended to emphasize a leading role for the government, others outlined what became known as the "network state". Daniel Okimoto, for example, argued that the ruling elite in Japan (encompassing senior managers, government bureaucrats and politicians) had a common social background that ensured an array of close, albeit informal, ties linking corporations to the ruling party and the state. This was undergirded by more formal institutional arrangements that provided sites for business and government representatives to interact regularly and develop common policies and ideas regarding economic development.[11] The work of Okimoto and others was influenced by and interacted with the theory of the developmental state that emerged in the 1980s. A key text in the emergence of the theory of the developmental state was Chalmers Johnson's 1982 study of the role of Ministry of International Trade and Industry in Japanese economic development between the 1920s and the 1970s.[12]

With the demise of the Soviet Union, vulgarized versions of the network state and/or the developmental state, along with other approaches that emphasized the close connection between government and business in Japan, were increasingly deployed in a fashion that represented Japan as a mysterious and irrational threat to US economic and even politico-military power.[13] For example, Karel Van Wolferen's book, *The Enigma of Japanese Power* (first published 1989), makes clear the way in which state-led industrialization and a tradition of technological borrowing facilitated the rise of Japan; however, he also falls back on orientalizing racial and cultural stereotypes. Van Wolferen represents the Japanese as irrational and illogical, and the immobilism of the Japanese political system is explained in reductionist cultural terms.[14] The powerful images of Japan as a threat to the US, and to the West more generally, which had gained influence by the end of the 1980s, meshed with long standing but fluctuating anxieties about both a non-specific "Yellow Peril" or a more specific Japanese "threat". The popular influence of this trend was reflected in the cinematic and publishing success of Michael Crichton's *Rising Sun*. In an afterword to the 1992 novel Crichton warned that: "sooner or later, the United States must come to grips with the fact that Japan has become the leading industrial nation in the world". He argued that "the Japanese have invented a new kind of trade – adversarial trade, trade like war, trade intended to wipe out the competition – which America has failed to understand for several decades". In his view it was time "for the United States to wake up, to see Japan clearly, and to act realistically" because "the Japanese are not our saviours" but "our competitors" and "we should not forget it".[15] This concern was taken even further in a novel by Tom Clancy that described how a US–Japanese trade war escalated into a real war in which a nuclear-armed Japan (with the support of the governments of China and India) set out to cripple the US financially and militarily, at the same time as it prepared to embark on the conquest of resource-rich Siberia.[16] The image of Japan (allied with India and China) as an undifferentiated oriental threat to the US and the West – which in Clancy's narrative also reincorporated Russia – was made somewhat problematic by the way his book portrayed the Japanese government as having been hijacked by a handful of powerful business and military men who had not forgotten their defeat by the US in 1945. However, in a 1994 interview, Clancy registered a more homogenous conception of the Japanese threat arguing that "the Japanese think we are fools" and they "still believe the master-race thing". In his view the US "pounded that out of the Germans, but not out of the Japanese" and "they still think they are the elected of God or Buddha or whatever. They just think they are better than everyone else."[17] Significantly, at the end of the 1990s, when, after a decade of economic decline, it was increasingly difficult to view Japan as a rising economic superpower, Clancy produced a novel that represented China not Japan as the primary threat to the United States (with Russia again represented as a US ally).[18]

"The Japan That Can Say No"

The racial/cultural reductionism of Crichton and Clancy in the early 1990s was often reinforced more than it was challenged by those commentaries and studies produced in Japan and East Asia that also deployed culture/race to explain Japan's post-1945 trajectory. But, despite Japan's special position in the transformation of Asia, and its growing influence in the region, Washington's continued role as the guarantor of Japanese security meant that most Japanese political leaders and intellectuals remained relatively circumspect in the international arena regarding the cause and significance of the resurgence of Japan and the rise of East Asia more generally.[19] Nevertheless, by the early 1990s, increasingly influential Japanese voices sought to speak for East Asia and/or to counter the dominant economic and political liberalism of the US-led globalization project. Representatives of the Japanese government increasingly sought to challenge the neo-liberal ascendancy at the World Bank in the late Cold War and early post-Cold War era. Meanwhile, important Japanese politicians and bureaucrats also sought to defend the state-centered Japanese model in more explicitly cultural if not racial terms. The most prominent articulator of a highly racialized vision of the Japanese model in this period was Ishihara Shintaro. A former member of the ruling Liberal Democratic Party (LDP), Ishihara stepped down from his seat in Parliament at the end of the 1990s and was subsequently elected governor of Tokyo. He is best known outside of Japan for his book, *The Japan That Can Say No: Why Japan Will Be First Among Equals*, that came out in English in 1991.[20] An earlier version, which was co-authored with Morita Akio, the head of Sony, was published in Japanese in 1989 as *No To Ieru Nihon*. While an unauthorized English-language edition that was financed by the US Department of Defence included Morita's contribution, he withdrew from the authorized North American edition.[21] Ishihara's understanding of US–Japan relations, and international relations more generally, clearly rested on racial categories. He characterized the US as a "Caucasian" power and the friction between the US and Japan as grounded in the way in which "racist attitudes are deeply entrenched in the Caucasian psyche" and "no matter how much non-whites object, Westerners will not soon shed their prejudices". At the same time he attributed South Korea and Taiwan's post-1945 success, and the economic failure of the Philippines, to their respective colonizers, implying Japanese cultural/racial superiority. Apart from viewing history as a struggle between races, Ishihara argued that Japan "must be part of Asia's future" because "as the Age of the Pacific dawns, the region will be even more vital to Japan's maturity than the United States" and Japan "must, when matters of crucial national interest warrant, articulate our position and say no to the United States".[22]

Another figure that emerged as a relatively outspoken, but much more moderate, advocate of the Japanese model in the 1990s was Sakakibara Eisuke. A senior official in the Japanese finance ministry in this period, eventually rising to the post of vice-minister of finance for international affairs, Sakakibara rejected the more traditional and racialized forms of Japanese nationalism (such as one associates with Ishihara) at the same time as he expressed a determination to protect what he thought was distinctively Japanese from the depredations of the West. Furthermore, in his book *Beyond Capitalism* (1993) he also represented the Japanese model as being "of great educational value for future economic development in areas such as Latin America, South-East Asia and Africa". He argued that Japan was a "non-capitalist market economy" insofar as companies competed in the market; however, they did not privilege profit over everything else and shareholders had virtually no power. From his perspective Japanese companies put people before profits, keeping loyal employees on the payroll even if there is an economic downturn, while the government worked to protect industry even at the expense of wider questions of economic efficiency. Sakakibara, who was also involved with a study group of Japanese politicians, academics and business leaders, held the Japanese model up in sharp contrast to the US model, and warned that if Japan went down the North American road the result would be "a wider gap in income distribution, rampant money worship and the vulgarization of culture".[23] In 1997, in the context of the onset of the Asian crisis, Sakakibara insisted that there was "a Japanese style of restructuring" that was "different from the Anglo-Saxon style".[24]

Meanwhile, the work of other Japanese politicians and academics complemented the populist cultural perspective on Japan's post-1945 success provided by Sakakibara. For example, in his now-standard work on the economic development of Japan, development economist Yoshihara Kunio emphasized the important role of Confucianism, particularly its emphasis on loyalty and filial piety, in explaining Japan's rise. Yoshihara argued that Confucianism was important in the Japanese case in the same way that Protestantism had, in his view, catalysed the rise of the West. He also argued that the best way to hasten economic development was through the intervention of the government or a developmental state that educates the people and initiates a dynamic private sector.[25] This interpretation reflected the wider popular narrative on the superiority of a Japanese and/or an Asian model based on a developmental state that commanded obedience and loyalty from the population of the nation. Yoshihara's emphasis on the lessons of the Japanese experience and their relevance for other nation-states in the region and beyond was reinforced, for example, by public statements by the former Prime Minister of Japan, Nakasone Yasuhiro, in 1995. Nakasone argued that post-1945 Japan was a new economic development model that had been central to the rise of East Asia and it represented "a profoundly important gift" to the rest of the world.[26]

The new Confucianism I: the Confucian ethic and the spirit of Asian capitalism

By the 1980s, with the dramatic rise of South Korea, Taiwan, Hong Kong and Singapore, the Confucian origins of Japan's success also began to enjoy greater emphasis. This trend was underpinned by conservative nostalgia for order and hierarchy in the region and beyond. Writers such as Hung-chao Tai argued that the "cultural setting" of Japan and the East Asian Newly Industrializing Countries (NICs) gave rise to what he described as an "Oriental" economic development model.[27] Meanwhile, Michio Morishima's influential book, *Why Has Japan Succeeded? Western Technology and the Japanese Ethos* (1989) emphasized that the key to Japan's success was closely linked to the wider Confucian heritage of East Asia.[28] This kind of approach exemplified the work of a growing band of academic observers, based inside and outside the region, which highlighted the role of culture generally, and Confucianism, or what Herman Kahn described as the "Confucian ethic", more specifically, in industrialization and national development.[29] Ironically, at the turn of the century, Max Weber, along with many others, had represented Confucianism as the key to China's historic decline and economic backwardness.[30] After the Second World War, the communist revolution in China and the rise of communism in Vietnam ensured that Confucianism was deployed in some cases to explain the region's susceptibility to communism.[31] By the 1980s, however, Confucianism was being held up as the key to capitalist success. For example, Roy Hofheinz and Kent Calder attached considerable importance to the Confucian legacy in relation to East Asian industrialization. They pointed to Lee Kuan Yew, former Prime Minister and now Senior Minister of Singapore, as a "quintessential Confucian leader", they linked high saving rates and hard work, as well as the "docility" of the work force, to Confucianism, arguing that the people of East Asia "tend to prefer compromise rather than confrontation, and the work-place is an arena for cooperation in the process of growth not for conflict over the spoils".[32] Undoubtedly one of the most well-known efforts to link Confucianism to the capitalist transformation of Asia after 1945 is S. Gordon Redding's *The Spirit of Chinese Capitalism* (1990).[33] Some earlier writers who emphasized the importance of Confucianism, such as Herman Kahn who explained the emergence of "neo-Confucian economies" in relation to wider changes in the 1970s, at least gestured towards the wider historical context. However, in Redding's study history is distinctly absent.[34] Instead, he uses a selective reading of Confucian (as well as Buddhist and Taoist) texts to construct a "cultural heritage" for Chinese entrepreneurs and businesses that he sees as having contributed "to their capacity to organize themselves so effectively" for business.[35]

The analysis provided by Redding reflects a widespread popular and journalistic device via which contemporary attitudes and practices are collapsed into Confucianism and other Asian cultural traditions. In this formulation, the contemporary economic success of East Asia is explained without recourse to history, but by turning instead to what the authors of the *New Asian Emperors* (1998), for example, present as the shared "philosophical and cultural roots" of the region.[36] The idea that Confucianism and/or Asian culture more generally were the key to the East Asian Miracle pervaded popular North American and Western European visions of the region by the 1990s. For example, the journalist and novelist Robert Elegant argued that "Neo-Confucian behaviour has produced the world's most dynamic nations: not only Taiwan, Korea, and, of course, Japan, but also the city-states of Singapore and Hong Kong." He went on to emphasize that "[e]xcept for Japan and Korea, they are also predominantly Chinese by race" at the same time as the "small overseas Chinese minority" spearheaded "the economic development of Southeast Asian nations, largely because of the Confucian work ethic".[37] Meanwhile, T. R. Reid produced a book-length study at the end of the 1990s, which celebrated "East Asia's social miracle". Reid, an Asia-based correspondent for *The Washington Post*, enthused that "Asians have built modern industrial societies characterized by the safest streets, the best schools and the most stable families in the world." He concluded that "a sense of civility and harmony that you can feel" had been "achieved ... primarily by holding to a set of ethical values – what they call Confucian values".[38] This celebration of Confucian values generally, and the work ethic of Chinese entrepreneurs more specifically, appears to have more to do with a conservative nostalgia for family and hierarchy in North America and a romantic vision of the way that hard work and entrepreneurial acumen (in a recapitulation of the romanticized conception of the role of Protestantism in the rise of the West) ostensibly provide the motor for capitalist transformation. The celebration and naturalization of neo-Confucian values and virtues has emerged out of the conjuncture of the economic rise of East Asia and the nostalgic and romantic response by outside observers. It has also flowed out of various efforts by elites in the region to selectively draw on their cultural legacy to consolidate their leadership in a time of dramatic change.

Promoting the New Asian Renaissance II

The new Confucianism II: Singapore

If it is possible to see the idea of the "New Asian Renaissance" as having been formally launched then it was done by Noordin Sopiee, the convenor of the Commission for a New Asia, who was also head of the Institute of Strategic Studies in Kuala Lumpur and a member of the Board of Directors of the Central Bank and the National Economic Action Council (NEAC) in Malaysia. Noordin argued that "Towards a New Asia", a document that was published in December 1993 by the Commission for a New Asia, was a veritable "manifesto for a new Asian Renaissance".[39] Noordin's grand vision reflected the fact that from the late 1980s until 1997 some of the most vocal proponents of the New Asian Renaissance, were to be found in Southeast Asia, especially Malaysia and Singapore, which, as already noted, were particularly central to the promotion of Asian values and the New Asian Renaissance. This was partly a result of the fact that English remains an important language in these former British colonies, which meant that the views of politicians and intellectuals were more easily projected to the international media. Furthermore, the multi-ethnic character of these erstwhile colonies has meant that ruling elites have been attracted to political strategies based on appeals to Asian unity, although strategies that emphasized ethnic or religious differences have also been used. The new strength of these elite voices celebrating a New Asian Renaissance and Asian values was apparent in the lead-up to the Vienna Human Rights Conference held on June 14–25 1993.[40] Prior to the Conference a growing number of Asian leaders were already expressing dissatisfaction with dominant international conceptions of human rights, arguing in favor of particularly Asian notions of human rights. A central criticism has been that ideas of human rights based on the individual are Western and therefore irrelevant to Asia where individual rights are secondary to the community and the wider society. This is a distinction that was often made in this period by Singaporean leaders such as Lee Kuan Yew and Goh Chok Tong, who succeeded Lee as Prime Minister in the early 1990s.[41] While the explanation for, and the lessons of, the rise of East Asia articulated by Lee Kuan Yew and the Singaporean elite are often expansive and vague in both spatial and temporal terms, they are grounded in Singapore's particular historical circumstances. The colonial division of labor and the highly racialized social formation that grew up under British rule laid the foundations for race, ethnicity and religion to serve as key social markers in the postcolonial period.[42] Since the early 1960s the People's Action Party (PAP), under Lee Kuan Yew, has built a strong state aimed at a high level of political and social control, at the same time as it has provided rising living standards and dramatic economic growth. As the Singaporean state, under the PAP, embarked on an economic development program, based after 1965 around export-oriented industrialization (EOI), it developed and extended its institutional power and the PAP-state emerged as a key element in the shaping of national identity and ethnic consciousness. In this context the notion of Asian values was increasingly deployed by Lee Kuan Yew and the Singaporean elite to legitimate and maintain the power of the PAP-state and generate unity amongst a multi-ethnic population.[43]

The PAP pointed to the West with ever increasing frequency by the 1970s, as the source of political unrest and social decay in the city-state. In his speech on National Day in 1978, Lee Kuan Yew argued that Singapore had, in effect, "already been infected" by the West and the "antidote" was the "strong assertion of the Asian values common to all Singapore's ethnic groups, stressing the virtues of individual subordination to the community so as to counteract the disruptive individualism of western liberalism". In the 1980s the elite increasingly represented Singapore as the embodiment of the communitarian, organic, and corporatist social order that was believed to have underpinned the political stability and economic development of the other Asian NICs and Japan. Clearly demonstrating the complementary relationship between cultural/racial explanations for the rise of East Asia provided by Anglo-American discourses and East Asian narratives, Lee Kuan Yew and Goh Chok Tong both referred in this period to a book edited by George Lodge and Ezra Vogel, entitled *Ideology and National Competitiveness* (1987), in which a neo-Confucian developmental state was held out as the key to the rise of East Asia.[44] There were also a number of high profile conferences in Singapore, including one in September 1987 co-sponsored by the China-based China Foundation of Confucius and the Institute of East Asian Philosophies at the National University of Singapore, on the relationship between Confucianism and industrialization. Key participants in these events included William Theodore de Bary of Columbia University and the Harvard-based specialist on Confucianism, Tu Wei-ming.[45] Scholars such as de Bary and Tu did not necessarily support the Singaporean government's efforts (or those of other governments in the region, such as China) to legitimate authoritarian political arrangements.[46] However, their emphasis on the value and importance of neo-Confucian ideas in education complemented the Singapore government's concerted promotion of Confucian values and the Mandarin language via the school curriculum and advertising campaigns by the 1980s. Chineseness was represented as a way of life that rested on Confucianism and Mandarin, and the government emphasized the values of obedience to authority, discipline and community. From this perspective Confucianism was not linked particularly with China, but to East Asia more generally. This made it possible to represent Confucianism as a key element in a wider Asian Renaissance. In late 1988 Goh Chok Tong proposed that the "Asian values common to" all of the ethnic groups of Singapore should be "specified in a National Ideology" which would "help Singaporeans keep their Asian bearings as they approach the 21st century".[47]

With the end of the Cold War the Singaporean elite gained a higher regional and international profile for its continued emphasis on Confucianism and Asian values. In the early post-Cold War era, Asian values and related formulations were repeatedly deployed to generate unity amongst different ethnic groupings and loyalty to the state in Singapore. Ideas about the necessity of putting the community before the individual, and fixed cultural/racial conceptions of Asia *vis-à-vis* the West, were key aspects of the dominant narrative on Singaporean identity and Asian values in this period. For example, Lee Kuan Yew emphasized, on more than one occasion, that the key to Singapore's success lay in the way they "used the family to push economic growth". From his perspective, Singapore was "fortunate" because it "had this cultural backdrop, the belief in thrift, hard work, filial piety and loyalty in the extended family, and most of all, the respect for scholarship and learning". At the same time his explanation for Singapore's continuing success was very quickly extrapolated to Asia as a whole: he emphasized that "Eastern societies believe that the individual exists in the context of his family."[48] The Singaporean leader also linked this to Confucianism, arguing that a "Confucianist view of order between subject and ruler" actually facilitates "the rapid transformation of society" because "you fit yourself into society – the exact opposite of the American rights of the individual".[49] Elsewhere Lee emphasized that central to the Asian values on which Singapore's success rested was the importance of discipline rather than democracy. In his view "democracy" led to "indiscipline and disorderly conduct" as this was "inimical to development".[50]

In 1994 the Chinese government appointed Lee Kuan Yew honorary chairman of the the newly established International Confucius Association (ICA), by which time in many parts of Asia the West was being represented as caught up in a process of "massive social decay".[51] However, with the onset of the Asian crisis (1997–1998), if not somewhat before, the emphasis being placed on Asian values by Lee Kuan Yew and the PAP subsided. Between the 1960s and the 1990s Singaporeans experienced a process of state-guided national development that courted foreign investment and enthusiastically supported free trade, while seeking to mobilize the population around a national identity and a political system with authoritarian characteristics and increasingly grounded in ostensibly Asian values. However, in the wake of the financial crisis, the PAP dramatically accelerated the process of economic liberalization and de-regulation, while increasingly urging Singaporeans to be more "creative" and in effect to discard some of the key Asian values that had been encouraged for a generation. The Singapore government's efforts to find a new direction in the post-Asian crisis era, via reinventing the city-state as an ever more globalized polity, is at odds with the "disciplinary modalities" and strident Asian cultural nationalism that had increasingly grounded Singapore's state-mediated national trajectory from 1965 to 1997.[52]

"The Asia That Can Say No": Malaysia

East Asian triumphalism of the late Cold War and early post-Cold War era, as the above discussion has suggested, was clearly not monolithic, and what constituted Asian values were contested from within and between elite groupings (and from below). For example, the Prime Minister of Malaysia, Mahathir Mohamad's reading of the rise of East Asia and his vision of the future was often at odds with the more Confucian orientation centered on Singapore. Of course, his vision was even more of a challenge to the visions of regional integration centered on the

Asia-Pacific Economic Cooperation forum (APEC). At the end of 1990 Mahathir sought to explicitly counter the APEC initiative with a proposal that Japan and other East Asian nation-states form an East Asian Economic Group (EAEG) which would exclude the US, Canada, Australia and New Zealand, as well as countries such as Mexico and Chile which are all members of APEC. The EAEG did not come into being, but Mahathir succeeded in having an East Asian Economic Caucus (EAEC) formed that operates within APEC. Mahathir's vision of an exclusive Asia in this period was linked to both domestic political contingencies and regional trends, and rested on fixed racial categories that flowed from the highly racialized politics of both the colonial and postcolonial eras. The importance of fixed cultural/racial categories to his vision of national development was foreshadowed in his early political testament. *The Malay Dilemma*, which Mahathir authored in the late 1960s – while he was cooling his heels in the political background following his expulsion from the United Malays National Organization (UMNO) for publicly criticizing the leadership of Tunku Abdul Rahman – is replete with theories of genetic inbreeding and the use of reductionist cultural/racial explanations for the subordinate educational and employment position of Malays in the country at that time.[53] From the moment he became Prime Minister, if not before, Mahathir has articulated an anti-Western position that was grounded in an explicitly racial conception of national and international power relations. In this context Mahathir has increasingly positioned himself as the voice, not just of Malaysia, but also of Asia (and even the Third World).[54] Mahathir's approach came at a time when the memories of the colonial era were still relatively fresh, while the role of Britain and the US during the Cold War era was littered with arrogant and racist incidents. Against this backdrop the leader of a political party that had held power in Malaysia without interruption for over thirty years (and who had personally been Prime Minister for over a decade by the early 1990s) was able to successfully represent himself as a revolutionary nationalist fighting against Western imperialism and racism. At the same time, his growing Pan-Asianism, centered on Japan, rested on explicitly racialized conceptions of Asia and Asians that reinforced and meshed with wider cultural/racial explanations for the rise of East Asia.

These increasingly powerful narratives on Pan-Asianism and the New Asian Renaissance that emerged in the 1980s and 1990s ultimately have to be understood in terms of the dynamics and imperatives of particular national trajectories in the context of the changing regional and global political economy. For example, Mahathir's effort to encourage a regional economic bloc, the East Asian Economic Caucus (EAEC), centered on Japan, was clearly grounded in the exigencies of Malaysian industrialization, a process in which the Japanese state and Japanese capital increasingly played a key role. At the end of 1980, while still Malaysia's Minister of Trade and Industry, Mahathir laid down what became known as Malaysia's "Look East" policy that dramatically re-oriented Malaysia's political economy towards using state-run enterprises to spearhead the diversification of the country's domestic industrial base by embarking on a range of import-substitution and capital-intensive industries which would complement private sector consumer and capital goods industries. Mahathir's shift made explicit reference to Japan and South Korea as models for Malaysia.[55] From the second half of the 1980s there was a significant increase in Japanese and East Asian investment flows into Malaysia, as well as Indonesia and Thailand, driven by the improved investment climate in Southeast Asia and a range of push factors linked to the rising cost of production in Northeast Asia and the wider financial and economic changes wrought by the rise of the US-led globalization project. In this period Mahathir presided over a major privatization process. Thirty-seven privatization projects were completed between 1983 and 1990. Significantly, although foreign investors, especially Japanese corporations, played a role, the privatization process worked to consolidate UMNO's power, as most of the major privatization projects involved the sale and transfer of public companies to individuals and companies closely connected to the ruling party.[56] Meanwhile, it was probably the decline of the value of the dollar in relation to the yen in particular, as a result of the Plaza Accord of 1985, which resulted in the dramatic increase in Japanese corporate investment southward. Before 1985 Japanese foreign direct investment (FDI) to the member countries of the Association of Southeast Asian Nations (ASEAN) totalled around US$900 million a year. By 1989 the figure was US$6.4 billion and a total of US$15 billion between 1988 and 1991.[57]

The end of the Cold War and renewed pressure for liberalization provided the context for a reorientation in Mahathir's national and regional visions of progress. A key aspect of Mahathir's developmental narrative in the 1990s was his promulgation and subsequent elaboration of Vision 2020. First announced in February 1991, Vision 2020 mapped out the Malaysian government's intention to engage in a large-scale process of national development and wealth creation. It sought to mobilize Malaysian citizens behind his government, garnering support and legitimacy through a powerful populist and nationalist vision of collective prosperity to be achieved by 2020. The goals of Vision 2020 were implemented via the Sixth Malaysia Plan (1991–1995). It was also facilitated in 1991 by the New Development Policy (NDP), an updating of the New Economic Policy (NEP), that had been implemented at the beginning of the 1970s to give preferential treatment to *Bumiputeras* (Malays and other people "indigenous" to Malaysia) in an effort to improve their overall social and economic position *vis-à-vis* the Chinese population of Malaysia. The Second Outline Perspective Plan (OPP2 – 1991–2000) was also aimed at implementing Vision 2020. The policy emphasis was on setting industrial targets, improving education and training, developing science and technology and maintaining strong links between the public and private sectors towards the overall goal of an annual economic growth rate of 7 percent. More broadly Vision 2020 sought to mobilize people around a collective national project holding out the promise of future reward. So powerful was the Vision 2020 concept that even the 1997–1998 financial crisis could not completely undermine its appeal and its long-term promise of prosperity. Vision 2020 also intersected with Mahathir's earlier exhortations to "Look East" and his emphasis on a regional economic grouping with shared Asian values in the 1990s.[58]

Mahathir's commitment to an exclusive Asian regional group was reflected in the fact that he declined to attend the APEC summit in Seattle in late 1993.[59] While he did attend the annual APEC conference in Bogor, Indonesia in mid-November 1994, he spent some time prior to the conference in Japan seeking to convert the Japanese to his East Asian Economic Caucus (EAEC) as an alternative to APEC. He also attended the November 1995 APEC meeting in Osaka, Japan, but like many other leaders, after the now ritual commitment to free trade within the region by 2010 for developed countries and 2020 for developing countries had been made, he was quick to qualify his government's support for this goal. Meanwhile, in 1994, prior to his visit to Japan he told the visiting Japanese Prime Minister that Japan ought to stop apologizing for its role in the Second World War and get on with business. This gesture was not sufficient to endear Mahathir's plan to the Japanese government, although undeterred Mahathir continued to try and sell his message on Japanese television and in the print media. His biography appeared in Japanese in 1994 and he also reached out to conservative forces in Japan by co-authoring a book in Japanese with Ishihara Shintaro, which also first appeared in 1994. The Japanese title is generally translated as "The Asia That Can Say No: A Policy to Combat Europe and America"; however, the English language version, which was published in 1995, was more diplomatically, but far less modestly, entitled *The Voice of Asia: Two Leaders Discuss the Coming Century*, although the actual content appears to be as unrestrained as the earlier Japanese edition.[60] In his section of the book Mahathir emphasized that the region and the world was at a turning point. He argued that: "it is possible for Asia to create a cultural region of unmatched historical greatness. What is important is that we consciously strive to maintain our value systems. If we do so, we will never come under European domination again".[61] Mahathir warned that: "the West would do well to learn from the success of East Asia and to some extent 'Easternize'. It should accept our values not the other way around". From his perspective, "Asians" permitted themselves "to be overtaken by the West" failing "to maintain and develop the achievements" of their "forebears". He concluded that Asia was "awakening to a new era, and there is no reason we cannot regain our former glory. If we preserve our distinctive values and cultures as we master modern technology, I am convinced Asia will again be great".[62]

Meanwhile, Ishihara's section of the book reinforced Mahathir's message, emphasizing that "Asia has a diverse and old civilisation and culture in contrast to a much shorter one in the United States" and that "it may be necessary" for governments in Asia to form "an anti-American Asian front on the issue of values".[63] Ishihara argued that the Japanese government should identify itself more with Asia and speak up more for the region even if that involved conflict with the US and Western Europe. He rested this on the argument that "Japan is an Asian country of Asian people with Asian blood" and "it ought to realize that it exists for Asia rather than for America".[64] Mahathir and Ishihara's views enjoyed wide, although not necessarily deep, appeal amongst the general population in Japan in this period. The latter's successful election as governor of

Tokyo at the end of the 1990s suggests his views are not a political liability. The "Asia-first" approach emphasized by Mahathir and Ishihara certainly meshed with the views of other members of the Japanese elite. Japan's Ministry of International Trade and Industry (MITI), a ministry that used to be central to Japan's economic development, but that has seen its influence decline steadily, had plans in the early 1990s to boost its profile in the region and establish a new position of director-general for Asian affairs, while the Tokyo-based Asia-Pacific Club entertained the idea of an Asia-centered policy as articulated by Mahathir. This emphasis was also popular in this period at the Asia Bureau of the foreign ministry. But other sections of the Japanese bureaucracy were more ambivalent and members of the Japanese elite continued to be aware that the US provides the military basis for Japan's economic power at the same time as Japanese-based industry and finance have important interests in North America and Western Europe, well outside the boundaries of Mahathir's proposed EAEC.[65] Furthermore, Mahathir's enthusiasm for an East Asian Economic Group led by Japan has little appeal in South Korea or China (as well as a number of other countries in the region) where attitudes towards Japan are far more ambivalent.[66]

In the 1990s Mahathir's call for an exclusive regional grouping grounded in a purportedly shared Asian cultural/racial heritage was increasingly challenged by commentators inside and outside the region in favor of what they described as a new East–West synthesis. For example, in 1996 Mahathir's own Deputy Prime Minister, Anwar Ibrahim, foreshadowing the rift with Mahathir that would lead to Anwar's incarceration in 1998, argued for a "Symbiosis Between East and West". Anwar suggested that the "renewed self-esteem" in Asia and the growing international awareness that Asia was "a force to be reckoned with" ought to "lead to greater interdependence and genuine mutual consultation in the years to come".[67] Mahathir himself remained less conciliatory in the lead up to, and in the aftermath of, the financial crisis. In *A New Deal for Asia*, published in 1999, Mahathir represented the IMF-led response to the Asian crisis as part of an effort by the West to ensure that Asia remained subordinate. He said that the crisis of 1997–1998 provided an "opportunity" for the West to "force open" Asian economies and "allow domination by more powerful nations".[68] With the onset of the crisis in 1997, Mahathir had denounced international currency speculators, such as George Soros, as "racists" who sought to destroy the Malaysian economy. Initialling establishing a rescue fund, he moved to prop up some of the more important Malaysian corporations, while rejecting an IMF bailout package and the advice that went with it. Mahathir's unwillingness to respond to the crisis in the same way as the governments of Thailand, South Korea and Indonesia drew widespread condemnation from the international media. In this context, Anwar emerged as a conciliator of foreign and domestic interests. With Mahathir's apparent approval Anwar presided over a series of budgetary reforms and confidence-building measures in late 1997 and early 1998 that mollified key business interests, as well as the IMF and the US, while avoiding direct IMF intervention. In January 1998, Anwar observed that the "great lesson" that had been learned from the crisis was the need for "greater transparency, greater accountability and for greater democracy". By mid-1998, the Malaysian economy was continuing to decline. The increasing differences over how to deal with the financial crisis, as part of a wider split within UMNO, prompted Mahathir to get rid of his deputy and main rival. This led to Anwar's arrest in the second half of 1998 and his eventual trial and conviction for corruption and sodomy.[69]

It was this turn of events in Malaysia that prompted the famous excoriation of Mahathir's handling of the economic crisis and the lack of democracy in Malaysia by US Vice-President Al Gore in a speech to the annual APEC meeting, which, significantly, was hosted by Mahathir and held in Kuala Lumpur in mid-November 1998. Gore sought to make a direct connection between liberal economics, democratic politics, and the successful management of the crisis. In his speech, the Vice-President pursued the argument that liberal democracies are better able to solve economic crises. Gore asserted that: "from Thailand to South Korea, Eastern Europe to Mexico, democracies have done better in coping with economic crises than nations where freedom is suppressed".[70] Of course, by the very end of the 1990s, Malaysia, and most other NICs (Indonesia excepted), had undergone a partial economic recovery, while Mahathir's resort to a more authoritarian form of rule had resolved the country's political crisis in the short term.[71] Meanwhile, the new "war on terrorism" has strengthened Mahathir's ability to contain his opponents at the same time as his relationship with the US has also improved. Mahathir quickly moved to align his government with the war on terrorism after September 11, arresting suspected terrorists under the Internal Security Act and garnering praise from Washington.[72] At the same time, often using more moderate language, Mahathir has continued to emphasize that "with the global economy in trouble, Asian countries should intensify their regional cooperation in trade and finance, including such initiatives as an East Asian Economic Grouping and a regional monetary fund".[73] In post-crisis Asia, Mahathir's conception of Asian regionalism has gained renewed purchase in the form of organizations such as ASEAN+3.[74] Significantly, and this is something that will be discussed at greater length in the conclusion, the widely felt sense of resentment about the way the Asian financial crisis and its aftermath unfolded, particularly the central role of the US and the IMF in that process, has been a key factor in regional mobilization and the basis for various regionally oriented policy initiatives by East Asian elites.[75]

The new Confucianism III: China

In economic and geo-political terms and in less-quantifiable cultural terms, China is central to the incipient post-crisis regionalism in Asia. In the 1980s, China (or Greater China) was increasingly perceived as another East Asian success story and by the 1990s it was being represented as a "new superpower".[76] In the early 1990s the Chinese Economic Area (CEA), which encompassed Hong Kong,

Taiwan and China, accounted for a share of world trade that was exceeded only by the national output of five of the major economic powers, the United States, Germany, Japan, France and Great Britain.[77] These trends have, of course, also been closely connected to the growing perception that China represents a long-term threat to US hegemony in the region and beyond. Despite China's dramatic economic growth in the 1980s and 1990s (a growth that was far less affected by the Asian crisis than other parts of the region), the delivery of material benefits (which was a highly uneven process) did not provide sufficient legitimacy for the aging leadership at the top of the Chinese Communist Party (CCP). The rise of neo-Confucianism (*ruxue fuxing*) in China, in the second half of the 1980s, represented a more or less explicit attempt by the Chinese Communist Party to find an alternative ideological vision in the context of the fading fortunes of Marxism in China and beyond. The rehabilitation of Confucius is seen to have begun with a Symposium on Confucianism at Shandong University in 1978, the same year that Deng's reformist agenda was launched. At the outset it appeared as if the Confucian revival was primarily an academic reassessment carried out under the watchful eye of the CCP. However, by the late 1980s, in the context of the growing regional and international discovery of Confucianism as a key to the rise of East Asia, neo-Confucianism took on new significance as a legitimating narrative in China. In the waning years of the Cold War, Chinese intellectuals and government officials embarked on an enthusiastic attempt to revive Confucianism in an effort to conflate a hierarchical social structure centered on the emperor with the contemporary political system centered on the CCP. In October 1986 a government-sponsored national meeting spent a week discussing the official promotion of philosophy and the social sciences that launched a national initiative on the study of "Modern Neo-Confucian Thought". As mentioned previously, in September 1987 the China Foundation of Confucius was joint sponsor, with the Institute of East Asian Philosophies in Singapore, of an international conference in the city-state at which Confucianism was explicitly portrayed as a key component in the economic success of many of the nation-states of East Asia. This was followed by another major international conference in Beijing in October 1989 that coincided with the 2,540th anniversary of Confucius's birth.[78]

By the 1990s, China was the site of an array of neo-nationalist efforts that drew directly or indirectly on the Confucian legacy and wider ideas about a New Asian Renaissance.[79] In October 1994, as already mentioned, the Chinese government held the inaugural meeting of the International Confucius Association (ICA), attended by scholars and political leaders from the US, Western Europe, and East and Southeast Asia. In an opening speech, Gu Mu, a one-time high-ranking party and government official, and now head of the ICA, argued that while China had benefited from Confucianism, it was also possible for the West to benefit. This was dutifully followed by an article in *The People's Daily* emphasizing that Confucianism had played an important role in the modernization of East Asia, and that it represented a solution to Western problems "because it is a non-religious humanism that can provide a basis for morals and the value of life". The article concluded that a culture based on Confucianism and science "better suits the future era" and "it will thrive particularly well in the next century and will replace modern and contemporary Western culture".[80] In the second half of the 1990s, the official government version of this modernized form of Confucianism was increasingly absorbed by the concept of "Socialist spiritual civilization", which was formally promulgated by then-President Jiang Zemin. An explicit response to the CCP's crisis of legitimacy, "Socialist spiritual civilization" had initially been outlined under Deng. However, the plan to formally promote "Socialist spiritual civilization" emerged from an October 1996 meeting of the CCP's Central Committee. It emphasized the importance of centralized power, Confucian deference to those in authority, and market-based competition but also of avoiding the excesses of Western capitalism. By the time the Asian crisis was sweeping the region, the Chinese leadership had embarked on an effort to link neo-Confucianism to a wider nationalist mobilization around a concern with the future of Taiwan, the role of Japan and of the United States in post-Cold War Asia.[81] Meanwhile, against the backdrop of confrontation with the US over Taiwan early in 1996, there was an apparent upsurge in highly nationalistic publications and rhetoric in China. Well-known publications, such as *China Can Say No*, attacked the US as a decadent imperial power that sought to undermine a rising China.[82] While not necessarily officially sanctioned, these virulently nationalistic interpretations of US–China relations enjoyed some tacit support from within the upper echelons of the CCP. In a broader sense these nationalistic soundings complemented the government's effort in the economic sphere to continue to try and pursue a developmental path that still emphasized economic nationalism and owed a great deal to the model of the developmental state pioneered by the governments of Japan and South Korea in the Cold War era.[83]

At the same time, the increased integration with, and dependence on, transnational economic interests is also fundamentally reconfiguring and constraining the Chinese leadership's ability to follow a path charted in an earlier era by Japan and South Korea. A key manifestation of this process is China's accession to the World Trade Organization (WTO). The WTO exemplifies the sort of decentered hegemony of liberal economic ideas and practices that is central to the expansion and consolidation of global capitalism. The Chinese government is clearly seeking to finesse some of the required reforms. However, the long-term significance of embracing the new regulatory regime is becoming increasingly clear. Organizations such as the WTO reflect the concerted effort to construct a legally enshrined order that provides the long-term political foundation for the interests of capital on a global scale. As emphasized in chapter 4, US–Chinese relations in post-Cold War Asia are simply the latest round in an ongoing cycle of Great Power confrontations. In fact, the transformation that is occurring in China and the dynamics of US–China relations are part and parcel of the major structural changes in the organization of China's economy including the growing role of transnational corporations and the increasing influence of transnational institutions like the

WTO, and the gradual and very uneven adoption of a new, globally oriented ideological, legal and institutional framework centered on the US-led globalization project. As already suggested in chapter 4, contemporary China is characterized by a crisis of state-mediated national development that not only involves national reorientation, but also encompasses an incipient crisis of the Chinese nation-state itself. As will be discussed in more detail in chapter 9, the Chinese trajectory reflects both the historical specificity of nation-state formation and the wider problems of the nation-state, even large nation-states, in the early twenty-first century. This is the context for the deployment of neo-Confucianism and neo-nationalism as the Chinese Communist Party attempts to retain a monopoly on political power in the shadow of political, social, environmental and economic crises grounded in rapid and uneven capitalist development.

Conclusion: the vicissitudes of the New Asian Renaissance

By the end of the Cold War a growing number of observers had begun to explain the rise of East Asia primarily in terms of Confucianism or other perceived cultural/racial characteristics. Explicitly racial discourses that regarded the rise of East Asia, especially Japan (and now China), as a threat to the West also emerged. In the late 1980s and early 1990s these representations of the New Asian Renaissance were both challenged and complemented by a variety of Pan-Asian narratives generated from within the region that located the capitalist success of East Asia in cultural/racial attributes said to be characteristic of, and even unique to, Asia. This chapter has outlined the way in which the promotion of a New Asian Renaissance is best explained in terms of its relationship to particular state-mediated national development projects in the context of the wider transformation of Asia and the changing global order. The continued, albeit shifting, importance of fixed notions of culture/race in this process has also been highlighted. Ultimately these cultural/racial explanations tell us more about the national and geo-political contexts in which their writers were operating than they do about the processes they were ostensibly seeking to explain. More broadly, while the Asian financial crisis initially weakened the cultural and racial explanations for Asian success that had complemented influential Pan-Asian visions of the region's future, the growing irrelevance of APEC, the increasing economic importance of China, the IMF's handling of the Asian financial crisis and the emergence of ASEAN+3, have all provided the basis for revised forms of Pan-Asianism, an issue that will be taken up in the conclusion of this book.

Notes

1 M. T. Berger, "Yellow Mythologies: The East Asian Miracle and Post-Cold War Capitalism" *positions: east asia cultures critique* vol. 4, no. 1, 1996.
2 F. Godement, *The New Asian Renaissance: From Colonialism to the Post-Cold War*, London: Routledge, 1997.

3 M. T. Berger, "A New East–West Synthesis? APEC and Competing Narratives of Regional Integration in the Post-Cold War Asia-Pacific" *Alternatives: Social Transformation and Humane Governance* vol. 23, no. 1, 1998.

4 E. F. Vogel, *Japan As Number One: Lessons for America*, Cambridge, MA: Harvard University Press, 1979.

5 W. W. Lockwood, "Japan's New Capitalism" in W. W. Lockwood, ed., *The State and Economic Enterprise in Japan*, Princeton: Princeton University Press, 1965, p. 503.

6 E. O. Reischauer, J. K. Fairbank and A. Craig, *East Asia: Tradition and Transformation*, Boston: Houghton Mifflin, 1973, pp. 829–30.

7 R. Katz, *Japan, the System that Soured: The Rise and Fall of the Japanese Economic Miracle*, Armonk: M. E. Sharpe, 1998, pp. 290–3.

8 H. Patrick and H. Rosovsky, "Japan's Economic Performance: An Overview" and "Prospects for the Future and Some Other Implications" in H. Patrick and H. Rosovsky, eds, *Asia's New Giant: How the Japanese Economy Works*, Washington, DC: Brookings Institution, 1976.

9 H. Patrick, "The Future of the Japanese Economy: Output and Labor Productivity" *Journal of Japanese Studies* vol. 3, no. 2, 1977, p. 239.

10 F. Gibney, *Miracle by Design: The Real Reasons behind Japan's Economic Success*, New York: Times Books, 1982; R. Dore, *Flexible Rigidities: Industrial Policy and Structural Adjustment in the Japanese Economy, 1970–1980*, Stanford: Stanford University Press, 1986; R. J. Samuels, *The Business of the Japanese State: Energy Markets in Comparative and Historical Perspective*, Ithaca: Cornell University Press, 1987; K. E. Calder, *Crisis and Compensation: Public Policy and Political Stability in Japan, 1949–1986*, Princeton: Princeton University Press, 1988; K. E. Calder, *Strategic Capitalism: Private Business and Public Purpose in Japanese Industrial Finance*, Princeton: Princeton University Press, 1993; T. Inoguchi and D. Okimoto, eds, *The Political Economy of Japan*, Stanford: Stanford University Press, 1988; D. Friedman, *The Misunderstood Miracle: Industrial Development and Political Change in Japan*, Ithaca: Cornell University Press, 1988; D. I. Okimoto and T. P. Rohlen, eds, *Inside the Japanese System: Readings on Contemporary Society and Political Economy*, Stanford: Stanford University Press, 1988.

11 D. Okimoto, *Between MITI and the Market: Japanese Industrial Policy for High Technology*, Stanford: Stanford University Press, 1989.

12 C. Johnson, *MITI and the Japanese Miracle: The Growth of Industrial Policy 1925–1975*, Stanford: Stanford University Press, 1982.

13 C. Prestowitz, *Trading Places: How We are Giving Our Future to Japan and How to Reclaim It*, 2nd edn, New York: Basic Books, 1989; P. Choate, *Agents of Influence: How Japan's Lobbyists in the United States Manipulate America's Political and Economic System*, New York: Alfred A. Knopf, 1990; C. Prestowitz, R. Morse and A. Tonelson, eds, *Powernomics: Economics and Strategy After the Cold War*, Washington, DC: Economic Strategy Institute, 1991; G. Friedman and M. Lebard, *The Coming War with Japan*, New York: St. Martin's Press, 1991; R. L. Kearns, *Zaibatsu America: How Japanese Firms Are Colonizing Vital U.S. Industries*, New York: Free Press, 1992; R. Harvey, *The Undefeated: The Rise, Fall and Rise of Greater Japan*, London: Macmillan, 1994; E. Fingleton, *Blindside: Why Japan is Still on Track to Overtake the US by the Year 2000*, New York: Simon and Schuster, 1995.

14 K. Van Wolferen, *The Enigma of Japanese Power: People and Politics in a Stateless Nation*, 2nd edn, London: Macmillan, 1990, pp. 1–10, 20–3.

15 M. Crichton, *Rising Sun*, London: Arrow, 1992, pp. 401–2.

16 T. Clancy, *Debt of Honor*, London: HarperCollins, 1994.

17 R. Cohen, "Master of War: Novelist Tom Clancy Keeps Making New Enemies" *Rolling Stone Yearbook*, 1994, p. 143; M. Walker, "Millionaire Minstrel of the Military" *The Guardian Weekly* December 25, 1994, p. 20.

18 T. Clancy, *The Bear and the Dragon*, New York: G. P. Putnam's Sons, 2000.

19 M. Woo-Cumings, "East Asia's America Problem" in M. Woo-Cumings and M. Loriaux, eds, *Past As Prelude: History in the Making of a New World Order*, Boulder: Westview, 1993, pp. 142–3.

20 S. Ishihara, *The Japan That Can Say No: Why Japan Will Be First Among Equals*, New York: Simon and Schuster, 1991.

21 S. Awanohara, "Japanese Pride and Prejudice" *Far Eastern Economic Review* February 21, 1991, p. 32.

22 Ishihara, *The Japan That Can Say No*, pp. 61–2, 82–3.

23 Sakakibara Eisuke cited in "Japan: The New Nationalists" *The Economist* January 14, 1995, p. 20; E. Sakakibara, *Beyond Capitalism: The Japanese Model of Market Economics*, Washington, DC: University Press of America, 1993.

24 He emphasized the absence of any significant "lay-offs" in the "Japanese style of restructuring". Cited in P. Landers, "American Accents" *Far Eastern Economic Review* July 31, 1997, p. 48. By the beginning of the twenty-first century Sakakibara, having left the MOF for a university post, was still taking the view that Japan should not "adopt the American system", but he was also urging the Koizumi government to move forward with its economic reform agenda. He argued that Japan needed "to have some corporate governance and there is nothing". Furthermore, corporate reform needed to be "combined" with financial reform. Although he "usually" would "endorse a gradualist approach at a time of crisis and we are approaching a state of crisis" Sakakibara argued that "a hard-landing scenario is necessary". M. Vatikiotis and D. Kruger, "Eisuke Sakakibara: He Wants a Revolution" *Far Eastern Economic Review* March 7, 2002, pp. 18–19.

25 K. Yoshihara, *Japanese Economic Development*, 3rd edn, Kuala Lumpur: Oxford University Press, 1994 (first published in 1977), pp. 196–7, 202. Also see K. Yoshihara, *The Rise of Ersatz Capitalism in Southeast Asia*, Singapore: Oxford University Press, 1988; K. Yoshihara, *The Nation and Economic Growth: The Philippines and Thailand*, Kuala Lumpur: Oxford University Press, 1994.

26 "Japan and the War: The Japan that Cannot Say Sorry" *The Economist* August 18, 1995, p. 21.

27 Hung-chao Tai, "The Oriental Alternative: An Hypothesis on Culture and Economy" in Hung-chao Tai, ed., *Confucianism and Economic Development: An Oriental Alternative?*, Washington, DC: Washington Institute Press, 1989, pp. 6–7.

28 M. Morishima, *Why has Japan Succeeded? Western Technology and the Japanese Ethos*, 2nd edn, Cambridge: Cambridge University Press, 1989. By the end of the 1990s, Morishima was seeking to explain Japan's "deadlock". See M. Morishima, *Japan at a Deadlock*, London: Macmillan, 2000.

29 H. Kahn, "The Confucian Ethic and Economic Growth" in M. A. Seligson, ed., *The Gap Between Rich and Poor: Contending Perspectives on the Political Economy of Development*, Boulder: Westview, 1984. Also see C. H. Chung, J. M. Shepard and M. J. Dollinger, "Max Weber Revisited: Some Lessons from East Asian Capitalistic Development" *Asia Pacific Journal of Management* vol. 6, no. 2, 1987; P. L. Berger, "An East Asian Development Model" in P. L. Berger and H. H. M. Hsiao, eds, *In Search of an East Asian Development Model*, New Brunswick: Transaction Books, 1988; R. Dore, *Taking Japan Seriously: A Confucian Perspective on Leading Economic Issues*, Stanford: Stanford University Press, 1988; G. Rozman, ed., *The East Asian Region: Confucian Heritage and its Modern Adaptation*, Princeton: Princeton University Press, 1991; E. F. Vogel, *The Four Little Dragons: The Spread of Industrialization in East Asia*, Cambridge, MA: Harvard University Press, 1991; Kim Kyong-Dong, "Confucianism and Capitalist Development in East Asia" in L. Sklair, ed., *Capitalism and Development*, London: Routledge, 1994.

30 M. Weber, *The Religion of China*, New York: Free Press, 1951 (first published in German in 1916).

31 For example, see F. FitzGerald, *Fire in the Lake: The Vietnamese and the Americans in Vietnam*, Boston: Little Brown, 1972, pp. 213–18.
32 R. Hofheinz, Jr and K. E. Calder, *The Eastasia Edge*, New York: Harper and Row, 1982, pp. 41–5, 58, 109–13, 121.
33 S. G. Redding, *The Spirit of Chinese Capitalism*, New York: Walter de Gruyter, 1990. For a good critique see S. Yao, *Confucian Capitalism: Discourse, Practice and the Myth of Chinese Enterprise*, London: Routledge, 2002.
34 D. C. Schak, "The Spirit of Chinese Capitalism: A Critique" *Tsing Hua Journal of Chinese Studes* (new series) vol. 25, no. 1, 1997.
35 Redding, *The Spirit of Chinese Capitalism*, p. 42. For a similar approach see E. Chen and G. G. Hamilton, "Introduction: Business Groups and Economic Development" in G. Hamilton, ed., *Asian Business Networks*, New York: Walter de Gruyter, 1996.
36 G. T. Haley, T. C. Tiong and U. C. V. Haley, *New Asian Emperors: The Overseas Chinese, their Strategies and Comparative Advantages*, Melbourne: Butterworth-Heinemann, 1998, p. 3.
37 R. Elegant, *Pacific Destiny: Inside Asia Today*, London: Headline, 1991 (first published 1990), pp. 35–6.
38 T. R. Reid, *Confucius Lives Next Door: What Living in the East Teaches us about Living in the West*, New York: Random House, 1999.
39 S. Noordin, *Towards A New Asia*, Commission for a New Asia, December 1993. Online at http://www.jaring.my/isis/asia.htm
40 S. Awanohara, M. Vatikiotis and S. Islam, "Vienna Showdown" *Far Eastern Economic Review* June 17, 1993, pp. 16–20.
41 M. Vatikiotis and R. Delfs, "Cultural Divide" *Far Eastern Economic Review* June 17, 1993, pp. 20–2.
42 G. Heng and J. Devan, "State Fatherhood: The Politics of Nationalism, Sexuality and Race in Singapore" in A. Parker, M. Russo, D. Sommer and P. Yaeger, eds, *Nationalisms and Sexualities*, London: Routledge, 1992.
43 On Lee Kuan Yew's ideas in the first decade and a half after independence see C. J. Christie, *Ideology and Revolution in Southeast Asia 1900–1980*, Richmond: Curzon, 2001, pp. 185–9.
44 Cited in D. Brown, *The State and Ethnic Politics in Southeast Asia*, London: Routledge, 1994, pp. 77–81, 84–6, 89–99, 106, 284–5; G. C. Lodge and E. F. Vogel, eds, *Ideology and National Competitiveness: An Analysis of Nine Countries*, Boston: Harvard Business School Press, 1987.
45 W. T. de Bary, ed., *A Forum on "The Role of Culture in Industrial Asia: The Relationship between Confucian Ethics and Modernisation"*, Singapore: Institute of East Asian Philosophies, 1988; Tu Wei-ming, *The Triadic Chord: Confucian Ethics, Industrial East Asia, and Max Weber – Proceedings of the 1987 Singapore Conference on "Confucian Ethics and the Modernisation of Industrial East Asia"*, Singapore: Institute of East Asian Philosophies, 1991.
46 W. T. de Bary and J. W. Chafee, eds, *Neo-Confucian Education: The Formative Stage*, Berkeley: University of California Press, 1989; Tu Wei-ming, ed., *Confucian Traditions in East Asian Modernity: Moral Education and Economic Culture in Japan and the Four Mini-Dragons*, Cambridge, MA: Harvard University Press, 1996. On Tu Wei-ming and Confucianism in Singapore see B.-H. Chua, *Communitarian Ideology and Democracy in Singapore*, London: Routledge, 1995, pp. 147–67.
47 Cited in D. Brown, *The State and Ethnic Politics in Southeast Asia*, London: Routledge, 1994, pp. 77–81, 84–6, 89–99, 106, 284–5; A. Ong, "Chinese Modernities: Narratives of Nation and of Capitalism" in A. Ong and D. Nonini, eds, *Ungrounded Empires: The Cultural Politics of Modern Chinese Transnationalism*, London: Routledge, 1997.
48 Cited in G. Lafitte, "Reorientations" *Arena Magazine* no. 12, 1994, pp. 13–15.

49 Cited in "Confucianism: New Fashion for Old Wisdom" *The Economist* January 27, 1995 p. 33.
50 Cited in "Democracy and Growth" *The Economist* August 27, 1994.
51 K. Mahbubani, "The Dangers of Decadence: What the Rest Can Teach the West" *Foreign Affairs* vol. 72, no. 4, 1993, p. 14. When this article, which was an explicit rejoinder to Huntington's "The Clash of Civilizations", was written Mahbubani was Deputy Secretary of Foreign Affairs and Dean of the Civil Service College in Singapore. He had earlier served as Singapore's Permanent Representative to the United Nations from 1984 to 1989.
52 C. J. W.-L. Wee, "The End of Disciplinary Modernisation? The Asian Economic Crisis and the Ongoing Re-Invention of Singapore" *Third World Quarterly: Journal of Emerging Areas* vol. 22, no. 6, 2001.
53 M. Mahathir, *The Malay Dilemma*, 2nd edn, Kuala Lumpur: Federal Publishers, 1982.
54 B. T. Khoo, *Paradoxes of Mahathirism: An Intellectual Biography of Mahathir Mohamad*, Kuala Lumpur: Oxford University Press, 1995, p. 332. Also see L Wong, "Cultural Claims on the New World Order: Malaysia as a Voice for the Third World?" in S. Yao, ed., *House of Glass: Culture, Modernity, and the State in Southeast Asia*, Singapore: Institute of Southeast Asian Studies, 2001.
55 K. J. Khoo, "The Grand Vision: Mahathir and Modernisation" in J. S. Kahn and F. Loh Kok Wah, eds, *Fragmented Vision: Culture and Politics in Contemporary Malaysia*, Sydney: Allen and Unwin, 1992.
56 J. Hilley, *Malaysia: Mahathirism, Hegemony and the New Opposition*, London: Zed Books, 2001, pp. 58–65.
57 R. Stubbs, "The Political Economy of the Asia-Pacific Region" in R. Stubbs and G. R. D. Underhill, eds, *Political Economy and the Changing Global Order*, London: Macmillan, 1994, pp. 371–2.
58 Hilley, *Malaysia*, pp. 4–7, 19–20, 36.
59 S. Burton, "The Stubborn Holdout" *Time: International* November 22, 1993, p. 27.
60 M. Mahathir and S. Ishihara, *The Voice of Asia: Two Leaders Discuss the Coming Century*, Tokyo: Kodansha International, 1995.
61 Cited in E. W. Desmond, "One Happy, Culturally Superior Family" *Time: Australia* November 21, 1994, p. 54.
62 M. Mahathir and S. Ishihara, "East Beats West" *Asiaweek* September 8, 1995, p. 41. Excerpted from M. Mahathir and S. Ishihara, *The Voice of Asia: Two Leaders Discuss the Coming Century*, Tokyo: Kodansha International, 1995.
63 The Japanese-language version of M. Mahathir and S. Ishihara, *The Asia That Can Say No: A Policy to Combat Europe and America* cited and discussed in R. McGregor, "Mahathir Fumes as Japan Plays Hard to Get" *The Weekend Australian* November 12–13, 1994, p. 16.
64 Cited in Desmond, "One Happy, Culturally Superior Family", p. 54.
65 "Saying No" *The Economist* November 25, 1994, p. 31.
66 G. Austin and S. Harris, *Japan and Greater China: Political Economy and Military Power in the Asian Century*, London: Hurst, 2001, pp. 42–79.
67 I. Anwar, *The Asian Renaissance*, Singapore: Times Books International, 1996, p. 45.
68 M. Mahathir, *A New Deal for Asia*, Subang Jaya: Pelanduk Publications, 1999, p. 61.
69 Cited in Hilley, *Malaysia*, pp. 65–77, 256.
70 Cited in J. Gittings, "Gore Lectures Leaders on Asian Democracy" *The Guardian Weekly* November 22, 1998, p. 4. Also see D. E. Sanger, "Tongue-Lashings and Backlashes" *The New York Times* November 22, 1998, p. 5.
71 M. Beeson, "Mahathir and the Markets: Globalisation and the Pursuit of Economic Autonomy in Malaysia" *Pacific Affairs* vol. 73, no. 3, 2000, pp. 343–5.
72 B. Wain, "Southeast Asia: Wrong Target" *Far Eastern Economic Review* April 18, 2002, pp. 15–16.

73 M. Mahathir, "Globalization: Challenges and Impact on Asia" in F. J. Richter and P. C. M. Mar, eds, *Recreating Asia: Visions for a New Century*, Singapore: John Wiley and Sons, 2002, p. 10.

74 R. Stubbs, "ASEAN Plus Three: Emerging East Asian Regionalism?", *Asian Survey* vol. 42, no. 3, 2002.

75 R. Higgott, "The Asian Economic Crisis: A Study in the Politics of Resentment" *New Political Economy* vol. 3, no. 3, 1998.

76 D. H. Perkins, *China: Asia's Next Economic Giant?*, 2nd edn, Seattle: University of Washington Press, 1989; W. H. Overholt, *The Rise of China: How Economic Reform is Creating a New Superpower*, New York: W. W. Norton, 1994; D. Shambaugh, ed., *Greater China: The Next Superpower?*, New York: Oxford University Press, 1995; M. Weidenbaum, *The Bamboo Network: How Expatriate Chinese Entrepreneurs Are Creating A New Economic Superpower in Asia*, New York: Martin Kessler Books, 1996; D. Wilson, *China: The Big Tiger – A Nation Awakes*, 2nd edn, London: Abacus, 1997; L. Brahm, *China As No. 1: The New Superpower Takes Center Stage*, Singapore: Butterworth-Heinemann, 1997.

77 S. Zhao, "China's Perceptions of NAFTA and Changing Roles in the Asia-Pacific" in S. Nishijima and P. H. Smith, eds, *Cooperation or Rivalry? Regional Integration in the Americas and the Pacific Rim*, Boulder: Westview, 1996, p. 234.

78 J. Wang, *High Culture Fever: Politics, Aesthetics, and Ideology in Deng's China*, Berkeley: University of California Press, 1996, pp. 64–5, 68–9, 300.

79 M. Forney, "Patriot Games" *Far Eastern Economic Review* October 3, 1996, pp. 22–8; B. Gilley, "Potboiler Nationalism" *Far Eastern Economic Review* October 3, 1996, p. 23.

80 Cited in F. Ching, "Confucius, the New Saviour" *Far Eastern Economic Review* November 10, 1994, p. 37.

81 R. MacFarquhar, "Demolition Man" *The New York Review of Books* vol. 44, no. 5, 1997, pp. 16–17; M. Forney, "New Chinese Man" *Far Eastern Economic Review* April 17, 1997, p. 30; F. Godemont, *The New Asian Renaissance: From Colonialism to the Post-Cold War*, London: Routledge, 1997, p. 16.

82 Q. Song *et al.*, eds, *Zhongguo keyi shuo bu: Lengzhanhou shidai de zhengzhi yu qinggan jueze (China Can Say No: The Political and Emotional Choice in the Post-Cold War Era)*, Beijing: Zhonghua gonshang lianhe chubanshe, 1996; Q. Song *et al.*, eds, *Zhongguo haishi neng shuo bu–Zhongguo keyi shuo bu xupin: Guoji guanxi bianshu yu women de xianshi yingfu (China Still Can Say No – The Sequel to China Can Say No: The Variables in International Relations and Our Realistic Responses)*, Beijing: Zhongguo wenlian chubanshe, 1996. Also see Q. Peng, M. Yang and D. Xu, *Zhongguo weishenmo shuo bu (Why Does China Say No?)*, Beijing: Xinshijie chubanshe, 1996; C. Xianwei, ed., *Zhongguo da zhanlue (China's Grand Strategy)*, Haikou: Hainan chubanshe, 1996. For a good overview of official and unofficial Chinese perceptions of US–China relations and China's position in the region and beyond see Y. Deng, "Conceptions of National Interest: Realpolitik, Liberal Dilemma and the Possibility of Change" in Y. Deng and F.-L. Wang, eds, *In the Eyes of the Dragon: China Views the World*, Lanham: Rowman and Littlefield, 1999. Also see F.-L. Wang, "Self-Image and Strategic Intentions: National Confidence and Political Insecurity" in Deng and Wang, eds, *In the Eyes of the Dragon*; T. J. Christensen, "Pride, Pressure and Politics: The Roots of China's Worldview" in Deng and Wang, eds, *In the Eyes of the Dragon*.

83 P. Nolan, *China and the Global Economy*, Basingstoke: Palgrave, 2001.

7 The rise and decline of the developmental state

Theories of the developmental state, which emphasized and elaborated the central role of state-directed industrial policy in successful national development, increasingly emerged to challenge the neo-liberal ascendancy in the late Cold War and early post-Cold War era. Like the emergent cultural explanations for the rise of East Asia, theories of the developmental state were closely connected to the wider battle for the East Asian Miracle. The emergence of a distinctive Anglo-American tradition of developmental state theory was also linked to the broader effort in various branches of the social sciences in North America to "bring the state back in". This chapter examines the rise and decline of theories of the developmental state in relation to the wider development debate and the changing global order. It is emphasized that most theories of the developmental state implicitly, if not explicitly, legitimated authoritarianism. This is a characteristic shared with many of the more culturally oriented approaches to capitalist transformation in East Asia and with the neo-liberalism that developmental state theorists sought to challenge. In fact, this chapter emphasizes that while developmental state theorists challenged neo-liberalism, they also shared many of the key assumptions on which neo-liberalism rested. Like neo-liberalism, theories of the developmental state routinized the nation-state and the nation-state system and produced explanations for the East Asian Miracle that were ahistorical and technocratic. While originating in part in important historically grounded studies of capitalist transformation, theories of the developmental state as they rose to prominence in the 1980s and 1990s have been increasingly domesticated to the dominant neo-liberal development discourse and are characterized by a failure to understand the wider historical significance of the universalization of the nation-state system, the capitalist transformation of East Asia and the emergence of the US-led globalization project.

The rise of the developmental state

Bringing the state back in I: "The Japanese Miracle"

The origins of the idea of the developmental state are complex.[1] Some commentators trace the idea of the developmental state to the work of Friedrich

List.[2] For other observers, the Japanese economist, Akamatsu Kaname, who was the originator of the "flying geese" theory of development in the 1930s, at a time when List's work was in the ascendant in Japan, provides a more recent point of origin for the idea of the developmental state in Asia.[3] In fact, as suggested in chapter 1, moderate and radical ideas in Japanese economic thought (which interacted with intellectual currents in Western Europe and North America) prior to 1945 provided an important setting for the emergence and codification of ideas about state-guided national development.[4] In earlier chapters, meanwhile, I have emphasized the importance of development economics as a precursor to the theory of the developmental state. The appearance of theories of the developmental state in the 1980s was also connected to the wider changes in political science and the social sciences, associated with the relative decline of political development theory and the revision of modernization theory (against the backdrop of the growing academic significance of dependency and world-system theory and Marxism) in the 1970s. As we have seen in chapter 3, modernization theory generally, and political development theory more specifically, were profoundly shaped in the 1950s and 1960s by the Social Science Research Council's (SSRC) Committee on Comparative Politics. In the context of the Cold War, the Committee played an important role in the establishment of the acceptable parameters of the professional study of politics and development and promulgated an alternative to Marxism that rested on an evolutionary, elite-oriented and unilinear conception of political and economic change grounded in a romanticized understanding of the history of the United States.[5] In particular, the Committee on Comparative Politics sought to effectively marginalize the conceptual use of the state in the post-war period.[6] Ironically, as we have also seen, the Committee on Comparative Politics played a role in "bringing the state back in" when it asked Charles Tilly to carry out a project that eventually resulted in the publication of *The Formation of National States in Western Europe* in 1975.[7] By assigning considerable importance to the role of violence in state formation and nation building, and by challenging the universalizing and ahistorical approach that was a key characteristic of political development theory, Tilly's book reinforced the process of theoretical and political diversification that was underway amongst political development theorists and in the social sciences more generally. In fact the Committee on Comparative Politics ceased operation in 1972. Tilly's book encapsulated the growing interest on the part of a number of North American social scientists in state-centered approaches to political, social and economic change.[8] This interest in the state was formalized with the formation of the SSRC's Committee on States and Social Structures in 1983, the body that sponsored the influential 1985 edited volume on "bringing the state back in" which included contributions by important proponents of the developmental state.[9]

At the same time, post-1945 Japan remains the crucial starting point for any effort to trace the medium- and short-term origins of the idea of the developmental state. As we have seen, up to the 1970s explanations for the economic resurgence of Japan generally centered on the idea that state intervention or close interaction between business and government had been crucial to the "Japanese Miracle".[10] By the time neo-liberalism rose to prominence at the end of 1970s there was far more contestation about the sources of Japan's success as influential commentators questioned the state-intervention or state-guided interpretation of Japanese success in the context of efforts to pressure Tokyo to adopt more liberal economic policies.[11] Into the 1980s, meanwhile, a growing number of academics conducted detailed studies that pointed to the complex, but clearly illiberal character of Japan's economic dynamism.[12] The resurgence of Japan, and the rise of East Asia more generally also fuelled the elaboration in the 1980s of a distinctive group of theories that characterized Japan and the NICs of Asia as developmental states. These commentators usually emphasized that South Korea and Japan in particular, and Taiwan and the other NICs in a more general fashion, were economically successful because they pursued comprehensive national industrial strategies based on direct state support for large corporations using high debt–equity ratios in an effort to gain competitive advantage in overseas markets. More broadly, a developmental state was increasingly defined as a state that derived its primary legitimacy from its effectiveness at promoting and sustaining high rates of economic growth via the restructuring of national production arrangements and its strategic engagement with the changing world economy.[13]

Chalmers Johnson's *MITI and the Japanese Miracle* (1982) is now widely regarded as the central text in the promotion of the developmental state approach to East Asian industrialization.[14] Johnson, who co-founded the Japan Policy Research Institute (JPRI) in 1994, served with the US Navy in the Pacific during the latter stages of the Korean War and then went on to study and then teach political science at the University of California (Berkeley) from the 1950s to the late 1980s. The central concern and argument of Johnson's foundational text is now well known. Writing retrospectively, Johnson himself has emphasized that he was primarily concerned to promote the notion of a "capitalist developmental state" as a way of moving beyond the distinction between the US and the Soviet economic models that had become central to the development debate during the Cold War. Researched and written in the 1970s, his book eventually appeared in 1982. The "essence" of his argument was that "credit" for the economic miracle in post-1945 Japan "should go primarily to the conscious and consistent governmental policies" that went back to the 1920s. In terms of the wider notion of a developmental state, which is drawn primarily from the final chapter of *MITI and the Japanese Miracle*, there is some irony in the fact that those parts of his 1982 book that have attracted the most attention over the years were included at the explicit direction of his publisher. Johnson himself was wary of drawing lessons from the Japanese trajectory (particularly the pre-1945 period). He was especially concerned that such an exercise could, in his words, lead to the conclusion "that fascism may be good for a nation". This concern was conveyed to his publisher in a letter in which he jokingly suggested that the final chapter of the book might be called "From the Wonderful Folks Who Brought You Pearl Harbour".[15] Given the direction in which the literature on the developmental state subsequently went, Johnson's concern about promoting the developmental state in a way that legitimated authoritarianism and militarism was, as we shall see, well founded.

By the end of the 1980s and the early 1990s, a number of approaches to capitalist development in East Asia, which emphasized the role of a developmental state in the process of national development and were inspired directly or indirectly by Johnson's work, had emerged and gained some influence. This revisionist Anglo-American work became increasingly policy-oriented in an effort to challenge the dominant neo-liberal approach to capitalist development.[16] This literature emerged as an important element in the wider struggle between the Japanese (state-centered) model and the US (market-oriented) model of capitalist development.[17] It also overlapped with the struggle at the World Bank, between the Japanese government on the one hand and supporters of neo-liberalism on the other. This period saw a growing interest on the part of proponents of the developmental state in identifying strong states (usually defined as states that had a high degree of coercive capability, relative independence or autonomy from certain classes or sectors of society and were capable of intervening to restructure society or direct the market) and extracting lessons from their developmental achievements. In the context of the neo-liberal ascendancy, developmental state theorists not only criticized free-market interpretations of the rise of East Asia, they often also emphasized that state intervention and protectionist policies had historically played far more of a role in the industrialization of Britain and the US than the idealized image of the rise of the West would suggest. For a number of writers their primary concern with studying the developmental states of East Asia generally, and Japan specifically, was the lessons that could be gleaned to improve US economic productivity and competitiveness. For example, in *In the Shadow of the Rising Sun: The Political Roots of American Economic Decline* (1991), William S. Dietrich, a steel executive with a PhD in Political Science from the University of Pittsburgh, lamented the "anti-statist tradition" in the United States. For Dietrich, the "only way" the US could "counter the Japanese challenge and regain world economic leadership" was "through the comprehensive use of industrial policy". He called for "fundamental institutional change" that would lead to the creation of "a strong central state and a top professional bureaucracy" in the United States.[18]

Meanwhile, as we have seen in chapter 6, vulgarized versions of the idea of the developmental state were also beginning to have some purchase on the popular debate about East Asian dynamism. An influential study that emphasized the important role of the state in capitalist development in Asia and beyond in this period was James Fallows's *Looking at the Sun: The Rise of the New East Asian Economic and Political System* (1994). Fallows, a US journalist, argued that: "in Anglo-American theory the state gets *in the way* of the economy's growth and the people's happiness", but "[i]n the Asian model it is an indispensable tool toward those ends".[19] His book was criticized for its cultural/racial reductionism. Fallows's analysis certainly meshed with and reinforced the fixed conceptions of culture/race that underpinned the popular cultural explanations for the rise of East Asia inside and outside the region in this period.[20] While the journalistic approach outlined by Fallows reflected the relative success of the theory of the developmental state, its main academic proponents adopted a broad institutional analysis of the developmental state that sought to avoid treating the state in monolithic terms and focused on the interaction between state institutions and the market. At the same time, developmental state theory continued to be challenged directly and indirectly by a more explicitly Marxist-derived (state and class) political economy.[21] While a growing number of theoretically sophisticated perspectives emerged out of the debate over the developmental state, developmental state theorists (with few exceptions) were increasingly constrained by their efforts to extract policy lessons from the East Asian experience without attempting to come to analyze why, in historical terms, strong institutions, or a developmental state, had emerged in East Asia. They collapsed space and time in their pursuit of technical and policy lessons. As will be discussed at the end of this chapter, even in recent work, such as Alice Amsden's *The Rise of "The Rest": Challenges to the West from Late-Industrializing Economies* (2001), proponents of revised versions of the developmental state (what Amsden, now a professor of political economy at the Massachusetts Institute of Technology, has called the "new developmentalism"), who seek to historicize late-industrialization, provide a highly selective analysis that continues to be ahistorical and technocratic.[22]

Bringing the state back in II: "Asia's Next Giant"

Amsden's work in the late 1980s was an important example of the academic studies of the developmental state that were influenced by Johnson's own work and/or by the SSRC's Committee on States and Social Structures. Amsden and others focused more on South Korea and Taiwan and the other NICs, than on Japan.[23] They were also generally more concerned with the significance of the rise of East Asia for the rest of the so-called Third World than for the United States.[24] They sought to find lessons that would allow developing nations elsewhere to replicate the success of South Korea and Taiwan. Amsden's book, *Asia's Next Giant: South Korea and Late Industrialization* (1989), had emerged as a key text in developmental state theory by the early 1990s. Amsden's overall argument that industrialization in South Korea flowed from "government initiatives and not the forces of the free market" and that this was "applicable to similar countries" was a clear and explicit challenge to neo-liberal interpretations of the South Korean trajectory and to the types of lessons that neo-liberalism sought to draw from the East Asian Miracle.[25] Her work, which extracted lessons from the distinctive South Korean experience and then emphasized their relevance for "similar countries", also clearly embodied the technocratic and ahistorical assumptions that were at the center of the developmental state tradition as it was codified and consolidated by the end of the 1980s.

This problem was also apparent in the work of a group of authors at the Institute of Development Studies at the University of Sussex in Britain with whom Amsden's perspective intersected. Robert Wade, a onetime employee of the World Bank, became the most well-known of the so-called Sussex School. His book-length study of industrial policy and performance in East Asia, which appeared in 1990, established him as one of the key writers in the developmental state tradition. In *Governing the Market*, Wade (now based at the Development Studies Institute at the London School of Economics and Political Science) sought to develop a theory of the "governed market" that clearly built on the developmental state approach and on ideas about development that flowed from development economics.[26] Although, as we have seen, development economics had declined dramatically by the end of the 1970s, its influence survived in the academy, while the careers of some of the main theorists of the developmental state, such as Wade and Sanjaya Lall, were clearly influenced by their work as development economists for the World Bank (the former was a staff member at the World Bank for a period in the 1970s and 1980s, while the latter worked there during the years 1965–1968 and 1985–1987) at a time, or times, when it was central to the shift from development economics to neo-classical economics.[27]

The emergence of state-centered challenges to neo-classical explanations for the rise of East Asian capitalism was an important complement to the relative recovery of development economics and the growing significance of political economy as a sub-discipline of political science by the second half of the 1980s. However, developmental state theory, like neo-liberalism, increasingly perpetuated an elite-oriented ahistorical approach to capitalist development as it moved away from an emphasis on *la longue durée* that was apparent in Johnson's excavation of the role of MITI in Japanese economic development between 1925 and 1975. For example, the first part of Linda Weiss and John Hobson's 1995 comparative study of states and economic development provides a history of the rise of Western Europe in which they argue in favor of a model of change that centers on a conflict between the state and the "dominant class". They emphasize that conflict between subordinate and dominate classes played a minimal role in state formation in Europe up to the eighteenth century. While this emphasis can be debated, the first part of the book does attempt to take an historical approach. However, the second part of the book, on East Asia since 1945, contains very little that can be described as historical analysis and narrowly defines the impact of the US in order to argue that the US role was irrelevant and may even have been detrimental to development efforts in South Korea and Taiwan after 1945. They frame the debate in terms of US intentions and define the US role in narrow economic terms.[28] Then, in putting their case, they make very selective, but repeated, use of the influential 1991 book on South Korea by Jung-En Woo (Meredith Woo-Cumings).[29] It is ironic that Weiss and Hobson drew so heavily on Woo's book as it (like her other work) provides a particularly detailed historical analysis that emphasizes the central importance of Japanese colonialism and of US Cold War imperatives in providing the overall context for the rise of an authoritarian, developmental and national security state in South Korea.[30] In fact, Woo-Cumings's emphasis on the state and finance in South Korea draws particular attention to the way internal shifts and initiatives were conditioned and interacted with external influences such as US geo-political and economic considerations and the dynamics of the Cold War generally.

Bringing the state back in III: "Pathways from the Periphery"

As in the case of Woo-Cumings's work, the importance of the wider international context was central to the approach taken by some proponents of the developmental state. In fact, some writers who became key theorists of the developmental state, such as Peter Evans, emerged directly from revisionist trends in dependency theory, an approach that focused primarily on the international context. His early work on Latin America, particularly Brazil, exemplified the link between the revision of classical dependency theory and the theory of the developmental state. His work also reflected the intersection between developmental state theory and the growing interest by the 1980s in comparing national paths to industrialization in East Asia with national trajectories in Latin America.[31] Classical dependency theory assumed that the international political economy was hierarchical and the relations of dominance and subordination within the world system reproduced and entrenched inequality between and within nation-states. The work of early dependency theorists (exemplified by the books written by André Gunder Frank in the 1960s and early 1970s) had failed to explain industrialization on the periphery because the model it subscribed to assumed that development on the periphery could not take place without a complete break with the capitalist order.[32] This resulted in a range of revisions to dependency theory in the 1970s and 1980s that sought to retain many of its insights, while providing a more nuanced approach to the dynamics of capitalist transformation.[33] By the 1970s, Immanuel Wallerstein's world-system theory had emerged as the most important single trend in radical social science and radical development theory.[34] At the same time, against the backdrop of the relative developmental success of East Asia by the 1970s and 1980s, dependency theory and world-system theory gained far more purchase in Latin American studies and African studies than they did in Asian studies.[35]

World-system theory ultimately rested on the assumption that the modern world-system has an historical significance as a totality. At the core of world-system theory is the notion that a particular nation-state's internal development can be understood only with reference to the position it occupies in the modern world-system as a whole. From this perspective the world economy is a singular entity, yet within it there are a number of political entities. World-system theorists trace the historical development of capitalism by focusing on the emergence and functioning of an international market comprising three levels, the periphery, semi-periphery and the core, and attempt to chart the trajectories of nation-states as a function of the logic of the emergence and expansion of this global capitalist economy. Inequality emerges and is maintained as a systemic characteristic because different regions within the world-system produce commodities for exchange using different labor control systems. The economic stagnation of the periphery, and the continued and even expanding gap between it and the core of the world-economy, were seen to flow from the privileged position held by core polities because of the historical terms under which they initially entered the world economy.[36]

Not surprisingly, world-system theory prompted considerable debate.[37] The emphasis on international economic relations left world-system theorists open to charges of economic determinism. Their model has also been understood to imply that the history of classes and nation-states is driven by the world capitalist system itself. Actors rarely appear to act in the system, but are acted on by it. The conception of power used by world-system theorists saw power as located in the structure of the international economy itself, particularly in the upper levels of the international order, in contrast to a more orthodox Marxist conception of power as flowing from class relationships and state structures. As a result world-system theory, or at least some influential strands of it, tended to represent change as a function of elite decision-making, or of the system itself, rather than holding out social struggles or nation-state interactions and initiatives as the cause of change.[38] Furthermore, despite its concern to take on a perspective that transcends the focus on the nation-state (which is still conceptually central to development theory and the social sciences generally), world-system theory used the nation-state as its basic unit of analysis in a fashion which facilitated the routinization of the nation-state and the nation-state system.

Dependency theory and world-system theory were increasingly being challenged and revised by the late 1970s to provide both a greater sense of regional and national specificity and to better explain successful industrialization on the periphery, particularly in key nation-states in Latin America prior to the 1980s and the NICs of Asia.[39] For example, in the late 1970s Peter Evans wrote an important book on Brazil that built on Fernando Enrique Cardoso's notion of "dependent development". Evans's study, which is regarded as a major contribution to the revision of dependency theory, represented late-industrialization in Brazil as a strategy of successful "dependent development". He emphasized that the increasing involvement of transnational capital in the Brazilian import-substitution industrialization process had to be understood as part of a "triple alliance" between foreign companies, local companies and the state.[40]

An important text that reflected the influence of dependency and world-system theory on the work of some theorists of the developmental state was Stephan Haggard's *Pathways from the Periphery* (1990).[41] This was Haggard's main contribution to the ongoing revision of dependency and world-system theory at the same time as it also represented an important contribution to the theory of the developmental state. A key argument of Haggard's book was that the "international context" was an important key to "understanding the policy choices of relatively weak states". He emphasized the significance of the size of the nation-state, the role of "great powers" and the impact of "macroeconomic shocks". At the same time, he argued that theories that sought to ascertain policy choices based exclusively on an assessment of the "configuration of social forces" (using interest group approaches or class analysis) had "fundamental" problems in theoretical and empirical terms. He emphasized that, while the impact of social forces on policy-making is beyond dispute, it is invariably mediated by institutional contexts. In some late-industrializing nation-states governing elites have inherited or erected institutions and organizations that make it very difficult for other social forces to have a significant impact on the political process and on economic policy. His third key argument was that, while the international setting can often stimulate, and the overall social structure within a particular nation conditions, particular policy shifts, they are also "heavily conditioned by the interests of political elites" in putting together and retaining "bases of support". He argued that the development strategies adopted by particular nation-states and the way in which they are carried out flows more from the "politically driven choices of state elites: the tactical give-and-take and coalition building characteristic of political life" than it does from the overall dynamics of social change. Finally, he argued that the "state" is not just "an actor but a set of institutions that exhibit continuity over time; a field of play that provides differential incentives for groups to organize". As a result of differences in the structure of institutions, political elites possess disparate capacities for organizing the population and pursuing developmental or other objectives. This "institutional variation" is crucial to any explanation for the type of development policies pursued by particular nation-states. For Haggard "political explanations" for economic development needed to focus on "the intersection between choice and institutional constraint".[42]

Despite Haggard's emphasis on context and conjuncture, as the 1990s progressed most writers in the developmental state tradition ended up treating the developmental state in a relatively narrow fashion as a policy-making body. There was and is insufficient recognition of the complicated and contested social relations in which it was embedded (and even when this was addressed by writers such as Peter Evans, the results remained ahistorical and technocratic). For proponents of the developmental state, economic development ultimately involved the subordination or containment of major social actors to state power, while complicated historical processes were regularly reinvented as technocratic and managerial practices.[43] The ahistorical character of much of their analysis and the way in which theories of the developmental state, like their neo-liberal counterparts, became increasingly implicated in a vision of the East Asian Miracle that had discovered the key to continued prosperity and progress was thrown into sharp relief by the Asian crisis.

The decline of the developmental state

The Asian crisis and after I: "The Myth of the Powerless State"

While many observers saw the Asian crisis as an indictment of the developmental state, defenders of state-guided development (and even some proponents of neo-classical economics) argued that the crisis needed to be understood primarily in terms of unregulated financial markets of which boom-bust cycles are a normal element, rather than as a result of an excess of state intervention or "crony capitalism". For example, in a major work of developmental state theory, which was published in the midst of the Asian crisis and entitled *The Myth of the Powerless State* (1998), Linda Weiss emphasized the need to differentiate between "state *involvement*" and "state *transformative capacity*", arguing that if the state was "part of the problem" in the Asian crisis it was as a result of "*too little state capacity*, rather than too much state involvement".[44] Certainly the Asian crisis needs to be understood in terms of unregulated financial markets, and in terms of state capacity rather than state involvement *per se*. Nevertheless, the events of 1997–1998 profoundly weakened the increasingly technocratic and ahistorical image of a developmental state presiding over steady economic growth and widening prosperity, which was central to the narrative on East Asia produced by proponents of the theory of the developmental state.[45] In fact, the actual developmental states in East Asia were in disarray well before the crisis. As we will see in chapter 8, the state-guided national development project in South Korea (that emerged as a paradigmatic developmental state) was being undone by its own success and by the wider historical context in which it operated by the late 1980s and early 1990s if not before. The developmental state in South Korea was able to pursue certain developmental objectives for many years because the state was particularly well insulated from the wider social order, especially from those social classes that might have challenged or undermined its developmental goals. The relative autonomy of the South Korean state, and its ability to spearhead a particularly successful national development effort, was grounded in the particular history of the Korean peninsula in the twentieth century. However, the success of the developmental state in South Korea led to a strengthening of various social classes whose growing political demands had dramatically weakened state autonomy by the second half of the 1980s. When this change intersected with the increasingly global, but still highly uneven, shift from national development to globalization against the backdrop of the waning of the Cold War, the result was the retreat of the developmental state in South Korea.[46] This process was repeated, with important variations, in Taiwan and elsewhere.[47]

Furthermore, the identification of developmental states such as South Korea as a more general model by writers such as Weiss and Amsden also provided implicit, if not explicit, justification for authoritarianism and militarism, highlighting the connection between theories of the developmental state and early theories of military-led modernization. While Samuel Huntington and the military modernization theorists were preoccupied with security and political order, advocates of the developmental state focused on the state's capacity to bring about economic development, setting out successful development under state auspices as the best guarantee for strengthening the power of the state. But they both emphasized that the power and capacity of the state was the basis for social and economic development.[48] For example, in *The Myth of the Powerless State*

(1998), Weiss criticized the way in which "the South Koreans have increasingly *relinquished* state control over the past decade".[49] This approach sidestepped the authoritarian character of the state prior to the late 1980s and the way in which the South Koreans "relinquished state control" over the economy was linked to wider political and social struggles and the transition from authoritarian to parliamentary politics. Meanwhile, Adrian Leftwich recently provided an even more explicit attempt to legitimate authoritarian developmental states and argue that "democracy" is an obstacle to development. He revived Gunnar Myrdal's distinction between "soft" and "hard" states (which was discussed in chapter 2). Myrdal's distinction had been part of a wider lament about how "democracy" (a "soft" state) had been an obstacle to development in the 1950s and 1960s in India and Indonesia, leading him to argue in favor of a "hard" state.[50] What is of particular significance here is the way in which theories of the developmental state ultimately remained part of the dominant economic policy discourse and perpetuated a technocratic and ahistorical approach to capitalist development. Like earlier theories of development and modernization and like their neo-liberal opponents, they are oriented towards government officials, politicians and planners.[51] Symptomatic of the retreat from historical analysis that characterizes most studies of the developmental state is the way that proponents of the developmental state have either naturalized culture/race, or treated it as irrelevant. For example, Jung-En Woo, whose work is far more historically grounded than most other writers in the developmental state tradition, argued that the rise of South Korea was "neither a miracle nor a cultural mystery, but the outcome of a misunderstood political economy". In her book she sought to "merge Korea with the stream of world history by discovering universal aspects of its development".[52] Although she implied that the South Korean trajectory was best understood as a variation on a universally applicable state-centered late-industrializing model, her book provided a detailed and historically particular analysis of the roots and rise of the South Korean developmental state.

By the 1990s most proponents of the developmental state perpetuated a technocratic, ahistorical approach to capitalist development in South Korea and beyond. Contrary to the view outlined by proponents of the developmental state such as Linda Weiss and Robert Wade, the rise of the US-led globalization project and the end of the Cold War have dramatically altered the capacity of states to guide national development, or revitalize national developmentalism.[53] One of the particular weaknesses of Weiss's analysis is that she defines globalization primarily, if not exclusively, in economic terms in an effort to minimize its significance.[54] Following an examination of trade patterns and capital flows, she concludes that there has not been nearly as much globalization as its proponents claim.[55] In a similar vein, Robert Wade notes that: "in the bigger national economies, more than 80 per cent of production is for domestic consumption and more than 80 per cent of investment by domestic investors".[56] However, it should not be assumed that trade and investment flows within national economies can simply be described as *national*, while trade and investment that moves between nation-states is *global*. As Martin Shaw has observed, what Weiss and Wade's exercise demonstrates is that trade and capital movements are "still measured in national and international terms".[57] I will cite just one example, to illustrate the problem associated with measuring the extent of globalization in this way. In Malaysia, as in many other parts of the world, hypermarkets owned by multinational corporations are increasingly displacing small locally owned shops and shopping centers. One of the main chains, Carrefour, which is head-quartered in France, now operates half a dozen large stores in Malaysia and purchases almost 80 percent of its merchandise within the national economy of Malaysia.[58] However, the fact that Carrefour buys the bulk of its goods in Malaysia tells us nothing about the wider economic, social and cultural signifi-cance of the spread of hypermarkets in Malaysia and beyond, even though this trend clearly reflects important changes that are directly linked to the rise of the US-led globalization project.

Building on her argument that the extent of globalization has been exagger-ated, Weiss also asserts that most states have far more capacity than is generally assumed and that this capacity could be deployed as part of a wider renewal of state-mediated national development.[59] Meanwhile Wade argues that: "there is more scope for government action to boost the productivity of firms operating within their territory than is commonly thought".[60] This approach fails to address the serious internal contradictions that were apparent in national development projects worldwide by the 1970s, and the growing external pressures associated with the US-led globalization project by the 1980s. Most importantly for the argument being outlined here, globalization is an uneven, heterogenous and multi-faceted process of political, social and cultural change that is conditioned, but not determined, by processes in which the state is increasingly oriented towards intervening in economic activity in a globalizing, rather than a national developmental, capacity.[61] The celebration of the market and the anti-statism of the dominant neo-liberal narrative have often obscured the changing, but impor-tant, role of nation-states in the US-led globalization project. Many developmental state theorists compounded this problem by focusing in an ahistor-ical fashion on the strength of developmental states in East Asia (or Northwest Europe) in contrast to the perceived relative absence or weakness of the state in the Anglo-American trajectories. However, this formulation obscures the way that the globalization project is being consolidated via the nation-state system and the way that the US state is central to, and one of the strongest states in, the highly uneven transformation of nation-states into neo-liberal states.[62] The US-led glob-alization project emerged following the universalization of the nation-state system and is now engaged in the dramatic reorientation of the nation-state system which has even more fundamental implications than in the past regarding what kind of intervention specific nation-states are able to carry out.

The Asian crisis and after II: "The Rise of the 'The Rest'"

As we have seen in chapter 5, the World Bank did not embrace the develop-mental state in its 1993 Report; however, under pressure from Japan and elsewhere, it did revise its neo-classical perspective in a direction that sought increasingly as the 1990s progressed to find some sort of common ground with the model promoted by the Japanese government and by theorists of the developmental state. In turn, since 1993 some writers broadly in the developmental state tradition have sought to revise their work, by engaging with, or drawing on, the new institutionalism and the new political economy that contributed to the revision of neo-liberalism in the 1990s. This process of revision is apparent in the later work of Alice Amsden and Peter Evans who had both gained considerable prominence in academic and policy circles by the 1990s. Amsden and Evans were both keynote speakers at the post-Asian crisis "High-level Roundtable on Trade and Development: Directions for the Twenty-first Century" at the United Nations Conference on Trade and Development (UNCTAD) X held in Bangkok in early February 2000. One of the most widely reported aspects of the Conference was the valediction delivered to the assembled UN representatives and guests, by Michael Camdessus (the retiring head of the IMF), praising the Thai government for its fealty to the IMF-mandated approach to the financial crisis, in contrast to its southern neighbor, Malaysia. The "High-level Roundtable", meanwhile, received less attention. It featured a range of academic luminaries of development theory, and a leavening of former officials of national and international financial bodies, presenting papers to government representatives of the member nations of the UN and an assortment of accredited guests. The paper-presenters covered a wide range. There were advocates of the free market who continued to argue that the solutions to virtually all development problems were to be found in neo-classical economics and neo-liberal policies. At the same time, there were also proponents of an updated form of the developmental state. For example, in her address Amsden called for a "new developmentalism" and continued to extract universal lessons from the historically specific experience of South Korea. While most participants wondered whether the market had gone too far, there were no serious challenges made to the neo-liberal framework. At the same time, the presentations by Amsden and Evans were indicative of the revision of the theory of the developmental state that had occurred in some quarters by the second half of the 1990s against the backdrop of the continued elaboration and amplification of the US-led globalization project.[63]

Evans and Amsden's presentations at the "High-level Roundtable on Trade and Development" reflected the key themes of their published (or soon-to-be-published) work. By the mid-1990s, for example, Peter Evans's focus had shifted in the context of the wider changes in the development debate. His work reflected the effort to move beyond "state" versus "market" explanations.[64] This was occurring in the context of the interaction between theories of the developmental state and rational choice theory (particularly the new political economy and the new institutionalism).[65] This concern was also reflected in books such as *Beyond the Developmental State* (1998), which aspired to be an exercise in "bringing the society back in". The editors argued that explanations for the economic success of a number of national trajectories in East Asia did not lie with either/or propositions about the state and the market. They also emphasized the way in which the developmental states had been weakened, undermined or dramatically reoriented by the social changes that accompanied the wider transformation over which they had presided.[66] In a similar vein Evans insisted that "sterile debates" about the level of state intervention needed to give way to debates about the type of intervention and its results. He emphasized that the involvement of the state "is a given" and the main issue is "not 'how much' but 'what kind' " of involvement. His point of departure in understanding different forms of state involvement was that states differ significantly in terms of their institutional character and the types of connections they have to society. This results in "different capacities for action" and distinct limits on "the range of roles that the state is capable of playing". Evans divided states into what he called "two historically grounded ideal types". These were predatory and developmental states. Predatory states, in his typology, exploited the vast majority of the people living within their territorial boundaries, actively undermining development, in both the broad social sense of the term and in the much narrower sense of basic capital accumulation. Developmental states, meanwhile, facilitated industrial transformation on a broad scale. He characterized his perspective as a "comparative institutional approach", emphasizing the need to avoid analyzing the state as a "reified monolith". Evans directly challenged the neo-liberal idea ("neo-utilitarian" in his terminology) that "state power" was "the cause of predation" and that the curbing of that power was the solution. He argued that developmental states demonstrated that "state capacity" could serve as an "antidote to predation". At the same time, state transformative capacity also depended on "state–society relations". While states that had very high degrees of autonomy from society could be exceedingly predatory, developmental states had to be "immersed in a dense network of ties that bind them to societal allies with transformative goals". According to Evans, it is "embedded autonomy, not just autonomy" that "gives the developmental state its efficacy". As with earlier theorists of the developmental state, Evans argued that "close ties to key social groups" is "fundamental to developmental efficacy". He concluded that, while "markets work only if they are 'embedded' in other forms of social relations, it seems likely that states must be 'embedded' in order to be effective".[67] While Evans's shift away from a focus on intervention *per se* to types of intervention was important, his analysis also worked to legitimize authoritarianism and his discussion of questions of "state capacity" and his comparative framework continued to naturalize the nation-state. Ultimately his approach reflected the increasingly technocratic and ahistorical direction of developmental state theory by the second half of the 1990s.

The connection between Evans and Amsden's work, meanwhile, is readily apparent. They come from a similar generation and milieux: both were involved (as editor and/or contributor) with the 1985 volume *Bringing the State Back In* and both point to the same intellectual influences on their work, such as Alexander Gerschenkron.[68] Like Evans, Amsden's earlier work had strong links to Johnson and Wade. At the same time, her book-length study, *The Rise of the "The Rest"*, which appeared in 2001, reflected her ongoing promotion and revision of the developmental state, or what she called the "new developmentalism" in her address in Bangkok in 2000. In *The Rise of the "The Rest"* Amsden observed that "one of the most" debated questions in relation to the rise of *"the rest"* (the group of "backward countries" that were already distinguished from *"the remainder"* by 1945 because of their possession of "manufacturing experience") was the "role played by government". She argued that the governments (she uses "government" interchangeably with "state" and "country") in this group of late-industrializing nation-states (which in her analysis includes: India, China, Korea, Taiwan, Malaysia, Indonesia, Thailand, Argentina, Brazil, Chile, Mexico and Turkey) all deliberately and systematically intervened in the market because there were "too few knowledge-based assets" within their borders to allow for successful competition in the world economy. She characterized her analysis as an "assets approach to industrial development". Explicitly building on, but revising Gerschenkron, she argues that there is not necessarily more "government intervention" in situations of late-industrialization, but it is quite likely to be *"different"*.[69]

Reflecting a direct engagement with rational choice theory, in the form of the new political economy and the new institutionalism, Amsden based her analysis of late-industrialization on three main assumptions, which are grounded in, but also reflect important departures from, the work of Douglass North.[70] First, for Amsden, the security of "property rights" was seen as "a necessary but an insufficient condition for industrializing late" (she also notes that property rights do not have to be private to be secure). By contrast, for new institutionalists, such as North, "secure" and private "property rights" and "perfect information" are assumed to be a "sufficient condition of growth". However, as she observed, "even if 'information'" (which she defined as "publicly accessible facts") was "perfect", "imperfect 'knowledge'" (which she characterized as "proprietary concepts") might result in "production costs" for "learners" greater than was the case for "incumbents". Against this backdrop she emphasized that successful late-industrialization *"involves moving from one set of distortions that is related to the rigidities of underdevelopment and primary product production to another set of distortions that is knowledge-based"*. Second, while many theories of economic growth assume that the structure and size of firms is not relevant, Amsden argued that late-industrialization could not occur without the creation of *"large-scale firms"*. Finally, her assets approach assumed that macroeconomic policies "do not matter in *the very long run"* (her book covered the periods from 1850–1950 and 1950–1980). Following on from a key argument of her earlier book on South Korea, she observed that "wildly wrong prices" made industrialization more difficult, "but the 'right' prices were not a precondition for industrialization: ironically, they were a constraint". Meanwhile, she also divided the countries in "the rest" into two possible sub-models that have emerged since the 1980s and might be followed by the nation-states of "the remainder". These are what she calls the "independent" approach, followed by South Korea, Taiwan, India and China, and the "integrationist" approach that has characterized Mexico, Chile and

Argentina (and less obviously Turkey). The independent model is based on "getting the institutions 'right'" and "building skills"; however, the integrationist model is grounded in "getting the prices 'right'" and "buying skills". She clearly regarded the former as having far greater "promise" than the latter.[71] Despite the ostensibly historical character of Amsden's analysis her use of history is very selective and her overall approach is technocratic. While she continues to challenge the dominant neo-liberal narrative, she also shares many of its main assumptions. In particular, like neo-liberalism she treats complex national trajectories as natural and nation-states as routine. These same criticisms can also be made of the influential work of Ha-Joon Chang, assistant direct of development studies at Cambridge University, who has worked as a consultant for the Asian Development Bank and the World Bank. His work has been celebrated, by journalists such as Michael Lind, as a powerful assault on the ahistorical character of the dominant development discourse.[72] However, his book, *Kicking Away the Ladder: Development Strategy in Historical Perspective*, wields "history" like a blunt instrument to defend state-mediated national development.[73] His work, like developmental state theorists generally, fails to come to grips with the universalization and transformation of the nation-state system in the second half of the twentieth century, or with the implications of the rise of the US-led globalization project. It is these world-historical changes, combined with the more particular capitalist transformation and Cold War history of East Asia, that are the backdrop for the rise and decline of the developmental state.

Conclusion: the rise and decline of the developmental state

This chapter has looked at the rise and decline of theories of the developmental state. It has been argued that theories of the developmental state have increasingly become ahistorical and/or technocratic in their efforts to explain capitalist success in Asia. It has further been argued that despite the revisions to the theory of the developmental state carried out by writers such as Peter Evans, Alice Amsden and Ha-Joon Chang, the deeper problems relating to the legitimation of authoritarianism and the continued commitment to an ahistorical and technocratic approach that seeks to extract universal lessons from discrete historical experiences have increasingly undermined the efforts by proponents of developmental state theory to challenge the globalization project. Ultimately, the theory of the developmental state is constrained by the same problems that beset the dominant neo-liberal narrative it seeks to challenge. These influential theories of development have all worked to routinize the nation-state with little or no regard for the complex history of the universalization and transformation of the nation-state system after 1945. In an attempt to move beyond the ahistorical and technocratic character of the dominant narratives on development in East Asia, the final two chapters turn to a historically grounded analysis of the transformation of Asia between the 1940s and the 1990s. The emphasis will be on the way in which the region was profoundly shaped by the uneven and destructive (as well as creative) processes of capitalist transformation. In this context there is a need to continue to emphasize social class, but in a historically and culturally contingent fashion. Linked to this is a need also to historicize rather than naturalize the nation-state and the nation-state system. At the same time, the changing role of the state in the shift from national development to globalization (and in capitalist transformation more generally) will also be foregrounded. The administrative and coercive institutions of government have been critical to shaping the cultural, social and economic spheres and attempting to define and redefine the very idea of the nation and what it means to be a citizen of the nation, at the same time as states are under increasing pressure to play an ever more globalizing role. Such a perspective allows for a critical and historically grounded approach to the transformation of Asia that highlights the historical specificity and contingent character of national trajectories. Furthermore, specific national trajectories are placed in the context of the wider history of decolonization and the important regional and global trends of the Cold War and post-Cold War eras.

Notes

1 B. Cumings, "Webs With No Spiders, Spiders With No Webs: The Genealogy of the Developmental State" in M. Woo-Cumings, ed., *The Developmental State*, Ithaca: Cornell University Press, 1999.

2 F. List, *The National System of Political Economy*, London: Longmans, Green and Company, 1916 (first published 1844).

3 P. Korhonen, "The Theory of the Flying Geese Pattern of Development and its Interpretations" *Journal of Peace Research* vol. 31, no. 1, 1994; E. Terry, *How Asia Got Rich: Japan, China and the Asian Miracle*, Armonk: M. E. Sharpe, 2002, pp. 46–101.

4 T. Morris-Suzuki, *A History of Japanese Economic Thought*, 2nd edn, London: Routledge, 1991.

5 N. Gilman, *Mandarins of the Future: Modernization Theory in Cold War America*, Baltimore: Johns Hopkins University Press, 2003; M. E. Latham, *Modernization as Ideology: American Social Science and "Nation Building" in the Kennedy Era*, Chapel Hill: University of North Carolina Press, 2000.

6 T. Mitchell, "The Limits of the State: Beyond Statist Approaches and their Critics" *American Political Science Review* vol. 85, no. 1, 1991, pp. 78–9.

7 C. Tilly, ed., *The Formation of National States in Western Europe*, Princeton: Princeton University Press, 1975.

8 S. Heydemann, "War, Institutions, and Social Change in the Middle East" in S. Heydemann, ed., *War, Institutions, and Social Change in the Middle East*, Berkeley: University of California Press, 2000, pp. 5–7, 28–9.

9 T. Skocpol, "Bringing the State Back In: Strategies of Analysis in Current Research" in P. B. Evans, D. Rueshemeyer and T. Skocpol, eds, *Bringing the State Back In*, New York: Cambridge University Press, 1985.

10 For example, see W. W. Lockwood, "Japan's New Capitalism" in W. W. Lockwood, ed., *The State and Economic Enterprise in Japan*, Princeton: Princeton University Press, 1965, p. 503; E. O. Reischauer, J. K. Fairbank and A. Craig, *East Asia: Tradition and Transformation*, Boston: Houghton Mifflin, 1973, pp. 829–30.

11 H. Patrick and H. Rosovsky, "Japan's Economic Performance: An Overview" and "Prospects for the Future and Some Other Implications" in H. Patrick and H. Rosovsky, eds, *Asia's New Giant: How the Japanese Economy Works*, Washington, DC: Brookings Institution, 1976.

214   *The globalization project*

12 R. Dore, *Flexible Rigidities: Industrial Policy and Structural Adjustment in the Japanese Economy,
    1970–1980*, Stanford: Stanford University Press, 1986; R. J. Samuels, *The Business of
    the Japanese State: Energy Markets in Comparative and Historical Perspective*, Ithaca: Cornell
    University Press, 1987; K. E. Calder, *Crisis and Compensation: Public Policy and Political
    Stability in Japan, 1949–1986*, Princeton: Princeton University Press, 1988; T. Inoguchi
    and D. Okimoto, eds, *The Political Economy of Japan*, Stanford: Stanford University
    Press, 1988; D. Friedman, *The Misunderstood Miracle: Industrial Development and Political
    Change in Japan*, Ithaca: Cornell University Press, 1988; D. I. Okimoto and T. P.
    Rohlen, eds, *Inside the Japanese System: Readings on Contemporary Society and Political
    Economy*, Stanford: Stanford University Press, 1988; D. Okimoto, *Between MITI and the
    Market: Japanese Industrial Policy for High Technology*, Stanford: Stanford University Press,
    1989; K. E. Calder, *Strategic Capitalism: Private Business and Public Purpose in Japanese
    Industrial Finance*, Princeton: Princeton University Press, 1993; R. J. Samuels, *"Rich
    Nation, Strong Army": National Security and Ideology in the Technological Transformation of
    Japan*, Ithaca: Cornell University Press, 1994.
13 M. Castells, "Four Asian Tigers with a Dragon Head: A Comparative Analysis of the
    State, Economy and Society in the Asian Pacific Rim" in R. P. Appelbaum and J.
    Henderson, eds, *States and Development in the Asian Pacific Rim*, Newbury Park: Sage,
    1992, p. 56.
14 C. Johnson, *MITI and the Japanese Miracle: The Growth of Industrial Policy 1925–1975*,
    Stanford: Stanford University Press, 1982. Also see C. Johnson, *Japan: Who Governs?
    The Rise of the Developmental State*, New York: W. W. Norton, 1995.
15 C. Johnson, "The Developmental State: Odyssey of a Concept" in M. Woo-Cumings,
    ed., *The Developmental State*, Ithaca: Cornell University Press, 1999, pp. 32, 37–40.
16 For good overviews of developmental state theory see J. Henderson and R. P.
    Appelbaum, "Situating the State in the East Asian Development Process" in R. P.
    Appelbaum and J. Henderson, eds, *States and Development in the Asian Pacific Rim*,
    Newbury Park: Sage, 1992; M. Woo-Cumings "Introduction: Chalmers Johnson and
    the Politics of Nationalism and Development" in M. Woo-Cumings, ed., *The
    Developmental State*, Ithaca: Cornell University Press, 1999.
17 F. Fajnzylber, "The United States and Japan as Models of Industrialisation" in G.
    Gereffi and D. L. Wyman, eds, *Manufacturing Miracles: Paths of Industrialisation in Latin
    America and East Asia*, Princeton: Princeton University Press, 1990.
18 W. S. Dietrich, *In the Shadow of the Rising Sun: The Political Roots of American Economic
    Decline*, University Park: Pennsylvania State University Press, 1991, p. 248.
19 J. Fallows, *Looking at the Sun: The Rise of the New East Asian Economic and Political System*,
    New York: Pantheon, 1994, pp. 216–17 (italics in original). Also see J. Fallows, *More
    Like Us: Making America Great Again*, Boston: Houghton Mifflin, 1989.
20 Chalmers Johnson defended Fallows shortly after the book appeared. In a review in
    the influential magazine, *The Atlantic Monthly*, Johnson argued that it was now over-
    whelmingly obvious that in Japan and East Asia the state and the private sector have
    worked closely together to produce "safe, sane societies with astonishingly high levels
    of evenly distributed income". He also emphasized that Japan and China were the
    "only two" nation-states that "could threaten the national security of the United
    States" if Washington's current relationships with them broke down. C. Johnson,
    "Intellectual Warfare" *The Atlantic Monthly* January, 1995, pp. 99–104.
21 K. Hewison, R. Robison and G. Rodan, eds, *Southeast Asia in the 1990s: Authoritarianism,
    Democracy and Capitalism*, Sydney: Allen and Unwin, 1993.
22 A. H. Amsden, *The Rise of "The Rest": Challenges to the West from Late-Industrializing
    Economies*, New York: Oxford University Press, 2001.
23 For example, see A. H. Amsden, "Taiwan's Economic History" *Modern China* vol. 5,
    no. 3, 1979; A. H. Amsden, "The State and Taiwan's Economic Development" in P.
    B. Evans, D. Rueshemeyer and T. Skocpol, eds, *Bringing the State Back In*, New York:
    Cambridge University Press, 1985; T. B. Gold, *State and Society in the Taiwan Miracle*,

London: M. E. Sharpe, 1986; R. Wade, "State Intervention in 'Outward-Looking' Development: Neoclassical Theory and Taiwanese Practice" in G. White, ed., *Developmental States in East Asia*, London: Macmillan, 1988; H. Koo and E. M. Kim, "The Developmental State and Capital Accumulation in South Korea" in R. P. Appelbaum and J. Henderson, eds, *States and Development in the Asian Pacific Rim*, Newbury Park: Sage, 1992; A. H. Amsden, "Taiwan in International Perspective" in N. T. Wang, ed., *Taiwan's Enterprises in Global Perspective*, Armonk: M. E. Sharpe, 1992.

24 A. H. Amsden, "Third World Industrialization: 'Global Fordism' or a New Model?" *New Left Review (I)* no. 182, 1990; A. H. Amsden, "Diffusion of Development: The Late Industrializing Model and Greater East Asia" *American Economic Review* vol. 81, no. 2, 1991.

25 A. Amsden, *Asia's Next Giant: South Korea and Late Industrialization*, New York: Oxford University Press, 1989, p. 27.

26 R. Wade, *Governing the Market: Economic Theory and the Role of Government in East Asian Industrialization*, Princeton: Princeton University Press, 1990, p. 26.

27 S. Lall, *Learning from the Asian Tigers: Studies in Technology and Industrial Policy*, London: Macmillan, 1996.

28 L. Weiss and J. Hobson, *States and Economic Development: A Comparative Historical Analysis*, Cambridge: Polity Press, 1995, pp. 52–3, 158, 189–90.

29 J.-E. Woo, *Race to the Swift: State and Finance in Korean Industrialization*, New York: Columbia University Press, 1991.

30 M. Woo-Cumings, "The Political Economy of Growth in East Asia: A Perspective on the State, Market, and Ideology" in M. Aoki, H.-K. Kim and M. Okuno-Fujiwara, eds, *The Role of Government in East Asian Economic Development: Comparative Institutional Analysis*, New York: Oxford University Press, 1997; J.-E. Woo-Cumings, "National Security and the Rise of the Developmental State in South Korea and Taiwan" in H. S. Rowen, ed., *Behind East Asian Growth: The Political and Social Foundations of Prosperity*, London: Routledge, 1998.

31 P. Evans, "Class, State, and Dependence in East Asia: Lessons for Latin Americanists" in F. C. Deyo, ed., *The Political Economy of the New Asian Industrialism*, Ithaca: Cornell University Press, 1987; G. Gereffi, "Paths of Industrialization: An Overview" in G. Gereffi and D. L. Wyman, eds, *Manufacturing Miracles: Paths of Industrialisation in Latin America and East Asia*, Princeton: Princeton University Press, 1990; R. Jenkins, "Learning from the Gang: Are There Lessons for Latin America from East Asia" *Bulletin of Latin American Research* vol. 10, no. 1, 1991; R. Jenkins, "The Political Economy of Industrialization: A Comparison of Latin American and East Asian Newly Industrializing Countries" *Development and Change* vol. 22, no. 2, 1991; G. Gereffi, "Rethinking Development Theory: Insights from East Asia and Latin America" in A. D. Kincaid and A. Portes, eds, *Comparative National Development: Society and Economy in the New Global Order*, Chapel Hill: University of North Carolina Press, 1994; J. Borrego, A. A. Bejar and K. S. Jomo, eds, *Capital, the State, and Late Industrialization: Comparative Perspectives on the Pacific Rim*, Boulder: Westview, 1997. Also see N. Birdsall and F. Jaspersen, eds, *Pathways to Growth: Comparing East Asia and Latin America*, Washington, DC: Inter-American Development Bank, 1997.

32 A. G. Frank, *Capitalism and Underdevelopment in Latin America: Historical Studies of Chile and Brazil*, 2nd edn, New York: Monthly Review Press, 1969; A. G. Frank, *Latin America: Underdevelopment or Revolution: Essays on the Development of Underdevelopment and the Immediate Enemy*, 2nd edn, New York: Monthly Review Press, 1970; A. G. Frank, *Lumpen-Bourgeoisie, Lumpen-Development: Dependence, Class and Politics in Latin America*, New York: Monthly Review Press, 1972; A. G. Frank, *World Accumulation 1492–1789*, London: Macmillan, 1978; A. G. Frank, *Dependent Accumulation and Underdevelopment*, London: Macmillan, 1978.

33 For example, the work of Samir Amin represented an important revision of classical dependency theory in the 1970s and 1980s. S. Amin, *Accumulation on a World Scale: A*

Critique of the Theory of Underdevelopment, Sussex: Harvester Press, 1974; S. Amin, *Unequal Development: An Essay on the Social Formations of Peripheral Capitalism*, New York: Monthly Review Press, 1976; S. Amin, *Imperialism and Unequal Development*, New York: Monthly Review Press, 1977. See D. F. Ruccio and L. H. Simon, "Perspectives on Underdevelopment: Frank, the Modes of Production School and Amin" in C. K. Wilber and K. P. Jameson, eds, *The Political Economic of Development and Underdevelopment*, 5th edn, New York: McGraw-Hill, 1992.

34 I. Wallerstein, *The Modern World-System – I: Capitalist Agriculture and the Origins of the European World-Economy in the Sixteenth Century*, New York: Academic Press, 1974; I. Wallerstein, *The Modern World-System – II: Mercantilism and the Consolidation of the European World-Economy 1600–1750*, New York: Academic Press, 1980; I. Wallerstein, *The Modern World-System – III: The Second Era of Great Expansion of the Capitalist World-Economy 1730–1840s*, San Diego: Academic Press, 1989; I. Wallerstein, *Historical Capitalism with Capitalist Civilization*, London: Verso, 1995. Wallerstein was influenced by dependency theory and by the work of Fernand Braudel and the Annales School. The influence was a two-way affair insofar as volume three of Braudel's *Civilization and Capitalism* drew heavily on Wallerstein's modern world-system. F. Braudel, *Civilization and Capitalism 15th–18th Century: Volume Three, The Perspective of the World*, New York: Harper and Row, 1984, pp. 69–70; C. Ragin and D. Chirot, "The World System of Immanuel Wallerstein: Sociology and Politics as History" in T. Skocpol, ed., *Vision and Method in Historical Sociology*, Princeton: Princeton University Press, 1984, pp. 276–83, 311. On the Annales School see P. Burke, *The French Historical Revolution: The Annales School 1929–1989*, Cambridge: Polity Press, 1990.

35 In North America the particular centrality of language and culture to Asian Studies and the relative resilience of anti-Marxism and revised forms of modernization theory, along with the liberal structures of the North American university system, acted to prevent dependency and world-system theory from making significant inroads in Asian Studies. For a variety of reasons, to do with the oil boom and the centrality of the Middle East to US policy, dependency theory and world-system theory also had limited purchase in Middle Eastern studies in comparison to other sectors of area studies. See I. Gendzier, *Managing Political Change: Social Scientists and the Third World*, Boulder: Westview, 1985; M. T. Berger, *Under Northern Eyes: Latin American Studies and US Hegemony in the Americas 1898–1990*, Bloomington: Indiana University Press, 1995.

36 For a detailed overview of world-system theory and its impact see T. R. Shannon, *An Introduction to the World-System Perspective*, 2nd edn, Boulder: Westview, 1996.

37 See, for example, R. Brenner, "The Origins of Capitalist Development: A Critique of Neo-Smithian Marxism" *New Left Review (I)* no. 104, 1977; T. Skocpol, "Wallerstein's World Capitalist System: A Theoretical and Historical Critique" *American Journal of Sociology* vol. 82, no. 5, 1977; A. Brewer, *Marxist Theories of Imperialism: A Critical Survey*, London: Routledge and Kegan Paul, 1980, pp. 158–81; C. H. George, "The Origins of Capitalism: A Marxist Epitome and a Critique of Immanuel Wallerstein's Modern World-System" *Marxist Perspectives* vol. 3, no. 2, 1980; P. Worsley, "One World or Three? A Critique of the World-System Theory of Immanuel Wallerstein" *The Socialist Register 1980*, London: Merlin, 1980.

38 A book by Wallerstein and his colleagues in the late 1980s partially addressed this problem and gave greater agency to a range of actors in the modern world-system. G. Arrighi, T. K. Hopkins and I. Wallerstein, *Antisystemic Movements*, London: Verso, 1989.

39 Of course, there were writers who continued to argue into the 1980s that industrialization in Southeast Asia, at least, was "ersatz". For Yoshihara Kunio capitalism in Southeast Asia remained "ersatz" because the region remained dependent on foreign capital and technology and a strong local capitalist elite had not yet been consolidated. K. Yoshihara, *The Rise of Ersatz Capitalism in Southeast Asia*, Singapore: Oxford

University Press, 1988, pp. 3–4, 122–31. Meanwhile, Chris Dixon, argued in a similar fashion that the "sustainability" of economic growth in Southeast Asia in the 1990s was "open to serious question" and the various economies in Southeast Asia "remain locked into wider regional and international structures over which the countries collectively or individually have little control". C. Dixon, *Southeast Asia in the World-Economy: A Regional Geography*, Cambridge: Cambridge University Press, 1991, pp. 1–34, 218. Also see J. Clad, *Behind the Myth: Business, Money and Power in Southeast Asia*, 2nd edn, London: Grafton, 1991.

40 P. Evans, *Dependent Development: The Alliance of Multinational, State and Local Capital in Brazil*, Princeton: Princeton University Press, 1979. See F. H. Cardoso, "Associated Dependent Development: Theoretical and Practical Implications" in A. Stepan, ed., *Authoritarian Brazil*, New Haven: Yale University Press, 1973. By the 1980s other important new dependency work included the "post-imperialism" school of writers. See D. G. Becker, *The New Bourgeoisie and the Limits of Dependency*, Princeton: Princeton University Press, 1983; D. G. Becker, "Development, Democracy and Dependency in Latin America: A Post-Imperialist View" *Third World Quarterly: Journal of Emerging Areas* vol. 6, no. 2, 1984; D. G. Becker, J. Frieden, S. P. Schatz and R. L. Sklar, *Postimperialism: International Capitalism and Development in the Late Twentieth Century*, Boulder: Lynne Rienner, 1987; D. G. Becker and R. L. Sklar, "Introduction" in D. G. Becker and R. L. Sklar, eds, *Postimperialism in World Politics*, New York: Praeger, 1999.

41 S. Haggard, *Pathways from the Periphery: The Politics of Growth in the Newly Industrializing Countries*, Ithaca: Cornell University Press, 1990.

42 Haggard, *Pathways from the Periphery*, pp. 3–4, 15–17.

43 A. H. Choi, "Statism and Asian Political Economy: Is There a New Paradigm?" *Bulletin of Concerned Asian Scholars* vol. 30, no. 3, 1998, pp. 51, 55–6.

44 L. Weiss, *The Myth of the Powerless State: Governing the Economy in a Global Era*, Cambridge: Polity Press, 1998, pp. xii–xiii (italics in original).

45 D. C. Kang, *Crony Capitalism: Corruption and Development in South Korea and the Philippines*, Cambridge: Cambridge University Press, 2002, pp. 2–3.

46 J. Minns, "Of Miracles and Models: The Rise and Decline of the Developmental State in South Korea" *Third World Quarterly: Journal of Emerging Areas* vol. 22, no. 6, 2001.

47 For example, see M.-C. Tsai, "Dependency, the State and Class in the Neoliberal Transition of Taiwan" *Third World Quarterly: Journal of Emerging Areas* vol. 22, no. 3, 2001.

48 J. Martinussen, *Society, State and Market*, London: Zed Books, 1997, p. 239.

49 Weiss, *The Myth of the Powerless State*, pp. xiii–xiv (italics in original).

50 A. Leftwich, *States of Development: On the Primacy of Politics in Development*, Cambridge: Polity Press, 2000, pp. 15, 80–1. See G. Myrdal, *Asian Drama: An Inquiry into the Poverty of Nations*, volume 1, London: Penguin, in association with the Twentieth Century Fund, 1968, pp. 47, 66–7.

51 P. W. Preston, *Rethinking Development: Essays on Development in Southeast Asia*, London: Routledge and Kegan Paul, 1987, p. 43.

52 Woo, *Race to the Swift*, pp. ix, 2–4.

53 L. Weiss, "Globalization and the Myth of the Powerless State" *New Left Review (I)* no. 225, 1997. Also see L. Weiss, "Managed Openness: Beyond Neoliberal Globalism" *New Left Review (I)* no. 238, 1999. Göran Therborn has also argued that, at least in "the developed democracies", the "state's capacity to pursue policy targets" has not "diminished". What he fails to emphasize is the fact that this capacity has usually been dramatically reoriented towards increasingly neo-liberal policy goals. See G. Therbon, "Into the 21st Century: The New Parameters of Global Politics" *New Left Review (II)* no. 10, 2001, p. 91.

54 Weiss, *The Myth of the Powerless State*, pp. 167–87.

55 One of Weiss's targets is K. Ohmae, *The End of the Nation-State: The Rise of Regional Economies*, London: HarperCollins, 1995.

56 R. Wade, "Globalization and Its Limits: Reports of the Death of the National Economy are Greatly Exaggerated" in S. Berger and R. Dore, eds, *National Diversity and Global Capitalism*, Ithaca: Cornell University Press, 1996, pp. 60–1.

57 M. Shaw, *Theory of the Global State: Globality as an Unfinished Revolution*, Cambridge: Cambridge University Press, 2000, pp. 14, 72–3, 81–2.

58 C. Prystay, "Malaysia: The Retail-Shopping War" *Far Eastern Economic Review* April 25, 2002, pp. 36–7.

59 Weiss, *The Myth of the Powerless State*, pp. 1–40, 188–212.

60 Wade, "Globalization and Its Limits", pp. 60–1.

61 J. H. Mittelman, *The Globalization Syndrome: Transformation and Resistance*, Princeton: Princeton University Press, 2000, pp. 15–26. This shift involves a host of complexities associated with domestication, accommodation and resistance. A. Appadurai, *Modernity at Large: Cultural Dimensions of Globalization*, Minneapolis: University of Minnesota Press, 1996.

62 L. Panitch, "The New Imperial State" *New Left Review (II)* no. 2, 2000, pp. 6–8, 14–15. S. Sassen, *Losing Control: Sovereignty in an Age of Globalization*, New York: Columbia University Press, 1996, p. 18.

63 I attended the "High-level Roundtable on Trade and Development". For details of my impressions see M. T. Berger, "Delusions of Development: The Contradictions of the Nation-State and the Challenges of Globalization" *Center for Advanced Studies Update* August, Singapore: National University of Singapore, 2000, pp. 10–11.

64 For example, by the mid-1990s, many writers influenced by the theory of the developmental state were emphasizing the compexity of the relationship between the state and the market (or government and business) rather than foregrounding the importance of one or the other. See A. MacIntyre, "Business, Government and Development: Northeast and Southeast Asian Experience" in A. MacIntyre, ed., *Business and Government in Industrialising Asia*, Sydney: Allen and Unwin, 1994; I. Islam, "Between the State and the Market: The Case for Eclectic Neo-Classical Political Economy" in MacIntyre, ed., *Business and Government in Industrialising Asia*; S. Haggard, "Business, Politics and Policy in Northeast and Southeast Asia" in MacIntyre, ed., *Business and Government in Industrialising Asia*.

65 Alex Choi has divided the developmental state literature as it proliferated in the 1990s into "rational choice statism" and "sociological statism". The former rests on the assumption that individual and collective action flows from rational self-seeking calculations, while the latter is somewhat more historically and sociologically grounded, seeing individual and institutional behaviour as "embedded" in historical processes. Choi, "Statism and Asian Political Economy", pp. 50, 58.

66 S. Chan, C. Clark and D. Lam, "Looking beyond the Developmental State" in S. Chan, C. Clark and D. Lam, eds, *Beyond the Developmental State: East Asia's Political Economies Reconsidered*, London: Macmillan, 1998. Also see C. Clark and S. Chan, "The Developmental Roles of the State: Moving Beyond the Developmental State in Conceptualizing Asian Political Economies" *Governance: An International Journal of Policy and Administration* vol. 7, no. 4, 1994; X. Huang, ed., *The Political and Economic Transition in East Asia: Strong Market, Weakening State*, Washington, DC: Georgetown University Press, 2000.

67 P. Evans, *Embedded Autonomy: States and Industrial Transformation*, Princeton: Princeton University Press, 1995, pp. 10–12, 17–19, 41, 248–50.

68 A. Gerschenkron, *Economic Backwardness in Historical Perspective: A Book of Essays*, Cambridge, MA: Harvard University Press, 1962. Evans explicitly located his approach in a tradition that he saw as running from Max Weber to economic historians such as Karl Polanyi, Alexander Gerschenkron and Albert O. Hirschman and to political economists (both exponents of the new political economy and developmental

state theorists) such as Robert H. Bates, Chalmers Johnson, Robert Wade and Alice Amsden. He also acknowledged a debt to the work of Fernando Henrique Cardoso, Clive Y. Hamilton, and Thomas Gold among others. Evans, *Embedded Autonomy*, pp. 10–19.

69 Amsden, *The Rise of "The Rest"*, pp. 1–2, 284–6 (italics in original).
70 D. C. North, *Institutions, Institutional Change and Economic Performance*, Cambridge: Cambridge University Press, 1990.
71 In Amsden's estimation, the countries in *"the remainder"* that "are most likely to follow in the immediate footsteps of 'the rest' are those" that have "manufacturing experi- ence" and "the ability to construct a reciprocal control mechanism that subsidizes learning … while giving nothing away for free". Amsden, *The Rise of "The Rest"*, pp. 286–93 (italics in original).
72 M. Lind, "Free Trade Fallacy" *Prospect* no. 82 (January), 2003, pp. 34–7.
73 H.-J. Chang, *Kicking Away the Ladder: Development Strategy in Historical Perspective*, London: Anthem, 2002.

Part III
The transformation of Asia

As the Cold War progressed, the notion that U.S. economic favours to Japan would keep it from falling to Communism segued into a much larger concept – that modernization itself constituted a defense against China and the Soviet Union, which by the mid-1950s were actively proselytizing their economic systems to the developing world.

Edith Terry,
How Asia Got Rich: Japan, China and the Asian Miracle,
Armonk: M. E. Sharpe, 2002, p. 359

A central preoccupation of American policy is to shape and channel China's position in the world market, so as to block the emergence of "another Japan" and the deep meaning and intent of the American and IMF response to the Asian liquidity crisis is to close the historical chapter in which the sheltered "developmental states" have prospered.

Bruce Cumings,
"The Korean Crisis and the End of 'Late' Development"
New Left Review no. 231 (September–October), 1998, pp. 51–2

8 The communist challenge and the changing global order

The decolonization of a growing number of former colonies in Asia and their emergence as sovereign independent nation-states was increasingly shaped by the interaction of the United States, Japan (which was Washington's key post-1945 client-ally in Asia), the Peoples Republic of China (Washington's main concern in the region after 1949) and Beijing's erstwhile patron-ally, the Soviet Union. The Cold War and the way it interacted with specific political and social struggles and wider capitalist dynamics are central to any understanding of the transformation of Asia after the Second World War. In the years immediately after 1945 the US emerged as the dominant global power, accounting for almost 50 percent of world economic output.[1] The only power anywhere that even began to rival the US in military, although not economic, terms was the Soviet Union. Furthermore, as already emphasized, while there was often an important connection between earlier imperial ideas and practices and the elaboration of new hegemonic strategies and tactics, both the US and the Soviet Union wielded power in a world increasingly made up of formally sovereign nation-states. Washington's grand strategy in the Cold War provided a crucial foundation for the emergence of various, usually authoritarian, but often developmental states in Asia at the same time as it imposed a range of constraints on the autonomy and sovereignty of virtually all nation-states in the region. Capitalist nation-states in Asia were increasingly incorporated into the post-1945 world order on terms that allowed for considerable autonomy over many issues within their territorial borders, at the same time as their sovereignty was limited with regard to issues that related to the Cold War and international affairs. Furthermore, in contrast to Europe the US was unwilling and unable to establish a significant multilateral political and military framework in Asia, relying on a growing range of bilateral defense treaties and arrangements. This chapter provides a historical interpretation of the transformation of Asia with a focus on the period from 1947–1975, but in some cases, such as the detailed examinations of the South Korean and Indonesian trajectories, it covers the period up to the late 1990s.

Consolidating capitalism in Asia I

Containing the communist challenge I: the Korean War, US hegemony and the historical political economy of the Cold War

At the center of US hegemony and the management of the alliances and arrangements that came into being in the Cold War era was an array of agencies and departments that made up the US national security state.[2] This emerging national security state reflected a general agreement in top US military and civilian circles in this period that Washington had to contain the USSR specifically, and international communism more generally, for reasons of national security and geo-politics. This goal was closely connected to the maintenance and expansion of North American access to markets, investment opportunities and raw materials. In this context the US had a crucial stake in the capitalist reconstruction of as much of Europe and Asia as possible and the extension of this process to the rest of the world. In 1947 the Marshall Plan for Western Europe (which also involved aid for Japan, South Korea and Saudi Arabia – an early pointer to what are still regarded by Washington as the most geo-politically significant regions) demonstrated US economic power and commitment in the emerging Cold War.[3] The conflict in Europe intensified after 1947 and the division of Europe into US and Soviet spheres of influence was institutionalized with the establishment of a US-led military alliance, the North Atlantic Treaty Organization (NATO), in 1949–1950 and the Soviet-led Warsaw Pact in May 1955. More broadly, despite the fact that a narrow conception of political advantage would have calculated that the US would benefit more from bilateral ties with specific nation-states in Western Europe, Washington encouraged multilateral defense arrangements and also encouraged the push in Europe for some form of economic and eventually political integration. In the immediate post-1945 era, policy-makers in Washington assumed that the US and Western European governments would have complementary interests in relation to most geo-political issues, while economic integration would strengthen economic progress and industrial development in Europe.[4] Meanwhile, by the end of the 1940s the US had also embarked on a full-scale effort to facilitate the industrial rebirth of Japan, as part of what would become a wider effort to turn as much of Northeast Asia (and later Southeast Asia) as possible into a capitalist bulwark against the USSR and Mao's China.[5]

With the Chinese Communist Party's victory in October 1949, followed soon after by the Korean War (1950–1953), the governmental and military institutions and bureaucratic structures of the US national security state were increasingly consolidated as instruments of regional and global power.[6] In terms of institutionalizing and amplifying Washington's commitment to the Cold War, the Korean War was an unequivocal turning point. While the Korean War was sparked by a northern attack on the south, the roots of the conflict are to be found in the complex and chaotic series of events that followed on from the collapse of Japanese colonial power at the end of the Second World War.[7] The end of Japanese colonialism on the peninsula was followed by the emergence of the Democratic People's Republic of Korea under Kim Il Sung (1948–1994) in the north and the Republic of Korea (ROK) under Syngman Rhee (1948–1960) in the south. Both regimes laid claim to the entire Korean peninsula, but by late 1948/early 1949 they had established separate institutions and structures, while continuing to deny the legitimacy of the other regime. In September 1947 the US had placed the Korean question before the General Assembly of the United Nations, which subsequently made a formal call for the unification of what was at that point a Korea divided between a northern government allied to the Soviet Union (and later the People's Republic of China – PRC) and a southern government allied to the United States. Following the outbreak of war between the north and the south on 25 June 1950, the Security Council quickly began organizing a UN military force, under US leadership, to intervene in Korea. This was made possible by the fact that Moscow had been boycotting the Security Council since the start of 1950. The Soviet Union was protesting the fact that China's permanent seat on the Security Council continued to be held by the KMT government that had been confined to Taiwan since the Chinese Communist Party's triumph on the mainland at the end of 1949. In this context the resolutions of the General Assembly on Korean unification were soon being used to justify a full-scale military effort against the North Korean regime. The initial aim of US/UN intervention, to achieve the limited goal of ending Northern aggression, was quickly transformed into a wider set of aims, centered on the reunification of the peninsula under a pro-US/UN government. The ensuing conflict eventually brought the People's Republic of China directly into the war and fighting continued until the signing of an armistice agreement on 27 July 1953. The Korean War resulted in civilian and military deaths of 1.3 million in the south and at least 1.5 million in the north.[8]

While devastating the Korean peninsula, the Korean War provided a crucial stimulus to industrial production in Japan as a result of the dramatic increase in US purchasing of military equipment and war-related products. From a figure of zero in 1949, US procurement of supplies from Japanese manufacturers for the war on the peninsula went to almost US$600 million in 1951 and reached US$850 million in 1952. In 1952 over 60 percent of exports from Japan went to the US-led war effort in Korea. As a result of Japan's strategic location the US continued to spend almost US$600 million annually in Japan in the 1950s in relation to the operation of bases and related military activities. Between 1952 and 1956, US defense spending financed more than 25 percent of imports to Japan. It was the Korean War that acted as the catalyst for industrial recovery in Japan at the same time as it paved the way for the US provision of technology to Japan's reindustrialization efforts.[9] As we shall see in chapter 9, these trends combined with the limiting of Japanese defense spending to 1 percent and the re-directing of revenue into economic reconstruction to ensure that the Japanese economy underwent a major revitalization in the 1950s.

US nation-building policies in Japan (and later South Korea and Taiwan) in the immediate post-1945 period were clearly shaped by the US experience of the New Deal in the 1930s and many of the key figures in the Occupation of Japan were "New Dealers".[10] This initially led to the encouragement of major land reform and support for the strengthening of trade unions. This also involved an initial commitment to dismantling the *zaibatsu* (conglomerates) that had been central to the Japanese economy up to and during the war. In the countryside, US advisers such as Wolf Ladejinsky played a key role in the process of land reform that redistributed land to a large number of peasants and also strengthened tenure rights for peasants who rented land.[11] At the outset US policy in Japan sought to democratize the political system and stabilize the capitalist order by giving peasants and workers a greater stake in the overall Japanese political economy. At the same time, by the end of the 1940s the US fear of communist revolution in Asia had led to the shelving of US plans to break up the industrial conglomerates with direct links to the pre-war imperial government. This resulted in the effective restoration of much of Japan's pre-1945 elite minus the most well-known militarists and imperialists. This reversal did not significantly affect the course of land reform, but at the national level political leaders with close ties to the *zaibatsu* and other businesses were able to regain their positions of power. While the *zaibatsu* had been officially dismantled, they often reappeared as *keiretsu*, as the relationship between business and government that had underpinned Japan's initial rise to Great Power status prior to 1945 was reoriented to fit the circumstances of the Cold War. The old *zaibatsu* like Mitsui, Sumitomo and Mitsubishi re-emerged in a modified fashion, while large new firms, such as Toyota, Toshiba, Nissan and Hitachi, which were established along the lines of the old *zaibatsu*, also took root and went on to reap the economic benefits of the Korean War.[12]

The beneficial economic impact of the Korean War was also felt in Southeast Asia. The concern that the war on the Korean peninsula might spread to Southeast Asia (which will be discussed in more detail below), combined with efforts by the major actors in the Cold War to increase their stockpiles of strategic raw materials, caused a significant increase in the price of commodities such as rubber and tin. The price of the former increased by 400 percent while the latter rose by 200 percent. The benefits from this commodity boom went particularly to British Malaya (renamed Malaysia after independence in 1957), which was the biggest rubber- and tin-producer in the world in the early 1950s. At the same time, the British colonial entrepot of Singapore, which served as the main port for the outward shipment of rubber and tin, was also well positioned and the commodity boom ensured that profits in the colony's commercial sector rose significantly, while the total tax revenue received by the government trebled throughout the British-ruled peninsula. Driven forward by a determination to defeat the guerrilla insurgency led by the Malayan Communist Party, Malaya's colonial rulers embarked on the extension and improvement of the colony's railroad and highway system in order that the army and the police would be able to operate more effectively throughout the countryside. At the same time, the colonial administrations in Singapore and Malaya used their rising revenues to upgrade port facilities and construct new power plants. Despite the fact that the

Korean War boom was confined to the period 1950–1953, its significance for Singapore and Malaya was considerable. The boom contributed directly to the expansion and deepening of social and economic infrastructure, and of government capabilities, which were subsequently used to tame the labor movement and more or less successfully impose the top-down corporatist arrangements that subsequently underpinned the state-guided national development projects that emerged in Singapore and Malaysia during the Cold War.[13]

At the same time, if there was a newly-industrializing country (NIC) that reflected the historical particularity of successful industrialization, and as a result pointed unequivocally to the problems associated with seeking to draw lessons from the distinctive national trajectories of Asia and applying those lessons to another place at another time, it would be Singapore. The former British colonial entrepots of Singapore and Hong Kong are particularly atypical HPAEs, to use World Bank parlance, and can be dismissed with relative ease as development models with significant lessons for other nation-states. Singapore, as a city-state, has benefited from the absence of a peasantry and a rural sector of any significance and therefore had no "agrarian question" in contrast to the vast majority of nation-states in Asia, Latin America and Africa. Singapore and Hong Kong's role in the British colonial empire is important to understanding their economic development experience. Their position as financial centers, as well as their long history as commercial ports, ensured them a relative advantage in any effort to industrialize and grow economically after 1945.[14] The Malaysian trajectory, meanwhile, never followed the South Korean or Taiwanese version of the developmental state very closely either. Throughout the high period of economic growth in Malaysia, economic development was certainly state-regulated and often state-guided and, under Mahathir, as we have seen, South Korea and Japan were looked to and invoked as models to be emulated, but the Malaysian state remained highly dependent on foreign (often Japanese) investment, while primary commodity exports also remained very important. The heavy reliance on foreign investment underlined the "fragility of the Malaysian miracle" even prior to 1997.[15] Meanwhile, the nation-states' highly racialized politics also conditioned the distinctive Malaysian trajectory in important ways.[16] In the 1980s and 1990s, as Mahathir responded to growing pressure for privatization of the public sector, the privatization process was increasingly used by the ruling party, United Malays National Organization (UMNO), to consolidate its economic power. As discussed in chapter 6, the majority of the successful privatization initiatives in this period involved selling public sector assets to companies in which individuals or groups with close connections to UMNO had an important or controlling interest.[17]

The South Korean trajectory and the transformation of Asia I: 1945–1979

Following a dramatic recovery from the devastation of the Korean War, South Korea, which had almost ceased to exist as a territorial entity in the early months of the war, emerged as the greatest success story of the wider East Asian Miracle by the late 1970s. At the beginning of the 1960s the country's GDP per capita was comparable to the newly independent former Belgian colony of the Congo and many South Koreans viewed the idea of South Korea catching up economically to the Philippines – regarded at the time as one of the new nation-states in Asia with the most economic potential – as impossible. By the eve of the Asian crisis, however, the South Korean economy was the twelfth biggest in the world and South Korea had become a member of the Organization for Economic Cooperation and Development (OECD).[18] After the Korean War the sustained US economic and military aid, and capital, that went to South Korea and Taiwan in the 1950s and 1960s played a major role in strengthening the capabilities of these emergent authoritarian developmental and national security states.[19] This is not to deny other factors in the rise of South Korea and Taiwan as NICs, but the emergence of capitalist, and authoritarian, developmental states in Northeast Asia after 1945 was grounded explicitly in US Cold War imperatives. For example, a comparative analysis of over thirty nation-states has pointed to the "positive effect" of US military aid on national economic development (in the period up to the early 1970s) in those instances where levels of aid were particularly high as a result of geo-political considerations. Of the thirty-two countries examined the four success stories were South Korea, Taiwan, Greece and Turkey.[20] US miliary aid to South Korea between 1946 and 1979 was US$7 billion. At the same time, geo-politics also ensured high levels of economic aid (of course the distinction between economic and military aid often becomes very blurred in practice). US economic aid to South Korea from 1946 to 1979 was more than US$6 billion dollars. In the 1950s more than 80 percent of South Korean imports were financed by US economic assistance. Most of the economic aid was disbursed in grant form prior to 1965. By the 1970s aid was being provided to the South Korean government primarily in the form of concessional loans and only very small quantities of aid were disbursed from the second half of the 1970s onwards.[21]

The figure for US military and economic aid to Taiwan over more or less the same period was US$5.6 billion. This does not, of course, include the aid from Japan, or from international financial institutions.[22] As much as 75 percent of Taiwan's infrastructure investment came from US economic aid in the 1950s. Taiwan and South Korea received more US economic aid than all the US economic aid to Africa and half the figure for all of Latin America over the same period. The growing power of the national security and emergent developmental states in South Korea and Taiwan was also linked to the relative weakness of capitalist elites and the undercutting of large landowners after 1945, as a result of the implementation of land reforms, under US auspices. As in Japan, the land reform initiatives were already in place by the late 1940s and early 1950s, before the more conservative Eisenhower administration increasingly discarded the remnants of the New Deal's influence on US aid policy. This ensured that subsequent US-sponsored land reform in South Vietnam and elsewhere had far more limited momentum, or favored landlords, in the context of a wider commitment to the status quo.[23] Meanwhile, in the 1950s and increasingly in the 1960s, manufacturers based in South Korea and Taiwan (and, of course, Japan, Singapore and Hong Kong) also gained privileged access to the North American market, at the same time as the US tolerated South Korea and Taiwan's protected markets and their governments' tight controls on foreign investment. Furthermore, South Korea, Taiwan, Singapore and Hong Kong all entered the world export markets in the 1960s when a consumer boom was under way. Meanwhile, Japanese-based corporations had begun to emerge as a key element in the wider US-centered Cold War political economy of Asia by the late 1950s. And, in the 1960s and 1970s, under US auspices, Japanese companies avoided the rising cost of labor in Japan by relocating operations to their former colonies.[24] At the same time, by the 1970s Japanese trading companies controlled 50–70 percent of the international trade of South Korea and Taiwan. In this period Japanese corporations also provided a substantial portion of the machinery and the other components needed for industrialization in South Korea and Taiwan, and they were also an important source of technology licenses.[25]

Apart from the important role of Japanese companies in South Korea and Taiwan in the post-1945 era, Japan also represented a model for its one-time colonies. Japanese colonialism laid the foundations for authoritarian developmentalism prior to 1945, at the same time as it provided a pattern for capitalist development.[26] Park Chung Hee, who ruled South Korea from 1961 until his assassination in 1979, had been an officer in the Japanese Kwantung Army during the Pacific War. His thinking was clearly influenced by the Japanese colonial industrial pattern, most importantly the state's close links with the *zaibatsu*.[27] Under Park, a relatively narrow, but extremely powerful, alliance between the military regime and a small group of *chaebol* (*jaebol*), the Korean term for *zaibatsu* or conglomerates, was at the center of South Korea's capitalist trajectory. After coming to power in 1961, Park quickly legitimated his rule via rigged elections that provided a constitutional smoke screen for his regime. At the same time, he purged the bureaucracy, getting rid of incompetent and corrupt officials. He established the Economic Planning Board (EPB) that quickly emerged as a crucial economic decision-making body that was thoroughly insulated from other branches of government and from private business. After 1960 the country's financial system was restructured: banks were nationalized and the Bank of Korea (the central bank) was put under the direct control of the Ministry of Finance. National economic development was held up as the top priority (a veritable "sacred mission"). Export-oriented industrialization (EOI) increasingly became the centerpiece of the state's overall development strategy by the mid-1960s. The power of the state was strengthened by the inflow of public and private loans from overseas and the Park regime directed these loans to private producers according to its overall economic plan. Almost 90 percent of all foreign loans had to be backed up by government guarantees that ensured that the government controlled the disbursement of these monies. An even more significant instrument of state control over private industry was government ownership of the domestic banks, which had been in private hands prior to the coup in 1961. As a result of the overall structure of investment in the context of changing market conditions internationally, authoritarian developmentalism in South Korea entered a major crisis of export-oriented industrialization in the late 1960s. Between 1969 and 1971 the South Korean government took over numerous poorly managed businesses, assuming their foreign debts. Under IMF auspices Park imposed a range of stabilization measures, which exacerbated the financial problems of those companies that already had debt problems. The crisis of the late 1960s was also linked to rising levels of labor unrest, while Park's efforts to extend his period in office beyond the limit of two four-year terms, allowed for by the constitution, resulted in a growing number of confrontations with students and opposition politicians.[28]

The Park regime entered a new phase in the early 1970s. This was a period of deepening intensity for the authoritarian developmental state in South Korea. This process was reflected in a range of new and increasingly draconian measures as South Korea entered the high period of what has been described as a bureaucratic-authoritarian industrializing regime (BAIR).[29] To begin with, the military regime imposed an even more repressive framework on organized labor and launched a number of measures to control finance capital. These measures paved the way for a particularly ambitious set of initiatives that were central to the political economy of South Korea in the 1970s and early 1980s. In January 1973 the Park regime promulgated a Heavy and Chemical Industrialization Plan. The South Korean state chose what it regarded as six strategic industries (steel, electronics, petrochemicals, shipbuilding, machinery and nonferrous metals) that were to be the focus of national development. This shift towards heavy industry and chemical production was made for a number of reasons, associated with changes in Washington's geo-political and geo-economic calculations, which have been discussed in chapter 4 and will be discussed further in chapter 9. At this juncture it should simply be noted that: first, the global financial system had become unstable following the breakdown of the Bretton Woods system in the early 1970s. Second, Japanese companies were moving into high-tech industries, which led to the relinquishing of important, and labor-intensive, sectors of heavy industry. Third, the broader Cold War context was shifting and, as we have seen, the Nixon administration was presiding over a major reorientation in US policy in the region.[30] However, one of the most significant reasons for the shift flowed from circumstances in South Korea itself. By the beginning of the 1970s South Korea had become a much more highly differentiated society than in the 1950s, while levels of political activity far exceeded what they had been at the time of Park's rise to power. Labor conflicts were on the increase, the student movement was growing and the activities of opposition politicians had expanded significantly. Workers in the agricultural sector were also disaffected, while the official opposition party had gained unexpected prominence under Kim Dae Jung (Gim Daejung). This was the social context for the imposition of an even more authoritarian politico-economic system in the 1970s.[31]

The South Korean trajectory and the transformation of Asia II: 1979–1997

In the second half of the 1970s the authoritarian developmental state (or bureaucratic-authoritarian industrializing regime) in South Korea was at its height in terms of its coercive capacity and its intervention in the economy. The BAIR in South Korea exercised a high degree of control over the distribution of capital and "industrial targeting" was a common practice. In the 1970s the country's ten largest *chaebol* (*jaebol*), with the backing of the state, consolidated large and sprawling economic empires. At the same time, by 1979 the South Korean economy was confronted by a number of structural problems. In 1979 the Second Oil Crisis was a serious blow to the South Korean economy. With the onset of the Debt Crisis in the early 1980s, South Korea's foreign debt levels were so high that, as in many other parts of the world (see chapter 4), a number of international banks became concerned about its "creditworthiness" (the overall foreign debt in South Korea went from US$2 billion in 1970 to US$35.8 billion in 1985). Meanwhile, the dramatic expansion in chemical production and heavy industry led to serious over-capacity problems and many large corporations found themselves in deteriorating financial circumstances, while ongoing problems associated with high debt levels, combined with declining exports, drove a number of companies, especially in the construction and shipping industries, to the brink. In April 1979 the Park government, with IMF support, introduced the Comprehensive Stabilization Plan. Among other things this involved a freeze on wages, the curbing of low-interest commercial loans and the cutting back on various subsidies to the farming sector. This was soon met by a widening strike by labor, with the support of the opposition party and students, which led to violent confrontations across the country. In the face of this crisis the regime split. Park Chung Hee was gunned down on October 26 1979 by the head of the South Korean Central Intelligence Agency.[32] A tumultuous transition, under General Chun Doo Hwan (1980–1988), which included the bloody suppression of the Kwangju Rebellion, ensued.

Between the early 1960s and the early 1980s authoritarian developmentalism in South Korea had rested on a close relationship between the national security state and the country's burgeoning conglomerates, at the same time as workers and trade unions were controlled via repression and top-down corporatist arrangements. However, what also needs to be emphasized is the way that important, and historically specific, cultural practices and nationalist ideas emerged as constitutive elements of authoritarian developmentalism in South Korea. During the Cold War, South Korea's corporate elite, and their allies in the national security state, sought to advance their economic interests by deploying selected aspects of Korean culture to mobilize employees and the population generally, while downplaying cultural traditions that might contribute to resistance to their rule. For example, the corporate managers justified their control via the use of selected elements of popular knowledge about father–son relations and they represented the founding and operation of the *chaebol* (*jaebol*) as an integral part of a wider national project for the benefit of all citizens, effectively imposing a "moral duty" on their employees which blurred the boundaries between employee of the company and citizen of the nation-state.[33] In the Cold War era the authoritarian developmental state, or BAIR, in South Korea was legitimized via appeals to a potent combination of ideas selected from Confucianism, militarism, anti-communism and Korean nationalism, backed up by a coercive national security apparatus. It also needs to be emphasized further that the South Korean state remained on a war footing, in the wake of what was an uneasy truce at the end of the Korean War. The results were highly militarized societies in both the south and the north. By the second half of the 1960s, as noted in chapter 3, hundreds of thousands of young South Korean men had received basic military training as well as completing various military courses.[34] This contributed to the wider militaristic and authoritarian character of nationalism in South Korea. Despite, or because of, these authoritarian efforts to emphasize hierarchy and harmony, the history of South Korea in this period was also a history of ongoing social and political struggles.

The rapid economic growth of the 1960s and 1970s, and the dramatic social changes of this era, paved the way for the decline of the authoritarian developmental state in South Korea in the 1980s. Domestic pressures for political and economic liberalization worked to undermine the state-centered authoritarian approach to capitalist development. At the same time, Washington increasingly began to question the financial and trading practices of Cold War allies such as South Korea. The liberalization of the political system was closely connected to the liberalization of the economy and Kim Young Sam, the first civilian president of South Korea in over three decades, made globalization (*segyehwa*) the centerpiece of his administration (1993–1997).[35] However, it was not until the Asian crisis in 1997 that the pressure for economic liberalization dramatically increased on the peninsula, and even in post-crisis South Korea the nationalist predisposition, and many of the mechanisms, for state-mediated national development remain significant. The IMF loan to South Korea, an unprecedented US$58 billion (as well as the smaller but still substantial loans to Thailand and Indonesia) was conditional on the implementation of a range of austerity measures and economic reforms. IMF officials demanded the setting-up of new regulatory procedures, the shutting-down of a range of banks and financial institutions and the liberalization of capital markets. The IMF also demanded that public enterprises be privatized and cartels be broken up. At the same time, the Fund pushed for the introduction of flexible labor markets. It initially found a willing ally in the newly elected government of Kim Dae Jung (Gim Daejung), whose political and economic goals were strengthened by the early IMF demands.[36] Kim was as committed as his predecessor to globalization, while the combination of the crisis and his assumption of the presidency in early 1998 was seen as opportunity to undermine key aspects of the collusion between the *chaebol* (*jaebol*) and the political elite that had been central to the developmental state in South Korea. While the crisis and Kim's efforts at reform have laid low key aspects of the developmental state, many of the arrangements and practices remain in place.[37] Nevertheless, in the context of the dramatic decline in the size of the South Korean economy in 1997–1998, there was a major, albeit still uneven, opening to foreign investors and foreign manufactures, complemented by legislative changes that liberalized the labor market and weakened job security.[38] The process of national reorientation in South Korea is also complicated by the fact that North and South Korean soldiers are still lined up along the 38th parallel and the US remains forward-deployed in support of its South Korean ally. As a result South Korea's prospects remained inextricably bound up with the increasingly decrepit character of the North Korean regime and the uncertainty surrounding the continued division of the peninsula, a direct legacy of the Cold War.[39]

Consolidating capitalism in Asia II

Containing the communist challenge II: the Vietnam War, US hegemony and the historical political economy of the Cold War

The Cold War was also central to the dynamics of capitalist transformation in Southeast Asia. In 1948, by which time it was becoming clear that Washington's long-term support for Chiang Kai-shek's nationalist regime in China was going to be insufficient to prevent the Chinese Communist party from coming to power, communist-led insurgencies were also growing in significance in the Philippines and Malaya, while the Viet Minh's struggle against the French in Indochina was gaining strength. The Indonesian Communist Party also launched an unsuccessful military challenge for the leadership of Sukarno's emergent Republic of Indonesia in 1948. The rise of the Chinese Communist Party was interpreted by the US, and the European colonial governments seeking to regain or retain their possessions in Southeast Asia, as emblematic of a vigorous international communist movement that operated as a monolithic force under the direction of Moscow and was about to spread to Southeast Asia. However, in the case of the Malayan Communist Party (MCP), for example, the evidence suggests that "little international stimulus" was required to "prompt" the organization to launch its insurgency in 1948. In relation to the much-debated question of the role of the decisions of the Calcutta Youth Conference in early 1948, the shift towards armed struggle in Soviet and Cominform policy, with which the conference in Calcutta is generally associated, simply "spurred" the leadership of the MCP to "follow a course it was already disposed to adopt".[40] Nevertheless, from the point of view of policy-makers in Washington the colonies and the emerging nation-states of Southeast Asia were interchangeable pieces on the chessboard of Cold War geo-politics and the major concern was with their stability and their role in the wider effort to contain communism. At the same time, the future of the colonies in Southeast Asia had a direct influence on the security and economic reconstruction of Britain, France and the Netherlands and the need for them to play a full role in the Cold War alliance arrangements being set up in Western Europe. In the case of the Dutch in

Southeast Asia, by late 1948 they controlled most of their former territory including all the main urban centers, while Sukarno (who had been declared president of an independent Indonesia in 1945) and other leading Indonesian nationalists had been detained. However, the Dutch still faced highly localized popular military resistance, especially on Sumatra and Java. This, combined with Dutch war-weariness, and strong US diplomatic and financial pressure, led to a breakthrough at the end of 1949, and the government of the Netherlands capitulated and formally transferred power to the independent United States of Indonesia.[41] In the interests of wider geo-politics, meanwhile, Washington was more willing to support the French effort to retain control in Indochina against a nationalist movement led by Ho Chi Minh that was more identifiably communist in its orientation. The US was also was more than willing to let the colonial authorities in British Malaya set the pace of decolonization.[42]

By 1950 the communist insurgency in British-ruled Malaya (the Federation of Malaya after 1948) had grown in significance; however, as we have seen the Korean War indirectly facilitated a major improvement in the colonial government's counter-insurgency efforts. Ultimately, the Korean War was a turning point for the British colonial government's counter-insurgency campaign against the Malayan Communist Party (MCP) and contributed directly to the expansion and deepening of social and economic infrastructure, and of the newly independent government's capabilities generally.[43] As discussed in chapter 3, the apparent success of the British colonial authorities against the Malayan communists by the second half of the 1950s (along with what was also understood to have been a counter-insurgency success in the Philippines) influenced the ill-fated US counter-insurgency and nation-building effort in South Vietnam in the late 1950s and early 1960s.[44] At the beginning of the 1950s Washington's assistance to France's embattled attempt to hold on to Indochina emerged as the focal point of the wider US commitment to challenge communism in Southeast Asia. Up to the end of 1950 the US had already disbursed at least US$133 million to the French colonial authorities for their war effort. This figure was dwarfed by US$316.5 million in military supplies scheduled to be provided for the 1951 fiscal year. US assistance went on by late 1952 to make up 40 percent of the overall cost of the French government's war effort in Indochina, while by the beginning of 1954 the US contribution had risen to 80 percent. In February 1955, following the dramatic military defeat of the French at Dien Bien Phu in May 1954, the US presided over the establishment of the South-East Asia Treaty Organization (SEATO) which was comprised of the governments of the United States, Australia, New Zealand, Britain, France, Pakistan, Thailand and the Philippines. A number of military exercises were arranged and conducted under the auspices of SEATO, but the organization never assumed an active military role even at the height of the Vietnam War. SEATO, with its headquarters in Bangkok, nevertheless symbolized the formalization of the US commitment to Southeast Asia, at a time when the Eisenhower administration had embarked on an increasingly costly attempt to help establish a stable non-communist nation-state in the southern part of Vietnam. For Eisenhower, and for his immediate successor (John F. Kennedy), the regime of Ngo Dinh Diem (1955–1963) was to be a "showcase for democracy" and the site for a definitive nation-building effort that would make clear the pre-eminence of North American institutions and values.[45]

As discussed in chapter 1, the growing geo-political importance of Southeast Asia intersected with the inauguration of the Colombo Plan For Cooperative Economic Development in Asia and the Pacific. Set up in 1951, following the Colombo Conference (held in the capital of Ceylon, renamed Sri Lanka in 1972) in January 1950, it sought to promote alternative development strategies to those being advanced by the communist parties of the region.[46] While the US did not send a delegation to the original conference, Washington had joined by 1951. At the conference in Colombo at the beginning of 1950 the British government sought to ensure that the emphasis was on economic development, technical assistance and a regional approach, which it thought would distract attention from the different, and even opposing, political positions of the governments in attendance, not to mention the communist parties in the region. The delegates to the conference eventually reached unanimous agreement in support of a draft resolution that called on the Commonwealth governments to provide whatever technical and financial aid they could to the governments of South and Southeast Asia. This was to take place via existing organizations and newly established bilateral arrangements. The actual implementation of various initiatives was the work of the Colombo Plan Secretariat and the Secretary-General of the Colombo Plan. At the outset it was agreed that the member governments of the Commonwealth in Asia should produce development plans for the six-year period from July 1 1950 to June 30 1956, and that invitations to participate in the Colombo initiative should be extended to other governments in the region. By 1957, 1,500 students had gone to Britain for training and education under the Colombo Plan, while 600 went to Canada, 375 to New Zealand and 4,000 to Australia. The Plan also involved the facilitation of public investment and infrastructure projects.[47] By the second half of the 1950s, the Asian governments that were members of the Colombo Plan had expanded from Ceylon, Pakistan and India to encompass Burma, Cambodia, Indonesia, Laos, Nepal, the Philippines, Thailand and South Vietnam.[48]

Of course, in Southeast Asia, South Vietnam increasingly emerged as the main focus of US policy in the region. Between 1954 and the end of Eisenhower's presidency at the beginning of 1961, his administration disbursed over US$2 billion worth of military and economic aid to the government of South Vietnam. As the 1960s began the Diem regime was the fifth highest recipient of US foreign aid worldwide (and it was the third highest recipient – after South Korea and Taiwan – amongst non-NATO countries). When Kennedy entered the White House in 1961, over 1,500 US citizens were already based in Saigon, employed in various public administration posts or serving with the Military Assistance and Advisory Group (MAAG), which advised and trained the Army of the Republic of Vietnam (ARVN). By the time of the new president's inauguration, Saigon had also become the site of the headquarters of the biggest

US economic aid program in the world.[49] Meanwhile, US-based foundations and North American universities (most prominently Michigan State University which was involved in the training of public administrators and police for the Diem government) were also participating in the burgeoning nation-building effort in South Vietnam.[50] As suggested previously, although the experience of nation-building in Japan, South Korea and Taiwan loomed over South Vietnam, by the mid-1950s the role of land reform, which is often seen as central to the success of those earlier efforts, had been marginalized or reoriented. From the outset, the Diem regime in South Vietnam was closely identified with large landowners. His vice-president, Nguyen Ngoc Tho, was one of the most powerful landowners in the Mekong Delta, while other members of his government were also major landlords, including the head of the Land Reform ministry. This, combined with the US shift away from any serious commitment to reformism (especially land reform), dramatically undermined any potential appeal the Diem regime would have had for the peasantry and hobbled all subsequent reform and nation-building efforts in South Vietnam.[51]

With the US build-up in South Vietnam there were important economic benefits for Washington's allies in Asia. In the same way that the Korean War represented an important turning point for Japan's post-war economic take-off, the Vietnam War was a major turning point for South Korea and Taiwan. US aid to South Korea and Taiwan went up at the end of the 1950s and early 1960s. Taiwan's economy also benefited from major US purchases of industrial and agricultural products, the repairing of US equipment at bases in Taiwan and the clearly mixed benefits of providing "rest and recreation" for US soldiers. Taiwanese companies received major contracts for work in Vietnam, while South Korean *chaebol* (*jaebol*), such as Hyundai and Daewoo, also gained major war-related construction contracts. The South Korean role in the Vietnam War was more direct than Taiwan's. Over 300,000 ROK troops had served in Vietnam by the time the US pulled out. On a per capita basis this level of involvement was higher than the US participation rate. The US paid for the wages and equipment for these troops. Although the sum of over US$1 billion that the Korean government received directly for its participation in the Vietnam War may have been relatively insignificant for the US, according to Meredith Woo-Cumings it "went a long way to finance Korea's take-off".[52] In the case of Japan, the Vietnam War was also an important economic turning point, pulling Japanese industry out of a slump it had entered in 1965. The deepening of the war in Southeast Asia lifted profits for major Japanese companies by more than US$1 billion annually between 1966 and 1971. It also directed funds to a number of crucial "infant export industries" and facilitated increased access to both North American and Southeast Asian markets for Japanese manufactures.[53]

With the escalation of US involvement in Southeast Asia in the 1960s, trade between Singapore and South Vietnam, particularly in petroleum products, increased precipitously, going from US$21.5 million to US$146 million between 1964 and 1969.[54] This reflected the wider rise in the tropical city-state's entrepot trade. And, like Taiwan, Singapore and Hong Kong, and especially Thailand, experienced the mixed benefits that flowed from the provision of "rest and recreation" for the large number of US soldiers stationed in Southeast Asia. Thailand's role in the "rest and recreation" economy was directly linked to its position as a major staging area for the war in Vietnam.[55] In fact, since the mid-1950s, geo-politicians in Washington had viewed Thailand as a key domino in the wider effort to contain communism in Southeast Asia. US military aid augmented the capabilities of the Thai state under military stewardship. US aid and the security imperatives of the Cold War led to a dramatic improvement in the country's communication and transportation networks. As US involvement in Vietnam intensified, there was a dramatic increase in US spending on everything from the building and operation of US military and airforce bases to the rest and recreation activities of US personnel. The total amount of US war-related spending in Thailand went from about US$27 million dollars in 1963 to US$318 million dollars by 1968. This is thought to be have been the equivalent of over 8.5 percent of the country's GNP. From the mid-1950s to the mid-1970s, US expenditures in Thailand totalled at least US$3.5 billion, much of it at the height of the Vietnam War. This Cold War foundation was a critical factor in what became known as the Thai boom.[56]

By the end of the 1960s, there was a massive US presence in Vietnam and Southeast Asia. At its peak, in January 31 1969, the number of US personnel stationed in South Vietnam was 542,400. Nevertheless, US hegemony in Southeast Asia and beyond was increasingly constrained by the limits on its military effort to build a stable and modern South Vietnam.[57] In the wake of the Tet Offensive, by which time the NLF had broken the power of the large landowners in most areas of South Vietnam, the US approach shifted to a more reformist land reform policy against the backdrop of impending military defeat. This led to the "Land-to-the-Tiller" Program, which began to be implemented in late 1970. On paper this program resembled the land reform programs that the US had supported in Japan, South Korea and Taiwan some twenty years earlier; however, in the context of the war-torn countryside its implementation was very uneven. With an increasingly corrupt political system in the south, landlords easily found ways around the reform process, while elsewhere the NLF had already won the battle for "hearts and minds".[58] By the end of the Vietnam War the number of US personnel killed totalled more than 50,000, while the military and civilian casualties amongst the Vietnamese population numbered in the millions.

The failure of US nation-building efforts in South Vietnam certainly can be attributed, in part, to major differences in approach compared to Northeast Asia. There were also important contextual differences related to the French colonial legacy on the one hand and the Japanese colonial legacy on the other. Although the US-led modernization project of the Cold War era provided the overall framework for the rise of authoritarian developmental states, US hegemony clearly needs to be seen as a necessary rather than a sufficient condition for successful national development along capitalist and industrial lines in Asia. For example, the Philippines was also a major Cold War ally of the US and, as already noted, it was seen to have the best economic prospects of virtually any nation-state in Southeast Asia in the 1950s. However, it never received the levels of aid and support that went to South Korea and Taiwan, nor were New Deal-style land reforms ever tried in the Philippines. By the 1970s, the Philippines had succumbed to the increasingly predatory ministrations of Ferdinand Marcos (1965–1986), a long-time client of Washington, who was eventually ousted by a broad-based populist revolt in 1986.[59] Every government since independence in 1946, including Marcos and his successors, has promised to implement land reform, but none has ever delivered. In the 1990s the Philippine Congress, a body that continues to be dominated by large landowners, suspended all proposed land reforms until 2020 on the distinctly Orwellian grounds that the implementation of land reform would act as a brake on industrial development.[60]

By the late 1960s, then, the US-led modernization project had reached its limits and these limits were most obviously apparent in Washington's failure in South Vietnam, despite a massive military and economic commitment over almost two decades. In broader diplomatic terms the limits of US hegemony in the region were reflected in Washington's inability to even gain or retain more widespread multilateral support for its involvement in Vietnam. SEATO, for example, was disabled from the outset by internal differences and an absence of any underlying strategic interest around which its members could unite. The government of Pakistan began to drift away at an early stage because of a lack of support for its conflict with India. Pakistan eventually withdrew from SEATO in November 1972. The French government was clearly against the escalation of US military involvement in Vietnam in the 1960s, while the British government failed to provide any real military support for that conflict. In fact, in July 1967 Britain formally announced its military disengagement from affairs to the east of Suez. Other SEATO members, such as the Australian, Thai and Filipino governments, did send troops to South Vietnam, but this was not done under the umbrella of SEATO. The treaty organization was further weakened by the Nixon administration's historic rapprochement with China in early 1972. With the waning of the Vietnam War (particularly after the Paris Peace Agreements of January 1973) SEATO lost any vestige of relevance and its military structures were abolished in February 1974. The organization as a whole was disbanded on June 30 1977.[61]

The Indonesian trajectory and the transformation of Asia I: 1945–1965

The rise of an authoritarian and ostensibly developmental state in Indonesia under General Suharto (1965–1998) also needs to be located in the wider context of decolonization and the Cold War.[62] By the early 1990s Suharto's New Order was regarded by the World Bank as one of the eight High Performing Asian Economies (HPAEs).[63] In 1996, Hal Hill, an influential Australian-based economist, characterized Indonesia as *Southeast Asia's Emerging Giant*.[64] However, the Asian crisis in 1997–1998 precipitated a major political crisis that led to the resignation of Suharto. Subsequent governments have restored a modicum of stability; however, the sprawling archipelago continues to be characterized by an ongoing economic and social crisis that has profound implications for the future of Indonesia and for the region.[65] Suharto's New Order state as it was consolidated in the 1960s and early 1970s followed on from two decades of national independence under Sukarno (1945–1965). Independent Indonesia generally and Suharto's New Order more specifically was the immediate successor to the complex historical amalgam that was the Dutch colonial state. East Timor aside, Indonesia continues to lay claim to the former Dutch colonial boundaries as they were consolidated by the beginning of the twentieth century.[66] Apart from the same boundaries, the historic connection between the New Order and the colonial era is apparent in socio-ethnic terms insofar as the Javanese *priyayi* (the hereditary petty aristocracy of Java) continued to reproduce itself and play a central role in the bureaucratic (and military) structures of the modern Indonesia state. This flowed from the history of Dutch colonialism and the overall character of the archipelago's pre-colonial social formations. Even before the Dutch conquest Java was heavily populated, agriculturally significant and a regional power center. In the context of Dutch colonial expansion the petty aristocracy of Java was transformed into a bureaucratic elite and incorporated into the colonial state apparatus.[67] Already well entrenched in the colonial system, the *priyayi* benefited the most from the expansion of the colonial education system at the end of the nineteenth century. As a result the Javanese elite took up most of the administrative jobs in the growing colonial state at the same time as a number of the early Dutch-educated leaders of the Indonesian nationalist movement also came from *priyayi* backgrounds. In this period the number of *priyayi* grew dramatically, through both birth and recruitment, as they reproduced and consolidated themselves as a relatively distinctive social class. While the *priyayi* dominated the lower and middle ranks of the Dutch colonial state, their influence was much weaker in the emerging nationalist movement. Anti-colonial nationalism did not take hold in the Netherlands East Indies until the early twentieth century, but throughout the colonial period local and regional rebellions and acts of resistance had shaped the wider historical trajectory in important ways.[68] However, they rarely threatened Dutch colonial rule as a whole. Even the emergent nationalist movement of the 1920s, over which the colony's nascent labor movement and the Indonesian Communist Party (PKI) exercised considerable influence, was unable to overcome the myriad forms of accommodation and co-optation or the repressive capacity, deployed by an increasingly powerful colonial state.[69]

In 1934, by which time urban intellectuals dominated the nationalist movement, Sukarno (who would become independent Indonesia's first president) and many other major nationalist leaders were banished to remote islands where they languished until the Japanese invasion in 1942. The Japanese advance into Southeast Asia dealt a blow to European colonialism in Asia generally, while their occupation of the Netherlands East Indies led to the release and encouragement of the gaoled nationalist leaders. The Japanese gave Sukarno and Hatta, as well as other Indonesian nationalists, important opportunities in the form of various mass-based political organizations to reach out to the people in the rural areas. The Japanese army also set up auxiliary armies in Sumatra, Java and Bali, using local officers, thus providing the nationalists with a future source of military power. They encouraged greater use of bahasa Indonesia as a national language as well as providing jobs in the bureaucracy for an increased number of "Indonesians" (the use of the term Indonesia to describe the Dutch colony was first taken up in the early 1920s by young legal students in the Netherlands who derived the word from anthropology courses at Leiden University). On the eve of Japanese defeat, Sukarno, Hatta and the Japanese high command for Southeast Asia promulgated a plan that laid the groundwork for an independent republic of Indonesia. On August 17 1945, just after the Japanese surrender, Indonesia declared its independence. While the new government, with Sukarno as the first President and Hatta as Vice-President, received wide support from many important political sectors of the new nation, what followed was a four-year battle for control of the archipelago.[70]

Between 1945 and 1949 there were two states effectively operating in what remained of the Dutch colony: the apparatus of the new republic and the Dutch colonial administration.[71] By the end of 1948 most of the former colonial administration was in Dutch hands as were all the main urban centers, while Sukarno, Hatta and other leading nationalists had been detained. At the same time, the Dutch still faced highly localized popular military resistance, especially on Sumatra and Java. This, combined with strong US diplomatic and financial pressure and Dutch war-weariness, led to a breakthrough at the end of 1949 at which time the Netherlands formally transferred power to the independent United States of Indonesia.[72] By 1950 the initial decentralized federal system had been replaced by a unitary republic that fell much more under direct Javanese control. Between 1950 and 1957 this fragile entity (fragile as a state and as a nation) was governed by a number of elected administrations that sought to stabilize and unify the archipelago and reintegrate a state structure, the "collective memory" of which kept the pre-1949 struggles alive. The overall coherence of the state was also undermined by the way successive administrations dramatically expanded the size of the civil service along patronage lines. At the same time between 1950 and 1957 all governments were coalition administrations, further facilitating departmental fragmentation.[73] From 1950 to 1957 the Indonesian state sought (under the overall supervision of Sukarno) to escape the economic structures of Dutch colonial rule via the encouragement of *pribumi* (indigenous, that is non-Chinese) capitalists. By the second half of the 1950s, as the republic lurched towards the populist authoritarianism that Sukarno called Guided Democracy, it was apparent that *pribumi* capitalists were unable to compete effectively with Dutch and other foreign corporations, not to mention the powerful Indonesian-Chinese business groups. Many of the new *pribumi* capitalists increasingly cooperated with established Indonesian-Chinese businesses, with the former providing the political linkages rather than anything resembling business acumen. As of 1957, at least 70 percent of the plantation agriculture on Sumatra and Java remained foreign-controlled, while 19 percent was Indonesian-Chinese owned and operated. In most instances where foreign capital had left Indonesia it was Indonesian-Chinese capital that had taken its place. At the same time, very little expansion of the industrial sector had occurred, and the share of the GDP that flowed from manufacturing actually fell from 12 percent in 1953 to 11 percent in 1958.[74] Between independence and the late 1950s a series of increasingly weak coalition governments grappled unsuccessfully with the new nations economic problems, while military and civilian officials increasingly sought to mesh their political dominance with wider social and economic power.[75]

By 1957 Indonesia had clearly turned to an "intensified nationalist strategy" which involved increased state intervention to restructure the economy and the take-over of a great deal of Dutch-owned property. At this point, more than 90 percent of the productive plantation sector, 60 percent of the previously foreign controlled export trade, along with almost 250 factories, numerous banks and mining companies, not to mention shipping businesses and various service industries, came under the direct control of the Indonesian state. By the second half of the 1950s the central government was also confronting serious rebellions in the Outer Islands, which were often colored by ethno-religious opposition to Javanese dominance. By the early 1960s, although the Outer Islands rebellions had been contained, they had resulted in further increases in power for the Indonesian Army (ABRI) and the enhancement of their ability to stifle political opposition under the umbrella of Sukarno's Guided Democracy. With important implications for the emergence of the New Order in 1965, ABRI also assumed a dramatically expanded economic role with direct control of large sectors of the economy after 1957. In the specific context of the expansion and deepening of its commitment to the politico-economic management of Indonesia under Sukarno, reflected in the promulgation of *dwifungsi* in 1958, by the early 1960s the Indonesian military had become central to the process of national unification and state-building. *Dwifungsi*, dual function, is an explicit enunciation that the military has a socio-political as well as a military role to play in Indonesia.[76] Apart from the military, Sukarno's Guided Democracy rested on a complex web of political alliances that revolved around the nationalist party (PNI), the PKI and a major Muslim party. He played these parties off against each other, at the same time as he pitted the mainly anti-communist military against the PKI. Guided Democracy (underpinned by Sukarno's strident anti-Western nationalism and idiosyncratic socialism) represented an explicitly state-led attempt at capitalist development. The Indonesian state directed earnings from the primary export sector into the primarily state-owned and operated manufacturing sector. Export earnings were also directed towards public works, health, food production, education and transportation, not to mention as payment on foreign debts. At the same time the state sought to attract new foreign loans in an effort to further expand the country's industrial base and its infrastructure. By the early 1960s, however, stagnation and decline in the sugar and rubber sectors, combined with falling commodity prices, had resulted in a shortage of funds and a serious balance of payments problem. Furthermore, the nationalization of large parts of the economy had done little to attract foreign investment. By the first half of the 1960s Indonesia's economy was on the brink of collapse. Inflation was hitting 600 percent annually, foreign debt was climbing rapidly and statistics on income and food intake per capita rivalled some of the poorest countries in the world.[77]

At the same time Sukarno had become very ill by mid-1964. By early 1965 it was increasingly apparent that the country's fragile power structure was in crisis and rumours of military coups and/or a PKI-led putsch became regular occurrences. The sequence of events during the fateful years of 1965 and 1966 is complex and many aspects are hotly debated. Contrary to the official version, which lays the blame at the door of the PKI, it appears that an attempt by a general in the Palace Guard to seize power on September 30 1965, ostensibly to pre-empt an expected coup against Sukarno, sparked off a series of events, driven by the splits in the military, which led to the marginalization of Sukarno and the effective elimination of the PKI. Although Sukarno was nominally still in charge in late 1965, the Indonesian military, with US military aid and CIA support, and the direct participation of a host of paramilitary Muslim youth groups, turned on the PKI and its supporters, in what the US ambassador described at the time as "wholesale killings". By mid-1966 the CIA and the State Department were estimating that anywhere between 250,000 and 500,000 alleged PKI members had been killed (in mid-1965 the PKI was reckoned to have 3 million members as well as 12 million people in associated organizations). Other estimates put the figure at over a million, and some estimates range as high as 1.5 million dead. The official Indonesian figures released in the mid-1970s were 450,000 to 500,000 dead. At the same time at least 200,000 people were imprisoned with about 55,000 of them still in jail a decade later.[78] It was out of the bloodshed, crisis and turmoil of the mid-1960s that the New Order emerged.

The Indonesian trajectory and the transformation of Asia II: 1965–1997

The bloody foundation of Suharto's New Order in the mid-1960s coincided with the deepening of the US presence in the region at the same time as it marked a restoration of conservative social forces in Indonesia which had been partially marginalized during the early national period under Sukarno. At the outset, the official interpretation of the ousting of Sukarno and the violent transition of 1965–1966 became a key element in the state-centered discourse on the communist threat. It was instrumental to the social reorganization of the New Order around a version of Indonesian nationalism grounded in anti-communism and a complex mix of politico-cultural ideas that emphasized the relevance of "Eastern" and "Indonesian" traditions, in contrast to unsuitable "Western" ideas such as Marxism and liberalism.[79] The vision of the Indonesian nation as an "Eastern" polity in which liberalism and Marxism were inappropriate and irrelevant was reinforced by the dramatic deepening of military involvement in the political system, the economy and in society.[80] Meanwhile, Suharto's elimination of the *Partai Komunis Indonesia* (Communist Party of Indonesia – PKI), and his regime's anti-communist credentials, ensured that the US and its allies quickly embarked on the reincorporation of Indonesia into the US-centered regional order. This included generous quantities of aid and a considerable amount of debt rescheduling. Under the guidance of a group of US-trained technocrats – the so-called Berkeley Mafia – the New Order solicited foreign investment, particularly from the US and Japan. From the mid-1960s, until at least the early 1980s, the New Order regime pursued an import-substitution industrialization (ISI) strategy financed by growing foreign investment, as well as by foreign aid and some domestic investment. Until the mid-1970s, Suharto was indebted to the US-backed international agencies particularly, and a range of foreign investors more generally; however, the dramatic increase in oil prices in the 1970s provided the New Order with the means to move to a far more state-centered approach to capitalist development. This trend was short-lived, however, and the decline in oil prices in the 1980s resulted in increasing debt and a decreased capacity on the part of the state to facilitate local capital accumulation, while greater use of foreign loans and foreign aid led to greater leverage on the part of the World Bank, the IMF and foreign investors. By the second half of the 1980s, important liberalizing reforms, centered on a turn to export-oriented industrialization (EOI), were underway. This shift in economic policy facilitated an increase in the influx of foreign capital in the late 1980s, much of it from Japan (as well as South Korea and Taiwan), and the rapid rise of an export-industry sector, especially on Java.[81]

With the deepening of the authoritarian structures of the Indonesian state by the 1970s, the New Order increasingly sought to rework and entrench Pancasila (the five principles of belief in one God, humanitarianism, nationalism, consensus, democracy and social justice which had first been promulgated in 1945 as the philosophical basis for an independent Indonesia) as a national ideology. While the impact of Pancasila ideology should not be exaggerated, insofar as many Indonesians were clearly aware of its contradictions long before Suharto stepped down in early 1998, it has acted as a powerful complement to the more overtly coercive aspects of state power and helped to constrain political debate in Indonesia for many years.[82] By 1975, the New Order rested on a comprehensive surveillance and security network and a narrow and tightly controlled political system that had eliminated or completely reorganized the country's political parties. This was complemented by a large and growing state bureaucracy, linked from top to bottom to the military and centered on President Suharto himself, who had an overwhelming range of patronage and control mechanisms at his disposal. In the case of labor, for example, a state-sanctioned and corporatist trade union body was set up, while the ideas on which it was grounded were increasingly infused with Pancasila ideology. Along with the denial of the right to independent organization, workers in New Order Indonesia were generally denied the right to strike. In 1974 Pancasila Industrial Relations (HIP – Hubungan Industrial Pancasila) was promulgated. This served to legitimate widespread state intervention, at the same time as it nullified the legitimacy of strike action via its emphasis on familial and harmonious relations between labor, capital and the state. The military also played an important role in the trade unions and labor relations (not least being the practice of retired army officers taking up positions in the official trade union movement).[83] While the importance of loyalty to the New Order was increasingly mediated through state-defined ideas about Pancasila, against the backdrop of an image of the Indonesian nation as a united and harmonious family (with Suharto as the father), a related aspect was the production of a powerful Indonesian develop-ment (*pembangunan*) discourse, which exhorted Indonesians to work together to develop the nation and bring about economic take-off, under the leadership of Suharto, the "father of development" (*Bapak Pembangunan*).[84]

As far as his own children were concerned, Suharto was an exemplary "father of development", and the president's offspring took up a direct and increasingly dominant role in commerce. When the Asian financial crisis began in mid-1997 it acted as a major catalyst for a looming social and political crisis centered on the rent-seeking and corruption of the Suharto family itself.[85] By early 1998 the Indonesian economy was on the verge of hyperinflation as unemployment esca-lated. Then, in May 1998, major student protests broke out, demanding Suharto's resignation. However, the transfer of power to Suharto's vice-president and protégé, B.J. Habibie, was met with more political unrest. His administration failed to restore economic stability while, in the context of rising inequality, social and ethnic cleavages were exacerbated. Estimates of the increased poverty levels by the end of 1998 and 1999 varied widely. The ILO calculated that the percentage of the Indonesian population living in poverty went from 48.2 to 66.3 percent of the population between December 1998 and December 1999, while a second set of estimates concluded that 20 percent of the population was living in poverty by the latter part of 1998, up from around 10 percent before the crisis.[86] Elections in June 1999 brought Abdurrahman Wahid to the presi-dency, followed by his replacement, in July 2001, by his vice-president, Megawati Sukarnoputri. Wahid's presidency was increasingly characterized by inconsis-tency and a lack of transparency at the same time as the end of Suharto's New Order quickly invigorated secessionist movements in various parts of Indonesia. Less than two years after Suharto's resignation in May 1998, East Timor had already achieved independence as a new nation-state. Meanwhile, secessionist movements in Aceh and Irian Jaya (Papua) have grown dramatically since the end of the Suharto era. The rise of these secessionist movements is grounded in the dynamics of state-guided national development of the Cold War era. More specifically, the secessionist movements were strengthened, to a considerable extent, by the brutal and inequitable way in which Suharto's New Order state pursued national development.[87]

The post-Suharto state also appears to be inclined to resort to military force to retain the territorial unity of Indonesia. The history of the New Order era suggests that this will only encourage and strengthen secessionist sentiment, aggravating the crisis of the Indonesian nation-state. Since assuming the presidency in 2001, Megawati, as "mother of the nation", has sought to map out a comforting and secure vision of the future in the context of political instability and economic decline. Her brand of populist nationalism lends itself to both an authoritarian style of politics and a potential commitment to neo-liberal austerity.[88] In fact, a more authoritarian political style may also provide comfort to IMF officials, who expressed concern, in the context of the end of the Suharto era, that "too much" democracy could be a potential threat to liberal economic reform.[89] Certainly, Megawati's government has continued to receive considerable support from the IMF. In early 2002, the Paris Club, with IMF support, agreed to a generous rescheduling of over US$5 billion in Indonesian government debt which involved the suspension of payments on the principal and the interest until the end of 2003.[90] But, while she appointed a well-regarded team of ministers to manage the economy and has clearly ushered in much improved relations with the IMF, the prognosis for the Indonesian economy is not good.[91] At the same time, the US-led "war on terrorism", although focused on the Middle East and Central Asia, has serious implications for the complex political dynamics in Indonesia, given its status as the largest Muslim nation in the world. The new global "war on terrorism" is already strengthening the military's position in Indonesia, while the small but active radical Islamic groups in the country draw attention to the various destabilizing ways the global confrontation could be played out in Indonesia and Southeast Asia more generally. For example, the implications for the secessionist struggle in Aceh, given its radical Islamic tone, could be significant.[92] In the wake of September 11 2001, and the Bali bombings of October 12 2002, there is little doubt that Megawati's government is intent on maintaining "national unity" via centralized political and military means and has embarked on various efforts to strengthen its relationship with, and the position of the military in the wider political system, following a certain amount of downgrading of its position in the immediate post-Suharto era.[93]

Conclusion: the communist challenge and the changing global order

This chapter has examined the history of the Cold War to draw out the way in which it provided the overall context for the consolidation and deepening of capitalism in Asia after 1945. In particular it has been emphasized that the Cold War and US geo-political and economic strategies played an important role in the rise and overall character of authoritarian state-guided national development projects in Asia. Furthermore, the Cold War framework placed significant limits on the sovereignty of all nation-states in the region. In Asia, the nation-states that emerged from decolonization and became allies/clients of the US had relative autonomy in relation to "national" affairs, but there were often serious constraints on any initiatives that were seen as relating directly or indirectly to US geo-political concerns and wider international arrangements. This was exemplified by the fact that, unlike US relations with its allies/clients in Western Europe,

Washington relied far more heavily on bilateral defense treaties and agreements in Asia. Meanwhile, the growing pressures on state-guided national development – as discussed in detail in relation to South Korea and Indonesia – against the backdrop of the shift in the 1970s from the US-led modernization project to the globalization project resulted in significant national reorientation and the waning of the authoritarian developmental state in South Korea in the 1980s. Indonesia, despite the anticipation by the mid-1990s on the part of some economists that it was the "emerging giant" of Southeast Asia, had entered into a widening crisis by 1997 that not only parallelled the dramatic process of national reorientation that was taking place in South Korea – setting aside the important and unresolved question of the future of North Korea and the prospects for and impact of reunification with the south – but also involves increasing conflict over the territorial boundaries of the nation-state itself. The wider context for the growing pressure on state-guided national development in South Korea and Indonesia was the major reorientation of the geo-political economy of the Cold War that was taking place by the 1970s. It is to this trend and the wider transformation of Asia between the 1970s and the 1990s that we now turn.

Notes

1 D. W. White, *The American Century: The Rise and Decline of the United States as a World Power*, New Haven: Yale University Press, 1996, p. 383. (This percentage is based on GNP estimates.)

2 M. P. Leffler, *A Preponderance of Power: National Security, the Truman Administration and the Cold War*, Stanford: Stanford University Press, 1992; M. J. Hogan, *A Cross of Iron: Harry S. Truman and the Origins of the National Security State, 1945–1954*, Cambridge: Cambridge University Press, 1998.

3 M. J. Hogan, *The Marshall Plan: America, Britain, and the Reconstruction of Western Europe, 1947–1952*, 2nd edn, Cambridge: Cambridge University Press, 1989.

4 G. Lundestad, *"Empire" By Integration: The United States and European Integration*, New York: Oxford University Press, 1998; J. G. Giauque, *Grand Designs and Visions of Unity: The Atlantic Powers and the Reorganization of Western Europe, 1955–1963*, Chapel Hill: University of North Carolina Press, 2002.

5 B. Cumings, "Japan in the World-System" in A. Gordon, ed., *Post-War Japan as History*, Berkeley: University of California Press, 1993; D. Kelly, *Japan and the Reconstruction of East Asia*, Basingstoke: Palgrave, 2002, pp. 33–64.

6 R. L. McGlothlen, *Controlling the Waves: Dean Acheson and U.S. Foreign Policy in Asia*, New York: W. W. Norton, 1993.

7 B. Cumings, *The Origins of the Korean War I: Liberation and the Emergence of Separate Regimes 1945–1947*, 2nd edn, Princeton: Princeton University Press, 1989; B. Cumings, *The Origins of the Korean War II: The Roaring of the Cataract 1947–1950*, Princeton: Princeton University Press, 1990.

8 W. Stueck, *The Korean War: An International History*, Princeton: Princeton University Press, 1997.

9 R. Stubbs, "War and Economic Development: Export-Oriented Industrialization in East and Southeast Asia" *Comparative Politics* vol. 31, no. 3, 1999, p. 344; W. S. Borden, *The Pacific Alliance: United States Foreign Economy Policy and Japanese Trade Recovery*, Madison: University of Wisconsin Press, 1984, p. 146; A. Forsberg. *America and the Japanese Miracle: The Cold War Context of Japan's Postwar Economic Revival, 1950–1960*, Chapel Hill: University of North Carolina Press, 2000.

10 T. Cohen, *Remaking Japan: The American Occupation as New Deal*, New York: Free Press, 1987.

11 N. Wiegersma and J. E. Medley, *US Economic Development Policies Towards the Pacific Rim: Successes and Failures of US Aid*, London: Macmillan, 2000, pp. 17–19.

12 W. LaFeber, *The Clash: U.S.–Japanese Relations throughout History*, New York: W. W. Norton, 1997, pp. 269, 293–5. The term *keiretsu*, which was the new word for *zaibatsu* (which were formally dissolved by the US Occupation authorities), can be translated as a group of affiliated companies and enterprises. There are a number of different types of *keiretsu*: these include, *kin'yuu keiretsu*, which are companies that are affiliated through financing; *shihon keiretsu*, which are affiliated companies with a single parent company; and *kigyoo keiretsu*, which are subcontractors.

13 R. Stubbs, "The Political Economy of the Asia-Pacific Region" in R. Stubbs and G. R. D. Underhill, eds, *Political Economy and the Changing Global Order*, London: Macmillan, 1994, p. 368.

14 M. Castells, "Four Asian Tigers with a Dragon Head: A Comparative Analysis of the State, Economy and Society in the Asian Pacific Rim" in R. P. Appelbaum and J. Henderson, eds, *States and Development in the Asian Pacific Rim*, Newbury Park: Sage, 1992.

15 A. Bowie, "The Dynamics of Business–Government Relations in Industrializing Malaysia" in A. MacIntyre, ed., *Business and Government in Industrializing Asia*, Sydney: Allen and Unwin, 1994, pp. 190–2.

16 P. M. Lubeck, "Malaysian Industrialization, Ethnic Divisions and the NIC Model: The Limits of Replication" in R. P. Appelbuam and J. Henderson, eds, *States and Development in the Asian Pacific Rim*, Newbury Park: Sage, 1992, pp. 176–98.

17 J. Hilley, *Malaysia: Mahathirism, Hegemony and the New Opposition*, London: Zed Books, 2001, pp. 58–65.

18 J. Minns, "Of Miracles and Models: The Rise and Decline of the Developmental State in South Korea" *Third World Quarterly: Journal of Emerging Areas* vol. 22, no. 6, 2001, p. 1025.

19 J.-E. Woo-Cumings, "National Security and the Rise of the Developmental State in South Korea and Taiwan" in H. S. Rowen, ed., *Behind East Asian Growth: The Political and Social Foundations of Prosperity*, London: Routledge, 1998.

20 C. Chase-Dunn, *Global Formation: Structures of the World-Economy*, Oxford: Basil Blackwell, 1989, p. 253.

21 K. S. Kim and M. Roemer, *Growth and Structural Transformation* (Studies in the Modernization of the Republic of Korea: 1945–1975), Cambridge, MA: Harvard University Press, 1979, p. vi.

22 M. Woo-Cumings, "The Political Economy of Growth in East Asia: A Perspective on the State, Market, and Ideology" in M. Aoki, H.-K. Kim and M. Okuno-Fujiwara, eds, *The Role of Government in East Asian Economic Development: Comparative Institutional Analysis*, Oxford: Clarendon Press, 1997, p. 334.

23 Wiegersma and Medley, *US Economic Development Policies Towards the Pacific Rim*, pp. 17, 20, 35–49.

24 Kelly, *Japan and the Reconstruction of East Asia*, pp. 67–105.

25 Stubbs, "The Political Economy of the Asia-Pacific Region", pp. 366–8.

26 B. Cumings, "The Legacy of Japanese Colonialism in Korea" in R. H. Myers and M. R. Peattie, eds, *The Japanese Colonial Empire 1895–1945*, Princeton: Princeton University Press, 1984.

27 J.-E. Woo, *Race to the Swift: State and Finance in Korean Industrialization*, New York: Columbia University Press, 1991, pp. 7–8, 20–1, 40.

28 H. Koo and E. M. Kim, "The Developmental State and Capital Accumulation in South Korea" in R. P. Appelbaum and J. Henderson, eds, *States and Development in the Asian Pacific Rim*, Newbury Park: Sage, 1992, pp. 124–31.

29 B. Cumings, "The Origins and Development of the Northeast Asian Political Economy: Industrial Sectors, Product Cycles and Political Consequences" in F. C.

Deyo, ed., *The Political Economy of the New Asian Industrialism*, Ithaca: Cornell University Press, 1987.

30 Koo and Kim, "The Developmental State and Capital Accumulation in South Korea", pp. 131–5.

31 M. Hart-Landsberg, *The Rush to Development: Economic Change and Political Struggle in South Korea*, New York: Monthly Review Press, 1993.

32 Koo and Kim, "The Developmental State and Capital Accumulation in South Korea", pp. 136–9.

33 R. L. Janelli (and D. Yim), *Making Capitalism: The Social and Cultural Construction of a South Korean Conglomerate*, Stanford: Stanford University Press, 1993, pp. 232–4, 238–9.

34 J. P. Lovell and C. I. E. Kim, "The Military and Political Change in Asia" in H. Bienen, ed., *The Military and Modernization*, Chicago: Aldine Atherton, 1971, pp. 108–11.

35 S. S. Kim, "Korea and Globalization (*Segyehwa*): A Framework for Analysis" in S. S. Kim, ed., *Korea's Globalization*, Cambridge: Cambridge University Press, 2000, pp. 2–4.

36 H.-J. Chang, "Korea: The Misunderstood Crisis" *World Development* vol. 26, no. 8, 1998, p. 1560.

37 C. S. E. Kang, "*Segyehwa* Reform of the South Korean Developmental State" in S. S. Kim, ed., *Korea's Globalization*, Cambridge: Cambridge University Press, 2000, pp. 97–101.

38 South Korea's GNP was almost US$500 billion, while its per capita GNP was approximately US$11,000 in November 1997. By the beginning of 1998 its GNP had dropped precipitously to US$312 billion (in per capita terms the figure was US$6,600). Over the same period it went from being the eleventh biggest industrial economy in the world to the seventeenth. Minns, "Of Miracles and Models", p. 1038.

39 M. Hart-Landsberg, *Korea: Division, Reunification and U.S. Foreign Policy*, New York: Monthly Review Press, 1998; M. Noland, *Avoiding the Apocalypse: The Future of the Two Koreas*, Washington, DC: The Institute for International Economics, 2000; S. S. Harrison, *Korean Endgame: A Strategy for Reunification and U.S. Disengagement*, Princeton: Princeton University Press, 2002.

40 N. Tarling, *Britain, Southeast Asia and the Onset of the Cold War 1945–1950*, Cambridge: Cambridge University Press, 1998, pp. 265, 310–11.

41 R. J. McMahon, *Colonialism and Cold War: The United States and the Struggle for Indonesian Independence 1945–1949*, Ithaca: Cornell University Press, 1981.

42 A. J. Stockwell, "The United States and Britain's Decolonization of Malaya, 1942–1957" in D. Ryan and V. Pungong, eds, *The United States and Decolonization: Power and Freedom*, London: Macmillan, 2000, pp. 196–7.

43 R. Stubbs, *Hearts and Minds in Guerrilla Warfare: The Malayan Emergency 1948–1960*, Singapore: Oxford University Press, 1989, especially pp. 107–14, 260–4. The long-term significance of the Malayan Emergency (1948–1960) for the coercive capacity of the postcolonial state in Malaysia is also linked to the way in which the government of newly independent Malaysia used the "detention without trial" provisions of the Emergency Act after 1957. In 1960 the Emergency Act became the basis of the Internal Security Act (ISA), which ensured that "preventive detention" was used by the state on terms that were "considerably more repressive" than under the earlier Emergency Regulations. A. Munro-Kua, *Authoritarian Populism in Malaysia*, London: Macmillan, 1996, pp. 32–3, 53.

44 D. M. Shafer, *Deadly Paradigms: The Failure of US Counterinsurgency Policy*, Princeton: Princeton University Press, 1988, pp. 240, 274–5.

45 R. J. McMahon, *The Limits of Empire: The United States and Southeast Asia since World War II*, New York: Columbia University Press, 1999, pp. 60–8; also see pp. 69–79.

46 J. E. Williams, "The Colombo Conference and Communist Insurgency in South and South East Asia" *International Relations* vol. 4, no. 1, 1972, pp. 94–107.

47 P. Gifford, "The Cold War across Asia" in D. Goldsworthy, ed., *Facing North: A Century of Australian Engagement with Asia*, Melbourne: Melbourne University Press, 2001.

48 As of 2001, the member states of the Colombo Plan included Afghanistan, Australia, Bangladesh, Bhutan, Cambodia, Fiji, India, Indonesia, Iran, Japan, Korea, Laos, Malaysia, the Maldives, Myanmar, Nepal, New Zealand, Pakistan, Papua New Guinea, the Philippines, Singapore, Sri Lanka, Thailand, and the United States. Mongolia is a provisional member. Online at http://www.colombo-plan.org/

49 C. A. Thayer, *War by Other Means: National Liberation and Revolution in Viet-Nam 1954–1960*, Sydney: Allen and Unwin, 1989, p. 123; D. C. Dacy, *Foreign Aid, War, and Economic Development: South Vietnam, 1953–1975*, Cambridge: Cambridge University Press, 1986.

50 J. Ernst, *Forging A Fateful Alliance: Michigan State University and the Vietnam War*, East Lansing: Michigan State University, 1998.

51 Wiegersma and Medley, *US Economic Development Policies Towards the Pacific Rim*, pp. 17, 20, 71–2, 75–9.

52 Woo-Cumings, "The Political Economy of Growth in East Asia", p. 335.

53 T. R. H. Havens, *Fire Across the Sea: The Vietnam War and Japan 1965–1975*, Princeton: Princeton University Press, 1987, p. 96.

54 Stubbs, "The Political Economy of the Asia-Pacific Region", p. 368.

55 R. Bishop and L. S. Robinson, *Night Market: Sexual Cultures and the Thai Economic Miracle*, London: Routledge, 1998, pp. 198–201.

56 Stubbs, "The Political Economy of the Asia-Pacific Region", pp. 368–9; R. J. Muscat, *Thailand and the United States: Development, Security, and Foreign Aid*, New York: Columbia University Press, 1990; D. Fineman, *A Special Relationship: The United States and Military Government in Thailand, 1947–1958*, Honolulu: University of Hawaii Press, 1997.

57 G. Kolko, *Anatomy of a War: Vietnam, the United States and Modern Historical Experience*, 2nd edn, New York: New Press, 1994, pp. 303–37, 341–55.

58 Wiegersma and Medley, *US Economic Development Policies Towards the Pacific Rim*, pp. 80–93.

59 A. F. Celoza, *Ferdinand Marcos and the Philippines: The Political Economy of Authoritarianism*, New York: Praeger, 1998.

60 D. C. Kang, *Crony Capitalism: Corruption and Development in South Korea and the Philippines*, Cambridge: Cambridge University Press, 2002, pp. 27–9.

61 The actual treaty that gave rise to SEATO was retained because it was the only formal military agreement between the United States and the government of Thailand. L. Buszynski, *SEATO: The Failure of an Alliance Strategy*, Singapore: Singapore University Press, 1984.

62 M. T. Berger, "Old State and New Empire in Indonesia: Debating the Rise and Decline of Suharto's New Order" *Third World Quarterly: Journal of Emerging Areas* vol. 18, no. 2, 1997.

63 World Bank, *The East Asian Miracle: Economic Growth and Public Policy*, Oxford: Oxford University Press for the World Bank, 1993.

64 H. Hill, *The Indonesian Economy Since 1966: Southeast Asia's Emerging Giant*, Cambridge: Cambridge University Press, 1996. The sub-title was, not surprisingly, dropped from the second edition that appeared in 2000. See H. Hill, *The Indonesian Economy*, 2nd edn, Cambridge: Cambridge University Press, 2000.

65 J. Bresnan, "Indonesia" in R. Chase, E. Hill and P. Kennedy, eds, *The Pivotal States: A New Framework for U.S. Policy in the Developing World*, New York: W. W. Norton, 1999.

66 B. Anderson, "Old State, New Society: Indonesia's New Order in Comparative Historical Perspective" in B. Anderson, *Langauge and Power: Exploring Political Cultures in Indonesia*, Ithaca: Cornell University Press, 1990, pp. 96–9.

67 H. Sutherland, *The Making of a Bureaucratic Elite: The Colonial Transformation of the Javanese Priyayi*, Sydney: Allen and Unwin, 1979.

68 For example, see A. L. Stoler, *Capitalism and Confrontation in Sumatra's Plantation Belt 1870–1979*, New Haven: Yale University Press, 1985, pp. 14–92.
69 R. von Albertini, *Decolonization: The Administration and Future of the Colonies 1919–1960*, New York: Greenwood Press, 1982, pp. 487–513.
70 Anderson, "Old State, New Society", pp. 99–100.
71 This was in part a result of the way the Dutch colonial state apparatus had been fractured during the Japanese Occupation. From 1942 to 1945 Java was ruled by the 16th Army, Sumatra by the 25th Army, while the eastern islands fell under the control of the Japanese navy. Anderson, "Old State, New Society", p. 100.
72 McMahon, *Colonialism and Cold War*.
73 Anderson, "Old State, New Society", pp. 100–3.
74 R. Robison, *Indonesia: The Rise of Capital*, Sydney: Allen and Unwin, 1986, pp. 42–4, 57.
75 R. Robison, "Structures of Power and the Industrialization Process in Southeast Asia" *Journal of Contemporary Asia* vol. 19, no. 4, 1989, pp. 383–4.
76 B. Magenda, "Ethnicity and State-Building in Indonesia: The Cultural Base of the New Order" in R. Guidieri, F. Pellizzi and S. J. Tambiah, eds, *Ethnicities and Nations: Processes of Interethnic Relations in Latin America, Southeast Asia and the Pacific*, Austin: University of Texas Press, 1988, pp. 350–3.
77 C. Dixon, *South East Asia in the World-Economy: A Regional Geography*, Cambridge: Cambridge University Press, 1991, pp. 191–2.
78 G. Kolko, *Confronting the Third World*, New York: Pantheon, 1988, pp. 173–85. Also see R. Cribb, ed., *The Indonesian Killings 1965–1966: Studies from Java and Bali*, Clayton: Centre for Southeast Asian Studies, Monash University, 1990.
79 D. Bourchier, "Indonesianising Indonesia: Conservative Indigenism in an Age of Globalisation" *Social Semiotics* vol. 8, nos. 2/3, 1998, pp. 203–4, 212–13.
80 H. Crouch, *The Army and Politics in Indonesia*, revised edition, Ithaca: Cornell University Press, 1988 (first published 1978).
81 J. A. Winters, *Power in Motion: Capital Mobility and the Indonesian State*, Ithaca: Cornell University Press, 1996, pp. 47–94.
82 D. E. Ramage, *Politics in Indonesia: Democracy, Islam and the Ideology of Tolerance*, London: Routledge, 1995, pp. 1–44, 184–202.
83 V. R. Hadiz, *Workers and the State in Indonesia*, London: Routledge, 1997, pp. 59–109.
84 M. T. Berger, "Post-Cold War Indonesia and the Revenge of History: The Colonial Legacy, Nationalist Visions, and Global Capitalism" in M. T. Berger and D. A. Borer, eds, *The Rise of East Asia: Critical Visions of the Pacific Century*, London: Routledge, 1997, p. 179.
85 "The Family Firm: Suharto Inc." *Time: The Weekly Newsmagazine* May 24, 1999, pp. 36–48.
86 Hill, *The Indonesian Economy*, 2nd edn, pp. 271–2.
87 E. Aspinall and M. T. Berger, "The Breakup of Indonesia? Nationalisms after Decolonization and the Limits of the Nation-State in Post-Cold War Southeast Asia" *Third World Quarterly: Journal of Emerging Areas* vol. 22, no. 6, 2001.
88 E. Aspinall, "Mother of the Nation" *Inside Indonesia*, no. 68 (October–December), 2001.
89 D. Murphy, "The Mod Squad" *Far Eastern Economic Review* August 19, 1999, pp. 10–11.
90 S. Dhume, "Indonesia: Helping Hand" *Far Eastern Economic Review* April 25, 2002, p. 39.
91 S. Dhume, "Indonesia: On Shaky Ground" *Far Eastern Economic Review* September 27, 2001, p. 51.
92 J. McBeth, "The Danger Within" *Far Eastern Economic Review* September 27, 2001, pp. 20–3.
93 J. McBeth and M. Vatikiotis, "Indonesia: An About Turn on the Military" *Far Eastern Economic Review* April 25, 2002, pp. 12–15.

9 The Asian challenge and the changing global order

The transformation of Asia between the 1940s and the 1970s had an important relationship to the reorientation of US hegemony in the late 1960s and early 1970s. At the same time, as in the rest of the world, the subsequent overall direction of the national trajectories in the region was profoundly affected by the changes in the political economy of the Cold War in this period. In fact, for some observers, the Nixon administration's dramatic geo-political shifts in the 1970s were of greater significance in Asia than the end of the Cold War in 1989. Nevertheless, the demise of the Soviet Union was also an important turning point in the region – it altered the dynamics of the US–China relationship, while the post-Cold War era also saw increased friction in Washington's relationship with Tokyo around economic questions and around renewed efforts by Washington to promote neo-liberalism in the region. This latter trend came to a head with the Asian crisis in 1997–1998. The crisis facilitated US efforts to wind back state-guided national development as it had emerged in various forms in Asia. At the same time the Asian financial crisis weakened post-Cold War forms of inclusive regionalism, like the Asia Pacific Economic Cooperation forum (APEC), in favor of the possible invigoration of exclusive Pan-Asian regionalism long advocated by the Prime Minister of Malaysia, Mahathir Mohamad.[1]

This chapter focuses on the period from 1975 to the late 1990s, particularly the post-Cold War era, although where required it looks at trends prior to 1975. It begins by looking at Asia in the final decades of the Cold War with a focus on the overall changes in this period. It then turns to the Japanese and Chinese trajectories with an emphasis on the period since 1975. The second part of the chapter turns to an examination of post-Cold War regional trends, particularly inter-state struggles over economic and security issues and the countervailing trend towards the strengthening of established, or the consolidation of new, regional organizations. This is followed by a discussion of the Japanese and Chinese trajectories in the post-Cold War era. These are particularly important nation-states and their present circumstances and future directions have major regional and global implications. The processes of national reorientation and crisis in Japan and China are closely connected to the continued and/or increased potential for inter-state conflict and to a shift towards new or reconfigured regional economic and political groupings of nation-states in Asia and elsewhere. The passing, or dramatic weakening, of state-mediated national development, ostensibly grounded in inclusive social goals (the record of which was exceedingly uneven in Asia and elsewhere), has important implications for inter-state conflict.

Reorientation I

Managing the Asian challenge I: Cold War Asia and the changing global order

As emphasized in chapter 4, the immediate origins of the shift from national development to globalization are to be found in the geo-political and economic policies of President Richard Nixon (1969–1974). The reorientation of US hegemony in this period, which paved the way for the rise of the globalization project, has a particular significance in relation to East Asia, insofar as the Vietnam War and US relations with China were central to the dramatic reorientation in US policy in the early 1970s. At the beginning of 1969, Nixon assumed the presidency with the promise that his administration would find an "honourable solution" to the war in Southeast Asia. He outlined the Nixon Doctrine, which centered on his ideas about a new US role in Asia and was primarily aimed at avoiding direct US military intervention.[2] In the 1970s Washington sought to manage the numerous reformist and revolutionary challenges to US hegemony in Asia and elsewhere, via increased reliance on covert activities, military aid and unquestioning support for authoritarian regimes. The Nixon Doctrine was explicitly aimed at avoiding another Vietnam; however, it did little to alter a deeply rooted Cold War outlook (which saw the Soviet Union as the major threat to US power). Central to Washington's geo-political shifts in the 1970s were US overtures to China leading to significantly improved relations between Beijing and the US by the late 1970s.[3]

The Nixon administration's decision to normalize relations with China in 1972 became known in Japan as the second "Nixon Shock" (the first "Nixon Shock" was the end of the Bretton Woods arrangements the previous year). As this formulation makes clear, the dramatic shift in US foreign policy towards China came as a surprise to the Japanese government. In fact, Washington's strategic *démarche* fuelled resentment in Tokyo over the United States' continuing lack of consultation with its main ally in the region. In fact, by the late 1960s, as we have seen, Washington had already become wary of Japan and West Germany's successful post-1945 exercises in state-guided national development, a factor that contributed to the first "Nixon Shock". But, despite the floating of the US dollar and the suspension of its convertibility to gold, as well as a new 10 percent surcharge on all imports into the United States that led to the Smithsonian Agreement and the re-valuation of the yen by 16.88 percent against the dollar, the Japanese trade surplus with the United States continued to rise during the 1970s.[4] At the same time, the "Nixon Shocks" weakened the position of Prime Minister Sato Eisaku. In particular, he was a major proponent of closer Japanese links to Taiwan, which had, of course, emerged over the preceding decades as a key ally of Washington and a major geo-political counter-weight to the People's Republic of China (Taiwan occupied "China's" permanent seat on the UN Security Council until 1972). But the US–China rapprochement included Washington's recognition of the People's Republic of China (PRC) rather than Taiwan as the rightful occupant of the "Chinese" seat as a permanent member of the UN Security Council. Following the Nixon administration's dramatic tilt towards Beijing, Sato resigned and his successor, Tanaka Kakuei, quickly sought to shift Japan's policy to take into account the reorientation of US policy toward China, particularly the marginalization of Taiwan that had resulted. Following meetings in Beijing, the Japanese government offered a formal apology to Beijing for "acts of war against China", and officially recognized the People's Republic as the legitimate government of China. Japan did not go so far as to break off diplomatic relations with Taiwan, however, nor did Beijing insist that it do so. Not surprisingly, the KMT government of Taiwan was less understanding and it cut diplomatic relations with Japan. However, Taiwan relied on investment and trade from Japan ,and informal connections were retained, while trade between Japan and Taiwan actually rose in the years after 1972.[5]

By the time of Washington's geo-political and economic reo-orientation in the 1970s, the US had been eclipsed by Japan as Asia's most significant source of foreign aid and investment. Between the 1940s and the 1970s, the Japanese government and Japan-based corporations, with US sponsorship, had gradually re-built their linkages with Northeast and Southeast Asia.[6] The growing regional economic significance of Japan, against the backdrop of the country's post-1945 economic boom, was complemented by renewed efforts on the part of Japanese officials and commentators to encourage regional integration and the creation of a "Pacific Community". In Japan, visions of a Pacific community can be traced to the end of the nineteenth century when Japanese intellectuals began to anticipate a "Pacific Age" in global history.[7] This was also connected to celebratory accounts of Japan's industrial rise and its emergence as a major colonial power by the early twentieth century.[8] However, it was the promulgation of an "Asia-Pacific policy" by the Japanese Foreign Ministry in late 1966 (in the wake of the establishment earlier in the year of the Asian Development Bank under the auspices of the Japanese government with support from the US) that is seen to have signalled the start of Japan's effort to build a regional trade organization. Against the backdrop of its new Asia-Pacific policy the Japanese government put forward a proposal for a "Pacific Free Trade Area". This represented an explicit reaction to the emergence of the European Economic Community (EEC), now the European Union (EU). This initiative did not gain widespread support, but it did ease the way for the creation of the Pacific Basin Economic Council (PBEC) in April 1967, which is comprised of nationally based business organizations. Meanwhile, at the beginning of 1968 a regional organization for economists, the Pacific Trade and Development Conference (PAFTAD), had its first meeting in Tokyo.[9] During the 1970s, the Japanese government, with Australian support, floated the idea of a Pan-Pacific trade organization made up of as many of the governments in the region as possible. This led to the formation of the Pacific Economic Cooperation Conference (PECC), later Council, which had its first meeting in Canberra in late 1980, and included representatives from the US, Japan, Canada, Australia, New Zealand, Korea, Malaysia, Thailand, Indonesia, Singapore and the Philippines. During the 1980s the governments of China, Taiwan, Brunei and the South Pacific Forum also began sending delegates to the PECC. While the PECC brought together academics, business and government officials, a key characteristic of its operation was the unofficial role played by governments. Although the PECC has produced a host of reports and recommendations over the years, they are not binding.[10]

Meanwhile, as touched upon in chapter 8, following the lifting of a number of restrictions on the export of capital in the late 1960s, foreign direct investment (FDI) from Japan moved into manufacturing in Taiwan and South Korea and into raw material extraction and shipment in Southeast Asia. By the first half of the 1970s, four times as much FDI was going to South Korea from Japan as from the United States. From the mid-1970s to the mid-1980s, investment by Japanese corporations in Northeast and Southeast Asia continued to increase at a steady rate, as Japanese manufacturers continued to expand their activities in South Korea, Taiwan, Singapore, Hong Kong and beyond, and corporations involved in resource-extraction dramatically increased their involvement in Indonesia. Then, within three years of the ratification of the Plaza Accord in September 1985 – which represented a successful Washington-led effort to wind back a growing US trade deficit with Japan by getting the major G-5 central banks to increase the value of the Japanese yen against the US dollar – the value of the yen in relation to the dollar went from 238 to 128 percent. This encouraged a growing number of Japanese corporations to move their operations offshore. Southeast Asia's proximity to Japan and the fact that the economic down-turn of the mid-1980s had encouraged greater interest in attracting FDI on the part of governments in Southeast Asia – along with the fact that Japanese corporations perceived countries such as Thailand, Malaysia and Singapore to have the requisite infrastructure and workforce, as well as generally stable and efficient administration and a commitment to export-oriented industrialization – combined to bring about a dramatic rise in the amount of Japanese investment flowing into Southeast Asia in the second half of the 1980s. In the early 1980s Japanese investment in the ASEAN nation-states was about US$900 million annually. Following a slight drop, the figure rose to US$4.6 billion for 1989 and US$15 billion for the period from 1988–1991. While much of this FDI went initially to the expansion of the electronics and industrial sectors in Thailand and Singapore, Japanese manufacturers subsequently turned to Malaysia and Indonesia. South Korean and Taiwan-based companies also expanded into Southeast Asia and coastal China in this period. In 1990 and 1991 Taiwan-based companies invested more in Malaysia than their counterparts in Japan, while Hong Kong-based investors also directed attention at Malaysia and Thailand, and of course southern China.[11]

The rising Japanese investment in South Korea and Taiwan in the 1960s had been bolstered by Japanese government aid.[12] The subsequent arrival of a growing number of Japanese investors in China and Southeast Asia in the 1970s also coincided with the transfer from Tokyo of large quantities of development aid into the region. In this period the governments of Thailand, the Philippines, Malaysia and Indonesia were given approximately one-third of all Japanese bilateral aid. In the wake of the dramatic rise of Japanese investment in Southeast Asia, the total amount of Japanese aid going to the region also rose dramatically going from US$914 million in 1986 to US$2.3 billion in 1990. For China the figures were US$497 million in 1986 and US$832 million in 1989.[13] The spread of Japanese corporations to South Korea and Taiwan, and subsequently to Southeast Asia and China, resulted in the regionalization of certain structural aspects of Japanese industry. It represented an attempt, which was only ever partially realized, to build a "regional production alliance", which would mirror the domestic political economy of Japan, and was grounded in the use of an array of flexible medium and small subcontractors.[14] Trade within the Asian region also increased dramatically. For example, in 1986 the nation-states of ASEAN exported US$15.2 billion worth of goods to Japan (13.75 percent of these were manufactured goods), but by 1991 the figure was US$30.26 billion (31.7 percent of which were manufactures).[15] By the 1980s East Asia generally had become a major site for the relocation of manufacturing, particularly from Japan, but also from North America and Western Europe. This geographical restructuring of the world economy was directly linked to the rise of the US-led globalization project and the passing of the high period of national development in North America, Western Europe and Japan.[16] It was also linked, however, to the countervailing trend towards selective industrial protectionism in the 1980s aimed at curbing the expansion of Japanese manufactures into the markets of North America and Western Europe. This latter trend led to the continued deepening of economic and political ties between the various nation-states of Asia and Japan.

The Japanese trajectory and the transformation of Asia: 1945–1989

As emphasized, the deepening of regional economic integration centered on Japan was directly linked to the end of almost two decades of "high-speed" economic growth and an important shift in the Japanese economy in the 1970s. As we have seen in chapter 8, with the end of the US occupation of Japan in 1952 the foundations for a resurgent capitalist nation-state had been laid. Between the mid-1950s and the early 1970s the Japanese economy boomed, growing at an average of 10 percent a year in the 1960s.[17] In this period the wider Cold War context interacted with practices and arrangements in Japan that reinforced the post-war resurgence. Between the 1950s and the 1970s there was an emphasis on austerity that facilitated the subordination of consumption to production.[18] This needs to be set against the backdrop of the complex relationship between the dominant national narratives in Japan and the state-directed national development project.[19] The emphasis on austerity and the imperatives of national reconstruction and development were closely linked to a labor relations system that kept wages down and production up. While the cooperative labor relations system that emerged in Japan in the 1950s is often characterized as a "class compromise" between capital and labor, it was firmly grounded in labor's subordination to capital following the defeat of the militant labor movement in the 1940s, a process that was facilitated by the United States. Meanwhile, as we have seen, the reversal of Washington's plans to dismantle Japan's pre-war *zaibatsu* ensured their reappearance alongside a number of new conglomerates.[20] Industrial production and foreign trade were actively promoted by the Ministry of International Trade and Industry (MITI) and other government agencies using interest rate subsidies and special tax rates to ensure that capital, labor and raw materials went to conglomerates producing goods for export. There was also a high degree of economic concentration in the Japanese economy generally and in the export sector especially. In this period, ten very large Japanese cartels presided over more than 50 percent of the total export trade. At the end of the 1940s, Japanese exports had been almost non-existent, rising by the beginning of the 1960s to 3.2 percent of all world exports in 1961 and reaching 10 percent by the mid-1980s. Up to the 1970s and beyond two key aspects of the post-1945 global order facilitated the Japanese boom. First, Japanese exports had relatively open access to world markets in the context of the wider General Agreement on Tariffs and Trade (GATT). In this situation, Japanese manufacturers targeted a small number of important markets selling manufactured goods at prices only a little above and even, on occasion, the same as the cost of production. At the same time, assured access to low priced foodstuffs and raw materials, and particularly energy, was crucial to the boom up to the 1970s. Furthermore, between 1945 and the beginning of the 1970s, the prices for commodities remained very low in comparison to the prices for manufactured goods.[21]

During much of the 1970s and 1980s Japan's economy expanded at a rate of about 4 percent per year.[22] In this period, Japanese companies started to shift their efforts towards technology-intensive production. As discussed earlier, the labor-intensive industries, as well as iron and steel and shipbuilding, that had been central to the 1950s and 1960s were often moved from Japan to elsewhere in Asia (although they were still characterized by the involvement of and ownership by Japanese companies). By the early 1980s, Japan was exporting technology-intensive merchandise (computers, office machines, telecommunications equipment and electrical goods) around the world.[23] At the same time, the access to world markets and to inexpensive sources of raw materials and energy that had grounded the country's spectacular export-driven industrial expansion came under a cloud in the 1970s. The dramatic rise in world oil prices was a serious threat to a nation-state that had oil reserves. Also threatening were the protectionist initiatives of the 1970s and the early 1980s emanating from North America and Western Europe (that coincided ironically with the rise of neo-liberalism). By the 1980s, the European Economic Community (EEC, later the

EU) had introduced selective barriers on Japanese imports, while US-based producers of video equipment, televisions and automobiles were able to exert pressure in Washington that resulted in the Japanese government agreeing to "voluntary export restraints". The Japanese government sought to compensate by broadening and deepening the various economic connections with the nation-states of Asia in particular (although Latin America also became a growing focus of trade and investment from Japan). As we have seen, the Japanese government increasingly directed large quantities of foreign aid to key nation-states in Asia as part of a wider strategy to encourage economic cooperation in the region. Japanese corporations followed Tokyo's lead as direct investments flowed into petroleum and mining in Southeast Asia (and Australia) in an effort to secure access to fossil fuels and minerals and open up new markets for Japanese manufactured goods to counter the possibility of increased protectionism emanating from North America and Western Europe. Japanese corporations also shifted labor-intensive manufacturing from Japan to a number of nation-states in Asia where wages were considerably lower ensuring access to markets for a variety of low-priced manufactures in the region and beyond. During the 1980s the Japanese government sought, with some success, to ameliorate the suspicions many people in the region still harbored as a result of the brutality of Japanese empire-building in the lead up to, and during, the Second World War. As we have also seen, a number of nation-states in Asia, such as Malaysia, not only accepted Japan as a major source of investment and trade, they viewed it as a state-led development model to be emulated.[24]

In Japan the 1980s is now described as the era of the "bubble economy" (referring to the incredible asset price inflation of this period) during which the Japanese government, in the view of some commentators, "lost control of the economy". Deregulation in the financial sector by the 1980s had permitted a number of major Japanese corporations to alter the way in which they raised funds. In the past Japanese companies had procured capital primarily by taking out loans from banks; however, with the changes of the 1970s, they increasingly raised funds by selling warrants and convertible bonds to investors. The corporations then put some of the money raised this way into "high-yielding financial assets" (these were often also high risk). At the same time, the banks required new clients to fill the gap left by the decline in borrowing on the part of the big corporations. This role was increasingly assumed by land investors, which contributed to the dramatic inflation of real estate prices. The Japanese government attempted, but failed, to curb this trend. The property boom was also aggravated by other developments. For example, the Japanese government had begun running "budget deficits" in the mid-1960s to cover the rising cost of various subsidies and its commitment-to-spending initiatives aimed at stimulating economic growth. With the oil crisis of the 1970s this trend increased. By the end of the 1970s the Japanese government had one of the largest public debts of any government in the world. The Ministry of Finance pushed for reduced government spending, especially on infrastructure, and for tax increases. The government's income from taxes also went up as a result of the property boom, leading to declining public debt and budget surpluses. As the government also became a less significant absorber of new loans, the banks redoubled their loans to the real estate industry. Real estate and share prices boomed and Japan-based investors became increasingly reckless in their purchases of real estate and other trophy investments inside and outside of Japan.[25] This trend was symbolized by the purchase of the Rockefeller Center in New York by Mitsubishi Real Estate for US$850 million in the late 1980s. Not to mention the 1989 purchase of Columbia Pictures by Sony for US$3.4 billion, and the controlling interest in MCA acquired by Matsushita in 1990 at a cost of US$6.59 billion. By the end of the 1980s it was calculated that one-third of all commercial real estate in Los Angeles was owned by Japan-based investors.[26] This was clearly the background for Michael Crichton's novel, *Rising Sun*, and the subsequent movie of the same name, which was set in Los Angeles and, as discussed in chapter 6, embodied the crude racialized fears that Japan was "invading" the United States.

The Chinese trajectory and the transformation of Asia: 1949–1989

By the 1980s, meanwhile, China had become a major focus of economic activity as it increasingly emerged as the new "workshop of the world" in contrast to Japan's assumption of the role of "banker to the world". Coastal China in particular began to experience a light-manufacturing boom that effectively continues to this day. The earlier improvement in US–China relations had increasingly coincided with important changes to the developmental orientation of the CCP-state. The approach to development in China between 1949 and the end of the Cold War has gone through a number of phases against the backdrop of changes in Beijing's relationships with the USSR and the United States. From 1949 to about 1960, the PRC was closely aligned with the USSR and this coincided with the rise and fall of the PRC's commitment to a technocratic Soviet-style industrial development model. In this period, the CCP received a relatively small amount of aid from the Soviet Union, although the aid and assistance was important to the implementation of the Soviet model in China. Experts were despatched from the Soviet Union to help with over 150 industrial and infrastructure projects. Soviet financial assistance, meanwhile, amounted to about US$430 million in loans and this money and technological assistance was central to the First Five-Year Plan (1953–1957), which sought to expand China's industrial base substantially from that already created during the KMT era. By the second half of the 1950s many members of the Chinese leadership had started to point to problems in the operation of the Soviet model in China. In particular, they were concerned about low levels of agricultural growth and excessive centralization. This was the context for the launch of the Great Leap Forward (1958–1961). While the mobilization and decentralization in the countryside involved in the Great Leap Forward represented a departure from the Soviet Model, the Chinese Communist Party (CCP) continued to draw directly on Soviet or Stalinist conceptions of planning and property ownership, continuing to direct their surplus to heavy industry, while emphasizing the importance of gross output rather than productivity. Like Stalin's regime in the 1930s, the Great Leap Forward had a horrific impact on the peasantry – the unrelenting diversion of resources to industry led to starvation in the countryside. The loss of life from famine between 1958 and 1961 is now calculated to run upwards of 30 million people.[27] Even in the wake of the formal Sino-Soviet split in 1961 and the exit of Soviet advisers and development planners from China, the general framework of state-guided development in China remained Stalinist in its overall contours. Both the Chinese leadership and most outside observers took the view that up to the second half of the 1970s China's economy remained grounded in the Soviet model. Only with Mao's death were many basic Stalinist economic concepts challenged even if the Soviet model had been domesticated to Chinese practice at least two decades earlier.[28]

With the Sino-Soviet split in 1960, Beijing was positioned internationally in conflict with both superpowers at the same time as its development path followed a rural-oriented communism based on mass mobilization culminating in the social and economic upheaval of the Cultural Revolution in the late 1960s and early 1970s. The USSR and the United States signed a nuclear test ban treaty in 1963, which was roundly criticized by Mao, and China successfully tested its own nuclear weapon in 1964. At the same time, as the Chinese leadership's war of words with Moscow and Washington escalated and China sought to position itself as a key nation-state in, if not the leader of, a wider Third Worldist challenge to the First World (centered on the US) and the Second World (centered on the Soviet Union), Mao was also increasingly caught up in a power struggle within the CCP. This led to the Great Proletarian Cultural Revolution (1966–1976) and massive social and economic disruption and dislocation.[29] By 1969 the most disruptive period of the Cultural Revolution had passed and the People's Liberation Army (PLA) was being used to restore or maintain order and suppress any imagined or real opposition to Mao's leadership. Meanwhile, a report was produced by four retired senior Chinese military officers – in the wake of a series of military clashes on the Soviet–Chinese border in 1969 and a threat by Moscow to use nuclear weapons – that portrayed the Soviet Union as a more serious military threat to China than the United States. This led Mao to approve initial contacts between US and Chinese officials and paved the way on the Chinese side for Richard Nixon's historic visit to Beijing in 1972.[30]

The rapprochement with Washington in the 1970s also provided the context for a major developmental reorientation on the part of the CCP-state.[31] The passing of Mao from the Chinese political stage in 1976, and the widespread awareness regarding the disastrous social and economic impact of the Soviet model, the Great Leap Forward and the Cultural Revolution, paved the way for the rise of Deng Xiaoping.[32] After 1978 China's central planning system was gradually wound back in favor of market mechanisms. There was also a dramatic opening to foreign capital and technology, foreign consumer goods and external export markets. China's return to capitalism in the late 1970s can be read as a "victory", of sorts, for the critics of state-socialism in

Cold War Asia, insofar as it marked an implicit acknowledgment of the relative success of capitalism generally, and of the post-war capitalist dynamism of
Japan, South Korea and Taiwan more particularly.[33] However, the CCP has,
of course, continued to argue that China is actually now pursuing "market
socialism", or "Socialism with Chinese characteristics". Furthermore, the
"victory" was ambiguous because China's rediscovery of capitalism actually
did little to alter Washington's long-term assessment of the PRC as a major
military threat, second only to the USSR/Russia.[34] The death of Mao and the
rise of Deng coincided with a "crisis of faith" in relation to state-socialism in
China that was more profound than the subsequent "crisis of faith" in the
Soviet Union with the passage from the Brezhnev to the Gorbachev era in the
mid-1980s. In response, Deng and his colleagues set out a new global role for
the Chinese state that involved a major political opening to the world. Deng
represented China as "Great Power", but not as superpower; as a member of
the UN Security Council, but also a leader of the Third World. The PRC's
political reassertion was paralleled by its dramatic economic opening to overseas markets, foreign investment and technology: under Deng's leadership,
coastal China in particular entered the world economy on terms that reflected
an emphasis on comparative advantage. Local and foreign investors increasingly sought to tap the country's vast labor supply to produce light industrial
goods for overseas markets. Within twenty years of Mao's death the total
foreign investment in China had risen from a negligible amount in the late
1970s to more than US$360 billion by 1997. Meanwhile, China had a trade
surplus of US$40 billion by 1997.[35]

While the PRC sought to attract foreign investment it also sought to emulate
the earlier experience of the Japanese and South Korean developmental states
and their use of state intervention to facilitate the emergence of large, globally
competitive Chinese corporations. China's dramatic post-1978 economic growth
is often seen to have rested with a coterie of small, often *de facto* private companies (township and village enterprises, or TVEs).[36] However, large companies
were also central to the process. In the context of tight political control and
economic experimentation that increasingly sought by the 1990s to avoid the
trajectory followed by Russia, the Chinese government encouraged the emergence of a "national team" of large Chinese enterprises that would be global
competitors. The focus was on sectors of the economy seen to be "strategic",
and included automobile manufacturing, coal mining, electricity generation,
aerospace, pharmaceuticals, iron and steel, electronics, chemicals, construction
materials, and transport. However, the post-1978 state-guided national development project in China was distinct from earlier East Asian developmental states
in important ways. First, unlike the Japanese and South Korean trajectories, the
Chinese leadership emphasized the need for the large enterprises in the
"national team" to continue to be primarily publicly owned. The central government was wary of large Chinese corporations becoming too resistant to
bureaucratic intervention. Second, the state structures that the Chinese leadership were using to carry out an industrial policy centered on the creation of large

globally competitive firms was far bigger, in relative and absolute terms, than South Korea and Japan, at the same time as the Chinese effort lacked the nationalist intensity and commitment that the leadership in South Korea (in the context of its position as a front-line state in the Cold War) and in Japan (in the wake of a traumatic military defeat) had successfully mobilized in an earlier era. Third, the effort to initiate China's capitalist national development project and encourage the emergence of large corporations that would be globally competitive coincided with dramatic changes in the practices of the increasingly large oligopolistic transnational corporations with which the Chinese firms were expected to compete. By contrast in the early Cold War era – when the Japanese and South Korean states had promoted the interests of their large corporations – the global context had been very different. After twenty years of effort by the Chinese state – beginning in the late Cold War era and extending into the post-Cold War era – against the backdrop of the elaboration of the US-led globalization project, the large Chinese companies that have been singled out as potential global competitors are clearly still a long way from realizing the developmental dreams of the Chinese leadership, particularly in areas such as aerospace and pharmaceuticals.[37]

Reorientation II

Managing the Asian challenge II: post-Cold War Asia and the changing global order

The steady, albeit uneven, elaboration of the US-led globalization project also saw the emergence in the post-Cold War era of new or reinvigorated regional economic and politico-military organizations in various parts of the world.[38] This trend was manifested in Asia by the establishment of the Asia Pacific Economic Cooperation forum (APEC) in 1989.[39] In the context of the rise of neo-liberalism in the 1980s, influential member-governments of APEC, such as the US and Australia, ensured that APEC was oriented from the outset towards trade liberalization and globalization. This contrasted with the emphasis placed on trade cooperation in the 1980s by the Japanese government, which as we have seen was a long-standing proponent of some form of regional organization. While the Japanese government, which played a key role in the establishment of APEC, conceded to the neo-liberal agenda, the organization was vigorously challenged by Prime Minister Mahathir Mohamad of Malaysia. As an alternative to APEC, Mahathir proposed the establishment of a trading bloc, initially called the East Asian Economic Bloc (EAEB), which would exclude the United States, Australia and New Zealand and all other "non-Asian" nation-states. As noted in chapter 6, to underline his opposition to APEC, Mahathir refused to attend the organization's first heads of government meeting in Seattle in 1993. However, by the time of the annual summit in November 1998, which was held in Kuala Lumpur (KL), he was the presiding host, and his East Asian Economic Bloc had been effectively folded into APEC as the East Asian Economic Caucus.[40]

APEC emerged at the start of the 1990s out of the geo-political and economic complexities of the transition from Cold War Asia to post-Cold War Asia as the major institutional expression of the idea of a "Pacific Century" that had taken hold in this period.[41] As the Cold War came to an end, elites in Northeast and Southeast Asia had become increasingly concerned that the post-Cold War international political economy was shifting towards economic blocs centered on Western Europe (EU) and North America (North American Free Trade Agreement – NAFTA). Concerns were also being expressed about changes in the US approach to security issues in the post-Cold War era. At the outset Washington was preoccupied with the situation in Europe, but in a 1991 visit to East Asia, George Bush's Secretary of State, James Baker, reaffirmed a US commitment to the region emphasizing the continued importance of Washington's bilateral security arrangements. These arrangements maintained, in a somewhat revised fashion, the basic bilateral politico-military architecture of the Cold War.[42] This did not necessarily mean that the US actively opposed regional and multinational initiatives; however, it was the Australian government that had taken the lead, with Japanese encouragement, in the establishment of APEC less than two years before. As already noted, although the Japanese government was more interested in trade cooperation than trade liberalization, APEC quickly emerged as a forum for the latter. From the outset APEC was portrayed by its officials and its supporters as being committed to "open region-alism" in contrast to the preferential trading practices that characterize the EU and NAFTA.[43] The Eminent Persons Group (EPG), which laid down much of the early organizational framework for APEC, made it clear that APEC would "not be a community" like the European Union, which is "characterised by acceptance of the transfer of sovereignty, deep integration and extensive institutionalization". By contrast it emphasized that APEC would "be a community in the popular sense of a 'big family' of like minded economies" that are "committed to friendship, cooperation and the removal of barriers to economic exchange among members in the interest of all".[44] At the same time, C. Fred Bergsten (former chair of the EPG and Director of the Washington-based Institute for International Economics) emphasized that the organization should not only play a central role in regional trade liberalization, but it should also act as a "force for world-wide liberalisation".[45] This perspective reflected a wider elite-driven view that APEC could play a key role in the global diffusion of economic liberalism.[46] This vision was readily apparent at the first major meeting in Seattle in late 1993, and the second major meeting in Bogor, Indonesia in November 1994. On the final day of the Bogor meeting the leaders from the eighteen member countries agreed in principle to the virtual elimination of tariff barriers and obstacles to capital flows within the APEC region by the year 2020 (2010 for developed nations and 2020 for developing nations).[47]

On the eve of the Bogor summit President Clinton emphasized his "vision of a new Asia-Pacific community with no artificial dividing line down the middle of the Pacific".[48] This meshed with an increasingly influential strand of the Pacific Century narrative that was grounded in the idea of a synthesis between East and

West. The public articulation of synthetic visions of the region's future by prominent politicians and intellectuals facilitated consensus-building aimed at easing tensions in and around APEC. In 1992 Mark Borthwick outlined a version of this new vision in *Pacific Century: The Emergence of Modern Pacific Asia*. Borthwick, who worked as US director of the Pacific Economic Cooperation Council (PECC), argued that, with the end of the Cold War, Japan now "aspires to the leadership of a Pacific economic renaissance" in alliance with the US which continues to work to "bind the region to its global political and economic foreign policy".[49] And, by the mid-1990s, the idea of a new East–West synthesis for which the US–Japan alliance served as the explicit or implicit cornerstone had become widespread. For example, in 1995, Tommy Koh, former Singaporean representative to the United Nations, argued that the new "Pacific Community" would be founded on a fusion of values and practices drawn from Asia and the West.[50] Meanwhile, another senior Singaporean government figure, George Yeo, argued, "an East Asian consciousness without the softening effect of Western liberal ideas will not gel".[51] The emerging East–West synthesis in all its vagueness and ambiguity could be discerned in a book written by John Naisbitt (while he was a fellow at the Institute of Strategic and International Studies in Kuala Lumpur). According to Naisbitt, a "new network of nations based on economic symbiosis" was "emerging" which was founded on both a "spirit of working together for mutual economic gain" and a new Asian consciousness. The "catalyst" for all this, he said, was the "free market", but the "modernization of Asia" was not the "Westernization of Asia, but the modernization of Asia in the 'Asian Way'".[52] As we have seen in chapter 6, Anwar Ibrahim (former Deputy Prime Minister and Finance Minister of Malaysia, who was widely viewed as Mahathir's successor until the late 1990s) also called for a synthesis of East and West in his 1996 book, *The Asian Renaissance*.[53]

An important example of the East–West synthesis was *Asia Pacific Fusion: Japan's Role in APEC* (1995) by Yoichi Funabashi, the former Chief Diplomatic Correspondent for *Asahi Shimbun*. Funabashi's book was, in part, a reply to Samuel Huntington who, as discussed in detail in chapter 4, had warned of the potential for a "clash of civilizations" in the post-Cold War Asia-Pacific and elsewhere.[54] Funabashi, who has close links to the Institute for International Economics in Washington and had served as head of *Asahi Shimbun*'s Washington, DC bureau, argued that "the Asia-Pacific experiment to bring the greatest civilizations of the world into one dynamic sphere of confluence will lead to a new era of prosperity into the next century". He emphasized that "the economic and cultural dynamics in the Asia-Pacific, suggest that in at least this region, economic interdependence and cross-fertilization among civilizations can perhaps transcend the barriers of race and ideology". He concluded that: "the growing fusion of the Asia Pacific is offering Japan" and other countries in the region "more room to harness elements of both East and West".[55] These sorts of exercises in cultural diplomacy suggest that APEC was emerging, prior to the East Asian crisis, as not just an organizational attempt to facilitate trade liberalization and advance the neo-liberal project, but as a possible embodiment of a new vision of the Pacific Century that ostensibly synthesized East and West. This view was particularly apparent at the annual APEC summit in Osaka, Japan in November 1995. The Japan meeting produced an "Action Agenda" which eschewed binding trade agreements in favor of what Fidel Ramos (president of the Philippines) called the "Asian Way". This amounted to verbal assurances by all member governments that they would make every effort to meet the economic liberalization goals of APEC.[56] The representation of this result as evidence of the "Asian Way" at work was significant. Regardless of the alleged antipathy between East and West, APEC had emerged as a site for a wider process of elite integration in the Asia-Pacific, and this was facilitated by the domestication of influential East Asian narratives of progress to the dominant neo-liberal discourse in the name of a new East–West synthesis. Despite the continued prevalence of conflicting ideas about Eastern versus Western modes of capitalist development, rising elites also sought to merge vague and ostensibly culturally specific formulations with the dominant international neo-liberal discourses. In this sense, the establishment of APEC was indicative of the post-Cold War transition to a reconfigured form of neo-liberalism that accommodated ostensibly Asian ideas and practices against the backdrop of the continued resilience of US hegemony. As we have seen in chapter 5, this process was also apparent at the World Bank, which played a very significant role in domesticating the East Asian Miracle to the influential neo-liberal narratives of progress in the 1980s and 1990s.[57]

In the post-Cold War era the dominant interpretations of the East Asian Miracle and the coming of the Pacific Century were promoted, and the APEC process unfolded, in the context of an international political economy in which the United States was the hegemonic power. Furthermore, despite the efforts at elite consensus building and the emerging East–West synthesis, the end of the Cold War and the continued spread of economic liberalism contributed to considerable tension. For example, in the post-Cold War era, relations between the US and Japanese governments, the key axis of the new East–West synthesis and the wider APEC process, continued to be beset by friction on a range of economic issues especially related to trading practices. At the same time, the ostensibly consensual character of agreements made at APEC meetings also pointed to the real limitations of such an organization, as no enforcement mechanisms were set up and no legally binding commitments were made. While the annual meeting in the Philippines in November 1996 proceeded much as earlier meetings, the organization's lack of formal and binding decision-making and its diverse membership were about to face a serious challenge far beyond the capabilities of APEC to deal with. Prior to 1997 the dominant neo-liberal narratives on the Pacific Century rested on the assumption that the rise of East Asia and the end of the Cold War had produced increased opportunities for greater regional integration and the spreading and deepening of economic prosperity and political stability. APEC was grounded in these optimistic visions and directly implicated in the view that the economic trends that were carrying the region forward were going to continue indefinitely, delivering prosperity to an ever-growing number of people. This celebratory view of the Pacific Century specifically, and the history of capitalism more generally, was dramatically challenged as the financial crisis which began in Thailand in July 1997 rapidly engulfed the region.

Shortly after the precipitous fall of the Thai baht in July 1997, which was followed by equally dramatic nosedives on the part of the Indonesian rupiah and the South Korean won, Kishore Mahbubani (a prominent advocate of the new East–West synthesis) warned that the crisis could "split" the Pacific Ocean "down the middle" and create "an east–west divide."[58] As long as the various leaders who attended APEC's annual summits were only being called upon to agree to relatively distant trade liberalization targets, the meetings had proceeded with few serious problems. However, by the time of the annual meeting in Vancouver in November 1997 the East Asian crisis presented regional leaders with a serious and immediate problem. Not surprisingly, given its size and organizational fraility, the Vancouver meeting produced nothing of substance: with the crisis, APEC rapidly became irrelevant, now serving primarily as an opportunity for the region's leaders to get together to hold a range of bilateral meetings on specific issues while going through the motions of reaffirming their commitment to the non-binding economic goals of the organization. After 1997, the IMF played a high-profile role in the management of the crisis providing the United States with the opportunity to pursue economic liberalization and deregulation in the region far more effectively than could ever be achieved via APEC. In the second half of 1997, as APEC drifted to the sidelines, the IMF embarked on major efforts to restore financial stability to the region via loan packages to the governments of Thailand, Indonesia and South Korea. IMF loans were conditional on the implementation of a range of austerity measures and liberal economic reforms. The IMF set out to remake the financial systems of the various countries. It demanded the setting-up of new regulatory procedures, the shutting-down of a range of banks and financial institutions, and the liberalization of capital markets. This included allowing foreign capital to embark on hostile acquisitions and mergers. The IMF's solution to the crisis also resulted in an extended period of deflation and an ongoing region-wide liquidity crisis because it insisted on tight restrictions on public expenditure and high interest rates for domestic borrowers. At the same time, the IMF reassured foreign bankers that they would be able to collect the entirety of their outstanding debts. In concert with the US Treasury and Japan's Ministry of Finance, the Fund brokered the conversion of considerable short-term debt to long-term debt primarily by forcing the governments concerned to socialize private debt. The IMF also demanded that public enterprises be privatized and cartels broken up. In South Korea – as we have seen in chapter 8 – where the Fund also pushed for the introduction of flexible labor markets, it initially found a willing ally in the government of President Kim Dae Jung, whose political and economic goals were strengthened by the early IMF demands. The same cannot be said of the cutting of food subsidies carried out by the Indonesian government, with IMF encouragement. The IMF's austerity packaged not only represented an assault on patrimonial capitalism in Indonesia, it also added dramatically to the millions and millions of people who already lived at, or below, the poverty line.[59]

The overall approach taken by the IMF reflected the dominant neo-liberal perspective that the crisis flowed from the inefficiencies and distortions that were characteristic of the various state-centered approaches to capitalist development that prevailed in East Asia ("crony capitalism").[60] Not surprisingly, Prime Minister Mahathir of Malaysia was quick to dispute the IMF's explanations, at the same time as his government sought to avoid IMF support and interference. Mahathir and a number of other politicians and commentators placed the blame for the region's problems at the door of foreign currency speculators. They argued that foreign currency traders had deliberately acted to undermine the economies of East Asia. In particular, Mahathir singled out the well-known fund manager, George Soros, who he charged with masterminding a deliberate and pre-meditated attempt to sabotage the economic dynamism of Malaysia and the other countries of the region.[61] He also criticized the IMF's approach. As outlined in chapter 6, Mahathir and numerous other government officials and regional ideologues had begun to question the relevance of so-called Western ideas and practices to the region long before the onset of the crisis. These critiques were linked to the rising Pan-Asianism that interpreted the Pacific Century in terms of a New Asian Renaissance in which Asia would return to center stage in world affairs unfettered by the West generally and the US more specifically. Mahathir reaffirmed this view at the first Asia–Europe Summit (ASEM) in Bangkok in early March 1996, when he reversed the dominant tendency to universalize "Western" liberalism and asserted that "Asian values are universal values", while "European values are European values".[62] The idea of a New Asian Renaissance and the resurgence of Pan-Asianism provided an important backdrop to Mahathir's promotion of an East Asian Economic Bloc (EAEB) in the immediate post-Cold War period on the grounds that Malaysia and other nation-states in Asia would lose out in any larger grouping such as APEC. While Mahathir's initiative flowed from concerns about the membership and orientation of APEC, as well as the rise of NAFTA and the EU, it also represented an attempt to curb the growing flow of Chinese-Malaysian capital to China by linking China more tightly into a regional economic coopera- tion network. The EAEC proposal, which the ASEAN secretariat had put forward at Mahathir's instigation, envisioned a caucus that enjoyed considerable indepen- dence within the framework of APEC and was made up of the governments of ASEAN plus Japan, South Korea and China. This line-up apparently reflected the perception in ASEAN that Japan and South Korea were the driving economic forces in the region, both of which were the source of major investment flows, while China was the main destination for overseas Chinese capital moving out of ASEAN. The exclusion of Hong Kong and Taiwan from this list also catered to Beijing's sensitivities. At the same time, Mahathir's vision remained focused on Japan as the leading economic power in the region, and a major economic force internationally: he foresaw the Japanese government acting as the "voice of Asia" at meetings of the G-7.[63] Furthermore, as we have seen in chapter 6, Mahathir continues to emphasize the need for and the prospect of an exclusive regional organization.[64] In post-crisis Asia, ASEAN+3 (which will be discussed in the conclusion) has increasingly emerged, in the view of some observers, as the potential organizational realization of Mahathir's Pan-Asian vision.

The Japanese challenge and US hegemony in post-Cold War Asia

Regardless of the increasing regional economic integration centered on Japan, which was apparent by the end of the Cold War, there were important constraints on Japan's ability to become a hegemonic power in East Asia. Trade within East Asia had risen to surpass trade between the US and East Asia, but the North American market remained very important to all the economies in the region. Although, as we have seen, in the early 1990s influential narratives continued to generate an image of Japan as a rising capitalist developmental state that represented a challenge to, or a model for, the US and beyond, this perception was already misleading well before the onset of the East Asian crisis. The end of the Cold War coincided with, and reinforced, a growing array of economic problems linked to the decrepit character of Japanese politics. In fact, the relative inertia of domestic politics and the waning of the Japanese "economic miracle" often overshadowed wider concerns in Japan about its position in post-Cold War Asia.[65] Up to the end of the Cold War the long-term implications of the rise of the US-led globalization project for the Japanese trajectory were not clear. At the end of the 1980s, interest rates were driven up causing a dramatic drop in the stock market at the beginning of 1990. The Ministry of Finance imposed so-called "total quantity restrictions" on banks and financial institutions ending the disbursement of new loans for real estate, triggering a dramatic drop in property prices by the end of 1990. In the context of a burgeoning recession, the holders of various warrants and bonds confronted higher interest rates on assets with a dramatically declining value. Because they had often been purchased with borrowed funds, banks confronted a rise in non-performing loans, while the drop in the price of real estate also increased non-performing loans in relation to other financial transactions as well. Some banks collapsed and a number of bank mergers were arranged in an effort to keep the financial system afloat in the context of a vigorous political debate in the early 1990s about how to address the economic malaise. Throughout the 1990s various government efforts to kick-start the Japanese economy via lower interest rates, tax cuts and public spending continued to be unsuccessful. With a political system driven by money and a commitment to the status quo, the prospects for a Japanese economic resurgence prior to 1997, without major political and social change, were already limited. Of course, some commentators continue to believe that MITI and the MOF would have the resilience and acumen to bring about a reverse course, and it was hoped that the long-established patterns of cooperation between business, government and organized labor could still provide the framework for a Japanese economic resurgence and expansion into Asia and beyond.[66]

With the onset of a full-scale economic crisis in the region in 1997, the Japanese economy came under increased pressure. While six of the top ten companies in the world (measured by market capitalization) were based in Japan in 1990, by 1998 there were no Japanese companies in the top ten. By 1998 the Japanese share of global stock market value had dropped to 10.5 percent from 41.5 percent in 1990. By 1998, eighteen of the top fifty companies in the world (measured by total sales) were in Japan, but only one Japanese company was in the top fifty on the basis of profits. By 1999 there was some suggestion that restructuring was beginning to occur in Japan's major companies. A number of corporations began to carry out significant downsizing. For example, Mitsubishi Electric foreshadowed a 10 percent reduction in its workforce and the closure of a number of loss-making parts of its operations. This was followed by similar announcements at Japan Airlines, NEC and Mitsubishi Chemical, among others. Meanwhile, a number of large mergers occurred in the country's banking system in response to similar mergers in the banking systems in North America and Western Europe. For example, Fuji Bank merged with Dai-Ichi Kangyo and Industrial Bank of Japan. This precipitated Fuji Bank's withdrawal as the lead Bank in the Fuyo *keiretsu*, which led in turn to companies in the *keiretsu* focusing on the bond and equity markets to raise new funds rather than getting loans from the banks in the Fuyo *keiretsu*, as had been standard practice in the past. There have also been some important mergers and/or takeovers between Japanese and foreign companies. The most well-known was the purchase of a controlling share of Nissan by Renault, an acquisition that has resulted in major organizational changes at Nissan under Carlos Ghosn, the new CEO appointed by Renault. By the end of the twentieth century the *keiretsu* system and the wider Japanese political economy were undergoing a major reorientation, but even though the role of the Japanese state has certainly been wound back and Japanese corporations have undergone significant changes, the process has been very uneven.[67] And, as in China, the banking system in Japan is in a chronic state of crisis. Estimates of the size of non-performing loans in relation to total assets held by Japan-based banks ranged up to a figure of almost 40 percent according to a report prepared by Goldman Sachs at the end of 2001.[68]

The ongoing economic malaise, centered on the banking system, has meant that the Japanese government and Japanese corporations have been unable to play as significant a role in the region in the post-Cold War era as many had anticipated or intended. The prevailing view in Japan prior to 1997 was that the end of the Cold War, combined with the economic dynamism of much of the rest of the region (if not of Japan itself), made it possible for the Japanese government to be "internationalist" and "Asianist" simultaneously. In the post-Cold War era, despite ongoing friction between Washington and Tokyo over trade issues, it was widely assumed amongst Japanese policy-makers that the Japanese economic presence could be extended ever more deeply into the region, without challenging either the US–Japan alliance or liberal forms of economic regionalism represented by APEC and advocated by the United States.[69] In the aftermath of the Asian crisis, the new Koizumi government committed itself to both neo-liberal reform and the strengthening of its alliance with the US. His government combined an appeal to conservative and populist neo-nationalist ideas with an in-principle commitment to the neo-liberal restructuring of the Japanese developmental state of the Cold War era.[70] However, it was soon apparent that the pace of Koizumi's planned reforms for the Japanese banking system and other areas of the economy would be slow.[71] At the same time the Japanese government was quick to support the US in its effort to build a global coalition to carry out its "war on terrorism". However, the exact character of that support was relatively minimal and it did not, of course, involve an actual Japanese military commitment.[72] The US-led war in Iraq in early 2003 also quickly garnered a statement of support from Tokyo, reflecting Japan's continued acquiescence to the US and a desire to maintain the bilateral ally/client relationship of the Cold War era. Against the backdrop of the economic decline and crisis of the 1990 s and the early years of the twenty-first century, the Japanese government is unlikely in the foreseeable future to play a leading role in the creation of an economic, and certainly not a politico-military, framework aimed at both greater regional integration and greater autonomy from the United States. Of course, at the outset of the Asian crisis, the Japanese government had attempted to play a leadership role. In September 1997 at a G-7 finance minister meeting, Japan's Finance Minister, Hiroshi Mitsuzuka, first proposed the concept of an Asian Monetary Fund as a means of countering economic instability without the conditions attached to the IMF packages.[73] While Mahathir was attacking currency speculators at the annual IMF–World Bank meeting in Hong Kong in mid-1997, the Japanese government again floated the Asian Monetary Fund idea, proposing that upwards of 100 billion dollars be set aside and that the institutional infrastructure to administer it be created, in order to be prepared for any future crises of the kind that were destabilizing Southeast Asia.[74] Not surprisingly, representatives from the US, Europe, and the IMF voiced strong opposition, while officials from Hong Kong, Malaysia, and Thailand expressed considerable enthusiasm.[75] In a gesture of support, Thai Finance Minister Thanong Bidaya announced his government's intention of lobbying for a single ASEAN currency at the December 1997 ASEAN summit in Kuala Lumpur.[76] Meanwhile, other East Asian leaders, particularly those of Singapore and Malaysia, made clear their frustration with the IMF's approach to the crisis.[77]

   The Asian Monetary Fund proposal was notable in that there were to be no conditions attached. It would have maintained the restrictions on foreign ownership of financial institutions and sustained the economic practices that East Asian elites associate with rapid capitalist development. However, when the Asian Monetary Fund was tabled at the November 1997 APEC Finance Minister's meeting in Manila it failed to get sufficient support and by the time of the ASEAN summit in Kuala Lumpur the following month, the majority of the governments of Southeast Asia had decided, albeit reluctantly in some cases, to endorse the IMF's plan for the crisis.[78] Prior to the annual APEC meeting in 1998 the idea of an Asian Monetary Fund was again raised.[79] However, as in late 1997, the proposal was rejected, leaving the IMF in control of the overall management of the crisis.[80] The 1998 APEC meeting made abundantly clear that its role would remain marginal.[81] At the same time it was also clear that ASEAN did not have the institutional capability or the stature to react to the crisis effectively. The organization's founding principle of non-intervention in relation to the domestic issues of member governments prevented a "comprehensive collective response", with or without Japanese support.[82] All this points to the fact that the US remains the only truly world power in military and economic terms, at the same time as it exercises a broad and diffuse political and cultural influence. US hegemony is mediated through an array of complex power relations, economic arrangements, social structures and cultural practices; however, Washington maintains effective control over the important aspects of the international political economy. In East Asia, US hegemony continues to rest on the alliance conditions and arrangements that the Japanese and South Korean states accepted during the Cold War era (and which also constrain virtually all other states in the region). Nor, at this juncture, does China represent a serious politico-military or economic threat to US hegemony and the likelihood of China achieving economic superpower status (and thus becoming a politico-military "threat" to the US) needs to be set against the complex centrifugal forces that confront the present Chinese leadership's pursuit of national and regional greatness.

The Chinese challenge and US hegemony in post-Cold War Asia

The Chinese trajectory reflects both the historical specificity of nation-state formation and the wider problems of the nation-state system in post-Cold War Asia and beyond. As already suggested, despite the historical specificity of the sustained, but still uneven, transformation of particular state-mediated national development projects into globalizing states, two generalized trajectories have been postulated. While Japan fits the first, which involves a process of national reorientation and a crisis of national development, China fits the second, which is characterized by a crisis of state-mediated national development that not only involves national reorientation, but also results in increasing conflict over the ethnic or religious content and/or territorial boundaries (usually, but not always, at the margins rather than the center) of the nation-state itself. At this juncture national fragmentation and a full-scale crisis of the nation-state in China is not necessarily imminent. However, the Chinese leadership's pursuit of national development and/or regional hegemony continues to be profoundly constrained by looming political, social, environmental and economic crises grounded in rapid and uneven capitalist development and characterized by increasingly stark divisions between the booming coastal regions and the impoverished interior. In urban centers as well there are now millions of disgruntled workers who have lost their formerly secure jobs at state-owned enterprises that have begun to respond to market pressures to be more competitive. As this process unfolds the re-employment rate has declined steadily from 50 percent in 1998 to 9 percent for the first part of 2002.[83] This is not to mention the complicated issue of the future of Taiwan and restive provinces such as Tibet and Xinjiang.[84] Meanwhile, the crisis in the banking system in China, centered on the four large state-owned institutions, which are said to be presiding over non-performing loans worth 28 percent of their total assets (independent observers put the figure at 50 percent or more), suggests the prospects for the successful emergence of a "national team" of large, globally competitive Chinese companies are remote.[85] This is all set against the backdrop of the Chinese state's domestication to, and resistance against, the US-led globalization project as manifested by Beijing's induction into the WTO in September 2001.

US–China relations are at the center of any equation regarding the changing regional and global order. For almost two decades from the early 1970s until 1989, US–China relations rested on what has been called a "Grand Bargain". The explicit and implicit elements of this Grand Bargain included an agreement by both sides that the issue of the status of Taiwan was to be set aside and dealt with at some unspecified time in the future. While Deng said it would be addressed fifty years in the future, Mao had earlier talked about a 100-year moratorium on the Tawian problem. Second, because the Chinese government was primarily concerned with gaining US support against the USSR, policy-makers in Beijing also accepted the US–Japan security alliance as central to the wider containment of the Soviet Union. At the same time, while both Washington and Beijing wanted improved trade relations, as long as a mutual concern about Moscow prevailed any problems related to investment or trade relations were relegated to the background. The end of the Cold War, which coincided with improving relations between Beijing and Moscow, meant the disappearance of the main reason both the PRC and the US had for ignoring or downplaying areas of contention between them. The brutal repression of protestors in Tiananmen Square in 1989 also undermined the Grand Bargain. At the same time, a range of other trends ensured that, by the beginning of the 1990s, the US–China relationship had entered a new and more difficult era in contrast to the previous two decades. First, as already suggested, the PRC had emerged by the late 1980s as a particularly successful economic modernizer, resulting in more economic friction between Beijing and Washington than had been anticipated when the initial Chinese turn to the market had been executed. Second, in the case of Taiwan, the island had made a transition from authoritarian military rule in the 1970s to parliamentary democracy by the late 1980s and politicians on Taiwan increasingly began to intrude into US–China relations challenging Beijing's continued claims to the island and/or US equivocation on the issue. Third, in the post-Vietnam era, the US Congress has sought to scrutinize and examine US foreign policy in Asia generally and towards China more particularly, making US–China relations an important concern for domestic politics in the United States. Fourth, the growing flow of information and news across the Pacific and around the world, as a result of the technological and economic changes of the previous decades, has meant that the communication and information flows associated with globalization had added a whole new dimension to US–China relations. Fifth, the first Gulf War highlighted the so-called "revolution in military affairs" at the beginning of the 1990s and the Chinese leadership increasingly sought to come to grips with these changes by increased defense spending, military reorientation and upgrading, resulting in changes to the military balance in the region.[86]

With the passing of the Grand Bargain, China-watchers increasingly drew attention to Beijing's effort to inherit the mantle of state-guided capitalist developmentalism exemplified by the Japanese and South Korean trajectories in earlier decades, representing a rising China as the main economic and military threat to US hegemony in the region. Books such as *The Coming Conflict With China* emphasized the PRC's growing military significance while also noting that its economic transformation was linked to "state capitalism" and its use of "methods pioneered by Japan".[87] The Clinton administration (1992–2000) sought, not always consistently, to pursue a policy of "engagement" and "enlargement" rather than "containment" or confrontation towards China.[88] During Clinton's years in office, US–China relations were punctuated by major ups and downs. "Engagement" and "enlargement" were reflected in Clinton's elimination of the connection between Most-Favored-Nation (MFN) trading status for China and its record on human rights, a link that his administration had insisted upon the previous year. By 1995–1996, Washington and Beijing were drifting towards the brink of military and naval confrontation in the Taiwan straits, as Beijing sought to use live-fire military maneuvers off Taiwan to influence elections on the island. By the late 1990s relations had improved and there was considerable discussion of the establishment of a "constructive strategic partnership". The second half of 1999 again saw a downturn in relations, beginning with the failure to reach agreement in April of that year over China's entry into the WTO. This was followed by, among other things, the US bombing of Beijing's embassy in Belgrade, a US Congressional report detailing a wide-ranging series of espionage activities in the US by Chinese agents, while the issue of Taiwan continued to simmer.[89] Under these circumstances, and in the context of the growing political debate in the US about China by the second half of the 1990s, and particularly in the lead up to the 2000 election, the Clinton administration was not always as committed to "engagement" and "enlargement" as its original pronouncements on the subject might suggest.[90] Nevertheless, the administration continued to argue that engaging rather than containing Beijing would enhance security. For example, in a speech delivered in early 2000 to the United States Military Academy at West Point, US Trade Representative (USTR) Charlene Barshefsky emphasized the close connection between US national security and China's accession to the WTO.[91]

By contrast, in the lead up to, and immediately following, his election as president at the end of 2000, George W. Bush emphasized that China was a long-term military threat in the wider context of the new administration's efforts to reassert Washington's regional and global military power, but avoid the entanglements that had characterized the Clinton era.[92] During its first six months in office, the Bush administration explicitly identified the Chinese state –

which has been regarded by US China-watchers and strategic planners as *the* major military "threat" to the US and its interests in the Asia-Pacific for a number of years – as a major focus of a reoriented US military effort.[93] Meanwhile, the initial commitment of the Bush administration to focus more on containing China, rather than engaging China, now appears to have been tempered by the somewhat improved US–China relations that followed the resolution of the US spy plane incident earlier in 2001 and the shift in US foreign policy to Central Asia and the Middle East. Nevertheless, a major *Quadrennial Defence Review Report* published by the US government at the end of September 2001 (that is shortly after September 11) reversed the order of importance of the three key regions that are the focus of US military and strategic orientation. Previous reviews had emphasized Europe, the Gulf and Central Asia, and East Asia, but the latest review has moved East Asia to first place, followed by the Gulf and Central Asia and then Europe.[94] In the lead-up to President Bush's February 2002 visit to China, a Rand Corporation, China specialist observed that the "war on terrorism" has "encouraged a shift toward the notion of tactical cooperation with China"; however, no one appeared to be "talking about a strategic shift". Meanwhile, according to the deputy director of the Institute of American Studies at the Chinese Academy of Social Sciences, "the parameters of the relationship haven't changed".[95]

Conclusion: the Asian challenge and the changing global order

While examining the Japanese and Chinese trajectories since the 1940s in some detail, this chapter has focused on national reorientations and regional changes from the mid-1970s to the late 1990s, particularly the post-Cold War era. Across Asia and beyond, the end of the Cold War, followed in less than a decade by the Asian financial crisis, facilitated the continued weakening of state-guided national development, even in the key developmental states of East Asia, such as Japan. At the same time, it has been emphasized that the Japanese trajectory reflects the uneven character of the rise of the US-led globalization project in Asia – Japan was pivotal to the transformation of Asia after 1945 and it remains central to the overall future of the region. At the moment Japan is undergoing a prolonged crisis of national development and a particularly drawn-out process of national politico-economic reorientation. Meanwhile, in China, the transition from state-socialism to capitalist-developmentalism is increasingly linked to a crisis of the Chinese nation-state that not only includes a process of dramatic national reorientation and crisis, but also involves struggles over the territorial boundaries and the cultural and ideological content of the erstwhile socialist nation-state. Japan and China are particularly important nation-states and their present circumstances and future directions have major regional and global implications. The processes of national reorientation and/or crisis are closely connected to the continued and/or increased potential for inter-state conflict and the shift towards new or reconfigured regional economic and political groupings in Asia and elsewhere. The 1990s saw the rise and the decline of APEC, while post-crisis Asia has been characterized by the strengthening of ASEAN+3. The question of Asian regionalism, particularly ASEAN+3, and the prospects for the nation-states of East Asia, in the wake of the Asian financial crisis and against the backdrop of the war on terrorism and the changing global order in the early twenty-first century, are taken up in the conclusion.

Notes

1 The member governments of APEC in 1989 were Australia, Brunei, Canada, Indonesia, Japan, Malaysia, New Zealand, the Philippines, Singapore, South Korea, Thailand, and the United States. China, Hong Kong and Taiwan joined in 1991. Mexico and Papua New Guinea joined in 1993 and Chile joined in 1994.
2 G. Kolko, *Anatomy of a War: Vietnam, the United States and Modern Historical Experience*, 2nd edn, New York: New Press, 1994, pp. 303–37, 341–55.
3 R. S. Litwak, *Détente and the Nixon Doctrine: American Foreign Policy and the Pursuit of Stability 1969–1976*, 2nd edn, Cambridge: Cambridge University Press, 1986, pp. 193–4.
4 R. Brenner, "Uneven Development and the Long Downturn: The Advanced Capitalist Economies from Boom to Stagnation, 1950–1998" *New Left Review (I)*, no. 229, 1998, pp. 116–24.
5 W. LaFeber, *The Clash: U.S.–Japanese Relations Throughout History*, New York: W. W. Norton, 1997, p. 358.
6 D. Kelly, *Japan and the Reconstruction of East Asia*, Basingstoke: Palgrave, 2002, pp. 67–105.
7 P. Korhonen, "The Pacific Age in World History" *Journal of World History* vol. 7, no. 1, 1996.
8 M. R. Peattie, "Japanese Attitudes towards Colonialism, 1895–1945" in R. H. Myers and M. R. Peattie, eds, *The Japanese Colonial Empire, 1895–1945*, Princeton: Princeton University Press, 1984.
9 T. Terada, "The Origins of Japan's APEC Policy: Foreign Minister Takeo Miki's Asia-Pacific Policy and Current Implications" *The Pacific Review* vol. 11, no. 3, 1998. On Japan's role in the formation of a Pacific Community between the late 1960s and the late 1990s see P. Korhonen, *Japan and Asia Pacific Integration: Pacific Romances 1968–1996*, London: Routledge, 1998.
10 Hong Kong and then Mexico, Chile and Peru had all joined the PECC by 1991–1992, while a number of other Latin American countries, along with the USSR (Russia after 1991), hold observer status. L. T. Woods, *Asia-Pacific Diplomacy: Nongovernmental Organisations and International Relations*, Vancouver: UBC Press, 1993, pp. 41–65.
11 R. Stubbs, "The Political Economy of the Asia-Pacific Region" in R. Stubbs and G. R. D. Underhill, eds, *Political Economy and the Changing Global Order*, London: Macmillan, 1994, pp. 371–2.
12 D. Yasutomo, *The Manner of Giving: Strategic Aid and Japanese Foreign Policy*, New York: D. C. Heath, 1986.
13 T. Shiraishi, "Japan and Southeast Asia" in P. J. Katzenstein and T. Shiraishi, eds, *Network Power: Japan and Asia*, Ithaca: Cornell University Press, 1997, pp. 187–8.
14 W. Hatch and K. Yamamura, *Asia in Japan's Embrace: Building a Regional Production Alliance*, Cambridge: Cambridge University Press, 1996.
15 Stubbs, "The Political Economy of the Asia-Pacific Region", p. 373.

16 I. Wallerstein, "The Rise of East Asia, or the World-System in the Twenty-First Century" in I. Wallerstein, *The End of the World As We Know It: Social Science for the Twenty-First Century*, Minneapolis: University of Minnesota Press, 1999, pp. 36–7.

17 F. B. Tipton, *The Rise of Asia: Economics, Society and Politics in Contemporary Asia*, London: Macmillan, 1998, p. 412.

18 See S. Garon, *Molding Japanese Minds: The State in Everyday Life*, Princeton: Princeton University Press, 1997.

19 B. Gao, "The Search for National Identity and Japanese Industrial Policy, 1950–1969" *Nations and Nationalism* vol. 4, no. 2, 1998.

20 Brenner, "Uneven Development and the Long Downturn", pp. 76–9.

21 The literature on the high period of state-guided national development was discussed in chapters 6 and 7. For a good synthesis see W. K. Tabb, *The Post-War Japanese System: Cultural Economy and Economic Transformation*, New York: Oxford University Press, 1995.

22 Tipton, *The Rise of Asia*, p. 415.

23 T. Morris-Suzuki, *The Technological Transformation of Japan: From the Seventeenth to the Twenty-First Century*, Cambridge: Cambridge University Press, 1994, pp. 161–208.

24 E. Terry, *How Asia Got Rich: Japan, China and the Asian Miracle*, Armonk: M. E. Sharpe, 2002.

25 Tipton, *The Rise of Asia*, pp. 418–19.

26 P. Hartcher, *The Ministry*, New York: HarperCollins, 1997, p. 63; G. Arrighi, *The Long Twentieth Century: Money, Power, and the Origins of Our Times*, London: Verso, 1994, pp. 17–18.

27 M. Goldman and A. J. Nathan, "Searching for the Appropriate Model for the People's Republic of China" in M. Goldman and A. Gordon, eds, *Historical Perspectives on Contemporary East Asia*, Cambridge, MA: Harvard University Press, 2000, pp. 298–9, 302–3.

28 N. P. Halpern, "Creating Socialist Economies: Stalinist Political Economy and the Impact of Ideas" in J. Goldstein and R. O. Keohane, eds, *Ideas and Foreign Policy: Beliefs, Institutions and Political Change*, Ithaca: Cornell University Press, 1993, pp. 101–2.

29 F. C. Teiwes, "The Chinese State During the Maoist Era" in D. Shambaugh, ed., *The Modern Chinese State*, Cambridge: Cambridge University Press, 2000, pp. 139–48.

30 Goldman and Nathan, "Searching for the Appropriate Model for the People's Republic of China", pp. 305–7.

31 C. Jian, *Mao's China and the Cold War*, Chapel Hill: University of North Carolina Press, 2001, pp. 49–84, 238–76.

32 R. Baum, *Burying Mao: Chinese Politics in the Age of Deng Xiaoping*, Princeton: Princeton University Press, 1994.

33 A. Dirlik, *After the Revolution: Waking to Global Capitalism*, London: Wesleyan University Press, 1994, p. 44.

34 S. Sestanovich, "US Policy Toward the Soviet Union, 1970–1990: The Impact of China" in R. Ross, ed., *China, the United States and the Soviet Union: Tripolarity and Policy Making in the Cold War*, London: M. E. Sharpe, 1993.

35 Goldman and Nathan, "Searching for the Appropriate Model for the People's Republic of China", pp. 308–9.

36 J. Oi, *Rural China Takes Off: Institutional Foundations of Economic Reform*, Berkeley: University of California Press, 1999.

37 P. Nolan, *China and the Global Economy*, Basingstoke: Palgrave, 2001, pp. 15–20, 93–4, 155, 186–8. Also see P. Nolan, *China's Rise, Russia's Fall: Politics, Economics and Planning in the Transition from Stalinism*, London: Macmillan, 1995; P. Nolan, *China and the Global Business Revolution*, Basingstoke: Palgrave, 2001.

38 A. Payne and A. Gamble, "Introduction: The Political Economy of Regionalism and World Order" in A. Gamble and A. Payne, eds, *Regionalism and World Order*, London: Macmillan, 1996.

39 J. Ravenhill, *APEC and the Construction of Pacific Rim Regionalism*, Cambridge: Cambridge University Press, 2001.

40 M. T. Berger, "APEC and its Enemies: The Failure of the New Regionalism in the Asia-Pacific" *Third World Quarterly: Journal of Emerging Areas* vol. 20, no. 5, 1999.

41 S. B. Linder, *The Pacific Century: Economic and Political Consequences of Asian-Pacific Dynamism*, Stanford: Stanford University Press, 1986; D. Aikman, *Pacific Rim: Area of Change, Area of Opportunity*, Boston: Little Brown, 1986; W. McCord, *The Dawn of the Pacific Century: Implications for Three Worlds of Development*, New Brunswick: Transaction Publishers, 1991; S. Winchester, *Pacific Rising: The Emergence of a New World Culture*, New York: Prentice Hall, 1991; F. Gibney, *The Pacific Century: America and Asia in a Changing World*, New York: Macmillan, 1992. For critical analysis of the idea of a Pacific Century see R. A. Palat, "Pacific Century: Myth or Reality?" *Theory and Society* vol. 25, no. 3, 1996; M. T. Berger and D. A. Borer, "Introduction – The Rise of East Asia: Critical Visions of the Pacific Century" in M. T. Berger and D. A. Borer, eds, *The Rise of East Asia: Critical Visions of the Pacific Century*, London: Routledge, 1997. M. T. Berger, "A New East–West Synthesis? APEC and Competing Narratives of Regional Integration in the Post-Cold War Asia-Pacific" *Alternatives: Social Transformation and Humane Governance* vol. 23, no. 1, 1998.

42 S. Yamakage, "Japan's National Security and Asia-Pacific's Regional Institutions in the Post-Cold War Era" in P. J. Katzenstein and T. Shiraishi, eds, *Network Power: Japan and Asia*, Ithaca: Cornell University Press, 1997, pp. 291–2; J. A. Baker, "America in Asia: Emerging Architecture for a Pacific Community" *Foreign Affairs* vol. 70, no. 6, 1991.

43 "Open regionalism" is a much-debated term. It is most commonly, and narrowly, defined as a concerted and unilateral process of trade liberalization along MFN – most favored nation – lines. See P. Drysdale, D. Vines and B. House, "Europe and East Asia: A Shared Global Agenda?" in P. Drysdale and D. Vines, eds, *Europe, East Asia and APEC: A Shared Global Agenda?*, Cambridge: Cambridge University Press, 1998, pp. 6–9.

44 Cited in M. Beeson and K. Jayasuriya, "The Political Rationalities of Regionalism: APEC and the EU in Comparative Perspective" *The Pacific Review* vol. 11, no. 3, 1998, p. 327.

45 C. F. Bergsten, "APEC and the World Economy: A Force for Worldwide Liberalisation" *Foreign Affairs* vol. 73, no. 3, 1994.

46 For example, see R. Garnaut, *Open Regionalism and Trade Liberalisation: An Asia-Pacific Contribution to the World Trade System*, Singapore: Institute of Southeast Asia Studies, 1996.

47 J. Walsh, "Toward the Pacific Age" *Time: International* November 22, 1993, pp. 22–7; "A Dream of Free Trade" *The Economist* November 25, 1994, pp. 29–30.

48 Cited in M. Gordon, "APEC's Great Leap Forward?" *The Weekend Australian* November 12–13, 1994, p. 21.

49 M. Borthwick (with contributions by selected scholars), *Pacific Century: The Emergence of Modern Pacific Asia*, Boulder: Westview, 1992, pp. 1–3, 543–5.

50 T. T. B. Koh, *The United States and East Asia: Conflict and Co-operation*, Singapore: Institute of Policy Studies, 1995, pp. 107–8. Also see K. Mahbubani, "The Pacific Way" *Foreign Affairs* vol. 74, no. 1, 1995, p. 107.

51 G. Yeo, "A New Greater East Asia Co-Prosperity Sphere" in G. Sheridan, ed., *Living With Dragons: Australia Confronts its Asian Destiny*, Sydney: Allen and Unwin, 1995, p. 179.

52 J. Naisbitt, *Megatrends Asia: The Eight Asian Megatrends that are Changing the World*, London: Nicholas Brealy, 1995, pp. ix–x.

53 A. Ibrahim, *The Asian Renaissance*, Singapore: Times Books International, 1996, p. 45.

54 S. P. Huntington, "The Clash of Civilizations?" *Foreign Affairs* vol. 72, no. 3, 1993; S. P. Huntington, *The Clash of Civilizations and the Remaking of World Order*, New York: Simon and Schuster, 1996.

55 Y. Funabashi, *Asia Pacific Fusion: Japan's Role in APEC*, Washington, DC: Institute for International Economics, 1995, pp. 10–11.

56 F. Ching, "APEC Moving Along 'Asian Way' " *Far Eastern Economic Review* December 7, 1995, p. 48.

57 M. T. Berger and M. Beeson, "Lineages of Liberalism and Miracles of Modernisation: The World Bank, the East Asian Trajectory and the International Development Debate" *Third World Quarterly: Journal of Emerging Areas* vol. 19, no. 3, 1998.

58 Cited in P. Hartcher and M. Dwyer, "East versus West: How the Markets are Uniting Asia Against the US" *The Australian Financial Review* September 27, 1997. Online at http://www.afr.com.au

59 H.-J. Chang, "Korea: The Misunderstood Crisis" *World Development* vol. 26, no. 8, 1998, p. 1560; R. Robison and A. Rosser, "Contesting Reform: Indonesia's New Order and the IMF" *World Development* vol. 26, no. 8, 1998.

60 International Monetary Fund, *Interim Assessment of the World Economic Outlook*, Washington, DC: International Monetary Fund, December 1997.

61 "Too Late for a Gentle Landing" *The Economist*, September 6, 1997, pp. 69–70; A. Brummer, "Malaysian Tiger Takes a Mauling" *The Guardian Weekly*, September 7, 1997, p. 19; "Mahathir, Soros and the Currency Markets" *The Economist*, September 27, 1997, p. 93.

62 Mahathir cited in "Asia and Europe: Friends Apart" *The Economist*, March 9, 1996, p. 27.

63 G. Hook, "Japan and the Construction of Asia-Pacific" in A. Gamble and A. Payne, eds, *Regionalism and World Order*, London: Macmillan, 1996, pp. 194–5.

64 M. Mahathir, "Globalization: Challenges and Impact on Asia" in F.-J. Richter and P. C. M. Mar, eds, *Recreating Asia: Visions for a New Century*, Singapore: John Wiley and Sons, 2002, p. 10.

65 H. Fukui and S. N. Fukai, "The End of the Miracle: Japanese Politics in the Post-Cold War Era" in M. T. Berger and D. A. Borer, eds, *The Rise of East Asia: Critical Visions of the Pacific Century*, London: Routledge, 1997.

66 Tipton, *The Rise of Asia*, pp. 415–20.

67 Nolan, *China and the Global Economy*, pp. 129–31.

68 T. Holland, "Banking in Asia: Japan" *Far Eastern Economic Review*, October 4, 2001, pp. 66–9. Also see "Japanese Banks: Abandon Hope" *The Economist*, September 22, 2001, p. 66; "Japanese Economy: The Ghosts of Reforms Past" *The Economist* November 2, 2002, pp. 67–9.

69 Shiraishi, "Japan and Southeast Asia", pp. 191–4.

70 K. M. Campbell, "Koizumi as Japan's Reagan" *Far Eastern Economic Review*, August 23, 2001, p. 29.

71 "Japan: Reform on Hold" *The Economist* September 8, 2001, pp. 29–30.

72 "Japan and the United States: On Board?" *The Economist* September 22, 2001, p. 32.

73 M. Dwyer, "Japan Backs $133bn Asia Fund" *The Australian Financial Review* September 22, 1997. Online at http://www.afr.com.au. Mitsuzuka subsequently resigned over a corruption scandal at the Ministry of Finance.

74 "Rumpus in Hong Kong" *The Economist* September 27, 1997, p. 15; "An Asian IMF" *The Economist* September 27, 1997, p. 84.

75 Dwyer and Hartcher, "East versus West".

76 S. Chupaka and K. Chaipipat, "ASEAN Currency Bid Launched" *The Nation* (Thailand) September 19, 1997.

77 "Asian Crisis – Global Crisis" *Pacific Rim Review* December 20, 1997. Online at http://pacificrim.bx.com/articles/12–20asian_crisis.htm

78 R. Wade and F. Veneroso, "The Gathering World Slump and the Battle Over Capital Controls" *New Left Review (I)* no. 231, 1998, pp. 20–1, 30, 41–2.
79 R. Wade and F. Veneroso, "The Resources Lie Within" *The Economist* November 7, 1998, pp. 19–21; K. Hamada, "Keeping Alive the Asian Monetary Fund" *Capital Trends* vol. 3, no. 10, 1998, pp. 8–9; M. Shiroyama, "With IMF Cash-Strapped, Room for Asian Monetary Fund" *Capital Trends* vol. 3, no. 10, 1998, p. 10.
80 D. D. Hale, "The IMF, Now More Than Ever" *Foreign Affairs*, vol. 77, no. 6, 1998, pp. 12–13; R. Wade and F. Veneroso, "The Asian Crisis: The High Debt Model Versus the Wall Street-Treasury-IMF Complex" *New Left Review (I)* no. 228, 1998, pp. 18–19. At the end of 1998 C. Fred Bergsten proposed the establishment of an Asia-*Pacific* Monetary Fund as a compromise. C. F. Bergsten, "Pursuing the Asia-*Pacific* Monetary Fund" *Capital Trends*, vol. 3, no. 13, 1998.
81 "APEC's Family Feud" *The Economist*, November 21, 1998, p. 41; D. E. Sanger, "Tongue-Lashings and Backlashes" *The New York Times*, November 22, 1998, p. 5.
82 Y. Funabashi, "Tokyo's Depression Diplomacy" *Foreign Affairs* vol. 77, no. 6, 1998, p. 28.
83 D. Murphy, "Urban Poverty: Nothing More to Lose" *Far Eastern Economic Review* November 7, 2002, pp. 30–3.
84 There are links between the Uighur militants in Xinjiang and the Taliban regime in Afghanistan, with the latter providing training for the former. The Chinese government saw possible "benefits" from a US-led attack on Afghanistan if it weakened or overthrew the Taliban and thus undermined its support for the Islamic militants in Xinjiang. D. Murphy and S. V. Lawrence, "Beijing Hopes to Gain from U.S. Raids on Afghanistan" *Far Eastern Economic Review* October 4, 2001, p. 18; "Muslims in China: Tarred with Bin Laden's Brush" *The Economist* March 30, 2002, pp. 63–4.
85 D. Lague, "Banking in Asia: China" *Far Eastern Economic Review* October 4, 2001, pp. 70–2; D. Lague, "China: On the Road to Ruin" *Far Eastern Economic Review* November 14, 2002, pp. 32–5.
86 D. M. Lampton, *Same Bed, Different Dreams: Managing U.S.–China Relations 1989–2000*, Berkeley: University of California Press, 2001, pp. 2–4.
87 R. Bernstein and R. H. Munro, *The Coming Conflict with China*, New York: Alfred A. Knopf, 1997, p. 136.
88 Office of the President of the United States, *A National Security Strategy of Engagement and Enlargement*, Washington, DC: US Government Printing Office, 1996. Online at http://www.fas.org/spp/military/docops/national/1996stra.htm
89 Lampton, *Same Bed, Different Dreams*, pp. 15–16, 30–1, 39–45, 46, 55, 62–3.
90 R. K. Betts, "Wealth, Power, and Instability: East Asia and the United States after the Cold War," *International Security*, vol. 18, no. 3 (Winter), 1993/1994, pp. 34–77; D. Shambaugh, "Containment or Engagement of China? Calculating Beijing's Responses" *International Security* vol. 21, no. 2 (Fall), 1996, pp. 180–209; R. S. Ross, "Beijing as a Conservative Power" *Foreign Affairs* March–April, 1997, pp. 33–44; J. Nye, Jr, "The Case Against Containment: Treat China Like an Enemy and That's What It Will Be" *Global Beat* June 22, 1998. Online at http://www.nyu.edu/global-beat/asia/china/06221998nye.html
91 C. Barshefsky, "The Case of China's WTO Accession" Olin Distinguished Lecture In National Security Issues at the United States Military Academy, West Point, New York, April 12, 2000. Online at http://gos.sbc.edu/b/barshefsky3.html
92 The popular and academic literature on the China threat is now extensive. See, for example, J. J. Mearsheimer, *The Tragedy of Great Power Politics*, New York: W. W. Norton, 2001, pp. 372–7, 384–92, 396–402; J. J. Mearsheimer, "The Future of the American Pacifier" *Foreign Affairs* vol. 80, no. 5, 2001. Also see S. W. Mosher, *Hegemon: China's Plan to Dominate Asia and the World*, San Francisco: Encounter Books, 2000.
93 "Bush's Asian Challenge" *The Economist* March 17, 2001, p. 13; "China, America and Japan: The Uneasy Triangle" *The Economist* March 17, 2001, pp. 21–6; "A Hint of the

Cold War over the South China Sea" *The Economist* April 7, 2001, pp. 31–2. Also see G. Achcar, "The Strategic Triad: The United States, Russia, and China" *New Left Review (I)* no. 228, 1998, pp. 102–5, 115–26.

94 R. Halloran, "U.S. Defence Policy: Eastern Threat" *Far Eastern Economic Review* October 18, 2001, p. 32.

95 James Mulvenon (Rand Corporation) and Tao Wenzhao (Chinese Academy of Social Sciences) cited in "It Takes More to Make a Revolution" *Far Eastern Economic Review* February 14, 2002, p. 28.

Conclusion

The battle for Asia

The early twenty-first century has seen important changes in Asia and the world. These have occurred against the backdrop of a series of systemic financial crises that began with the Asian crisis in 1997–1998 and culminated by 2000–2001 in the end of the decade-long US-centered economic boom. The Al Qaeda suicide bombings in New York and Washington on September 11 2001 and the subsequent war on terrorism – followed in early 2003 by the US-led war in Iraq and the ouster of the regime of Saddam Hussein – have also had a major impact on the direction and dynamics of the US-led globalization project, with important implications for the Asia-Pacific and the rest of the world. At one level, the US-led globalization project is currently in the midst of an economic crisis linked to a US-centered economic downturn and the increasingly unequal distribution of wealth in North America and around the world. At another level, the attacks on the World Trade Center and the Pentagon crystallized the transition from the Cold War to the post-Cold War order that had been underway since the first Gulf War at the beginning of the 1990s. The reorientation in US foreign policy and the wider changes in the global political economy and the nation-state system in the wake of September 11 2001 suggest that the world is in the midst of a geo-political and economic shift as significant as the shift in international politics and economic structures that attended the end of the Second World War – and led to the establishment of the United Nations, the onset of the Cold War, the dramatic spread of the nation-state system and the rise of Third Worldism between the mid-1940s and the mid-1950s. Furthermore, although the reorientation of the US-led globalization project at the start of the twenty-first century is currently focused on the Middle East, Asia and the Asia-Pacific continues to be of particular significance to the changing global order of the post-Cold War era.

A major theme of this book has been the relationship between the geo-politics of economic development and the elaboration of the nation-state system in Asia after 1945. This has been set against the wider history and political economy of the changing global order between the 1940s and the 1990s. Adopting a critical perspective on the transformation of Asia over the past fifty years, I have sought in particular to locate the history of economic development in the context of the world-historical shift from decolonization to globalization. The universalization of the nation-state system and the uneven, and destructive as well as creative, processes of capitalist transformation (along with major state-socialist challenges to capitalism) profoundly conditioned the emergence and elaboration of state-led national development after 1945. Apart from an examination of the influential theories of development that were consolidated and revised in the context of decolonization and the Cold War, there has been a particular focus on the Asian development debate between the 1970s and the 1990s. I have also provided a synthetic overview of Asian and international history from the 1940s to the 1990s with a discussion of specific national trajectories, such as India, Indonesia, China, Japan, South Korea and, to a lesser extent, Taiwan, Malaysia, Singapore, South Vietnam, the Philippines and Thailand. This has ensured that the historical specificity and contingent character of national trajectories has been set against the backdrop of the capitalist transformation of Asia and the changing global order. At the same time, the altered role of the state in the shift from national development to globalization (and in capitalist transformation more generally) has also been foregrounded. Particular emphasis has been placed on the way the US-led globalization project emerged in the wake of a major wave of decolonization in Asia and Africa that had resulted in the effective universalization of the nation-state system. The global spread of the nation-state system increasingly exposed the limits of the nation-state as an instrument of social advance and economic development. While the contradictions of state-mediated national development became increasingly apparent between the 1940s and the 1970s, the rise of the US-led globalization project has further exposed the limits of the nation-state and the nation-state system in an era of increasingly global oligopolistic capitalism.

The Asian crisis and the subsequent economic crises in Brazil and Russia in 1998 and Argentina at the beginning of the twenty-first century are symptoms of the wider boom-bust character of the oligopolistic capitalism at the heart of the US-led globalization project. This boom-bust cycle was further underlined by the economic downturn and recession that was underway in the United States by 2000–2001, following a decade-long economic boom centered on the unsustainable expansion of the stockmarket, particularly in the information technology sector. While the causes of the Asian financial crisis (1997–1998) are the subject of considerable debate, at the broadest level the crisis flowed from the relative regulatory weaknesses of the international financial system that was increasingly displacing what were often also deeply flawed national regulatory frameworks. At the same time, as in earlier periods of economic crisis that have punctuated the history of the US-led globalization project, the response has been to push for greater globalization. From the outset the Asian crisis was characterized by the effort by the IMF, under the direct guidance of the US Treasury, to deepen the trend towards deregulation, privatization and liberalization in Asia. At the same time, the Asian crisis, and particularly the IMF's handling of the crisis, may have strengthened, rather than weakened, the promotion of a form of Asian regionalism that seeks to protect important instrumentalities associated with the developmental state and the Asian development model that the US-led globalization project has increasingly displaced. As mentioned in previous chapters,

ASEAN+3 has taken on new significance in post-crisis Asia and continues to represent an important site for at least the partial institutionalization of the Pan-Asian vision associated with regional leaders such as Prime Minister Mahathir Mohamad of Malaysia. Certainly the role of the IMF, and of the US more generally, in the region during and after the Asian financial crisis worked to fuel a great deal of resentment that was channelled and mobilized by regional elites in support of the strengthening of regional economic integration via organizations such as ASEAN+3 more specifically. The influential narratives on the Asian Renaissance (which had complemented wider Pan-Asian perspectives) were obviously undermined by the Asian financial crisis. At the same time, the IMF's management of the crisis, the speedy marginalization of APEC combined with the steadily growing economic significance of the People's Republic of China have facilitated the emergence of revised forms of Pan-Asianism centered on ASEAN+3.

Despite the incipient twenty-first century Pan-Asian regionalism of ASEAN+3, neither Beijing nor Tokyo (both of which have substantial monetary reserves) has sought to provide regional leadership in the area of financial and monetary affairs, which was at the heart of the Asian crisis. While the communist leadership in Beijing played an important role in the provision of regional financial stability during the crisis, and while the Japanese state and Japan-based corporations continue to become ever more central to the production networks and trade relations of the region, both nation-states have carefully avoided asserting regional leadership. The relative lack of increased regional financial integration under the auspices of China or Japan, or both, does not appear to be primarily a result of any significant conflict between the region's two economic and political titans. The main reason that the Japanese and Chinese governments continue to leave the management of monetary relations in Asia to the IMF apparently flows from a concern on the part of the respective governments to avoid open-ended commitments to the other governments in the region in relation to currency-swap arrangements. Tokyo and Beijing, despite all the expectations or fears about their respective potential as regional leaders and major challengers to US hegemony, remain focused on their national monetary and financial interests and this is a brake on any move in the near future towards regional monetary cooperation.

This situation flows to a considerable degree from the limits of the wider global order centered on US power. Central to the US-led globalization project has been the elaboration of an increasingly global economic framework that involves a growing disjuncture between a deregulated international financial system on the one hand and the "real" economy of the production of goods and services on the other. In this situation, unless there is a systematic and region-wide effort to introduce capital controls (such as was pursued for a while in Malaysia during the Asian crisis) even the political elites presiding over the largest and most independent national economies are profoundly limited in their ability to prevent the conflation of the interests of "Wall Street" and the financial markets on the one hand with the macroeconomic policy settings of governments around the world on the other. US power, therefore, mediated through key financial sector institutions, such as the IMF, continues to impose limits on specific national development trajectories in East Asia and on regional integration as a whole. And these limits flow both from the politico-military alliances and other arrangements that were laid down during the Cold War and from the international economic structures that underpin the globalization project. At this juncture, neither China nor Japan is in a position to challenge US hegemony. China's growing military significance as a result of its dramatic economic growth is balanced by the fact that even a Japan that has been in economic recession for over a decade remains a crucial economic force in the region. Furthermore, China's military potential not only needs to be set against the significant US military presence in the region, but also against the large standing armies of South Korea, Taiwan and Vietnam (the first two being integral to the wider US military and naval position in the region). Meanwhile, Japan has been, and continues to be, subordinate in both military and politico-economic terms to the United States. While the Chinese leadership is seeking to manage its integration into the global capitalist economy via membership of the World Trade Organization, and the government of Japan remains focused on its ongoing economic difficulties, the prospects for major advances in regional economic and political integration centered on Beijing or Tokyo or both, in a fashion that would challenge US hegemony, seems remote. In fact, the recent resurgence of bilateral trade arrangements in the region and beyond points not only to the passing of APEC, but the relative weakness of economic multilateralism in the region more generally. At the same time, the ASEAN nation-states continue to be concerned about the economic and politico-military influence of China and Japan (and to a lesser extent South Korea).

The US-led overthrow of the Taliban in Afghanistan, and the uncertainty surrounding the future of Iraq and the Middle East more generally since the overthrow of the regime of Saddam Hussein in early 2003, have highlighted the relative importance of military power to the US-led globalization project under George W. Bush. The Bush administration's vigorous pursuit of unassailable global military supremacy in the context of the increased emphasis on security and the ongoing "war on terrorism", while contributing to a military build-up in the Asian region generally, also serves to further underwrite US hegemony in the region even as it contributes in important ways to regional instability. There is an ongoing crisis centered on North Korea, which has profound implications for its immediate neighbors and is a legacy of the Cold War era. At the other end of the region there is a quasi-permanent crisis afflicting the nation-state of Pakistan, the roots of which are to be found in the timing and character of decolonization and its relations with post-1947 India against the backdrop of the Cold War. As far as Northeast and Southeast Asia are concerned, it is possible that as the post-Cold War/post-9/11 order takes shape regional elites will use ASEAN+3 to try and overcome intra-regional tensions and to challenge US hegemony. Nevertheless, the waning of state-mediated national development and/or looming inter-state conflicts cannot easily be ameliorated by regional organizations (centered on nation-states), which reproduce at a regional level all the problems associated with the nation-state. The fragmentation, turmoil, and inequality of the post-Cold War era, which is being reinforced and aggravated by the worldwide politico-military shift facilitated by the suicide bombing of the World Trade Center and the Pentagon, reflects the profound limits on the ability of the nation-state and the nation-state system to provide the framework for social advance, individual freedom and human dignity in an era of globalization. The transition from decolonization to globalization, which has been a central trend in the history of the second half of the twentieth century and the early years of the twenty-first century, has entered a new phase. It is hoped that in this new phase "the battle for Asia" will be played out in ways that avoid the tragedy and destruction that has characterized previous decades.

Bibliography

Abdulgani, R., *Bandung Spirit: Moving on the Tide of History*, Djakarta: Prapantja, 1964.

Abe, S., "Prospects for Asian Economic Integration" in S. Nishijima and P. H. Smith, eds, *Cooperation or Rivalry? Regional Integration in the Americas and the Pacific Rim*, Boulder: Westview, 1996.

Abernethy, D. B., *The Dynamics of Global Dominance: European Overseas Empires 1415–1980*, New Haven: Yale University Press, 2000.

Abu-Lughod, J., *Before European Hegemony: The World System A.D. 1250–1350*, New York: Oxford University Press, 1989.

Achcar, G., "The Strategic Triad: The United States, Russia, and China" *New Left Review (I)* no. 228, 1998.

—— *The Clash of Barbarisms: Sept 11 and the Making of the New World Disorder*, New York: Monthly Review Press, 2002.

Adams, F., *Dollar Diplomacy: United States Economic Assistance to Latin America*, Aldershot: Ashgate, 2000.

Adriano, F. D., "A Critique of the Bureaucratic Authoritarian State Thesis: The Case of the Philippines" *Journal of Contemporary Asia* vol. 14, no. 4, 1984.

Aikman, D., *Pacific Rim: Area of Change, Area of Opportunity*, Boston: Little Brown, 1986.

Allen, D., "Antiwar Asian Scholars and the Vietnam/Indochina War" *Bulletin of Concerned Asian Scholars* vol. 21, nos. 2–4, 1989.

Allison, J. M., "Indonesia: Year of the Pragmatists" *Asian Survey* vol. 9, no. 2, 1969.

—— "Indonesia: The End of the Beginning?" *Asian Survey* vol. 10, no. 2, 1970.

Almond, G. A., *The Appeals of Communism*, Princeton: Princeton University Press, 1954.

Amin, S., *Accumulation on a World Scale: A Critique of the Theory of Underdevelopment*, Sussex: Harvester Press, 1974.

—— *Unequal Development: An Essay on the Social Formations of Peripheral Capitalism*, New York: Monthly Review Press, 1976.

—— *Imperialism and Unequal Development*, New York: Monthly Review Press, 1977.

—— *Re-reading the Postwar Period: An Intellectual Itinerary*, New York: Monthly Review Press, 1994.

Amsden, A. H., "Taiwan's Economic History" *Modern China* vol. 5, no. 3, 1979.

—— "The State and Taiwan's Economic Development" in P. B. Evans, D. Rueshemeyer and T. Skocpol, eds, *Bringing the State Back In*, New York: Cambridge University Press, 1985.

—— *Asia's Next Giant: South Korea and Late Industrialization*, New York: Oxford University Press, 1989.

——— "Third World Industrialization: 'Global Fordism' or a New Model?" *New Left Review (I)* no. 182, 1990.

——— "Diffusion of Development: The Late Industrializing Model and Greater East Asia" *American Economic Review* vol. 81, no. 2, 1991.

——— "Taiwan in International Perspective" in N. T. Wang, ed., *Taiwan's Enterprises in Global Perspective*, Armonk: M. E. Sharpe, 1992.

——— "Why Isn't the Whole World Experimenting with the East Asian Model to Develop? Review of The East Asian Miracle" *World Development* vol. 22, no. 4, 1994.

——— *The Rise of "The Rest": Challenges to the West from Late-Industrializing Economies*, New York: Oxford University Press, 2001.

Anderson, B., "Old State, New Society: Indonesia's New Order in Comparative Historical Perspective" *Journal of Asian Studies* vol. 42, no. 2, 1983.

——— "Old State, New Society: Indonesia's New Order in Comparative Historical Perspective" in B. Anderson, *Langauge and Power: Exploring Political Cultures in Indonesia*, Ithaca: Cornell University Press, 1990.

——— *The Spectre of Comparison: Nationalism, Southeast Asia and the World*, London: Verso, 1998.

Anderson, P., *Lineages of the Absolutist State*, London: New Left Books, 1974.

——— *The Origins of Postmodernity*, London: Verso, 1998.

Ansprenger, F., *The Dissolution of the Colonial Empires*, London: Routledge, 1989.

Anwar, I., *The Asian Renaissance*, Singapore: Times Books International, 1996.

APEC Eminent Persons Group, *A Vision for APEC: Towards an Asia Pacific Economic Community*, Singapore: APEC Secretariat, October 1993.

——— *Achieving the APEC Vision: Free and Open Trade in the Asia Pacific*, Singapore: APEC Secretariat, August 1994.

——— *Implementing the APEC Vision*, Singapore: APEC Secretariat, August 1995.

Appadorai, A., *The Bandung Conference*, New Delhi: Indian Council of World Affairs, 1955.

Appadurai, A., *Modernity at Large: Cultural Dimensions of Globalization*, Minneapolis: University of Minnesota Press, 1996.

Arnason, J. P., *The Future That Failed: Origins and Destinies of the Soviet Model*, London: Routledge, 1993.

Arndt, H. W., *Economic Development: The History of an Idea*, Chicago: University of Chicago Press, 1987.

Arrighi, G., *The Long Twentieth Century: Money, Power, and the Origins of Our Times*, London: Verso, 1994.

——— "The Rise of East Asia and the Withering Away of the Interstate System" in C. Bartolovich and N. Lazarus, eds, *Marxism, Modernity and Postcolonial Studies*, Cambridge: Cambridge University Press, 2002.

Arrighi, G., Hopkins, T. K. and Wallerstein, I., *Antisystemic Movements*, London: Verso, 1989.

Arrighi, G., Ikeda, S. and Irwan, A., "The Rise of East Asia: One Miracle or Many?" in R. A. Palat, ed., *Pacific-Asia and the Future of the World-System*, Westport: Greenwood Press, 1993.

Arrighi, G., Hamashita, T. and Selden, M., *The Resurgence of East Asia: 500, 150 and 50 Year Perspectives*, London: RoutledgeCurzon, 2003.

Asia Monitor Resource Centre, *Everyone's State? Redefining an 'Effective State' in East Asia*, Hong Kong: Asia Monitor Resource Centre, 1997.

Aspinall, E., "Mother of the Nation" *Inside Indonesia* no. 68 (October–December), 2001.

Aspinall, E. and Berger, M. T., "The Breakup of Indonesia? Nationalisms after Decolonization and the Limits of the Nation-State in Post-Cold War Southeast Asia" *Third World Quarterly: Journal of Emerging Areas* vol. 22, no. 6, 2001.

Austin, G. and Harris, S., *Japan and Greater China: Political Economy and Military Power in the Asian Century*, London: Hurst, 2001.

Awanohara, S., "Japanese Pride and Prejudice" *Far Eastern Economic Review*, 21 February, 1991.

Awanohara, S., Vatikiotis, M. and Islam, S., "Vienna Showdown" *Far Eastern Economic Review* June 17, 1993.

Babb, S., *Managing Mexico: Economists from Nationalism to Neoliberalism*, Princeton: Princeton University Press, 2001.

Bacevich, A. J., *American Empire: The Realities and Consequences of U.S. Diplomacy*, Cambridge, MA: Harvard University Press, 2002.

Badie, B., *The Imported State: The Westernization of the Political Order*, Stanford: Stanford University Press, 2000.

Baily, S. L., *The United States and the Development of South America 1945–1975*, New York: Franklin Watts, 1976.

Baker, J. A., "America in Asia: Emerging Architecture for a Pacific Community" *Foreign Affairs* vol. 70, no. 6, 1991.

Balassa, B., *The Newly Industrializing Countries in the World Economy*, New York: Pergamon Press, 1981.

—— "The Lessons of East Asian Development: An Overview" *Economic Development and Cultural Change* vol. 36, no. 3, supplement, 1988.

Baldwin, D. A., *Economic Development and American Foreign Policy 1943–1962*, Chicago: University of Chicago Press, 1966.

Bamyeh, M. A., *The Ends of Globalization*, Minneapolis: University of Minnesota Press, 2000.

Barlow, T. E., "Colonialism's Career in Postwar China Studies" in T. E. Barlow, ed., *Formations of Colonial Modernity in East Asia*, Durham: Duke University Press, 1997.

Barshefsky, C., "The Case of China's WTO Accession" Olin Distinguished Lecture In National Security Issues at the United States Military Academy, West Point, New York, April 12, 2000. Online at http://gos.sbc.edu/b/barshefsky3.html

Bates, R. H., *Markets and States in Tropical Africa: The Political Basis of Agricultural Policies*, Berkeley: University of California Press, 1981.

—— *Essays on the Political Economy of Rural Africa*, Berkeley: University of California Press, 1987.

—— *Beyond the Miracle of the Market: The Political Economy of Agrarian Development in Kenya*, Cambridge: Cambridge University Press 1989.

Bauer, P. T., *The Rubber Industry: A Study in Competition and Monopoly*, Cambridge, MA: Harvard University Press, 1948.

—— *West African Trade: A Study of Competition, Oligopoly and Monopoly in a Changing Economy*, Cambridge: Cambridge University Press, 1954.

—— *Equality, the Third World, and Economic Delusion*, Cambridge, MA: Harvard University Press, 1981.

—— *Reality and Rhetoric: Studies in the Economics of Development*, London: Weidenfeld and Nicolson, 1984.

—— "Remembrance of Studies Past: Retracing First Steps" in G. M. Meier and D. Seers, eds, *Pioneers in Development*, Oxford: Oxford University Press for the World Bank, 1984.

Baum, R., *Burying Mao: Chinese Politics in the Age of Deng Xiaoping*, Princeton: Princeton University Press, 1994.

Bayart, J.-F., *The State in Africa: The Politics of the Belly*, London: Longman, 1993 (first published in 1989 in French as *L'Etat en Afrique*).

Beaucage, P., "The Third Wave of Modernization: Liberalism, Salinismo, and Indigenous Peasants in Mexico" in L. Philips, ed., *The Third Wave of Modernization in Latin America: Cultural Perspectives on Neoliberalism*, Wilmington, DE: Scholarly Resources, 1998.

Becker, D. G., *The New Bourgeoisie and the Limits of Dependency*, Princeton: Princeton University Press, 1983.

—— "Development, Democracy and Dependency in Latin America: A Post-Imperialist View" *Third World Quarterly: Journal of Emerging Areas* vol. 6, no. 2, 1984.

Becker, D. G. and Sklar, R. L., "Introduction" in D. G. Becker and R. L. Sklar, eds, *Postimperialism in World Politics*, New York: Praeger, 1999.

Becker, D. G., Frieden, J., Schartz, S. P. and Sklar, R. L., *Postimperialism: International Capitalism and Development in the Late Twentieth Century*, Boulder: Lynne Rienner, 1987.

Beckett, A., *Pinochet in Piccadilly: Britain and Chile's Hidden History*, London: Faber, 2002.

Beeson, M., "Mahathir and the Markets: Globalisation and the Pursuit of Economic Autonomy in Malaysia" *Pacific Affairs* vol. 73, no. 3, 2000.

Beeson, M. and Berger, M. T., "The Paradoxes of Paramountcy: Regional Rivalries and the Dynamics of US Hegemony in East Asia" *Global Change, Peace & Security* vol. 15. no. 1, 2003.

Beeson, M. and Jayasuriya, K., "The Political Rationalities of Regionalism: APEC and the EU in Comparative Perspective" *The Pacific Review* vol. 11, no. 3, 1998.

Benda, H. J., "Communism in Southeast Asia" *The Yale Review* vol. 45, 1956.

—— "Reflections on Asian Communism" *The Yale Review* vol. 56, 1966.

Benjamin, J. R., "The Framework of US Relations with Latin America in the Twentieth Century: An Interpretive Essay" *Diplomatic History* vol. 11, no. 2, 1987.

Berger, M. T., "Post-Cold War Capitalism: Modernization and Modes of Resistance After the Fall" *Third World Quarterly: Journal of Emerging Areas* vol. 16, no. 4, 1995.

—— *Under Northern Eyes: Latin American Studies and US Hegemony in the Americas 1898–1990*, Bloomington: Indiana University Press, 1995.

—— "Southeast Asian Trajectories: Eurocentrism and the History of the Modern Nation-State" *Bulletin of Concerned Asian Scholars* vol. 28, nos. 3–4, 1996.

—— "Yellow Mythologies: The East Asian Miracle and Post-Cold War Capitalism" *positions: east asia cultures critique* vol. 4, no. 1, 1996.

—— "Old State and New Empire in Indonesia: Debating the Rise and Decline of Suharto's New Order" *Third World Quarterly: Journal of Emerging Areas* vol. 18, no. 2, 1997.

—— "Post-Cold War Indonesia and the Revenge of History: The Colonial Legacy, Nationalist Visions, and Global Capitalism" in M. T. Berger and D. A. Borer, eds, *The Rise of East Asia: Critical Visions of the Pacific Century*, London: Routledge, 1997.

—— "A New East–West Synthesis? APEC and Competing Narratives of Regional Integration in the Post-Cold War Asia-Pacific" *Alternatives: Social Transformation and Humane Governance* vol. 23, no. 1, 1998.

—— "APEC and its Enemies: The Failure of the New Regionalism in the Asia-Pacific" *Third World Quarterly: Journal of Emerging Areas* vol. 20, no. 5, 1999.

—— "Bringing History Back In: The Making and Unmaking of the East Asian Miracle" *Internationale Politik Und Gesellschaft* no. 3, 1999.

—— "Delusions of Development: The Contradictions of the Nation-State and the Challenges of Globalization" *Centre for Advanced Studies Update* August, Singapore: National University of Singapore, 2000.

—— "The Nation-State and the Challenge of Global Capitalism" *Third World Quarterly: Journal of Emerging Areas* vol. 22, no. 6, 2001.

—— "The Rise and Demise of National Development and the Origins of Post-Cold War Capitalism" *Millennium: Journal of International Studies* vol. 30, no. 2, 2001.

—— "Battering Down the Chinese Walls: The Antinomies of Anglo-American Liberalism and the History of East Asian Capitalism in the Shadow of the Cold War" in C. J. W.-L. Wee, ed., *Local Cultures and the "New Asia": The State, Culture and Capitalism in Southeast Asia*, Singapore: Institute of Southeast Asian Studies, 2002.

—— "Decolonizing Southeast Asia: Nationalism, Revolution and the Cold War" in M. Beeson, ed., *Contemporary Southeast Asia: Regional Dynamics, National Differences*, Basingstoke: Palgrave Macmillan, 2003.

—— "The Cold War and National Liberation in Southern Africa: The United States and the Emergence of Zimbabwe" *Intelligence and National Security: An Inter-Disciplinary Journal* vol. 18, no. 1, 2003.

—— "The New Asian Renaissance and Its Discontents: National Narratives, Pan-Asian Visions and the Changing Post-Cold War Order" *International Politics: A Journal of Transnational Issues and Global Problems* vol. 40, no. 2, 2003.

—— "After the Third World? History, Destiny and the Fate of Third Worldism" *Third World Quarterly: Journal of Emerging Areas*, vol. 25, no. 1, 2004.

Berger, M. T. and Beeson, M., "Lineages of Liberalism and Miracles of Modernisation: The World Bank, the East Asian Trajectory and the International Development Debate" *Third World Quarterly: Journal of Emerging Areas* vol. 19, no. 3, 1998.

Berger, M. T. and Beeson, M., "APEC, ASEAN+3 and American Power: The Limits of the New Regionalism in the Asia-Pacific" in M. Boas, M. Marchand and T. Shaw, eds, *New Regionalisms in the New Millennium*, Basingstoke: Palgrave Macmillan, 2003.

—— "Miracles of Modernisation and Crises of Capitalism: The World Bank, Liberal Hegemony and East Asian Development" in D. Moore, ed., *Banking on Hegemony: Critical Essays on the World Bank's Development Discourse*, Pietermaritzburg: University of Natal Press/London: Zed Books, 2003.

Berger, M. T. and Borer, D. A., "Introduction: The Rise of East Asia: Critical Visions of the Pacific Century" in M. T. Berger and D. A. Borer, eds, *The Rise of East Asia: Critical Visions of the Pacific Century*, London: Routledge, 1997.

Berger, P. L., "An East Asian Development Model" in P. L. Berger and H. H. M. Hsiao, eds, *In Search of an East Asian Development Model*, New Brunswick: Transaction Books, 1988.

Bergsten, C. F., "APEC and the World Economy: A Force for Worldwide Liberalisation" *Foreign Affairs* vol. 73, no. 3, 1994.

—— "Pursuing the Asia-*Pacific* Monetary Fund" *Capital Trends* vol. 3, no. 13, 1998.

Bernard, M., "States, Social Forces, Regions and Historical Time in the Industrialization of Eastern Asia" *Third World Quarterly: Journal of Emerging Areas* vol. 17, no. 4, 1996.

—— "East Asia's Tumbling Dominoes: Financial Crises and the Myth of the Regional Model" in L. Panitch and C. Leys, eds, *Socialist Register 1999: Global Capitalism Versus Democracy*, New York: Monthly Review Press, 1999.

Bernard, M. and Ravenhill, J., "Beyond Product Cycles and Flying Geese: Regionalisation, Hierarchy and the Industrialisation of East Asia" *World Politics* vol. 47, no. 1, 1995.

Bernstein, R. and Munro, R. H., *The Coming Conflict with China*, New York: Alfred A. Knopf, 1997.

Bethell, T., *The Noblest Triumph: Property and Prosperity Through the Ages*, New York: St. Martin's Press, 1998.

Betts, R. F., *Decolonization*, London: Routledge, 1998.

Betts, R. K., "Wealth, Power, and Instability: East Asia and the United States after the Cold War", *International Security*, vol. 18, no. 3 (Winter), 1993/1994.

Bienen, H., "The Background to Contemporary Study of Militaries and Modernization" in H. Bienen, ed., *The Military and Modernization*, Chicago: Aldine Atherton, 1971.

Birdsall, N. and Jaspersen, F. eds, *Pathways to Growth: Comparing East Asia and Latin America*, Washington, DC: Inter-American Development Bank, 1997.

Bishop, R. and Robinson, L.S., *Night Market: Sexual Cultures and the Thai Economic Miracle*, London: Routledge, 1998.

Blumenthal, S., *The Rise of the Counter-Establishment: From Conservative Ideology to Political Power*, New York: Times Books, 1986.

Borden, W. S., *The Pacific Alliance: United States Foreign Economic Policy and Japanese Trade Recovery, 1947–1955*, Madison: University of Wisconsin Press, 1984.

Borrego, J., Bejar, A. A. and Jomo, K.S. eds, *Capital, the State, and Late Industrialization: Comparative Perspectives on the Pacific Rim*, Boulder: Westview, 1997.

Borthwick M. (with contributions by selected scholars), *Pacific Century: The Emergence of Modern Pacific Asia*, Boulder: Westview, 1992.

Bose, S., "Instruments and Idioms of Colonial and National Development: India's Historical Experience in Comparative Perspective" in F. Cooper and R. Packard, eds, *International Development and the Social Sciences: Essays on the History and Politics of Knowledge*, Berkeley: University of California Press, 1997.

Boswell, T. and Chase-Dunn, C., *The Spiral of Capitalism and Socialism: Toward Global Democracy*, Boulder: Lynne Rienner, 2000.

Bourchier, D., "Indonesianising Indonesia: Conservative Indigenism in an Age of Globalisation" *Social Semiotics* vol. 8, nos. 2/3, 1998.

Bowie, A., "The Dynamics of Business–Government Relations in Industrializing Malaysia" in A. MacIntyre, ed., *Business and Government in Industrializing Asia*, Sydney: Allen and Unwin, 1994.

Brahm, L., *China As No. 1: The New Superpower Takes Center Stage*, Singapore: Butterworth-Heinemann, 1997.

Brands, H. W., *The Specter of Neutralism: The United States and the Emergence of the Third World, 1947–1960*, New York: Columbia University Press, 1990.

—— *The Strange Death of American Liberalism*, New Haven: Yale University Press, 2001.

Brandt, W., *North–South: A Programme for Survival – Report of the Independent Commission on International Development Issues*, London: Pan, 1980.

Braudel, F., *Civilization and Capitalism 15th–18th Century: Volume One, The Structures of Everyday Life*, New York: Harper and Row, 1981.

—— *Civilization and Capitalism 15th–18th Century: Volume Two, The Wheels of Commerce*, New York: Harper and Row, 1982.

—— *Civilization and Capitalism 15th–18th Century: Volume Three, The Perspective of the World*, New York: Harper and Row, 1984.

Brenner, R., "The Origins of Capitalist Development: A Critique of Neo-Smithian Marxism" *New Left Review (I)* no. 104, 1977.

—— "Agrarian Class Structure and Economic Development in Pre-Industrial Europe" in T. H. Aston and C. H. E. Philpin, eds, *The Brenner Debate: Agrarian Class Structure and*

Economic Development in Pre-Industrial Europe, Cambridge: Cambridge University Press, 1987.

—— "Uneven Development and the Long Downturn: The Advanced Capitalist Economies from Boom to Stagnation, 1950–1998" *New Left Review (I)* no. 229, 1998.

Bresnan, J., *Managing Indonesia: The Modern Political Economy*, New York: Columbia University Press, 1993.

—— "Indonesia" in R. Chase, E. Hill and P. Kennedy, eds, *The Pivotal States: A New Framework for U.S. Policy in the Developing World*, New York: W. W. Norton, 1999.

Brewer, A., *Marxist Theories of Imperialism: A Critical Survey*, London: Routledge and Kegan Paul, 1980.

Browitt, J., "Capital Punishment: The Fragmentation of Colombia and the Crisis of the Nation-State" *Third World Quarterly: Journal of Emerging Areas* vol. 22, no. 6, 2001.

Brown, C., " 'Really Existing Liberalism' and International Order" *Millennium: Journal of International Studies* vol. 21, no. 3, 1992.

Brown, D., *The State and Ethnic Politics in Southeast Asia*, London: Routledge, 1994.

Brown, M. B., *Africa's Choices: After Thirty Years of the World Bank*, London: Penguin, 1995.

Brown, M. E., Lynn-Jones, S. M. and Miller, S. E. eds, *Debating the Democratic Peace*, Cambridge, MA: MIT Press, 1996.

Brown, W. N., *The United States and India and Pakistan*, Cambridge, MA: Harvard University Press, 1953.

Brummer, A., "Malaysian Tiger Takes a Mauling" *The Guardian Weekly* September 7, 1997.

Budiman, A., "The State and Industrialisation in Indonesia" in K. Kyong-Dong, ed., *Dependency Issues in Korean Development*, Seoul: National University Press, 1987.

Bulmer-Thomas, V., *The Economic History of Latin America Since Independence*, Cambridge: Cambridge University Press, 1994.

Bundy, M., "The Battlefields of Power and the Searchlights of the Academy" in E. A. G. Johnson, ed., *Dimensions of Diplomacy*, Baltimore: Johns Hopkins University Press, 1964.

Burke, P., *The French Historical Revolution: The Annales School 1929–1989*, Cambridge: Polity Press, 1990.

Burton, S., "The Stubborn Holdout" *Time: International* November 22, 1993.

Buszynski, L., *SEATO: The Failure of an Alliance Strategy*, Singapore: Singapore University Press, 1984.

Butler, L. J., *Britain and Empire: Adjusting to a Post-Imperial World*, London: I. B. Tauris, 2002.

Byres, T. J., "The Agrarian Question and Differing Forms of Capitalist Agrarian Transitions: An Essay with Reference to Asia" in J. Breman and S. Mundle, eds, *Rural Transformation in Asia*, New Delhi: Oxford University Press, 1991.

Cai, X. ed., *Zhongguo da zhanlue (China's Grand Strategy)*, Haikou: Hainan chubanshe, 1996.

Calder, K. E., *Crisis and Compensation: Public Policy and Political Stability in Japan, 1949–1986*, Princeton: Princeton University Press, 1988.

—— *Strategic Capitalism: Private Business and Public Purpose in Japanese Industrial Finance*, Princeton: Princeton University Press, 1993.

Campbell, K. M., "Koizumi as Japan's Reagan" *Far Eastern Economic Review* August 23, 2001.

Cammack, P., *Capitalism and Democracy in the Third World: The Doctrine of Political Development*, London: Leicester University Press, 1997.

—— "Attacking the Global Poor" *New Left Review (II)* no. 13, 2002.

Campos, J. E., and Root, H. L., *The Key to the Asian Miracle: Making Shared Growth Credible*, Washington, DC: Brookings Institution, 1996.

Cannadine, D., *Ornamentalism: How the British Saw their Empire*, London: Penguin, 2001.

Cardoso, F. H., "Associated Dependent Development: Theoretical and Practical Implications" in A. Stepan, ed., *Authoritarian Brazil*, New Haven: Yale University Press, 1973.

Carothers, T., *Aiding Democracy Abroad: The Learning Curve*, Washington, DC: Brookings Institution, 1999.

Carter, M. R., "Intellectual Openings and Policy Closures: Disequilibria in Contemporary Development Economics" in F. Cooper and R. Packard, eds, *International Development and the Social Sciences: Essays on the History and Politics of Knowledge*, Berkeley: University of California Press, 1997.

Castells, M., "Four Asian Tigers with a Dragon Head: A Comparative Analysis of the State, Economy and Society in the Asian Pacific Rim" in R. P. Appelbaum and J. Henderson, eds, *States and Development in the Asian Pacific Rim*, Newbury Park: Sage, 1992.

—— *The Rise of Network Society* (*The Information Age: Economy, Society and Culture*, volume 1), Oxford: Blackwell, 1996.

—— *The Power of Identity* (*The Information Age: Economy, Society and Culture*, volume 2), Oxford: Blackwell, 1997.

—— *End of Millennium* (*The Information Age: Economy, Society and Culture*, volume 3), Oxford: Blackwell, 1998.

Caufield, C., *Masters of Illusion: The World Bank and the Poverty of Nations*, New York: Henry Holt, 1996.

Celoza, A. F., *Ferdinand Marcos and the Philippines: The Political Economy of Authoritarianism*, New York: Praeger, 1998.

Chakrabarty, D., *Provincializing Europe: Postcolonial Thought and Historical Difference*, Princeton: Princeton University Press, 2000.

Chakravarty, S., *Development Planning: The Indian Experience*, Oxford: Clarendon Press, 1987.

Chamberlain, M. E., *Decolonization: The Fall of the European Empires*, 2nd edn, Oxford: Blackwell, 1999.

Chan, S., Clark, C. and Lam, D., "Looking beyond the Developmental State" in S. Chan, C. Clark and D. Lam, eds, *Beyond the Developmental State: East Asia's Political Economies Reconsidered*, London: Macmillan, 1998.

Chandra, B., "Colonial India: British versus Indian Views of Development" *Review: A Journal of the Fernand Braudel Center* vol. 14, no. 1, 1991.

Chang, H.-J., "Korea: The Misunderstood Crisis" *World Development* vol. 26, no. 8, 1998.

—— "The Economic Theory of the Developmental State" in M. Woo-Cumings, ed., *The Developmental State*, Ithaca: Cornell University Press, 1999.

—— ed., *Joseph Stiglitz and the World Bank: The Rebel Within*, London: Anthem, 2002.

—— *Kicking Away the Ladder: Development Strategy in Historical Perspective*, London: Anthem, 2002.

Chase-Dunn, C., *Global Formation: Structures of the World-Economy*, Oxford: Basil Blackwell, 1989.

Chatterjee, P., *Nationalist Thought and Colonial World: A Derivative Discourse?*, London: Zed Books, 1986.

Chen, E. K. Y., *Hyper-Growth in Asian Economies: A Comparative Study of Hong Kong, Japan, Korea, Singapore and Taiwan*, London: Macmillan, 1979.

Chen, E. and Hamilton, G. G., "Introduction: Business Groups and Economic Development" in G. Hamilton, ed., *Asian Business Networks*, New York: Walter de Gruyter, 1996.

Chen, H. C., "America in East Asia" *New Left Review (II)* no. 12, 2001.

—— "Introduction: The Decolonization Question" in H. C. Chen ed., *Trajectories: Inter-Asia Cultural Studies*, London: Routledge, 1998.

Chen, H. C., Shepard, J. M. and Dollinger, M. J., "Max Weber Revisited: Some Lessons from East Asian Capitalistic Development" *Asia Pacific Journal of Management* vol. 6, no. 2, 1987.

Chen, K.-H., "America in East Asia" *New Left Review (II)* no. 12, 2001.

Ching, F., "Confucius, the New Saviour" *Far Eastern Economic Review*, November 10, 1994.

—— "APEC Moving Along 'Asian Way' " *Far Eastern Economic Review* December 7, 1995.

Ching, L., "Globalizing the Regional, Regionalizing the Global: Mass Culture and Asianism in the Age of Late Capital" *Public Culture* vol. 12, no. 1, 2000.

Choate, P., *Agents of Influence: How Japan's Lobbyists in the United States Manipulate America's Political and Economic System*, New York: Alfred A. Knopf, 1990.

Choi, A. H., "Statism and Asian Political Economy: Is There a New Paradigm?" *Bulletin of Concerned Asian Scholars* vol. 30, no. 3, 1998.

Christensen, T. J., "Pride, Pressure and Politics: The Roots of China's Worldview" in Y. Deng and F.-L. Wang, eds, *In the Eyes of the Dragon: China Views the World*, Lanham: Rowman and Littlefield, 1999.

Christie, C. J., *Ideology and Revolution in Southeast Asia 1900–1980*, Richmond: Curzon, 2001.

Chua, B.-H., *Communitarian Ideology and Democracy in Singapore*, London: Routledge, 1995.

Chupaka, S. and Chaipipat, K., "ASEAN Currency Bid Launched" *The Nation* (Thailand) September 19, 1997.

Citino, N.J., *From Arab Nationalism to OPEC: Eisenhower, King Saud, and the Making of U.S.–Saudi Relations*, Bloomington: Indiana University Press, 2002.

Clad, J., *Behind the Myth: Business, Money and Power in Southeast Asia*, 2nd edn, London: Grafton, 1991.

Clancy, T., *Debt of Honor*, London: HarperCollins, 1994.

—— *The Bear and the Dragon*, New York: G. P. Putnam's Sons, 2000.

Clark, C. and Chan, S., "The Developmental Roles of the State: Moving Beyond the Developmental State in Conceptualizing Asian Political Economies" *Governance: An International Journal of Policy and Administration* vol. 7, no. 4, 1994.

Clinton, B., "World Without Walls: How Do We Defeat Global Terrorism?" *The Guardian (Saturday Review)* January 26, 2002.

Coates, D., *Models of Capitalism: Growth and Stagnation in the Modern Era*, Cambridge: Polity Press, 2000.

Cockett, R., *Thinking the Unthinkable: Think-Tanks and the Economic Counter-Revolution 1931–1983*, Hammersmith: HarperCollins, 1995.

Cohen, R., "Master of War: Novelist Tom Clancy Keeps Making New Enemies" *Rolling Stone Yearbook*, 1994.

Cohen, S. P. and Ganguly, S., "India" in R. Chase, E. Hill and P. Kennedy, eds, *The Pivotal States: A New Framework for U.S. Policy in the Developing World*, New York: W. W. Norton, 1999.

Cohen, T., *Remaking Japan: The American Occupation as New Deal*, New York: Free Press, 1987.

Cole, D. C. and Lyman, P. N., *Korean Development: The Interplay of Politics and Economics*, Cambridge, MA: Harvard University Press, 1971.

Coleman, J. S., "The Political Systems of the Developing Areas" in G. Almond and J. S. Coleman, eds, *The Politics of the Developing Areas*, Princeton: Princeton University Press, 1960.

Collier, D., "The Bureaucratic-Authoritarian Model: Synthesis and Priorities for Future Research" in D. Collier, ed., *The New Authoritarianism in Latin America*, New York: Columbia University Press, 1979.

Connor, W., *Ethnonationalism: The Quest for Understanding*, Princeton: Princeton University Press, 1990.

Cooper, F., *Decolonization and African Society: The Labor Question in French and British Africa*, Cambridge: Cambridge University Press, 1996.

—— "Modernizing Bureaucrats, Backward Africans, and the Development Concept" in F. Cooper and R. Packard, eds, *International Development and the Social Sciences: Essays on the History and Politics of Knowledge*, Berkeley: University of California Press, 1997.

—— *Africa Since 1940: The Past of the Present*, Cambridge: Cambridge University Press, 2002.

Cooper, F. and Packard, R., "Introduction" in F. Cooper and R. Packard, eds, *International Development and the Social Sciences: Essays on the History and Politics of Knowledge*, Berkeley: University of California Press, 1997.

—— eds, *International Development and the Social Sciences: Essays on the History and Politics of Knowledge*, Berkeley: University of California Press, 1997.

Constantine, S., *The Making of British Colonial Development Policy 1914–1940*, London: Frank Cass, 1984.

Corbo, V., Krueger, A. O. and Ossa, F., *Export-Oriented Development Strategies*, Boulder: Westview, 1985.

Corbridge, S. and Harriss, J., *Reinventing India: Liberalization, Hindu Nationalism and Popular Democracy*, Cambridge: Polity Press, 2000.

Cowen, M. P. and Shenton, R. W., *Doctrines of Development*, New York: Routledge 1996.

Cox, R. W., *Production, Power and World Order: Social Forces in the Making of History*, New York: Columbia University Press, 1987.

Cribb, R. ed., *The Indonesian Killings 1965–1966: Studies from Java and Bali*, Clayton: Centre for Southeast Asian Studies, Monash University, 1990.

Crichton, M., *Rising Sun*, London: Arrow, 1992.

Cronin, J. E., *The World the Cold War Made: Order, Chaos and the Return of History*, London: Routledge, 1996.

Crouch, H., *The Army and Politics in Indonesia*, 2nd edn, Ithaca: Cornell University Press, 1988.

Cullather, N., "Development? Its History" *Diplomatic History* vol. 24, no. 4, 2000.

—— "Parable of Seeds: The Green Revolution in the Modernizing Imagination" in M. Frey, R. W. Pruessen and T. T. Yong, eds, *The Transformation in Southeast Asia: International Perspectives on Decolonization*, Armonk: M. E. Sharpe, 2003.

Cumings, B., "The Legacy of Japanese Colonialism in Korea" in R. H. Myers and M. R. Peattie, eds, *The Japanese Colonial Empire 1895–1945*, Princeton: Princeton University Press, 1984.

—— "The Origins and Development of the Northeast Asian Political Economy: Industrial Sectors, Product Cycles and Political Consequences" *International Organization* vol. 38, no. 1, 1984 (reprinted in Deyo, F. C., ed., *The Political Economy of the New Asian Industrialism*, Ithaca: Cornell University Press, 1987).

—— "The Origins and Development of the Northeast Asian Political Economy: Industrial Sectors, Product Cycles and Political Consequences" in F. C. Deyo, ed., *The Political Economy of the New Asian Industrialism*, Ithaca: Cornell University Press, 1987.

—— *The Origins of the Korean War I: Liberation and the Emergence of Separate Regimes 1945–1947*, 2nd edn, Princeton: Princeton University Press, 1989.

—— *The Origins of the Korean War II: The Roaring of the Cataract 1947–1950*, Princeton: Princeton University Press, 1990.

—— "The Wicked Witch of the West is Dead. Long Live the Wicked Witch of the East" in M. J. Hogan, ed., *The End of the Cold War: Its Meaning and Implications*, Cambridge: Cambridge University Press, 1992.

—— "Japan in the World-System" in A. Gordon, ed., *Post-War Japan as History*, Berkeley: University of California Press, 1993.

—— "Bringing Korea Back In: Structured Absence, Glaring Presence, and Invisibility" in W. I. Cohen, *Pacific Passage: The Study of American-East Asian Relations on the Eve of the Twenty-First Century*, New York: Columbia University Press, 1996.

—— "Japan and Northeast Asia into the Twenty-First Century" in P. J. Katzenstein and T. Shiraishi, eds, *Network Power: Japan and Asia*, Ithaca: Cornell University Press, 1997.

—— "Boundary Displacement: Area Studies and International Studies During and After the Cold War" in C. Simpson, ed., *Universities and Empire: Money and Politics in the Social Sciences During the Cold War*, New York: New Press, 1998.

—— "Still the American Century" *Review of International Studies* vol. 25, supplement, 1999.

—— "Webs With No Spiders, Spiders With No Webs: The Genealogy of the Developmental State" in M. Woo-Cumings, ed., *The Developmental State*, Ithaca: Cornell University Press, 1999.

Dacy, D. C., *Foreign Aid, War, and Economic Development: South Vietnam, 1953–1975*, Cambridge: Cambridge University Press, 1986.

Daniel, D. C. F. and Ross, A. L., "U.S. Strategic Planning and the Pivotal States" in R. Chase, E. Hill and P. Kennedy, eds, *The Pivotal States: A New Framework for U.S. Policy in the Developing World*, New York: W. W. Norton, 1999.

Darby, P., *Three Faces of Imperialism: British and American Approaches to Asia and Africa 1870–1970*, New Haven: Yale University Press, 1987.

de Bary, W. T., "The Association for Asian Studies: Nonpolitical but Not Unconcerned" *Journal of Asian Studies* vol. 29, no. 4, 1970.

—— ed., *A Forum on "The Role of Culture in Industrial Asia: The Relationship between Confucian Ethics and Modernisation"*, Singapore: Institute of East Asian Philosophies, 1988.

de Bary, W. T. and Chafee, J. W. eds, *Neo-Confucian Education: The Formative Stage*, Berkeley: University of California Press, 1989.

Deng, Y., "Conceptions of National Interest: Realpolitik, Liberal Dilemma and the Possibility of Change" in Y. Deng and F.-L. Wang, eds, *In the Eyes of the Dragon: China Views the World*, Lanham: Rowman and Littlefield, 1999.

De Rivero, O., *The Myth of Development: The Non-Viable Economies of the 21st Century*, London: Zed Books, 2001.

Desai, P., "Introduction" in P. Desai, ed., *Going Global: Transition from Plan to Market in the World Economy*, Cambridge, MA: MIT Press, 1997.

Desai, R., "Second-Hand Dealers in Ideas: Think-Tanks and Thatcherite Hegemony" *New Left Review (I)* no. 203, 1994.

Desmond, E. W., "One Happy, Culturally Superior Family" *Time: Australia* November 21, 1994.

Deyo, F. C., *Beneath the Miracle: Labor Subordination in the New Asian Industrialism*, Berkeley: University of California Press, 1989.

Dhume, S., "Indonesia: On Shaky Ground" *Far Eastern Economic Review* September 27, 2001.

—— "Indonesia: Helping Hand" *Far Eastern Economic Review* April 25, 2002.

Dietrich, W. S., *In the Shadow of the Rising Sun: The Political Roots of American Economic Decline*, University Park: Pennsylvania State University Press, 1991.

Dirlik, A., *After the Revolution: Waking to Global Capitalism*, London: Wesleyan University Press, 1994.

Dixon, C., *South East Asia in the World Economy: A Regional Geography*, Cambridge: Cambridge University Press, 1991.

Dore, R., *Flexible Rigidities: Industrial Policy and Structural Adjustment in the Japanese Economy, 1970–1980*, Stanford: Stanford University Press, 1986.

—— *Taking Japan Seriously: A Confucian Perspective on Leading Economic Issues*, Stanford: Stanford University Press, 1988.

Dore, R. P. ed., *Aspects of Social Change in Modern Japan*, Princeton: Princeton University Press, 1967.

Dower, J. W., "E. H. Norman, Japan and the Uses of History" in J. W. Dower, *Origins of the Modern Japanese State: Selected Writings of E. H. Norman*, New York: Pantheon Books, 1975.

—— *Embracing Defeat: Japan in the Wake of World War II*, New York: W. W. Norton, 1999.

Drysdale, P., Vines, D. and House, B., "Europe and East Asia: A Shared Global Agenda?" in P. Drysdale and D. Vines, eds, *Europe, East Asia and APEC: A Shared Global Agenda?*, Cambridge: Cambridge University Press, 1998.

Duffield, M., *Global Governance and the New Wars: The Merging of Development and Security*, London: Zed Books, 2001.

Dunkerley, J, *The Pacification of Central America: Political Change in the Isthmus 1987–1993*, London: Verso, 1994.

Dutt, N. K., "The United States and the Asian Development Bank" *Journal of Contemporary Asia* vol. 27, no. 1, 1997.

Dwyer, M., "Japan Backs $133bn Asia Fund" *The Australian Financial Review* September 22, 1997. Online at http://www.afr.com.au

Dwyer, M. and Hartcher, P., "East versus West: How the Markets are Uniting Asia Against the US" *The Australian Financial Review* September 27, 1997. Online at http://www.afr.com.au

Easterly, W., *The Elusive Quest for Growth: Economists' Adventures and Misadventures in the Tropics*, Cambridge, MA: MIT Press, 2001.

Easton, D., *The Political System: An Inquiry into the State of Political Science*, 2nd edn, Chicago: University of Chicago Press, 1981.

Economist, The, "Democracy and Growth" *The Economist* August 27, 1994.

—— "A Dream of Free Trade" *The Economist* November 25, 1994.

—— "Saying No" *The Economist* November 25, 1994.

—— "Japan: The New Nationalists" *The Economist* January 14, 1995.

—— "Confucianism: New Fashion for Old Wisdom" *The Economist* January 27, 1995.

—— "Japan and the War: The Japan that Cannot Say Sorry" *The Economist* August 18, 1995.

—— "Asia and Europe: Friends Apart" *The Economist* March 9, 1996.

—— "Too Late for a Gentle Landing" *The Economist* September 6, 1997.

—— "An Asian IMF" *The Economist* September 27, 1997.

—— "Mahathir, Soros and the Currency Markets" *The Economist* September 27, 1997.

—— "Rumpus in Hong Kong" *The Economist* September 27, 1997.

—— "Asia's Spreading Shadow" *The Economist* November 1, 1997.

—— "APEC's Family Feud" *The Economist*, November 21, 1998.

—— "A Bad Time to be an Ostrich" *The Economist*, December 19, 1998.

—— "ASEAN Looks to the New Year" *The Economist* December 19, 1998.

—— "Liberalism Lives" *The Economist* January 2, 1999.

—— "Bush's Asian Challenge" *The Economist* March 17, 2001.

—— "China, America and Japan: The Uneasy Triangle" *The Economist* March 17, 2001.

—— "A Hint of the Cold War over the South China Sea" *The Economist* April 7, 2001.

—— "Japan: Reform on Hold" *The Economist* September 8, 2001.

—— "Japan and the United States: On Board?" *The Economist* September 22, 2001.

—— "Japanese Banks: Abandon Hope" *The Economist* September 22, 2001.

—— "Help in the Right Places" *The Economist* March 16, 2002.

—— "Foreign Aid: A Feast of Giving" *The Economist* March 23, 2002.

—— "Muslims in China: Tarred with Bin Laden's Brush" *The Economist* March 30, 2002.

—— "When Trade and Security Clash" *The Economist* April 6, 2002.

—— "Japanese Economy: The Ghosts of Reforms Past" *The Economist* November 2, 2002.

Elegant, R., *Pacific Destiny: Inside Asia Today*, 2nd edn, London: Headline, 1991.

Engerman, D. C., "Modernization from the Other Shore: American Observers and the Costs of Soviet Economic Development" *American Historical Review* vol. 105, no. 2, 2000.

—— "West Meets East: The Center for International Studies and Indian Economic Development" in D. Engerman, N. Gilman, M. Haefele and M. Latham, eds, *Staging Growth: Modernization, Development and the Global Cold War*, Amherst: University of Massachusetts Press, 2003.

—— *Modernization from the Other Shore: American Intellectuals and Russian Development*, Cambridge, MA: Harvard University Press, 2003.

—— *Staging Growth: Modernization, Development and the Global Cold War*, Amherst: University of Massachusetts Press, 2003.

Ernst, J., *Forging A Fateful Alliance: Michigan State University and the Vietnam War*, East Lansing: Michigan State University, 1998.

Ertman, T., *Birth of the Leviathan: Building States and Regimes in Medieval and Early Modern Europe*, Cambridge: Cambridge University Press, 1997.

Escobar, A., *Encountering Development: The Making and Unmaking of the Third World*, Princeton: Princeton University Press, 1995.

Evans, P., *Dependent Development: The Alliance of Multinational, State and Local Capital in Brazil*, Princeton: Princeton University Press, 1979.

—— "Class, State, and Dependence in East Asia: Lessons for Latin Americanists" in F. C. Deyo, ed., *The Political Economy of the New Asian Industrialism*, Ithaca: Cornell University Press, 1987.

—— *John Fairbank and the American Understanding of Modern China*, Oxford: Basil Blackwell, 1988.

—— *Embedded Autonomy: States and Industrial Transformation*, Princeton: Princeton University Press, 1995.

Fairbank, J. K., *The United States and China*, Cambridge, MA: Harvard University Press, 1948.

Fajnzylber, F., "The United States and Japan as Models of Industrialisation" in G. Gereffi and D. L. Wyman, eds, *Manufacturing Miracles: Paths of Industrialisation in Latin America and East Asia*, Princeton: Princeton University Press, 1990.

Fallows, J., *More Like Us: Making America Great Again*, Boston: Houghton Mifflin, 1989.

—— *Looking at the Sun: The Rise of the New East Asian Economic and Political System*, New York: Pantheon, 1994.

Far Eastern Economic Review, "It Takes More to Make a Revolution", February 14, 2002.

Feith, H., *The Decline of Constitutional Democracy in Indonesia*, Ithaca: Cornell University Press, 1962.

Fieldhouse, D. K., "Decolonization, Development, and Dependence: A Survey of Changing Attitudes" in P. Gifford and W. R. Louis, eds, *The Transfer of Power in Africa: Decolonization, 1940–1960*, New Haven: Yale University Press, 1982.

Fineman, D., *A Special Relationship: The United States and Military Government in Thailand, 1947–1958*, Honolulu: University of Hawaii Press, 1997.

Fingleton, E., *Blindside: Why Japan is Still on Track to Overtake the US by the Year 2000*, New York: Simon and Schuster, 1995.

Finnemore, M., "Redefining Development at the World Bank" in F. Cooper and R. Packard, eds, *International Development and the Social Sciences*, Berkeley: University of California Press, 1997.

Fisher, D., *Fundamental Development of the Social Sciences: Rockefeller Philanthropy and the United States Social Science Research Council*, Ann Arbor: University of Michigan Press, 1993.

FitzGerald, F., *Fire in the Lake: The Vietnamese and the Americans in Vietnam*, Boston: Little Brown, 1972.

Forney, M., "Patriot Games" *Far Eastern Economic Review* October 3, 1996.

—— "New Chinese Man" *Far Eastern Economic Review* April 17, 1997.

Forsberg, A., *America and the Japanese Miracle: The Cold War Context of Japan's Postwar Economic Revival, 1950–1960*, Chapel Hill: University of North Carolina Press, 2000.

Frank, A. G., *Capitalism and Underdevelopment in Latin America: Historical Studies of Chile and Brazil*, 2nd edn, New York: Monthly Review Press, 1969.

—— *Latin America: Underdevelopment or Revolution: Essays on the Development of Underdevelopment and the Immediate Enemy*, 2nd edn, New York: Monthly Review Press, 1970.

—— *Lumpen-Bourgeoisie, Lumpen-Development: Dependence, Class and Politics in Latin America*, New York: Monthly Review Press, 1972.

—— *Dependent Accumulation and Underdevelopment*, London: Macmillan, 1978.

—— *World Accumulation 1492–1789*, London: Macmillan, 1978.

—— *ReOrient: Global Economy in the Asian Age*, Berkeley: University of California Press, 1998.

Frankel, F. R., *India's Green Revolution: Economic Gains and Political Costs*, Princeton: Princeton University Press, 1973.

—— *India's Political Economy, 1947–1977: The Gradual Revolution*, Princeton: Princeton University Press, 1978.

Freedman, L., *Kennedy's Wars: Berlin, Cuba, Laos and Vietnam*, New York: Oxford University Press, 2000.

Friedman, D., *The Misunderstood Miracle: Industrial Development and Political Change in Japan*, Ithaca: Cornell University Press, 1988.

Friedman, E., "The Challenge of a Rising China: Another Germany?" in R. J. Lieber, ed., *Eagle Adrift: American Foreign Policy at the End of the Century*, New York: Longman, 1997.

Friedman, G. and Lebard, M., *The Coming War with Japan*, New York: St. Martin's Press, 1991.

Friedman, M. and Friedman, R., *Free to Choose: A Personal Statement*, New York: Harcourt Brace Jovanovich, 1980.

Friedman, T., *The Lexus and the Olive Tree*, New York: HarperCollins, 1999.

Fromkin, D., *A Peace to End All Peace: The Fall of the Ottoman Empire and the Creation of the Modern Middle East*, 2nd edn, New York: Henry Holt, 2001.

Fukui, H. and Fukai, S. N., "The End of the Miracle: Japanese Politics in the Post-Cold War Era" in M. T. Berger and D. A. Borer, eds, *The Rise of East Asia: Critical Visions of the Pacific Century*.

Fukuyama, F., "The End of History?" *The National Interest* vol. 16, no. 8, 1989.

—— *The End of History and the Last Man*, London: Hamish Hamilton, 1992.

Funabashi, Y., *Asia Pacific Fusion: Japan's Role in APEC*, Washington, DC: Institute for International Economics, 1995.

—— "Tokyo's Depression Diplomacy" *Foreign Affairs* vol. 77, no. 6, 1998.

Gaddis, J. L., *The Long Peace: Inquiries into the History of the Cold War*, New York: Oxford University Press, 1987.

—— "Living in Candlestick Park" *The Atlantic Monthly* vol. 283, no. 4, 1999.

Galenson, W. ed., *Foreign Trade and Investment: Economic Growth in the Newly Industrializing Asian Countries*, Madison: University of Wisconsin Press, 1985.

Gao, B., "The Search for National Identity and Japanese Industrial Policy, 1950–1969" *Nations and Nationalism* vol. 4, no. 2, 1998.

Gardner, L. C., *Approaching Vietnam: From World War II Through Dienbienphu*, New York: W. W. Norton, 1988.

Garnaut, R., *Open Regionalism and Trade Liberalization: An Asia-Pacific Contribution to the World Trade System*, Singapore: Institute of Southeast Asia Studies, 1996.

Garon, S., *Molding Japanese Minds: The State in Everyday Life*, Princeton: Princeton University Press, 1997.

Garten, J. E., *The Big Ten: The Big Emerging Markets and How They Will Change Our Lives*, New York: Basic Books, 1997.

—— "From New Economy to Siege Economy: Globalization, Foreign Policy and the CEO Agenda" *Business and Strategy* no. 26, 2002.

Gates, H., *China's Motor: A Thousand Years of Petty Capitalism*, Ithaca: Cornell University Press, 1996.

Geddes, B., "Paradigms and Sand Castles in Comparative Politics of Developing Areas" in W. Crotty, ed., *Comparative Politics, Policy, and International Relations (Political Science: Looking to the Future, vol. 2)*, Evanston: Northwestern University Press, 1991.

Geertz, C., "The Integrative Revolution: Primordial Sentiments and Civil Politics in the New States" in C. Geertz, ed., *Old Societies and New States: The Quest for Modernity in Asia and Africa*, London: Macmillan, 1963.

Gendzier, I. L., *Managing Political Change: Social Scientists and the Third World*, Boulder: Westview, 1985.

George, C. H., "The Origins of Capitalism: A Marxist Epitome and a Critique of Immanuel Wallerstein's Modern World-System" *Marxist Perspectives* vol. 3, no. 2, 1980.

Gereffi, G., "Paths of Industrialization: An Overview" in G. Gereffi and D. L. Wyman, eds, *Manufacturing Miracles: Paths of Industrialisation in Latin America and East Asia*, Princeton: Princeton University Press, 1990.

—— "Rethinking Development Theory: Insights from East Asia and Latin America" in A. D. Kincaid and A. Portes, eds, *Comparative National Development: Society and Economy in the New Global Order*, Chapel Hill: University of North Carolina Press, 1994.

Gerschenkron, A., *Economic Backwardness in Historical Perspective: A Book of Essays*, Cambridge, MA: Harvard University Press, 1962.

Giauque, J. G., *Grand Designs and Visions of Unity: The Atlantic Powers and the Reorganization of Western Europe, 1955–1963*, Chapel Hill: University of North Carolina Press, 2002.

Gibney, F., *Miracle by Design: The Real Reasons behind Japan's Economic Success*, New York: Times Books, 1982.

—— *The Pacific Century: America and Asia in a Changing World*, New York: Macmillan, 1992.
Gifford, P., "The Cold War across Asia" in D. Goldsworthy, ed., *Facing North: A Century of Australian Engagement with Asia*, Melbourne: Melbourne University Press, 2001.
Gill, S., *American Hegemony and the Trilateral Commission*, Cambridge: Cambridge University Press, 1990.
—— "Globalisation, Market Civilisation, and Disciplinary Neo-Liberalism" *Millennium: Journal of International Studies* vol. 24, no. 3, 1995.
—— *Power and Resistance in the New World Order*, Basingstoke: Palgrave Macmillan, 2003.
Gilley, B., "Potboiler Nationalism" *Far Eastern Economic Review* October 3, 1996.
Gills, B., "The Hegemonic Transition in East Asia: A Historical Perspective" in S. Gill, ed., *Gramsci, Historical Materialism and International Relations*, Cambridge: Cambridge University Press, 1993.
Gilman, N., "Paving the World with Good Intentions: The Genesis of Modernization Theory", unpublished PhD thesis, Berkeley: University of California, 2000.
—— *Mandarins of the Future: Modernization Theory in Cold War America*, Baltimore: Johns Hopkins University Press, 2003.
Gilpin, R., *Global Political Economy: Understanding the International Economic Order*, Princeton: Princeton University Press, 2001.
Gittings, J., "Gore Lectures Leaders on Asian Democracy" *The Guardian Weekly* November 22, 1998.
Glassburner, B., "Economic Policy-Making in Indonesia, 1950–1957" and "Indonesian Economic Policy after Sukarno" in B. Glassburner, ed., *The Economy of Indonesia: Selected Readings*, Ithaca: Cornell University Press, 1971.
—— "Political Economy and the Suharto Regime" *Bulletin of Indonesian Economic Studies* vol. 14, no. 3, 1978.
Gluck, C., "The Past in the Present" in A. Gordon, ed., *Postwar Japan as History*, Berkeley: University of California Press, 1993.
Glyn, A., Hughes, A., Lipietz, A. and Singh, A., "The Rise and Fall of the Golden Age" in S. A. Marglin and J. B. Schor, eds, *The Golden Age of Capitalism: Interpreting the Postwar Experience*, 2nd edn, New York: Oxford University Press, 1991.
Godement, F., *The New Asian Renaissance: From Colonialism to the Post-Cold War*, London: Routledge, 1997.
Gold, T. B., *State and Society in the Taiwan Miracle*, London: M. E. Sharpe, 1986.
Goldman, M. and Nathan, A. J., "Searching for the Appropriate Model for the People's Republic of China" in M. Goldman and A. Gordon, eds, *Historical Perspectives on Contemporary East Asia*, Cambridge, MA: Harvard University Press, 2000.
Goldstein, A., "Great Expectations: Interpreting China's Arrival" in M. E. Brown, O. R. Coté, Jr, S. M. Lynn-Jones and S. E. Miller, eds, *The Rise of China*, Cambridge, MA: MIT Press, 2000.
Goodson, L. P., *Afghanistan's Endless War: State Failure, Regional Politics, and the Rise of the Taliban*, Seattle: University of Washington Press, 2001.
Gordon, M., "APEC's Great Leap Forward?" *The Weekend Australian* November 12–13, 1994.
Goss, J., "Postcolonialism: Subverting Whose Empire?" *Third World Quarterly: Journal of Emerging Areas* vol. 17, no. 2, 1996.
Goss, J. and Burch, D., "From Agricultural Modernisation to Agri-Food Globalisation: The Waning of National Development in Thailand" *Third World Quarterly: Journal of Emerging Areas* vol. 22, no. 6, 2001.

Gowan, P., *The Global Gamble: Washington's Faustian Bid for World Dominance*, London: Verso, 1999.

—— "After America?" *New Left Review (II)* no. 13, 2002.

Graham, W. G., "Communism in South Asia" *The Pacific Spectator: A Journal of Interpretation* vol. 5, no. 2, 1951.

Gray, J., *False Dawn: The Delusions of Global Capitalism*, 2nd edn, New York: New Press, 2000.

—— "Goodbye to Globalisation" *The Guardian Weekly* March 14, 2001.

—— "The Decay of the Free Market" *New Statesman* March 25, 2002.

Green, D. P. and Shapiro, I., *Pathologies of Rational Choice Theory: A Critique of Applications in Political Science*, New Haven: Yale University Press, 1994.

Greenfield, G., "Fragmented Visions of Asia's Next Tiger: Vietnam and the Pacific Century" in M. T. Berger and D. A. Borer, eds, *The Rise of East Asia: Critical Visions of the Pacific Century*, London: Routledge, 1997.

Greenfeld, L., *The Spirit of Capitalism: Nationalism and Economic Growth*, Cambridge, MA: Harvard University Press, 2002.

Griffin, K., "Foreign Aid After the Cold War" *Development and Change* vol. 22, no. 4, October, 1991.

Grimes, W. W., *Unmaking the Japanese Miracle: Macroeconomic Politics, 1985–2000*, Ithaca: Cornell University Press, 2001.

Gunnell, J. G., "The Declination of the 'State' and the Origins of American Pluralism" in J. Farr, J. S. Dryzek and S. T. Leonard, eds, *Political Science in History: Research Programs and Political Traditions*, Cambridge: Cambridge University Press, 1995.

Gupta, A., *Postcolonial Developments: Agriculture in the Making of Modern India*, Durham: Duke University Press, 1998.

Gurr, T. R., "Ethnic Warfare on the Wane" *Foreign Affairs* vol. 79, no. 3, 2000.

Gutteridge, W., *Armed Forces in the New States*, London: Oxford University Press, 1962.

—— *Military Institutions and Power in the New States*, New York: Praeger, 1965.

Guyatt, N., *Another American Century? The United States and the World After 2000*, London: Zed Books, 2000.

Gyohten, T., "Japan and the World Bank" in D. Kapur, J. P. Lewis and R. Webb, eds, *The World Bank: Its First Half Century, Volume 2: Perspectives*, Washington, DC: Brookings Institution, 1997.

Haas, E. B., *Nationalism, Liberalism and Progress: (Volume 1) The Rise and Decline of Nationalism*, Ithaca: Cornell University Press, 1997.

—— *Nationalism, Liberalism and Progress: (Volume 2) The Dismal Fate of New Nations*, Ithaca: Cornell University Press, 2000.

Hadiz, V. R., *Workers and the State in Indonesia*, London: Routledge, 1997.

Haggard, S., *Pathways From the Periphery: The Politics of Growth in the Newly Industrializing Countries*, Ithaca: Cornell University Press, 1990.

Haggard, S., "Business, Politics and Policy in Northeast and Southeast Asia" in A. MacIntyre, ed., *Business and Government in Industrialising Asia*, Sydney: Allen and Unwin, 1994.

Hahn, P. L., *The United States, Great Britain and Egypt, 1945–1956: Strategy and Diplomacy in the Early Cold War*, Chapel Hill: University of North Carolina Press, 1991.

Hale, D. D., "The IMF, Now More Than Ever" *Foreign Affairs*, vol. 77, no. 6, 1998.

Haley, G. T., Tiong, T. C. and Haley, U. C. V., *New Asian Emperors: The Overseas Chinese, their Strategies and Comparative Advantages*, Melbourne: Butterworth-Heinemann, 1998.

Hall, J. W., "Foreword" in M. B. Jansen, ed., *Changing Japanese Attitudes toward Modernization*, Princeton: Princeton University Press, 1965.

—— "Changing Conceptions of the Modernization of Japan" in M. B. Jansen, ed., *Changing Japanese Attitudes toward Modernization*, Princeton: Princeton University Press, 1965.

Hall, R. B., *National Collective Identity: Social Constructs and International Systems*, New York: Columbia University Press, 1999.

Hall, S., "The West and the Rest: Discourse and Power" in S. Hall and B. Gieben, eds, *Formations of Modernity*, Milton Keynes: Open University Press, 1992.

Halliday, F., *The Making of the Second Cold War*, London: Verso, 1986.

Halloran, R., "U.S. Defence Policy: Eastern Threat" *Far Eastern Economic Review* October 18, 2001.

Halpern, N. P., "Creating Socialist Economies: Stalinist Political Economy and the Impact of Ideas" in J. Goldstein and R. O. Keohane, eds, *Ideas and Foreign Policy: Beliefs, Institutions and Political Change*, Ithaca: Cornell University Press, 1993.

Hamada, K., "Keeping Alive the Asian Monetary Fund" *Capital Trends* vol. 3, no. 10, 1998.

Harcourt, M., "India: From Stable Underdevelopment to Turbulent Growth" in J. Ingleson, ed., *Third World Update*, Sydney: University of New South Wales, 1986.

Hardgrave, R. L., Jr, *India Under Pressure: Prospects for Political Stability*, Boulder: Westview, 1984.

Hardt, M. and Negri, A., *Empire*, Cambridge, MA: Harvard University Press, 2000.

Harris, N., *The End of the Third World: Newly Industrializing Countries and the Decline of an Ideology*, London: I. B. Tauris, 1986.

Harrison, S. S., *Korean Endgame: A Strategy for Reunification and U.S. Disengagement*, Princeton: Princeton University Press, 2002.

Harriss, J., Hunter, J. and Lewis, C. M., "Introduction: Development and the Significance of New Institutional Economics" in J. Harriss, J. Hunter and C. M. Lewis, eds, *The New Institutional Economics and Third World Development*, 2nd edn, London: Routledge, 1997.

Hartcher, P., *The Ministry*, New York: HarperCollins, 1997.

Hartcher, P. and Dwyer, M., "East versus West: How the Markets are Uniting Asia Against the US" *The Australian Financial Review* September 27, 1997. Online at http://www.afr.com.au

Hart-Landsberg, M., *The Rush to Development: Economic Change and Political Struggle in South Korea*, New York: Monthly Review Press, 1993.

—— *Korea: Division, Reunification and U.S. Foreign Policy*, New York: Monthly Review Press, 1998.

Harvey, D., *The Condition of Postmodernity: An Enquiry into the Origins of Cultural Change*, London: Basil Blackwell, 1989.

Harvey, R., *The Undefeated: The Rise, Fall and Rise of Greater Japan*, London: Macmillan, 1994.

Hatch, W. and Yamamura, K., *Asia in Japan's Embrace: Building a Regional Production Alliance*, Cambridge: Cambridge University Press, 1996.

Havens, T. R. H., *Fire Across the Sea: The Vietnam War and Japan 1965–1975*, Princeton: Princeton University Press, 1987.

Havinden, M. and Meredith, D., *Colonialism and Development: Britain and its Tropical Colonies 1850–1960*, London: Routledge, 1993.

Hayek, F. A., *The Road to Serfdom*, Chicago: University of Chicago Press, 1994 (first published 1944).

Hefner, R. W., "Introduction: Society and Morality in the New Asian Capitalisms" in R. W. Hefner, ed., *Market Cultures: Society and Morality in the New Asian Capitalisms*, Boulder: Westview, 1998.

Heiss, M. A., *Empire and Nationhood: The United States, Great Britain, and Iranian Oil, 1950–1954*, New York: Columbia University Press, 1997.

Henderson, J. and Appelbaum, R. P., "Situating the State in the East Asian Development Process" in R. P. Appelbaum and J. Henderson, eds, *States and Development in the Asian Pacific Rim*, Newbury Park: Sage, 1992.

Heng, G. and Devan, J., "State Fatherhood: The Politics of Nationalism, Sexuality and Race in Singapore" in A. Parker, M. Russo, D. Sommer and P. Yaeger, eds, *Nationalisms and Sexualities*, London: Routledge, 1992.

Henry, C. M. and Springborg, R., *Globalization and the Politics of Development in the Middle East*, Cambridge: Cambridge University Press, 2001.

Herring, R. J., "Embedded Particularism: India's Failed Developmental State" in M. Woo-Cumings, ed., *The Developmental State*, Ithaca: Cornell University Press, 1999.

Hettne, B., *Development Theory and the Three Worlds*, London: Longman, 1990.

Hewison, K., *Bankers and Bureaucrats: Capital and the Role of the State in Thailand*, New Haven: Yale University Press, 1989.

Hewison, K., Robison, R. and Rodan, G. eds, *Southeast Asia in the 1990s: Authoritarianism, Democracy and Capitalism*, Sydney: Allen and Unwin, 1993.

Heydemann, S., "War, Institutions, and Social Change in the Middle East" in S. Heydemann, ed., *War, Institutions, and Social Change in the Middle East*, Berkeley: University of California Press, 2000.

Higgott, R., "The Asian Economic Crisis: A Study in the Politics of Resentment" *New Political Economy* vol. 3. no. 3, 1998.

Higgott, R. and Robison, R., "Theories of Development and Underdevelopment: Implications for the Study of Southeast Asia" in R. Higgott and R. Robison, eds, *Southeast Asia: Essays in the Political Economy of Structural Change*, London: Routledge and Kegan Paul, 1985.

Hilderbrand, R. C., *Dumbarton Oaks: The Origins of the United Nations and the Search for Postwar Security*, Chapel Hill: University of North Carolina Press, 1990.

Hill, H., *The Indonesian Economy Since 1966: Southeast Asia's Emerging Giant*, Cambridge: Cambridge University Press, 1996.

—— *The Indonesian Economy*, 2nd edn, Cambridge: Cambridge University Press, 2000.

Hilley, J., *Malaysia: Mahathirism, Hegemony and the New Opposition*, London: Zed Books, 2001.

Hirschman, A. O., "The Rise and Decline of Development Economics" in A. O. Hirschman, *Essays in Trespassing: Economics to Politics and Beyond*, Cambridge: Cambridge University Press, 1981.

Hobsbawm, E., *The Age of Empire 1875–1914*, 2nd edn, London: Abacus, 1994.

Hodgson, G. M., *Economics and Evolution: Bringing Life Back into Economics*, Ann Arbor: University of Michigan Press, 1993.

—— *How Economics Forgot History*, London: Routledge, 2001.

Hoffmann, S., *World Disorders: Troubled Peace in the Post-Cold War Era*, Lanham: Rowman and Littlefield, 1998.

Hofheinz, R., Jr and Calder, K. E., *The Eastasia Edge*, New York: Harper and Row, 1982.

Hogan, M. J., *The Marshall Plan: America, Britain, and the Reconstruction of Western Europe, 1947–1952*, 2nd edn, Cambridge: Cambridge University Press, 1989.

—— *A Cross of Iron: Harry S. Truman and the Origins of the National Security State, 1945–1954*, Cambridge: Cambridge University Press, 1998.

Holland, T., "Banking in Asia: Japan" *Far Eastern Economic Review* October 4, 2001.

Hook, G., "Japan and the Construction of Asia-Pacific" in A. Gamble and A. Payne, eds, *Regionalism and World Order*, London: Macmillan, 1996.

Horowitz, I. L. ed., *The Rise and Fall of Project Camelot: Studies in the Relationship between Social Science and Practical Politics*, Cambridge, MA: MIT Press, 1967.

—— *Beyond Empire and Revolution: Militarization and Consolidation in the Third World*, New York: Oxford University Press, 1982.

Horsman, M. and Marshall, A., *After the Nation-State: Citizens, Tribalism and the New World Disorder*, London: HarperCollins, 1994.

Huang, X. ed., *The Political and Economic Transition in East Asia: Strong Market, Weakening State*, Washington, DC: Georgetown University Press, 2000.

Hughes, H. ed., *Achieving Industrialization in East Asia*, Cambridge: Cambridge University Press, 1988.

Hunt, D., *Economic Theories of Development: An Analysis of Competing Paradigms*, Brighton: Harvester Wheatsheaf, 1989.

Hunt, R. A., *Pacification: The American Struggle for Vietnam's Hearts and Minds*, Boulder: Westview, 1995.

Huntington, S. P., *The Soldier and the State: The Theory and Politics of Civil–Military Relations*, Cambridge, MA: Harvard University Press, 1957.

—— ed., *Changing Patterns of Military Politics*, New York: Free Press, 1962.

—— "Political Development and Political Decay" *World Politics* vol. 17, no. 3, 1965.

—— "Social Science and Vietnam" *Asian Survey* vol. 7, no. 8, 1967.

—— *Political Order in Changing Societies*, New Haven: Yale University Press, 1968.

—— "The Bases of Accommodation" *Foreign Affairs* vol. 46, no. 3, 1968.

—— "The U.S. – Decline or Renewal?" *Foreign Affairs* vol. 67, no. 2 (Winter), 1988/1989.

—— "The Clash of Civilizations?" *Foreign Affairs* vol. 72, no. 3, 1993.

—— "The West: Unique, not Universal" *Foreign Affairs* vol. 75, no. 6 (November/December), 1996.

—— *The Clash of Civilizations and the Remaking of World Order*, New York: Simon and Schuster, 1996.

—— "The Erosion of American National Interests" *Foreign Affairs* vol. 76, no. 5 (September/October), 1997.

—— "The Lonely Superpower" *Foreign Affairs* vol. 78, no. 2, 1999.

Huntington, S. P., Crozier M. and Watanuki, J., *The Crisis of Democracy: Report on the Governability of Democracies to the Trilateral Commission*, New York: New York University Press, 1975.

Hutton, W., *The World We're In*, Boston: Little Brown, 2002.

Ikenberry, G. J., "Creating Yesterday's New World Order: Keynesian 'New Thinking' and the Anglo-American Postwar Settlement" in J. Goldstein and R. O. Keohane, eds, *Ideas and Foreign Policy: Beliefs, Institutions and Political Change*, Ithaca: Cornell University Press, 1993.

Inikori, J. E., *Africans and the Industrial Revolution in England: A Study in International Trade and Economic Development*, Cambridge: Cambridge University Press, 2002.

Inoguchi, T. and Okimoto, D. eds, *The Political Economy of Japan*, Stanford: Stanford University Press, 1988.

International Monetary Fund, *Interim Assessment of the World Economic Outlook*, Washington, DC: International Monetary Fund, December 1997.

Iriye, A., "Reischauer, Fairbank and American–Asian Relations" *Diplomatic History* vol. 12, no. 3, 1988.

Ishihara, S., *The Japan That Can Say No: Why Japan Will Be First Among Equals*, New York: Simon and Schuster, 1991.

Islam, I., "Between the State and the Market: The Case for Eclectic Neo-Classical Political Economy" in A. MacIntyre, ed., *Business and Government in Industrialising Asia*, Sydney: Allen and Unwin, 1994.

Islam, I. and Chowdhury, A., *The Political Economy of East Asia: Post-Crisis Debates*, New York: Oxford University Press, 2000.

Jackson, R. H., *Quasi-states: Sovereignty, International Relations and the Third World*, 2nd edn, Cambridge: Cambridge University Press, 1993.

Jalal, A., *The State of Martial Rule: The Origins of Pakistan's Political Economy of Defence*, Cambridge: Cambridge University Press, 1990.

James, W. E., Naya, S. and Meier, G. M., *Asian Development: Economic Success and Policy Lessons*, Madison: University of Wisconsin Press, 1989.

Janelli, R. L. (and D. Yim), *Making Capitalism: The Social and Cultural Construction of a South Korean Conglomerate*, Stanford: Stanford University Press, 1993.

Janowitz, M., *The Military in the Political Development of New Nations: An Essay in Comparative Analysis*, Chicago: University of Chicago Press, 1964.

Jenkins, R., "Learning from the Gang: Are There Lessons for Latin America from East Asia" *Bulletin of Latin American Research* vol. 10, no. 1, 1991.

—— "The Political Economy of Industrialization: A Comparison of Latin American and East Asian Newly Industrializing Countries" *Development and Change* vol. 22, no. 2, 1991.

Jessop, B., *State Theory: Putting Capitalist States in Their Place*, University Park: Pennsylvania University Press, 1990.

—— "Narrating the Future of the National Economy and the National State: Remarks on Remapping Regulation and Reinventing Governance" in G. Steinmetz, ed., *State/Culture: State-Formation after the Cultural Turn*, Ithaca: Cornell University Press, 1999.

—— *The Future of the Capitalist State*, Cambridge: Cambridge University Press, 2003.

Jian, C., *Mao's China and the Cold War*, Chapel Hill: University of North Carolina Press, 2001.

Johnson, C., *MITI and the Japanese Miracle: The Growth of Industrial Policy 1925–1975*, Stanford: Stanford University Press, 1982.

—— "Intellectual Warfare" *The Atlantic Monthly* January, 1995.

—— *Japan: Who Governs? The Rise of the Developmental State*, New York: W. W. Norton, 1995.

—— "The Developmental State: Odyssey of a Concept" in M. Woo-Cumings, ed., *The Developmental State*, Ithaca: Cornell University Press, 1999.

Johnson, J. J. ed., *The Role of the Military in Underdeveloped Countries*, Princeton: Princeton University Press, 1962.

Jones, E. L., *The European Miracle: Environments, Economies and Geopolitics in the History of Europe and Asia*, 2nd edn, Cambridge: Cambridge University Press, 1992.

Kahin, A. R. and Kahin, G. McT., *Subversion as Foreign Policy: The Secret Eisenhower and Dulles Debacle in Indonesia*, New York: New Press, 1995.

Kahin, G. McT., *Nationalism and Revolution in Indonesia*, Ithaca: Cornell University Press, 1952.

—— *The Asian-African Conference, Bandung, Indonesia, April 1955*, Ithaca: Cornell University Press, 1956.

—— ed., *Major Governments of Asia*, 2nd edn, Ithaca: Cornell University Press, 1963.

306 *Bibliography*

—— *Governments and Politics of Southeast Asia*, 2nd edn, Ithaca: Cornell University Press, 1964.

—— *Intervention: How America Became Involved in Vietnam*, New York: Alfred A. Knopf, 1986.

—— *Southeast Asia: A Testament*, London: RoutledgeCurzon, 2003.

Kahin, G. McT. and Lewis, J. W., *The United States in Vietnam*, 2nd edn, New York: Dial Press, 1969.

Kahn, H., "The Confucian Ethic and Economic Growth" in M. A. Seligson, ed., *The Gap Between Rich and Poor: Contending Perspectives on the Political Economy of Development*, Boulder: Westview, 1984.

Kaldor, M., *New and Old Wars: Organized Violence in a Global Era*, 2nd edn, Cambridge: Polity Press, 2001.

Kang, C. S. E., "*Segyehwa* Reform of the South Korean Developmental State" in S. S. Kim, ed., *Korea's Globalization*, Cambridge: Cambridge University Press, 2000.

Kang, D. C., *Crony Capitalism: Corruption and Development in South Korea and the Philippines*, Cambridge: Cambridge University Press, 2002.

Kaplan, R. D., *Balkan Ghosts: A Journey through History*, New York: Vintage, 1994.

—— *The Ends of the Earth: A Journey to the Frontiers of Anarchy*, New York: Vintage, 1997.

—— *The Coming Anarchy: Shattering the Dreams of the Post-Cold War*, New York: Vintage, 2000.

—— "Looking the World In The Eye" *The Atlantic Monthly* vol. 288, no. 5, 2001.

—— *Soldiers of God: With Islamic Warriors in Afghanistan and Pakistan*, 2nd edn, New York: Vintage, 2001.

—— *Warrior Politics: Why Leadership Demands a Pagan Ethos*, New York: Random House, 2001.

Kapur, D., Lewis, J. and Webb, R., *The World Bank: Its First Half-Century, Volume 1: History*, Washington, DC: Brookings Institution, 1997.

Karsh, E. and Karsh, I., *Empires of the Sand: The Struggle for Mastery in the Middle East, 1789–1923*, Cambridge, MA: Harvard University Press, 1999.

Katz, R., *Japan, the System that Soured: The Rise and Fall of the Japanese Economic Miracle*, Armonk: M. E. Sharpe, 1998.

Kearns, R. L., *Zaibatsu America: How Japanese Firms Are Colonizing Vital U.S. Industries*, New York: Free Press, 1992.

Keegan, W., *The Spectre of Capitalism: The Future of the World Economy After the Fall of Communism*, 2nd edn, London: Vintage, 1993.

Kelly, D., *Japan and the Reconstruction of East Asia*, Basingstoke: Palgrave, 2002.

Kelly, J. D. and Kaplan, M., *Represented Communities: Fiji and World Decolonization*, Chicago: University of Chicago Press, 2001.

Kennan, G. F., "Review of Current Trends, U.S. Foreign Policy" PPS/23 (Top Secret) in *Department of State, Foreign Relations of the United States, 1948*, Washington, DC: Government Printing Office, 1976.

Kennedy, P., *The Rise and Fall of the Great Powers: Economic Change and Military Conflict 1500 to 2000*, 2nd edn, London: HarperCollins, 1989 (first published 1987).

—— "Maintaining American Power: From Injury to Recovery" in S. Talbott and N. Chanda, eds, *The Age of Terror: America and the World After September 11*, Oxford: Perseus Press, 2001.

Kenski, H. C. and Kenski, M. G., *Teaching Political Development and Modernization at American Universities: A Survey*, Tucson: University of Arizona Press, 1974.

Khilnani, S., *The Idea of India*, New York: Farrar Straus Giroux, 1997.

Khoo, B. T., *Paradoxes of Mahathirism: An Intellectual Biography of Mahathir Mohamad*, Kuala Lumpur: Oxford University Press, 1995.

Khoo, K. J., "The Grand Vision: Mahathir and Modernisation" in J. S. Kahn and F. Loh Kok Wah, eds, *Fragmented Vision: Culture and Politics in Contemporary Malaysia*, Sydney: Allen and Unwin, 1992.

Kim, K.-D., "Confucianism and Capitalist Development in East Asia" in L. Sklair, ed., *Capitalism and Development*, London: Routledge, 1994.

Kim, K. S. and Roemer, M., *Growth and Structural Transformation* (Studies in the Modernization of the Republic of Korea: 1945–1975), Cambridge, MA: Harvard University Press, 1979.

Kim, S. S., "Korea and Globalization (*Segyehwa*): A Framework for Analysis" in S. S. Kim, ed., *Korea's Globalization*, Cambridge: Cambridge University Press, 2000.

King, D. Y., "Indonesia's New Order as a Bureaucratic Polity, a Neopatrimonial Regime, or a Bureaucratic-Authoritarian Regime: What Difference Does It Make?" in B. Anderson and A. Kahin, eds, *Interpreting Indonesian Politics: Thirteen Contributions to the Debate*, Ithaca: Cornell Modern Indonesia Project, Cornell University, 1982.

Kingston-Mann, E., *In Search of the True West: Culture, Economics and Problems of Russian Development*, Princeton: Princeton University Press, 1999.

Knutsen, T. L., *The Rise and Fall of World Orders*, Manchester: Manchester University Press, 1999.

Kofas, J. V., "Stabilization and Class Conflict: The State Department, the IMF and the IBRD in Chile, 1952–1958" *The International History Review* vol. 21, no. 2 (June), 1999.

Koh, T. T. B., *The United States and East Asia: Conflict and Co-operation*, Singapore: Institute of Policy Studies, 1995.

Kohli, A., *The State and Poverty in India: The Politics of Reform*, London: Cambridge University Press, 1987.

Kolko, G., *Confronting the Third World: United States Foreign Policy 1945–1980*, New York: Pantheon Press, 1988.

—— *Anatomy of A War: Vietnam, the United States and the Modern Historical Experience*, 2nd edn, New York: New Press, 1994.

Komer, R. W., *Bureaucracy At War: U.S. Performance in the Vietnam Conflict*, Boulder: Westview, 1986.

Koo, H. and Kim, E. M., "The Developmental State and Capital Accumulation in South Korea" in R. P. Appelbaum and J. Henderson, eds, *States and Development in the Asian Pacific Rim*, Newbury Park: Sage, 1992.

Korhonen, P., "The Theory of the Flying Geese Pattern of Development and its Interpretations" *Journal of Peace Research* vol. 31, no. 1, 1994.

—— "The Pacific Age in World History" *Journal of World History* vol. 7, no. 1, 1996.

—— *Japan and Asia Pacific Integration: Pacific Romances 1968–1996*, London: Routledge, 1998.

Krueger, A. O., "Asian Trade and Growth Lessons" *American Economic Review* vol. 80, no. 2, 1990.

Krugman, P., *Strategic Trade Policy and the New International Economics*, Cambridge, MA: MIT Press, 1986.

—— "The Myth of Asia's Miracle" *Foreign Affairs* vol. 73, no. 6, 1994.

—— *Pop Internationalism*, 2nd edn, Cambridge, MA: MIT Press, 1997.

—— "Saving Asia: It's Time to Get Radical" *Fortune* September 7, 1998.

—— "The Fall and Rise of Development Economics" in P. Krugman, *Development, Geography and Economic Theory*, 2nd edn, Cambridge, MA: MIT Press, 1999.

Kupchan, C., *The End of the American Era: U.S. Foreign Policy After the Cold War*, New York: Alfred A. Knopf, 2002.

Kwon, J., "The East Asian Challenge to Neoclassical Orthodoxy" *World Development* vol. 22, no. 4, 1994.

LaFeber, W., *Inevitable Revolutions: The United States in Central America*, 2nd edn, New York: W. W. Norton, 1993.

—— *The Clash: U.S.–Japanese Relations throughout History*, New York: W. W. Norton, 1997.

Lafitte, G., "Reorientations" *Arena Magazine* no. 12, 1994.

Lague, D., "Banking in Asia: China" *Far Eastern Economic Review* October 4, 2001.

—— "China: On the Road to Ruin" *Far Eastern Economic Review* November 14, 2002.

Lake, A., "From Containment to Enlargement" *U.S. Department of State Dispatch* vol. 4, no. 39 (September 27), 1993.

Lal, D., *The Poverty of Development Economics*, 2nd edn, Cambridge, MA: Harvard University Press, 1985.

—— *Unintended Consequences: The Impact of Factor Endowments, Culture and Politics in Long-Run Economic Performance*, Cambridge, MA: MIT Press, 1998.

Lall, S., "'The East Asian Miracle' Study: Does the Bell Toll for Industrial Strategy?" *World Development* vol. 22, no. 4, 1994.

—— *Learning from the Asian Tigers: Studies in Technology and Industrial Policy*, London: Macmillan, 1996.

Lampton, D. M., *Same Bed, Different Dreams: Managing U.S.–China Relations 1989–2000*, Berkeley: University of California Press, 2001.

Landers, P., "American Accents" *Far Eastern Economic Review* July 31, 1997.

Landes, D. S., *The Unbound Prometheus: Technological Change and Industrial Development in Western Europe from 1750 to the Present*, Cambridge: Cambridge University Press, 1969.

—— *The Wealth and Poverty of Nations; Why Some Are So Rich and Some So Poor*, New York: W. W. Norton, 1998.

Larrain, J., *Theories of Development: Capitalism, Colonialism and Dependency*, London: Polity Press, 1989.

Latham, M. E., "Ideology, Social Science and Destiny: Modernization and the Kennedy-Era Alliance for Progress" *Diplomatic History* vol. 22, no. 2, 1998.

—— *Modernization as Ideology: American Social Science and "Nation-Building" in the Kennedy Era*, Chapel Hill: University of North Carolina Press, 2000.

Latham, R., *The Liberal Moment: Modernity, Security and the Making of Postwar International Order*, New York: Columbia University Press, 1997.

Latouche, S., *The Westernization of the World: The Significance, Scope and Limits of the Drive towards Global Uniformity*, Cambridge: Polity Press, 1996.

Lee, J. M., *Colonial Development and Good Government: A Study of the Ideas Expressed by the British Official Classes in Planning Decolonization 1939–1964*, Oxford: Clarendon Press, 1967.

—— *The Colonial Office, War, and Development Policy: Organisation and the Planning of A Metropolitan Initiative, 1939–1945*, London: Institute of Commonwealth Studies, 1982.

Leffler, M. P., *A Preponderance of Power: National Security, the Truman Administration and the Cold War*, Stanford: Stanford University Press, 1992.

Leftwich, A., *States of Development: On the Primacy of Politics in Development*, Cambridge: Polity Press, 2000.

Leger, J. M., "The Boom: How Asians Started the 'Pacific Century' Early" *Far Eastern Economic Review* November 24, 1994.

LeoGrande, W. M., *Our Own Backyard: The United States in Central America, 1977–1992*, Chapel Hill: University of North Carolina Press, 1998.

Lerner, D., *The Passing of Traditional Society: Modernizing the Middle East*, New York: Free Press, 1958.

Leslie, S. W., *The Cold War and American Science: The Military–Industrial–Academic Complex at MIT and Stanford*, New York: Columbia University Press, 1993.

Lev, D. S., *The Transition to Guided Democracy: Indonesian Politics 1957–1959*, Ithaca: Cornell Modern Indonesia Project Monograph, 1966.

Lewis, W. A., "Economic Development with Unlimited Supplies of Labour" *Manchester School* May 22, 1954.

—— *The Theory of Economic Growth*, London: Allen and Unwin, 1955.

—— "Development Economics in the 1950s" in G. M. Meier and D. Seers, eds, *Pioneers in Development*, Oxford: Oxford University Press for the World Bank, 1984.

—— "The State of Development Theory" *American Economic Review* vol. 74, no. 1, 1984.

Leys, C., "Samuel Huntington and the End of Classical Modernization Theory" in H. Alavi and T. Shanin, eds, *Introduction to the Sociology of "Developing Societies"*, London: Macmillan, 1983.

—— *The Rise and Fall of Development Theory*, Bloomington: Indiana University Press, 1996.

Lind, M., "Free Trade Fallacy" *Prospect* no. 82 (January), 2003.

Linder, S. B., *The Pacific Century: Economic and Political Consequences of Asian-Pacific Dynamism*, Stanford: Stanford University Press, 1986.

List, F., *The National System of Political Economy*, London: Longmans, Green and Company, 1916 (first published 1844).

Little, I. M. D., "An Economic Reconnaissance" in W. Galenson, ed., *Economic Growth and Structural Change in Taiwan: The Post-War Experience of the Republic of China*, Ithaca: Cornell University Press, 1979.

—— "The Experiences and Causes of Labour-Intensive Development in Korea, Taiwan Province, Hong Kong and Singapore and the Possibilities of Emulation" in E. Lee, ed., *Export Processing Zones and Industrial Employment in Asia*, Bangkok: International Labour Organization/Artep, 1981.

—— *Economic Development: Theory, Policy and International Relations*, New York: Basic Books, A Twentieth Century Fund Book, 1982.

Litwak, R. S., *Détente and the Nixon Doctrine: American Foreign Policy and the Pursuit of Stability 1969–1976*, 2nd edn, Cambridge: Cambridge University Press, 1986.

Lizée, P. P., *Peace, Power and Resistance in Cambodia: Global Governance and the Failure of International Conflict Resolution*, London: Macmillan, 2000.

Lockwood, W. W. ed., *The State and Economic Enterprise in Japan*, Princeton: Princeton University Press, 1965.

—— "Japan's New Capitalism" in W. W. Lockwood, ed., *The State and Economic Enterprise in Japan*, Princeton: Princeton University Press, 1965.

Lodge, G. C. and Vogel, E. F. eds, *Ideology and National Competitiveness: An Analysis of Nine Countries*, Boston: Harvard Business School Press, 1987.

Loewenstein, K., "Report on the Research Panel on Comparative Government" *American Political Science Review* vol. 38, no. 2, 1944.

Louis, W. R., *The British Empire in the Middle East 1945–1951: Arab Nationalism, the United States and Postwar Imperialism*, Oxford: Clarendon Press, 1984.

Love, J. L., *Crafting the Third World: Theorizing Underdevelopment in Rumania and Brazil*, Stanford: Stanford University Press, 1996.

Lovell, J. P. and Kim, C. I. E., "The Military and Political Change in Asia" in H. Bienen, ed., *The Military and Modernization*, Chicago: Aldine Atherton, 1971.

Low, D. A., *Eclipse of Empire*, Cambridge: Cambridge University Press, 1991.

—— *The Egalitarian Moment: Asia and Africa 1950–1980*, Cambridge: Cambridge University Press, 1996.

Lubeck, P. M., "Malaysian Industrialization, Ethnic Divisions and the NIC Model: The Limits of Replication" in R. P. Appelbuam and J. Henderson, eds, *States and Development in the Asian Pacific Rim*, Newbury Park: Sage, 1992.

Lundestad, G., *"Empire" By Integration: The United States and European Integration*, New York: Oxford University Press, 1998.

—— *East, West, North, South: Major Developments in International Politics Since 1945*, 4th edn, New York: Oxford University Press, 1999.

Lustig, N., *Mexico: The Remaking of an Economy*, Washington, DC: Brookings Institution, 1998.

McBeth, J., "The Danger Within" *Far Eastern Economic Review* September 27, 2001.

McBeth, J. and Vatikiotis, M., "Indonesia: An About Turn on the Military" *Far Eastern Economic Review* April 25, 2002.

McCarthy, J., *The Ottoman Peoples and the End of Empire*, New York: Oxford University Press, 2001.

McCaughey, R. A., *International Studies and Academic Enterprise: A Chapter in the Enclosure of American Learning*, New York: Columbia University Press, 1984.

McCord, W., *The Dawn of the Pacific Century: Implications for Three Worlds of Development*, New Brunswick: Transaction Publishers, 1991.

McCormick, T. J., *America's Half Century: United States Foreign Policy in the Cold War*, Baltimore: Johns Hopkins University Press, 1989.

Macfarlane, A., *The Origins of English Individualism: The Family, Property and Social Transition*, Oxford: Blackwell, 1978.

—— *The Culture of Capitalism*, Oxford: Blackwell, 1987.

—— "The Cradle of Capitalism: The Case of England" in J. Baechler, J. A. Hall and M. Mann, eds, *Europe and the Rise of Capitalism*, 2nd edn, Oxford: Basil Blackwell, 1989.

—— *The Riddle of the Modern World: Of Liberty, Wealth and Equality*, Basingstoke: Palgrave, 2001.

MacFarquhar, R., "Demolition Man" *The New York Review of Books* vol. 44, no. 5, 1997.

McGlothlen, R. L., *Controlling the Waves: Dean Acheson and U.S. Foreign Policy in Asia*, New York: W. W. Norton, 1993.

MacIntyre, A., "Business, Government and Development: Northeast and Southeast Asian Experience" in A. MacIntyre, ed., *Business and Government in Industrialising Asia*, Sydney: Allen and Unwin, 1994.

—— "South-East Asia and the Political Economy of APEC" in G. Rodan, K. Hewison and R. Robison, eds, *The Political Economy of South-East Asia: An Introduction*, Melbourne: Oxford University Press, 1997.

McMahon, R. J., *Colonialism and Cold War: The United States and the Struggle for Indonesian Independence 1945–1949*, Ithaca: Cornell University Press, 1981.

—— *The Cold War on the Periphery: The United States, India and Pakistan*, New York: Columbia University Press, 1994.

—— "U.S.–Vietnamese Relations: A Historiographical Survey" in W. I. Cohen, ed., *Pacific Passage: The Study of American–East Asian Relations on the Eve of the Twenty-First Century*, New York: Columbia University Press, 1996.

—— *The Limits of Empire: The United States and Southeast Asia since World War II*, New York: Columbia University Press, 1999.

McMichael, P., "Rethinking Comparative Analysis in a Post-Develolpmentalist Context" *International Social Science Journal* no. 133, 1992.

—— *Development and Social Change: A Global Perspective*, 2nd edn, Thousand Oaks: Pine Forge Press, 2000.

McNamara, R. S., *One Hundred Countries, Two Billion People: The Dimensions of Development*, New York: Henry Holt, 1973.

McWilliam, M., *The Development Business: A History of the Commonwealth Development Corporation*, London: Palgrave, 2001.

McWilliams, W. C. ed., *Garrisons and Governments: Politics and the Military in New States*, San Francisco: Chandler, 1967.

Magenda, B., "Ethnicity and State-Building in Indonesia: The Cultural Base of the New Order" in R. Guidieri, F. Pellizzi and S. J. Tambiah, eds, *Ethnicities and Nations: Processes of Interethnic Relations in Latin America, Southeast Asia and the Pacific*, Austin: University of Texas Press, 1988.

Mahathir, M., *The Malay Dilemma*, 2nd edn, Kuala Lumpur: Federal Publishers, 1982.

—— *A New Deal for Asia*, Subang Jaya: Pelanduk Publications, 1999.

—— "Globalization: Challenges and Impact on Asia" in F.-J. Richter and P. C. M. Mar, eds, *Recreating Asia: Visions for a New Century*, Singapore: John Wiley and Sons, 2002.

Mahathir, M. and Ishihara, S., *The Voice of Asia: Two Leaders Discuss the Coming Century*, Tokyo: Kodansha International, 1995.

—— *The Asia That Can Say No: A Policy to Combat Europe and America* cited and discussed in R. McGregor, "Mahathir Fumes as Japan Plays Hard to Get" *The Weekend Australian* November 12–13, 1994.

—— "East Beats West" *Asiaweek* September 8, 1995.

Mahbubani, K., "The Dangers of Decadence: What the Rest Can Teach the West" *Foreign Affairs* vol. 72, no. 4, 1993.

—— "The Pacific Way" *Foreign Affairs* vol. 74, no. 1, 1995.

Mann, M., *The Sources of Social Power Volume I: A History of Power from the Beginning to A.D. 1760*, Cambridge: Cambridge University Press, 1986.

—— *The Sources of Social Power Volume II: The Rise of Classes and Nation-States, 1760–1914*, Cambridge: Cambridge University Press, 1993.

Martinussen, J., *Society, State and Market: A Guide to Competing Theories of Development*, London: Zed Books, 1997.

Marx, K. and Engels, F., *The Communist Manifesto*, New York: Penguin, 1986 (this translation first published 1888).

Mazower, M., *Dark Continent: Europe's Twentieth Century*, London: Allen Lane, 1998.

Mearsheimer, J. J., "The Future of the American Pacifier" *Foreign Affairs* vol. 80, no. 5, 2001.

—— *The Tragedy of Great Power Politics*, New York: W. W. Norton, 2001.

Mehmet, O., *Westernizing the Third World: The Eurocentricity of Economic Development Theories*, 2nd edn, London: Routledge, 1999.

Meier, G. M., and Seers, D. eds, *Pioneers in Development*, Oxford: Oxford University Press for the World Bank, 1984.

Meier, G. M., Stiglitz, J. E. and Stern, N. eds, *The Frontiers of Development Economics: The Future in Perspective*, New York: Oxford University Press, 2000.

Menzel, U., "The Newly Industrialising Countries of East Asia: Imperialist Continuity or a Case of Catching Up?" in W. J. Mommsen and J. Osterhammel, eds, *Imperialism and After: Continuities and Discontinuities*, London: Allen and Unwin, 1986.

Merrill, D., *Bread and the Ballot: The United States and India's Economic Development, 1947–1963*, Chapel Hill: University of North Carolina Press, 1990.

Miliband, R., *The State in Capitalist Society*, London: Weidenfeld and Nicolson, 1969.

Millikan, M. F. and Blackmer, D. L. M. eds, *The Emerging Nations: Their Growth and United States Policy*, Boston: Little, Brown and Company, 1961.

Minns, J., "Of Miracles and Models: The Rise and Decline of the Developmental State in South Korea" *Third World Quarterly: Journal of Emerging Areas* vol. 22, no. 6, 2001.

Mirowski, P., "Doing What Comes Naturally: Four Metanarratives on What Metaphors Are For" in P. Mirowski, ed., *Natural Images in Economic Thought: "Markets Read in Tooth and Claw"*, Cambridge: Cambridge University Press, 1994.

Mitchell, T., "The Limits of the State: Beyond Statist Approaches and their Critics" *American Political Science Review* vol. 85, no. 1 (March), 1991.

—— "Society, Economy, and the State Effect" in G. Steinmetz, ed., *State/Culture: State-Formation after the Cultural Turn*, Ithaca: Cornell University Press, 1999.

Mittelman, J. H., "The Globalization Challenge: Surviving at the Margins" *Third World Quarterly: Journal of Emerging Areas* vol. 15, no. 3, 1994.

—— *The Globalization Syndrome: Transformation and Resistance*, Princeton: Princeton University Press, 2000.

Miyoshi, M., "A Borderless World? From Colonialism to Transnationalism and the Decline of the Nation-State" *Critical Inquiry* vol. 19, no. 4, 1993.

Moertopo, A., *Some Basic Thoughts on the Acceleration and Modernization of 25 Years' Development*, Jakarta: Centre for Strategic and International Studies, 1972.

Mokyr, J., *The Lever of Riches: Technological Creativity and Economic Progress*, New York: Oxford University Press, 1990.

Moore, B., Jr, *Social Origins of Dictatorship and Democracy: Lord and Peasant in the Making of the Modern World*, Boston: Beacon Press, 1966.

Moore, D., "Neo-Liberal Globalisation and the Triple Crisis of 'Modernisation' in Africa: Zimbabwe, The Democratic Republic of the Congo and South Africa" *Third World Quarterly: Journal of Emerging Areas* vol. 22, no. 6, 2001.

Moore, D. B. and Schmitz, G. J. eds, *Debating Development Discourse: Institutional and Popular Perspectives*, London: Macmillan, 1995.

Morawetz, D., *Twenty-Five Years of Economic Development 1950–1975*, Baltimore: Johns Hopkins University Press for the World Bank, 1977.

Morgan, D. J., *The Official History of Colonial Development* (5 volumes), London: Macmillan, 1980.

Morishima, M., *Why has Japan Succeeded? Western Technology and the Japanese Ethos*, 2nd edn, Cambridge: Cambridge University Press, 1989.

—— *Japan at a Deadlock*, London: Macmillan, 2000.

Morley, J. W. ed., *Dilemmas of Growth in Prewar Japan*, Princeton: Princeton University Press, 1971.

Morris-Suzuki, T., *A History of Japanese Economic Thought*, 2nd edn, London: Routledge, 1991.

—— *The Technological Transformation of Japan: From the Seventeenth to the Twenty-First Century*, Cambridge: Cambridge University Press, 1994.

Morse, E. L. and Richard, J., "The Battle for Energy Dominance" *Foreign Affairs* vol. 81, no. 2, 2002.

Mortimer, R., *Showcase State: The Illusion of Indonesia's "Accelerated Modernisation"*, Sydney: Angus and Robertson, 1973.

Mortimer, R. A., *The Third World Coalition in World Politics*, Boulder: Westview, 1984.

Mosher, S. W., *Hegemon: China's Plan to Dominate Asia and the World*, San Francisco: Encounter Books, 2000.

Mosley, P., Harrigan, J. and Toye, J., *Aid and Power: The World Bank and Policy-based Lending* (volume 1: Analysis and Policy Proposals), London: Routledge, 1991.

—— *Aid and Power: The World Bank and Policy-Based Lending* (volume 2: Case Studies), London: Routledge, 1991.

Moulder, F. V., *Japan, China and the Modern World Economy: Toward a Reinterpretation of East Asian Development ca. 1600 to ca. 1918*, 2nd edn, Cambridge: Cambridge University Press, 1979.

Munro-Kua, A., *Authoritarian Populism in Malaysia*, London: Macmillan, 1996.

Muravchik, J., *Exporting Democracy: Fulfilling America's Destiny*, Washington, DC: American Enterprise Institute, 1991.

Murphy, D., "The Mod Squad" *Far Eastern Economic Review* August 19, 1999.

—— "Urban Poverty: Nothing More to Lose" *Far Eastern Economic Review* November 7, 2002.

Murphy, D. and Lawrence, S. V., "Beijing Hopes to Gain from U.S. Raids on Afghanistan" *Far Eastern Economic Review* October 4, 2001.

Muscat, R. J., *Thailand and the United States: Development, Security, and Foreign Aid*, New York: Columbia University Press, 1990.

Myrdal, G., *Economic Theory and Underdeveloped Regions*, New York: Harper, 1957.

—— *Asian Drama: An Inquiry into the Poverty of Nations*, volume I, London: Penguin, in association with the Twentieth Century Fund, 1968.

—— "International Inequality and Foreign Aid in Retrospect" in G. M. Meier and D. Seers, eds, *Pioneers in Development*, Oxford: Oxford University Press for the World Bank, 1984.

Nafziger, E. W., *Learning from the Japanese: Japan's Pre-War Development and the Third World*, Armonk: M. E. Sharpe, 1995.

Naisbitt, J., *Megatrends Asia: The Eight Asian Megatrends that are Changing the World*, London: Nicholas Brealy, 1995.

Nau, H. R., *The Myth of America's Decline: Leading the World Economy into the 1990s*, New York: Oxford University Press, 1990.

Needell, A., "Project Troy and the Cold War Annexation of the Social Sciences" in C. Simpson, ed., *Universities and Empire: Money and Politics in the Social Sciences During the Cold War*, New York: New Press, 1998.

Nesadurai, H. E. S., "APEC: a tool for US regional domination?" *The Pacific Review* vol. 9, no. 1, 1996.

Newman, R. P., *Owen Lattimore and the "Loss" of China*, Berkeley: University of California Press, 1992.

Nolan, P., *China's Rise, Russia's Fall: Politics, Economics and Planning in the Transition from Stalinism*, London: Macmillan, 1995.

—— *China and the Global Business Revolution*, Basingstoke: Palgrave, 2001.

—— *China and the Global Economy*, Basingstoke: Palgrave, 2001.

Noland, M., *Avoiding the Apocalypse: The Future of the Two Koreas*, Washington, DC: Institute for International Economics, 2000.

North, D. C., *Structure and Change in Economic History*, New York: W. W. Norton, 1981.

—— *Institutional Change and Economic Performance*, Cambridge: Cambridge University Press, 1990.

—— *Understanding the Process of Economic Change*, London: Institute of Economic Affairs, 1999.

North, D. C. and Paul, R., *The Rise of the Western World: A New Economic History*, Cambridge: Cambridge University Press, 1973.

Now, "Indian Plan, U.S. Model", December 25, 1964.

Nye, J. S., Jr, *Bound to Lead: The Changing Nature of American Power*, New York: Basic Books, 1990.

—— "The Case Against Containment: Treat China Like an Enemy and That's What It Will Be" *Global Beat* June 22, 1998. Online at http://www.nyu.edu/globalbeat/asia/china/06221998nye.html

—— "America's Power: The New Rome Meets the New Barbarians" *The Economist* March 23, 2002.

—— *The Paradox of American Power: Why the World's Only Superpower Can't Go It Alone*, New York: Oxford University Press, 2002.

Nzongola-Ntalaja, G., *The Congo From Leopold to Kabila: A People's History*, London: Zed Books, 2002.

O'Brien, D. C., "Modernization, Order, and the Erosion of a Democratic Ideal: American Political Science 1960–1970" in D. Lehmann, ed., *Development Theory: Four Critical Essays*, London: Frank Cass, 1979.

O'Donnell, G. A., *Modernization and Bureaucratic-Authoritarianism: Studies in South American Politics*, Berkeley: University of California Institute of International Studies, 1973.

—— "Modernization and Military Coups: Theory, Comparisons and the Argentine Case" in A. F. Lowenthal, ed., *Armies and Politics in Latin America*, New York: Holmes and Meier, 1976.

—— "Corporatism and the Question of the State" in J. M. Malloy, ed., *Authoritarianism and Corporatism in Latin America*, Pittsburgh: University of Pittsburgh Press, 1977.

—— "Reflections on the Patterns of Change in the Bureaucratic-Authoritarian State" *Latin American Research Review* vol. 13, no. 1, 1978.

—— "Tensions in the Bureaucratic-Authoritarian State and the Question of Democracy" in D. Collier, ed., *The New Authoritarianism in Latin America*, New York: Columbia University Press, 1979.

—— *Bureaucratic-Authoritarianism: Argentina, 1966–1973, in Comparative Perspective*, Berkeley: University of California Press, 1988.

Office of the President of the United States, *A National Security Strategy of Engagement and Enlargement*, Washington, DC: US Government Printing Office, 1996. Online at http://www.fas.org/spp/military/docops/national/1996stra.htm

Ohmae, K., *The End of the Nation-State: The Rise of Regional Economies*, London: Harper-Collins, 1995.

Oi, J., *Rural China Takes Off: Institutional Foundations of Economic Reform*, Berkeley: University of California Press, 1999.

Okimoto, D., *Between MITI and the Market: Japanese Industrial Policy for High Technology*, Stanford: Stanford University Press, 1989.

Okimoto, D. I. and Rohlen, T. P. eds, *Inside the Japanese System: Readings on Contemporary Society and Political Economy*, Stanford: Stanford University Press, 1988.

Ong, A. "Chinese Modernities: Narratives of Nation and of Capitalism" in A. Ong and D. Nonini, eds, *Ungrounded Empires: The Cultural Politics of Modern Chinese Transnationalism*, London: Routledge, 1997.

Overholt, W. H., *The Rise of China: How Economic Reform is Creating a New Superpower*, New York: W. W. Norton, 1994.

Owen, R., "Egypt" in R. Chase, E. Hill and P. Kennedy, eds, *The Pivotal States: A New Framework for U.S. Policy in the Developing World*, New York: W. W. Norton, 1999.

Pacific Rim Review, "Asian Crisis – Global Crisis", December 20, 1997. Online at http://pacificrim.bx.com/articles/12–20asian_crisis.htm

Packenham, R. A., *Liberal America and the Third World: Political Development Ideas in Foreign Aid and Social Science*, Princeton: Princeton University Press, 1973.

—— *The Dependency Movement: Scholarship and Politics in Development Studies*, Cambridge, MA: Harvard University Press, 1992.

Paige, J. M., *Agrarian Revolution: Social Movements and Export Agriculture in the Underdeveloped World*, New York: Free Press, 1978.

—— "The East Asian Miracle: An Introduction" *World Development* vol. 22, no. 4, 1994.

—— *Coffee and Power: Revolution and the Rise of Democracy in Central America*, Cambridge, MA: Harvard University Press, 1997.

Palat, R. A., "Pacific Century: Myth or Reality?" *Theory and Society* vol. 25, no. 3, 1996.

Panitch, L., "The New Imperial State" *New Left Review (II)* no. 2 (March–April), 2000.

Pastor, R. A., *Latin America's Debt Crisis: Adjusting to the Past or Planning for the Future*, Boulder: Lynne Rienner, 1987.

Patrick, H., "The Future of the Japanese Economy: Output and Labor Productivity" *Journal of Japanese Studies* vol. 3, no. 2, 1977.

Patrick, H. and Rosovsky, H., "Japan's Economic Performance: An Overview" in H. Patrick and H. Rosovsky, eds, *Asia's New Giant: How the Japanese Economy Works*, Washington, DC: Brookings Institution, 1976.

—— "Prospects for the Future and Some Other Implications" in H. Patrick and H. Rosovsky, eds, *Asia's New Giant: How the Japanese Economy Works*, Washington, DC: Brookings Institution, 1976.

Pauker, G. J., "Southeast Asia as Problem Area in the Next Decade" *World Politics* vol. 11, no. 3, 1959.

—— "Indonesia: The Age of Reason?" *Asian Survey* vol. 8, no. 2, 1968.

Payer, C., *The World Bank: A Critical Analysis*, New York: Monthly Review Press, 1982.

Payne, A. and Gamble, A., "Introduction: The Political Economy of Regionalism and World Order" in A. Gamble and A. Payne, eds, *Regionalism and World Order*, London: Macmillan, 1996.

Pearce, K. C., *Rostow, Kennedy, and the Rhetoric of Foreign Aid*, East Lansing: Michigan State University Press, 2001.

Peattie, M. R., "Japanese Attitudes towards Colonialism, 1895–1945" in R. H. Myers and M. R. Peattie, eds, *The Japanese Colonial Empire, 1895–1945*, Princeton: Princeton University Press, 1984.

Pempel, T. J., "Regional Ups, Regional Downs" in T. J. Pempel, ed., *The Politics of the Asian Economic Crisis*, Ithaca: Cornell University Press, 1999.

Pender, J., "From 'Structural Adjustment' to 'Comprehensive Development Framework': Conditionality Transformed?" *Third World Quarterly: Journal of Emerging Areas* vol. 22, no. 3 (June), 2001.

Peng, Q., Yang, M. and Xu, D., *Zhongguo weishenmo shuo bu (Why Does China Say No?)*, Beijing: Xinshijie chubanshe, 1996;

Perelman, M., *The Invention of Capitalism: Classical Political Economy and the Secret History of Primitive Accumulation*, Durham: Duke University Press, 2000.

Perkins, D., "There Are At Least Three Models of East Asian Development" *World Development* vol. 22, no. 4, 1994.

Perkins, D. H., *China: Asia's Next Economic Giant?*, 2nd edn, Seattle: University of Washington Press, 1989.

Petras, J. and Morley, M., *Empire or Republic? American Global Power and Domestic Decay*, New York: Routledge, 1995.

Philpott, D., *Revolutions in Sovereignty: How Ideas Shaped Modern International Relations*, Princeton: Princeton University Press, 2001.

Philpott, S., *Rethinking Indonesia: Postcolonial Theory, Authoritarianism and Identity*, London: Macmillan, 2000.

Pinches, M., "Cultural Relations, Class and the New Rich in Asia" in M. Pinches, ed., *Culture and Privilege in Capitalist Asia*, London: Routledge, 1999.

Polanyi, K., *The Great Transformation*, Boston: Beacon Press, 1944.

Pomeranz, K., *The Great Divergence: China, Europe and the Making of the Modern World Economy*, Princeton: Princeton University Press, 2001.

Popper, K. R., *The Open Society and Its Enemies: Volume I Plato*, 5th edn, Princeton: Princeton University Press, 1966.

—— *The Open Society and Its Enemies: Volume II Hegel and Marx*, 5th edn, Princeton: Princeton University Press, 1966.

Porter, M., *The Competitive Advantage of Nations*, London: Macmillan, 1990.

Poulantzas, N., *Political Power and Social Classes*, London: Verso, 1973 (first published in French in 1968 as *Pouvoir politique et classes sociales*).

Powelson, J. P., *Centuries of Economic Endeavor: Parallel Paths in Japan and Europe and Their Contrast with the Third World*, Ann Arbor: University of Michigan Press, 1994.

Prebisch, R., *The Economic Development of Latin America and Its Principal Problems*, New York: United Nations, 1949.

—— "Five Stages in My Thinking on Development" in G. M. Meier and D. Seers, eds, *Pioneers in Development*, New York: Oxford University Press for the World Bank, 1984.

Preston, P. W., *Rethinking Development: Essays on Development in Southeast Asia*, London: Routledge and Kegan Paul, 1987.

—— *Development Theory: An Introduction*, Oxford: Blackwell, 1996.

Prestowitz, C., *Trading Places: How We are Giving Our Future to Japan and How to Reclaim It*, 2nd edn, New York: Basic Books, 1989.

Prestowitz, C., Morse, R. and Tonelson, A. eds, *Powernomics: Economics and Strategy After the Cold War*, Washington, DC: Economic Strategy Institute, 1991.

Prystay, C., "Malaysia: The Retail-Shopping War" *Far Eastern Economic Review* April 25, 2002.

Pye, L., *Guerrilla Communism in Malaya: Its Social and Political Meaning*, Princeton: Princeton University Press, 1956.

Pye, L. W., "The Politics of Southeast Asia" in G. A. Almond and J. S. Coleman, eds, *The Politics of Developing Areas*, Princeton: Princeton University Press, 1960.

—— *Politics, Personality and Nation-Building: Burma's Search for Identity*, New Haven: Yale University Press, 1962.

—— "Political Development and Foreign Aid", November 1963, Bell Papers, box 23, "AID's Advisory Committee on Economic Development (Mason Committee) 1963–1964" JFKL.

—— *Asian Power and Politics: The Cultural Dimensions of Authority*, Cambridge, MA: Harvard University Press, 1985.

Rabe, S. G., *The Most Dangerous Area in the World: John F. Kennedy Confronts Communist Revolution in Latin America*, Chapel Hill: University of North Carolina Press, 1999.

Rachman, G., "Containing China" *Washington Quarterly* vol. 19, no. 1, 1996.

Ragin, C. and Chirot, D., "The World System of Immanuel Wallerstein: Sociology and Politics as History" in T. Skocpol, ed., *Vision and Method in Historical Sociology*, Princeton: Princeton University Press, 1984.

Ramage, D. E., *Politics in Indonesia: Democracy, Islam and the Ideology of Tolerance*, London: Routledge, 1995.

Ramirez-Faria, C., *The Origins of Economic Inequality Between Nations: A Critique of Western Theories of Development and Underdevelopment*, London: Unwin Hyman, 1991.

Randall, V. and Theobald, R., *Political Change and Underdevelopment: A Critical Introduction to Third World Politics*, London: Macmillan, 1985.

Ranis, G. and Fei, J. C. H., "Development Economics: What Next?" in G. Ranis and T. P. Schultz, eds, *The State of Development Economics: Progress and Perspectives*, Oxford: Basil Blackwell, 1988.

Raudzens, G., *Empires: Europe and Globalization 1492–1788*, Gloucestershire: Sutton, 1999.

Ravenhill, J., *APEC and the Construction of Pacific Rim Regionalism*, Cambridge: Cambridge University Press, 2001.

Redding, S. G., *The Spirit of Chinese Capitalism*, New York: Walter de Gruyter, 1990.

Reich, S., *The Fruits of Fascism: Postwar Prosperity in Historical Perspective*, Ithaca: Cornell University Press, 1990.

Reid, T. R., *Confucius Lives Next Door: What Living in the East Teaches us about Living in the West*, New York: Random House, 1999.

Reischauer, E. O., "What Went Wrong?" in J. W. Morley, ed., *Dilemmas of Growth in Prewar Japan*, Princeton: Princeton University Press, 1971.

—— *My Life Between Japan and America*, New York: Harper and Row, 1986.

Reischauer, E. O., Fairbank, J. K. and Craig, A., *East Asia: Tradition and Transformation*, Boston: Houghton Mifflin, 1973.

Remmer, K. L. and Merkx, G. W., "Bureaucratic-Authoritarianism Revisited" *Latin American Research Review* vol. 17, no. 2, 1982.

Reynolds, D., *One World Divisible: A Global History Since 1945*, New York: W. W. Norton, 2000.

Ricci, D. M., *The Tragedy of Political Science: Politics, Scholarship, and Democracy*, New Haven: Yale University Press, 1984.

Rich, B., *Mortgaging the Earth: The World Bank, Environmental Impoverishment and the Crisis of Development*, Boston: Beacon Press, 1994.

Rist, G., *The History of Development: From Western Origins to Global Faith*, London: Zed Books, 1997.

Rizvi, H.-A., "Pakistan" in R. Chase, E. Hill and P. Kennedy, eds, *The Pivotal States: A New Framework for U.S. Policy in the Developing World*, New York: W. W. Norton, 1999.

Robin, R., *The Making of the Cold War Enemy: Culture and Politics in the Military–Intellectual Complex*, Princeton: Princeton University Press, 2001.

Robinson, W. I., *Promoting Polyarchy: Globalization, US Intervention and Hegemony*, Cambridge: Cambridge University Press, 1996.

Robison, R., *Indonesia: The Rise of Capital*, Sydney: Allen and Unwin, 1986.

—— "Structures of Power and the Industrialization Process in Southeast Asia" *Journal of Contemporary Asia* vol. 19, no. 4, 1989.

—— "Indonesia: Tensions in State and Regime" in K. Hewison, R. Robison and G. Rodan, eds, *Southeast Asia in the 1990s: Authoritarianism, Democracy and Capitalism*, Sydney: Allen and Unwin, 1993.

—— "Indonesia: Crisis, Oligarchy and Reform" in G. Rodan, K. Hewison and R. Robison, eds, *The Political Economy of South-East Asia: Conflicts, Crises and Change*, 2nd edn, New York: Oxford University Press, 2001.

Robison, R. and Rosser, A., "Contesting Reform: Indonesia's New Order and the IMF" *World Development* vol. 26, no. 8, 1998.

Robison, R., Rodan, G. and Hewison, K., "Introduction" in G. Rodan, K. Hewison and R. Robison, eds, *The Political Economy of South-East Asia: An Introduction*, Melbourne: Oxford University Press, 1997.

Rodan, G., *The Political Economy of Singapore's Industrialization*, London: Macmillan, 1989.

Romulo, C. P., *The Meaning of Bandung*, Chapel Hill: University of North Carolina Press, 1956.

Roorda, E. P., *The Dictator Next Door: The Good Neighbor Policy and the Trujillo Regime in the Dominican Republic, 1930–1945*, Durham: Duke University Press, 1998.

Rosen, G., *Western Economists and Eastern Societies: Agents of Change in South Asia, 1950–1970*, Baltimore: Johns Hopkins University Press, 1985.

Rosenberg, J., *The Follies of Globalisation Theory: Polemical Essays*, London: Verso, 2000.

Rosenberg, N., and Birdzell, L. E., Jr, *How the West Grew Rich: The Economic Transformation of the Industrial World*, New York: Basic Books, 1986.

Rosenstein-Rodan, P. N., "Problems of Industrialization of Eastern and South-Eastern Europe" *Economic Journal* vol. 53, 1943.

—— "The International Development of Economically Backward Areas" *International Affairs* vol. 20, no. 2, 1944.

Ross, E. B., *The Malthus Factor: Poverty, Politics and Population in Capitalist Development*, London: Zed Books, 1998.

Ross, R. S., "Beijing as a Conservative Power" *Foreign Affairs* March–April, 1997.

Rostow, W. W., *The Stages of Economic Growth: A Non-Communist Manifesto*, New York: Cambridge University Press, 1960.

—— "Development: The Political Economy of the Marshallian Long Period" in G. M. Meier and D. Seers, eds, *Pioneers in Development*, Oxford: Oxford University Press for the World Bank, 1984.

—— *Theories of Economic Growth From David Hume to the Present*, 2nd edn, New York: Oxford University Press, 1992.

Rotter, A. J., *Comrades at Odds: The United States and India, 1947–1964*, Ithaca: Cornell University Press, 2000.

Roy, O., *Islam and Resistance in Afghanistan*, Cambridge: Cambridge University Press, 1986.

Rozman, G. ed., *The East Asian Region: Confucian Heritage and its Modern Adaptation*, Princeton: Princeton University Press, 1991.

Ruccio, D. F. and Simon, L. H., "Perspectives on Underdevelopment: Frank, the Modes of Production School and Amin" in C. K. Wilber and K. P. Jameson, eds, *The Political Economic of Development and Underdevelopment*, 5th edn, New York: McGraw-Hill, 1992.

Rudolph, L. I. and Rudolph, S. H., *The Modernity of Tradition: Political Development in India*, Chicago: University of Chicago Press, 1967.

—— *In Pursuit of Lakshmi: The Political Economy of the Indian State*, Chicago: University of Chicago Press, 1987.

Rueschemeyer, D., Stephens, E. H. and Stephens, J. D., *Capitalist Development and Democracy*, Chicago: University of Chicago Press, 1992.

Sachs, J., "Global Capitalism: Making It Work" *The Economist* September 12, 1998.

—— "The IMF and the Asian Flu" *The American Prospect* no. 37, 1998.

Sakakibara, E., *Beyond Capitalism: The Japanese Model of Market Economics*, Washington, DC: University Press of America, 1993.

Salter, M. B., *Barbarians and Civilization in International Relations*, London: Pluto Press, 2002.

Samuels, R. J., *The Business of the Japanese State: Energy Markets in Comparative and Historical Perspective*, Ithaca: Cornell University Press, 1987.

——— *"Rich Nation, Strong Army": National Security and Ideology in the Technological Transformation of Japan*, Ithaca: Cornell University Press, 1994.

Sanger, D. E., "Tongue-Lashings and Backlashes" *The New York Times* November 22, 1998.

Sassen, S., *Losing Control: Sovereignty in an Age of Globalization*, New York: Columbia University Press, 1996.

Schak, D. C., "The Spirit of Chinese Capitalism: A Critique" *Tsing Hua Journal of Chinese Studies* (new series) vol. 25, no. 1, 1997.

Schmitz, D. F., *Thank God They're On Our Side: The United States and Right-Wing Dictatorships, 1921–1965*, Chapel Hill: University of North Carolina Press, 1999.

Schonberger, H. B., *Aftermath of War: Americans and the Remaking of Japan 1945–1952*, Kent: Kent State University Press, 1989.

Schudson, M., "Culture and the Integration of National Societies" *International Social Science Journal* no. 139, 1994.

Scott, D., *Refashioning Futures: Criticism After Postcoloniality*, Princeton: Princeton University Press, 1999.

Scott, J. C., *Seeing Like A State: How Certain Schemes to Improve the Human Condition Have Failed*, New Haven: Yale University Press, 1998.

Seers, D., "The Birth, Life, and Death of Development Economics" *Development and Change* vol. 10, no. 4, 1979.

——— *The Political Economy of Nationalism*, Oxford: Oxford University Press, 1983.

Selden, M., "China, Japan, and the Regional Political Economy of East Asia, 1945–1995" in P. J. Katzenstein and T. Shiraishi, eds, *Network Power: Japan and Asia*, Ithaca: Cornell University Press, 1997.

Sestanovich, S., "US Policy Toward the Soviet Union, 1970–1990: The Impact of China" in R. Ross, ed., *China, the United States and the Soviet Union: Tripolarity and Policy Making in the Cold War*, London: M. E. Sharpe, 1993.

Seth, S., *Marxist Theory and Nationalist Politics: The Case of Colonial India*, New Delhi: Sage, 1995.

Seybold, P. J., "The Ford Foundation and the Triumph of Behavioralism in American Political Science" in R. F. Arnove, ed., *Philanthropy and Cultural Imperialism: The Foundations at Home and Abroad*, Bloomington: Indiana University Press, 1982.

Shafer, D. M., *Deadly Paradigms: The Failure of US Counterinsurgency Policy*, Princeton: Princeton University Press, 1988.

Shambaugh, D. ed., *Greater China: The Next Superpower?*, New York: Oxford University Press, 1995.

——— "Containment or Engagement of China? Calculating Beijing's Responses" *International Security* vol. 21, no. 2 (Fall), 1996.

Shannon, T. R., *An Introduction to the World-System Perspective*, 2nd edn, Boulder: Westview, 1996.

Shaw, M., *Theory of the Global State: Globality as an Unfinished Revolution*, Cambridge: Cambridge University Press, 2000.

Shiraishi, T., "Japan and Southeast Asia" in P. J. Katzenstein and T. Shiraishi, eds, *Network Power: Japan and Asia*, Ithaca: Cornell University Press, 1997.

Shiroyama, M., "With IMF Cash-Strapped, Room for Asian Monetary Fund" *Capital Trends* vol. 3, no. 10, 1998.

Shively, D. H. ed., *Tradition and Modernization in Japanese Culture*, Princeton University Press, 1971.

Sklair, L., *The Transnational Capitalist Class*, Oxford: Blackwell Publishers, 2001.

Skocpol, T., "Wallerstein's World Capitalist System: A Theoretical and Historical Critique" *American Journal of Sociology* vol. 82, no. 5, 1977.

—— "Bringing the State Back In: Strategies of Analysis in Current Research" in P. B. Evans, D. Rueshemeyer and T. Skocpol, eds, *Bringing the State Back In*, New York: Cambridge University Press, 1985.

Smith, J. A., *The Idea Brokers: Think Tanks and the Rise of the New Policy Elite*, New York: Free Press, 1991.

Smith, M., *Burma: Insurgency and the Politics of Ethnicity*, 2nd edn, London: Zed Books, 1999.

Smith, P. H., "The Rise and Fall of the Developmental State in Latin America" in M. Vellinga, ed., *The Changing Role of the State in Latin America*, Boulder: Westview, 1998.

Smith, T., *America's Mission: The United States and the Worldwide Struggle for Democracy in the Twentieth Century*, Princeton: Princeton University Press, 1994.

So, A. Y. and Chiu, S. W. K., *East Asia and the World Economy*, Thousand Oaks: Sage, 1995.

Song, Q. et al., eds, *Zhongguo keyi shuo bu: Lengzhanhou shidai de zhengzhi yu qinggan jueze (China Can Say No: The Political and Emotional Choice in the Post-Cold War Era)*, Beijing: Zhonghua gonshang lianhe chubanshe, 1996.

Song, Q., et al., eds, *Zhongguo haishi neng shuo bu–Zhongguo keyi shuo bu xupin: Guoji guanxi bianshu yu women de xianshi yingfu (China Still Can Say No – The Sequel to China Can Say No: The Variables in International Relations and Our Realistic Responses)*, Beijing: Zhongguo wenlian chubanshe, 1996.

Sopiee, N., *Towards a New Asia*, Commission for a New Asia, December 1993. Online at http://www.jaring.my/isis/asia.htm

Springhall, J., *Decolonization Since 1945: The Collapse of European Overseas Empires*, Basingstoke: Palgrave Macmillan, 2001.

Steven, R., *Japan's New Imperialism*, Armonk: M. E. Sharpe, 1990.

Stiglitz, J. E. and Yusuf, S. eds, *Rethinking the East Asian Miracle*, New York: Oxford University Press, 2001.

—— *Globalisation and Its Discontents*, New York: W. W. Norton, 2002.

Stockwell, A. J., "The United States and Britain's Decolonization of Malaya, 1942–1957" in D. Ryan and V. Pungong, eds, *The United States and Decolonization: Power and Freedom*, London: Macmillan, 2000.

Stokes, G., "The Fate of Human Societies: A Review of Recent Macrohistories" *The American Historical Review* vol. 106, no. 2, 2001.

Stoler, A. L., *Capitalism and Confrontation in Sumatra's Plantation Belt 1870–1979*, New Haven: Yale University Press, 1985.

Stone, D., *Capturing the Political Imagination: Think Tanks and the Policy Process*, London: Frank Cass, 1997.

Stubbs, R., *Hearts and Minds in Guerrilla Warfare: The Malayan Emergency 1948–1960*, Singapore: Oxford University Press, 1989.

—— "The Political Economy of the Asia-Pacific Region" in R. Stubbs and G. R. D. Underhill, eds, *Political Economy and the Changing Global Order*, London: Macmillan, 1994.

—— "War and Economic Development: Export-Oriented Industrialization in East and Southeast Asia" *Comparative Politics* vol. 31, no. 3, 1999.

—— "ASEAN Plus Three: Emerging East Asian Regionalism?" *Asian Survey* vol. 42, no. 3, 2002.

Stueck, W., *The Korean War: An International History*, Princeton: Princeton University Press, 1997.

Sutherland, H., *The Making of a Bureaucratic Elite: The Colonial Transformation of the Javanese Priyayi*, Sydney: Allen and Unwin, 1979.

Tabb, W. K., *The Amoral Elephant: Globalization and the Struggle for Social Justice in the Twenty-First Century*, New York: Monthly Review Press, 2001.

Tahir-Kheli, S. R., *India, Pakistan, and the United States: Breaking with the Past*, New York: Council on Foreign Relations Press, 1997.

Tai, H.-C., "The Oriental Alternative: An Hypothesis on Culture and Economy" in H.-C. Tai, ed., *Confucianism and Economic Development: An Oriental Alternative?*, Washington, DC: Washington Institute Press, 1989.

Tarling, N., *Britain, Southeast Asia and the Onset of the Cold War 1945–1950*, Cambridge: Cambridge University Press, 1998.

Terry, E., *How Asia Got Rich: Japan, China and the Asian Miracle*, Armonk: M. E. Sharpe, 2002.

Thatcher, M., "The Triumph of Trade" *Far Eastern Economic Review* September 2, 1993.

Thayer, C. A., *War by Other Means: National Liberation and Revolution in Viet-Nam 1954–1960*, Sydney: Allen and Unwin, 1989.

Therbon, G., "Into the 21st Century: The New Parameters of Global Politics" *New Left Review (II)* no. 10, 2001.

Thomas, J. N., *The Institute of Pacific Relations: Asian Scholars and American Politics*, Seattle: University of Washington Press, 1974.

Thompson, R., *Defeating Communist Insurgency: Experiences from Malaya and Vietnam*, London: Chatto and Windus, 1966.

Thurow, L., *Head To Head: The Coming Economic Battle Among Japan, Europe and America*, Sydney: Allen and Unwin, 1992.

Tilly, C. ed., *The Formation of National States in Western Europe*, Princeton: Princeton University Press, 1975.

Time: The Weekly Newsmagazine, "The Family Firm: Suharto Inc.", May 24, 1999.

Tinker, H., *Men Who Overturned Empires: Fighters, Dreamers and Schemers*, Madison: University of Wisconsin Press, 1987.

Todaro, M. P., *Economic Development in the Third World*, 4th edn, London: Longman, 1989.

—— *Economic Development*, 5th edn, New York: Longman, 1994.

Toye, J., *Dilemmas of Development*, Oxford: Blackwell, 1987.

Tripp, C. A., *A History of Iraq*, Cambridge: Cambridge University Press, 2000.

Tsai, M.-C., "Dependency, the State and Class in the Neoliberal Transition of Taiwan" *Third World Quarterly: Journal of Emerging Areas* vol. 22, no. 3, 2001.

Tu, W.-M., *The Triadic Chord: Confucian Ethics, Industrial East Asia, and Max Weber – Proceedings of the 1987 Singapore Conference on "Confucian Ethics and the Modernisation of Industrial East Asia"*, Singapore: Institute of East Asian Philosophies, 1991.

—— ed., *Confucian Traditions in East Asian Modernity: Moral Education and Economic Culture in Japan and the Four Mini-Dragons*, Cambridge, MA: Harvard University Press, 1996.

Tucker, V., "The Myth of Development: A Critique of a Eurocentric Discourse" in R. Munck and D. O'Hearn, eds, *Critical Development: Contributions to a New Paradigm*, London: Zed Books, 1999.

United Nations, *Measures for the Economic Development of Underdeveloped Countries*, New York: United Nations, 1951.

—— *Declaration on the Right to Development* (Resolution 41/128 of the United Nations General Assembly, 1976).

United Nations Development Programme, *Human Development Report 1999*, New York: Oxford University Press, 1999.

United States Agency for International Development, "Agency Objectives". Online at http://www.usaid.gov/democracy/dgso.html

—— *Private Enterprise Development*, Washington, DC: Bureau for Program and Policy Coordination, US Agency for International Development, November 9, 1984. Online at http://www.usaid.gov

United States Department of Defense, *National Military Strategy of the United States*, Washington, DC: US Government Printing Office, January, 1992.

United States Department of Defense, Office of International Security Affairs, *United States Security Strategy for the East Asia and Pacific Region*, Washington, DC: US Department of Defense, February 1995.

Valdés, J. G., *Pinochet's Economists: The Chicago School in Chile*, Cambridge: Cambridge University Press, 1995.

Van Creveld, M., *The Rise and Decline of the State*, Cambridge: Cambridge University Press, 1999.

Van Wolferen, K., *The Enigma of Japanese Power: People and Politics in a Stateless Nation*, London: Macmillan, 1990 (first published 1989).

Vatikiotis, M. and Delfs, R., "Cultural Divide" *Far Eastern Economic Review*, June 17, 1993.

Vatikiotis, M. and Kruger, D., "Eisuke Sakakibara: He Wants a Revolution" *Far Eastern Economic Review* March 7, 2002.

Vitalis, R. and Heydemann, S., "War, Keynesianism and Colonialism: Explaining State–Market Relations in the Postwar Middle East" in S. Heydemann, ed., *War, Institutions, and Social Change in the Middle East*, Berkeley: University of California Press, 2000.

Vogel, E. F., *Japan As Number One: Lessons for America*, Cambridge, MA: Harvard University Press, 1979.

—— *The Four Little Dragons: The Spread of Industrialization in East Asia*, Cambridge, MA: Harvard University Press, 1991.

von Albertini, R., *Decolonization: The Administration and Future of the Colonies 1919–1960*, New York: Greenwood Press, 1982.

von Hippel, K., *Democracy By Force: US Military Intervention in the Post-Cold War World*, Cambridge: Cambridge University Press, 2000.

Wade, R., "State Intervention in 'Outward-Looking' Development: Neoclassical Theory and Taiwanese Practice" in G. White, ed., *Developmental States in East Asia*, London: Macmillan, 1988.

—— *Governing the Market: Economic Theory and the Role of Government in East Asian Industrialization*, Princeton: Princeton University Press, 1990.

—— "Globalization and Its Limits: Reports of the Death of the National Economy are Greatly Exaggerated" in S. Berger and R. Dore, eds, *National Diversity and Global Capitalism*, Ithaca: Cornell University Press, 1996.

—— "Japan, the World Bank, and the Art of Paradigm Maintenance: The East Asian Miracle in Political Perspective" *New Left Review (I)* 217, 1996.

—— "The Asian Crisis and the Global Economy: Causes, Consequences, and Cure" *Current History* vol. 97, no. 622, 1998.

Wade, R. and Veneroso, F., "The Asian Crisis: The High Debt Model Versus the Wall Street–Treasury–IMF Complex" *New Left Review (I)* no. 228, 1998.

—— "The Gathering World Slump and the Battle Over Capital Controls" *New Left Review (I)* no. 231, 1998.

—— "The Resources Lie Within" *The Economist* November 7, 1998.

Wain, B., "Southeast Asia: Wrong Target" *Far Eastern Economic Review* April 18, 2002.

Waldon, A., "Deterring China" *Commentary* vol. 100, no. 4, 1995.

Walker, M., "Millionaire Minstrel of the Military" *The Guardian Weekly* December 25, 1994.

—— "Pentagon Trapped in Political Crossfire" *The Guardian Weekly* July 16, 1995.

Wall, I. M., *France, the United States and the Algerian War*, Berkeley: University of California Press, 2001.

Wallerstein, I., *The Modern World-System – I: Capitalist Agriculture and the Origins of the European World-Economy in the Sixteenth Century*, New York: Academic Press, 1974.

—— *The Modern World-System – II: Mercantilism and the Consolidation of the European World-Economy 1600–1750*, New York: Academic Press, 1980.

—— *The Modern World-System – III: The Second Era of Great Expansion of the Capitalist World-Economy 1730–1840s*, San Diego: Academic Press, 1989.

—— "The Concept of National Development 1917–1989" *American Behavioural Scientist* vol. 35, nos. 4–5, 1992.

—— *After Liberalism*, New York: New Press, 1995.

—— *Historical Capitalism with Capitalist Civilization*, London: Verso, 1995.

—— "The Unintended Consequences of Cold War Area Studies" in A. Schiffrin, ed., *The Cold War and the University: Toward an Intellectual History of the Postwar Years*, New York: New Press, 1997.

—— "The Rise of East Asia, or the World-System in the Twenty-First Century" in I. Wallerstein, *The End of the World As We Know It: Social Science for the Twenty-First Century*, Minneapolis: University of Minnesota Press, 1999.

—— "The Eagle Has Crash Landed" *Foreign Policy* July/August, 2002.

Walsh, J., "Toward the Pacific Age" *Time: International* November 22, 1993.

Wang, F.-L., "Self-Image and Strategic Intentions: National Confidence and Political Insecurity" in Y. Deng and F.-L. Wang, eds, *In the Eyes of the Dragon: China Views the World*, Lanham: Rowman and Littlefield, 1999.

Wang, J., *High Culture Fever: Politics, Aesthetics, and Ideology in Deng's China*, Berkeley: University of California Press, 1996.

Ward, R. E., *Political Development in Modern Japan*, Princeton University Press, 1968.

Weber, M., *The Religion of China*, New York: Free Press, 1951 (first published in German in 1916).

Wedel, J. R., *Collision and Collusion: The Strange Case of Western Aid to Eastern Europe 1989–1998*, New York: St. Martin's Press, 1998.

Wee, C. J. W.-L., "The End of Disciplinary Modernisation? The Asian Economic Crisis and the Ongoing Re-Invention of Singapore" *Third World Quarterly: Journal of Emerging Areas* vol. 22, no. 6, 2001.

—— "Introduction: Local Cultures, Economic Development and Southeast Asia" in C. J. W.-L.Wee, ed., *Local Cultures and the "New Asia": The State, Culture and Capitalism in Southeast Asia*, Singapore: Institute of Southeast Asian Studies, 2002.

Weidenbaum, M., *Greater China: The Next Economic Superpower?*, St. Louis: Washington University Center for the Study of American Business, Contemporary Issues Series 57, February 1993.

Weidenbaum, M. and Hughes, S., *The Bamboo Network: How Expatriate Chinese Entrepreneurs are Creating a New Economic Superpower in Asia*, New York: Martin Kessler Books, 1996.

Weiner, M., *Party Politics in India: The Development of a Multi-Party System*, Princeton: Princeton University Press, 1957.

—— "The Politics of South Asia" in G. A. Almond and J. S. Coleman, eds, *The Politics of Developing Areas*, Princeton: Princeton University Press, 1960.

—— *Party Building in a New Nation: The Indian National Congress*, Chicago: University of Chicago Press, 1967.

—— *The Politics of Scarcity: Public Pressure and Political Response in India*, 3rd edn, Chicago: University of Chicago Press, 1968.

Weiss, L., "Globalization and the Myth of the Powerless State" *New Left Review (I)* no. 225, 1997.

—— *The Myth of the Powerless State: Governing the Economy in a Global Era*, Cambridge: Polity Press, 1998.

—— "Managed Openness: Beyond Neoliberal Globalism" *New Left Review (I)* no. 238, 1999.

Weiss, L. and Hobson, J., *States and Economic Development: A Comparative Historical Analysis*, Cambridge: Polity Press, 1995.

Wesley, M., *Casualties of the New World Order: The Causes of Failure of UN Missions to Civil Wars*, London: Macmillan, 1997.

Wessell, D. and Davis, B., "Currency Controls Gain a Hearing as Crisis in Asia Takes Its Toll" *The Wall Street Journal* September 4, 1998.

Westad, O. A., "The New International History of the Cold War" *Diplomatic History* vol. 24, no. 4, 2000.

White, D. W., *The American Century: The Rise and Decline of the United States as a World Power*, New Haven: Yale University Press, 1996.

Whitehead, L., "Debt, Diversification and Dependency: Latin America's International Political Relations" in K. J. Middlebrook and C. Rico, eds, *The United States and Latin America in the 1980s: Contending Perspectives on a Decade of Crisis*, Pittsburgh: University of Pittsburgh Press, 1986.

Wiarda, H., *Ethnocentrism in Foreign Policy: Can We Understand the Third World?*, Washington, DC: American Enterprise Institute, 1985.

Wiebe, R.H., *Who We Are: A History of Popular Nationalism*, Princeton: Princeton University Press, 2002.

Wiegersma, N. and Medley, J. E., *US Economic Development Policies Towards the Pacific Rim: Successes and Failures of US Aid*, London: Macmillan, 2000.

Willetts, P., *The Non-Aligned Movement: The Origins of a Third World Alliance*, London: Macmillan, 1978.

Williams, D., "Constructing the Economic Space: The World Bank and the Making of *Homo Oeconomicus*" *Millennium: Journal of International Studies* vol. 28, no. 1, 1999.

Williams, J. E., "The Colombo Conference and Communist Insurgency in South and South East Asia" *International Relations* vol. 4, no. 1, 1972.

Williamson, J., "The Progress of Policy Reform in Latin America" in J. Williamson, ed., *Latin American Adjustment: How Much Has Happened?*, Washington, DC: Institute for International Economics, 1990.

Wilson, D., *China: The Big Tiger – A Nation Awakes*, 2nd edn, London: Abacus, 1997.

Wilson, H. S., *African Decolonization*, London: Edward Arnold, 1994.

Winchester, S., *Pacific Rising: The Emergence of a New World Culture*, New York: Prentice Hall, 1991.

Winichakul, T., *Siam Mapped: A History of the Geo-Body of A Nation*, Honolulu: University of Hawaii Press, 1994.

Winks, R. W., *Cloak and Gown: Scholars in the Secret War 1939–1961*, New Haven: Yale University Press, 1987.

Winters, J. A., *Power in Motion: Capital Mobility and the Indonesian State*, Ithaca: Cornell University Press, 1996.

Wise, D. and Ross, T. B., *The Invisible Government: The CIA and US Intelligence*, New York: Vintage, 1974 (first published 1964).

Wolf, C., "Blame Government for the Asian Meltdown" *Asian Wall Street Journal* February 5, 1998.

Wolf, E., *Europe and the Peoples Without History*, Berkeley: University of California Press, 1982.

Wolfensohn, J. D., "People First", Paul Hoffman Lecture, New York, May 29, 1997. Online at http://www.worldbank.org

Wong, L., "Cultural Claims on the New World Order: Malaysia as a Voice for the Third World?" in S. Yao, ed., *House of Glass: Culture, Modernity, and the State in Southeast Asia*, Singapore: Institute of Southeast Asian Studies, 2001.

Wong, R. B., *China Transformed: Historical Change and the Limits of European Experience*, Ithaca: Cornell University Press, 1997.

Woo, J.-E. (M. Woo-Cumings), *Race to the Swift: State and Finance in Korean Industrialization*, New York: Columbia University Press, 1991.

Woo-Cumings, J.-E., "National Security and the Rise of the Developmental State in South Korea and Taiwan" in H. S. Rowen, ed., *Behind East Asian Growth: The Political and Social Foundations of Prosperity*, London: Routledge, 1998.

Woo-Cumings, M., "East Asia's America Problem" in M. Woo-Cumings and M. Loriaux, eds, *Past As Prelude: History in the Making of a New World Order*, Boulder: Westview, 1993.

—— "The Political Economy of Growth in East Asia: A Perspective on the State, Market, and Ideology" in M. Aoki, H.-K. Kim and M. Okuno-Fujiwara, eds, *The Role of Government in East Asian Economic Development: Comparative Institutional Analysis*, Oxford: Clarendon Press, 1997.

—— "Introduction: Chalmers Johnson and the Politics of Nationalism and Development" in M. Woo-Cumings, ed., *The Developmental State*, Ithaca: Cornell University Press, 1999.

—— ed., *The Developmental State*, Ithaca: Cornell University Press, 1999.

Wood, E. M., *The Pristine Culture of Capitalism*, London: Verso, 1991.

—— *The Origin of Capitalism: A Longer View*, London: Verso, 2002.

Woodall, P., "Frozen Miracle: A Survey of East Asian Economies" *The Economist* March 7, 1998.

Woods, L. T., *Asia-Pacific Diplomacy: Nongovernmental Organisations and International Relations*, Vancouver: UBC Press, 1993.

World Bank, *World Development Report 1980*, Washington, DC: World Bank, 1980.

—— *Accelerated Development in Sub-Saharan Africa: An Agenda for Action*, Washington, DC: World Bank, 1981.

—— *Korea's Experience with the Development of Trade and Industry: Lessons for Latin America*, Washington, DC: World Bank, 1988.

—— *World Development Report 1991: The Challenge of Development*, Washington, DC: World Bank, 1991.

—— *The East Asian Miracle: Economic Growth and Public Policy*, Oxford: Oxford University Press for the World Bank, 1993.

—— *World Development Report 1997: The State in a Changing World*, New York: Oxford University Press, 1997.

Worsley, P., "One World or Three? A Critique of the World-System Theory of Immanuel Wallerstein" *The Socialist Register 1980*, London: Merlin, 1980.

Yamakage, S., "Japan's National Security and Asia-Pacific's Regional Institutions in the Post-Cold War Era" in P. J. Katzenstein and T. Shiraishi, eds, *Network Power: Japan and Asia*, Ithaca: Cornell University Press, 1997.

Yanagihara, T., "Anything New in the Miracle Report? Yes and No" *World Development* vol. 22, no. 4, 1994.

Yao, S., *Confucian Capitalism: Discourse, Practice and the Myth of Chinese Enterprise*, London: Routledge 2002.

Yasutomo, D., *The Manner of Giving: Strategic Aid and Japanese Foreign Policy*, New York: D. C. Heath, 1986.

Yeo, G., "A New Greater East Asia Co-Prosperity Sphere" in G. Sheridan, ed., *Living With Dragons: Australia Confronts its Asian Destiny*, Sydney: Allen and Unwin, 1995.

Yergin D. and Stanislaw, J., *The Commanding Heights: The Battle between Government and the Marketplace that is Remaking the Modern World*, New York: Simon and Schuster, 1998.

Yoshihara, K., *The Rise of Ersatz Capitalism in Southeast Asia*, Singapore: Oxford University Press, 1988.

—— *Japanese Economic Development*, 3rd edn, Kuala Lumpur: Oxford University Press, 1994.

—— *The Nation and Economic Growth: The Philippines and Thailand*, Kuala Lumpur: Oxford University Press, 1994.

Young, A., "A Tale of Two Cities: Factor Accumulation and Technical Change in Hong Kong and Singapore" in O. J. Blanchard and S. Fischer, eds, *NBER Macroeconomics Annual 1992*, Cambridge, MA: MIT Press, 1992.

—— "Lessons from the East Asian NICs: A Contrarian View" *European Economic Review* no. 38, 1994.

Young, R. J. C., *Postcolonialism: An Historical Introduction*, Oxford: Blackwell, 2001.

Zakaria, F., "Speak Softly, Carry a Veiled Threat" *New York Times Magazine* February 18, 1996.

Zhao, S., "China's Perceptions of NAFTA and Changing Roles in the Asia-Pacific" in S. Nishijima and P. H. Smith, eds, *Cooperation or Rivalry? Regional Integration in the Americas and the Pacific Rim*, Boulder: Westview, 1996.

Zolberg, A., *Creating Political Order: The Party-States of West Africa*, New York: Rand McNally, 1965.

Index

Asia–Europe Summit (ASEM) 266
Asia–Pacific Club 187
Asia–Pacific Economic Cooperation forum
    (APEC) 4, 160, 184, 251, 261, 263,
    264–5, 282, 283; summits 186, 188,
    264, 269–70
Asia–Pacific integration 263–4, 280
Asian crisis (1997–1998) 4, 6, 11–12, 22,
    133, 149, 163, 166–7, 190, 191, 265–6,
    280, 281; and after 205–12; effects in
    Indonesia 238–9; IMF-led response
    187–8, 281–2; and neo-liberalism 251
Asian Development Bank (ADB) 43, 253
Asian Dragons/Tigers 3, 156
Asian Drama (Myrdal) 76–7
Asian Miracle *see* East Asian Miracle
Asian Monetary Fund proposal 269–70
Asian Renaissance, The (Ibrahim) 263
Asian Studies 86, 90–2
Asian Survey 105
Asian–African Conferences 48, 49
Asia's New Giant (Patrick and Rosovsky)
    175–6
*Asia's Next Giant: South Korea and Late
    Industrialization* (Amsden) 201
Association for Asian Studies (AAS) 90, 91,
    101–2; Conference on Modern Japan
    (1958) 93
Association of Southeast Asian Nations *see*
    ASEAN
Australia 53, 238; and establishment of
    APEC 261, 262; government 160
authoritarian developmentalism 77, 229,
    230, 231
authoritarianism 14, 99, 106, 166, 197;
    and developmental state 199–200;
    regimes 45, 105, 164–5

Bacevich, Andrew J. 117
Baker, James 262
Balassa, Bela 158
Bali 240; terrorist bombing (2002) 245
Bandung Conference (Indonesia 1955) 48,
    49, 52
"Bandung Era" 16–17, 37–8, 47–9;
    regimes 53, 78–9; and Third Worldism
    49–55, 123
Bank of America 154
Bank of Japan 161
Bank of Korea 229
banking systems: Chinese/Japanese 267,
    268, 271; international 120, 122–3;
    regional development 43; US 121–2

Barshefsky, Charlene 272
Bates, Robert H. 78, 164
Batista, Fulgencio 46
Bauer, Peter T. 63, 152
Belgian Congo *see* Democratic Republic of
    the Congo
Belgium 18
Bell, Bernard 73
Benda, Harry J. 96
Berg, Elliot 154
Berg Report 154–5
Bergsten, C. Fred 160, 262
Bernard, Mitchell 11–12
Bevin, Ernest 44
Beyond Capitalism (Sakakibara) 178
Beyond the Developmental State (Chan, Clark
    and Lam) 209–10
Bhutto, Zulfikar Ali 127
Bismarck, Otto von 10
Blackmer, Donald 66
Borthwick, Mark 263
Bosnia-Herzegovina 140
Boutros-Ghali, Boutros 140–1; "Agenda for
    Peace" 140
Bowles, Chester 68
Braudel, Fernand 8
Brazil 53, 124, 133, 203, 204
Brenner, Robert 8
Bretton Woods meeting (1944) 120; post-
    Bretton Woods order 121–2; system 21,
    42, 120, 154, 230, 252
Brezhnev, Leonid 127
Bringing the State Back In (Evans,
    Rueshemeyer and Skocpol) 107, 210
Britain 18; Colombo Plan (1950) 44;
    colonial development 39, 50, 63;
    Colonial Office/Research Committee
    39, 63, 64; and neo-liberalism 68, 150;
    Thatcher government 22, 55, 122; and
    Vietnam War 238
British Malaya 95–6, 100–1; communist
    insurgency 234; economic effects from
    Korean War 226–7, 234, *see also*
    Malaysia
Brown, W. Norman 90
Bundy, McGeorge 90
bureaucratic-authoritarian industrializing
    regimes (BAIR) 11, 230, 231
bureaucratic-authoritarianism theory 106
Burma 48, 49, 138; transitional problems
    97–9
Bush, George Snr: administration 23, 129;
    "New World Order" 136

Republic of Korea (ROK) 225, *see also* South Korea
Revolutionary Government of the Republic of Indonesia (PPRI) 99
Reynolds, David 21
Rhee, Syngman 225
Rhodesia (Zimbabwe) 50
Rise and Fall of the Great Powers (Kennedy) 134
Rise of "The Rest", The (Amsden) 201, 210–11
Rising Sun (Crichton) 176–7, 258
Robin, Ron 95
Robison, Richard 9–10, 12
Rockefeller Foundation 73, 152
Root, Hilton L. 164, 165
Rosenberg, Justin 20
Rosenstein-Rodan, Paul N. 38–9, 62–3, 66, 69, 72
Rosovsky, Henry 175
Rostow, Walt Whitman 64, 65–6, 68, 100
Royal Institute of International Affairs (Nuffield College, UK) 62
Rueschemeyer, Dietrich 8
Russia 133; economic crisis 133, 281; and national development 38; nuclear capability 128; oil exports 128; US aid 128, 129
Russian Revolution 38
Rwanda 140

Sachs, Jeffrey 167
Sakakibara Eisuke 178
Salinas de Gortari, Carlos 124
Sao Tome 50
Sato Eisaku 252–3
Saudi Arabia: oil exports/reserves 128, 129; US aid/relations 41, 129
Second World (Soviet-centred) 18, 51, 79, 259
Second World War 8, 39, 62; and Asian Studies 90; effects on North American political science 89
Shastri, Lal Bahadur 71, 73, 74, 79
Shaw, Martin 207–8
Shenton, R.W. 38
Shils, Edward 88
Shiratori, Masaki 159
Shively, Donald H. 93
Singapore 3, 4, 50, 67, 107, 137, 281; and authoritarianism 164–5; and cultural integration 132; and Debt Crisis 124; and economic development 156, 179; industrialization 227; and ISI–EOI shift

158; Korean War boom 226–7; and New Asian Renaissance 181–3; People's Action Party (PAP) 181–2
Sino–Soviet split 49
Skocpol, Theda 8
Smith, Adam 6–7
Smithsonian Agreement (1971) 120, 252
Social Origins of Dictatorship and Democracy (Moore) 8
Social Science Research Council (SSRC) 87, 95; Committee on Comparative Politics 86–7, 88–9, 95, 105, 106, 198; Committee on States and Social Structures 107, 198, 201; Foreign Area Fellowship Program (FAFP) 95, 107
social sciences 19, 61
socialism 14, 16, 53, 54; market 260; and national development 18, 241; Nehruvian 69–71, 73–5, *see also* state-socialism
Soldier and the State, The (Huntington) 103
Somalia 140
Somoza family 46
Soros, George 187
South Africa 48, 49, 50
South Asia: and Colombo Plan 44; and economic development 77; and nation-building 101–2; US aid/policies 44, 72, 127
South Asian Studies 90, 91
South Korea 3, 4, 11, 46, 50, 133, 137, 187, 227–33, 246, 281; and authoritarianism/militarism (BAIR) 164–5, 206, 230, 231; *chaebol (jaebol)* 229, 231, 232, 236; Comprehensive Stabilization Plan 231; and Debt Crisis 122, 124, 125, 231; and developmental state 152, 156, 178, 179, 206–8, 231; economic growth/development 227–33; foreign debts 231; Heavy and Chemical Industrialization Plan 230; and IMF 167, 230, 231, 233; industrialization 201; and ISI–EOI shift 158, 229–30, 243; Kwangju Rebellion 231; and liberalization 157, 232; military education system 105, 232; modernization 67; as NIC 5, 107, 227–8; Park regime 229–30, 231; and postcolonialism 16; US aid/relations 41, 42, 46, 66–7, 129, 228–9; and Vietnam War 236–7, *see also* Korean War
South Vietnam 281; appeal of communism 104; Diem regime 100–1,

studies/publications 158–9; and US
interests/influence 154
World Development journal 162
World Development Reports 5–6, 161, 164
World Health Organization (WHO) 43
World Trade Organization (WTO) 190–1,
271; "Battle for Seattle" 22
world-system theory 11, 203–5

Xinjiang 271

Yasushi Mieno 161

Yeo, George 263
Yom Kippur War (1973) 120
Yoshihara Kunio 178–9
Young, Alwyn 163
Yugoslavia 49

Zaire *see* Democratic Republic of the
Congo
Zakaria, Fareed 134–5
Zambia 49
Zia ul-Haq, Mohammad 127
Zimbabwe 49, 50